Rocks & Minerals
of The World

Rocks & Minerals of The World

Text by Rudolf Ďuďa
and Luboš Rejl

TIGER

Topaz (p. 2) – idiomorphic crystal (9 mm); Thomas Range (USA)

Designed and produced by Aventinum Publishers, Prague,
Czech Republic
Text by Rudolf Ďuďa and Luboš Rejl
Translated by Zdenka Náglová
Photographs by Dušan Slivka
Line drawings by František Rejl
Graphic design by Dušan Slivka

Copyright © 1990 AVENTINUM NAKLADATELSTVÍ, s.r.o.

This edition published in 1998 by
Tiger Books International PLC,
Twickenham, UK

ISBN 1-84056-025-8
Printed in the Czech Republic by Polygrafia, a.s., Prague
3/19/01/51-04

Contents

Foreword

In recent times a revival of interest in the relationship of Man to Nature has taken place. Increasing numbers of people are interested in the study, identification and collecting of different natural objects, among the most popular of which are minerals. Their popularity is to some extent due to their aesthetic aspect (colour, crystal form, lustre, the ability to take a polish or to be cut into attractive shapes), but it is also associated with Man's endeavours to protect nature and learn as many of its secrets as possible. The aim of this colour guide to minerals is to supply the reader with information on well-known as well as rare minerals, their physical and chemical properties, the mode of their collecting, identification and application.

The book is divided into three parts: the first contains a short introduction to general mineralogy, a description of origin and the minerals' most important features, and methods of identification, collection and preservation. We do not presume that all the described methods will be required for the identification of the minerals. The diagnostic features may be either based on sight recognition or with the help of very simple tests, some of which may be carried out directly in the field. In this introduction, techniques requiring more thorough professional studies and a specially equipped laboratory have been deleted; these include such topics as the internal structure of crystals, optics and chemistry. The description of crystallographic forms is limited as well, because ideal crystallographic forms are very rare in nature. Nevertheless, fundamental crystallographic forms and typical crystal forms of some minerals have been included in the descriptive section or in the identification tables. Those interested in more thorough studies of the above aspects of mineralogy will find a list of specialist literature in the Appendix.

The descriptive and pictorial section includes 602 minerals, both common and less frequently encountered species. Their choice was primarily based on the established mineral groups, but the interests of collectors of precious stones, ore minerals and other specialities were not neglected. The illustrated section shows attractive mineral specimens in their typical naturally developed forms.

Minerals, in the descriptive as well as the illustrated section, are arranged according to their hardness, specific gravity (with some exceptions), and mineral group. Hardness was established as the main identification clue, because it can be determined easily by some simple means directly in situ. After this initial information, most minerals can usually be identified by the identification tables, in combination with some other common identification clues, which are included in the Appendix.

The determination of other properties can be carried out later at home after separation of the mineral sample from its matrix or associated minerals. A fresh, unweathered mineral sample is desirable. Problems in the identification of a mineral can be eliminated by the combination of different properties described in the identification tables, so that most mineral specimens can be identified correctly. Sometimes, however, we cannot identify a mineral. The specimen may either be non-homogeneous, heavily altered, or not included in this compendium. In such a case another specimen must be used for identification, or sometimes more complicated laboratory equipment is required. In this case advice should be asked from a more experienced mineralogist.

The description of individual minerals is arranged in this order too. Firstly, features that can be recognized either by sight or by very simple tests in situ (hardness, streak, colour, transparency, lustre, cleavage, fracture, crystal morphology) are given. Secondly, other features are described that can be determined only by means of laboratory tests, apparatus or special equipment (specific gravity, crystal form, magnetism, luminescence, radioactivity, optical and chemical properties). The description also includes important information on handling and cleaning individual minerals. Usually, distilled water as a cleaning substance is mentioned for minerals less resistant to chemicals, where its application may result in the etching of crystal faces or whole specimens. Lastly, data on the genesis, associated minerals, occurrence and application are included.

The tabulated section includes identification tables combining both specific and common features, so that the mineral under examination can be identified directly. It also gives a list of minerals with distinctive properties or special application. This is aimed at those specialising in collecting only certain types of minerals.

The list of reference books and recommended literature is arranged according to individual specializations. A separate group lists the most often used mineralogical periodicals.

Illustrations show mineral specimens from the Moravian Museum in Brno, and from the Technical University, the National Museum, and the Faculty of Natural Sciences at the Charles University, all in Prague. However, some mineral specimens were borrowed from private collections.

Mineralogy in general

Man started using natural resources from the very beginning of his existence on Earth. The first things in which he became interested in inorganic nature were minerals and rocks which he could apply, with little modification, to daily use. Later, when he became acquainted with ores (gold, copper, tin, iron, etc.), he began looking eagerly for all minerals containing these essential ores. Such ores gave names to individual ages, such as the Bronze Age and the Iron Age.

Archaeological history shows that minerals were systematically extracted by the Babylonians, Celts and Greeks. The oldest written records come from the Greek philosopher and scientist Aristotle (384—322 B.C.) and from Pliny Senior (23—79 A.D.). The first classification of known minerals and rocks was given by Avicena-Ibn Sina (980—1037). In Europe minerals and ores were mentioned for the first time by Albertus Magnus (1193—1280). Later, all known facts about mining, metallurgy, mineralogy and ores were recorded by Georg Bauer, under the name of Georgius Agricola (1494—1555). The most intense period of development of all branches of geology, including mineralogy, has taken place since the eighteenth century.

Mineralogy (*minera* -- ore) is a science concerned with the study of minerals — their morphology, composition, physical and chemical properties, and the conditions of their origin. Minerals are natural chemical compounds often very complicated, less often pure elements and alloys (eg C, Au, Ag), which began through different geological processes. The majority of minerals are inorganic in composition, only rarely are compounds of organic origin included with the minerals. There are some 3,000 known mineral species, the commonest of which contain silicon. The major part of minerals found in the Earth's crust are called rock-forming minerals, among the commonest being quartz, feldspars, amphiboles, pyroxenes, micas, olivine and calcite. These minerals form rocks, and rocks are the basic building blocks of the earth's crust. Some rocks comprise several minerals (granite or basalt), others are composed of a single mineral (limestone or dolomite). Other minerals, in comparison with the rock-forming minerals, are comparatively rare. The science of studying rocks is called petrography (from the Greek *petros* — rock and *graphein* — to write).

System of mineral classification

As in all other branches of natural science, mineralogists arrange minerals under certain headings, thus providing easier identification and comparison. During the development of mineralogy the criteria of mineral classification have changed several times. Mineralogists started to classify minerals according to their chemical composition and internal atomic lattice structure. Generally this system has been accepted and almost all large mineral collections are arranged according to it. The same method is recommended as well for arranging smaller private collections. However, the crystallochemical classification includes many problems and difficulties. Most minerals have a constant chemical composition which may be expressed easily by a chemical formula. On the other hand, a number of minerals have a variable chemical composition, yet their crystal structure remains unchanged (isomorphism). Minerals with similar chemical compositions, internal structure and physical properties form mineral species. Minerals containing some impurities, or minerals of like chemical composition and structure, but varying in other features, form varieties.

On the basis of the above-mentioned criteria all known minerals are divided into several classes and groups, starting with elements and continuing from the simple to the more complicated inorganic compounds. The last group is formed by organic compounds. H. Strunz (1970) divided minerals into nine classes:

1. Native elements
2. Sulphides, selenides, tellurides, arsenides, antimonides and bismuthides
3. Halides
4. Oxides and hydroxides
5. Nitrates, carbonates and borates
6. Sulphates, chromates, molybdates and wolframates
7. Phosphates, arsenates and vanadates
8. Silicates
9. Organic substances.

These classes are further divided into subclasses, orders, groups, species and varieties. The Strunz classification system has been used to classify the minerals in this book as well.

Origin and occurrence of minerals

In order to gain some knowledge of the minerals formed and still forming on the surface or within the Earth's crust, it is important to learn the geological conditions prevailing at the time of their origin. The long geological evolution of the Earth has been affected by many successive complicated processes. Roughly, they may be divided into magmatic, sedimentary and metamorphic (Fig. 1).

In a magmatic process the minerals originate from a glowing, liquid, molten silicate mass called magma, rich in volatile compounds. The magma originates within the Earth's crust or in its upper mantle. Under the influence of com-

plicated tectonic processes (eg folding and faulting) it is driven upwards to cooler layers where it solidifies gradually. On its way upwards it carries with it parts of the adjacent rocks which dissolve and change the chemistry of the magma. The cooling of the magma is accompanied by a gradual filterpress action (ie separating of fluids from solid substances) and by magmatic differentiation. The lighter minerals remain in the upper levels and the heavier ones sink slowly. The minerals first separated out crystallize in the molten silicate mass in the form of perfectly developed crystals; other minerals adapt to the shape of those previously crystallized.

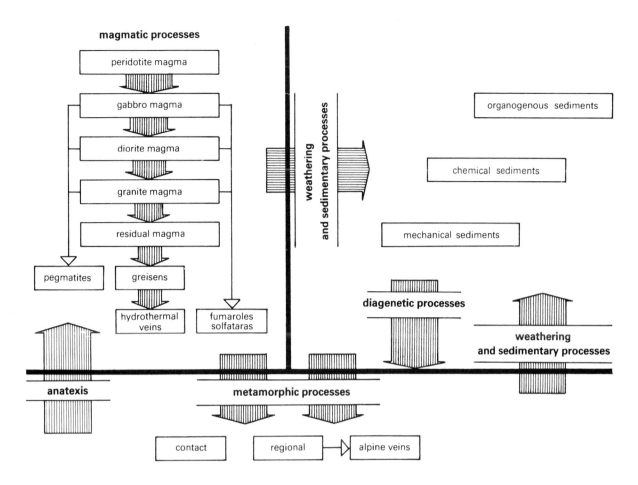

magmatic processes

peridotite magma

gabbro magma

diorite magma

granite magma

residual magma

pegmatites

greisens

hydrothermal veins

fumaroles solfataras

weathering and sedimentary processes

organogenous sediments

chemical sediments

mechanical sediments

diagenetic processes

weathering and sedimentary processes

anatexis

metamorphic processes

contact

regional

alpine veins

Fig. 1 Scheme of origin of minerals

Magmatic differentiation produces rocks with different chemical and mineral compositions. Thus we may speak of ultrabasic rocks (eg peridotite and picrite) rich in MgO and FeO but low in SiO_2. They are composed, for instance, of olivines, pyroxenes and amphiboles. Basic rocks (eg gabbro and basalt), comprising more SiO_2, Al_2O_3 and CaO, are formed eg of feldspars, pyroxenes and amphiboles. Acidic rocks (eg. granites and rhyolites) are rich in SiO_2, and enriched by Na_2O and K_2O but poorer in CaO, FeO and MgO. They are mostly composed of quartz, feldspars, micas and, occasionally, of pyroxenes and amphiboles.

In the course of magmatic differentiation some minerals can form large accumulations. In this way, rich heavy mineral deposits are formed, such as those of magnetite, ilmenite, chromite, pyrrhotite, chalcopyrite, pentlandite and platinum. A characteristic feature of these deposits is their irregular streak or nest-shaped development.

In the final phase of magma consolidation the molten residual silicate mass often forms coarse-grained irregular bodies, lenticles and veins, the so-called pegmatites. They occur either within the magmatic body or in its upper layer. Pegmatites are accompanied by many minerals of economic value, such as feldspars, quartz and micas, often in crystals of considerable size. Apart from these lithium minerals, such as lepidolite, spodumene or rubellite, and concentrations of zircon, xenotime, monazite, cassiterite, columbite, tantalite, allanite, emerald, sapphire, topaz, aquamarine, apatite or garnet may be found.

In the early post-magmatic process of mineral formation the main part is played by residual magmatic solutions enriched by volatile substances, such as boron, fluorite and lithium. These hot solutions together with gases and water vapour escape through rock fissures and cracks to the surface of the Earth. Meanwhile, the original hot solutions become cooler, and new minerals crystallize on the walls of the fissures. This process is known as the hydrothermal formation of such minerals as quartz, dolomite and calcite. If elements of heavy metals are present in the solutions, ore veins are formed.

The process of a direct separation of minerals, such as tourmaline, topaz and wolframite from hot gases and vapour, is called pneumatolysis or pneumatolytic mineral formation.

In places where gases and hot solutions affect the adjacent rocks the so-called contact-metasomatic minerals originate (eg vesuvianite, magnetite, pyrrhotite and chalcopyrite).

If, during volcanic activity, molten magma reaches the Earth's surface, its solidification conditions are very different from those in the interior of the Earth. Due to a faster cooling and a decrease in pressure and escape of volatile substances, the magma solidifies very quickly. If it consolidates near the surface of the earth, a part of it crystallizes in the form of phenocrysts, the remaining part only achieving the form of tiny crystals. The closer to the surface the faster the cooling rate of the magma, which finally results in a glassy mass (obsidian). As a result of gases escaping from the cooling magma, cavities are often formed, filled at a later stage with different minerals, such as calcite, quartz and chalcedony. Many minerals arise from gas escaping from fumaroles and solfataras, eg sulphur, sassolite, alunogen and sal-ammoniac. Volcanic thermal water, together with percolating surface water, jets forth forming both cold and hot mineral springs, mostly acidic. Also they give rise to various minerals, such as aragonite, calcite, chalcedony and cinnabar.

On the surface of the Earth all minerals are constantly subjected to the effects of atmosphere (O_2, CO_2) and hydrosphere (H_2O), temperature variations or biological processes which alter them so radically that new minerals are formed. This gradual, irrevocable and continuous process is called weathering. New accumulations of decomposed or secondarily-formed minerals are called sedimentary deposits.

Rock surfaces are affected mechanically by changing temperature (eg sunshine and frost) and by the shattering effect of frost (eg water and ice). As a result, the individual minerals resulting from the decomposition of the rocks are concentrated either in the place of their origin or they slide down slopes because of gravitational effects (ie talus accumulations). In this way only those minerals which are insoluble and less prone to oxidation, such as gold, platinum, cassiterite, wolframite, magnetite or garnet, become concentrated.

Furthermore, they may be transported by water or wind to locations far away from their place of origin. At the same time, weathered particles are separated according to their grain size and specific gravity. Minerals deposited by water solutions form placer deposits where heavy minerals, solid and resistant to weathering, became concentrated. Minerals also may be accumulated in seas and lakes to which they have been transported by water. In this way lacustrine or marine placers (eg sand on a beach) are formed, such as deposits of gold, monazite or ilmenite. Lighter, non-metallic minerals, such as quartz or feldspars, may also be found in large deposits and are of industrial importance.

Chemical weathering is caused by water, atmospheric oxygen, mechanical weathering and biological agents. As a result, profound changes or dissolution takes place in minerals, and new, secondary minerals are formed.

In the process of leaching of mineral deposits by surface water, parts of the soluble minerals are carried away by water, whereas insoluble minerals remain in their original location. In this way residual deposits originate; eg concentrations of minerals are formed by lateritic weathering in warm and tropical areas, such as the accumulation of limonite, Ni-silicates and iron. In residual deposits kaolinite may also be found; this is a product of chemical weathering of feldspar rocks. Other examples of residual deposits are those of phosphates, gypsum, manganese and bauxite. Sometimes the leached substances coagulate in deeper levels and form so-called infiltration deposits of minerals, such as those of iron, manganese, copper, vanadium, uranium, phosphates, borates, gypsum and magnesite. Both residual and infiltration deposits are often closely associated, which can be demonstrated by an example of certain ore concentrations. As a result of the weathering of the upper oxidation zone, sulphur compounds (eg pyrite, chalcopyrite, galena and sphalerite) change into oxygen salts (eg malachite, azurite, goethite, cerrusite and smithsonite). In these deposits they concentrate in so-called gossans (ie iron caps or iron hats), or are carried away. Such metals as Cu, Ag and Zn often pass from a lower oxidation zone to a deeper cementation zone where, after their reaction with primary minerals, they give rise to new sulphides (eg chalcosine, bornite and covellite).

Products of chemical weathering which are deposited in lakes and seas often coagulate by further chemical processes and form new minerals. In this way comparatively large deposits of halite (ie rock salt), sylvite, carnallite, mirabilite, anhydrite, gypsum, borax, ulexite, limonite, siderite, psilomelane and pyrolusite have originated.

Living organisms also take an active part in the process of mineral weathering and in the origin of new deposits. On the surface of the earth, minerals are mechanically disturbed by plant roots. Minerals arise by the accumulation of decomposed animal (ie phosphor) or plant remains or products (ie fossil resin, peat, coal, naphtha or earth wax). A number of minerals may be formed from substances dissolved in water with the assistance of living organisms (limestone, diatomites, phosphorites or sulphur).

Under the influence of external as well as internal conditions, minerals are subjected to frequent changes. For instance, changes of sedimentary deposits occur as a result of the dehydration of aqueous oxides or because of the carbonization or silicification of organic remains. These changes are called diagenetic changes and occur at normal temperatures on the earth's surface.

More intensive changes take place as a result of changes in the physico-chemical conditions found more deeply in the earth's interior or at contact with magma or hydrothermal springs.

In this process the molten magma affects rocks by its temperature, pressure or chemical reactions. As a result, rocks change their appearance as well as their physical and chemical properties. This process is called metamorphism, when new associated minerals originate.

We distinguish contact-metamorphism, which affects rocks found near volcanic rocks (ie scarna or erlans), and regional metamorphism, affecting large areas. Different minerals arise in different stages of this process. In metamorphic changes of a regional extent, important deposits of iron, manganese and graphite are formed.

In metamorphic rocks veins, of what is referred to as alpine type, are formed in the process of hydrothermal changes, and are of a similar composition as adjacent rocks. They are characterized by druses of perfectly developed crystals, such as smoky quartz, rock crystal, rutile, titanite and adularia.

A special group is represented by meteorites formed by minerals of extra-terrestrial origin. We distinguish between iron and stony meteorites. Up to the present time more than 50 minerals of this type have been described.

Associated minerals

Individual minerals may originate under different conditions and in many different ways. In natural conditions a mineral seldom occurs by itself; almost always it is associated with several other minerals in groups characteristic of certain processes of mineral origin. Such a mineral association is called a paragenesis (*para* – beside and *genesis* – origin).

A thorough knowledge of associated minerals is very important in a mineralogical study since it makes it possible to predict the existence of a certain mineral deposit or rock, and eliminate the occurrence of some others. Examples of associated minerals are shown in the Tables on pp. 494–497.

Properties of minerals

Hardness

From the physical point of view, hardness is not a precisely defined characteristic. It includes a whole series of properties based upon the cohesion of minerals and depending to a great extent upon cleavage. If the cleavage plane is vertical to the plane under inspection, the hardness is lowest in the direction parallel to the cleavage rifts. Perpendicular to them it is highest. The cohesion between individual grains in polycrystalline minerals plays an important part in the hardness determination. Considerable hardness differences are found in polymorphic minerals, such as graphite and diamond, the size of their atoms and ions and the bonding between them plays an important part. Minerals with smaller atoms and ions tend to be harder; and those with larger atoms and ions tend to be softer. Hardness is one of the most helpful diagnostic features for obtaining quick identification of minerals in the field.

Hardness is the resistance offered by a mineral to mechanical abrasion. For its determination, a hardness scale was established by Friedrich Mohs. It has ten grades represented by a set of standard minerals producing a white streak. They are arranged in order of increasing hardness. The difference in hardness between neighbouring minerals in the Mohs' scale varies from small differences among the lowest grades to larger differences among the last minerals (see Fig. 2). More precise methods of determining the hardness based on the resistance of minerals to abrasion (Rosiwal), and to scratching with a diamond point, are applied mainly in testing metals and in the ceramics industry.

The hardness of a mineral may be tested by scratching it with the sharp edge of another mineral from the scale, and vice versa. The edges of a mineral are used because they are harder than its cleavage planes. The hardness of the mineral in question and the scale sample is the same if they scratch each other. If the mineral under determination can scratch the mineral sample, but cannot itself be cut by it, it is harder and the test may proceed to the next lower grade. Not much force on the scratching point is needed — it only needs to be sharp. The scratch is then wiped clean and investigated with a lens.

In field work, however, this method is not always practical. Minerals of hardness 1 and 2 can be scratched by the finger nail, and have

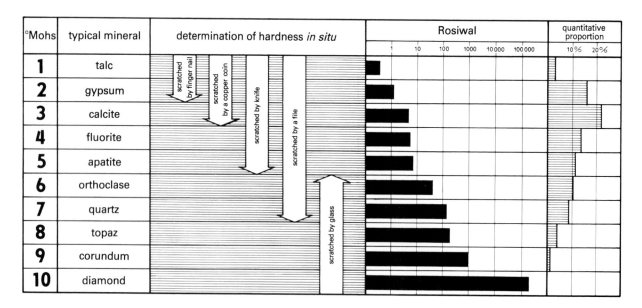

Fig. 2 Absolute and relative hardness of minerals and their quantitative proportion in individual hardness grades

a soft greasy feel. A copper coin scratches minerals up to the hardness of 3, a pocket knife up to the hardness of 5, a steel file up to the hardness of 7. Minerals with a hardness 6 and over can scratch window glass.

Hardness tests should be applied to fresh and sufficiently large mineral specimens. The surfaces to be scratched should be flat. Mineral aggregates or weathered minerals have usually a lower hardness than the single or unaltered crystals of the same mineral. For instance, hematite (hardness 6) will have a lower hardness in the radiating or earthy form than in individual crystals. An incorrect determination of hardness can easily be made in needle-shaped, fibrous and foliated minerals, where the apparent change in hardness is caused by disturbed cohesion, or in brittle minerals by fracturing. On the other hand some compact aggregates show an increasing hardness when compared with their isolated crystals. For instance, a finely granular aggregate of gypsum compared with an isolated crystal can only be scratched by a finger nail with difficulty. Owing to the fact that hardness is a directional property and depends upon the mineral's internal crystal structure, some show a different hardness in different directions. Therefore, we must test the hardness of minerals both on different surfaces and in different directions. This property is seen most clearly in columnar kyanite (see Fig. 3) or calcite. Crystals intended for collections should be tested very carefully to avoid visible damage to their crystal faces.

Colour

Colour is one of the most characteristic but not always the most reliable clue for identifying minerals. Many minerals occur in nature in various shades of colour or in quite different colours at the same time. For instance, fluorite may be colourless, white, blue, green, yellow or violet. However, there are many other minerals which are colourless in their pure state, yet if they do contain impurities may be of quite different colours, (eg quartz, rock crystal, amethyst and smoky quartz). Nevertheless, a number of minerals have a typical colour and are named after that colour, eg chlorite − green, azurite − azure blue, albite − white. Colours of other minerals have become characteristic of a well-defined shade of colour; some familiar examples are malachite green, emerald green, turquoise blue.

On the basis of their colour, minerals may be divided into the following four groups:

1. Achromatic (colourless) − with perfect transmission of light rays without being absorbed into the visible part of the spectrum (eg rock crystal, achroite, diamond and goshenite).

2. Idiochromatic − with their own, unchangeable colour owing to the presence of a definite element in the mineral, eg Cu−blue − azurite; Mn−pink − rhodonite; U−yellow − autunite; Cr−orange − crocoite; Fe−yellow − goethite; Co−pink − erythrite.

3. Allochromatic − of variable colours. Their colouring is due to the presence of elements which form different impurities, pigments, mineral inclusions and, occasionally, small traces of other elements, such as some varieties of quartz, rock salt, beryl or tourmaline. The colouring may also be caused by so-called colour zones formed in the absence of atoms on certain sites leading to defects in the crystal lattice, eg smoky quartz, amethyst, fluorite or diamond. A special kind of colouring is due to colour interpositions, the distribution of very small foreign mineral particles (eg inclusions of chlorite and hematite in jasper).

Allochromatic minerals display other characteristics in their colouring associated with the character of individual crystals or their crystal structure, eg colour distributed in regular bands or zones. Some minerals change their colour with a change of illumination; eg alexandrite is green in sunlight, whereas it is rose-violet in artificial light. There are also minerals which change their colour when held up to the light and rotated, eg cordierite and zoisite tanzanite. Such minerals are called pleochroic.

4. Pseudochromatic − apparently coloured

minerals. Their colouring is due to various optical properties, such as refraction, reflection, diffraction, dispersion or interference of light. Cleavage planes or rifts of predominantly transparent minerals of a glassy lustre exhibit a special colouring which is called iridescence and is caused by the diffraction of light. Iridescent tarnish is also exhibited by opaque minerals of metallic lustre, such as chalcopyrite or bornite, as a result of oxidation of their surface. Asterism exhibited by a suitably cut diopside or corundum is due to the reflection of light from tiny inclusions in the crystal's interior in certain definite directions. In sapphire it is often brought about by rod-like inclusions of rutile growing from the base plane at 120°. As a result, in a cabochon-cut stone it reflects light in a six-pointed star (Fig. 4). A special glitter caused by the reflection of light may also be observed on the inclusions of thin mica plates in aventurine. The bluish glitter of adularia is because of the dispersion of light in the stratified structure of feldspars. Precious opal exhibits a brilliant play of colours called opalescence. It is caused by the refraction and diffraction of light on fine sections containing minute beads of SiO_2 with a variable portion of water. In crocidolites the light dispersed by reflection from closely packed, almost parallel, needles and tubes produces patterns resembling animals' eyes (eg tiger's eye or cat's eye).

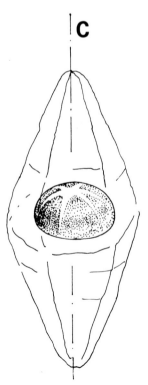

Fig. 4 Cut corundum crystal exhibiting asterism

The results of investigations into the physical properties of solid substances carried out in the last twenty years, together with the application of the quantum theory, have elucidated the reasons for the colouring of minerals. Twelve colour-forming agents have been defined but, for practical use, this classical division given above will be sufficient.

In determining the colour of a mineral, it is necessary to ensure that the true colour of the mineral is seen. Minerals exhibit different colours in sunlight and in artificial light. Their colour must always be tested on a fresh surface. As a result of weathering, some minerals show their so-called iridescent tarnish which sometimes completely obscures their original colour. Minerals containing silver react sensitively to light and slowly become coated by a thin black film (eg silver, proustite, acanthite and pyrargyrite). In the presence of light, realgar reacts in a similar way, changing from red to light yellow; topaz changes from blue to green. Amethyst, rose quartz and emerald become paler in sunlight. In museum collections such minerals must be carefully protected from light. In some agates, on the other hand, a longer exposure to light results in colour regeneration. Changes in colour may also be brought about by the effects of continued weathering, eg ankerite weathers to limonite, becoming brown in the process; pink-rose rhodochrosite turning into black Mn oxides. Due to the dehydration of their surfaces some minerals, such as melanterite and chalcanthite become paler, and it is advisable to store them in plastic bags.

A special kind of colour change is that caused or speeded up by man. In this way, some minerals display new colours or richer colour shades. Quite popular is the artificial 'colouring' of agates by aniline dyes, or the heating of amethysts from which yellow citrines, or Madeira topazes, may be obtained. By heating, yellow carnelian and tiger's eye become red, green aquamarine turns blue. Recently, diamond, corundum and topaz have been found to display richer colour shades under radioactive or ultraviolet rays. In this way too, smoky quartz is produced from rock crystal.

Streak

In the identification of minerals it is very important to distinguish between the true colour of the mineral and its apparent colouring. The true colour of a mineral is found by determining its streak, which is the colour of the fine powder produced by scratching the mineral. It may be obtained quite easily and is very useful in identifying opaque or semi-transparent minerals which have rich colours. Some minerals are named from the colour of their streak, such as hematite – blood, crocoite – saffron and xanthocone – yellow. The powder may be obtained by scratching the mineral with a sharp point or rubbing it on a streak plate, ie a piece of unglazed porcelain or the back of a tile. The mineral can be rubbed against its rough surface or may alternatively be scratched by the sharp edge of a plate. On a white plate its colour shows clearly. However, it must not be forgotten that the hardness of porcelain is 6–6.5. Therefore, minerals harder than this must be rubbed to powder in a mortar or on a steel plate, and after that on the streak plate. In some metallic minerals a dark plate (lydite) may be used for better determination of the streak colour. Coloured minerals always produce a coloured streak which is a little lighter than the true colour of the mineral, eg gold – yellow, sulphur – yellow or cinnabar – red. Large differences between the true colour and the streak of a mineral appear in some minerals, such as yellow pyrite which produces a greenish-black streak, grey galena giving a black streak, and black cassiterite a white streak. Generally, colourless and discoloured minerals produce a white or light-grey streak. The colour of the streak will vary if the mineral is tested in its crystal form or in compact, earthy pieces. When determining streak only those parts of the mineral which do not contain admixtures of foreign minerals should be used.

Transparency

Transparency is the ability of minerals to transmit light, which is most important, particularly in precious stones. The following degrees of transparency (see Fig. 5) are recognised:

Transparent minerals – when writing can be read through a thick section of them, eg calcite, rock crystal, topaz or diamond.

Semi-transparent minerals (subtransparent) – when writing seen through them appears indistinct, eg rose quartz and most emeralds.

Translucent minerals – in even thicker sections, minerals transmit light, but cannot be seen through, eg sulphur, orpiment or milk quartz.

Non-transparent minerals – do not transmit light when cut into thicker slabs; in powder form under magnification or when cut into very thin sections, they become translucent to transparent, eg amphibole or augite.

Opaque minerals – do not transmit light even in its powder form or in thin sections, eg magnetite or pyrite.

In granular aggregates transparent minerals become only translucent, eg calcite, marble, mica or gypsum aggregates. Under magnification, however, individual grains or thin sections of finely granular aggregates are transparent. Varieties of the same mineral may also display some differences. Transparency may also become lower because of mechanical effects – small rifts often appear on the surface of minerals (some can arise during the preparation of the mineral for testing). Owing to internal pressure they gradually enlarge, become more distinct and cause light dispersion and discolouration of the mineral.

Lustre

Lustre is the ability of minerals to reflect light from their surface. It depends upon various factors, particularly on the number of rays absorbed or reflected, and on the character of the mineral surface (ie even or rough). The lustre of a mineral increases for these minerals with a high refractive index, and becomes less intense with a higher light absorption, and a rough surface, but it is not dependent on the colour of the mineral.

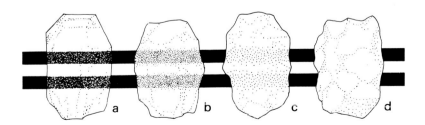

Fig. 5 Transparency of identically thick plates of rock crystal – a, smoky quartz – b, opal – c, and jasper – d

The kinds of lustre to be distinguished are as follows:

Metallic lustre (splendent, full) — characteristic of the majority of opaque minerals. It is best seen on freshly fractured surfaces and cleavage planes, eg galena, chalcopyrite or magnetite.

Submetallic lustre occurs on transparent or semi-transparent (subtransparent) minerals with a refractive index of 2.6—3.0, such as cinnabar and cuprite.

Adamantine lustre (shining) occurs only on transparent and translucent minerals with a refractive index of 1.92 and over, because of the total reflection of light, such as cerussite, zircon and diamond.

Vitreous or glassy lustre resembles the lustre of glass. It is typical of transparent as well as translucent minerals with a refractive index of 1.3—1.9, such as fluorite, quartz and corundum.

Greasy lustre is a self-explanatory term. This is shown particularly by minerals displaying numerous microscopic inclusions, such as opal and cordierite.

Pearly lustre — typical of transparent or semi-transparent minerals with a perfect cleavage, such as gypsum, muscovite or stilbite.

Silky lustre — is peculiar to minerals having a parallel, fine-fibrous structure, such as asbestos and crocidolite.

Dull (glimmering) lustre — typical of minerals of an earthy character, such as kaolinite and pyrolusite.

Lustre is observed in daylight on even, unweathered and clean surfaces. A particular mineral does not always have the same lustre. In granular aggregates the lustre is less evident than in individual crystals. For instance, magnetite has a metallic lustre on its crystal faces but a dull lustre in a granular mass. The lustre of granular minerals can be studied under magnification or by means of a microscope. Cleavage planes have a brighter lustre than crystal faces. It is sometimes very difficult to determine the lustre of dark minerals. However, an experienced collector can specify the type of lustre fairly reliably by comparing other selected types of lustre.

Cleavage

Cleavage is the ability of minerals to separate readily into definite directions. Like hardness, cleavage is one of the properties of mineral cohesion. Cleavage is a good identification feature particularly in well crystallized but imperfectly developed minerals. Cleavage depends on the internal crystal structure and remains constant for a given mineral. Crystals always cleave in the direction of least cohesion, ie in the direction of the smallest force, which binds the molecules together. It can be seen to best advantage when the mineral is struck with a hammer (see Fig. 6a). Bodies obtained by cleaving some minerals, bounded on all sides by cleavage planes, are called cleavage forms (eg in rock salt, calcite or fluorite). Some minerals possess a good cleavage along the crystallographic planes (eg rock salt or calcite); some others cleave only along certain cleavage planes (eg aragonite). Many minerals are named by their typical cleavage. Orthoclase exhibits a cleavage along straight planes and plagioclase cleaves obliquely, while euclase has a perfect cleavage.

The following types of cleavage are recognised:

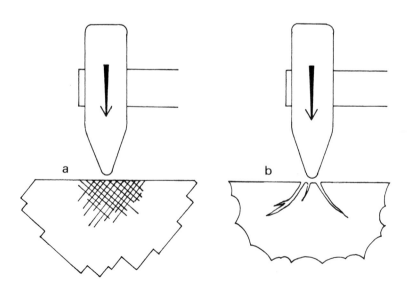

Fig. 6 Cleavage — a, and fracture — b of minerals

16

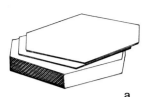

Fig. 7 Examples of typical cleavage of muscovite – a, galena – b, and calcite – c

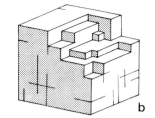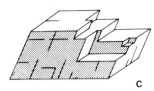

Perfect cleavage – when a mineral separates easily into thin laminae usually in one direction (eg graphite, gypsum, chlorite and muscovite, see Fig. 7a).

Good (or distinct) cleavage – when crystals, reduced to smaller fragments, always retain the shape of, eg a cube (such as galena or rock salt, see Fig. 7b), or a rhombohedron (such as calcite, see Fig. 7c).

Indistinct cleavage – cleavage planes are less distinct and not always quite even (eg feldspars, amphiboles or pyroxenes).

Difficult cleavage – cleavage planes have an uneven surface (eg sulphur, apatite or cassiterite).

Imperfect cleavage – a complete absence of cleavage. Minerals of imperfect cleavage exhibit uneven fracture surfaces generally known as fracture (see Fig. 6b).

According to the character of the surface, the following types of fracture may be distinguished:
– conchoidal (eg quartz or opal);
– uneven (eg arsenopyrite or pyrite);
– hackly (eg silver, gold or acanthite);
– splintery (eg nephrite or garnet);
– earthy (eg aluminite or kaolinite).

The types of cleavage may be determined by the force necessary to split a mineral. Evidence of a perfect cleavage is given by the pearly lustre of the cleavage planes, a good cleavage by vitreous lustre. Cleavage may be best observed on thin laminae or sheets. By the determination of an approximate angle between the cleavage planes, it may be possible to distinguish some similar minerals, such as amphiboles (120°) and pyroxenes (90°). Some minerals can have a less easy cleavage than indicated in the tables, and in many cases cleavage is absent.

The property of parting should not be confused with cleavage; it is either due to a twin growth of crystals or to the presence of layered inclusions of foreign minerals. The divisibility becomes more apparent by weathering.

Other physical properties dependent upon cohesion

Apart from cleavage and fracture, some minerals show further properties of cohesion. Ductile or malleable minerals, such as native metals, can be flattened by hammering into thin plates, eg copper and gold. Soft minerals such as aluminite and talc split into powder under a hammer blow, while brittle minerals, such as pyrite and quartz, crumble into small fragments when struck. A thin plate of mica can be bent, and if the pressure is removed it returns to its original shape. Such minerals are called elastic. Others, such as gypsum, chlorites, or ductile minerals do not spring back to their original position; they are called flexible. On the basis of these properties we can easily distinguish between suitable specimens of the elastic micas and the flexible chlorites.

Morphology

Morphology is a science dealing with the shapes of crystallised minerals, from which some of them have obtained their names, such as anatase (elongation), scapolite (rod), actinolite (ray), sanidine (plate), staurolite (cross). Minerals bounded by a number of flat surfaces with their external form related to their internal structure, are called crystals. Crystals usually occur with imperfectly developed faces, but nevertheless with a regular internal structure. Minerals lacking an essential atomic structure are rare and are called amorphous (opal). Apart from their chemistry, the crystal form is one of the most important clues in the identification of minerals.

The following growth forms of crystals are recognised:

– Free, embedded crystals, restrained in growth on all sides. They are most common in intrusive rocks (eg amphibole, augite, orthoclase and garnet), in argillaceous rocks (eg gypsum) and in sandstones (eg quartz).

– Attached crystals (ie druses, geodes,

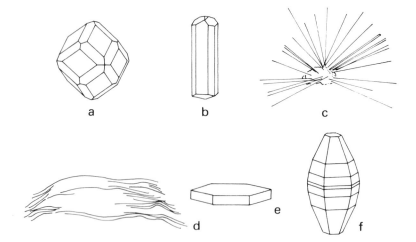

Fig. 8 Morphological forms of crystals: isometric – a, columnar – b, acicular – c, fibrous – d, platy – e, barrel-shaped – f

aggregates) occur in veins, cavities or vugs, nodules (ie concretions) and clay deposits.

The following terms are used in describing the shapes of crystals:

– euhedral (idiomorphic) crystals – bound only by crystal faces;
– subeuhedral (hypiodiomorphic) crystals – having distinctive crystal faces;
– xenomorphic crystals – deformed; this deformation is caused by a limited space for the growth of the crystal.

There are other types of habit, such as barrel-shaped (see Fig. 8f) which is between the isometric and elongated types (eg anatase or sapphire).

A characteristic morphological feature of the growth of crystals in some minerals is the growth of twin crystals or aggregates, which is regulated by certain definite laws (eg gypsum, fluorite, rutile, orthoclase, cassiterite and staurolite, Fig. 9).

Crystal aggregates (see Fig. 10) may attain different forms according to the arrangement of their crystals:

– granular aggregates (ie coarse- and fine-grained). In compact aggregates no individual grains can be usually seen by the naked eye;
– columnar aggregates (eg aragonite), fibrous aggregates (eg sillimanite), may be parallels, radiating or irregular;
– lamellar aggregates, typical of micas and chlorites;
– oolitic aggregates, typical of chamosite;
– concretions are egg-shaped, sometimes with a kidney-shaped surface (eg gypsum and diadochite);
– dendritic aggregates are developed in branching or fern-like growths, typical of copper, gold and psilomelane;
– porous, foamy or spongy aggregates are typical of limonite and calcite;
– crusty, drop-shaped and colloidal aggregates occur predominantly in aragonite, limonite, pyrite, marcasite, in various kinds of opals and in hyalite;

Pseudomorphs are crystals which have altered from another mineral but retained their original shape. At times a younger mineral of different composition can be deposited on the surface of another and thereby enclose it completely. This is called perimorphism.

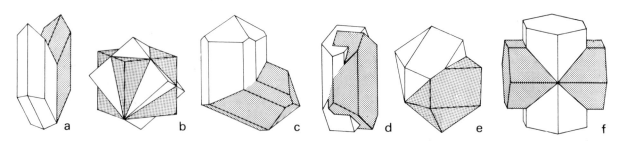

Fig. 9 Characteristic twinning of crystals in gypsum – a, fluorite – b, rutile – c, orthoclase – d, cassiterite – e, and staurolite – f

18

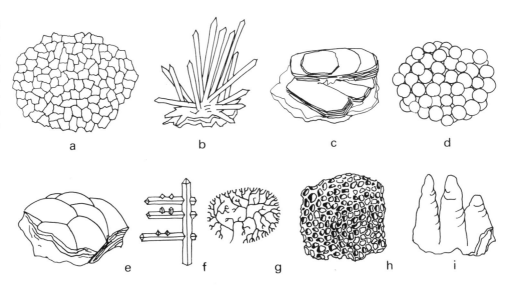

Fig. 10 Crystalline aggregates of minerals: granular — a, rodlike — b, spathic — c, oolitic — d, concretions — e, dendritic (arborescent) — f, g, porous — h, stalactitic — i

Sometimes the original mineral dissolved and the resulting cavity filled with a substitute. Another kind of pseudomorph is a paramorph, in which the mineral retains its form as well as its chemical composition, but changes its atomic structure.

A whole series of minerals, such as gypsum, calcite and quartz occur in different crystal forms or aggregates pertaining to the conditions of their origin. Sometimes, crystals and aggregates attain a typical form that becomes an important identification feature (ie needle-shaped natrolite). Some deformation in the growth of individual crystals or their faces may serve as an important clue for identification. These are divided into external (ie irregular development of crystal faces, parallel overgrowth, phantoms, cavernous crystals, skeletal crystals), and internal (ie liquid, gaseous and solid inclusions, such as inclusions of sagenite in quartz).

Solubility

The fact that many minerals dissolve in water or in different acids may be used as an aid in their identification. For instance, rock salt and chalcanthite dissolve readily in water, whereas other minerals dissolve slowly. However, most minerals, are completely insoluble in water.

Many minerals, however, are soluble in acids. In cold dilute hydrochloric acid (HCl), calcite dissolves with effervescence, whereas other minerals of similar appearance, such as dolomite, remain unchanged. In field work only dilute acids may be used. In testing their reaction with carbonates care must be taken to avoid damaging good crystals.

Other properties

In field work, other properties of minerals, called physiological properties, become apparent. Minerals soluble in water, such as rock salt, epsomite and others, have a characteristic taste, being respectively saline and bitter. However, some soluble minerals such as witherite, are poisonous. Some minerals can be identified by the characteristic odour particularly when heated or rubbed, eg sulphur and some sulphides such as pyrite or marcasite produce an odour of sulphur, while arsenopyrite gives off a garlicky smell.

Some minerals, especially those of low hardness such as kaolinite, feel rough; others (eg talc) feel greasy and smooth. An experienced mineralogist can distinguish minerals according to their heat conductivity, for instance, feeling them against his forehead. Experienced stone polishers are able to distinguish real gemstones from glass imitations in this way.

Specific gravity

Another physical property of minerals, used in their identification, is specific gravity. In minerals of constant chemical composition, it is always the same at fixed temperatures and pressures, its exact determination frequently helps in their identification. It depends upon the chemical composition of the mineral, on its atomic weight and the molecular size and arrangement; in crystalline substances it depends upon their crystal structure. Minerals, in single crystal form, have higher specific gravities than their polycrystalline equivalents.

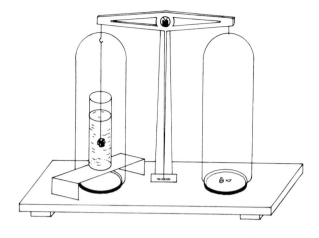

Fig. 11 A balance used to measure specific gravity

An experienced collector can estimate the approximate specific gravity by simply holding the mineral and guessing its weight. There are light minerals of a specific gravity 1–2 (some bitumens), medium-heavy minerals of a specific gravity 2–4 (gypsum and quartz), heavy minerals of a specific gravity 4–6 (sphalerite and barytes), and very heavy minerals of a specific gravity of more than 6 (galena and cassiterite). Native metals, such as gold (15–16) and platinum (14–20) have the highest specific gravities.

A quick determination of specific gravity may be obtained by the suspension method. The relative specific gravity of minerals is determined when a piece of unweathered mineral (about 1 gm) is submerged in a liquid of known density. If the mineral sinks to the bottom, its specific gravity is higher than that of the liquid; if it floats, its specific gravity is lower.

For a more accurate measurement, the liquid is either diluted or concentrated until it achieves the density at which the mineral just floats. Then, it is easy to determine the specific gravity of the liquid by means of a densimeter (ie hydrometer) or pycnometer. A suitable liquid is bromoform $CHBr_3$ with a density of 2.904 (diluted by ether or benzol), acetylene tetrabromide $C_2H_2Br_4$ of a density of 3 (diluted by benzol), methylene iodide CH_2I_2 of a density of 3.33 (diluted in alcohol, ether or benzol). The only disadvantage of this method is that liquids of higher density are not readily available, or easy to handle and most of them are harmful.

For a quick and exact determination of the specific gravity of a sample, it can be weighed twice, in air and then in water. This method can be applied best to non-porous minerals.

A laboratory balance specially adapted for this purpose can be used (see Fig. 11). On a small hook above one of the scales is hung a small container on a silk thread, which is balanced on the other scale. The mineral sample is placed in the container and weighed in air. To estimate its weight in water, a beaker containing distilled water is placed under the container so that it is complety immersed. With water-soluble minerals the immersion medium should be oil or alcohol.

When the weight of the mineral is known, its specific gravity can be calculated by means of the formula:

$$S_m = \frac{m_t \cdot S_k}{m_t - m_t'}$$

where m_t is the weight of the sample in the air
m_t' is the weight of the sample in the liquid
S_k is the density of the liquid (density of H_2O at 20 °C = 0.9982 = 1 g/cm^3).

For an exact determination of the specific gravity of very small mineral fragments the pycnometric method can be applied. The sample is placed in a glass bottle (ie pycnometer) of known volume, which is then filled with a density fluid. The volume of the sample is determined by weighing. Its specific gravity can be calculated using the formula:

$$S_m = \frac{(m_2 - m_1)S_k}{(M_1 - M_2) + (m_2 - m_1)}$$

where m_1 = weight of the empty pycnometer
m_2 = weight of pycnometer with sample
M_1 = weight of pycnometer with liquid
M_2 = weight of pycnometer with sample and liquid
S_k = density of the fluid.

The specific gravity of minerals may fluctuate considerably in weathered and damaged specimens. Isomorphous admixtures of foreign minerals, and occluded gases and liquids may influence the result of the measurement. Therefore, each sample should be examined prior to the tests by means of a lens or binocular microscope. This method requires skilful manipulation of the small grains.

Crystals and crystal systems

Most minerals exist in nature as crystals ranging in size from macroscopic to microscopic size. Crystals of individual minerals have characteristic forms which are the outward expression of their internal structure, which depends on the arrangement of their constituent atoms. These are arranged in

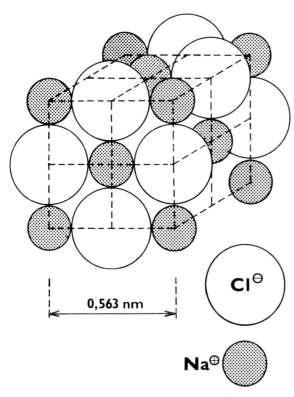

 placed above — figure.

0,563 nm

Cl⁻

Cl$^\ominus$

Na$^\oplus$

Fig. 12 Model of crystal lattice of halite (rock salt)

a geometrical pattern forming a crystal or space lattice. Several types of lattices are formed, according to the arrangement of the atoms. Some minerals, such as rock salt, display comparatively simple space lattices (see Fig. 12), whereas in other minerals very complicated space lattices occur. As a geometric shape a crystal is bounded by faces and angles with which the same faces intersect are identical in all crystals of one mineral irrespective of their size. This is known as the Law of Constancy of Angle.

The faces bounding the crystal may be symmetrical about a centre, axis or plane. These are the elements of crystal symmetry:

a) The plane of symmetry divides the crystal into two symmetrical halves. There exist 1, 2, 3, 4, 5, 6, 7 and 9 planes of symmetry in specific crystals.

b) The axis of symmetry is an imaginary line assumed to pass through the ideal centre of each crystal. Rotated about this axis through a definite angle the crystal reaches a position identical with its original position. The axes of symmetry are divided into diad, triad, tetrad and hexad axes.

c) The centre of symmetry is the point dividing all intersecting faces, edges and angles into halves. Each crystal face has a similar, parallel counterface.

In all there are 32 crystal classes into which all

crystals can be placed. Each class includes crystals of an identical geometrical and physical symmetry. According to a number of common features, the 32 crystal classes are grouped into 7 major divisions, the seven Crystal Systems (see Fig. 13). The common feature, a three-dimensional axial cross, permits a precise determination of the location of every crystal face. The smallest number of symmetry elements is found in the triclinic system, the largest in the cubic system.

To enable individual crystal faces to be designated, crystallographic symbols or indexes are introduced. Most often Miller's crystallographic symbols, expressing the relationship between the specific parameters and the axial cross, are used. They enable the designation of all crystal faces by integral numbers, the first number indicating the front-to-rear, the second the right-to-left, and the third number the vertical axis. In the hexagonal system the vertical axis is designated by the fourth number. If the face intersects the axial cross in a negative direction, it is marked with the negative (−) symbol above the respective index (see Fig. 14).

Each crystal system is characterized by certain basic crystal shapes. Minerals crystallizing in the triclinic, monoclinic or orthorhombic system appear in the form of pedions, pinacoids, prisms and pyramids, or their combinations. Minerals crystallizing in the trigonal system display the rhombohedral form. Minerals in the cubic system crystallize in cubes, tetrahedra, octahedra, hexahedra and their combinations.

Each mineral species belongs to a single class and consequently has a definite type of lattice. However, some minerals of identical chemical composition, having originated under quite different conditions, can crystallize in two or more classes. Such minerals are called polymorphs. For example, diamond (602) − graphite (2); calcite (217) − aragonite (221); rutile (464) − brookite (353) − anatase (352); quartz (534) − tridymite (461) − cristobalite (462); sphalerite (181) − wurtzite (184); pyrite (436) − marcasite (437). Sometimes minerals of a different chemical composition but similar crystal lattice can alter into one another; examples are calcite (217) − magnesite (302) − siderite (306) − rhodochrosite (304), or albite (493) − anorthite (498). They are called isomorphic minerals.

Owing to the fact that crystals do not always exhibit ideal forms, an exact description and

Crystal system (number of classes)	Axial cross	Basic parametres and inter-axial angles	Some characteristic crystal forms
triclinic (2)	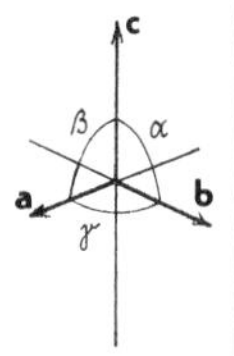	$a \neq b \neq c$ $\alpha \neq \beta \neq \gamma \neq 90°$	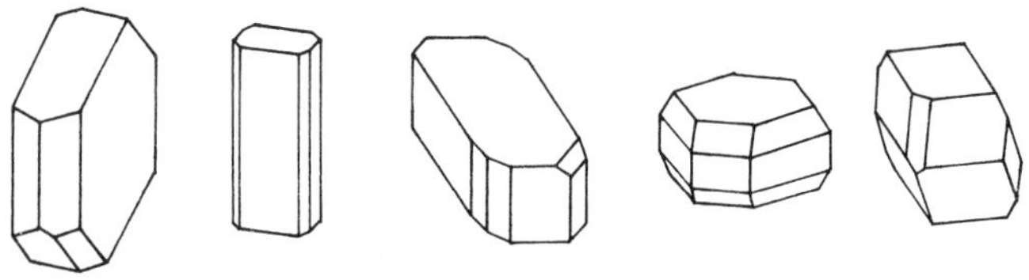 albite · kyanite · chalcanthite · sassolite · rhodonite
monoclinic (3)	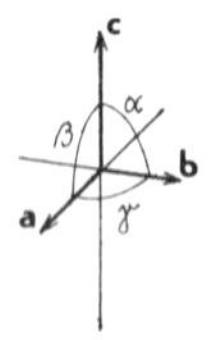	$a \neq b \neq c$ $\alpha = \gamma = 90°$ $\beta \neq 90°$	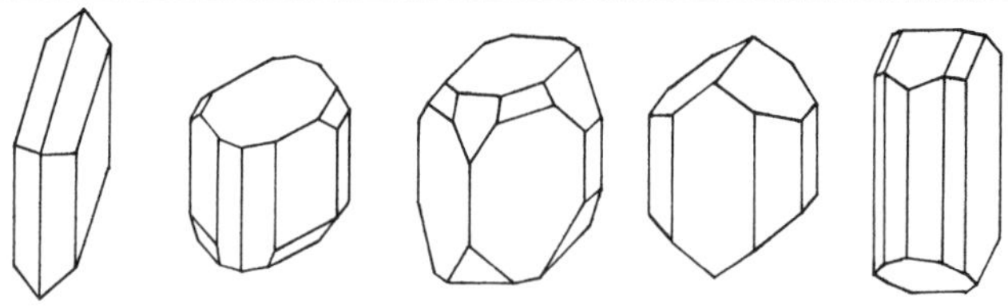 gypsum · realgar · melanterite · augite · orthoclase
orthorhombic (3)	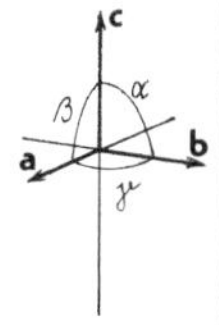	$a \neq b \neq c$ $\alpha = \beta = \gamma = 90°$	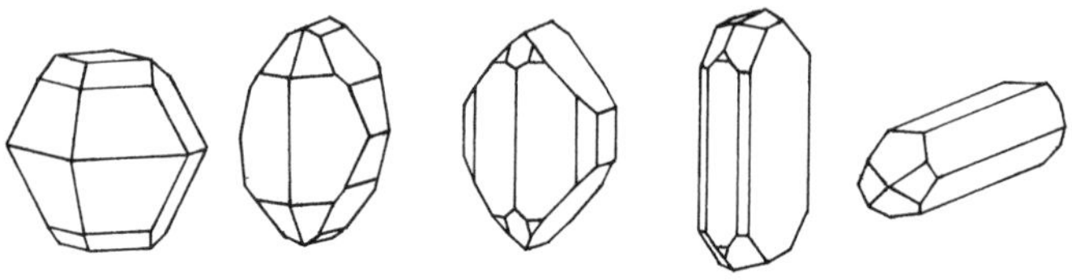 sulphur · cerussite · olivine · enstatite · baryte
tetragonal (7)	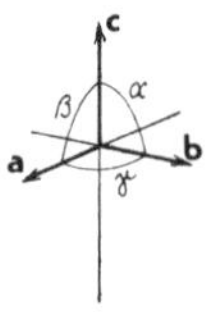	$a = b \neq c$ $\alpha = \beta = \gamma = 90°$	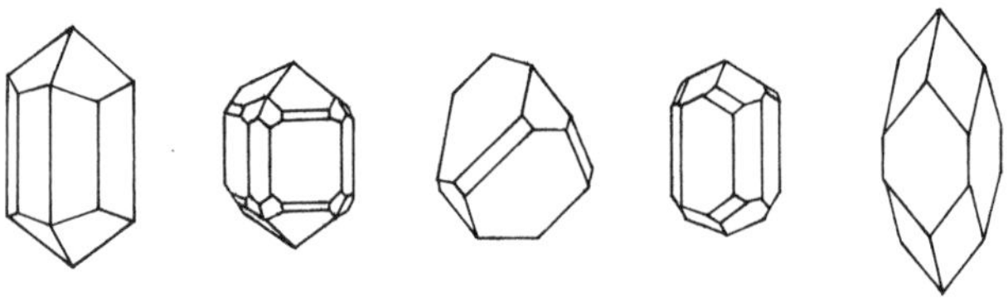 rutile · zircon · chalcopyrite · scapolite · apophyllite
hexagonal (7)	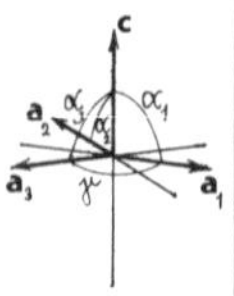	$a_1 = a_2 = a_3 \neq c$ $\alpha = \beta = 90°$ $\gamma = 120°$	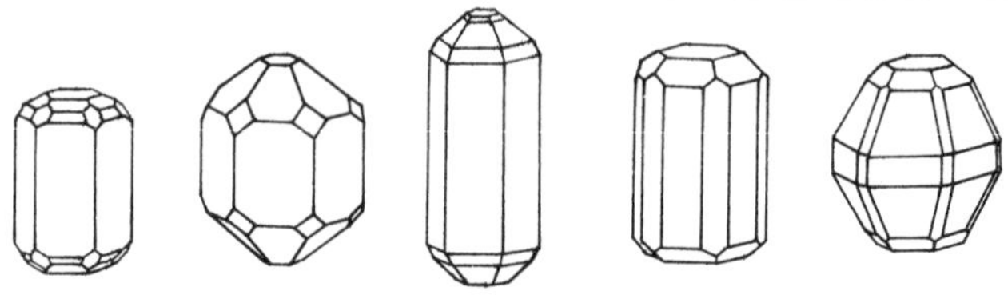 beryl · apatite · vanadinite · nepheline · pyrrhotite
trigonal (5)	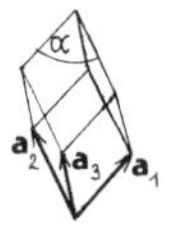	$a \; a_2 = a_3$ $\alpha_1 = \alpha_2 = \alpha_3 \neq 90°$	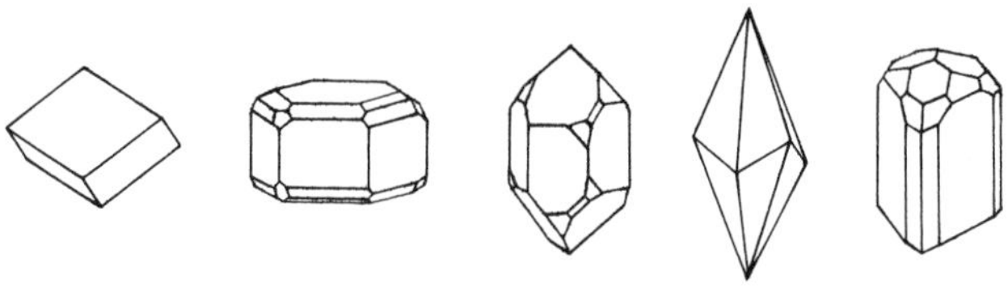 calcite · cinnabar · quartz · aragonite · tourmaline
cubic (5)	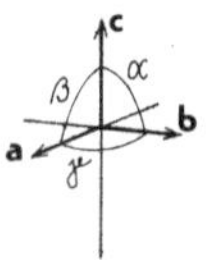	$a = b = c$ $\alpha = \beta = \gamma = 90°$	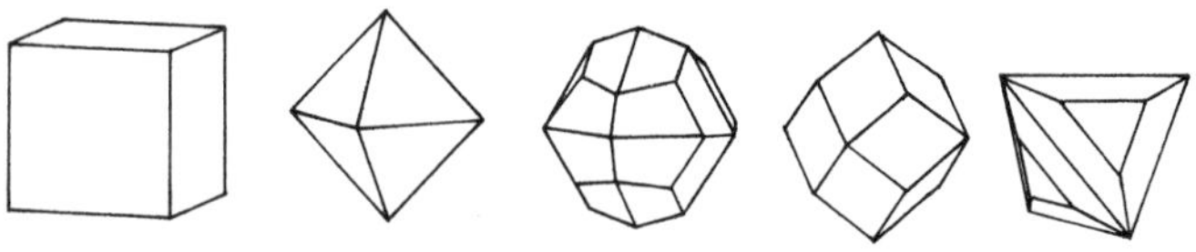 galena · magnetite · pyrite · almandine · tetrahedrite

Fig. 13 Examples of characteristic crystal forms of the seven crystal systems

Fig. 14 Miller's indices and their orientation to crystal axes

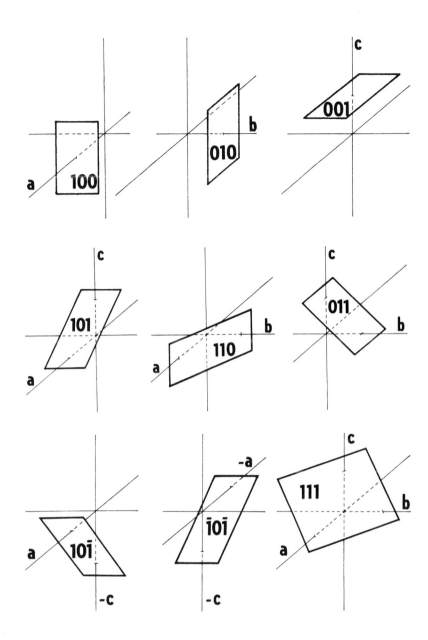

classification of a crystal in a certain definite class or crystal system requires a thorough knowledge of crystallography, and sometimes also requires study by special (X-ray) apparatus.

Special optical properties

Apart from lustre, transparency and colour, which can usually be observed directly, some other optical properties of minerals may be also used in their identification, such as the index of refraction of light, the optical isotropy or anisotropy of minerals, which are very important in the determination, for instance, between silicate minerals of similar appearance. A polarizing microscope is very useful for these determinations, but is rather expensive and needs some expertise in its use. Since the

description of its application is beyond the scope of this book, those interested in a more detailed study are referred to more specialized literature.

For our purposes the simplest microscope equipped with two polarizing filters will be sufficient in the study of optical properties of minerals.

On a solid plate or in an agate mortar a small fragment of the mineral sample is crushed, and with a dampened brush some of the powder is mounted on a slide in a drop of water and covered with the cover-slip.

The first thing to notice when examining a mineral under a microscope is its colour. As was mentioned previously, it depends upon the absorption of light by minerals. In isotropic minerals (ie those exhibiting identical physical properties in all crystallographic directions,

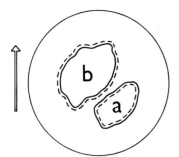

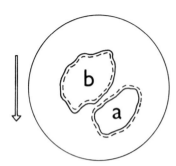

and including minerals of the cubic system and amorphous substances), light transmittance takes place in all directions with an identical speed; also the absorption of light is the same in all directions. Isotropic minerals therefore always have the same colour. In anisotropic minerals the absorption of light as well as colour depends upon the crystallographic directions. Therefore, the colour of mineral grains in the same specimen can differ greatly when seen in transmitted light in different directions. This property is called pleochroism.

In some minerals the change of colour may be seen by the naked eye, eg cordierite and tourmaline. In the majority of minerals, however, it is discernible only through a microscope. Under the microscope condenser place a polarizing filter, and put another piece of foil above the eyepiece so that the field of view is as dark as possible. If all fragments of the isotropic mineral remain dark in the viewing field, the mineral is amorphous (eg glass, amber, opal), or it belongs to the cubic system (eg garnet). If at least part of the fragment glistens in the dark field, the mineral is anisotropic. Sometimes the mineral fragment displays layers of different colour shades or alternating coloured and colourless zones. This is called colour zonation.

The refractive index is determined on a finely crushed sample of the mineral which is placed on the microscope slide. A drop of immersion liquid is added — the refractive index of the liquid should be near to the suspected value for the mineral. The microscope is stopped down as far as possible. As the microscope tube is raised a white ring appears along the border of the mineral grains (the so-called Becke's line) and tends to move into the higher refractive index medium. If the inspected mineral has a higher refractive index than the immersion liquid, the white ring disappears and forms a light point within the mineral grains. If the specimen includes some fluid bubbles of a lower refractive index than the liquid, the white ring adheres to the bubbles as the microscope tube is raised. A similar effect occurs in minerals with a lower refractive index than that of the liquid except that, when the microscope tube is raised, the line moves in the opposite direction (see Fig. 15).

Successive tests with different refractive index liquids enables an almost exact determination of the refractive index of the mineral. If the whole set of immersion liquids is not available, a mixture of two liquids can be used. Some immersion liquids are as follows: olive oil (refraction index n = 1.470), rape oil (n = 1.476), castor oil (n = 1.478), flax-seed oil (n = 1.486), benzene (n = 1.500), cedar oil (n = 1.505), ethylene bromide (n = 1.536), clove oil (n = 1.537), nitrobenzene (n = 1.554), cinnamon oil (n = 1.605) and acetylene tetrabromide (n = 1.636).

Luminescence

Some minerals exhibit luminescence. It is caused by the conversion of different forms of energy (mechanical, chemical, thermal or electromagnetic) into luminous energy. It occurs in a number of minerals in which the crystal lattices contain admixtures of foreign atoms (eg rare earths, Ag, Cr, Mn, S, $[UO_2]^{3+}$) which are called luminescent substances. On the other hand, luminescence does not exist if some other atoms are present in the crystal lattice (eg Fe, Ni); these are called luminescent screens. In minerals in which the luminescent substance is part of the crystal lattice, luminescence is a regular phenomenon (eg fluorite, scheelite, willemite, uranium minerals or zircon). As the content of these admixtured elements may vary in minerals from different localities, the luminescence is not constant (eg sphalerite, calcite, opal or topaz), and the phenomenon cannot therefore be considered a reliable clue for mineral identification in these cases.

Basically, there are the following types of luminescence: triboluminescence — induced by crushing or rubbing some minerals, such as fluorite, willemite, quartz. Thermoluminescence is the ability of some minerals to emit light after heating (eg fluorite and diamond). Photoluminescence may be seen on some minerals when they are exposed to light, or to invisible short- or long-wave ultraviolet radiation. If luminescence shows only while irradiation takes place (eg some fluorites, scheelite, sodalite), it is called fluorescence; if it persists for a time after irradiation has ceased, it is called phosphorescence (eg strontianite and diamond). Exposure to ultraviolet light induces luminescence from organic minerals and bitumens, and from all minerals containing them as inclusions (eg opals). Luminescence can best be observed when a mineral is irradiated by an ultraviolet lamp with a dark filter. Take care when using an ultraviolet lamp, as radiation can harm the eyes.

Minerals showing luminescence are marked with a symbol in the text. A list with their typical luminescence colour is given in the identification table on p. 490.

Magnetism

Strong magnetism is actually shown only by the mineral magnetite; to a lesser extent by pyrrhotite, hematite and wolframite. A large number of minerals are attracted to a strong magnet, particularly when they contain iron, manganese and nickel. Magnetism is shown also by some other minerals, such as cassiterite, when they contain submicroscopic particles of ferro-magnetic minerals. In mineralogy this property of minerals may be used in gravel and sand separation.

Electrical conductivity

In some instances electrical conductivity may be of help in identifying minerals. Conducting minerals can be distinguished from non-conducting minerals by a simple test. The specimen is placed on a zinc plate and immersed in a solution of copper sulphate. In minerals which are good electrical conductors a thin layer of Cu appears on their mineral surfaces at the points of contact with the zinc plate.

Radioactivity

Some minerals containing uranium, thorium and radium, such as torbernite and uraninite, show radioactive properties. They emit an invisible radiation (ie alpha, beta and gamma rays), and in this way give rise to numerous isotopes. A typical example of a radioactive mineral is uraninite UO_2, containing a certain portion of UO_3 and Pb. UO_3 is the product of oxidation and Pb of radioactive decay of UO_2.

The radioactive radiation affects photographic plates and substances showing luminescence. The radioactivity may be measured by a Geiger-Müller counter. Some minerals containing uranium and thorium are subject to metamictal decay; ie although the external crystal form remains unchanged, the internal structure of the crystal is damaged by radiation (eg allanite). These minerals gradually become opaque, then black, with glassy amorphous atomic structure. Their cleavages disappear, they show a greasy or resinous lustre, and their fractures become conchoidal. To a lesser extent minerals containing radioactive trace elements are radioactive, such as zircon, which forms an isomorphous mixture with thorite.

It is not advisable for amateurs to maintain collections of radioactive minerals without appropriate safety precautions.

Minerals exhibiting radioactivity are marked in the text with a symbol. A list is given in the identification table on p. 493.

Chemical properties

The chemical composition of minerals plays an important part in their classification. It is determined by chemical analysis. A simple technique, dry analysis, may be applied. It is applicable particularly to ore-bearing minerals because of its speed and simplicity, but is not always reliable. Wet analysis, on the other hand, gives very reliable results, but is very time-consuming and does require some special laboratory equipment.

Dry analysis methods include the following tests:

- determination of fusibility and flame colour;
- tube test: heating minerals in closed or open tubes;
- blowpipe tests: heating minerals on a charcoal block; and
- bead tests with borax powder.

For these chemical tests, a Bunsen (or Mecker) gas burner (see Fig. 16) is required. Also needed are glass tubes of a diameter of approx. 7 mm, a blowpipe, a piece of platinum wire, chemical forceps and the following reagents: charcoal, hydrochloric acid (HCl), 10%

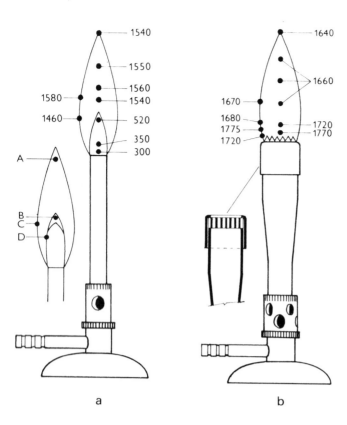

Fig. 16 Bunsen burner – a, and Mecker burner – b with temperatures of blowpipe flame in °C (A – flame for oxidizing beads, B – most effective reducing flame, C – most effective oxidizing flame, D – less effective reducing flame)

solution of cobalt nitrate $(Co(NO_3)_2)$, borax $(Na_2B_4O_7 . 10 H_2O)$, acidic sodium-ammonium phosphate, lime water and ammonia liquor.

To determine fusibility and flame colour: in these tests a thin sharp-edged sliver of the mineral is held by forceps directly in the dark part of a Bunsen burner flame. It should be noted whether it fuses easily, less easily, with difficulty (only thin edges), or not at all. To observe the colour of the flame, the surface of the specimen should be moistened with acid (HCl), and held in the dark flame (Table on p. 499–500). During these tests, contact of the forceps with the flame, (they may be soiled and can change its colour) should be avoided. Prior to the test, the specimen should not be touched with fingers as they may leave traces of rock salt on its surface, causing a yellow colouring of the flame by Na. The sample must be from a fresh mineral specimen as its outer surface might be contaminated.

Heating minerals in a closed tube: from a glass tube an 8 cm long piece is cut and heated until it forms a drop at one end. The tube is quickly drawn away from the flame, and shaped by blowing into a flask with a diameter of approx. 15 mm (see Fig. 17a). The specimen is inserted into the flask and heated slowly, gradually increasing the intensity of the flame. During this process observations can be made of the volatility, fusibility, spattering, changes of colour and luminescence. The specimen

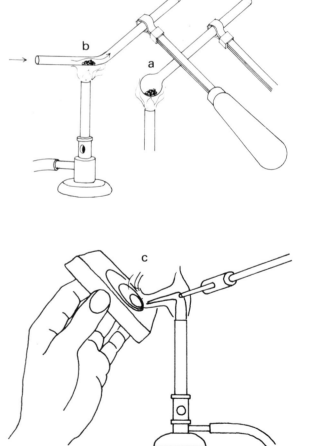

Fig. 17 Chemical tests in open – a, and closed – b tubes, and on a charcoal block – c

26

must be inserted in the flask carefully without touching its walls, because the sublimate forming on the walls during heating is an important diagnostical feature. Use each flask only once.

Heating powdered minerals in an open tube: a piece of glass tubing should be bent in the flame at approximately one third of its length, at an angle of ca. 30° (see Fig. 17b). The powdered mineral is inserted into the short end close to the bend and the specimen heated while held at a low angle. Air circulates through the open tube and oxidizes the mineral powder. Use only the minimum amount of mineral powder to carry out the test, and avoid clogging the tube and preventing air from circulating. Sublimates form in the top part of the tube.

Blowpipe tests: heating minerals on charcoal blocks. The small sample of the mineral is placed in a depression at one end of a charcoal block. The depression should not be so deep as to prevent the released fumes from striking its walls and escaping. Some water must be added to the powdered specimen to prevent it dispersing. Using a blowpipe, the flame of the gas burner is applied to the test specimen (see Fig. 17c). A charcoal block held above the specimen is used to capture the volatile substances. The test is carried out in the oxidizing flame (ie the tip of the blowpipe held in the flame) and in the reducing flame (ie the blowpipe held behind the flame). In the oxidizing flame the specimen is heated at the tip of the flame only where extra oxygen comes to it by air blown into the flame. In the reducing flame the whole specimen is put into the flame, whereby hot gases take oxygen from the specimen.

The sulphide reaction to charcoal (ie test for sulphur): mineral powder mixed with soda-ash in the ratio of 1 : 5, is heated in an oxidizing flame. The molten specimen is then placed on a silver plate or coin and 1–2 drops of water are added. If the specimen contains sulphur in any form, sodium sulphide forms in the course of heating and reacts with silver, giving rise to black silver sulphide (Se and Te react in the same way).

Reaction of the cobalt solution to charcoal: the test is carried out on minerals of light colour which do not fuse in the blowpipe flame. The specimen is heated prior to the test, then moistened with 2–3 drops of 10% cobalt nitrate solution, and heated again. During the test a change of colour by the specimen can be seen.

Bead tests: many oxides of metals when heated with borax flux or phosphoric salt dissolve in them and alter to a glassy substance of a characteristic colour. The borax flux or phosphoric salt is heated in a loop of platinum wire or a magnesium rod until a clear glassy bead is formed. The hot borax bead is touched onto a small quantity of the powdered mineral and is reheated in the oxidizing flame. During this test the colour of the bead is noted when hot and when cold (Table on p. 498).

Those with a microscope can complete the chemical identification methods by a microchemical reaction test. For this test a very small sample of the mineral is needed. It is dissolved and by means of a suitable flux a crystalline precipitate is produced and studied under the microscope. Certain elements may be identified by the characteristic form of its crystals and their optical features.

Other identification methods

For the exact identification of minerals, apart from other optical and chemical methods, X-ray analysis, differential thermal analysis, spectral analysis, infra-red spectroscopy, electron microprobe, scanning electron microscopy and energy dispersive X-ray analysis are applied in modern mineralogical laboratories.

However, these methods require complicated and expensive laboratory equipment, and trained staff.

To those collectors who are interested in specialized identification methods, a comprehensive literature list is recommended at the end of the book.

27

Basic collecting equipment

Before starting collecting minerals and their identification, it is necessary, apart from a theoretical preparation, to acquire basic equipment for mineral collectors.

The most useful tool in mineral collecting is a good geological hammer of medium size made of hard steel (approx. 900 gm). There are pointed hammers and hammers with sharp edges diagonal to the handle. To crush larger pieces of rock use a heavier, short hammer, but for the trimming of samples a small hammer. Apart from the hammer, at least two chisels of different sizes are needed which may be used for prising out minerals from the rock or for the initial trimming of the samples. Sometimes a field shovel or a pickaxe may be of use. An indispensable aid in field work is a lens, magnifying at least eight to ten times, by means of which characteristic features of minerals may be determined in situ, and the specimens selected for collection. Other indispensable aids are: a pocket knife for determining hardness, a piece of broad glass and a steel file; for determining streak colour, a plate of rough, hard porcelain; for determining carbonates, an unbreakable, hermetically-sealed bottle containing diluted hydrochloric acid (see Fig. 18).

Apart from these aids it is necessary to have a good geological map, a notebook, labels, pencils, newspaper, soft paper, cotton wool, and small cardboard boxes in which to place the brittle minerals, and some cement of the beeswax type. To transport minerals over long distances, it pays to have a good knapsack with a bamboo or steel supporting frame. Experience has shown that it is advisable for every mineral collector to carry a first-aid box in case of injury, protective spectacles and a helmet when collecting in dangerous places. The trimming of samples at home requires a small anvil or a steel plate, a hand vice, a pair of larger pincers, a set of preparation needles, a pair of forceps and for preparing specimens for optical and chemical tests a grinding mortar. Mineral specimens may be cleaned with different brushes; those soluble in water should be washed in kerosene or ethyl alcohol. For a precise determination of hardness a set of samples of the Mohs' Scale of Hardness, at least for the first 8 grades (which covers the hardness of the majority of minerals) is required. To determine

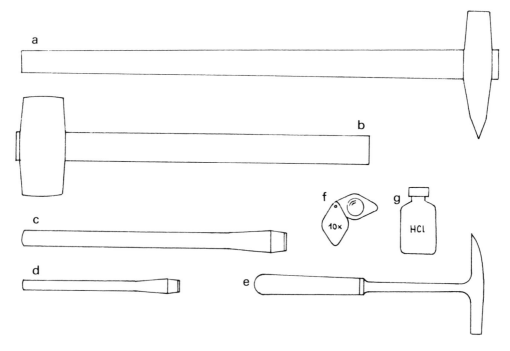

Fig. 18 Equipment for mineral collectors: geological hammer — a and e, mallet — b, chisel — c and d, lens — f, unbreakable bottle with diluted hydrochloric acid — g

28

specific gravity, optical and chemical properties, luminescence, electric conductivity and magnetism, the fundamental equipment should be supplemented with acids and chemicals mentioned earlier in the description of the testing methods.

Many minerals, especially precious stones, achieve their beauty when faceted or tumble-polished. This way of treating minerals has become very popular recently. There are many books and handbooks (for further reading, see page 513) describing in detail the art of treating minerals and precious stones. Precious stones mentioned in this book are marked with a symbol. Table on p. 501 gives a list and mode of treating.

When, where and how are minerals found?

Every collecting hobby requires a certain theoretical background, which may be acquired by studying the relevant literature, by advice from more experienced collectors or experts, and by viewing museum collections. By undertaking this preparation initial mistakes can be avoided which are due mostly to inexperience in searching, identifying and trimming minerals. Moreover, this practice provides valuable information about places to visit, becoming acquainted with minerals and the forms of their occurrence, and gaining a little knowledge of the character of the chosen locality which makes field work easier.

The time to visit individual localities is not of much importance; it depends above all on their character and location. In the course of time every collector will learn the most suitable time for collecting certain minerals. Localities where minerals might be found are dependent upon the geological structure of the area, ie on conditions favourable for the occurrence of associated minerals, and on exposures of the earth's crust either due to human activities or natural forces.

The most suitable localities for finding minerals are local stone quarries, abandoned shafts, mines, slag heaps, sand pits and clay fields, road and railway cuttings, tunnels, building excavations, melioration trenches, gas and oil pipeline trenches, natural exposures in mountain areas, rocky river and brook beds, rockbound lake and sea coasts, caves, erosion furrows originating after rain, and arable land. Minerals can be acquired from river beds by washing, and from coast sands by digging. Remember to ask local authorities for permission to enter an area and to collect minerals.

What the individual collects depends entirely upon his interest. The trimming of the specimens should be carried out directly in situ with regard to the required size and typical form. A uniform size allows an easier arrangement of specimens, adding much to the aesthetic aspect of the collection. Compact and crystalline minerals are usually trimmed in the shape of a rectangular. It is a good idea to take home smaller fragments of freshly broken minerals to study their physical, optical and chemical properties rather than remove crystals from better specimens. Some interesting fragments may be put aside for cutting. It is worthwhile collecting associated inconspicuous minerals because often they are frequently characteristic of a certain association of minerals, which may be a guide to the identification of the specimen. In situ, basic properties, such as hardness, colour, cleavage, morphology and solubility, should be determined if possible. All these data, together with a short description or a small sketch of the area should be put down in the notebook to facilitate work later. Every specimen should be provided with a provisional label bearing the name of the area, the name of the mineral, a short description of the actual place where it was found (ie quarry, erosion furrow, etc.), and the date of collection to prevent any subsequent confusion with the specimens. Each labelled specimen is then carefully wrapped up in newspaper. Fragile specimens, particularly those with delicate and brittle needle-shaped forms, should be transported in cardboard boxes embedded in crumpled soft paper or cotton wool.

Some minerals cannot be trimmed directly. Their trimming must be carried out at home by means of a hand vice, a pair of pincers, chisels and preparation needles. Mould, dust or secondary coatings are best removed by water. Minerals soluble in water, such as the nitrates, some hydroxides, carbonates, borates, sulphates, phosphates or arsenates are cleaned with fine brushes in kerosene or alcohol. Some coatings (ie carbonates) can be removed by different acids, such as acetic or hydrochloric acid. The black film typical of silver minerals can be removed with a diluted solution of NaCl. In places where no liquid can be applied, dust can simply be blown off by a stream of air. In modern laboratories some minerals are frequently cleaned in ultrasonic water baths. (The method recommended for cleaning individual minerals is given with their description.) Water-bearing minerals must never be exposed to excessive heat or direct sunshine to dry.

Minerals and their aggregates damaged during acquisition or trimming can be repaired by using glue or cement. Different pigments can be added to synthetic glues to achieve the required colour shade. When including such a specimen in a collection it is necessary to record the repair in the description of the mineral.

Specimens required for the determination of physical, optical and chemical properties must be chosen with great care. Only fresh, homogenous minerals without the admixture of other minerals should be used to avoid misleading measurements. Each specimen must be first thoroughly observed by means of a lens or a binocular microscope. Admixtures of foreign minerals and weathered parts must be separated out. The separation can be carried out mechanically, by means of a heavy liquid, or a magnet. Specimens for optical and chemical tests can be obtained by crushing or grinding in a mortar.

Plates

The ordinal number before the mineral name indicates the respective mineral in the Identification Tables.

The abbreviation **H** plus a number in the colour rectangle on the right side indicates the hardness of a group of minerals.

P = precious stone

L = luminescent mineral

R = radioactive mineral

31

Sulphur

Native element
S

1

P

Historical name

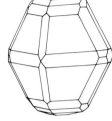

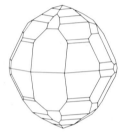

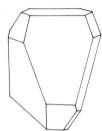

● Hardness: 1.5−2 (brittle) ● Streak: white, sometimes light yellow ● Colour: straw-yellow, honey-yellow, yellow-brown to yellow-green (according to admixture), whitish in loose crusts ● Transparency: translucent ● Lustre: adamantine on crystal faces, glimmering on fracture surfaces ● Cleavage: indistinct on (001) (110) and (111) ● Fracture: conchoidal, uneven ● Morphology: crystals, granular, earthy, reniform and powdery aggregates, deposits, stalactites ● Specific gravity: 2.05−2.08 ● Crystal system: orthorhombic at normal temperature, < 95.6 °C monoclinic: amorphous sulphurite ● Crystal form: bipyramidal, disphenoidal and coarsely tabular, sometimes in multi-planed crystals or twins ● Chemical composition: theoretically 100% S, admixtures: Se, Te, As and Tl ● Chemical properties: easily soluble in carbon disulphide, benzol, kerosene and concentrated nitric acid ● Handling: clean with water, HCl and H_2SO_4 ● Sulphur is very brittle, breaks easily when cleaned mechanically; crystals may crumble if held in a warm hand ● Similar minerals: in powder form − copiapite **(123)**, greenockite **(199)** and orpiment **(4)** ● Distinguishing features: low hardness, brittle, low melting point, easily inflammable: burns with a blue flame releasing a pungent gas, SO_2 ● Genesis: sedimentary rocks, by the action of organisms on solfataras and mofettas, as sublimation in hot springs, in oxidized zones of sulphide deposits ● Associated minerals: gypsum **(29)**, calcite **(217)**, dolomite **(218)**, strontianite **(222)**, celestite **(239)**, aragonite **(221)**, sal-ammoniac **(14)** ● Occurrence: common; in sedimentary deposits in Texas and Louisiana (USA), Tarnobrzeg region and Machów (Poland), Karakum Desert and Volgaland (Russia), Cádiz (Spain), Sicily (Italy). Sulphur of volcanic origin is found in Turkey, Mexico, Indonesia, Japan, Russia, Italy and Iceland. Sulphur found in oxidized zones of sulphatic deposits is unimportant − Urals (Russia), Kostajnik (Serbia) and Allchar (Macedonia). It also originates by sublimation in fires on coal tips or oil shales − California (USA). Perfect crystals have come from Sicily (Italy), (Poland) and (USA). Individual crystals have been found as large as 14×13×4 cm ● Application: in the production of sulphuric acid, chemical compounds, explosives, in paper, rubber and leather industries, agriculture.

Sulphur − aggregates of multi-faced crystals (the largest size 20 mm) in association with aragonite; Girgenti (Sicily, Italy)

Sulphur

Graphite (Plumbago, Black lead)

2

From the Greek *grafein* – to write

● Hardness: 1–1.5 ● Streak: dark steel-grey, glossy ● Colour: dark grey (crystals); black, steel-grey (aggregates) ● Transparency: opaque; in thin sections, translucent ● Lustre: shiny, metallic; in cryptocrystalline forms, dull ● Cleavage: perfect on (0001) ● Other features of cohesion: flexible but inelastic, sectile ● Morphology: crystals are rare; lamellar, scaly, spherical aggregates, earthy infillings ● Other properties: greasy feel ● Specific gravity: 2.25 (alternating due to impurities) ● Crystal system: hexagonal ● Crystal form: hexagonal plates; twinning is rare ● Electrical conductivity: good ● Chemical composition: theoretically 100% C, admixtures: N, H, CO_2, CH_4, SiO_2, Al_2O_3, etc ● Chemical properties: insoluble in acids, but reacts with HNO_3 when boiled ● Handling: clean with acids, water. Graphite is brittle when cleaned mechanically ● Similar minerals: molybdenite **(8)**, manganese minerals ● Distinguishing features: the streak of blue molybdenite is greenish. Graphite has a dull lustre and lower hardness, is infusible, acid-proof, good electrical conductor. Manganese minerals are never flocculent, soft or feel greasy ● Genesis: magmatic (pegmatites), a high-temperature metamorphic mineral ● Associated minerals: pyrite **(436)**, calcite **(217)**, marcasite **(437)** ● Occurrence: common; Clay region in Alabama (USA); Harz (FRG); Botogol deposit (Russia); metamorphic deposits are found near Passau (FRG), (Madagascar), southern Bohemia (Czech Republic); vein deposits are in (Sri Lanka), Quebec (Canada); crystalline forms occur in the pegmatites in (Sri Lanka) ● Application: metallurgy, in electrical industries, nuclear technology especially in reactors, manufacture of lubricants and lead pencils; artificially produced for engineering purposes.

Mercury (Quicksilver)

3

From the Arabic

● Hardness: liquid at normal temperature ● Colour: tin-white, grey-white ● Lustre: metallic ● Morphology: liquid drops ● Specific gravity: at normal temperature 13.6 ● Crystal system: trigonal (at −38.87 °C) ● Crystal form: rhombohedron ● Chemical composition: theoretically 100% Hg, admixtures Au, Ag ● Chemical properties: soluble in HNO_3, evaporates at normal temperature ● Handling: owing to its volatility, it should be kept in sealed bottles ● Genesis: hydrothermal, oxidized zones ● Associated minerals: cinnabar **(76)**, silver amalgam **(179)**, siderite **(306)** ● Occurrence: rare; Idria (Slovenia), Moschellandsberg (FRG), Almaden (Spain), Monte Amiata (Italy), Juan Cavelica (Peru), (USA) ● Application: chemistry, measuring instruments, electrical engineering, ore-working industry (extraction of Au).

---

1. **Graphite** – scaly aggregate from graphite deposits in Sri Lanka (width of field 80 mm) 2. **Mercury** – drops with metallic lustre (up to 2 mm) on cinnabar; Idria (Slovenia)

Graphite, mercury

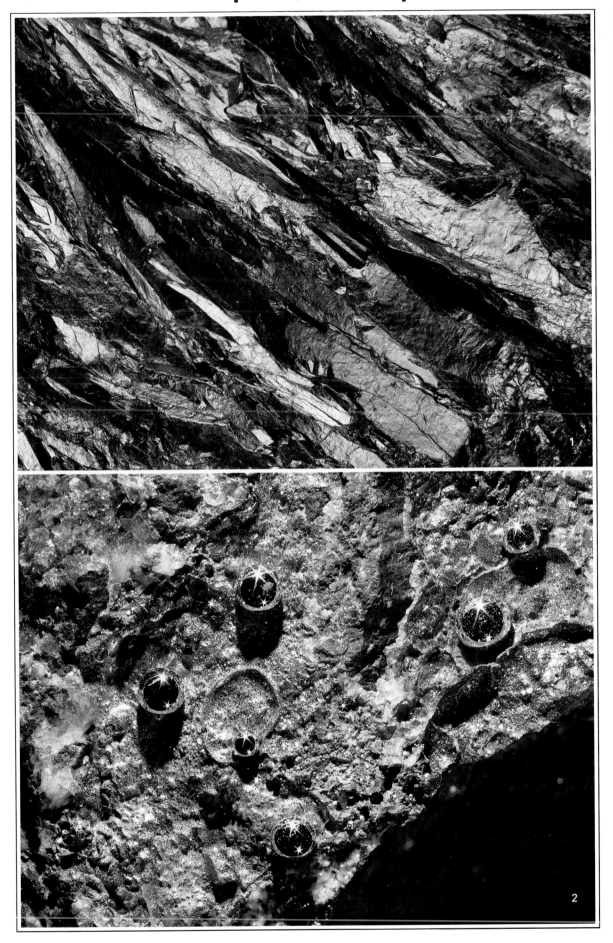

Orpiment

4

P

From the Latin *aurum* – gold and *pigmentum* – pigment (Agricola 1546)

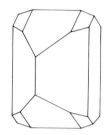

● Hardness: 1.5–2 ● Streak: light yellow ● Colour: gold-yellow, orange-yellow to brown ● Transparency: in thin, transparent lamellae ● Lustre: greasy, but pearly on fracture surfaces ● Cleavage: perfect on (010); lamellae partially flexible ● Morphology: crystals; lamellar aggregates; crusts; earthy, reniform and powdery aggregates ● Specific gravity: 3.48 ● Crystal system: monoclinic ● Crystal form: short prisms with uneven faces, twinning ● Chemical composition: As 60.91%, S 39.09%, admixtures Hg, Ge ● Chemical properties: soluble in KOH; easily fusible producing vapour with garlicky odour ● Handling: clean with water, HCl; oxidizes in the air; deadly poisonous ● Similar minerals: sulphur (1), greenockite (199) ● Distinguishing features: perfect cleavage, pearly lustre on fracture surfaces, fibrous and lamellar aggregates, higher hardness than in S ● Genesis: low-temperature; from hot springs, also secondary sulphide ● Associated minerals; realgar (5), cinnabar (76), stibnite (51) ● Occurrence: rare; Ratcha (Russia), Luchumi – Caucasus (Georgia), Allchar deposit (Macedonia), Mercur – Utah (USA), Juan Cavelica (Peru); large crystals (up to 60 cm and 30 kg) are found in Minkyule – Yakutia (Russia), St. Andreasberg – Harz (FRG), Imfeld and Binnental (Switzerland) ● Application: As ore (extraction of As), in dyes and paints, as decorative stone (Russia).

Realgar

5

From the Arabic *Rahj al ghár* – ore powder (Wallerius 1747)

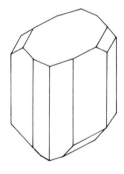

● Hardness: 1.5 ● Streak: orange-red to orange-yellow ● Colour: brown-red, orange-red ● Transparency: translucent to non-transparent ● Lustre: adamantine, greasy ● Cleavage: perfect on (010) ● Fracture: conchoidal ● Morphology: crystals, compact and finely granular aggregates, pulverulent, earthy or cakey crusts ● Specific gravity: 3.5 ● Crystal system: monoclinic ● Crystal form: prisms, often striated ● Chemical composition: As 70.08%, S 29.92% ● Chemical properties: partly soluble in acids and KOH; easily fusible releasing poisonous fumes with garlicky odour ● Handling: clean with water. In the presence of light it becomes yellow and crumbles, so keep in dark ● Similar minerals: crocoite (133), cinnabar (76), cuprite (209) ● Distinguishing features: low hardness, striation of prism faces, streak colour ● Genesis: hydrothermal; from hot springs, secondary ● Associated minerals: orpiment (4), cinnabar (76), stibnite (51), ores of As, Ag, Au ● Occurrence: rare; Allchar (Macedonia), Cavnic (Romania), Binnental (Switzerland), Luchumi – Caucasus – crystals up to 1.5 cm (Georgia), Getchell Mine – Nevada (USA) ● Application: ore (extraction of As), glass industry, medieval medicine.

---

1. Orpiment – fan-shaped aggregates of short, columnar crystals (up to 7 mm); Luchumi – Caucasus (Georgia). **2. Realgar** – idiomorphic crystal (3 mm) on calcite; Tajov (Slovakia)

Orpiment, realgar

Covelline (Indigo copper)

Sulphide
CuS

6

Named after the Italian mineralogist N. Covelli (1790–1829)
(Beudant 1832)

● Hardness: 1.5–2 (brittle) ● Streak: grey to black, dark blue when rubbed ● Colour: indigo blue, blue-violet ● Transparency: opaque ● Lustre: dull to resinous ● Cleavage: perfect on (0001) ● Other properties of cohesion: flexible lamellae, fragile ● Morphology: usually compact granular aggregates, coatings and pseudomorphs; crystals are rare ● Specific gravity: 4.68 ● Crystal system: hexagonal ● Crystal form: hexagonal plates ● Electrical conductivity: good ● Chemical composition: Cu 66.48%, S 33.52%, admixtures Fe, Se, Ag, Pb ● Chemical properties: soluble in hot HNO_3, fusible, thin plates burn with blue flame releasing SO_2 ● Handling: clean with water or by mechanical means ● Similar minerals: bornite (192), chalcocite (68) ● Distinguishing features: bright blue colour, low hardness, cleavage; in water turns violet immediately, when dry turns blue again ● Genesis: cementation zones of sulphidic deposits, hydrothermal ● Associated minerals: bornite (192), chalcocite (68), chalcopyrite (185), pyrite (436), enargite (187) ● Occurrence: frequent; hydrothermal covelline is found in Butte – Montana – fine crystals (USA), Tsumeb (Namibia), Bor (Yugoslavia), Baiţa (Romania), in Mansfeld copper-bearing shales (FRG), Badenweiler – Schwarzwald (FRG), in large masses in (Chile) and (Bolivia) ● Application: copper ore.

Kermesite (Red antimony, Pyrantimonite)

Sulphide
Sb_2S_2O

7

From the Persian *qurmizq* – dark red
(Chapman 1843)

● Hardness: 1–1.5 ● Streak: brown-red, orange after rubbing ● Colour: cherry-red, turning darker in time ● Transparency: translucent in fine needles ● Lustre: adamantine to submetallic ● Cleavage: perfect on (001) ● Morphology: crystals, fibrous and acicular aggregates, crusts, deposits ● Specific gravity: 4.7 ● Crystal system: triclinic ● Crystal form: long prisms with longitudinal striation ● Chemical composition: Sb 74.96%, S 20.04%, O 5.0% ● Chemical properties: soluble in HNO_3, when heated with blowpipe on charcoal forms sublimates of Sb_2O_3 ● Handling: clean with water, HCl; brittle; breaks easily ● Similar minerals: realgar (5), cinnabar (76) ● Distinctive features: streak colour, specific gravity ● Genesis: hydrothermal, secondary sulphide ● Associated minerals: stibnite (51), senarmontite (93), valentinite (94), stibiconite (292) ● Occurrence: rare; Bräunsdorf near Freiberg (FRG), Pereta – Tuscany (Italy), Djebel Hamimat (Algeria), Kadamdja (Kirgizia). Radiated drusses of 15 cm have been found at Pernek (Slovakia).

---

1. **Covellite** – granular aggregate from oxidation zone of ore veins (width of field 40 mm); Železník (Slovakia)
2. **Kermesite** – radiating fibrous aggregate in quartz (size of needles 12 mm); Bräunsdorf near Freiburg (Saxony, FRG)

Covelline, kermesite

Molybdenite (Molybdic ochre)

8

From the Greek
molybdos – lead
(Hielm 1782)

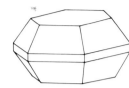

● Hardness: 1–1.5 ● Streak: blue-grey to green ● Colour: blue-grey, violet tint ● Transparency: opaque ● Lustre: metallic ● Cleavage: perfect on (0001) ● Other features of cohesion: flexible, inelastic laminae ● Morphology: scales, lamellar aggregates; crystals are rare ● Other properties: greasy feel ● Specific gravity: 4.7–4.8 ● Crystal system: hexagonal ● Crystal form: tabular ● Chemical composition: Mo 59.94%, S 40.06%; admixtures Re, Ag, Au ● Chemical properties: fusion difficult; slightly soluble in acids ● Handling: clean with water; easily wears off; soft ● Similar minerals: graphite **(2)**, specularite **(473)** ● Distinguishing features: graphite has a different streak and lustre and is a good electrical conductor; specularite has a different streak and hardness ● Genesis: magmatic, in pegmatites; hydrothermal; metasomatic ● Associated minerals: cassiterite **(548)**, wolframite **(369)**, scheelite **(310)**, quartz **(534)**, bismutite **(71)**, arsenopyrite **(344)** ● Occurrence: rare; in pegmatites with cassiterite and wolframite in Stavanger (Norway), in the Urals (Russia), in Bayerischer Wald (FRG); molybdenite crystals found in Edison – New Jersey (USA) and in Wakefield – Quebec (Canada); hydrothermal molybdenite found in Questa – New Mexico, Climax – Colorado and Bingham – Utah (USA); large plates in New South Wales (Australia); in scheelite scarns in Tyrny-Auz (Dagestan) and Azegour (Morocco); pneumatolytic molybdenite in Ore Mountains (FRG) and (Czech Republic); Cananea (Mexico) ● Application: manufacture of special steels, electronic, chemical industry.

Polybasite

9

From the Greek *poly*
– much and *basis* –
a base
(Rose 1829)

● Hardness: 1.5–2 ● Streak: black with reddish tint ● Colour: steel black ● Transparency: non-transparent, thin sections show dark red translucence ● Lustre: metallic, adamantine or glimmering ● Cleavage: poor on (001) ● Fracture: uneven ● Morphology: crystals, crusts, granular compact aggregates ● Specific gravity: 6–6.2 ● Crystal system: monoclinic ● Crystal form: pseudohexagonal plates showing characteristic triangular striations, twinning rare ● Chemical composition ● Cu 4.10%, Ag 69.47%, Sb 10.82%, S 15.61%; admixtures: As, Fe ● Chemical properties: easily fusible; soluble in HNO$_3$ ● Handling: clean with water ● Similar minerals: acanthite **(75)**, stephanite **(67)** ● Distinguishing features: hardness; crystal form ● Genesis: hydrothermal ● Associated minerals: acanthite, silver **(49)**, stephanite, pyrargyrite **(64)** ● Occurrence: rare; Freiberg, St. Andreasberg (FRG), Příbram (Czech Republic), (Chile), (Mexico), (USA) and (Russia) ● Application: silver ore.

---

1. Molybdenite – platy crystal (18 mm) embayed in quartz; Altenberg (FRG) **2. Polybasite** – black-grey plates (8 mm) in cavity of quartz-carbonate vein; Banská Štiavnica (Slovakia)

Molybdenite, polybasite

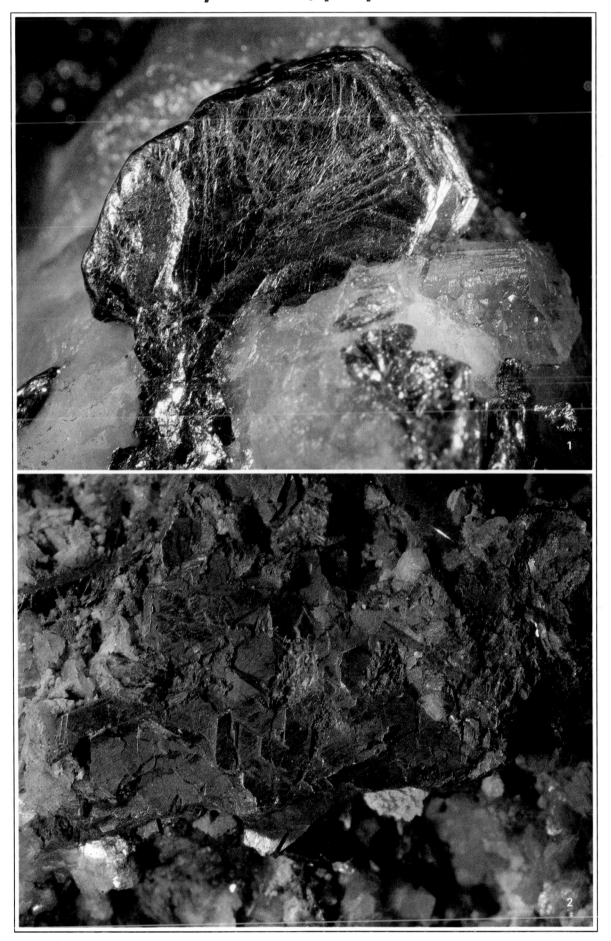

Tetradymite

Sulphide
Bi$_2$Te$_2$S

10

From the Greek
tetradymos – fourfold
(Haidinger 1831)

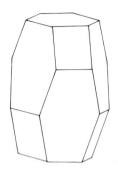

● Hardness: 1.5–2 ● Streak: steel-grey ● Colour: steel-grey to yellowish ● Transparency: opaque ● Lustre: metallic ● Cleavage: perfect on (0001) ● Other features of cohesion: flexible laminae ● Morphology: crystals, laminae, granular ● Specific gravity: 7.2–7.9 ● Crystal system: trigonal ● Crystal form: rhombohedron, twinning ● Chemical composition: Bi 59.27%, S 4.55%, Te 36.18%; admixtures: Se, Au, Cu and Pb ● Chemical properties: soluble in HNO$_3$ and H$_2$SO$_4$ ● Handling: clean with water ● Similar minerals: nagyagite **(11)** ● Distinguishing features: *see* nagyagite ● Genesis: hydrothermal ● Associated minerals: bismutite **(71)**, gold **(50)**, pyrite **(436)** ● Occurrence: rare; Ciclova (Romania), (USA), (Japan) ● Application: Te and Bi ore.

Nagyagite (Black tellurium)

Sulphide
Au(PbSbFe)$_8$(TeS)$_{11}$

11

Named after the deposit
Nagyág (now
Săcărâmb), Romania
(Haidinger 1845)

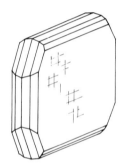

● Hardness: 1–1.5 ● Streak: grey-black ● Colour: dark lead-grey ● Transparency: opaque ● Lustre: metallic ● Cleavage: perfect on (010) ● Fracture: jagged ● Other features of cohesion: flexible laminae ● Morphology: crystals (rare), scaly, granular ● Specific gravity: 7.5 ● Crystal system: tetragonal ● Crystal form: plates; twinning ● Chemical composition: variable ● Chemical properties: readily fusible, soluble in HNO$_3$ ● Handling: clean with water ● Similar minerals: tetradymite **(10)** ● Distinguishing features: streak; test for Pb ● Genesis: hydrothermal ● Associated minerals: gold **(50)**, krennerite **(81)**, altaite **(78)** ● Occurrence: rare; Săcărâmb (Romania), Cripple Creek (USA) ● Application: Au ore.

Sylvanite

Sulphide
AgAuTe$_4$

12

Named after Transyl-
vania
(Necker 1835)

● Hardness: 1.5–2 ● Streak: steel-grey ● Colour: silver-white with yellowish tint ● Transparency: opaque ● Lustre: metallic ● Cleavage: perfect on (010) ● Morphology: crystals resembling hieroglyphs, skeletal, dendritic, granular ● Specific gravity: 8.2 ● Crystal system: monoclinic ● Crystal form: short prisms, coarse plates, twinning ● Chemical composition: Ag 13.22%, Au 24.19%, Te 62.59%; admixtures Sb, Pb, Cu ● Chemical properties: readily fusible, soluble in acids ● Handling: clean with water ● Similar minerals: krennerite **(81)** ● Distinguishing features: typical crystal form, chemical composition ● Genesis: hydrothermal ● Associated minerals: krennerite, petzite **(82)**, calaverite **(83)** ● Occurrence: rare; Săcărâmb, Baia de Aries (Romania), Kalgoorlie (Australia), Calaveras Co. (USA) ● Application: Au, Ag, Te ore.

---

1. **Tetradymite** – crystalline aggregate (crystals up to 3 mm) on andesite tuff; Župkov (Slovakia) 2. **Nagyagite** – lamellar crystals (up to 30 mm) in quartz; Săcărâmb (Romania) 3. **Sylvanite** – silver-white shining skeletal crystals (up to 5 mm) in fissure in quartz; Săcărâmb (Romania)

Tetradymite, nagyagite, sylvanite

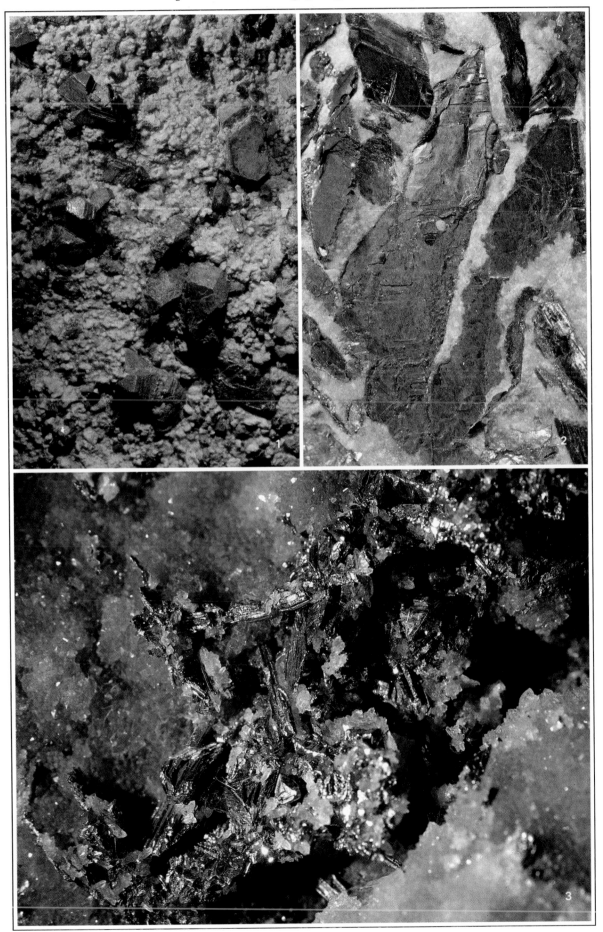

Hessite (Telluric silver)

Sulphide
Ag$_2$Te

13

Named after the Swiss chemist G. H. Hesse (1802–1850) (Fröbel 1843)

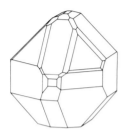

● Hardness: 1.5–2 ● Streak: light grey, glossy ● Colour: lead-grey, steel-grey, bluish to blackish tarnish ● Transparency: opaque ● Lustre: metallic ● Cleavage: imperfect on (100) ● Fracture: uneven ● Other properties of cohesion: cut with a knife ● Morphology: crystals, finely granular, compact ● Specific gravity: 8.4 ● Crystal system: monoclinic, > 155 °C cubic ● Crystal form: isometric, pseudocubic, often deformed ● Chemical composition: Ag 62.86%, Te 37.14%; admixtures: Au ● Chemical properties: soluble in HNO$_3$ and H$_2$SO$_4$, forming a raspberry-coloured solution; fusible, colouring a flame light green ● Similar minerals: acanthite **(75)** ● Distinguishing features: lighter colour, higher specific gravity ● Handling: clean with water ● Genesis: hydrothermal ● Associated minerals: gold **(50)**, nagyagite **(11)**, sylvanite **(12)** ● Occurrence: rare; Boteş (Romania), Zavodinsk — compact masses up to 200 kg (Russia), San Sebastian (Mexico), Coquimbo (Chile), Red Cloud (Colorado) and Calaveras Co. (California) (both in the USA) ● Application: rarely Ag and Te ore.

Sal-ammoniac (Salmiak)

Halide
NH$_4$Cl

14

Name from the original *salamoniarum* – Amon's salt (Agricola 1546)

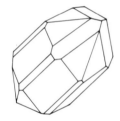

● Hardness: 1–2 ● Streak: white ● Colour: colourless, white, yellow, reddish ● Transparency: transparent ● Lustre: vitreous ● Cleavage: poor on (111) ● Morphology: multi-planed crystals, powdery, deposits, crusts, fanlike aggregates ● Other properties: soluble in water, tastes salty ● Specific gravity: 1.53 ● Crystal system: cubic ● Crystal form: tetragon-trioctahedron, rhombododecahedron ● Chemical composition: NH$_4$ 33.72%, Cl 66.28% ● Chemical properties: when heated with soda ash and acids it changes into ammonia, its characteristic odour ● Similar minerals: sylvite **(85)**, halite **(86)** ● Distinguishing features: gives off ammonia when heated with acids ● Genesis: volcanic activity, guano deposits, in fires on coal tips ● Associated minerals: sulphur **(1)**, halite **(86)** ● Occurrence: local; Vesuvius, Etna (Italy), Duttweiler, Oberhausen (FRG).

Calomel (Horn quicksilver)

Halide
HgCl

15

L

From the Greek *kalós* – beautiful and *mélas* – black (Werner 1789)

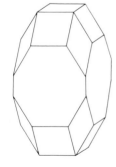

● Hardness: 1–2 ● Streak: white ● Colour: white, yellow-grey, grey, turns darker in air ● Transparency: transparent to translucent ● Lustre: adamantine ● Cleavage: poor on (100) and (011) ● Morphology: multi-planed crystals, crusts, earthy masses, bundle-shaped twins ● Specific gravity: 6.4–6.5 ● Crystal system: tetragonal ● Crystal form: prismatic, dipyramidal, platy, twinning (101) ● Luminescence: sometimes orange, rose or red ● Chemical composition: Hg 84.98%, Cl 15.02% ● Chemical properties: with KOH turns black, practically insoluble in acids, in tube tests forms sublimates ● Handling: clean with water ● Genesis: secondary ● Associated minerals: mercury **(3)**, cinnabar **(76)** ● Occurrence: rare; with cinnabar in Moschellandsberg (FRG), Almaden (Spain), Terlingua deposit – Texas (USA), (Mexico) and (Russia) ● Application: Hg ore.

---

1. Hessite – crystalline aggregate on quartz; Botesti (Romania – width of field 16 mm) **2. Sal-ammoniac** – aggregation of crystals from pile of a coal mine; Kladno (Czech Republic – width of field 15 mm) **3. Calomel** – brown-black crystals (up to 7 mm) in a cavity; Terlingua (USA)

Hessite, sal-ammoniac, calomel

Chlorargyrite (Horn silver)

Halide
AgCl

16

Named after its chemical composition (Weissbach 1875)

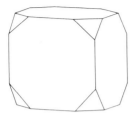

● Hardness: 1.5 ● Streak: white, glossy ● Colour: grey, yellowish, brownish to black ● Transparency: opaque ● Lustre: resinous, adamantine, dull ● Cleavage: absent ● Fracture: uneven ● Other properties of cohesion: plastic ● Morphology: crusts, deposits, waxy, granular, crystals ● Specific gravity: 5.5–5.6 ● Crystal system: cubic ● Crystal form: hexahedron, hexoctahedron, twinning ● Chemical composition: Ag 75.26%, Cl 24.74% ● Chemical properties: soluble in NH_4OH, readily fusible producing Ag ● Handling: clean with water; should be kept in darkness, turns dark when exposed ● Genesis: oxidation zones in arid areas ● Associated minerals: limonite **(355)**, acanthite **(75)**, bromargyrite, embolite ● Occurrence: rare; Johanngeorgenstadt (FRG), Dernbach (FRG), Leadvill and Treasury Hill – crystallic blocks (USA), Broken Hill – New South Wales (Australia), (Chile) ● Application: Ag ore.

Iodargyrite (Iodyrite)

Halide
AgI

17

Named after its chemical composition (Rammelsberg 1860)

● Hardness: 1–1.5 ● Streak: yellow, glossy ● Colour: yellow, yellow-green ● Transparency: transparent ● Lustre: greasy to adamantine ● Cleavage: perfect on (0001) ● Other properties of cohesion: flexible ● Morphology: crystals, scales, powdered ● Specific gravity: 5.7 ● Crystal system: hexagonal ● Crystal form: prismatic, platy, barrel-shaped ● Chemical composition: Ag 45.95%, I 54.05% ● Chemical properties: soluble in hot HNO_3 and H_2SO_4 ● Handling: clean in distilled water, should be kept in darkness ● Similar minerals: chlorargyrite **(16)**, bromargyrite ● Distinguishing features: perfect cleavage ● Genesis: secondary ● Associated minerals: limonite **(355)**, chlorargyrite, vanadinite **(263)**, descloizite **(260)** ● Occurrence: rare; Dernbach (FRG), (Chile), (Mexico), Broken Hill (New South Wales, Australia) ● Application: Ag ore.

Sassolite

Hydrated oxide
$B(OH)_3$

18

L

Named after Sasso in Italy (Karsten 1800)

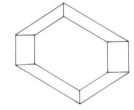

● Hardness: 1 ● Streak: white ● Colour: colourless, white, grey ● Transparency: transparent ● Lustre: vitreous, pearly ● Cleavage: perfect on (001) ● Other properties of cohesion: flexible ● Morphology: scales, crystals, coatings ● Other properties: soluble in hot water, greasy feel, bitter taste ● Specific gravity: 1.45 ● Crystal system: triclinic ● Crystal form: plates ● Luminescence: sometimes blue ● Chemical composition: B_2O_3 56.5%, H_2O 43.5% ● Chemical properties: produces water when heated in a flask, readily fusible, colours a flame green ● Handling: clean with alcohol ● Genesis: volcanic, hot springs ● Associated minerals: sulphur **(1)**, borates ● Occurrence: rare; Vulcano Island and Sasso (Italy), volcano Avchinskaya in Kamchatka (Russia), Wiesbaden region (FRG) ● Application: chemical, glass and food industries, and medicine.

---

1. Chlorargyrite – aggregation of yellowish crystals (the largest size 4 mm) from the oxidation zone of deposit; Leadville (USA) **2. Iodargyrite** – yellow-green aggregate of platy crystals from the oxidation zone of deposit; Broken Hill (Australia – width of field 20 mm) **3. Sassolite** – crystalline aggregate of platy crystals; Vulcano Island (Italy – width of field 32 mm)

Chlorargyrite, iodargyrite, sassolite

Ulexite

Borate
NaCa[B$_5$O$_6$(OH)$_6$] . 5 H$_2$O

19

L

P

Named after the German chemist G.L.Ulex (1811–1883) (Dana 1850)

● Hardness: 1 (brittle) ● Streak: white ● Colour: colourless, white ● Transparency: transparent ● Lustre: vitreous, silky in fibres ● Cleavage: perfect on (010) ● Morphology: fibrous and radiating aggregates ● Other properties: slightly soluble in hot water ● Specific gravity: 2.0 ● Crystal system: triclinic ● Crystal form: plates, fine needles ● Luminescence: white ● Chemical composition: Na$_2$O 7.7%, CaO 13.8%, B$_2$O$_3$ 43.0%, H$_2$O 35.5% ● Chemical properties: swells when heated, then fuses quickly, colours a flame yellow ● Handling: clean with cold water ● Similar minerals: colemanite **(301)**, inyoite **(100)**, hydroboracite ● Distinguishing features: crystal forms, hardness ● Genesis: borax lakes ● Associated minerals: borax **(97)**, colemanite, inyoite ● Occurrence: rare; borax lakes in Columbus Marsh (USA) ● Application: chemical industry, used as gemstone.

Natron

Carbonate
Na$_2$CO$_3$. 10 H$_2$0

20

Named from *natron* – soda (Wallerius 1747)

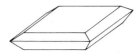

● Hardness: 1–1.5 ● Streak: white ● Colour: colourless, white, grey ● Transparency: translucent ● Lustre: vitreous ● Cleavage: very good on (100) ● Morphology: crystals, crusts, efflorescences ● Other properties: readily soluble in water, alkaline taste ● Specific gravity: 1.42–1.47 ● Crystal system: monoclinic ● Crystal form: tabular or platy ● Chemical composition : Na$_2$O 21.6%, CO$_2$ 15.4%, H$_2$O 63.0% ● Chemical properties: absorbs water, dehydrates readily when heated, colours a flame yellow ● Handling: clean with alcohol, preserve in plastic bags ● Similar minerals: mirabilite **(23)**, epsomite **(111)**, thenardite **(125)** ● Distinguishing features: dissolves effervescently in HCl ● Genesis: soda lakes ● Associated minerals: thermonatrite, mirabilite, trona **(102)** ● Occurrence: common ● Application: chemical industry.

Nitratite (Nitronatrite)

Nitrate
NaNO$_3$

21

Named after its chemical composition (Glocker 1847)

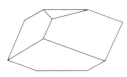

● Hardness: 1.5–2 ● Streak: white ● Colour: white, grey, red-brown, lemon-yellow ● Transparency: translucent ● Lustre: vitreous to dull ● Cleavage: perfect on (1011) ● Fracture: conchoidal ● Morphology: crystals, masses, efflorescences ● Other properties: soluble in water, sweetish, cool to the touch ● Specific gravity: 2.2–2.3 ● Crystal system: trigonal ● Crystal form: rhombohedron ● Chemical composition: Na$_2$O 36.5%, N$_2$O$_5$ 63.5% ● Chemical properties: fuses readily, tinges a flame yellow, slightly hygroscopic ● Genesis: sedimentary ● Associated minerals: gypsum **(29)**, mirabilite **(23)**, halite **(86)** ● Occurrence: rare; (Chile), (Russia) ● Application: fertilizers, metallurgy, food industry.

Stichtite

Carbonate
Mg$_6$Cr$_2$OH$_{16}$CO$_3$. 4 H$_2$O

22

P

Named after Robert Sticht, director of a mining corporation (Petterd 1910)

● Hardness: 1.5–2 ● Streak: white to violet ● Colour: pale violet ● Transparency: translucent ● Lustre: vitreous ● Cleavage: perfect on (0001) ● Morphology: scales, compact, fibrous, nodules ● Specific gravity: 2.2 ● Crystal system: trigonal ● Crystal form: plates, scales ● Chemical composition: MgO 36.98%, Cr$_2$O$_3$ 23.24%, CO$_2$ 6.73%, H$_2$O 33.05% ● Handling: clean with water ● Genesis: secondary ● Associated minerals: chromite **(371)**, serpentine **(273)** ● Occurrence: rare; (South Africa), (Tasmania).

---

1. **Ulexite** – radiating-fibrous aggregate; Bandirma (Turkey) 2. **Natron** – grey-brown porous aggregate; Chile (width of field 68 mm) 3. **Stichtite** – massive light violet occupying chamber in serpentinite; Barberton (RSA – width of field 42 mm)

Ulexite, natron, stichtite

Mirabilite (Glauber salt)

Sulphate
Na$_2$SO$_4$. 10 H$_2$O

L

Named after *sal mirabile Glauberi* – Glauber salt (Haidinger 1845)

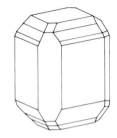

● Hardness: 1.5 ● Streak: white ● Colour: colourless, white, yellowish, greenish ● Transparency: transparent to translucent ● Lustre: vitreous to dull ● Cleavage: perfect on (100) ● Fracture: conchoidal ● Morphology: crystals, efflorescent crusts, granular, deposits ● Other properties: readily soluble in water, bitter, salty taste ● Specific gravity: 1.49 ● Crystal system: monoclinic ● Crystal form: short prisms ● Luminescence: white ● Chemical composition: Na$_2$O 19.3%, SO$_3$ 24.8%, H$_2$O 55.9% ● Chemical properties: soluble in acids, tinges a flame yellow ● Handling: clean with alcohol, preserve in plastic bags; when exposed to air it dehydrates and crumbles to white powder ● Similar minerals: natron (20) ● Distinguishing features: bitter, salty taste; in HCl no CO$_2$ is produced as in natron ● Genesis: salt lakes and ocean salt deposits ● Associated minerals: gypsum (29), halite (86), thenardite (125) ● Occurrence: local; salt deposits in Ischl, Hallstatt (Austria), (Egypt), Karabogaz Gulf in Caspian Sea (Turkmenistan) ● Application: production of soda, glass, dye and paint industries.

Tschermigite (Ammonium alum)

Sulphate
NH$_4$Al[SO$_4$]$_2$. 12 H$_2$O

24

Named after the locality Čermníky (Czech Republic) (Kobell 1853)

● Hardness : 1.5 ● Streak: white ● Colour: colourless, white ● Lustre: vitreous ● Cleavage: indistinct ● Fracture: conchoidal ● Morphology: crystals, fibrous aggregates ● Other properties: soluble in water ● Specific gravity: 1.65 ● Crystal system: cubic ● Crystal form: plates, needles, octahedrons ● Chemical composition: (NH$_4$)$_2$O 5.75%, Al$_2$O$_3$ 11.24%, SO$_3$ 35.32%, H$_2$O 47.69% ● Chemical properties: fuses in a flame, releasing ammonia ● Handling: clean with alcohol ● Similar minerals: mirabilite (23) ● Distinguishing features: cleavage ● Genesis: secondary in coal deposits and fumaroles ● Associated minerals: gypsum (29), clayey minerals ● Occurrence: rare; Čermníky (Czech Republic), Tokod (Hungary), Wackersdorf, Oberhausen (FRG).

Aluminite

Sulphate
Al$_2$(SO$_4$)(OH)$_4$. 7 H$_2$O

25

L

Named after its chemical composition (Haberle 1807)

● Hardness: 1 ● Streak: white ● Colour: white ● Transparency: translucent ● Lustre: dull ● Fracture: earthy ● Other properties of cohesion: sectile ● Morphology: mammillary and botryoidal nodules and powdered aggregates ● Other properties: clings to the tongue ● Specific gravity: 1.7 ● Crystal system: monoclinic ● Crystal form: needles ● Luminescence: sometimes white ● Chemical composition: Al$_2$O$_3$ 29.6%, SO$_3$ 23.3%, H$_2$O 47.1% ● Chemical properties: hygroscopic, when heated loses water, soluble in HCl ● Handling: clean with distilled water, preserve in plastic bags ● Similar minerals: alunogen (26) ● Distinguishing features: alunogen is soluble in water ● Genesis: secondary ● Associated minerals: alunogen, kaolinite (38), epsomite (111) ● Occurrence: rare; Halle (FRG), Newhaven and Brighton (Great Britain), Salt Range (Pakistan).

---

1. **Aluminite** – botryoidal nodular aggregate; Halle (FRG – width of field 95 mm) 2. **Mirabilite** – crystal aggregate; Halle (FRG) 3. **Tschermigite** – group of crystals (to 3 mm); Zastávka (Czech Republic)

Alunogen (Keramohalite)

Sulphate
$Al_2(SO_4)_3$. 18 H_2O

26

From the Latin *alumen* and the Greek *genos* – origin (Beudant 1832)

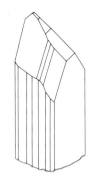

● Hardness: 1–2 ● Streak: white ● Colour: colourless, white-yellow, reddish ● Transparency: transparent ● Lustre: vitreous to silky and pearly ● Cleavage: perfect on (010) ● Morphology: acicular and laminated aggregates, crusts, crystals, powdery ● Solubility: soluble in water ● Other properties: bitter taste ● Specific gravity: 1.78 ● Crystal system: triclinic ● Crystal form: plates, prismatic ● Chemical composition: Al_2O_3 14.90%, SO_3 35.09%, H_2O 50.01% ● Handling: clean with alcohol ● Similar minerals: alunite **(232)** ● Distinguishing features: alunite is insoluble in water or HCl ● Genesis: secondary ● Associated minerals: halotrichite **(27)**, fibroferrite **(120)** and other sulphates ● Occurrence: rare; Friesdorf near Bonn (FRG); Dubník (Slovakia), Solfatara, Vesuvius (Italy), Alun Mnt – New Mexico – layers up to 3 m thick (USA)

Halotrichite (Iron alum, Feather alum)

Sulphate
$Fe^{2+}Al_2(SO_4)_4$. 22 H_2O

27

From the Latin *halotrichum* – hair salt (Glocker 1839)

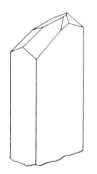

● Hardness: 1.5 ● Streak: lighter than its colour ● Colour: colourless, white, yellowish, greenish ● Transparency: translucent ● Lustre: vitreous to silky ● Cleavage: imperfect on (010) ● Morphology: crusts, fibres, coatings, crystals ● Solubility: soluble in water ● Specific gravity: 1.9 ● Crystal system: monoclinic ● Crystal form: acicular, prismatic ● Chemical composition: FeO 8.07%, Al_2O_3 11.45%, SO_3 35.97%, H_2O 44.51% ● Chemical properties: crumbles when exposed to air ● Handling: clean with alcohol, preserve in plastic bags ● Similar minerals: pickeringite **(28)** and other sulphates ● Distinguishing features: chemical properties ● Genesis: secondary ● Associated minerals: alunogen **(26)**, pickeringite, copiapite **(123)** ● Occurrence: rare; Reichenbach, Mörsfeld (FRG), Istria (Croatia), Dubník (Slovakia), Capiapo, (Chile), Alun Mnt – New Mexico (USA).

Pickeringite

Sulphate
$MgAl_2(SO_4)_4$. 22 H_2O

28

Named after J. Pickering (1777–1846) (Hayes 1844)

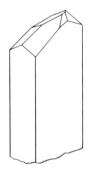

● Hardness: 1.5 ● Streak: lighter than its colour ● Colour: colourless, white, pinkish, reddish ● Transparency: transparent ● Lustre: vitreous to pearly and silky ● Cleavage: imperfect on (010) ● Morphology: crystals, crusts, coatings with reniform surface ● Solubility: soluble in water ● Specific gravity: 1.8 ● Crystal system: monoclinic ● Crystal form: needles, prismatic ● Chemical composition: MgO 4.69%, Al_2O_3 11.87%, SO_3 37.29%, H_2O 46.15%; admixtures Mn, Fe, Co ● Chemical properties: crumbles when exposed to air, when heated loses water ● Handling: clean with alcohol, preserve in plastic bags ● Similar minerals: halotrichite **(27)** ● Distinguishing features: chemical ● Genesis: secondary ● Associated minerals: halotrichite, alunogen **(26)** and other sulphates ● Occurrence: rare; Wetzelstein (FRG), Dubník (Slovakia), Elba (Italy), Bosjeman (SAR), Chuquicamata (Chile).

---

1. **Alunogen** – crust of small platy crystals; Dubník (Slovakia) 2. **Halotrichite** – globular aggregates of acicular crystals; Dubník (Slovakia – width of field 70 mm)

Alunogen, halotrichite

Gypsum

Sulphate
$CaSO_4 . 2 H_2O$

29

L

P

From the Greek *gyps* – gypsum

● Hardness: 1.5–2 ● Streak: white ● Colour: colourless when pure, with admixtures may be white, grey, yellow, brown, bluish ● Transparency: transparent to translucent ● Lustre: vitreous, pearly on (010) plane ● Cleavage: perfect on (010), distinct on (100) ● Other properties of cohesion: flexible ● Morphology: platy crystals (larger transparent plates – Maria Glass), fibrous aggregates (selenite), druses, fine fibrous aggregates, brown and rose with sand inclusions (desert rose), concretions, fine-grained up to massive (alabaster) ● Specific gravity: 2.3–2.4 ● Crystal system: monoclinic ● Crystal form: some 70 different types of form are known, most common being plates, prisms, nodular and lenticular forms, twinning (swallow-tails) ● Luminescence: sometimes in ultra-violet light yellow and green ● Chemical composition: CaO 32.57%, SO_3 46.50%, H_2O 20.93% ● Chemical properties: when heated becomes scaly, fuses and loses water; often contains impurities, such as bituminous and clayey substances; dissolves in hot HCl ● Handling: clean with cold water and alcohol ● Similar minerals: cryolite **(88)**, calcite **(217)**, anhydrite **(235)**, alabaster may be mistaken for marble, but feels warmer (is a poor heat conductor) ● Distinguishing features: hardness, cleavage in one direction, does not dissolve with effervescence in HCl, but slightly soluble in hot water ● Genesis: sedimentary, secondary, hydrothermal ● Associated minerals: sulphur **(1)**, halite **(86)**, aragonite **(221)**, anhydrite, celestine **(239)** important deposits are in permian and triassic rocks in FRG. Sedimentary deposits are in tertiary rocks in France and Italy, in the vicinity of Salzburg (Austria) and in the vicinity of Wieliczka and Bochnia near Cracow (Poland) – in combination with salt deposits. Large gypsum deposits occur in permian rocks in Russia (Bashkir and Tartary National Area); and associated with anhydrite and salt, gypsum occurs in New York, Kansas, Michigan, New Mexico, Colorado (USA). Perfect crystals and druses are found in Eisleben and Förste in Harz (FRG), fine Maria Glass is found in clay in Wiesloch – Baden (FRG). Crystals over 1 m were found in Naica and Chihuahua (Mexico) and in Braden (Chile). Fine alabaster for sculpture comes from Volterra (Italy) ● Application: in the manufacture of cement and building materials; alabaster is commonly used for decorative objects and souvenirs, less often for use in jewellery.

Gypsum – euhedral crystal (6 mm) with ingrown needle of antimonite in quartz-chalcedony vein containing Sb ochres; Zlatá Baňa (Slovakia)

Gypsum

Sideronatrite

Sulphate
$Na_2Fe^{3+}(SO_4)_2(OH) \cdot 3 H_2O$

30

Named after its chemical composition
(Raimondi 1878)

● Hardness: 1.5 ● Streak: yellow-white ● Colour: yellow, yellow-brown to orange ● Transparency: translucent ● Lustre: vitreous to dull ● Cleavage: perfect on (100) ● Morphology: fine fibrous, lumpy and nodular aggregates, crusts ● Solubility: soluble in hot water ● Specific gravity: 2.3 ● Crystal system: orthorhombic ● Crystal form: needles ● Chemical composition: Na_2O 16.99%, Fe_2O_3 21.87%, SO_3 43.87%, H_2O 17.27% ● Handling: clean with cold water ● Genesis: secondary ● Associated minerals: melanterite **(114)**, voltaite **(233)**, pyrite **(436)** ● Occurrence: rare; Tarapaca province (Chile), Potosí (Bolivia), islands in the Caspian Sea (Russia).

Struvite

Phosphate
$(NH_4)MgPO_4 \cdot 6 H_2O$

31

Named after the Russian diplomat, H. G. von Struve (1772–1851)
(Ulex 1846)

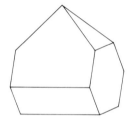

● Hardness: 1.5–2 ● Streak: white ● Colour: colourless, yellowish, brownish ● Transparency: transparent to translucent ● Lustre: vitreous to dull ● Cleavage: perfect on (100) ● Morphology: isometric, crystalline ● Solubility: slightly soluble in water ● Specific gravity: 1.7 ● Crystal system: orthorhombic ● Crystal form: short prisms, coarse plates, wedge-shaped, twinning ● Chemical composition: MgO 16.43%, $(NH_4)_2O$ 10.61%, P_2O_5 28.92%, H_2O 44.04% ● Chemical properties: readily fusible, when heated loses water and ammonia, on dehydration becomes dull, tinges a flame green, is soluble in acids ● Handling: clean mechanically, preserve in plastic bags ● Genesis: secondary ● Occurrence: rare; Hamburg, Braunschweig (FRG), Skipton Cave (Australia), Reunion Island (Indian Ocean), Saldanha Bay (RSA).

Tyrolite

Arsenate
$Ca_2Cu_9(AsO_4)_4(OH)_{10} \cdot 10 H_2O$

32

Named after the Tyrol (Austria)
(Haidinger 1845)

● Hardness: 1.5–2 ● Streak: lighter than its colour ● Colour: light green to blue-green, blue-grey ● Transparency: translucent ● Lustre: vitreous to pearly ● Cleavage: perfect on (001) ● Other properties of cohesion: flexible ● Morphology: crystals, laminated and fan-shaped, botryoidal aggregates, crusts ● Specific gravity: 3.2 ● Crystal system: orthorhombic ● Crystal form: plates, scales ● Electric conductivity: good ● Chemical composition: CaO 7.12%, CuO 36.32%, As_2O_5 39.39%, H_2O 17.17% ● Chemical properties: soluble in acids, when heated loses colour, fuses, smells garlicky ● Handling: clean with distilled water ● Similar minerals: strashimint **(151)** ● Distinguishing features: hardness, specific gravity ● Genesis: secondary ● Associated minerals: langite **(130)**, posnjakite **(131)**, brochantite **(228)**, chalcophillite **(138)**, malachite **(307)** ● Occurrence: rare; Bieber, Richelsdorf, Schneeberg, Saafeld (FRG), Linares (Spain), Poniky (Slovakia), Tintic district – Utah (USA).

1. **Sideronatrite** – long prismatic crystals associated with carbonate; Sierra Gorda (Chile) 2. **Tyrolite** – vein containing radiating lamellar crystals with fine plates of gypsum; Novoveská Huta (Slovakia – width of field 27 mm)

Sideronatrite, tyrolite

2

57

Montmorillonite

Silicate
$(Na,Ca)_{0.33}(Al,Mg)_2Si_4O_{10}(OH)_2 \cdot n\ H_2O$

33

Named after the locality, Montmorillon (France) (Mauduyt 1847)

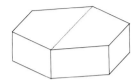

• Hardness: 1−2 • Streak: white • Colour: white, grey-white, yellow, brownish, greenish, pink, bluish • Transparency: opaque • Lustre: dull • Cleavage: perfect on (001) • Morphology: compact, massive, earthy and powdered aggregates • Specific gravity: 1.7−2.7 • Crystal system: monoclinic • Crystal form: scales, visible only when magnified • Chemical composition: variable • Chemical properties: soluble in acids, swells in water • Handling: clean with distilled water • Similar minerals: halloysite **(34)**, illite, kaolinite **(38)** • Distinguishing features: optical, X-rays, chemical, sometimes white luminescence • Genesis: secondary • Associated minerals: illite, halloysite, kaolinite, quartz **(534)** • Occurrence: very common; an important part of soils and clays. Large deposits in Montmorillon (France), Landshut (FRG), (Armenia), (Georgia), Florida, Georgia, California (USA). Rocks transformed from volcanic tuffs and composed mostly of montmorillonites are called bentonites. Their deposits occur in volcanic areas, such as Lastovce and Kuzmice (Slovakia), (Hungary), (Romania), Antrim (Northern Ireland), Caucasus (Ukraine), New Mexico, Arizona, Colorado (USA) • Application: ceramics manufacture, pharmaceutical, oil and rubber industries, cosmetics.

Halloysite

Silicate
$Al_2Si_2O_5(OH)_4$

34

L

Named after O. d'Halloy (1707−1789) (Berthier 1826)

• Hardness: 1−2 • Streak: white • Colour: white, yellowish, reddish, greenish, bluish • Transparency: translucent • Lustre: dull, greasy • Cleavage: absent • Fracture: earthy • Other properties of cohesion: scratching leaves shiny striation; when dry it crumbles into angular fragments • Morphology: powdered, earthy, gelatinous and compact aggregates • Other properties: when dry clings to tongue • Specific gravity: 2.0−2.2 • Crystal system: monoclinic • Crystal form: fine, tubular forms only visible when greatly magnified • Chemical composition: Al_2O_3 34.7%, SiO_2 40.8%, H_2O 24.5%, admixtures of Fe, Cr, Mg, Ni, Cu; changes into metahalloysite by dehydration • Chemical properties: soluble in HCl, crumbles in water but does not swell • Handling: clean with distilled water • Similar minerals: montmorillonite **(33)**, kaolinite **(38)** • Distinguishing features: optical, X-rays, chemical, white or blue luminescence • Genesis: low hydrothermal, secondary • Associated minerals: montmorillonite, kaolinite, marcasite **(437)** • Occurrence: common; Altenberg near Aachen (FRG), Angleur (Belgium), Michalovce (Slovakia), Tarnowice (Poland), Zaglinsk (Azerbaijan) • Application: manufacture of ceramics.

---

1. **Halloysite** − compact earthy aggregate; Cotas du More (France) 2. **Montmorillonite** − compact earthy aggregate coloured by Fe hydroxides; Montmorillon (France − width of field 60 mm)

Halloysite, montmorillonite

Saponite (Soapstone)

Silicate
$(Mg,Al,Fe)_3(Al,Si)_4O_{10}(OH)_2$

35

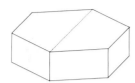

From the Latin *sapo* – soap (Svanberg 1840)

● Hardness: 1.5 ● Streak: white ● Colour: white, yellowish, greenish, reddish, bluish ● Transparency: opaque ● Lustre: greasy ● Cleavage: perfect on (001) ● Morphology: massive, finely granular ● Specific gravity: 2.3 ● Crystal system: monoclinic ● Crystal form: scales ● Chemical composition: variable ● Chemical properties: soluble in H_2SO_4 ● Handling: clean with distilled water ● Similar minerals: talc **(41)**, pyrophyllite **(42)** ● Distinguishing features: solubility in H_2SO_4 ● Genesis: secondary ● Associated minerals: serpentine **(273)** ● Occurrence: common; Cornwall (Great Britain), Transvaal (RSA), (USA), (Canada) ● Application: raw material for some carved objects.

Nontronite

Silicate
$Na_{0.33}Fe_2^{3+}(Si,Al)_4O_{10} \cdot n\ H_2O$

36

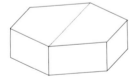

Named after Nontrone (France) (Bertier 1827)

● Hardness: 1–2 ● Streak: white ● Colour: green-yellow, brown-green, olive-green ● Transparency: non-transparent ● Lustre: dull, waxy ● Cleavage: perfect on (001) ● Morphology: earthy, cryptocrystalline aggregates ● Specific gravity: 2.3 ● Crystal system: monoclinic ● Crystal form: scales ● Chemical composition: variable ● Chemical properties: soluble in HCl, forming precipitation ● Handling: clean with distilled water ● Similar minerals: montmorillonite **(33)** ● Distinguishing features: chemical, optical ● Genesis: secondary ● Associated minerals: serpentine **(274)**, opal **(440)**, quartz **(534)** ● Occurrence: common; Nontrone (France), St. Andreasberg, Heppenheim (FRG), (Czech Republic), (Slovakia), (Mexico), (USA).

Vermiculite

Silicate
$(Mg,Fe^{2+},Al)_3(Al,Si)_4O_{10}(OH)_2 \cdot 4\ H_2O$

37

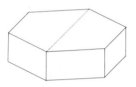

From the Latin *vermiculus* – little worm (Webb 1814)

● Hardness: 1.5 ● Streak: greenish ● Colour: yellow-brown, green-brown ● Transparency: translucent ● Lustre: pearly to bronze-like ● Cleavage: perfect on (001) ● Morphology: laminae, scales ● Specific gravity: 2.3–2.7 ● Crystal system: monoclinic ● Crystal form: pseudo-hexagonal scales ● Chemical composition: variable ● Chemical properties: swells when heated and enfoliates, from which it is named ● Handling: clean with water ● Similar minerals: biotite **(167)**, phlogopite **(168)** ● Distinguishing features: behaves differently when heated ● Genesis: secondary ● Associated minerals: biotite, phlogopite ● Occurrence: rare; Palabora (RSA), (Russia), Montana (USA), (Argentina), (Canada) ● Application: thermo-insulating material, sound insulation, lubricants, paper industry.

---

1. **Saponite** – fine scaly aggregate with greasy lustre; Canada 2. **Nontronite** – compact, yellow-green earthy aggregate; Strigom (Poland) 3. **Vermiculite** – spherical aggregates of lamellar crystals with rutile needles; Alps (Austria – width of field 62 mm)

Saponite, nontronite, vermiculite

H
0—2

61

Kaolinite

Silicate
$Al_2Si_2O_5(OH)_4$

38

Named after the locality, Kao-Ling (China) (Brongniart 1807)

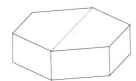

• Hardness: 1 • Streak: white • Colour: snow-white, yellowish, grey-green • Transparency: opaque to translucent • Lustre: dull, pearly • Cleavage: perfect on (001) • Morphology: polycrystalline, earthy • Specific gravity: 2.6 • Crystal system: triclinic • Crystal form: thin plates, rarely pseudo-hexagonal • Chemical composition: Al_2O_3 39.5%, SiO_2 46.5%, H_2O 14.0% • Chemical properties: soluble in H_2SO_4, when heated • Handling: clean with distilled water • Similar minerals: illite, halloysite **(34)**, dickite **(39)** • Distinguishing features: chemical, X-rays • Genesis: hydrothermal, secondary • Associated minerals: quartz **(534)**, K-feldspars, micas • Occurrence: common; Tirschenreuth, Schneittenbach, Aue (FRG), Podbořany and Sedlec (Czech Republic), (Great Britain), (France), (China) • Application: manufacture of ceramics, paper, dyes, paint and rubber.

Dickite

Silicate
$Al_2Si_2O_5(OH)_4$

39

Named after the Scottish chemist, A. B. Dick (1833–1926)

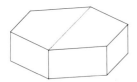

• Hardness: 1 • Streak: white • Colour: white, colourless, yellowish • Transparency: transparent • Lustre: pearly • Cleavage: perfect on (001) • Morphology: loose, crystals • Specific gravity: 2.6 • Crystal system: monoclinic • Crystal form: plates, scales • Chemical composition: Al_2O_3 39.5%, SiO_2 46.5%, H_2O 14.0% • Chemical properties: soluble in H_2SO_4 • Handling: clean with distilled water or alcohol • Similar minerals: kaolinite **(38)**, sericite **(165)** • Distinguishing features: from kaolinite by X-ray diffraction, from sericite by dissolving in H_2SO_4 • Genesis: hydrothermal • Associated minerals: sulphides, dolomite **(218)** • Occurrence: rare; Essen (FRG), Pike Co. – Arkansas (USA), Anglesey Island (Great Britain).

Nacrite

Silicate
$Al_2Si_2O_5(OH)_4$

40

From the French *nacre* – mother-of-pearl (Breithaupt 1832)

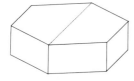

• Hardness: 1 • Streak: white • Colour: white, yellow, grey-white • Transparency: translucent • Lustre: pearly • Cleavage: perfect on (001) • Morphology: crystals, massive, fine, scaly, radiating • Specific gravity: 2.6 • Crystal system: monoclinic • Crystal form: plates • Chemical composition: Al_2O_3 39.5%, SiO_2 46.5%, H_2O 14.0% • Chemical properties: like kaolinite **(38)** • Handling: clean with distilled water • Similar minerals: kaolinite, dickite **(39)** • Distinguishing features: chemical, differential thermal analysis, X-rays • Genesis: hydrothermal, secondary • Associated minerals: calcite **(217)**, dolomite **(218)**, quartz **(534)** • Occurrence: rare; Brand-Erbisdorf near Freiberg (FRG), Colorado (USA), Slavkov (Czech Republic).

---

1. **Kaolinite** – earthy aggregate; Karlovy Vary (Czech Republic) 2. **Dickite** – powdered, with baryte in cavity in siderite; Beřovice (Czech Republic) 3. **Nacrite** – earthy aggregate in crack in granite; Golčův Jeníkov (Czech Republic – width of field 55 mm)

Kaolinite, dickite, nacrite

Talc

Silicate
Mg$_3$Si$_4$O$_{10}$(OH)$_2$

41

From the Arabic

● Hardness: 1 ● Streak: white ● Colour: light green, white, brownish, yellowish ● Transparency: transparent to translucent ● Lustre: vitreous, pearly ● Cleavage: perfect on (001) ● Other features of cohesion: forms flexible, inelastic scales ● Morphology: lamellar crystals, scaly, massive, granular ● Other properties: poor conductor of heat, feels greasy ● Specific gravity: 2.7–2.8 ● Crystal system: monoclinic ● Crystal form: plates ● Luminescence: sometimes white, green-white, yellow, creamy, brown, green, blue ● Chemical composition: MgO 31.7%, SiO$_2$ 63.5%, H$_2$O 4.8% ● Chemical properties: insoluble in acids, not fusible ● Handling: clean with water, acids ● Similar minerals: pyrophyllite **(42)** ● Distinguishing features: Mg test (rose colour) ● Genesis: hydrothermal, contact-metasomatic ● Associated minerals: chlorite **(158)**, dolomite **(218)**, serpentine **(273)**, magnesite **(302)** ● Occurrence: common; large deposits in (China), (North Korea), (Canada), (Russia), (Austria) and (Slovakia); also in Zöblitz – Saxony (FRG), St. Gotthard – crystals (Switzerland), Appalachian Mountains (USA) ● Application: lubricants, paper, rubber, textile and ceramic industries, cosmetics. Its compact variety, steatite, is carved into ornaments, particularly in China.

Pyrophyllite

Silicate
Al$_2$Si$_4$O$_{10}$(OH)$_2$

42

L

P

From the Greek *pyro* – fire and *fýllon* – leaf (Germann 1829)

● Hardness: 1–1.5 ● Streak: white ● Colour: white, grey, green, yellowish ● Transparency: translucent ● Lustre: vitreous, pearly ● Cleavage: perfect on (001) ● Morphology: scaly, massive, spherical, radial, lamellar aggregates ● Specific gravity: 2.8 ● Crystal system: monoclinic ● Crystal form: rare, in plates ● Luminescence: sometimes white, yellow, orange ● Chemical composition: Al$_2$O$_3$ 28.3%, SiO$_2$ 66.7%, H$_2$O 5.0% ● Chemical properties: insoluble in acids, when heated crumbles in flakes ● Handling: clean with water or acids ● Similar minerals: talc **(41)** ● Distinguishing features: reaction to Mg (talc), lustre ● Genesis: hydrothermal, metamorphic ● Associated minerals: talc, quartz **(534)** ● Occurrence: rare; Eifel, Ochsenkopf (FRG), Zermatt (Switzerland), Banská Štiavnica (Slovakia), Sutherland (Great Britain), Hirvivaara (Finland), Ottré (Belgium), Săcărâmb (Romania), Berezovsk, Urals (Russia), Tibet (China), Lincoln Co. – Georgia (USA) ● Application: its compact variety, agalmatolite, is carved into ornaments, particularly in China.

1. Talc – coarsely lamellar aggregate with greenish colour; Zillertal (Austria – width of field 51 mm) **2. Pyrophyllite** – group of radiating-lamellar aggregates; Zermatt (Switzerland)

Talc, pyrophyllite

Evenkite

Organic substance
$C_{24}H_{50}$

43

L

Named after the Evenk National Area (Russia) (Skropyshev 1953)

● Hardness: 1 ● Streak: white ● Colour: colourless, white, yellowish, yellow-green, grape-yellow ● Transparency: transparent to translucent ● Lustre: greasy, vitreous ● Cleavage: exfoliation parallel to basal plane ● Other features of cohesion: plastic, flexible ● Morphology: crystals, granular and massive aggregates, impregnations ● Specific gravity: 0.87 ● Crystal system: monoclinic ● Crystal form: plates ● Luminescence: strong in ultra-violet light, blue-white ● Chemical composition: C 85.09%, H 14.91% ● Chemical properties: soluble in warm water, readily fusible in acids, evaporates at temperatures over 45 °C ● Handling: clean with cold distilled water, protect from sunlight and heat ● Similar minerals: amber **(173)**, idrialine **(44)**, calcite **(217)** ● Distinguishing features: hardness, specific gravity, cleavage, fusibility ● Genesis: hydrothermal, postvolcanic ● Associated minerals: calcite, marcasite **(437)**, chalcedony **(449)**, idrialine ● Occurrence: rare; only in a few localities. Discovered initially in Russia in a mercury deposit in the drainage area of the Tunguska river, Evenk National Area; later in mercury deposits in Dubník and Merník (Slovakia).

Idrialine

Organic substance
$C_{22}H_{14}$

44

L

Named after the locality Idria (Slovenia) (Dumas 1832)

● Hardness: 1–1.5 (brittle) ● Streak: white ● Colour: yellow-green, green, grey, light brown, brown-black ● Transparency: transparent, translucent ● Lustre: vitreous to adamantine ● Cleavage: perfect on (001) ● Fracture: conchoidal ● Morphology: crystals, granular and massive aggregates, nodules, impregnations with cinnabar **(76)** ● Specific gravity: 1.23 ● Crystal system: orthorhombic ● Crystal form: plates ● Luminescence: in ultra-violet light – light blue (Idria), yellow-green to light green (Dubník, Skaggs Springs) ● Chemical composition: C 94.92%, H 5.08% ● Chemical properties: soluble in H_2SO_4, forms blue-green solution, fusible at 260–360 °C ● Handling: clean with distilled water ● Similar minerals: evenkite **(43)** ● Distinguishing features: specific gravity, melting point ● Genesis: hydrothermal, post-volcanic ● Associated minerals: evenkite, cinnabar, calcite **(217)**, marcasite **(437)**, chalcedony **(449)** ● Occurrence: rare; Idria (Slovenia), Ordejov, Merník, Dubník (Slovakia), Skaggs Springs (California, USA).

---

1. **Evenkite** – honey-coloured crystal (18 mm) on argillaceous andesite; Dubník (Slovakia) 2. **Idrialine** – yellow-green aggregate of platy and scaly crystals (size to 10 mm) on rhyodacite; Merník (Slovakia)

Evenkite, idrialine

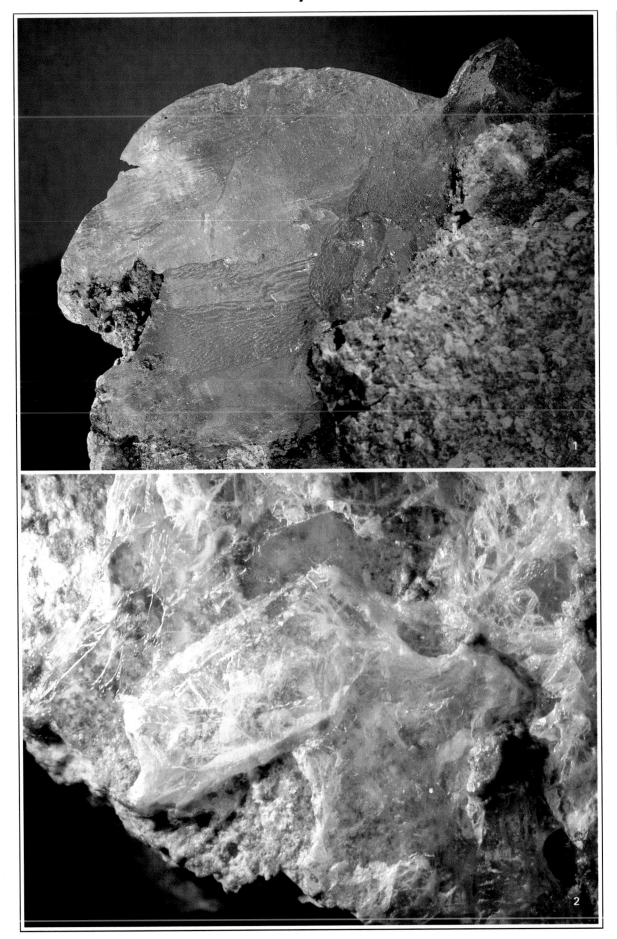

Selenium

45

From the Greek *Selene* – goddess of the Moon (Del Rio 1828)

● Hardness: 2 ● Streak: red ● Colour: grey or purple-grey ● Transparency: in thin sections translucent (reddish) ● Lustre: submetallic ● Cleavage: good on $(01\bar{1}2)$ ● Other features of cohesion: flexible ● Morphology: crystals, globular grains, fibrous aggregates, loose crusts ● Specific gravity: 4.81 ● Crystal system: trigonal ● Crystal form: prisms ● Chemical composition: theoretically, 100% Se ● Genesis: secondary ● Associated minerals: pyrite **(436)**, U-minerals, selenides ● Occurrence: rare; Colorado Plateau (USA), (Russia), Kladno (Czech Republic) ● Application: mineralogically important.

Tellurium

46

From the Latin *tellus* – earth (Müller/Reichenstein 1782)

● Hardness: 2–3 ● Streak: grey ● Colour: tin white ● Transparency: opaque ● Lustre: metallic ● Cleavage: perfect on (1010) ● Morphology: crystals are rare, sometimes finely granular or in minute hexagonal prisms ● Specific gravity: 6.1–6.3 ● Crystal system: trigonal ● Crystal form: prisms, needles ● Electric conductivity: good ● Chemical composition: theoretically, 100% Te; admixtures of Au, Ag, Se ● Chemical properties: soluble in HNO_3 and in hot H_2SO_4, solution turns red, tinges a flame green ● Handling: clean with water ● Similar minerals: arsenic **(176)** ● Distinguishing features: resembles arsenic but the latter, when heated, smells garlicky ● Genesis: hydrothermal, secondary ● Associated minerals: tellurides of Au and Ag, galena **(77)**, pyrite **(436)**, quartz **(534)** ● Occurrence: rare; (Romania), Cripple Creek (USA), (Australia).

Copper

47

From the Latin *cuprum* – Cyprus

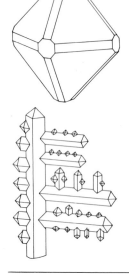

● Hardness: 2.5–3 ● Streak: copper-red ● Colour: light red, darkening copper-red and brown-red ● Transparency: opaque; in very thin laminae becomes translucent green ● Lustre: metallic ● Cleavage: absent ● Fracture: hackly, conchoidal ● Other properties of cohesion: sectile, malleable ● Morphology: rarely in crystals, plates, wiry, arborescent, massive, sometimes pseudo-morphous ● Specific gravity: 8.93 ● Crystal system: cubic ● Crystal form: hexahedron, tetrahedron, dodecahedron, rarely octahedron, often crystals developed only in one direction or as twins ● Electrical conductivity: very good ● Chemical composition: theoretically 100% Cu; admixtures of Ag, Fe, As, Bi ● Chemical properties: soluble in HNO_3, melts when heated ● Handling: clean with water ● Genesis: secondary, on contact of oxidized and cementation zone ● Associated minerals: cuprite **(209)**, azurite **(226)**, malachite **(307)** ● Occurrence: the most important locality for native copper is the southern shore of Lake Superior (USA) – the largest piece of copper weighed 420 tons. Native copper is also found in the Mansfeld slates in Zwickau, Wolf Mine (near Herdorf, Reichenbach, FRG), Bisbee, Georgetown, Keewenaw Peninsula (USA), Rudabánya (Hungary), Cananea (Mexico), Burra Burra (Australia), (Chile), Tsumeb (Namibia) ● Application: electrical industry, chemical engineering.

---

1. Selenium – coating of acicular crystals; Kladno (Czech Republic) **2. Tellurium** – fine granular aggregate with metallic lustre, on quartz; Fata Bai (Romania) **3. Copper** – arborescent group of euhedral crystals; Michigan (USA – height of specimen 70 mm)

Selenium, tellurium, copper

Bismuth

48

Probably from the Arabic *bi ismid* – having the properties of antimony

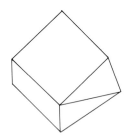

● Hardness: 2–2.5 ● Streak: lead-grey, glossy ● Colour: on a fresh cut – silver-white with yellowish or pinkish tinge, later turning red ● Transparency: opaque ● Lustre: metallic ● Cleavage: perfect on (0001) ● Other features of cohesion: brittle, sectile ● Morphology: crystals, often skeletal, granular, laminar ● Specific gravity: 9.7–9.8 ● Crystal system: trigonal ● Crystal form: rhombohedron, pseudo-cubic, polysynthetic twinning ● Electric conductivity: good ● Chemical composition: theoretically, 100% Bi; admixtures of Fe, Te, As, S, Sb ● Chemical properties: readily soluble in HNO_3, almost insoluble in HCl, readily smelted on charcoal ● Handling: clean with water ● Similar minerals: linnaeite **(342)**, niccolite **(351)** ● Distinguishing features: perfect cleavage, low hardness ● Genesis: pegmatitic, pneumatolytic, hydrothermal ● Associated minerals: bismutite **(71)**, molybdenite **(8)**, wolframite **(369)**, cassiterite **(548)** ● Occurrence: rare; Altenberg, Zinnwald, Schneeberg, Annaberg, Wittichen (FRG), Jáchymov (Czech Republic), Pozoblanco (Spain), (Bolivia), (Mexico), (Peru), (Chile), Cobalt (Canada) ● Application: Bi ore.

Silver

49

Historical name

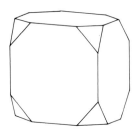

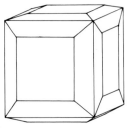

● Hardness: 2.5–3 ● Streak: white, glossy ● Colour: silver-white, gradually turning dull to black ● Transparency: opaque ● Lustre: metallic ● Cleavage: absent ● Fracture: hackly ● Other features of cohesion: malleable, ductile, flexible ● Morphology: crystals, dendrites, wires, plates, compact masses, pseudo-morphs after acanthite **(75)** and pyrargyrite **(64)** ● Specific gravity: 9.6–12, according to admixtures ● Crystal system: cubic ● Crystal form: hexahedron, octahedron, contact twinning (111), skeletal crystals developed in one direction ● Electric conductivity: excellent ● Chemical composition: theoretically, 100% Ag; admixtures: Au, Hg, Bi, Sb, Cu, As, Pt ● Chemical properties: melts when heated; soluble in HNO_3 and HCl; with H_2S turns black ● Handling: clean with distilled water; by electrolysis, black film can be removed using ultrasonic cleaning. Should be kept in the dark, and well separated from minerals containing sulphur ● Similar minerals: acanthite, dyscrasite **(204)**, platinum **(281)** ● Distinguishing features: colour, density, specific gravity ● Genesis: hydrothermal, supergene (cementation zone), sedimentary ● Associated minerals: pyrargyrite, acanthite, and other silver sulphides, galena **(77)**, nickel and cobalt arsenides ● Occurrence: rare; Schneeberg deposit (wires up to 40 cm long) and mines in Freiberg, Schwarzwald (FRG), Kongsberg (Norway), Jáchymov – wires up to 30 cm (Czech Republic), southern Arizona – one piece weighing 1,350 kg (USA), Cobalt – Ontario – one piece weighing 612 kg (Canada), (Mexico), (Bolivia) ● Application: precious metal, used in minting, jewellery, medicine, chemistry, photography, electrotechnology.

---

1. Bismuth – flat cockscomb formations; Schneeberg (Saxony, FRG – width of field 92 mm) **2. Silver** – wiry aggregates; Příbram (Czech Republic – width of field 26 mm)

Bismuth, silver

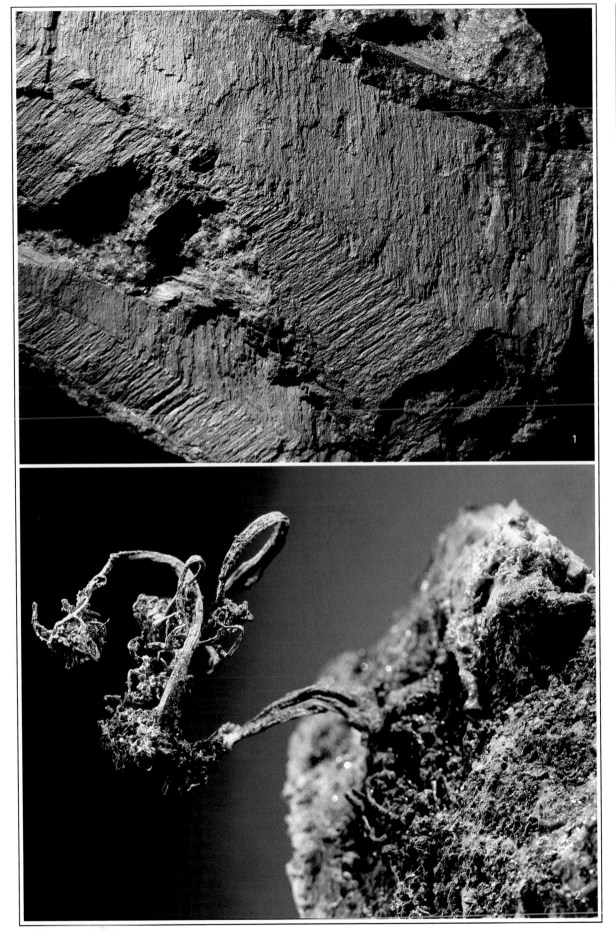

Gold

50

Historical name

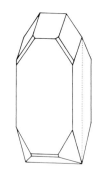

● Hardness: 2.5−3 ● Streak: yellow, shining ● Colour: gold-yellow, yellow-white ● Transparency: opaque; in thin laminae, translucent ● Lustre: metallic ● Cleavage: absent ● Fracture: hackly ● Other features of cohesion: ductile, flexible, malleable ● Morphology: crystals, plates, laminae, wires, dendrites, compact, grains, nuggets, cavernous ● Other properties: warm to the touch ● Specific gravity: 19.28 when pure (varies from 15.5 to 19.3, according to admixtures) ● Crystal system: cubic ● Crystal form: octahedron, dodecahedron, hexahedron, frequent twinning, crystals develop in one direction ● Electric conductivity: good ● Chemical composition: theoretically, 100% Au; admixtures: Ag (electrum variety, more than 20% Ag), Cu (cuproaurite variety), Pd (porpezite variety), Rh (rhodite variety), Ir (iraurite variety), Pt (platinum gold), Te, Se, Bi ● Chemical properties: soluble in agua regia, KCN, NaCN, reacts quickly with Hg, melts when heated and forms small, shiny globules ● Handling: clean with water; mechanically, with acids ● Similar minerals: chalcopyrite **(185)**, pyrite **(436)** ● Distinguishing features: colour, lower hardness, high density, malleability; chalcopyrite and pyrite are soluble in HNO_3 ● Genesis: hydrothermal, secondary in placers ● Associated minerals: stibnite **(51)**, chalcopyrite, arsenopyrite **(344)**, pyrite, quartz **(534)**, tellurides, Ag minerals ● Occurrence: rare; the largest gold deposits are in Witwatersrand (RSA), Berezovsk, Urals, Stepnyak, Siberia (Russia), Nevada, Colorado, California, Alaska (USA), (Mexico), (Canada), (Colombia). Gold deposits are also found in (Ghana), (Egypt), (Asia), (the Philippines), (India), (Australia) and (Fiji). In Europe, the most important gold deposits are in Baia de Arieş, Roşia Montana and Săcărâmb (Romania), Jílové (Czech Republic), Kremnica and Banská Štiavnica (Slovakia). In FRG gold is found in Brandholz-Goldkronach, in the area between Basle and Karlsruhe, in the Isar, Danube and Eder rivers. Historically, gold nuggets have been found of considerable size and weight, e.g. nuggets weighing 93 kg in Hill End (Australia), 70.9 kg in Dunotty and 153 kg in Chile. Classic placer deposits were found in the Klondike in the Yukon (Canada) and Sacramento – California (USA). Large nuggets are occasionally found in Siberia (Russia) ● Application: precious metal, in coins, jewellery and medicine.

Gold – skeletal twins on quartz; Săcărâmb (Romania – width of field 21 mm)

Gold

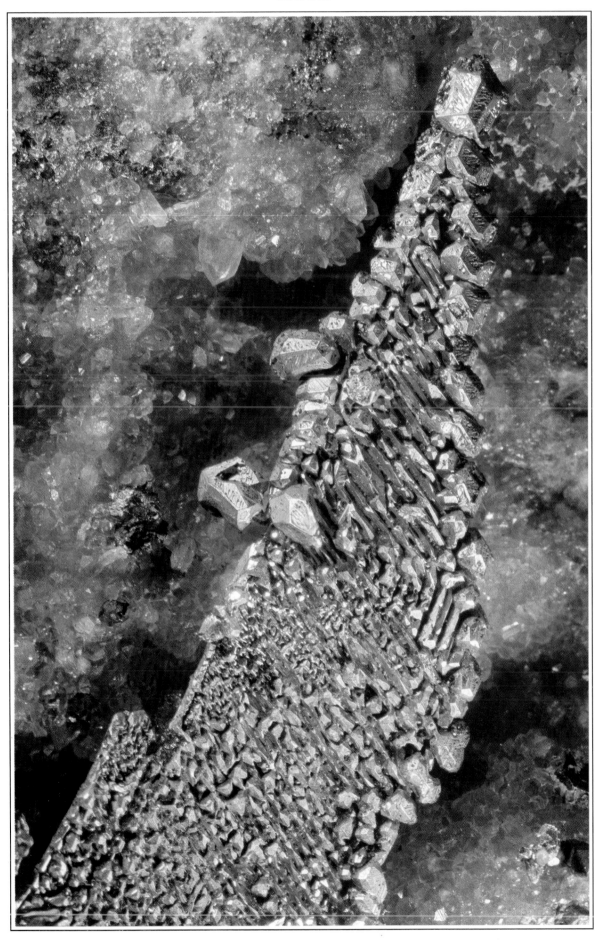

Stibnite
(Antimonite, Antimony glance, Grey antimony)

51

From the Greek
anthemon – flower (the
form of crystal druses)
(Haidinger 1845)

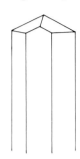

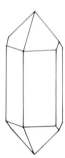

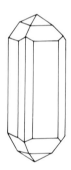

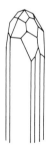

● Hardness: 2 ● Streak: lead-grey ● Colour: lead-grey, steel-grey, with a slight bluish tint, black aggregates (greasy). On the surface often dark-blue. Metastibnite is reddish ● Transparency: opaque ● Lustre: metallic ● Cleavage: perfect on (010), cleavage planes of highly metallic lustre ● Fracture: conchoidal ● Other features of cohesion: flexible ● Morphology: long-columnar crystals, radial in bunches, fibrous aggregates, sometimes felt-like similar to asbestos, granular, massive, compact ● Specific gravity: 4.6–4.7 ● Crystal system: orthorhombic; amorphous variety: metastibnite ● Crystal form: more than 100 different forms, mostly long prisms, vertically striated crystals, sometimes entangled, columnar, acicular, twinning ● Chemical composition: Sb 71.38%, S 28.62%; admixtures: As, Bi, Ag, Pb, Fe, Zn, Cu, Au ● Chemical properties: soluble in HNO$_3$ and in hot HCl, fusible, in oxidizing flame produces white deposit, turns black in KOH ● Handling: clean with water, fragile ● Similar minerals: berthierite **(52)**, bismuthite **(71)**, galena **(77)**, manganite **(295)**, pyrolusite **(474)** ● Distinguishing features: lower specific gravity than bismuthite; galena possesses perfect cleavage in three directions; manganite and pyrolusite exhibit a different streak colour and different hardness; berthierite differs chemically ● Genesis: hydrothermal ● Associated minerals: orpiment **(4)**, realgar **(5)**, gold **(50)**, berthierite, jamesonite **(53)**, cinnabar **(76)**, arsenopyrite **(344)**, marcasite **(437)** ● Occurrence: common; Wolfsberg in Harz (FRG), Casparizeche near Arnsberg (Westphalia, FRG), Milešov, Krásná Hora (Czech Republic), Magurka, Kremnica (Slovakia), Baia Sprie, Chiusbaia (Romania), Nikitovka, Khardarkan, Turgaysk, Uspensk (Russia), (France), Kostajnik (Serbia), Oporto (Portugal), Djebel Haminat (Algeria), (Mexico), (Bolivia), (USA), Tuscany and Sardinia (Italy), (Australia), Bau, Sarawak (Borneo). The most important deposits are in China; the largest and most beautiful crystals have been found in Ichinokawa (Shikoku Island, Japan). They reach a length of 60 cm and a width of 5 cm and are used to support flower pots or for miniature fences around gardens ● Application: in the production of different alloys and fireworks, the rubber and textile industries, glassmaking and medicine. In the Middle Ages it was used in the manufacture of cosmetics and medicines.

Stibnite – radiating aggregates (32 mm) with baryte; Baia Sprie (Romania)

Stibnite

Berthierite

Sulphide
FeSb$_2$S$_4$

52

Named after the French chemist, P. Berthier (1782–1861) (Haidinger 1827)

● Hardness: 2–3 ● Streak: brown-grey ● Colour: dark steel-grey with a brownish tint, frequently showing tarnish colours ● Transparency: opaque ● Lustre: metallic ● Cleavage: good in the direction of elongation ● Morphology: crystals, granular ● Specific gravity: 4.6 ● Crystal system: orthorhombic ● Crystal form: fine, needle-shaped prisms ● Electric conductivity: good ● Chemical composition: Fe 13.06%, Sb 56.95%, S 29.99%; admixtures: Cu, Pb, Ag ● Chemical properties: fusible (a slightly magnetic ball is formed on fusion), soluble in HNO$_3$ ● Handling: clean with water ● Similar minerals: stibnite **(51)**, jamesonite **(53)** ● Distinguishing features: chemical, X-rays ● Genesis: hydrothermal ● Associated minerals: stibnite, tetrahedrite **(190)**, arsenopyrite **(344)** ● Occurrence: Bräunsdorf near Freiberg (FRG), Auvergne (France), Příbram (Czech Republic), Baia Sprie, Chiusbaia (Romania), (Japan), (Peru), (Chile), Oruro (Bolivia). In Romania, deposits of berthierite needles reach a length of 15 cm.

Jamesonite

Sulphide
Pb$_4$FeSb$_6$S$_{14}$

53

Named after the Scottish mineralogist, R. Jameson (1774–1854) (Haidinger 1825)

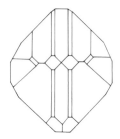

● Hardness: 2.5 (brittle) ● Streak: dark grey to black ● Colour: lead-grey, often showing tarnish colours ● Transparency: opaque ● Lustre: metallic ● Cleavage: perfect on (001) ● Fracture: uneven ● Morphology: crystals, granular and radial aggregates ● Specific gravity: 5.63 ● Crystal system: monoclinic ● Crystal form: long prisms with vertical striation, fibrous, twinning ● Chemical composition: Pb 40.16%, Fe 2.71%, Sb 35.39%, S 21.74%; admixtures: Cu, Zn, Ag, Bi (Bi-jamesonite) ● Chemical properties: soluble in HNO$_3$ and in hot HCl; fuses in flame of blowpipe ● Handling: clean with water; forms fibrous aggregates in an air stream ● Similar minerals: berthierite **(52)**, plagionite **(54)**, boulangerite **(55)** ● Distinguishing features: chemical, X-rays ● Genesis: hydrothermal ● Associated minerals: stibnite **(51)**, boulangerite, sphalerite **(181)** ● Occurrence: rare; St. Andreasberg (Waldsassen, FRG), Freiberg, Wolfsberg, Neudorf (FRG), Příbram (Czech Republic), Nižná Slaná – crystals up to 20 cm (Slovakia), Sala (Sweden), (Romania), Zapokrovsk, Smirnovsk, Darasun (Russia), Oruro (Bolivia), (USA), (Australia), Zimapan (Mexico), (Japan) ● Application: Sb and Pb ore.

---

1. Berthierite – radiating-acicular crystals; Auvergne (France – width of field 47 mm) **2. Jamesonite** – radiating-acicular aggregates on quartz; Příbram (Czech Republic – width of field 61 mm)

Berthierite, jamesonite

Plagionite

Sulphide
$Pb_5Sb_8S_{17}$

54

From the Greek *plagios* – oblique
(Rose 1833)

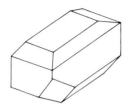

● Hardness: 2.5 (brittle) ● Streak: grey-black with a reddish tint ● Colour: black, grey-black ● Transparency: opaque ● Lustre: metallic ● Cleavage: perfect on (112) ● Fracture: uneven ● Morphology: crystals, finely tabular, often botryoidal aggregates, compact ● Specific gravity: 5.4–5.6 ● Crystal system: monoclinic ● Crystal form: plates ● Chemical composition: Pb 40.75%, Sb 37.78%, S 21.47% ● Chemical properties: fusible, soluble in hot HCl ● Handling: clean with water ● Similar minerals: semseyite **(56)**, jamesonite **(53)**, boulangerite **(55)** ● Distinguishing features: chemical, X-rays ● Genesis: hydrothermal ● Associated minerals: Pb-Sb sulphosalts ● Occurrence: rare; Wolfsberg, Goldkronach (FRG), Oruro (Bolivia), (Russia).

Boulangerite

Sulphide
$Pb_5Sb_4S_{11}$

55

Named after the French mining engineer, C. L. Boulanger (1810–1849)
(Thaulow 1837)

● Hardness: 2.5 (brittle) ● Streak: grey-black with reddish tint ● Colour: lead-grey to black ● Transparency: opaque ● Lustre: metallic ● Cleavage: imperfect on (100) ● Other features of cohesion: flexible needles ● Morphology: crystals, granular, fibrous to felt-like aggregates, compact ● Specific gravity: 5.8–6.2 ● Crystag system: monoclinic ● Crystal form: long prisms vertically striated, needle-shaped, filiform ● Chemical composition: Pb 55.42%, Sb 25.69%, S 18.89%; admixtures of Cu, Zn, Sn, Fe ● Chemical properties: soluble in hot HCl, slightly insoluble in HNO_3, melts when heated ● Handling: clean with water; fibrous aggregates should not be cleaned; protect from dust ● Similar minerals: stibnite **(51)**, jamesonite **(53)** ● Distinguishing features: chemical, X-rays; jamesonite more easily soluble in HNO_3 ● Genesis: hydrothermal ● Associated minerals: stibnite, jamesonite, plagionite **(54)**, sphalerite **(181)** ● Occurrence: rare; Sulzburg, Clausthal, Neudorf und Wolfsberg (FRG), Příbram (Czech Republic), Nižná Slaná (Slovakia), Sala and Boliden (Sweden), Nagolny Kryazh and Nerchinsk (Russia), Trepča (Serbia), (USA), (Canada).

Semseyite

Sulphide
$Pb_9Sb_8S_{21}$

56

Named after the Hungarian collector of minerals, A. Semsey (1833–1923)
(Krenner 1881)

● Hardness: 2.5 (brittle) ● Streak: black ● Colour: black ● Transparency: opaque ● Lustre: metallic ● Cleavage: good on (112) ● Morphology: crystals, radial and spherical aggregates ● Specific gravity: 6.1 ● Crystal system: monoclinic ● Crystal form: plates, prisms, twins ● Chemical composition: Pb 53.10%, Sb 27.73%, S 19.17% ● Chemical properties: reacts with HNO_3 and HCl ● Similar minerals: plagionite **(54)** ● Distinguishing features: chemical ● Handling: clean with water ● Genesis: hydrothermal ● Associated minerals: stibnite **(51)**, pyrrhotite **(283)** ● Occurrence: rare; Wolfsberg (FRG), Chiusbaia and Rodna (Romania), Oruro (Bolivia).

---

1. Plagionite – crystal aggregates in association with Pb-Sb sulphosalts; Oruro (Bolivia – width of field 20 mm)
2. Boulangerite – feather-like, filling a cavity in quartz; Příbram (Czech Republic – width of field 18 mm) **3. Semseyite** – spherical aggregates of platy crystals covered in some places by a limonite coating; Chiuzbaia (Romania – width of field 48 mm)

Plagionite, boulangerite, semseyite

Livingstonite

Sulphide
$HgSb_4S_8$

57

Named after the missionary, D. Livingstone (1813–1873)
(Barcena 1874)

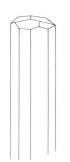

● Hardness: 2 ● Streak: red ● Colour: steel-grey ● Transparency: opaque, in thin fragments reddish translucence ● Lustre: metallic to adamantine ● Cleavage: perfect on (010) and on (100) ● Morphology: crystals, radiating, fibrous, and columnar aggregates ● Specific gravity: 4.9 ● Crystal system: monoclinic ● Crystal form: columnar, acicular ● Chemical composition: Hg 21.25%, Sb 51.59%, S 27.16% ● Chemical properties: soluble in hot HNO_3 ● Handling: clean with water ● Genesis: hydrothermal ● Associated minerals: cinnabar **(76)**, stibnite **(51)**, valentinite **(94)** ● Occurrence: rare; Huitzuco and Guadalcazar (Mexico), Chaidarkan (Kirgizia).

Cylindrite

Sulphide
$Pb_3Sn_4Sb_2S_{14}$

58

From the Greek *kylindros* – cylinder (Frenzel 1893)

● Hardness: 2.5 ● Streak: black ● Colour: dark lead-grey ● Transparency: opaque ● Lustre: metallic ● Cleavage: absent ● Morphology: cylindrical aggregates which separate under pressure into shells or folia resembling a scroll of paper ● Other properties: feels like graphite ● Specific gravity: 5.4 ● Crystal system: orthorhombic ● Crystal form: triclinic ● Chemical composition: Pb 30.59%, Sn 23.36%, Sb 23.96%, S 22.09% ● Chemical properties: slightly soluble in hot HCl and HNO_3 ● Handling: clean with water ● Genesis: hydrothermal ● Associated minerals: jamesonite **(53)**, franckeite **(59)**, stannite **(284)** ● Occurrence: rare; Santa Cruz near Poopó (Bolivia), Smirnovsk (Russia) ● Application: formerly Sn ore.

Franckeite

Sulphide
$Pb_5Sn_3Sb_2S_{14}$

59

Named after the mining engineers, C. and E. Francke
(Stelzner 1893)

● Hardness: 2 ● Streak: grey-black ● Colour: grey-black, sometimes showing iridescent tarnish ● Transparency: opaque ● Lustre: metallic ● Cleavage: perfect on (001) ● Other features of cohesion: flexible ● Morphology: crystals, massive, radiating, fibrous, flaky balls ● Specific gravity: 5.5–5.9 ● Crystal system: monoclinic ● Crystal form: thin plates ● Chemical composition: Pb 49.78%, Sn 17.10%, Sb 11.65%, S 21.47%; admixtures: Ag, Ge, In ● Chemical properties: soluble in hot HNO_3 and HCl ● Handling: clean with water ● Similar minerals: teallite ● Distinguishing features: darker colour of franckeite, X-rays, chemical ● Genesis: hydrothermal ● Associated minerals: boulangerite **(55)**, cylindrite **(58)**, wurtzite **(184)** ● Occurrence: rare; Chocaya, Colquechaca and Llallagua (Bolivia), Kalkar (USA), Smirnovsk (Russia).

---

1. **Livingstonite** – columnar crystals (to 26 mm) embayed in quartz; Huitzuco (Mexico) 2. **Cylindrite** – typical elongated cone-shaped crystals (size to 30 mm); Poopó (Bolivia) 3. **Franckeite** – aggregate of finely bladed crystals; Llallagua (Bolivia – width of field 29 mm)

Livingstonite, cylindrite, franckeite

Miargyrite

Sulphide
AgSbS$_2$

60

From the Greek *meyon* – smaller and *argyros* – silver (Rose 1829)

● Hardness: 2–2.5 (brittle) ● Streak: cherry-red ● Colour: steel-grey, lead-grey, black, in thin fragments blood-red ● Transparency: non-transparent ● Fracture: subconchoidal to uneven ● Lustre: metallic to adamantine ● Cleavage: imperfect on (010) ● Morphology: crystals often occur on pyrargyrite **(64)**, granular, massive aggregates, disseminated ● Specific gravity: 5.2 ● Crystal system: monoclinic ● Crystal form: coarse plates or isometric and wedge-shaped, striated, often multi-planed, sometimes twinned ● Chemical composition: Ag 36.72%, Sb 41.45%, S 21.83% ● Chemical properties: soluble in concentrated HNO$_3$, readily fusible ● Handling: clean with distilled water, protect from light ● Similar minerals: proustite **(63)** ● Distinguishing features: proustite when fused produces garlicky odour, is translucent; miargyrite does not cleave ● Genesis: hydrothermal ● Associated minerals: polybasite **(9)**, pyrargyrite, stephanite **(67)**, sphalerite **(181)** ● Occurrence: rare; Bräunsdorf near Freiberg (FRG), Příbram and Kutná Hora (Czech Republic), Baia Sprie (Romania), Hiendelaencina (Spain), Zacatecas and Molinares (Mexico), Silver City – Idaho – large crystals (USA).

Diaphorite

Sulphide
Pb$_2$Ag$_3$Sb$_3$S$_8$

61

From the Greek *diaphora* – difference (Zepharovich 1871)

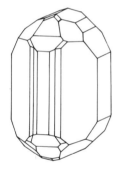

● Hardness: 2.5 (brittle) ● Streak: steel-grey ● Colour: steel-grey ● Transparency: opaque ● Lustre: metallic ● Cleavage: absent ● Fracture: uneven ● Morphology: crystals, granular aggregates ● Specific gravity: 6.0 ● Crystal system: monoclinic ● Crystal form: short prisms vertically striated, twinning ● Chemical composition: Pb 30.48%, Ag 23.78%, Sb 26.87%, S 18.87% ● Chemical properties: soluble in HNO$_3$, readily fusible in a candle flame ● Handling: clean with distilled water, protect from light ● Genesis: hydrothermal ● Associated minerals: boulangerite **(55)**, galena **(77)**, sphalerite **(181)** ● Occurrence: rare; Freiberg (FRG), Příbram – tiny crystals (Czech Republic), San Luis Potosí (Mexico), Baia Sprie (Romania), (USA), (Russia), (Colombia).

Stromeyerite

Sulphide
CuAgS

62

Named after the German chemist, F. Stromeyer (1776–1835) (Beudant 1832)

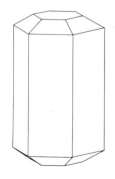

● Hardness: 2.5–3 (brittle) ● Streak: dark steel-grey ● Colour: dark steel-grey, light violet tint ● Transparency: opaque ● Lustre: metallic to dull (weathered) ● Cleavage: absent ● Fracture: conchoidal ● Morphology: granular and massive aggregates, crystals are rare ● Specific gravity: 6.2–6.3 ● Crystal system: dimorphous, below 78 °C orthorhombic, above 78 °C cubic ● Crystal form: pseudohexagonal prisms, sometimes twinned ● Chemical composition: Cu 31.19%, Ag 53.05%, S 15.76% ● Chemical properties: soluble in HCl and HNO$_3$ ● Handling: clean with distilled water, protect from light ● Similar minerals: chalcocite **(68)** ● Distinguishing features: chemical reaction to Ag ● Genesis: hydrothermal and secondary ● Associated minerals: chalcocite, acanthite **(75)**, bornite **(192)** ● Occurrence: rare; Czechanowiecz (Poland), Copiapó (Chile), Guanacevi (Mexico), Broken Hill – New South Wales (Australia) ● Application: Ag ore.

---

1. Miargyrite – coarse-bladed crystals (to 10 mm) in cavity in quartz; Příbram (Czech Republic) **2. Diaphorite** – short columnar, vertically striated crystals (5 mm) in association with carbonates; Příbram (Czech Republic)

Miargyrite, diaphorite

Proustite (Light red silver ore)

Sulphide
Ag$_3$AsS$_3$

63

Named after the French chemist, J. L. Proust (1755–1826) (Beudant 1832)

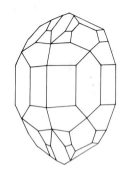

● Hardness: 2.5 (brittle) ● Streak: brick-red ● Colour: cinnabar-red, turns black with time ● Transparency: semi-transparent to translucent ● Lustre: adamantine ● Cleavage: good on (10$\bar{1}$1) ● Fracture: conchoidal ● Morphology: crystals, granular aggregates, dendrites, crusts, massive ● Specific gravity: 5.57 ● Crystal system: trigonal ● Crystal form: prisms, short columnar (seemingly scalenohedra), twinning ● Chemical composition: Ag 65.42%, As 15.14%, S 19.44%; admixtures: Sb ● Chemical properties: melts when heated, produces garlicky odour, soluble in HNO$_3$ ● Handling: clean with distilled water, protect from light ● Similar minerals: pyrargyrite **(64)** ● Distinguishing features: lighter streak and colour than pyrargyrite, chemical ● Genesis: mostly hydrothermal ● Associated minerals: silver **(49)**, acanthite **(75)**, arsenic **(176)** ● Occurrence: rare; Annaberg, Wittichen (FRG), Jáchymov (Czech Republic), Chañarcillo (Chile) ● Application: Ag ore.

Pyrargyrite (Dark red silver ore)

Sulphide
Ag$_3$SbS$_3$

64

From the Greek *pyr* – fire and *argyros* – silver (Glocker 1831)

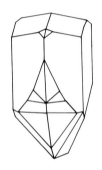

● Hardness: 2.5–3 (fragile) ● Streak: cherry-red ● Colour: dark red to grey-red ● Transparency: in thin plates, reddish translucence ● Lustre: adamantine, splendent, metallic ● Cleavage: good on (1011) ● Fracture: conchoidal to uneven ● Morphology: crystals, granular aggregates, massive, encrustations, pseudomorphs ● Specific gravity: 5.85 ● Crystal system: trigonal ● Crystal form: prisms (usually prisms with triangular cross-section), hemihedral with differently developed faces, rarely twinned ● Chemical composition: Ag 59.76%, Sb 22.48%, S 17.76%; admixtures: As ● Chemical properties: melts when heated, soluble in HNO$_3$, HCl and KOH ● Handling: clean with distilled water, protect from light ● Similar minerals: proustite **(63)**, cinnabar **(76)**, cuprite **(209)** ● Distinguishing features: of darker streak than proustite, chemical (granular aggregates) ● Genesis: hydrothermal ● Associated minerals: silver **(49)**, stephanite **(67)**, acanthite **(75)** ● Occurrence: rare; St. Andreasberg, Freiberg (FRG), Příbram, Jáchymov (Czech Republic), Hiendelaencina (Spain), Chañarcillo (Chile), Zacatecas and Guanajuato (Mexico), (USA), (Peru) ● Application: Ag ore.

Pyrostilpnite (Fire blende)

Sulphide
Ag$_3$SbS$_3$

65

From the Greek *pyr* – fire and *stilpnos* – shining (Dana 1868)

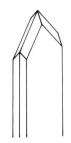

● Hardness: 2 ● Streak: orange-yellow ● Colour: hyacinth-red to orange-red (luminous red) ● Transparency: translucent ● Lustre: adamantine, pearly on (010) ● Cleavage: perfect on (010) ● Fracture: conchoidal ● Other features of cohesion: in thin plates, flexible ● Morphology: crystals, wisp-like and needle-shaped aggregates ● Specific gravity: 5.94 ● Crystal system: monoclinic ● Crystal form: elongated plates with vertical striation, rarely in twins ● Chemical composition: Ag 59.76%, Sb 22.48%, S 17.76% ● Chemical properties: soluble in HNO$_3$, melts when heated ● Handling: clean with distilled water, protect from light ● Similar minerals: cinnabar **(76)** ● Distinguishing features: specific gravity, chemical properties ● Genesis: hydrothermal ● Associated minerals: silver **(49)**, miargyrite **(60)**, pyrargyrite **(64)**, acanthite **(75)** ● Occurrence: rare; St. Andreasberg, Freiberg (FRG), Příbram (Czech Republic), Chañarcillo (Chile).

---

1. Proustite – prismatic crystal (9 mm) with calcite; Jáchymov (Czech Republic) **2. Pyrargyrite** – elongated crystals (up to 4 mm) in cavity in quartz; Banská Štiavnica (Slovakia)

Proustite, pyrargyrite

Xanthoconite

Sulphide
Ag_3AsS_3

66

From the Greek *xanthos* – yellow and *konis* – powder (Breithaupt 1840)

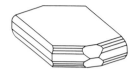

● Hardness: 2–3 (brittle). ● Streak: orange-yellow ● Colour: dark crimson red, dark orange to brown, in transmitted light lemon-yellow ● Transparency: translucent to transparent ● Lustre: adamantine, pearly on (001) ● Cleavage: on (001) ● Fracture: subconchoidal ● Morphology: crystals, earthy ● Specific gravity: 5.5–5.6 ● Crystal system: monoclinic ● Crystal form: plates, pseudorhombic ● Chemical composition: Ag 65.42%, As 15.14%, S 19.44% ● Chemical properties: when heated melts and produces garlicky odour, soluble in HNO_3 ● Handling: clean with distilled water, protect from light ● Similar minerals: proustite **(63)** ● Distinguishing features: streak, crystal form ● Genesis: hydrothermal ● Associated minerals: proustite, arsenic **(176)** ● Occurrence: rare; Freiberg, Wittichen (FRG), Jáchymov (Czech Republic), Chañarcillo (Chile).

Stephanite (Brittle silver ore)

Sulphide
Ag_5SbS_4

67

Named after the Austrian mining engineer, A. Stephan (1817–1867) (Haidinger 1845)

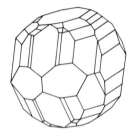

● Hardness: 2.5 (brittle) ● Streak: black, shining ● Colour: iron-black ● Transparency: opaque ● Lustre: metallic, when exposed to the light slowly becomes dull ● Cleavage: imperfect on (010) ● Fracture: conchoidal to uneven ● Morphology: crystals, granular aggregates, massive ● Specific gravity: 6.2–6.3 ● Crystal system: orthorhombic ● Crystal form: short prisms, often pseudohexagonal, multi-planed, coarse plates ● Chemical composition: Ag 68.33%, Sb 15.42%, S 16.25%; admixtures: As, Cu, Fe ● Chemical properties: melts when heated, soluble in hot HNO_3 ● Handling: clean with distilled water, protect from light ● Similar minerals: polybasite **(9)**, acanthite **(75)** ● Distinguishing features: crystal form, hardness, specific gravity ● Genesis: hydrothermal, secondary ● Associated minerals: silver **(49)**, pyrargyrite **(64)**, acanthite and other Ag minerals ● Occurrence: rare; Freiberg, St. Andreasberg (FRG), Příbram (Czech Republic), Comstock Lode (USA), Chañarcillo (Chile) ● Application: Ag ore.

Chalcocite (Copper glance)

Sulphide
Cu_2S

68

From the Greek *chalkos* – copper (Beudant 1832)

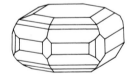

● Hardness: 2.5–3 (brittle) ● Streak: dark grey, metallic ● Colour: lead-grey, quickly becomes dark, with a bluish or greenish tint ● Transparency: opaque ● Lustre: on a fresh fracture metallic, becomes dull ● Cleavage: imperfect on (110) ● Fracture: conchoidal to uneven ● Morphology: crystals, rarely massive granular aggregates, earthy, pseudomorphs after bornite **(192)** ● Specific gravity: 5.7–5.8 ● Crystal system: dimorphic, < 103 °C orthorhombic, > 103 °C hexagonal ● Crystal form: coarse plates, short prisms, rarely dipyramidal, sometimes twins or even triplets ● Chemical composition: Cu 79.8%, S 20.2%; admixtures: Ag, Fe ● Chemical properties: spatters when heated, soluble in HNO_3 ● Handling: clean with water ● Similar minerals: acanthite **(75)**, tetrahedrite **(190)**, bornite ● Distinguishing features: when scratched shows a shining striation; specific gravity and crystal form ● Genesis: hydrothermal, secondary ● Associated minerals: copper **(47)**, chalcopyrite **(185)**, bornite, cuprite **(209)** ● Occurrence: common; primary in Redruth – Cornwall (Great Britain). The secondary mineral is found in Butte and Bisbee (USA), Chuquicamata (Chile) ● Application: Cu ore.

---

1. **Xanthoconite** – euhedral crystal (2 mm); Jáchymov (Czech Republic) 2. **Stephanite** – short columnar crystals (up to 4 mm) on quartz; Banská Štiavnica (Slovakia) 3. **Chalcocite** – druse of pseudohexagonal crystals (the largest blades 7 mm); Redruth (Great Britain)

Xanthoconite, stephanite, chalcocite

Emplectite

69

From the Greek *emplektos* – interwoven (Kenngott 1853)

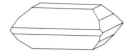

● Hardness: 2 (brittle) ● Streak: black ● Colour: tin-white to steel-grey with a greenish tint ● Transparency: opaque ● Lustre: metallic ● Cleavage: perfect on (010) ● Fracture: uneven ● Morphology: rodlike crystals, granular and massive aggregates ● Specific gravity: 6.4 ● Crystal system: orthorhombic ● Crystal form: elongated plates, needles, long prisms with longitudinal striations, twins ● Chemical composition: Cu 18.88%, Bi 62.08%, S 19.04% ● Chemical properties: melts when heated, soluble in HNO_3 ● Handling: clean with distilled water ● Similar minerals: wittichenite **(70)**, bismutite **(71)** and other Bi minerals ● Distinguishing features: specific gravity ● Genesis: hydrothermal Bi-Co-Ni formations ● Associated minerals: bismutite, chalcopyrite **(185)**, quartz **(534)** ● Occurrence: rare; Schwarzenberg, Wittichen (FRG), Baiţa (Romania), Krásno (Czech Republic), Cerro de Pasco (Peru), Copiapó (Chile).

Wittichenite

70

Named after its locality in Wittichen (FRG) (Kenngott 1853)

● Hardness: 2.5 (brittle) ● Streak: black ● Colour: lead-grey, frequently tarnished ● Transparency: opaque ● Lustre: metallic ● Cleavage: absent ● Fracture: conchoidal to uneven ● Morphology: crystals, massive aggregates ● Specific gravity: 6.3–6.7 ● Crystal system: orthorhombic ● Crystal form: columnar to nodular, elongated plates ● Chemical composition: Cu 38.46%, Bi 42.15%, S 19.39%; admixtures: Ag ● Chemical properties: melts when heated, soluble in HCl and HNO_3 ● Handling: clean with distilled water ● Similar minerals: emplectite **(69)**, bismutite **(71)** ● Distinguishing features: emplectite – cleavable, bismutite – cleavable, lower fusibility, chemical properties ● Genesis: hydrothermal ● Associated minerals: bismutite, tennantite **(189)**, baryte **(240)**, fluorite **(291)** ● Occurrence: rare; Wittichen (FRG), Tsumeb (Namibia), Butte (USA), Cornwall (Great Britain).

Bismutite

71

Named after its composition (Dana 1868)

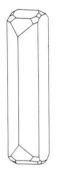

● Hardness: 2 ● Streak: grey, shining ● Colour: steel-grey with a slight yellowish or bluish tint ● Transparency: opaque ● Lustre: metallic ● Cleavage: perfect on (010) ● Fracture: uneven ● Other features of cohesion: flexible, sectile ● Morphology: crystals, radial, laminar and granular aggregates ● Specific gravity: 6.8–7.2 ● Crystal system: orthorhombic ● Crystal form: prisms, vertically striated, needle-shaped ● Chemical composition: Bi 81.30%, S 18.70%; admixtures: Se (seleno-bismutite), Sb (stibio-bismutite), Au, Pb, Cu ● Chemical properties: melts in candle flame, spattering when heated with a blow-pipe; soluble in HNO_3, in hot HCl and in alkaline substances ● Handling: clean with water ● Similar minerals: emplectite **(69)**, wittichenite **(70)**, cosalite **(72)** ● Distinguishing features: low fusibility, distinct cleavage, colouring ● Genesis: hydrothermal, pegmatites, contact-metasomatic ● Associated minerals: chalcopyrite **(185)**, arsenopyrite **(344)**, wolframite **(369)**, quartz **(534)**, cassiterite **(548)** ● Occurrence: rare; Schneeberg, Altenberg (FRG), Jáchymov (Czech Republic), Baiţa (Romania), Tasno (Bolivia), Cornwall (Great Britain) ● Application: Bi ore.

---

1. Emplectite – acicular crystals (up to 3 mm) in cavity in quartz; Oraviţa (Romania) **2. Bismutite** – prismatic crystals (to 20 mm) in siderite; Brosso (Italy) **3. Wittichenite** – long columnar crystals (21 mm) embayed in baryte; Wittichen (FRG)

Emplectite, bismutite, wittichenite

Cosalite

Sulphide
Pb₂Bi₂S₅

Sulphide
$Pb_2Bi_2S_5$

72

Named after the Cosala Mine (Mexico) (Genth 1877)

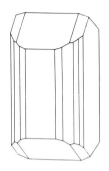

● Hardness: 2.5–3 ● Streak: black ● Colour: lead-grey to steel-grey ● Transparency: opaque ● Lustre: metallic ● Cleavage: good on (010) ● Fracture: uneven ● Morphology: radial and granular aggregates ● Specific gravity: 6.4–6.8 ● Crystal system: orthorhombic ● Crystal form: long prisms, vertically striated, hair-like ● Chemical composition: Pb 41.75%, Bi 42.10%, S 16.15%; admixtures: Cu, Ag, Sb, Se ● Chemical properties: fusible, soluble in HCl and HNO_3 ● Handling: clean with water ● Similar minerals: bismutite **(71)**, and other Bi sulpho-salts ● Distinguishing features: bismutite has a low fusibility; chemical properties ● Genesis: hydrothermal ● Associated minerals: Bi sulpho-salts with Pb, Cu ● Occurrence: rare; Baiţa (Romania), (Czech Republic), (Slovakia), Cosala Mine (Mexico), Cobalt (Canada), Kingsgate (Australia), Bukuka and Sochodo (Russia) ● Application: Bi ore.

Galenobismutite

Sulphide
PbBi₂S₄

Sulphide
$PbBi_2S_4$

73

Named after its chemical composition (Sjögren 1878)

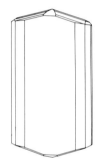

● Hardness: 2.5–3 ● Streak: grey-black, shining ● Colour: tin-white, light grey with yellowish and iridescent tarnished colours ● Transparency: opaque ● Lustre: metallic, full ● Cleavage: good on (110) ● Fracture: uneven ● Other features of cohesion: flexible ● Morphology: crystals, radial, fibrous and massive aggregates ● Specific gravity: 7.1 ● Crystal system: orthorhombic ● Crystal form: prisms, distorted, needles, plates ● Chemical composition: Pb 27.50%, Bi 55.48%, S 17.02%; admixtures: Se weibullite variety ● Chemical properties: fuses in a blowpipe flame, soluble in HNO_3 producing a yellow precipitate ● Handling: clean with water, but fibrous aggregates with a stream of air ● Similar minerals: bismutite **(71)**, cosalite **(72)** ● Distinguishing features: chemical properties: from bismutite by fusibility, from cosalite by cleavage ● Genesis: hydrothermal, fumaroles ● Associated minerals: bismuth **(48)**, gold **(50)**, bismutite, Au tellurides ● Occurrence: rare; Falun-Ko Mine (Sweden) – weibullite variety, Rammelsberg (FRG), Vulcano (Italy), Caribou (Canada) ● Application: Bi ore.

Berzelianite

Selenide
Cu₂Se

Selenide
Cu_2Se

74

Named after J. J. Berzelius (1799–1848) (Beudant 1832)

● Hardness: 2 ● Streak: shining ● Colour: on a fresh fractured surface silver-white with bluish tint, quickly becomes dull and black ● Transparency: opaque ● Lustre: on a freshly fractured surface metallic, turns dull ● Cleavage: absent ● Fracture: uneven ● Morphology: granular, massive aggregates, dendrites, impregnations ● Specific gravity: 6.7 ● Crystal system: cubic ● Crystal form: unknown ● Chemical composition: Cu 61.62%, Se 38.38%; admixtures: Ag and Tl ● Chemical properties: soluble in HNO_3 ● Handling: clean with water, protect from light ● Similar minerals: other selenides ● Distinguishing features: X-rays and chemical properties ● Genesis: hydrothermal ● Associated minerals: clausthalite **(79)**, tiemannite **(80)**, umangite **(201)** and other selenides ● Occurrence: rare; Lehrbach, Clausthal and Tilkerode (FRG), Skrikerum (Sweden), Předbořice, Petrovice and Bukov (Czech Republic), Sierra de Cacheuta (Argentina).

---

1. Cosalite – aggregate of acicular crystals (to 10 mm) in quartz-siderite vein; Prachovce (Slovakia) **2. Berzelianite** – irregular granular aggregations in carbonates; Bukov (Czech Republic – width of field 23 mm)

Cosalite, berzelianite

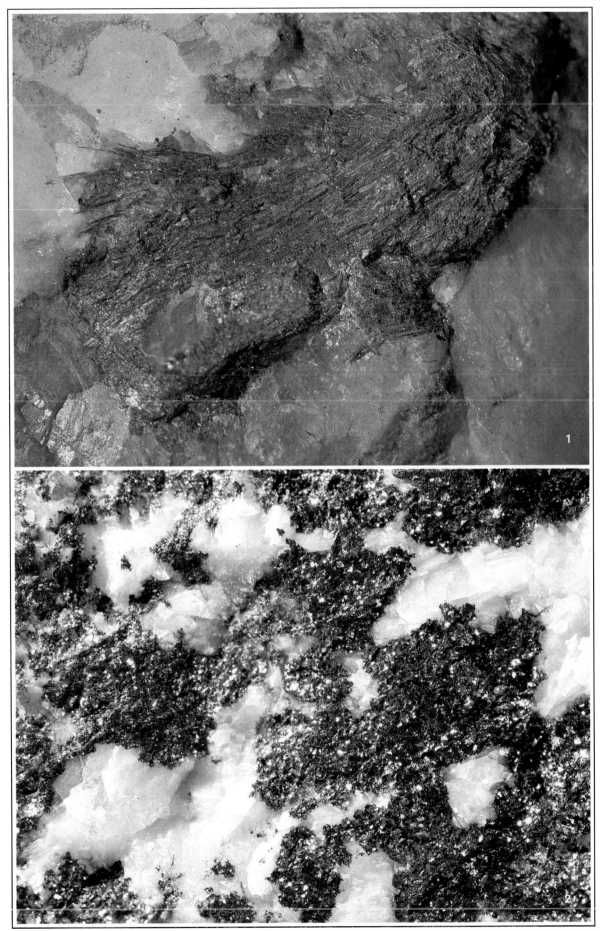

H
2—3

1

2

Acanthite – Argentite (Silver glance)

Sulphide
Ag$_2$S

75

From the Greek *akanta* – arrow (acanthite) (Kenngott 1855)

From the Latin *argentum* – silver (argentite) (Heidinger 1845)

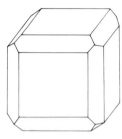

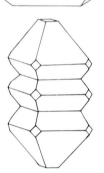

● Hardness: 2 ● Streak: black, submetallic ● Colour: lead-grey to black, becomes dull in the light ● Transparency: opaque ● Lustre: on freshly fractured surface metallic, otherwise dull ● Cleavage: imperfect on (100) ● Fracture: conchoidal, uneven ● Other features of cohesion: malleable, flexible, sectile ● Morphology: crystals, dendrites, skeletal, granular and massive aggregates, pseudomorphs ● Specific gravity: 7.3 ● Crystal system: dimorphic, > 179 °C stable acanthite (orthorhombic), < 179 °C argentite (cubic) ● Crystal form: octahedral, hexahedral, rhombododecahedral – **argentite;** often bent and uneven, twins, plates, isometric, columnar – **acanthite.** Acanthite often occurs as pseudomorphs after argentite ● Chemical composition: Ag 87.06%, S 12.94%; admixtures: Cu ● Chemical properties: soluble in HNO$_3$, HCl and ammonia ● Handling: clean with distilled water, protect from light ● Similar minerals: silver **(49)**, chalcocite **(68)**, galena **(77)** ● Distinguishing features: from chalcocite by specific gravity and crystal form; from silver by specific gravity; from galena by difficult cleavage, malleability ● Genesis: hydrothermal, secondary (cementation zone) ● Associated minerals: polybasite **(9)**, silver, proustite **(63)**, pyrargyrite **(64)**, stephanite **(67)**, galena ● Occurrence: rare; Schneeberg, Annaberg, Johanngeorgenstadt and Freiberg – crystals up to 4 kg (FRG), Jáchymov (Czech Republic), Banská Štiavnica (Slovakia), Kongsberg (Norway), Cornwall (Great Britain), Arispa – large crystals (Mexico), Comstock Lode – Nevada (USA) ● Application: important Ag ore.

Cinnabar

Sulphide
HgS

76

P

The name is probably of Persian origin (Theophrastus 315 BC)

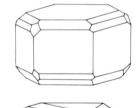

● Hardness: 2–2.5 (brittle) ● Streak: red ● Colour: red, brownish-red ● Transparency: translucent ● Lustre: on cleavage planes and crystal faces adamantine, otherwise dull ● Cleavage: perfect on (1010) ● Fracture: uneven, splintery ● Morphology: crystals, rarely granular, massive, loose-aggregates, pseudomorphs ● Specific gravity: 8.1 (varying according to admixtures) ● Crystal system: trigonal ● Crystal form: coarse plates, rhombohedra, trapezohedra, twins ● Chemical composition: Hg 86.21%, S 13.79%; admixtures: Se, Te, Sb, bitumens ● Chemical properties: evaporates when heated, insoluble in HNO$_3$ and H$_2$SO$_4$ ● Handling: clean with water and acids ● Similar minerals: realgar **(5)**, proustite **(63)**, cuprite **(209)**, rutile **(464)**, hematite **(472)** ● Distinguishing features: higher specific gravity, fusibility, chemical properties ● Genesis: hydrothermal, rarely secondary ● Associated minerals: stibnite **(51)**, pyrite **(436)**, marcasite **(437)**, chalcedony **(449)**, quartz **(534)** ● Occurrence: common; Moschellandsberg (FRG), Monte Amiata (Italy), Almaden (Spain), Idria (Slovenia), Rudňany (Slovakia), Nikitovka – twins (Ukraine), Terlingua, New Idria and New Almaden (USA), Wanshanchang deposit – Hu-nan – large crystals and twins measuring 4.5 cm (China) ● Application: important Hg ore; rarely faceted as a precious stone.

---

1. Acanthite – euhedral crystals (4 mm) on quartz; Jáchymov (Czech Republic) **2. Cinnabar** – carmine crystals (9 mm) on quartz; Almaden (Spain)

Acanthite — argentite, cinnabar

Galena (Lead glance, Blue lead)

Sulphide
PbS

77

The Roman naturalist, Pliny, used the name *galena* to describe lead ore

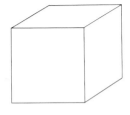

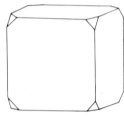

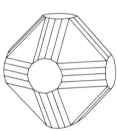

● Hardness: 2.5 (brittle) ● Streak: grey-black, bluish, shiny ● Colour: light or dark lead-grey, with a bluish tint on a fresh fracture ● Transparency: opaque ● Lustre: metallic, splendent on cleavage planes ● Cleavage: perfect on (100), poor on (111) ● Other features of cohesion: soft ● Morphology: crystals, granular, coarse-grained to compact, skeletal or stalactitic aggregates. Sometimes found grown with sphalerite **(181)** or as pseudomorph after pyromorphite **(262)** ● Crystal faces often are rough, broken by prominences; sometimes it is covered by quartz **(534)** or calcite crusts, sometimes overgrown with small crystals of chalcopyrite **(185)** ● Specific gravity: 7.2–7.6 ● Crystal system: cubic ● Crystal form: hexahedra, octahedra and their combinations, rarely plates and twins ● Chemical composition: Pb 86.60%, S 13.40%; admixtures: Ag, Sb, Bi, Se, Fe, Zn, Au ● Chemical properties: readily fusible, produces sulphidic vapours and tiny ductile globules; soluble in HNO_3 and HCl ● Similar minerals: compact massive stibnite **(51)**, altaite **(78)**, clausthalite **(79)**, bournonite **(193)** ● Distinguishing features: from stibnite and bournonite by a higher specific gravity, perfect cleavage, crystal forms and chemical properties; from altaite and clausthalite by a lower specific gravity and chemical properties ● Handling: clean with water; when cleaned mechanically cleavage should be observed. Calcite crusts can be removed by acetic acid ● Genesis: hydrothermal, rarely secondary, sedimentary, contact-metasomatic ● Associated minerals: sphalerite, calcite **(217)**, baryte **(240)**, fluorite **(291)**, pyrite **(436)**, quartz ● Occurrence: common: Bad Grund and Clausthal in Harz; Bensberg, Siegerland, Christian Levin Mine near Essen and Altenberg near Aachen, Freiberg and Neudorf (FRG), Příbram (Czech Republic – in the Stříbro deposit large hexahedral crystals measuring 12 cm long have been found), Banská Štiavnica (Slovakia), Trepča (Serbia), Linares and La Carolina (Spain), Cœur d'Alène – Idaho, Leadville and Aspen-Colorado, Joplin – Missouri (USA), Isle of Man (Great Britain – large crystals measuring 25 cm), Sadon and Turlan (Russia), Olkuz, Bytom and Trzebionka (Poland), Bleiberg (Austria), Raibl and Tarvizio (Italy), Bawdin Mine (Burma), Rosebery (Tasmania), Kabwe (Zambia) ● Application: most important Pb ore; because of a high content of Ag galena is one of the most important Ag ores.

Galena – druse of euhedral crystals (20 mm); Freiberg (FRG)

Galena

Altaite

78

Named after its locality in the Altai Mountains (Russia)
(Rose 1837)

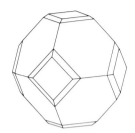

● Hardness: 2.5 (brittle) ● Streak: black ● Colour: tin-white with a yellowish tint, bronze tarnish colours ● Transparency: opaque ● Lustre: metallic ● Cleavage: perfect on (100) ● Fracture: conchoidal to uneven ● Morphology: crystals, granular, massive ● Specific gravity: 8.1–8.2 ● Crystal system: cubic ● Crystal form: hexahedral, octahedral ● Chemical composition: Pb 61.91%, Te 38.09%; admixtures: Ag, Au, Cu ● Chemical properties: soluble in HNO_3 and H_2SO_4 ● Handling: clean with distilled water ● Similar minerals: galena **(77)** ● Distinguishing features: altaite has a higher specific gravity and is a lighter colour ● Genesis: hydrothermal ● Associated minerals: silver **(49)**, gold **(50)**, galena, tetrahedrite **(190)** ● Occurrence: rare; Zavodinsk and Stepnyak (Russia), Săcărâmb (Romania), Stanislaus Mine (California, USA), Coquimbo (Chile) ● Application: sometimes a source of Te.

Clausthalite

79

Named after its source in Lorenz Mine (Clausthal, Harz, FRG)
(Beudant 1832)

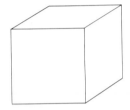

● Hardness: 2.5–3 ● Streak: grey-black ● Colour: lead-grey, slightly bluish ● Transparency: opaque ● Lustre: metallic ● Cleavage: perfect on (001) ● Morphology: granular, compact ● Specific gravity: 8.28 ● Crystal system: cubic ● Crystal form: unknown ● Chemical composition: Pb 72.34%, Se 27.66%; admixtures: Hg, Co, Cu ● Chemical properties: soluble in HNO_3 and H_2SO_4 ● Handling: clean with distilled water ● Similar minerals: galena **(77)**, altaite **(78)** ● Distinguishing features: reliably by chemical properties ● Genesis: hydrothermal ● Associated minerals: berzelianite **(74)**, tiemannite **(80)**, and other selenides ● Occurrence: rare; Clausthal, Lehrbach, Tilkerode (FRG), Předbořice, Zálesí, Petrovice and Bukov (Czech Republic), Cerro de Cacheuta (Argentina), Pacajaque (Boliva), (Sweden).

Tiemannite

80

Named after its discoverer, C. W. F. Tiemann (1848–1899)
(Naumann 1855)

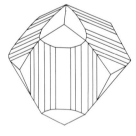

● Hardness: 2.5 (brittle) ● Streak: black ● Colour: dark lead-grey ● Transparency: opaque ● Lustre: metallic ● Cleavage: absent ● Fracture: uneven ● Morphology: crystals, granular, compact ● Specific gravity: 8.26 ● Crystal system: cubic ● Crystal form: tetrahedral (very rare) ● Chemical composition: Hg 71.70%, Se 28.30%; admixtures: Cd, Se ● Chemical properties: only soluble in aqua regia ● Handling: clean with water or acids ● Similar minerals: chalcocite **(68)** ● Distinguishing features: chemical properties, specific gravity, solubility in acids ● Genesis: hydrothermal ● Associated minerals: clausthalite **(79)**, umangite **(201)**, calcite **(217)**, baryte **(240)** ● Occurrence: rare; Clausthal, Lehrbach, Zorge, Tilkerode (FRG), Předbořice, Černý důl and Petrovice (Czech Republic), Marysville, Piute Co. – Utah and Clear Lake – California (USA).

---

1. Clausthalite – grey, finely granular irregular aggregates in carbonates; Lehrbach (FRG) **2. Tiemannite** – fine granular aggregation in association with carbonates and chalcopyrite; Clausthal (FRG – width of field 52 mm)

Clausthalite, tiemannite

97

Krennerite

Telluride
(Au,Ag)Te$_2$

81

Named after the Hungarian mineralogist, J. A. Krenner (1839–1920) (Rath 1877)

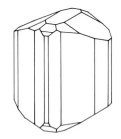

● Hardness: 2–3 (brittle) ● Streak: silvery-white ● Colour: silvery-white to light brass yellow ● Transparency: opaque ● Lustre: metallic ● Cleavage: perfect on (001) ● Morphology: crystals, granular aggregates ● Specific gravity: 8.62 ● Crystal system: orthorhombic ● Crystal form: short prisms, deeply striated ● Chemical composition: Au 32.99%, Ag 7.22%, Te 59.79 %; proportion of Au to Ag varies ● Chemical properties: soluble in HNO$_3$; when heated with H$_2$SO$_4$ the solution is tinged raspberry-red ● Handling: clean with water ● Similar minerals: sylvanite **(12)**, petzite **(82)**, calaverite **(83)** ● Distinguishing features: from calaverite and petzite by cleavage, lower specific gravity; from sylvanite by higher hardness ● Genesis: hydrothermal ● Associated minerals: sylvanite, calaverite, gold **(50)**, pyrrhotine **(283)**, pyrite **(436)** ● Occurrence: rare; Săcărâmb (Romania), Cripple Creek – Colorado (USA), Kalgoorlie (Australia) ● Application: Au ore.

Petzite

Telluride
Ag$_3$AuTe$_2$

82

Named after W. Petz (who first analysed it) (Haidinger 1845)

● Hardness: 2.5 (brittle) ● Streak: grey-black ● Colour: lead-grey to black ● Transparency: opaque ● Lustre: splendent, metallic ● Cleavage: absent ● Fracture: uneven ● Morphology: massive and granular aggregates ● Specific gravity: 9.13 ● Crystal system: cubic ● Crystal form: unknown ● Chemical composition: Ag 41.71%, Au 25.42%, Te 32.87% ● Chemical properties: soluble in HNO$_3$ (Au remains), in hot H$_2$SO$_4$ becomes a raspberry-red colour ● Handling: clean with water and HCl ● Similar minerals: coloradoite **(198)** ● Distinguishing features: chemical properties, hardness, specific gravity ● Genesis: hydrothermal ● Associated minerals: sylvanite **(12)**, tellurium **(46)**, calaverite **(83)** ● Occurrence: rare; Săcărâmb (Romania), Cripple Creek – Colorado (USA), Kalgoorlie (Australia) ● Application: Ag and Au ore.

Calaverite

Telluride
AuTe$_2$

83

Named after its source in Calaveras County (California, USA)

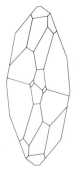

● Hardness: 2.5 (brittle) ● Streak: greenish-grey, yellowish-grey ● Colour: bronze-yellow to silver-white ● Transparency: opaque ● Lustre: metallic ● Cleavage: absent ● Fracture: uneven ● Morphology: rarely crystals, granular aggregates ● Specific gravity: 9.3 ● Crystal system: monoclinic ● Crystal form: prisms, multi-planed, striated, needle-shaped, twinning ● Chemical composition: Au 43.59%, Te 56.41%; admixtures: Ag ● Chemical properties: soluble in HNO$_3$ and H$_2$SO$_4$ ● Handling: clean with water ● Similar minerals: pyrite **(436)**, other tellurides ● Distinguishing features: from pyrite by lower hardness, form of crystals; from tellurides by chemical composition ● Genesis: hydrothermal ● Associated minerals: sylvanite **(12)**, gold **(50)** and other tellurides ● Occurrence: rare; Calaveras County – California and Cripple Creek – Colorado (USA), Kalgoorlie (Australia), (Romania), (Russia), (Mexico) ● Application: Au ore.

---

1. Petzite – granular aggregate in quartz; Săcărâmb (Romania – width of field 42 mm) **2. Krennerite** – short prismatic striated crystals (up to 2 mm) with quartz; Săcărâmb (Romania) **3. Calaverite** – intergrown columnar crystals in quartz with longitudinal striation; Cripple Creek (USA – width of field 12 mm)

Petzite, krennerite, calaverite

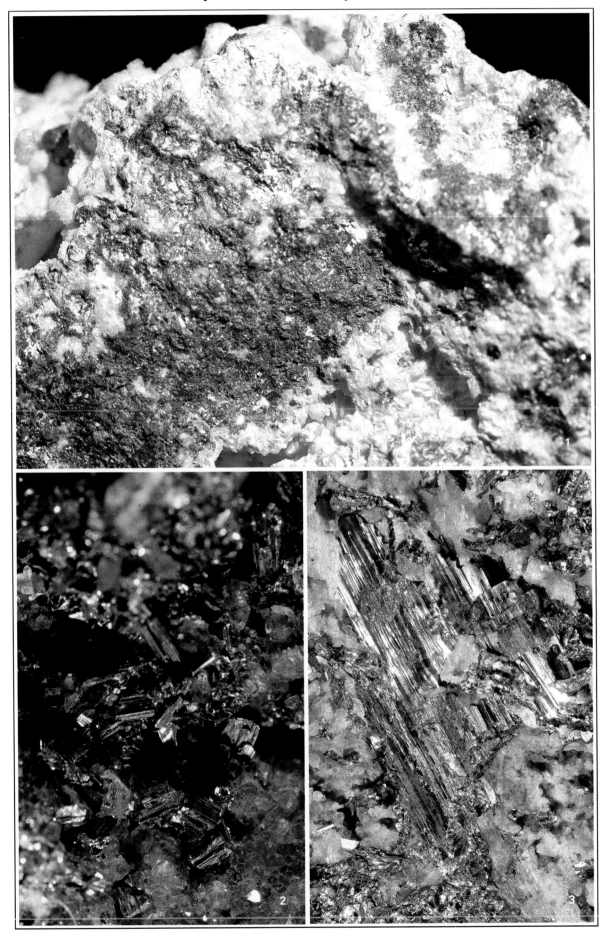

Carnallite

84

Named after the German mining engineer, R. von Carnall (1804–1874) (Rose 1856)

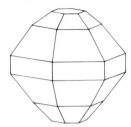

● Hardness: 2.5 ● Streak: white ● Colour: colourless, milky-white, yellowish, pinkish, brownish, rarely light green ● Transparency: transparent to translucent ● Lustre: vitreous, on fractured surface greasy ● Cleavage: absent ● Fracture: conchoidal ● Morphology: crystals are rare, granular and fibrous aggregates forming layers ● Solubility: readily soluble in water emitting creaking sound ● Other properties: bitter ● Specific gravity: 1.6 ● Crystal system: orthorhombic ● Crystal form: coarse plates, dipyramidal, pseudohexagonal ● Chemical composition: K 14.07%, Mg 8.75%, Cl 38.28%, H_2O 38.90%; admixtures: Na, Br, Cs, Rb, Li, Tl ● Chemical properties: readily fusible, tinges a flame violet ● Handling: hygroscopic, preserve in sealed bottles ● Similar minerals: sylvite **(85)**, halite **(86)** ● Distinguishing features: no cleavage, more fragile ● Genesis: in oceans and salt lakes ● Associated minerals: sylvite, halite ● Occurrence: frequent; Beienrod, Stassfurt (FRG), Kaluzh (Ukraine) ● Application: source of K, Mg, Br.

Sylvite

85

Named after the Dutch chemist, Sylvia de la Boë (1614–1672) (Beudant 1832)

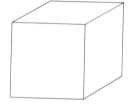

● Hardness: 2 ● Streak: white ● Colour: white, yellowish, reddish, grey, bluish ● Transparency: transparent to translucent ● Lustre: vitreous ● Cleavage: perfect on (100) ● Fracture: conchoidal ● Morphology: crystals, granular, fibrous, earthy aggregates, crusts ● Solubility: soluble in water ● Other properties: bitter-saline taste ● Specific gravity: 1.99 ● Crystal system: cubic ● Crystal form: hexahedral, octahedral, blunt ● Chemical composition: K 52.44%, Cl 47.56%; admixtures: Na ● Chemical properties: hygroscopic, fusible in candle flame, tinges a flame violet ● Handling: preserve in sealed bottles ● Similar minerals: halite **(86)** ● Distinguishing features: sylvite has a bitter-saline taste and tinges a flame violet ● Genesis: ocean salt deposits, salt lakes, volcanic emanations ● Associated minerals: carnallite **(84)**, halite ● Occurrence: rare; Hannover, Stassfurt (FRG), (USA) ● Application: source of K.

Halite (Rock salt)

86

L

From the Greek *halos* – salt and *líthos* – rock (Glocker 1847)

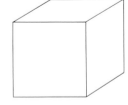

● Hardness: 2 (brittle) ● Streak: white ● Colour: white, greyish, pinkish, bluish, violet, orange ● Transparency: transparent to translucent ● Lustre: vitreous, greasy ● Cleavage: perfect on (100) ● Fracture: conchoidal ● Morphology: crystals, granular, fibrous aggregates, stalactitic ● Solubility: soluble in water ● Other properties: saline ● Specific gravity: 2.1–2.2 ● Crystal system: cubic ● Crystal form: hexahedral, rarely octahedral, skeletal crystals, rarely twins ● Chemical composition: Na 39.34%, Cl 60.66%; admixtures: I, Br ● Chemical properties: spatters when heated and tinges a flame yellow ● Handling: clean with alcohol, slightly hygroscopic, preserve in a dry place ● Similar minerals: sylvite **(85)**, anhydrite **(235)** ● Distinguishing features: saline, perfect cleavage ● Genesis: ocean salt deposits, salt lakes, volcanic emanations ● Associated minerals: gypsum **(29)**, carnallite **(84)**, sylvite ● Occurrence: frequent; Heilbronn, Stassfurt (FRG), Salzkammergut (Austria), Wieliczka (Poland), Great Salt Lake – Utah (USA) ● Application: food and chemical industries.

---

1. Carnallite – reddish granular aggregate; Solikamsk, Urals (Russia) **2. Sylvite** – granular aggregate of crystals of subhedral structure in association with halite; Buggingen (France – width of field 90 mm) **3. Halite** – druse of hexahedral crystals (the largest 21 mm); Salzkammer (Austria)

Carnallite, sylvite, halite

Villiaumite

Halide
NaF

87

Named after the French traveller, Villiaum (Lacroix 1908)

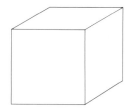

● Hardness: 2 ● Streak: white, pinkish ● Colour: crimson-red, dark cherry-red, colourless ● Transparency: transparent to translucent ● Lustre: vitreous ● Cleavage: perfect on (100) ● Morphology: rarely crystals, granular aggregates ● Solubility: readily soluble in cold water ● Specific gravity: 2.79 ● Crystal system: cubic ● Crystal form: imperfect hexahedra ● Chemical composition: Na 54.76%, F 45.24% ● Chemical properties: readily fusible ● Handling: clean with alcohol ● Genesis: alkaline eruptive rocks ● Associated minerals: astrophyllite **(278)**, nepheline **(397)**, sodalite **(393)** ● Occurrence: rare; Los Island (Guinea), Kola Peninsula, Lovozer Tundra − in an apatite deposit aggregates of several centimetres in size, and Khibiny Tundra (Russia), Ilimaussak (Greenland).

Cryolite

Halide
Na$_3$AlF$_6$

88

From the Greek *kryos* − ice and *lithos* − stone (Abildgaard 1799)

● Hardness: 2.5−3 (brittle) ● Streak: white ● Colour: white, grey, reddish, brownish ● Transparency: transparent to translucent ● Lustre: vitreous to greasy, pearly on (001) faces ● Cleavage: good on (001) ● Fracture: uneven ● Morphology: crystals, granular aggregates often arranged in a parqueting pattern ● Specific gravity: 2.95 ● Crystal system: monoclinic ● Crystal form: pseudotetragonal, pseudocubic, twinning ● Chemical composition: Na 32.86%, Al 12.84%, F 54.30% ● Chemical properties: readily fusible into colourless glass, soluble in H$_2$SO$_4$, and partly in HCl ● Handling: clean with water ● Similar minerals: anhydrite **(235)**, baryte **(240)** ● Distinguishing features: hardness, specific gravity ● Genesis: pegmatites ● Associated minerals: galena **(77)**, siderite **(306)**, pyrite **(436)**, quartz **(534)** ● Occurrence: rare; Ivigtut (Greenland) − in pegmatites, Pikes Peak − Colorado (USA), Mias, Urals (Russia), Kaffa granites (Nigeria) ● Application: glazing and optical glass; was extracted as Al ore in Ivigtut.

Diaboleite

Halide
2 Pb(OH)$_2$. CuCl$_2$

89

From the Greek *dia* − difference and the mineral *boleite* (Spenser 1923)

● Hardness: 2.5 (brittle) ● Streak: blue ● Colour: dark blue ● Transparency: transparent to translucent ● Lustre: adamantine ● Cleavage: perfect on (001) ● Fracture: conchoidal ● Morphology: crystals, grains, crusts ● Specific gravity: 5.48 ● Crystal system: tetragonal ● Crystal form: plates ● Chemical composition: Pb 67.18%, Cu 10.30%, Cl 11.49%, O 5.19%, H$_2$O 5.84 % ● Chemical properties: soluble in HNO$_3$ ● Handling: clean with water ● Similar minerals: linarite **(110)** ● Distinguishing features: more intense colour, higher specific gravity, lower hardness ● Genesis: secondary ● Associated minerals: boleite **(207)**, cerussite **(225)**, wulfenite **(243)** and other secondary minerals ● Occurrence: rare; Mendip Hills (Great Britain), Mammoth Mine − Arizona (USA), Christian Levin near Essen (FRG).

---

1. Villiaumite − fissile aggregate in nepheline syenite; Los Island (Guinea − width of field 34 mm) **2. Cryolite** − crystalline aggregate of parquet-like appearance; Ivigtut (Greenland − width of field 44 mm)

Villiaumite, cryolite

Gibbsite (Hydrargyllite)

Hydroxide
Al(OH)$_3$

90

L

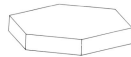

Named after the American collector, G. Gibbs (1776–1833) (Torrey 1822)

● Hardness: 2.5–3 ● Streak: white ● Colour: white, grey-white, green-white ● Transparency: transparent to translucent ● Lustre: vitreous, pearly on cleavage planes ● Cleavage: perfect on (001), scaly ● Morphology: crystals, scaly, cryptocrystalline, radial-fibrous and crusty aggregates ● Specific gravity: 2.3–2.4 ● Crystal system: monoclinic ● Crystal form: plates, scales, twins ● Luminescence: sometimes green or orange (short waves) ● Chemical composition: Al$_2$O$_3$ 65.4%, H$_2$O 34.6%; admixtures: Fe, Ga ● Chemical properties: soluble in hot acids and KOH, infusible, glowing, loses water, becomes white and hard ● Handling: clean with distilled water ● Similar minerals: muscovite **(165)**, diaspore **(463)** ● Distinguishing features: specific gravity, hardness ● Genesis: hydrothermal, secondary ● Associated minerals: boehmite **(208)**, limonite **(355)**, diaspore, corundum **(598)** ● Occurrence: frequent; Vogelsberg (FRG), Zlatoust – southern Urals – crystals up to 5 cm (Russia), Routivaare (Sweden), (USA), (Brazil), (France), (Hungary) ● Application: source of Al.

Brucite

Hydroxide
Mg(OH)$_2$

91

L

Named after the American mineralogist, A. Bruce (1777–1818) (Beudant 1824)

● Hardness: 2.5 ● Streak: white ● Colour: white, green ● Transparency: translucent to transparent ● Lustre: vitreous, pearly on cleavage planes ● Cleavage: perfect on (0001), scaly ● Other properties of cohesion: scales are flexible ● Morphology: crystals, scaly, fibrous or granular aggregates ● Specific gravity: 2.4 ● Crystal system: trigonal ● Crystal form: plates ● Luminescence: blue, blue-white ● Chemical composition: MgO 69%, H$_2$O 31%; admixtures: Mn, Fe ● Chemical properties: soluble in acids, infusible, shines when heated ● Handling: clean with distilled water ● Similar minerals: talc **(41)**, pyrophyllite **(42)**, gibbsite **(90)** ● Distinguishing features: solubility in HCl, hardness, X-rays, chemical properties ● Genesis: hydrothermal, secondary ● Associated minerals: chlorite **(158)**, hydromagnesite **(214)**, serpentine **(273)** ● Occurrence: frequent; Predazzo (Italy), (Kazakhstan), (Sweden), Texas (USA), Palabora (RSA), Asbestos – Quebec (Canada) ● Application: as a source of Mg.

Nemalite

Hydroxide
Mg(OH)$_2$

92

From the Greek *nema* – thread or yarn and *lithos* – stone (Fibrous variety of brucite)

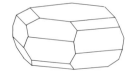

Physical and chemical properties are identical to those of brucite **(91)** from which it differs by a higher content of Fe and by fibrous structure of aggregates, resembling asbestos. It is usually coloured golden-yellow to yellowish-green; pearly to silky lustre ● Genesis and associated minerals are identical to brucite ● Occurrence: common; Asbestos – Quebec – fibres up to 50 cm long (Canada), Bazhenovsk – Urals (Russia), Jakobsberg (Sweden), Jaklovce (Slovakia) – associated with hydromagnesite in serpentines (USA).

---

1. Gibbsite – crusty aggregates partly coloured by Fe hydroxides; Gamba (Brazil) **2. Brucite** – massive aggregate of indistinct platy cleavages; Chromtau (Kazakhstan – width of field 52 mm) **3. Nemalite** (a fibrous variety of brucite) – fibrous aggregates (length of fibres to 30 mm); Hoboken (USA)

Gibbsite, brucite, nemalite

Senarmontite

Oxide
Sb_2O_3

93

Named after the French mineralogist, H. H. de Sénarmont (1808–1862) (Dana 1851)

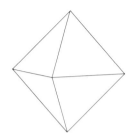

● Hardness: 2 (brittle) ● Streak: white ● Colour: white to grey-white ● Transparency: transparent to translucent ● Lustre: adamantine, silky to greasy ● Cleavage: imperfect on (111) ● Fracture: conchoidal to uneven ● Morphology: crystals, granular or massive aggregates ● Specific gravity: 5.2–5.3 ● Crystal system: cubic ● Crystal form: octahedral ● Chemical composition: Sb 83.54%, O 16.46% ● Chemical properties: readily soluble in HCl; heated on charcoal produces white deposit ● Handling: clean with water ● Similar minerals: fluorite **(291)** ● Distinguishing features: low hardness, higher specific gravity, easy solubility in HCl ● Genesis: secondary ● Associated minerals: kermesite **(7)**, stibnite **(51)**, valentinite **(94)**, cervantite **(294)** ● Occurrence: rare; Djebel-Hamimat (Algeria), Pernek and Dúbrava (Slovakia), Arnsberg (FRG), Baia Sprie (Romania), Sardinia (Italy), South Ham (Canada).

Valentinite (Antimony bloom)

Oxide
Sb_2O_3

94

Named after the German alchemist, B. Valentinus (16th century) (Haidinger 1845)

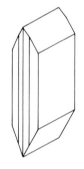

● Hardness: 2–3 (brittle) ● Streak: white ● Colour: white, grey, yellowish-grey to reddish ● Transparency: translucent ● Lustre: adamantine, on cleavage planes pearly ● Cleavage: perfect on (110) and (010) ● Morphology: crystals, often striated, fan-shaped, radiate-fibrous and granular aggregates ● Specific gravity: 5.6–5.8 ● Crystal system: orthorhombic ● Crystal form: prisms, rarely plates ● Chemical composition: Sb 83.54%, O 16.46%; admixtures: As ● Chemical properties: readily fusible; soluble in HCl and tartaric acid; when heated, also in HNO_3 ● Handling: clean with water ● Similar minerals: cerussite **(225)** ● Distinguishing features: lower specific gravity and hardness, crystal form and associated minerals ● Genesis: secondary ● Associated minerals: stibnite **(51)**, senarmontite **(93)**, cervantite **(294)** ● Occurrence: rare; Wolfsberg near Sangerhausen and Bräunsdorf near Freiberg (FRG), Příbram (Czech Republic), Pernek and Pezinok (Slovakia), Allemont (France), Sensa Mine (Algeria – extracted as Sb ore), Tatasi (Bolivia).

Minium (Red oxide of lead)

Oxide
Pb_3O_4

95

Named after the river Minius (north-west Spain)

● Hardness: 2–3 ● Streak: orange-yellow ● Colour: light red to brownish-red ● Transparency: non-transparent ● Lustre: dull to greasy ● Cleavage: perfect on (110) ● Fracture: earthy ● Morphology: scales, powdered or massive aggregates ● Specific gravity: 8.2 ● Crystal system: tetragonal ● Crystal form: microscopic scales ● Chemical composition: Pb 90.67%, O 9.33% ● Chemical properties: soluble in HCl and HNO_3 ● Handling: clean carefully with water ● Similar minerals: realgar **(5)**, cinnabar **(76)** ● Distinguishing features: from realgar by lower specific gravity and colour; from cinnabar by solubility in HNO_3 ● Genesis: secondary ● Associated minerals: galena **(77)**, cerussite **(225)** ● Occurrence: rare; Badenweiler and Bleialf (FRG), Mežica (Slovenia), Leadhills (Scotland, Great Britain), Bolanos (Mexico).

---

1. **Senarmontite** – octahedral crystal (4 mm) with a fan-shaped aggregate of stibnite; Pernek (Slovakia) 2. **Minium** – powdery coatings on carbonate; Bolanos (Mexico – width of field 29 mm) 3. **Valentinite** – rod-like druses with pearly lustre (rods to 14 mm); Příbram (Czech Republic)

Senarmontite, minium, valentinite

Ianthinite

Oxide
$UO_2(OH)_2$

96

R

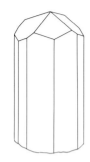

From the Greek
ianthinos – violet
(Schoep 1926)

● Hardness: 2–3 ● Streak: brown-violet ● Colour: black-violet, violet, purple-violet ● Transparency: translucent ● Lustre: vitreous to submetallic ● Cleavage: perfect on (100) ● Morphology: crystals, granular aggregates ● Specific gravity: 5.16 ● Crystal system: orthorhombic ● Crystal form: platy, prismatic to needle-shaped ● Chemical composition: UO_2 80.87%, H_2O 19.13% ● Chemical properties: soluble in HNO_3 (yellow solution), HCl and H_2SO_4 ● Handling: clean with water ● Similar minerals: mourite ● Distinguishing features: insoluble in H_2SO_4, slightly soluble in HCl ● Genesis: secondary ● Associated minerals: uraninite **(482)** ● Occurrence: rare; Wölsendorf (FRG), Shinkolobwe (Congo), Bigay, La Crouzille and Puy-de-Dôme (France).

Borax (Tincal)

Hydroxide
$Na_2B_4O_5(OH)_4 . 8 H_2O$

97

L

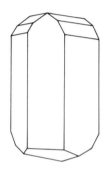

From the Arabic *buraq*
– white
(Wall 1848)

● Hardness: 2–2.5 (brittle) ● Streak: white ● Colour: colourless, white, grey, yellowish ● Transparency: transparent to translucent ● Lustre: vitreous, greasy ● Cleavage: perfect on (100) ● Fracture: conchoidal ● Morphology: crystals, earthy, compact ● Solubility: readily soluble in water ● Other properties: sweetish taste ● Specific gravity: 1.7–1.8 ● Crystal system: monoclinic ● Crystal form: prisms, rarely twinning ● Luminescence: sometimes blue green ● Chemical composition: Na_2O 16.26%, B_2O_3 36.51%, H_2O 47.23% ● Chemical properties: when heated fuses and forms a translucent ball; soluble in acids; when exposed to air quickly loses water, becomes dull and crumbles to fine powder (tincalconite) ● Handling: keep in sealed bottles or plastic bags ● Similar minerals: sassolite **(18)**, kernite **(101)** ● Distinguishing features: hardness, specific gravity, chemical properties ● Genesis: on edges of borate lakes ● Associated minerals: natron **(20)**, mirabilite **(23)**, halite **(86)** ● Occurrence: rare; western Tibet (China), Clear Lake and Borax Lake – California (USA), Tarapaca (Chile) ● Application: in chemical, food, paper and glass industries; in manufacture of fertilizers.

Gaylussite (Natrocalcite)

Carbonate
$CaNa_2(CO_3)_2 . 5 H_2O$

98

L

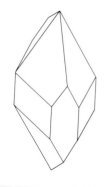

Named after the French
chemist and physicist,
J. L. Gay-Lussac
(1778–1850)
(Boussingault 1826)

● Hardness: 2.5 (brittle) ● Streak: grey-white ● Colour: white, yellowish-white ● Transparency: transparent to translucent ● Lustre: vitreous, dull ● Cleavage: very good on (110) ● Fracture: conchoidal ● Morphology: crystals prismatic or wedge-shaped ● Solubility: slightly soluble in water, effervesces in HCl ● Specific gravity: 1.99 ● Crystal system: monoclinic ● Crystal form: columnar, pseudo-octahedral ● Luminescence: sometimes creamy-white ● Chemical composition: CaO 18.94%, Na_2O 20.93%, CO_2 29.72%, H_2O 30.41% ● Chemical properties: soluble in acids; when exposed to the air it slowly crumbles ● Handling: keep in sealed bottles or plastic bags ● Genesis: in clays, occurring in soda lakes ● Associated minerals: natron **(20)**, borax **(97)**, calcite **(217)** ● Occurrence: rare; (East Africa – lakes), salt lakes in Gobi Desert (Mongolia), Searles Lake – California (USA), Mérida (Venezuela), (Namibia – large crystals in desert sands).

1. Borax – isolated crystals; Borax Lake (USA) **2. Gaylussite** – isolated crystals; Searles Lake (USA – width of field 36 mm)

1

2

Inderite

Borate
MgB$_3$O$_3$(OH)$_5$. 5 H$_2$O

99

Named after its source, Inder Lake (Kazakhstan), (Boldyreva 1937)

● Hardness: 2.5 ● Streak: white ● Colour: white, pinkish ● Transparency: transparent ● Lustre: vitreous ● Cleavage: good on (110) ● Fracture: uneven ● Morphology: crystals, massive aggregates ● Specific gravity: 1.8 ● Crystal system: monoclinic ● Crystal form: prisms, needle-shaped ● Chemical composition: MgO 14.41%, B$_2$O$_3$ 37.32%, H$_2$O 48.27% ● Chemical properties: soluble in diluted, warm HCl ● Handling: clean with water ● Similar minerals: inyoite **(100)**, ascharite **(213)** ● Distinguishing features: chemical properties (ascharite − different specific gravity) ● Genesis: borate lakes ● Associated minerals: hydroboracite ● Occurrence: rare; Inder (Kazakhstan), California − in borate lakes, crystals measuring 40 cm (USA) ● Application: in chemical industry.

Inyoite

Borate
CaB$_3$O$_3$(OH)$_5$. 4 H$_2$O

100

L

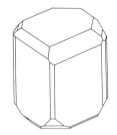

Named after its source in Inyo County (California, USA) (Shaller 1914)

● Hardness: 2 (brittle) ● Streak: white ● Colour: white, pinkish ● Transparency: translucent ● Lustre: vitreous ● Cleavage: good on (001) ● Fracture: uneven ● Morphology: crystals, massive and spherulitic aggregates ● Specific gravity: 1.87 ● Crystal system: monoclinic ● Crystal form: short prisms, plates ● Luminescence: sometimes yellow-white ● Chemical composition: CaO 20.20%, B$_2$O$_3$ 37.61%, H$_2$O 42.19% ● Chemical properties: soluble in warm water and diluted acids ● Handling: clean with cold water ● Similar minerals: inderite **(99)**, ascharite **(213)** ● Distinguishing features: chemical properties (ascharite − different specific gravity) ● Genesis: borate lakes ● Associated minerals: priceite **(212)**, colemanite **(301)** ● Occurrence: rare; Death Valley − California (USA), Inder (Kazakhstan), Hillsborough (Canada) ● Application: in chemical industry.

Kernite

Borate
Na$_2$B$_4$O$_6$(OH)$_2$. 3 H$_2$O

101

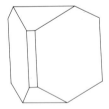

Named after its source in Kern County (California, USA) (Schaller 1927)

● Hardness: 2.5 ● Streak: white ● Colour: colourless, white ● Transparency: transparent or translucent ● Lustre: vitreous, pearly on cleavage planes ● Cleavage: perfect on (100) and on (001) ● Morphology: crystals, massive and fibrous aggregates ● Other properties of cohesion: flexible, elastic ● Solubility: slightly soluble in water ● Specific gravity: 1.95 ● Crystal system: monoclinic ● Crystal form: isometric twinning ● Chemical composition: Na$_2$O 22.68%, B$_2$O$_5$ 50.95%, H$_2$O 26.37% ● Chemical properties: soluble in acids ● Handling: keep in sealed bottles or plastic bags ● Similar minerals: borax **(97)** ● Distinguishing features: chemical properties ● Genesis: borate lakes on contact with intrusions ● Associated minerals: ulexite **(19)**, borax ● Occurrence: rare; Kern Co. − California (USA), Tincalaya − crystals measuring 1 × 2.5 m (Argentina), Sallent (Spain) ● Application: in chemical industry.

---

1. Inyoite − massive partly fissile aggregate; Panderma (Turkey) **2. Kernite** − grey-white fibrous aggregate; Kern Co. (California, USA − width of field 65 mm) **3. Inderite** − greyish massive aggregate; Kern Co. (California, USA)

Inyoite, kernite, inderite

Trona

Carbonate
$Na_3H(CO_3)_2 . 2 H_2O$

102

L

From Arabic origin –
natron
(Bagge 1773)

● Hardness: 2.5 ● Streak: white ● Colour: grey, white, yellowish ● Transparency: translucent ● Lustre: vitreous ● Cleavage: perfect on (100) ● Fracture: uneven to subconchoidal ● Morphology: crystals, fibrous to compact aggregates, crystal crusts ● Other properties: alkaline taste ● Solubility: soluble in water ● Specific gravity: 2.17 ● Crystal system: monoclinic ● Crystal form: prisms, plates ● Luminescence: sometimes white and blue ● Chemical composition: Na_2O 41.14%, CO_2 38.94%, H_2O 19.92% ● Chemical properties: effervescent in acids ● Handling: keep in sealed bottles or plastic bags ● Genesis: salt lakes, efflorescences ● Associated minerals: natron **(20)**, halite **(86)**, thenardite **(125)** ● Occurrence: common; (Tibet – salt lakes), (Iran), (Sudan), (Mongolia), Owens Lake and Searles Lake (USA) ● Application: manufacturing soda; in Egypt formerly used for building purposes.

Hydrozincite (Zinc bloom)

Carbonate
$Zn_5(CO_3)_2(OH)_6$

103

L

Named after its composition
(Kenngot 1853)

● Hardness: 2–2.5 (brittle) ● Streak: white ● Colour: white, light yellow, grey, pinkish, light blue ● Transparency: translucent, usually non-transparent ● Lustre: crystalline aggregates – pearly; massive – silky to dull ● Cleavage: perfect (100) ● Morphology: crystals, rarely massive, earthy, powdered aggregates, stalactitic, crusts ● Specific gravity: 3.2–3.8 ● Crystal system: monoclinic, rarely amorphous ● Crystal form: plates ● Luminescence: light blue ● Chemical composition: ZnO 74.12%, CO_2 16.03%, H_2O 9.85% ● Chemical properties: swells in acids ● Handling: clean with distilled water ● Similar minerals: smithsonite **(373)** ● Distinguishing features: lower specific gravity and hardness ● Genesis: secondary ● Associated minerals: aurichalcite **(106)**, sphalerite **(181)**, cerussite **(225)**, smithsonite ● Occurrence: rare; Bleiberg (Austria), Brilon (FRG), (Spain), (Poland), (Russia), (Algeria), Mina Ojuela (Mexico), (USA) ● Application: Zn ore.

Alumohydrocalcite

Carbonate
$CaAl_2(CO_3)_2(OH)_4 . 3 H_2O$

104

Named after its composition
(Bilibin 1926)

● Hardness: 2.5 (brittle) ● Streak: white ● Colour: white, blue-white, violet, light yellow ● Transparency: translucent ● Lustre: vitreous ● Cleavage: perfect (100) ● Morphology: crystals, fibrous aggregates, spherulites ● Specific gravity: 2.23 ● Crystal system: monoclinic ● Crystal form: fibrous, acicular ● Chemical composition: CaO 17.63%, Al_2O_3 32.05%, CO_2 27.67%, H_2O 22.65%; admixture: Cr ● Chemical properties: soluble in hot water and acids, effervescent in HCl ● Handling: clean with cold water ● Similar minerals: artinite **(105)**, dawsonite **(215)**, calcite **(217)**, wavellite **(247)** ● Distinguishing features: solubility in hot water, chemical properties ● Genesis: secondary ● Associated minerals: allophane **(266)**, wad, limonite **(355)** ● Occurrence: rare; (Russia), Ladomirov (Slovakia), Bergisch-Gladbach (FRG).

---

1. **Trona** – brownish fibrous aggregate; Searles Lake (USA) 2. **Alumohydrocalcite** – radiating white encrustations on sandstone; Ladomirov (Slovakia – width of field 85 mm) 3. **Hydrozincite** – stalactitic aggregate; Bleiberg (Austria)

Trona, alumohydrocalcite, hydrozincite

Artinite

105

Named after the Italian mineralogist, E. Artini (1866–1928) (Brugnatelli 1902)

● Hardness: 2.5 (brittle) ● Streak: white ● Colour: white ● Transparency: transparent ● Lustre: vitreous, silky ● Cleavage: perfect on (100), good on (001) ● Morphology: crystals, fibrous aggregates, spherulites, crusts ● Specific gravity: 2.03 ● Crystal system: monoclinic ● Crystal form: needles, fibres ● Chemical composition: MgO 41.0%, CO_2 22.37%, H_2O 36.63% ● Chemical properties: readily soluble in acids ● Similar minerals: dawsonite **(215)** ● Distinguishing features: chemical properties ● Genesis: low-hydrothermal ● Associated minerals: brucite **(91)**, hydromagnesite **(214)**, calcite **(217)**, aragonite **(221)** ● Occurrence: rare; Val Brutta (Italy), Gulsen near Kraubath and Styria (Austria), Hoboken, Long Island – New York – acicular crystals (USA).

Aurichalcite

106

Probably from the Greek *oreichalchos* – mountain copper (Böttger 1839)

● Hardness: 2 (brittle) ● Streak: lighter than its colour ● Colour: light blue, blue-green ● Transparency: translucent ● Lustre: pearly, silky ● Cleavage: perfect on (010) ● Morphology: crystals, crusty or granular aggregates ● Specific gravity: 3.9 ● Crystal system: orthorhombic ● Crystal form: needles, finely foliated and scaly crystals ● Chemical composition: CuO 19.92%, ZnO 54.08%, CO_2 16.11%, H_2O 9.89% ● Chemical properties: soluble in acids (effervesces) and in ammonia ● Handling: clean with distilled water ● Similar minerals: leadhillite **(108)**, cyanotrichite **(126)**, chrysocolla **(268)** ● Distinguishing features: specific gravity, chemical properties ● Genesis: secondary ● Associated minerals: hydrozincite **(103)**, limonite **(355)**, smithsonite **(373)**, hemimorphite **(403)** ● Occurrence: rare; Monteponi (Italy), Lávrion (Greece), Mapimí (Mexico), Tsumeb (Namibia), Nagato (Japan), (USA), (Russia), (Iran), (Romania).

Phosgenite (Horn lead)

107

From *phosgen* – $(COCl_2)$ (Breithaupt 1841)

● Hardness: 2.5–3 ● Streak: white ● Colour: white, grey, yellow, greenish, pink ● Transparency: transparent to translucent ● Lustre: adamantine, vitreous, greasy ● Cleavage: perfect on (110) and on (001) ● Fracture: conchoidal ● Morphology: crystals, granular and massive aggregates ● Other properties: readily sectile ● Specific gravity: 6–6.3 ● Crystal system: tetragonal ● Crystal form: short prisms, plates or pyramids (often multi-planed) ● Luminescence: light yellow ● Chemical composition: PbO 81.86%, Cl 13.00%, CO_2 5.14% ● Chemical properties: soluble in dilute HNO_3 (with effervescence), fusible ● Handling: clean with water ● Similar minerals: cerussite **(225)**, anglesite **(242)** ● Distinguishing features: chemical properties ● Genesis: secondary ● Associated minerals: cerussite, anglesite and other Pb minerals ● Occurrence: rare; Monteponi (Italy) – crystals measuring 12 cm, Matlock (Great Britain), Tarnów (Poland), Christian Levin Mine near Essen (FRG), (USA), (Argentina), (Tunisia), Tsumeb (Namibia).

---

1. **Aurichalcite** – elongated aggregates of bladed crystals in vesicles in limonite; Mapimí (Mexico – width of field 28 mm)
2. **Phosgenite** – short prismatic crystals (up to 12 mm); Monteponi (Italy)

Aurichalcite, phosgenite

H
2—3

Leadhillite

108

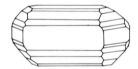

L

Named after its source in Leadhills (Scotland, Great Britain) (Beudant 1832)

● Hardness: 2.5 ● Streak: white ● Colour: colourless, white, grey, light green, light blue ● Transparency: transparent to translucent ● Lustre: adamantine, pearly to silky ● Cleavage: perfect on (001) ● Fracture: conchoidal ● Other properties of cohesion: readily sectile ● Morphology: crystals, granular, massive, sometimes bowl-shaped aggregates ● Specific gravity: 6.45–6.55 ● Crystal system: monoclinic ● Crystal form: plates, scales, rhombohedra, twinning, trillings ● Luminescence: sometimes yellowish ● Chemical composition: PbO 82.75%, SO_3 7.42%, CO_2 8.16%, H_2O 1.67% ● Chemical properties: fusible, soluble in hot water, in HNO_3 effervescent and crumbly ● Handling: clean with cold water ● Similar minerals: cerussite (225) ● Distinguishing features: hardness, chemical properties, solubility in hot water ● Genesis: secondary ● Associated minerals: caledonite (109), linarite (110), cerussite, anglesite (242) ● Occurrence: rare; Leadhills (Scotland, Great Britain), Iglesias and Monteponi (Italy), Djebel Ressa (Tunisia), Mammoth Mine – Arizona and Tintic – Utah (USA), Tsumeb (Namibia).

Caledonite

Carbonate
$Pb_5Cu_2(CO_3)(SO_4)_3(OH)_6$

109

Named after Caledonia (historical name of Scotland) (Beudant 1832)

● Hardness: 2.5–3 (brittle) ● Streak: greenish-white ● Colour: dark green, blue-green ● Transparency: translucent ● Lustre: vitreous, greasy ● Cleavage: good on (001) ● Fracture: uneven ● Morphology: crystals, massive, crusty, radiating-fibrous aggregates ● Specific gravity: 5.7 ● Crystal system: orthorhombic ● Crystal form: prisms (often striated), acicular ● Chemical composition: CuO 9.86%, PbO 69.17%, SO_3 14.89%, CO_2 2.73%, H_2O 3.35% ● Chemical properties: fusible, soluble in HNO_3 (swelling) ● Handling: clean with water ● Similar minerals: langite (130), posnjakite (131) ● Distinguishing features: chemical properties, X-rays ● Genesis: secondary ● Associated minerals: cerussite (225), anglesite (242), malachite (307) ● Occurrence: rare; Leadhills – Scotland (Great Britain), Mammoth Mine – Arizona (USA), Berezovsk (Russia), Toroku Mine (Japan), Tsumeb (Namibia), Challacallo (Chile), Baiţa (Romania).

Linarite

Sulphate
$PbCu(SO_4)(OH)_2$

110

Named after its source in Linares (Spain) (Brooke 1822)

● Hardness: 2.5 ● Streak: light blue ● Colour: sky-blue ● Transparency: translucent ● Lustre: vitreous ● Cleavage: perfect on (100) ● Fracture: conchoidal ● Morphology: crystals, granular and crusty aggregates ● Specific gravity: 5.3–5.5 ● Crystal system: monoclinic ● Crystal form: prisms (striated) and plates ● Chemical composition: CuO 19.85%, PbO 55.68%, SO_3 19.97%, H_2O 4.50% ● Chemical properties: soluble in diluted HNO_3 and HCl ● Handling: clean with distilled water ● Similar minerals: azurite (226), lazurite (392) ● Distinguishing features: hardness, specific gravity, in HCl produces white $PbCl_2$ ● Genesis: secondary ● Associated minerals: aurichalcite (106), cerussite (225), antlerite (227), malachite (307), hemimorphite (403) ● Occurrence: rare; Linares (Spain), Lölling (Austria), Schapbachtal (FRG), Nerchinsk (Russia), Red Gill (Great Britain), (Namibia), (USA), (Argentina).

---

1. **Leadhillite** – tabular, yellow-white crystals (5 mm); Tsumeb (Namibia) 2. **Linarite** – dark blue euhedral crystals (up to 10 mm) on quartz and limonite; Red Gill (Cumberland, Great Britain)

Leadhillite, linarite

Epsomite (Bitter salt)

Sulphate
$MgSO_4 \cdot 7 H_2O$

111

Named after its original locality in Epsom (Great Britain) (Beudant 1824)

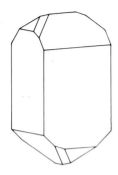

● Hardness: 2–2.5 (brittle) ● Streak: white ● Colour: white, yellowish, greenish, reddish, pink ● Transparency: transparent to translucent ● Lustre: vitreous, silky ● Cleavage: perfect on (010) ● Morphology: rarely crystals, fibrous aggregates, crusts, stalactites, encrustations, earthy or pulverulent masses ● Solubility: in water ● Other properties: bitter-saline taste ● Specific gravity: 1.68 ● Crystal system: orthorhombic ● Crystal form: prisms, needles ● Chemical composition: MgO 16.36%, SO_3 32.48%, H_2O 51.16% ● Chemical properties: on exposure to air loses water and becomes dull ● Handling: clean only with alcohol; keep in sealed bottles or plastic bags ● Similar minerals: halotrichite **(27)**, pickeringite **(28)**, kieserite **(231)** ● Distinguishing features: X-rays, chemical properties ● Genesis: secondary ● Associated minerals: halotrichite, melanterite **(114)**, kieserite and other sulphates ● Occurrence: common; Djaman-Klych and Djelon Lakes (Kazakhstan), Epsom (Great Britain), Death Valley – California, and salt lakes in Kruger Hills – Washington – crystals up to 2 m (USA), Hodruša near Banská Štiavnica (Slovakia) ● Application: in the past in medicine.

Hexahydrite

Sulphate
$MgSO_4 \cdot 6 H_2O$

112

Named after the number of water molecules *hexa* – six and *hydor* – water (Johnston 1911)

● Hardness: unknown, probably similar to epsomite ● Streak: white ● Colour: white, light green ● Transparency: transparent ● Lustre: pearly ● Cleavage: perfect on (100) ● Fracture: conchoidal ● Morphology: crystals, fibrous aggregates ● Solubility: in water ● Other properties: saline to bitter-saline taste ● Specific gravity: 1.76 ● Crystal system: monoclinic ● Crystal form: plates ● Chemical composition: MgO 17.64%, SO_3 35.04%, H_2O 47.32% ● Chemical properties: on exposure to air absorbs water and alters to epsomite **(111)** ● Handling: keep in sealed bottles or plastic bags ● Similar minerals: other Mg sulphates ● Distinguishing features: chemical properties and X-rays ● Genesis: salt lakes, secondary ● Associated minerals: epsomite ● Occurrence: common; Boleslaw (Poland), Saki salt lakes, Crimea near the Caspian Sea (Russia), Bonaparte River (Canada), Oroville – Washington (USA).

Goslarite

Sulphate
$ZnSO_4 \cdot 7 H_2O$

113

Named after its original locality in Goslar (FRG) (Haidinger 1845)

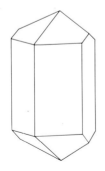

● Hardness: 2–2.5 ● Streak: white ● Colour: white, yellowish-white ● Transparency: transparent to translucent ● Lustre: vitreous ● Cleavage: perfect on (010) ● Morphology: stalactitic, crusts, pulverulent, granular or fibrous aggregates ● Solubility: in water ● Other properties: bitter, astringent taste ● Specific gravity: 2.0 ● Crystal system: orthorhombic ● Crystal form: acicular ● Chemical composition: ZnO 28.30%, SO_3 27.84%, H_2O 43.86% ● Chemical properties: on exposure to air loses water ● Handling: clean with alcohol; keep in sealed bottles or plastic bags ● Similar minerals: alunogen **(26)**, halotrichite **(27)** ● Distinguishing features: chemical properties, X-rays ● Genesis: secondary ● Associated minerals: epsomite **(111)**, melanterite **(114)** ● Occurrence: rare; Rammelsberg near Goslar, Freiberg and Altenberg (FRG), Banská Štiavnica (Slovakia), Falun (Sweden), (France), (Spain), (USA), (Peru), (Chile).

Epsomite – long acicular crystals (up to 28 mm) on quartz; Banská Štiavnica (Slovakia)

Epsomite

Melanterite (Copperas, Green vitriol)

Sulphate
$FeSO_4 . 7 H_2O$

114

From the Greek *melas* – black
(Beudant 1832)

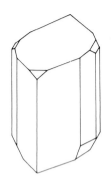

● Hardness: 2 ● Streak: white ● Colour: green, yellow-green, rarely brown-black ● Transparency: transparent to translucent ● Lustre: vitreous ● Cleavage: perfect on (001) ● Morphology: crystals, granular and crusty aggregates, stalactitic ● Solubility: water-soluble ● Other properties: tastes of ink ● Specific gravity: 1.9 ● Crystal system: monoclinic ● Crystal form: short prisms, plates, pseudorhombohedra ● Chemical composition: FeO 25.9%, SO_3 28.8%, H_2O 45.3%; admixtures: Cu (pisanite – **115**), Mg (kirovite) ● Chemical properties: on exposure to air loses water and crumbles to a powder ● Handling: keep in sealed bottles or plastic bags ● Similar minerals: goslarite **(113)** ● Distinguishing features: chemical properties, X-rays ● Genesis: secondary ● Associated minerals: alunogen **(26)**, halotrichite **(27)**, pyrrhotite **(283)**, pyrite **(436)** ● Occurrence: common; Rammelsberg (FRG), Río Tinto (Spain), Falun (Sweden), Smolník (Slovakia), Idria (Slovenia), Recsk (Hungary).

Pisanite (Melanterite variety)

Sulphate
$(Fe,Cu)SO_4 . 7 H_2O$

115

Named after the French chemist, F. Pisani (1831–1920)
(Kenngott 1860)

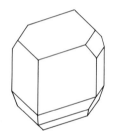

● Hardness: 2 ● Streak: white ● Colour: light green, light blue ● Transparency: translucent ● Lustre: vitreous ● Cleavage: perfect on (001) ● Morphology: granular, encrustations, crusts, stalactitic ● Solubility: water-soluble ● Specific gravity: 1.9 ● Crystal system: monoclinic ● Crystal form: short prisms, coarse plates ● Chemical composition: like melanterite, CuO from 9 to 18% ● Similar minerals: chalcanthite **(116)** ● Distinguishing features: chemical properties, X-rays ● Genesis: secondary ● Associated minerals: halotrichite **(27)**, melanterite **(114)** and other sulphates ● Occurrence: like melanterite.

Chalcanthite (Copper vitriol, Blue vitriol)

Sulphate
$CuSO_4 . 5 H_2O$

116

From the Greek *chalkos* – copper and *anthos* – flower
(Kobell 1853)

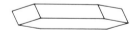

● Hardness: 2.5 ● Streak: white ● Colour: blue ● Transparency: transparent ● Lustre: vitreous ● Cleavage: imperfect on (110) ● Fracture: conchoidal ● Morphology: crystals, crusts, stalactitic, granular, reniform ● Solubility: water-soluble ● Other properties: poisonous ● Specific gravity: 2.2–2.3 ● Crystal system: triclinic ● Crystal form: coarse plates, short prisms ● Chemical composition: CuO 31.87%, SO_3 32.06%, H_2O 36.07%; admixtures: Fe, Mg, Co ● Chemical properties: on exposure to air loses water and crumbles to greenish-white powdered aggregates ● Handling: keep in sealed bottles or plastic bags ● Similar minerals: kröhnkite **(127)**, liroconite **(144)** ● Distinguishing features: pickeringite **(28)**, epsomite **(111)**, melanterite **(114)**, fibroferrite **(120)** ● Occurrence: rare; Rammelsberg and Goslar (FRG), Špania Dolina (Slovakia), Cornwall (Great Britain), Rio Tinto (Spain), Chuquicamata (Chile).

1. **Pisanite** – light to dark blue crystalline aggregate; Smolník (Slovakia) 2. **Melanterite** – stalactitic aggregate of green colour; Rammelsberg (FRG) 3. **Chalcanthite** – finely crystalline aggregate of blue colour; Rio Tinto (Spain – width of field 77 mm)

Pisanite, melanterite, chalcanthite

Bieberite

Sulphate
$CoSO_4 . 7 H_2O$

117

Named after its original locality in Bieber (Hessen, FRG) (Haidinger 1845)

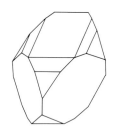

• Hardness: 2 • Streak: white • Colour: pink-red, flesh-pink • Transparency: translucent to non-transparent • Lustre: vitreous, dull because of dehydration • Cleavage: perfect on (001) • Morphology: stalactitic, crusts • Solubility: water-soluble • Specific gravity: 1.9 • Crystal system: monoclinic • Crystal form: only synthetic crystals are known • Chemical composition: CoO 26.66%, SO_3 28.48%, H_2O 44.86% • Chemical properties: on exposure to air loses water • Handling: keep in sealed bottles or plastic bags • Genesis: secondary • Associated minerals: pharmacolite **(139)**, erythrite **(141)** • Occurrence: rare; Bieber and Siegen (FRG), Chalanches (France), (USA), (Chile).

Morenosite (Nickel vitriol)

Sulphate
$NiSO_4 . 7 H_2O$

118

Named after Señor Moreno (Spain) (Casares 1851)

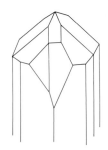

• Hardness: 2–2.5 • Streak: green-white • Colour: emerald green, green-white • Lustre: vitreous • Cleavage: good on (010) • Morphology: crystals, stalactitic, crusts • Solubility: water-soluble • Specific gravity: 2.0 • Crystal system: orthorhombic • Crystal form: acicular, synthetic crystals are prismatic • Chemical composition: NiO 26.59%, SO_3 28.51%, H_2O 44.90% • Chemical properties: on exposure to air loses water • Handling: keep in sealed bottles or plastic bags • Genesis: secondary • Associated minerals: erythrite **(141)**, annabergite **(142)** • Occurrence: rare; Cap Ortegal (Spain), Richelsdorf, Hessen and Lichtenburg (FRG), Jáchymov (Czech Republic), (Italy), (France), (USA), (Canada), (Peru).

Botryogen

Sulphate
$MgFe^{3+}(SO_4)_2(OH) . 7 H_2O$

119

From the Greek *botrys* – grape and *genos* – to yield (Haidinger 1828)

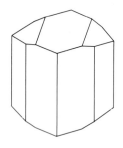

• Hardness: 2 • Streak: ochre-yellow • Colour: hyacinth-red • Transparency: translucent to transparent • Lustre: vitreous • Cleavage: perfect on (010), good on (110) • Morphology: crystals, botryoidal and radiating-fibrous aggregates • Specific gravity: 2–2.1 • Crystal system: monoclinic • Crystal form: long and short prisms • Chemical composition: MgO 9.64%, Fe_2O_3 19.28%, SO_3 38.55%, H_2O 32.53% • Chemical properties: soluble in hot water and HCl • Handling: clean with distilled water • Similar minerals: realgar **(5)**, cinnabar **(76)** • Distinguishing features: hardness distinguishes it from realgar, specific gravity from cinnabar • Genesis: secondary • Associated minerals: epsomite **(111)**, coquimbite **(121)**, copiapite **(123)**, voltaite **(233)** • Occurrence: rare; Rammelsberg near Goslar (FRG), Falun (Sweden), Smolník (Slovakia), Paracutin (Mexico), Chuquicamata (Chile), Knoxville – Tennessee (USA).

---

1. **Morenosite** – group of crystals; Cape Ortegal (Spain – width of field 24 mm) 2. **Botryogen** – globular aggregates on halotrichite (size of globules 2 mm); Smolník (Slovakia)

Morenosite, botryogen

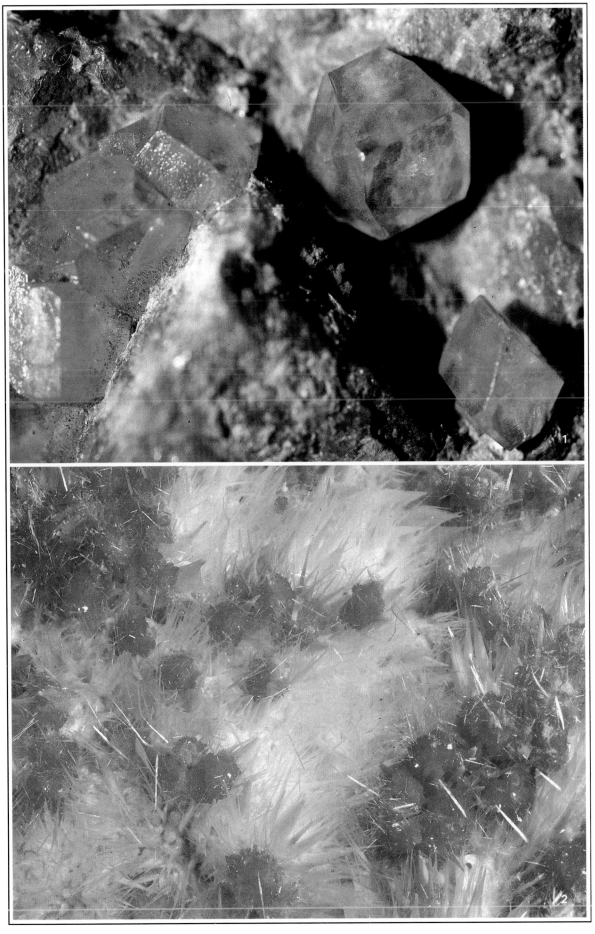

Fibroferrite (Stypticite)

Sulphate
$Fe^{3+}(SO_4)(OH) \cdot 5 H_2O$

120

From the Latin *fibra* – fibre and *ferrum* – iron (Rose 1833)

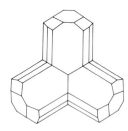

• Hardness: 2 • Streak: white • Colour: light yellow, white, green-grey to light green • Transparency: translucent • Lustre: silky, pearly • Cleavage: perfect on (001) • Morphology: crystals, massive, crusty, radiating-fibrous and botryoidal aggregates • Solubility: water-soluble • Specific gravity: 1.9 • Crystal system: orthorhombic • Crystal form: acicular • Chemical composition: Fe_2O_3 30.83%, SO_3 30.91%, H_2O 38.26% • Handling: keep in sealed bottles or plastic bags • Genesis: secondary • Associated minerals: alunogen **(26)**, halotrichite **(27)**, melanterite **(114)** and other sulphates • Occurrence: rare; Palières (France), Valachov (Czech Republic), Santa Elena Mines – 3 cm crusts of fibroferrite (Argentina), Tierra Amarilla (Chile), (Bolivia), (USA).

Coquimbite

Sulphate
$Fe_2^{3+}(SO_4)_3 \cdot 9 H_2O$

121

Named after the province of Coquimbo (Chile) (Breithaupt 1841)

• Hardness: 2 • Streak: white • Colour: greenish, bluish to light violet • Transparency: transparent • Lustre: vitreous • Cleavage: imperfect on $(10\bar{1}1)$ • Morphology: crystals, granular, and powdered aggregates • Other properties: bitter taste • Solubility: water-soluble • Specific gravity: 2.1 • Crystal system: hexagonal • Crystal form: coarse plates or short prisms • Chemical composition: Fe_2O_3 28.41%, SO_3 42.74%, H_2O 28.85%; admixtures: Al_2O_3 • Chemical properties: on exposure to air loses water and crumbles to a powder • Handling: keep in sealed bottles or plastic bags • Similar minerals: quenstedtite **(122)** • Distinguishing features: X-rays, chemical properties • Genesis: secondary • Associated minerals: quenstedtite, copiapite **(123)**, pyrite **(436)** and other sulphates • Occurrence: rare; Rammelsberg near Goslar (FRG), Smolník (Slovakia), Huelva on the Gulf of Cadiz (Spain), Chuquicamata and Copiapó (Chile), (USA).

Quenstedtite

Sulphate
$Fe_2^{3+}(SO_4)_3 \cdot 10 H_2O$

122

Named after the German mineralogist, F. A. Quenstedt (1809–1889) (Linck 1888)

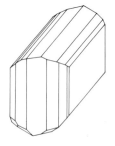

• Hardness: 2.5 • Streak: white, light violet • Colour: light violet to red-violet • Transparency: transparent • Lustre: vitreous • Cleavage: perfect on $(0\bar{1}0)$ • Morphology: crystals, granular aggregates • Solubility: water-soluble • Specific gravity: 2.14 • Crystal system: triclinic • Crystal form: plates, short prisms (often striated) • Chemical composition: Fe_2O_3 27.53%, SO_3 41.41%, H_2O 31.06% • Chemical properties: loses water and changes into coquimbite **(121)** • Handling: keep in sealed bottles or plastic bags • Similar minerals: coquimbite • Distinguishing features: X-rays, chemical properties • Genesis: secondary • Associated minerals: coquimbite, copiapite **(123)**, pyrite **(436)** • Occurrence: rare; Tierra Amarilla and Alcaparrosa (Chile).

---

1. Fibroferrite – radiate fibrous aggregates (up to 3 mm); Copiapó (Chile) **2. Coquimbite** – fine tabular to massive aggregates with grains of yellow copiapite; Coquimbo (Chile – width of field 70 mm)

Fibroferrite, coquimbite

Copiapite

Sulphate
$MgFe_4^{3+}(SO_4)_6(OH)_2 \cdot 18\,H_2O$

123

Named after its locality
Copiapó (Chile)
(Haidinger 1845)

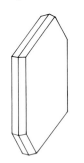

● Hardness: 2.5 ● Streak: lighter than colour ● Colour: yellow, yellowish-green, orange-yellow ● Transparency: transparent to translucent ● Lustre: pearly ● Cleavage: perfect on (010) ● Morphology: crystals, pulverulent or crusty aggregates ● Solubility: water-soluble ● Specific gravity: 2.1 ● Crystal system: triclinic ● Crystal form: plates ● Chemical composition: MgO 3.4%, Fe_2O_3 27.0%, SO_3 40.7%, H_2O 28.9%; admixtures: Cu (cuprocopiapite), Ca, Al ● Handling: keep in sealed bottles or plastic bags ● Genesis: secondary ● Associated minerals: halotrichite **(27)**, pickeringite **(28)**, pyrite **(436)**, marcasite **(437)** ● Occurrence: rare; Rammelsberg near Goslar (FRG), Dubník (Slovakia), Falun (Sweden), (France), (Spain), Copiapó and Chuquicamata (Chile), (USA).

Ferrinatrite

Sulphate
$Na_3Fe^{3+}(SO_4)_3 \cdot 3\,H_2O$

124

Named after its chemical composition
(Scharizer 1905)

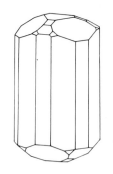

● Hardness: 2.5 ● Streak: white ● Colour: grey-white, light green, blue-green ● Transparency: transparent to translucent ● Lustre: vitreous ● Cleavage: perfect on (10$\bar{1}$0) ● Fracture: splintery ● Morphology: crystals, fibrous, cryptocrystalline masses, stellate crystal aggregates ● Solubility: water-soluble ● Specific gravity: 2.55 ● Crystal system: hexagonal ● Crystal form: short prisms ● Chemical composition: Na_2O 19.91%, Fe_2O_3 17.10%, SO_3 51.42%, H_2O 11.57% ● Chemical properties: in humid environment alters to sideronatrite **(30)** ● Handling: keep in sealed bottles or plastic bags ● Genesis: secondary ● Associated minerals: sideronatrite, copiapite **(123)** and other sulphates ● Occurrence: rare; areas with a dry climate: Sierra Gorda, Alcaparrosa and Chuquicamata (Chile), Vesuvius (Italy) − in fumaroles.

Thenardite

Sulphate
Na_2SO_4

125

Named after the French chemist, L. J. Thénard (1777−1857)
(Casaseca 1826)

● Hardness: 2.5 ● Streak: white ● Colour: grey-white, yellowish, reddish ● Transparency: transparent to translucent ● Lustre: vitreous to greasy ● Cleavage: perfect on (010) ● Fracture: splintery to uneven ● Morphology: crystals, crusts and encrustations, deposits ● Solubility: water-soluble ● Other properties: saline taste ● Specific gravity: 2.67 ● Crystal system: orthorhombic ● Crystal form: plates, dipyramidal, rarely prismatic, twinning ● Luminescence: yellowish-white, yellow, yellowish-brown ● Chemical composition: Na_2O 43.7%, SO_3 56.3% ● Handling: keep in sealed bottles or plastic bags ● Similar minerals: mirabilite **(23)** ● Distinguishing features: X-rays, chemical properties ● Genesis: salt lakes in tropical areas, fumaroles ● Associated minerals: mirabilite, gypsum **(29)**, epsomite **(111)** ● Occurrence: common; desert areas in (Chile), (Peru), (USA), (Azerbaijan), (Spain), Vesuvius − in fumaroles (Italy) ● Application: glass industry.

Copiapite − crystalline aggregate in association with halotrichite and Fe hydroxides; Copiapó (Chile − width of field 23 mm)

Copiapite

Cyanotrichite (Lettsomite)

Sulphate
$Cu_4Al_2(SO_4)(OH)_{12} \cdot 2 H_2O$

126

From the Greek *kyaneos* – blue and *triches* – hair (Glocker 1839)

● Hardness: about 2 (unknown) ● Streak: light blue ● Colour: dark blue ● Transparency: transparent ● Lustre: silky ● Cleavage: good, undefined ● Morphology: crystals, radiating-fibrous bristly aggregates ● Specific gravity: 2.7 ● Crystal system: orthorhombic ● Crystal form: needles ● Chemical composition: CuO 49.39%, Al_2O_3 15.82%, SO_3 12.42%, H_2O 22.37% ● Chemical properties: soluble in acids ● Handling: clean with distilled water ● Similar minerals: aurichalcite **(106)** ● Distinguishing features: specific gravity, X-rays ● Genesis: secondary ● Associated minerals: azurite **(226)**, malachite **(307)**, limonite **(355)** ● Occurrence: rare; Moldova Noua (Romania), La Garonne (France), Lávrion (Greece), Morenci and Majuba Hill (USA), Mednorudnyansk (Russia)

Kröhnkite

Sulphate
$Na_2Cu(SO_4)_2 \cdot 2 H_2O$

127

Named after B. Kröhnke, who was the first person to analyze it (Domeyko 1876)

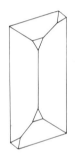

● Hardness: 2.5–3 ● Streak: white ● Colour: blue to light blue ● Transparency: transparent to translucent ● Lustre: vitreous ● Cleavage: perfect on (010) ● Fracture: conchoidal ● Morphology: crystals, fibrous and crusty aggregates, also granular or massive ● Solubility: water-soluble ● Specific gravity: 2.9 ● Crystal system: monoclinic ● Crystal form: prisms, pseudo-octahedral ● Chemical composition: Na_2O 18.36%, CuO 23.56%, SO_3 47.41%, H_2O 10.67% ● Similar minerals: chalcanthite **(116)** ● Distinguishing features: X-rays, chemical properties ● Genesis: secondary ● Associated minerals: chalcanthite, atacamite **(206)**, antlerite **(227)** ● Occurrence: rare; Chuquicamata and Quetena Mine (Chile).

Spangolite

Sulphate
$Cu_6Al(SO_4)(OH)_{12}Cl \cdot 3 H_2O$

128

Called after N. Spang, (USA) (Penfield 1890)

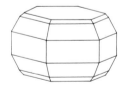

● Hardness: 2–3 (brittle) ● Streak: light green ● Colour: dark green, blue-green, emerald green ● Transparency: transparent to translucent ● Lustre: vitreous ● Cleavage: perfect on (0001) ● Fracture: conchoidal ● Morphology: crystals ● Specific gravity: 3.1 ● Crystal system: hexagonal ● Crystal form: short prisms, plates ● Chemical composition: CuO 59.82%, Al_2O_3 6.39%, SO_3 10.03%, Cl 4.44%, H_2O 20.32%, (less O ≡ Cl 1.00%) ● Chemical properties: readily soluble in acids, insoluble in water ● Handling: clean with distilled water ● Genesis: secondary ● Associated minerals: tyrolite **(32)**, azurite **(226)**, adamite **(258)**, malachite **(307)** ● Occurrence: rare; Moldova Noua (Romania), Lávrion (Greece), Arenas – Sardinia (Italy), St. Day – Cornwall (Great Britain), Blanchard Mine – New Mexico, Czar Mine – Arizona, Myler Mine – Nevada (USA).

---

1. Cyanotrichite – blue acicular aggregates grown on limonite; Moldova Noua (Romania – width of field 90 mm) **2. Kröhnkite** – inter-penetrating fibrous aggregate in a 13 mm thick veinlet; Chuquicamata (Chile) **3. Spangolite** – aggregate of tabular crystals (3 mm) of blue-green colour; Lávrion (Greece)

Cyanotrichite, kröhnkite, spangolite

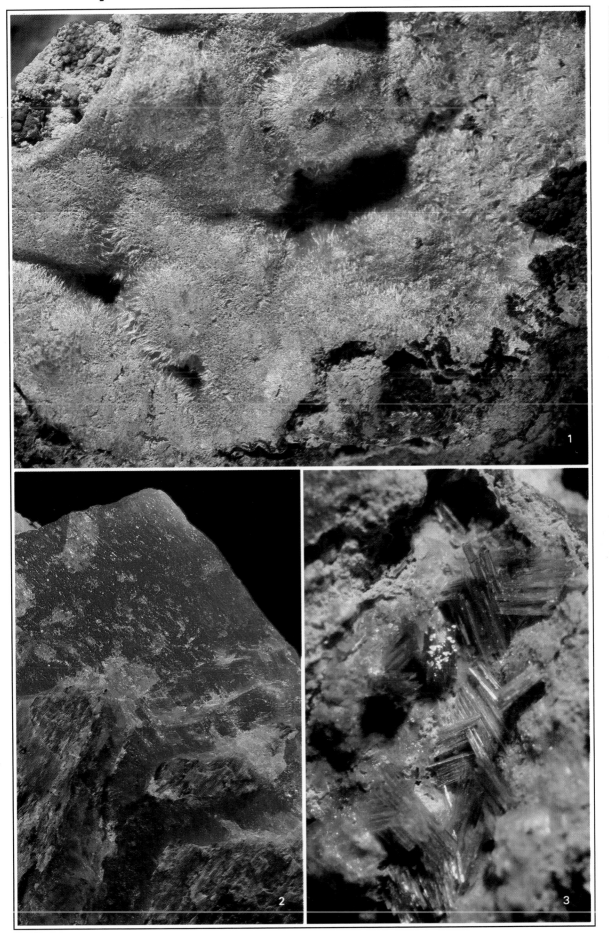

Devilline (Herrengrundite)

Sulphate
$CaCu_4(OH)_6(SO_4)_2 . 3 H_2O$

129

Named after the French chemist, H. E. S. C. Deville (1818–1881) (Pisani 1864)

● Hardness: 2.5 ● Streak: light green ● Colour: dark green, emerald green to blue-green ● Transparency: transparent ● Lustre: vitreous to pearly ● Cleavage: perfect on (001) ● Morphology: crystals, rose-shaped aggregates, crusts ● Specific gravity: 3.1 ● Crystal system: monoclinic ● Crystal form: plates ● Chemical composition: CaO 8.73%, CuO 49.53%, SO_3 24.92%, H_2O 16.82% ● Chemical properties: soluble in HNO_3, insoluble in water and concentrated H_2SO_4 ● Handling: clean with distilled water ● Genesis: secondary ● Associated minerals: gypsum **(29)**, azurite **(226)**, malachite **(307)** ● Occurrence: rare; Cornwall (Great Britain), Špania Dolina (Slovakia), Uspensk (Kazakhstan), Schwarz and the Tyrol (Austria), Montgomery – Pennsylvania (USA).

Langite

Sulphate
$Cu_3(SO_4)(OH)_4 . H_2O$

130

Named after the Viennese physicist, V. von Lang (1838–1921) (Maskelyne 1864)

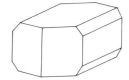

● Hardness: 2.5–3 ● Streak: blue-green ● Colour: blue-green to blue ● Transparency: translucent ● Lustre: vitreous ● Cleavage: perfect on (001) ● Morphology: crystals, crusty, earthy and fibrous aggregates ● Specific gravity: 3.5 ● Crystal system: orthorhombic ● Crystal form: isometric or elongated (100), twinning ● Chemical composition: CuO 67.66%, SO_3 15.32%, H_2O 17.02% ● Chemical properties: readily soluble in acids and ammonia; insoluble in water ● Handling: clean with distilled water ● Similar minerals: posnjakite **(131)** ● Distinguishing features: X-rays, chemical properties ● Genesis: secondary ● Associated minerals: gypsum **(29)**, chalcopyrite **(185)** ● Occurrence: rare; Mollau (France), St. Just and St. Blazey (Cornwall, Great Britain), Hagendorf (FRG), Eschbach (Austria), Špania Dolina (Slovakia), Ward Mine – Nevada (USA).

Posnjakite

Sulphate
$Cu_4(SO_4)(OH)_6 . H_2O$

131

Named after the geochemist, E. W. Posnjak (1888–1949) (Komkov 1967)

● Hardness: 2–3 ● Streak: bluish ● Colour: blue to dark blue ● Lustre: vitreous ● Cleavage: unknown ● Morphology: crystals, crusts ● Specific gravity: 3.4 ● Crystal system: monoclinic ● Crystal form: plates ● Chemical composition: CuO 67.66%, SO_3 17.02%, H_2O 15.32% ● Chemical properties: like langite **(130)** ● Handling: clean with distilled water ● Similar minerals: langite ● Distinguishing features: X-rays, chemical properties ● Genesis: secondary ● Associated minerals: gypsum **(29)**, aurichalcite **(106)**, langite ● Occurrence: rare; Nuratalkinsk (Kazakhstan), Špania Dolina (Slovakia), Wittichen (FRG).

---

1. Devilline – semi-globular aggregates of tabular crystals (up to 7 mm); Špania Dolina (Slovakia) **2. Langite** – small crystals (up to 2 mm); Ward Mine (USA) **3. Posnjakite** – dendritic aggregate of crystals in a crack in quartz (size of aggregate 11 mm); Richtárová (Slovakia)

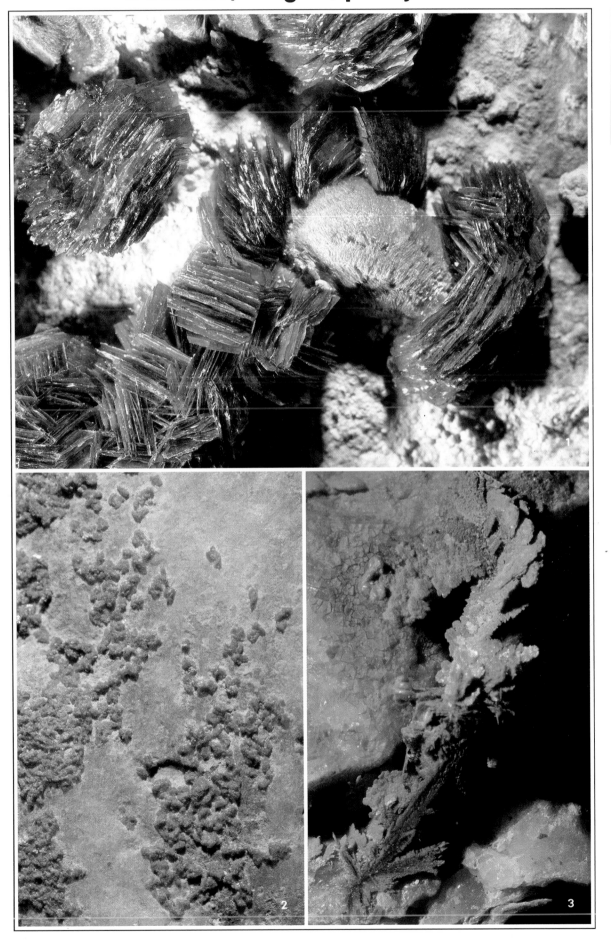

Ferrimolybdite

132

Named after its chemical composition (Filipenko 1914)

● Hardness: 2 ● Streak: light yellow ● Colour: yellow to canary yellow ● Lustre: adamantine to silky ● Cleavage: perfect on (001) ● Morphology: crystals, fibrous, scaly and earthy aggregates ● Specific gravity: 4–4.5 ● Crystal system: orthorhombic ● Crystal form: needles, scales ● Chemical composition: varying, Fe_2O_3 22.25%, MoO_3 60.17%, H_2O 17.58% ● Chemical properties: soluble in acids and ammonia, readily fusible ● Handling: clean with distilled water ● Genesis: secondary ● Associated minerals: molybdenite **(8)** ● Occurrence: common; Altenberg (FRG), Baveno (Italy), Schmirn (Austria), Hůrky (Czech Republic), Mt. Mulgine (Australia), Yeniseisk (Russia), Climax Mine near Leadville – Colorado (USA), Renfrew – Quebec (Canada).

Crocoite (Red lead ore)

133

L

P

From the Greek *krokos* – crocus (Breithaupt 1841)

● Hardness: 2.5–3 ● Streak: orange-yellow ● Colour: orange-red, dark orange, yellow-red ● Transparency: transparent ● Lustre: adamantine ● Cleavage: good on (110) ● Fracture: conchoidal to uneven ● Other properties of cohesion: sectile ● Morphology: crystals, massive, granular ● Specific gravity: 6.0 ● Crystal system: monoclinic ● Crystal form: prisms, rarely rhombohedral ● Luminescence: dark brown ● Chemical composition: PbO 69.06%, CrO_3 30.94% ● Chemical properties: soluble in hot HCl and KOH; tinges phosphoric and borax beads emerald green ● Handling: clean with distilled water or ultrasonically ● Similar minerals: realgar **(5)**, cinnabar **(76)** ● Distinguishing features: hardness, specific gravity, crystal form, solubility in acids ● Genesis: a secondary lead mineral ● Associated minerals: galena **(77)**, limonite **(355)**, quartz **(534)** ● Occurrence: rare; Gallenberg (FRG), Berezovsk (Russia), (Romania), Luzon Island (Philippines), Minas Gerais (Brazil), Dundas – Tasmania – crystals measuring 20 cm (Australia), (USA) ● Application: mineralogically important; sometimes used as a precious stone (facets, chabochons).

Stolzite

134

L

Named after J. A. Stolz (1803–1896) from Teplice (Czech Republic) (Haidinger 1845)

● Hardness: 2.5–3 (brittle) ● Streak: white ● Colour: reddish-brown, yellowish-brown, brown, greenish ● Transparency: transparent in thin laminae ● Lustre: greasy to sub-adamantine ● Cleavage: indistinct on (001) ● Fracture: conchoidal to uneven ● Morphology: crystals, granular ● Specific gravity: 7.9–8.2 ● Crystal system: tetragonal ● Crystal form: dipyramide, coarse plates ● Luminescence: green-white ● Chemical composition: PbO 49.04%, WO_3 50.96% ● Chemical properties: soluble in acids ● Handling: clean with distilled water ● Similar minerals: scheelite **(310)** ● Distinguishing features: hardness, specific gravity, luminescence ● Genesis: a secondary mineral of lead – tungsten deposits ● Associated minerals: scheelite, wolframite **(369)**, quartz **(534)**, cassiterite **(548)** ● Occurrence: rare; Oberwolfach (FRG), Domodossola and Piedmont (Italy), Cínovec (Czech Republic), Broken Hill – New South Wales – crystals measuring 2.5 cm (Australia), Huachuca Mts (USA), Abuja (Nigeria).

---

1. Ferrimolybdite – yellow aggregates and crusts on quartz; Climax (Colorado, USA – width of field 33 mm) **2. Crocoite** – long prismatic crystals (to 30 mm) on limonite; Dundas (Australia)

Ferrimolybdite, crocoite

Delvauxite

Phosphate
$Fe_2^{3+}(PO_4)(OH)_3 . 3 . 5 H_2O$

135

Named after the chemist, J. S. P. J. Delvaux de Feuffe (1782–?) (Haidinger 1845)

● Hardness: 2.5 ● Streak: yellow ● Colour: yellowish-brown, brown, reddish-brown, brownish-black ● Lustre: vitreous, greasy, waxy ● Transparency: non-transparent ● Cleavage: absent ● Fracture: conchoidal ● Morphology: concretions, stalactitic, crusts, gelatinous masses ● Solubility: effervescent in water, crumbly ● Specific gravity: 1.85–2.0 ● Crystal system: unknown ● Crystal form: unknown ● Chemical composition: Fe_2O_3 49.79%, P_2O_5 22.13%, H_2O 28.08% ● Chemical properties: breaks up when heated, turns black and alters to magnetic slag ● Genesis: secondary ● Associated minerals: limonite **(355)**, hematite **(472)** ● Occurrence: rare; Berneau near Liège (Belgium), Železník (Slovakia), Litošice (Czech Republic), Nassau (FRG), Peierbach (Austria), Kerch (Ukraine).

Vivianite (Blue iron earth)

Phosphate
$Fe_3(PO_4)_2 . 8 H_2O$

136

P

Named after the English mineralogist, J. G. Vivian (Werner 1817)

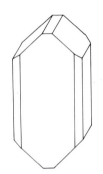

● Hardness: 2 ● Streak: white, changing immediately to indigo blue ● Colour: white, changing to blue-green, indigo blue or blackish-blue ● Transparency: translucent, opaque ● Lustre: vitreous, pearly, dull ● Cleavage: perfect on (010) ● Fracture: uneven ● Other properties of cohesion: sectile, flexible laminae ● Morphology: crystals, fibrous, spherical, earthy, radiating-fibrous aggregates ● Specific gravity: 2.6–2.7 ● Crystal system: monoclinic ● Crystal form: prisms, plates, isometric ● Chemical composition: FeO 42.96%, P_2O_5 28.31%, H_2O 28.73% ● Chemical properties: soluble in acids; when heated it turns red and alters to magnetic bead ● Handling: clean with distilled water ● Similar minerals: lazulite **(378)** ● Distinguishing features: hardness, solubility in acids, infusible ● Genesis: a secondary mineral of metallic deposits ● Associated minerals: siderite **(306)**, limonite **(355)** ● Occurrence: common; Bodenmais, Waldsassen and the Bavarian Forest (FRG), St. Agnes (Cornwall, Great Britain), Litošice (Czech Republic), Trepča (Serbia), Llallagua and Poopó deposits – crystals over 10 cm (Bolivia), Bingham Canyon – Utah – crystals over 15 cm (USA), N'gaoundere (Cameroon) – crystals over 0.5 m ● Application: dye; sometimes as a precious stone (facets, cabochons).

Symplesite

Arsenate
$Fe_3(AsO_4)_2 . 8 H_2O$

137

From the Greek *syn* – together and *plesiazein* – to associate (Breithaupt 1837)

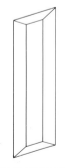

● Hardness: 2.5 (brittle) ● Streak: blue-white ● Colour: grass green to indigo-blue ● Transparency: fresh specimens transparent ● Lustre: vitreous, on cleavage planes pearly ● Cleavage: perfect on (110) ● Fracture: uneven ● Morphology: crystals, spheroidal aggregates, earthy ● Specific gravity: 3.0 ● Crystal system: triclinic ● Crystal form: imperfect prisms and platy crystals ● Chemical composition: FeO 36.56%, As_2O_5 38.99%, H_2O 24.45% ● Chemical properties: soluble in acids; when heated infusible but turning black and becoming magnetic ● Handling: clean with distilled water ● Genesis: secondary ● Associated minerals: pharmacosiderite **(140)**, erythrite **(141)**, annabergite **(142)**, scorodite **(254)**, limonite **(355)** ● Occurrence: rare; Lobenstein and Neustedtel (FRG), Lölling and Carinthia (Austria), Baia Sprie (Romania).

---

1. Delvauxite – nodules of red-brown colour; Kerch (Ukraine – width of field 52 mm) **2. Vivianite** – columnar crystals (to 20 mm); Ashio (Japan)

Delvauxite, vivianite

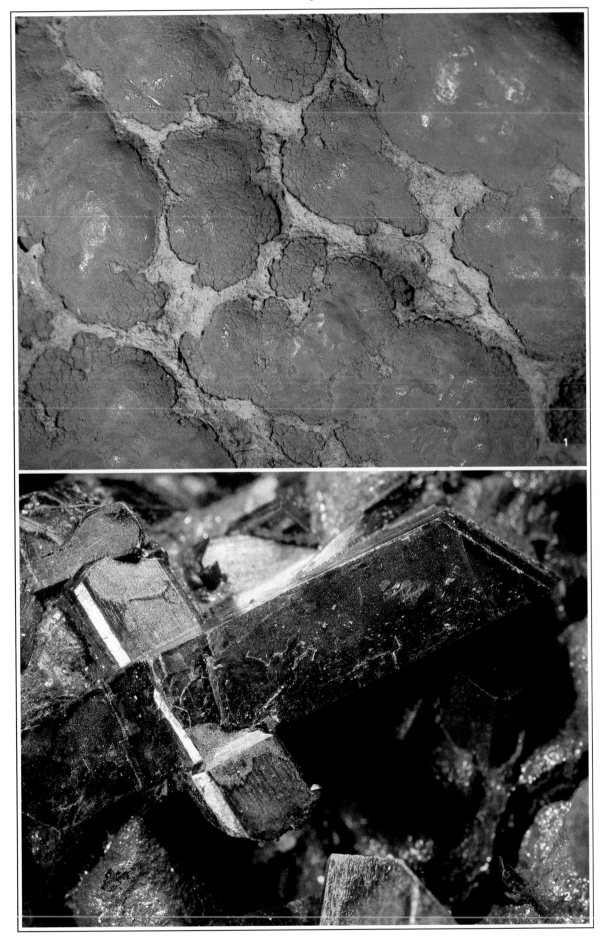

Chalcophyllite

Arsenate
$Cu_{18}Al_2(AsO_4)_3(SO_4)_3(OH)_{27} \cdot 36 H_2O$

138

From the Greek *chalkos* – copper and *fyllon* – leaf
(Breithaupt 1847)

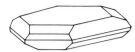

● Hardness: 2 ● Streak: lighter than the colour ● Colour: emerald green, blue-green to grass green ● Transparency: transparent to translucent ● Lustre: vitreous, adamantine, pearly ● Cleavage: perfect on (0001) ● Morphology: crystals, rose-shaped, massive aggregates ● Specific gravity: 2.4−2.6 ● Crystal system: trigonal ● Crystal form: plates ● Chemical composition: CuO 47.55%, Al_2O_3 3.39%, As_2O_5 11.45%, SO_3 7.98%, H_2O 29.63% ● Chemical properties: soluble in acids and ammonia, readily fusible ● Handling: clean with distilled water ● Genesis: secondary ● Associated minerals: azurite **(226)**, chrysocolla **(268)**, malachite **(307)**, limonite **(355)** ● Occurrence: rare; Clara Mine near Wolfach, Neubulach near Calw, and the Black Forest area (FRG), Schwaz – Tyrol (Austria), Redruth (Cornwall, Great Britain), Nizhni Tagil (Russia), Braden (Chile), Arizona – Utah (USA).

Pharmacolite

Arsenate
$CaH(AsO_4) \cdot 2 H_2O$

139

From the Greek *farmakon* – poison and *líthos* – stone
(Karsten 1800)

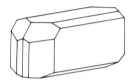

● Hardness: 2−2.5 ● Streak: white ● Colour: white, yellow, reddish ● Transparency: translucent ● Lustre: vitreous, silky ● Cleavage: good on (010) ● Fracture: uneven ● Other properties of cohesion: sometimes flexible ● Morphology: crystals, fibrous, botryoidal, stalactitic, pulverulent and crusty aggregates ● Solubility: water-soluble ● Specific gravity: 2.6 ● Crystal system: monoclinic ● Crystal form: needles ● Chemical composition: CaO 25.96%, As_2O_5 53.20%, H_2O 20.84% ● Chemical properties: soluble in acids ● Handling: clean with distilled water ● Genesis: secondary ● Associated minerals: erythrite **(141)**, annabergite **(142)**, gersdorffite **(343)**, niccolite **(351)** ● Occurrence: rare; Wittichen and St. Andreasberg (FRG), Jáchymov (Czech Republic), San Gabriel Canyon – California (USA).

Pharmacosiderite (Cube ore)

Arsenate
$KFe_4^{3+}(AsO_4)_3(OH)_4 \cdot 7 H_2O$

140

From the Greek *farmakon* – poison and *sideros* – iron
(Hausmann 1813)

● Hardness: 2.5 ● Streak: lighter than the colour ● Colour: olive green, emerald green to reddish-brown ● Transparency: transparent to translucent ● Lustre: adamantine to greasy ● Cleavage: indistinct on (100) ● Fracture: uneven ● Other properties of cohesion: sectile ● Morphology: crystals, granular, earthy ● Specific gravity: 2.8−2.9 ● Crystal system: cubic ● Crystal form: cubes, tetrahedra ● Chemical composition: K_2O 5.39%, Fe_2O_3 36.57%, As_2O_5 39.47%, H_2O 18.57% ● Chemical properties: when heated fusible, producing a magnetic bead; in ammonia turns red, but when immersed in dilute HCl it returns to its original colour ● Handling: clean with distilled water ● Genesis: secondary ● Associated minerals: scorodite **(254)**, arsenopyrite **(344)**, limonite **(355)** ● Occurrence: rare; Lobenstein, Wittichen, Clara Mine near Wolfach, Black Forest, and Neubulach (FRG), Cornwall (Great Britain), Nová Baňa (Slovakia), Majuba Hill – Nevada (USA), Victoria (Australia).

---

1. Chalcophyllite – aggregates of tabular crystals (2 mm) on azurite; Špania Dolina (Slovakia) **2. Pharmacolite** – white globular aggregates with erythrite (globules 1 mm); Dobšiná (Slovakia) **3. Pharmacosiderite** – pseudohexagonal crystals (to 6 mm) on limonite; Nová Baňa (Slovakia)

Erythrite (Cobalt bloom)

Arsenate
$Co_3(AsO_4)_2 \cdot 8\,H_2O$

141

L

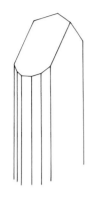

From the Greek *erythros* – red
(Beudant 1832)

● Hardness: 2 ● Streak: pink-red ● Colour: purple-red, pink-red, violet ● Transparency: pellucid to translucent ● Lustre: adamantine, pearly ● Cleavage: perfect on (010) ● Other properties of cohesion: sectile, flexible ● Morphology: crystals, radiate-fibrous, earthy, pulverulent aggregates ● Specific gravity: 3.07 ● Crystal system: monoclinic ● Crystal form: prisms, nodular (striated) ● Luminescence: orange ● Chemical composition: CoO 37.54%, As_2O_5 38.39%, H_2O 24.07% ● Chemical properties: soluble in HNO_3 (produces a pink-coloured solution), tinges a flame green; when heated fusible, altering to a grey ball with garlicky smell, loses water and turns blue ● Handling: clean with distilled water ● Genesis: secondary ● Associated minerals: pharmacolite **(139)**, annabergite **(142)**, chloanthite **(346)** ● Occurrence: rare; Schneeberg, Saalfeld, Thuringia, Richelsdorf, Hessen, Bieber and Wittichen (FRG), Allemont (France), Jáchymov (Czech Republic), Schladming (Austria), Cornwall (Great Britain), Cobalt – Ontario (Canada), Álamos (Mexico), Bou Azzer (Morocco).

Annabergite (Nickel bloom)

Arsenate
$Ni_3(AsO_4)_2 \cdot 8\,H_2O$

142

Named after its source in Annaberg (FRG)
(Brooke and Miller 1852)

● Hardness: 2 (brittle) ● Streak: light green ● Colour: green, green-white, apple-green ● Transparency: translucent to opaque ● Lustre: adamantine, pearly, dull ● Cleavage: perfect on (010) ● Morphology: crystals, earthy, pulverulent aggregates, crusts ● Specific gravity: 3.0–3.1 ● Crystal system: monoclinic ● Crystal form: prisms, needles ● Chemical composition: NiO 37.46%, As_2O_5 38.44%, H_2O 24.10%; admixtures: Mg (up to 6%), Ca, Zn, Fe ● Chemical properties: soluble in acids, readily fusible ● Handling: clean with distilled water ● Similar minerals: antlerite **(227)** ● Distinguishing features: hardness, specific gravity, solubility in acids, test for Ni ● Genesis: secondary ● Associated minerals: erythrite **(141)**, gersdorfite **(343)**, chloanthite **(346)** ● Occurrence: rare; Schneeberg, Annaberg, Wittichen and Richelsdorf (FRG), Lávrion (Greece), Jáchymov (Czech Republic), Dobšiná (Slovakia), Sierra Cabrera (Spain), Cobalt – Ontario (Canada), Allemont (France), (USA), (Chile), (Mexico).

Cabrerite (Annabergite variety)

Arsenate
$(Ni,Mg)_3(AsO_4)_2 \cdot 8\,H_2O$

143

Named after its locality Sierra Cabrera (Spain)
(Dana 1868)

● Hardness: 2 ● Streak: lighter than colour ● Colour: apple-green ● Transparency: translucent ● Lustre: adamantine, pearly ● Cleavage: perfect on (010) ● Morphology: crystals, powdered aggregates ● Specific gravity: 3.1 ● Crystal system: monoclinic ● Crystal form: prisms, needles ● Chemical composition: the same as in annabergite **(142)**; contains up to 6% MgO ● Chemical properties: as in annabergite ● Handling: clean with distilled water ● Genesis: secondary ● Associated minerals: as in annabergite ● Occurrence: rare; Sierra Cabrera (Spain), Lávrion (Greece), Hirt (Austria).

---

1. Erythrite – wisp-like crystals in quartz; Schneeberg (FRG) – width of field 85 mm) **2. Annabergite** – fan-shaped aggregate (12 mm) with calcite; Lávrion (Greece) **3. Cabrerite** – wisp-like aggregates (to 5 mm) on calcite; Lávrion (Greece)

Erythrite, annabergite, cabrerite

Liroconite

Arsenate
$Cu_2Al(AsO_4)(OH)_4 . 4 H_2O$

From the Greek *liros* – pale and *konia* – powder (Mohs 1820)

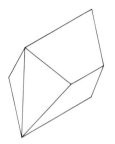

● Hardness: 2–2.5 ● Streak: light blue to green ● Colour: light blue to green ● Transparency: transparent to translucent ● Lustre: vitreous ● Cleavage: poor on (110) and on (011) ● Fracture: uneven to conchoidal ● Morphology: crystals, granular aggregates ● Specific gravity: 2.9–3.0 ● Crystal system: monoclinic ● Crystal form: flattened octahedra – lenticular ● Chemical composition: CuO 36.74%, Al_2O_3 11.77%, As_2O_5 26.53%, H_2O 24.96% ● Chemical properties: soluble in acids, readily fusible (fuses into dark grey glass) ● Handling: clean with distilled water ● Similar minerals: chalcanthite (116) ● Distinguishing features: streak, insoluble in water ● Genesis: secondary ● Associated minerals: chalcophyllite (138), malachite (307), limonite (355) ● Occurrence: rare; Cornwall (Great Britain), Sayda near Freiberg, Ullersreuth, Hirschberg, Siegen (FRG), California (USA), (Congo), N'Kana (Zambia).

Lavendulane

Arsenate
$(Ca,Na)_2Cu_5(AsO_4)_4Cl . 4-5 H_2O$

Named for its lavender colour (Breihaupt 1837)

● Hardness: 2.5 ● Streak: lighter than colour ● Colour: blue, lavender blue ● Transparency: transparent ● Lustre: vitreous to waxy, silky ● Cleavage: good on (001) ● Morphology: scales, fibrous and botryoidal aggregates, crusts ● Specific gravity: 3.54 ● Crystal system: orthorhombic ● Crystal form: plates ● Chemical composition: variable ● Genesis: secondary ● Associated minerals: erythrite (141), olivenite (257) ● Occurrence: rare; Jáchymov (Czech Republic), Annaberg (FRG), Wittichen and Müllenbach (FRG), San Juan (Chile), Gold Hill – Utah (USA).

Clinoclase

Arsenate
$Cu_3(AsO_4)(OH)_3$

From the Greek *klíneis* – to incline and *klas* – to break (Breithaupt 1830)

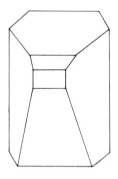

● Hardness: 2.5–3 (brittle) ● Streak: blue-green ● Colour: green-black, blue-green ● Transparency: transparent to translucent ● Lustre: vitreous, on cleavage planes pearly ● Cleavage: very good on (001) ● Fracture: uneven ● Morphology: crystals, fibrous, spherical aggregates, deposits, encrustations ● Specific gravity: 4.2–4.4 ● Crystal system: monoclinic ● Crystal form: prisms, plates, pseudorhombic ● Chemical composition: CuO 62.71%, As_2O_5 30.19%, H_2O 7.10% ● Chemical properties: readily fusible, soluble in acids and ammonia ● Handling: clean with distilled water ● Similar minerals: azurite (226) ● Distinguishing features: hardness, specific gravity; azurite effervesces in HCl ● Genesis: a secondary copper mineral ● Associated minerals: tyrolite (32), chalcophyllite (138), olivenite (257), cornwallite (320) ● Occurrence: rare; Sayda near Freiberg, Clara Mine near Oberwolfach and Freudenstadt (FRG), Novoveská Huta (Slovakia), Cornwall (Great Britain), Collahuasi (Chile), Tintic – Utah (USA).

1. **Liroconite** – druse of dark blue crystals (up to 10 mm); Wheal Gorland (Cornwall, Great Britain) 2. **Lavendulane** – fine crystalline crusts on limonite; San Juan (Chile – width of field 40 mm) 3. **Clinoclase** – tabular aggregates (plates to 6 mm); Cornwall (Great Britain)

Liroconite, lavendulane, clinoclase

Strashimirite

Arsenate
$Cu_8(AsO_4)_4(OH)_4 . 5 H_2O$

147

Named after the Bulgarian petrographer, Strashimir Dimitrov (Stefanova 1968)

• Hardness: 2.5–3 • Streak: lighter than colour • Colour: white, green • Transparency: translucent • Lustre: pearly, greasy • Cleavage: unknown • Morphology: crystals, fibrous aggregates, coatings • Specific gravity: 3.8 • Crystal system: monoclinic • Crystal form: needles, fibres • Genesis: secondary • Associated minerals: azurite **(226)**, euchroite **(256)** • Occurrence: rare; Zapacica (Bulgaria), Oberwolfach (FRG).

Autunite (Lime uranite)

Phosphate
$Ca(UO_2)_2(PO_4)_2 . 8-12 H_2O$

148

Named after its locality Autun (France) (Brooke 1852)

L

R

• Hardness: 2–2.5 • Streak: light yellow • Colour: yellow-green • Transparency: translucent • Lustre: pearly, vitreous • Cleavage: good on (001) • Morphology: crystals, scaly, crusty and earthy aggregates • Specific gravity: 3.2 • Crystal system: tetragonal • Crystal form: plates, subparallel twinning • Luminescence: striking yellow-green • Radioactivity: strong • Chemical composition: CaO 5.69%, UO_3 58.00%, P_2O_5 14.39%, H_2O 21.92% (for 12 H_2O) • Chemical properties: soluble in HNO_3, tinges a flame orange-red, reacts with borax on U • Handling: clean with distilled water • Similar minerals: torbernite **(149)** • Distinguishing features: chemical properties • Genesis: secondary • Associated minerals: other uranium micas • Occurrence: common; Hagendorf (FRG), Jáchymov (Czech Republic), Autun (France), Cornwall (Great Britain) • Application: U ore.

Torbernite (Copper uranite)

Phosphate
$Cu(UO_2)_2(PO_4)_2 . 8-12 H_2O$

149

Named after the Swedish chemist, Tornbern Bergmann (1735–1784) (Werner 1786)

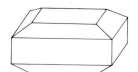

R

• Hardness: 2–2.5 (brittle) • Streak: lighter than colour • Colour: green • Transparency: translucent • Lustre: vitreous, pearly • Cleavage: perfect on (001) • Morphology: crystals, scaly and earthy aggregates • Specific gravity: 3.3 • Crystal system: tetragonal • Crystal form: plates, rarely dipyramidal • Chemical composition: CuO 7.88%, UO_3 56.65%, P_2O_5 14.06%, H_2O 21.41% (at 12 H_2O); admixture: Ca • Chemical properties: soluble in HNO_3; at a temperature of 45 °C alters to metatorbernite **(152)** • Handling: clean with distilled water • Similar minerals: autunite **(148)**, zeunerite **(153)** • Distinguishing features: luminescence, reaction with HNO_3, X-rays, chemical properties, strong radioactivity • Genesis: secondary • Associated minerals: uranium micas • Occurrence: frequent; Schneeberg (FRG), Jáchymov (Czech Republic), Cornwall (Great Britain) • Application: U ore.

Tyuyamunite

Vanadate
$Ca(UO_2)_2(VO_4)_2 . 5-8 H_2O$

150

Named after its deposit in Tyuya Muyun (Turkmenistan) (Nanadkevich 1912)

L

R

• Hardness: 1–2 • Streak: light yellow • Colour: yellow with greenish or orange tint • Transparency: transparent to non-transparent • Lustre: pearly to adamantine • Cleavage: perfect on (001) • Morphology: crystals, scaly or earthy aggregates, crusts, coatings • Specific gravity: 3.3–3.6 • Crystal system: orthorhombic • Crystal form: plates to scales • Luminescence: sometimes yellow-green • Radioactivity: strong • Genesis: secondary • Associated minerals: carnotite **(154)**, asphalt, vanadinite **(263)** • Occurrence: rare • Application: U and V ore.

---

1. **Autunite** – druse of tabular crystals (up to 7 mm) of light green colour; Autun (France) 2. **Torbernite** – tabular crystals in druses (to 4 mm); Cornwall (Great Britain) 3. **Tyuyamunite** – aggregates of tabular crystals of yellow colour (to 2 mm); Valencia Co. (Grants, USA)

Autunite, torbernite, tyuyamunite

Meta-autunite

Phosphate
$Ca(UO_2)_2(PO_4)_2 \cdot 2-6\,H_2O$

151

Like autunite but with a lower water content, with prefix *meta* (Gauber 1904)

• Hardness: 2–2.5 • Streak: lighter than its colour • Colour: yellow to yellow-green • Transparency: translucent to non-transparent • Lustre: pearly to dull • Cleavage: good on (001) • Morphology: crystals, pseudomorphs, crusts, powdered aggregates • Specific gravity: 3.45–3.55 • Crystal system: tetragonal • Crystal form: plates • Luminescence: lower than in autunite • Radioactivity: strong • Chemical composition: CaO 6.96%, UO_3 70.96%, P_2O_5 17.61%, H_2O 4.47% (with $2\,H_2O$) • Other properties identical as in autunite **(148)**.

Metatorbernite

Phosphate
$Cu(UO_2)_2(PO_4)_2 \cdot 8\,H_2O$

152

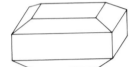

Like torbernite but with a lower water content, with prefix *meta* (Halimond, 1916)

• Hardness: 2.5 (brittle) • Streak: lighter than its colour • Colour: green to dark green • Transparency: translucent to transparent • Lustre: vitreous, pearly on (001) • Cleavage: good on (001) • Morphology: crystals, scales, rose-shaped aggregates, pseudomorphs after torbernite due to dehydration • Specific gravity: 3.7 • Crystal system: tetragonal • Crystal form: plates • Radioactivity: strong • Chemical composition: CuO 8.48%, UO_3 61.01%, P_2O_5 15.14%, H_2O 15.37% • Other properties identical as in torbernite **(149)**.

Zeunerite

Arsenate
$Cu(UO_2)_2(AsO_4)_2 \cdot 8-12\,H_2O$

153

Named after the German physicist, G. A. Zeuner (1828–1907) (Weisbach 1872)

• Hardness: 2.5 • Streak: lighter than its colour • Colour: green • Transparency: hydrated specimens are transparent • Lustre: vitreous • Cleavage: perfect on (001) • Morphology: crystals, scaly aggregates • Specific gravity: 3.4 • Crystal system: tetragonal • Crystal form: plates • Chemical composition: CuO 6.75%, UO_3 48.57%, As_2O_5 26.33%, H_2O 18.35% (with $12\,H_2O$) • Chemical properties: soluble in HNO_3, when heated on charcoal forms white sublimate of As_2O_3 • Handling: clean with distilled water • Similar minerals: torbernite **(149)** • Distinguishing features: X-rays, strong radioactivity, chemical properties • Genesis: secondary • Associated minerals: other U minerals • Occurrence: rare; Schneeberg, Wittichen (FRG), Dexter Mine – Utah (USA).

Carnotite

Vanadate
$K_2(UO_2)_2(VO_4)_2 \cdot 3\,H_2O$

154

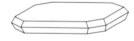

Named after the French chemist, M. A. Carnot (1839–1920) (Friedel 1899)

• Hardness: 2 • Streak: light yellow • Colour: canary yellow, green-yellow • Transparency: transparent • Lustre: aggregates – dull, earthy; crystals – pearly • Cleavage: perfect on (001), micaceous • Morphology: crystals, powdered, earthy and microcrystalline aggregates • Specific gravity: 3.7–4.7 • Crystal system: monoclinic • Crystal form: plates, rhombohedral • Chemical composition: K_2O 10.44%, UO_3 63.42%, V_2O_5 20.16%, H_2O 5.98% • Chemical properties: soluble in acids • Similar minerals: copiapite **(123)**, tyuyamunite **(150)** • Distinguishing features: strong radioactivity, specific gravity, optical and chemical properties • Genesis: secondary • Associated minerals: tyuyamunite, asphalt, vanadinite **(263)** and other secondary U micas • Occurrence: rare; Fergana (Uzbekistan), Radium Hill (Australia), (Congo).

---

1. **Meta-autunite** – fine yellow aggregate of minute crystals; Jáchymov (Czech Republic) 2. **Metatorbernite** – druse of green tabular crystals; Cornwall (Great Britain) 3. **Carnotite** – powdery yellow aggregates on quartz; Arizona (USA) 4. **Zeunerite** – emerald-green tabular crystals; Schneeberg (FRG – width of field 89 mm)

Meta-autunite, metatorbernite, carnotite, zeunerite

Sepiolite (Sea foam)

Silicate
$Mg_4Si_6O_{15}(OH)_2 . 6 H_2O$

155

L

P

From the Greek *sepia* – sepia and *lithos* – stone (according to colour and porosity) (Glocker 1847)

● Hardness: 2–2.5 ● Streak: white ● Colour: white, grey-white, yellowish, green-blue ● Transparency: non-transparent ● Lustre: dull ● Cleavage: unknown ● Fracture: conchoidal ● Morphology: cryptocrystalline, earthy, massive, porous, fibrous, aggregates ● Other properties: floats on water, clings to the tongue ● Specific gravity: 2 ● Crystal system: orthorhombic ● Crystal form: cryptocrystalline, fibrous, amorphous ● Luminescence: sometimes white-yellow or blue-white ● Chemical composition: MgO 24.88%, SiO_2 55.65%, H_2O 19.47% ● Chemical properties: not readily fusible, soluble in HCl ● Handling: clean with distilled water ● Genesis: secondary in serpentinites ● Associated minerals: serpentine **(273)**, magnesite **(302)**, opal **(440)** ● Occurrence: common; Eskisehir (Turkey), Vallecas (Spain), Samos (Greece) ● Application: electrotechnology, pharmaceuticals, decorative articles.

Palygorskite

Silicate
$(Mg,Al)_2Si_4O_{10}(OH) . 4 H_2O$

156

Named after its deposit in the Urals (Russia) (Savchenkov 1862)

● Hardness: 2–2.5 ● Streak: white ● Colour: white, grey, brownish ● Transparency: translucent to non-transparent ● Lustre: dull ● Cleavage: good on (110) ● Other features of cohesion: fine fragments are flexible ● Morphology: cryptocrystalline, fibrous, massive aggregates ● Other properties: very porous, floats on water ● Specific gravity: 2.1–2.2 ● Crystal system: monoclinic ● Crystal form: fibrous ● Chemical composition: variable ● Chemical properties: in a blowpipe flame fuses and alters into porous milkglass, soluble in HCl and hot H_2SO_4 ● Genesis: secondary ● Associated minerals: chlorite **(158)**, magnesite **(302)**, opal **(440)**, chalcedony **(449)** ● Occurrence: rare; Scotland (Great Britain), (France), (Czech Republic), (Slovakia), (Austria), (Russia), Georgia and Washington (USA) ● Application: insulation and soundproofing materials.

Garnierite (Noumeaite)

Silicate
$(Ni,Mg)_3Si_2O_5(OH)_4$

157

Named after the French engineer, J. Garnier (1839–1904) (Clarke 1874)

● Hardness: 2–4 (brittle) ● Streak: light-green ● Colour: green, blue-green ● Transparency: non-transparent ● Lustre: dull ● Cleavage: absent ● Fracture: uneven, conchoidal ● Morphology: cryptocrystalline, gelatinous, earthy and crusty aggregates ● Specific gravity: 2.2–2.7 ● Crystal system: monoclinic ● Crystal form: microscopic, subparallel fibrous aggregates ● Chemical composition: NiO 34.09%, MgO 18.39%, SiO_2 36.56%, H_2O 10.96% (when Ni:Mg = 1:1). Garnierite is a mixture of Ni hydrosilicates ● Chemical properties: soluble in hot HCl ● Handling: clean with distilled water ● Genesis: secondary ● Associated minerals: magnesite **(302)**, limonite **(355)**, opal **(440)**, chrysoprase **(457)** ● Occurrence: rare; St. Egedien (FRG), Ufalei (Russia), (Cuba), (Brazil), Nouméa (New Caledonia) ● Application: Ni ore.

---

1. Palygorskite – grey-white fibrous aggregate; Schneeberg (FRG) **2. Sepiolite** – fibrous aggregates on marble; Hejná (Czech Republic) **3. Garnierite** – massive light green aggregate on serpentinite; Szklary (Poland – width of field 76 mm)

Palygorskite, sepiolite, garnierite

Chlorites (group of minerals)

158

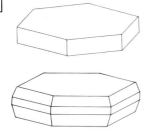

From the Greek *chloros* – green

● Hardness: 2–2.5 ● Streak: white to light green ● Colour: green, black-green, reddish, violet, white ● Transparency: transparent to translucent ● Lustre: vitreous to pearly ● Cleavage: perfect on (001) ● Other features of cohesion: flexible, but inelastic ● Morphology: crystals, massive, scaly and granular aggregates ● Specific gravity: 2.5–4.8 ● Crystal system: monoclinic ● Crystal form: plates ● Chemical composition: variable; they contain: Fe^{2+}, Fe^{3+}, Mg, Mn, sometimes Ni, Cr, Al. They include clinochlore **(159)**, pennine **(160)**, ripidolite **(161)**, kämmererite **(162)**, delessite **(163)**, thuringite **(164)** ● Chemical properties: usually soluble in acids ● Handling: clean with distilled water ● Genesis: magmatic, metamorphic, hydrothermal, sedimentary ● Associated minerals: calcite **(217)**, rutile **(464)**, quartz **(534)** ● Occurrence: common rock-forming minerals in crystalline schists and granodiorites.

Clinochlore

159

L

From the Greek *klino* – oblique and *chloros* – green
(Jeremiev 1861)

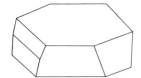

● Hardness: 2–2.5 ● Streak: white ● Colour: black-green, blue-green, white, yellow-green, olive-green ● Transparency: translucent ● Lustre: vitreous, pearly to greasy ● Cleavage: perfect on (001) ● Other features of cohesion: scales are flexible, but not elastic ● Morphology: crystals, scaly, granular, earthy aggregates ● Specific gravity: 2.55–2.75 ● Crystal system: monoclinic ● Crystal form: plates of hexagonal shape ● Luminescence: sometimes dull orange ● Chemical composition: complicated, variable; admixtures: Mn, Cr and Ca; varieties: leuchtenbergite and kotschubeite ● Chemical properties: dissolves in H_2SO_4, liberating heat ● Handling: clean with distilled water ● Similar minerals: other chlorites ● Genesis: metamorphic ● Associated minerals: calcite **(217)**, diopside **(505)**, epidote **(513)**, garnet **(577)** ● Occurrence: common; rock-forming mineral. Fine crystals are found in chloritic schists in Val d'Ala and Piedmont (Italy), Pfitsch and Zillertal (Austria), Akhmatov Mine near Zlatoust in the Urals (Russia), Westchester – Pennsylvania (USA).

Pennine

160

Named after its locality in Pennine Alps (Switzerland)
(Fröbel 1840)

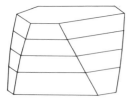

● Hardness: 2–2.5 ● Streak: white ● Colour: emerald-green, olive-green, white, yellow-white ● Transparency: translucent ● Lustre: vitreous, on cleavage planes pearly ● Cleavage: perfect on (001), micaceous ● Other features of cohesion: scales are flexible, but inelastic ● Morphology: crystals, scaly, massive and granular aggregates ● Specific gravity: 2.5–2.6 ● Crystal system: monoclinic ● Crystal form: plates, rhombohedra ● Chemical composition: complicated, variable; admixtures: Cr (kämmererite). Of the chlorites it contains most SiO_2 ● Chemical properties: soluble in HCl and H_2SO_4 ● Handling: clean with distilled water ● Similar minerals: other chlorites ● Genesis: metamorphic ● Associated minerals: actinolite **(413)**, epidote **(513)**, garnet **(577)** ● Occurrence: common; in crystalline schists; Rimpfischwäge and Zermatt (Switzerland), Zillertal (Austria), Val d'Ala and Piedmont (Italy), Urals (Russia).

---

1. Chlorite – fine scaly aggregate of black-green colour; Zillertal (Austria) **2. Clinochlore** – tabular crystals with hessonite; Val d'Ala (Italy – width of field 66 mm) **3. Pennine** – tabular crystals (to 70 mm); Passo di Vizze (Italy)

Chlorites, clinochlore, pennine

H
2—3

Ripidolite

$(Mg,Fe^{2+})_5Al(Si,Al)_4O_{10}(OH)_8$

161

From the Greek *rhipis* – fan and *lithos* – stone (Kobell 1839)

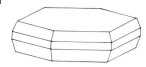

● Hardness: 2 ● Streak: light green ● Colour: black-green to brownish-green ● Transparency: transparent to translucent ● Lustre: pearly ● Cleavage: perfect on (001) ● Other features of cohesion: scales are flexible, but inelastic ● Morphology: crystals, massive, granular, scaly, often fan-shaped aggregates ● Specific gravity: 2.8–3.0 ● Crystal system: monoclinic ● Crystal form: plates ● Chemical composition: complicated and variable ● Chemical properties: soluble in H_2SO_4 ● Handling: clean with distilled water ● Genesis: metamorphic, in alpine veins ● Associated minerals: titanite **(430)**, albite **(493)**, quartz **(534)** ● Occurrence: common; Cornwall (Great Britain).

Kämmererite

Silicate

$(Mg,Cr)_6(Si,Al),O_{10}(OH)_8$

162

L

Named after the Russian mining engineer, A. A. Kämmerer (1789–1858) (Nordenskjöld) 1841)

● Hardness: 2–2.5 ● Streak: reddish ● Colour: red ● Transparency: translucent to transparent ● Lustre: vitreous ● Cleavage: perfect on (001), micaceous ● Other features of cohesion: scales are flexible ● Morphology: crystals, scaly aggregates ● Specific gravity: 2.64 ● Crystal system: monoclinic ● Crystal form: plates of hexagonal forms ● Luminescence: sometimes dull orange ● Chemical composition: complicated, variable ● Chemical properties: soluble in HCl and H_2SO_4 ● Handling: clean with distilled water ● Genesis: metamorphic ● Associated minerals: chromite **(371)**, uvarovite **(581)** ● Occurrence: rare; Sysersk (Russia), Guleman (Turkey), Texas (USA), Shetland Islands (Great Britain).

Delessite (Chamosite variety)

Silicate

$(Mg,Fe^{2+},Fe^{3+},Al)_6(Si,Al)_4O_{10}(O,OH)_8$

163

Named after the French mineralogist, A. E. Deless (1817–1881) (Naumann 1850)

● Hardness: 2–3 ● Streak: grey-green to olive-green ● Colour: green-black to black ● Cleavage: perfect on (001) ● Morphology: massive and scaly aggregates, radial-fibrous aggregates ● Specific gravity: 2.73 ● Crystal system: monoclinic ● Crystal form: plates ● Chemical composition: complicated and variable ● Chemical properties: soluble in acids ● Handling: clean with distilled water ● Similar minerals: iron chlorites ● Distinguishing features: X-rays, chemical ● Genesis: volcanic ● Associated minerals: calcite **(217)**, zeolites, quartz **(534)** ● Occurrence: rare; Idar and Oberstein (FRG).

Thuringite

Silicate

$(Fe^{2+},Fe^{3+},Mg)_6(Si,Al)_4O_{10}(OH)_8$

164

Named after its locality in Thuringia (Breithaupt 1832)

● Hardness: 2–2.5 ● Streak: green-grey ● Colour: olive-green, green-brown, dark brown ● Transparency: translucent ● Lustre: dull, pearly ● Cleavage: perfect on (001) ● Morphology: scaly, compact, cryptocrystalline aggregates ● Specific gravity: 3.2 ● Crystal system: monoclinic ● Crystal form: rarely scales ● Chemical composition: complicated and variable ● Chemical properties: When heated fuses and forms black magnetic glass; readily soluble in acids ● Handling: clean with distilled water ● Similar minerals: chamosite **(277)** ● Distinguishing features: chemical properties ● Genesis: metamorphic, sedimentary ● Associated minerals: siderite **(306)**, limonite **(355)**, magnetite **(367)** ● Occurence: rare; locally common; Thuringia (FRG), Zirmsee (Austria), Lake Superior – Michigan (USA) ● Application: iron ore.

---

1. **Kämmererite** – druse of crystals (to 3 mm); Erzincan (Turkey) 2. **Ripidolite** – druse of tabular crystals; Cornwall (Great Britain) 3. **Thuringite** – grey-black finely crystalline aggregate; Šternberk (Czech Republic – width of field 82 mm)

Kämmererite, ripidolite, thuringite

Muscovite (Common mica)

Silicate
$KAl_3Si_3O_{10}(OH,F)_2$

165

From the old English name of Moscow (Muscov) (Dana 1850)

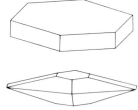

● Hardness: 2–2.5 ● Streak: white ● Colour: white, grey, silver-white, brownish, greenish, yellow-green ● Transparency: transparent to translucent ● Lustre: pearly, vitreous, silky ● Cleavage: perfect on (001), micaceous ● Other features of cohesion: flexible and elastic scales ● Morphology: crystals, scaly, massive aggregates, cryptocrystalline (sericite variety) ● Specific gravity: 2.7–2.8 ● Crystal system: monoclinic ● Crystal form: plates, prisms, pyramidal ● Chemical composition: complicated, variable. Varieties: hydromuscovite (contains more OH and less K), phengite (contains more Si and less H_2O), mariposite (contains more Si and about 1% Cr_2O_3), fuchsite (**166** – up to 5% Cr_2O_3) ● Chemical properties: insoluble in acids ● Handling: clean with diluted acids or water ● Similar minerals: other micas ● Distinguishing features: habit, X-rays, chemical properties ● Genesis: magnetic, pegmatitic, hydrothermal, metamorphic ● Associated minerals: feldspars, biotite **(167)**, quartz **(534)** ● Occurrence: quite abundant; fine and large crystals are found in pegmatites in (Norway), (Sweden), (Austria), (FRG), (Russia); spathic crystals (measuring 5 m² by 0.5 m long, weighing 85 tons) are found in Mamsk – Urals (Russia); crystals measuring 10 cm long are common in the pegmatites of Custer – South Dakota (USA) ● Application: electrical industry, insulating material, ceramics manufacturing.

Fuchsite (Muscovite variety)

Silicate
$K(Al,Cr)_2AlSi_3O_{10}(OH,F)_2$

166

Named after the German mineralogist, J. N. von Fuchs (1774–1856) (Schaffhäutel 1843)

P

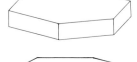

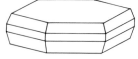

● Hardness: 2.5 ● Streak: light green to white ● Colour: emerald-green ● Transparency: translucent ● Lustre: pearly to silky ● Cleavage: perfect on (001), micaceous ● Morphology: scaly to massive aggregates ● Specific gravity: 2.8–2.9 ● Crystal system: monoclinic ● Crystal form: plates ● Chemical composition: like muscovite, contains up to 5% Cr_2O_3 ● Chemical properties: insoluble in acids ● Handling: clean with distilled water or diluted acids ● Genesis: hydrothermal ● Associated minerals: carbonates, quartz **(534)** ● Occurrence: rare; Schwarzenstein (Austria), Dobšiná and Rudňany (Slovakia), Lengenbach (Switzerland), Urals (Russia) ● Application: used in the production of decorative articles (Guatemala).

Muscovite – tabular crystal (50 mm) of pearly lustre from a pegmatite; Maršíkov (Czech Republic)

Muscovite

Biotite (Iron mica, Micaceous iron ore)

Silicate
$K(Mg,Fe^{2+})_3(Al,Fe^{3+})Si_3O_{10}(OH)_2$

167

Named after the French physicist, J. B. Biot (1774–1862) (Hausmann 1847)

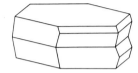

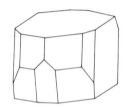

● Hardness: 2.5–3 ● Streak: white, grey ● Colour: dark brown, brown-green, brown-black ● Transparency: transparent to translucent ● Lustre: vitreous, pearly, opaque ● Cleavage: perfect on (001), micaceous ● Other features of cohesion: scales are flexible and fragile ● Morphology: crystals, scaly, massive, granular aggregates ● Specific gravity: 2.8–3.2 ● Crystal system: monoclinic ● Crystal form: plates, short prisms ● Chemical composition: complicated, variable; admixtures: Ti, Na, Li, Ba, Sr, Cs, Mn (manganophyllite), Fe (lepidomelane) ● Chemical properties: fuses with difficulty into black magnetic glass, soluble in concentrated H_2SO_4 (SiO_2 skeleton) ● Handling: clean with distilled water or diluted acids (except H_2SO_4) ● Similar minerals: phlogopite **(168)** ● Distinguishing features: when fused phlogopite does not form magnetic glass; X-rays, chemical tests ● Genesis: magmatic, in pegmatites, metamorphic, contact ● Associated minerals: feldspars, muscovite **(165)**, quartz **(534)** ● Occurrence: quite common; rock building mineral; Evje – crystals measuring 7 m² (Norway), Vesuvius (Italy), (Sweden), (Austria), Scotland (Great Britain), (Russia), (USA) ● Application: insulating material.

Phlogopite

Silicate
$KMg_3AlSi_3O_{10}(OH,F)_2$

168

From the Greek *flogopos* – resembling fire (Breithaupt 1841)

L

● Hardness: 2.0–2.5 ● Streak: white ● Colour: brown, grey, green, yellow, reddish-brown ● Transparency: transparent to translucent ● Lustre: pearly ● Cleavage: perfect on (001), micaceous ● Other features of cohesion: scales are flexible and elastic ● Morphology: crystals, scaly, granular aggregates ● Specific gravity: 2.7–2.9 ● Crystal system: monoclinic ● Crystal form: plates, short prisms, coarse scales ● Luminescence: sometimes dull yellow, sometimes fluorescent in short-wave UV ● Chemical composition: complicated, variable; admixtures: Ba, Fe, Mn and Cr ● Chemical properties: not readily fusible, soluble in concentrated acids (especially H_2SO_4) ● Handling: clean with diluted acids and distilled water ● Similar minerals: other micas ● Distinguishing features: habit, X-rays, chemical tests – muscovite **(165)** is insoluble in acids ● Genesis: in pegmatites, contact-metasomatic, magmatic (ultrabasic rocks) ● Associated minerals: calcite **(217)**, scapolite **(398)**, diopside **(505)** ● Occurrence: common: Pargas (Finland), Aker (Sweden), Campolungo (Italy), Slyudyanka – crystals measuring 5 m (Russia), Sydenham – Ontario (Canada), (southern Madagascar) ● Application: electronics.

Biotite – tabular crystal (12 mm); Alps (Austria)

Biotite

Lepidolite (Lithium mica)

Silicate
$K(Li,Al)_3(Si,Al)_4O_{10}(OH,F)_2$

169

L

P

From the Greek *lepidion* – scale and *líthos* – stone (Klaproth 1792)

● Hardness: 2.5–3 ● Streak: white, light pink ● Colour: violet, light red, grey, greenish, white ● Transparency: translucent to transparent ● Lustre: pearly ● Cleavage: perfect on (001) ● Other features of cohesion: scales are flexible and elastic ● Morphology: crystals, scaly, massive, granular aggregates ● Specific gravity: 2.8–2.9 ● Crystal system: monoclinic ● Crystal form: pseudohexagonal plates ● Luminescence: sometimes green ● Chemical composition: complicated, variable ● Handling: clean with water ● Similar minerals: zinnwaldite **(276)** ● Distinguishing features: habit, chemical properties ● Genesis: pegmatites, greisens ● Associated minerals: orthoclase **(486)**, quartz **(534)**, elbaite **(567)** ● Occurrence: rare; Rožná (Czech Republic), (Brazil), Madagascar) ● Application: Li ore.

Lamprophyllite

Silicate
$Na_3Sr_2Ti_3(Si_2O_7)_2(O,OH,F)_2$

170

From the Greek *lampros* – lustre and *fyllon* – leaf (Ramsay 1894)

● Hardness: 2.5 (brittle) ● Streak: white, brown-yellow ● Colour: yellow, brown ● Transparency: translucent ● Lustre: vitreous, on cleavage planes silky or submetallic ● Cleavage: good on (100) ● Fracture: uneven ● Morphology: crystals, stellate and radial-fibrous aggregates, acicular aggregates ● Specific gravity: 3.44 ● Crystal system: orthorhombic ● Crystal form: plates, rarely prisms ● Chemical composition: complicated, variable ● Handling: clean with distilled water ● Genesis: magmatic, pegmatitic ● Associated minerals: nepheline **(397)**, eudialite **(402)** ● Occurrence: very rare; Langesundsfjord (Norway), Montana (USA).

Chapmanite

Silicate
$Fe_2Sb(SiO_4)_2 . OH$

171

Named after the Canadian mineralogist, E. J. Chapman (1821–1904) (Walker 1924)

● Hardness: 2.5 ● Streak: identical with colour ● Colour: green-yellow, yellow, olive-green ● Lustre: dull ● Morphology: crystals, granular, powdered to earthy aggregates ● Specific gravity: 3.7 ● Crystal system: orthorhombic ● Crystal form: plates, prisms ● Chemical composition: Fe_2O_3 36.73%, Sb_2O_3 33.55%, SiO_2 27.65%, H_2O 2.07% ● Handling: clean with distilled water ● Genesis: hydrothermal or secondary ● Associated minerals: graphite **(2)**, silver **(49)**, stibnite **(51)** ● Occurrence: rare; Freiberg (FRG), Durango (Mexico), (Canada).

Uranophane

Silicate
$CaH_2(SiO_4)_2UO_2 . 5 H_2O$

172

R

L

From *uran* and *phanos* – to appear (Websky 1853)

● Hardness: 2.5 ● Streak: yellowish ● Colour: yellow, yellow-green ● Transparency: translucent to transparent ● Lustre: vitreous, earthy forms are dull ● Cleavage: perfect on (100) ● Morphology: crystals, earthy, cryptocrystalline, spherulitic and radial-fibrous aggregates ● Specific gravity: 3.9 ● Crystal system: monoclinic ● Crystal form: prisms, acicular ● Chemical composition: CaO 6.55%, UO_3 66.80%, SiO_2 14.03%, H_2O 12.62% ● Handling: clean with distilled water ● Genesis: pegmatites, secondary ● Associated minerals: U-minerals ● Occurrence: common; Wölsendorf (FRG), Jáchymov (Czech Republic), Kasolo (Congo), Ontario (Canada), South Dakota (USA) ● Application: U ore.

---

1. **Lepidolite** – pink-violet distorted scaly aggregates in Li pegmatites; Dobrá Voda (Czech Republic) 2. **Chapmanite** – yellow-green powdery crusts; Smilkov (Czech Republic) 3. **Uranophane** – fine yellow granular aggregates; Pankkajarraara (Finland – width of shot 120 mm)

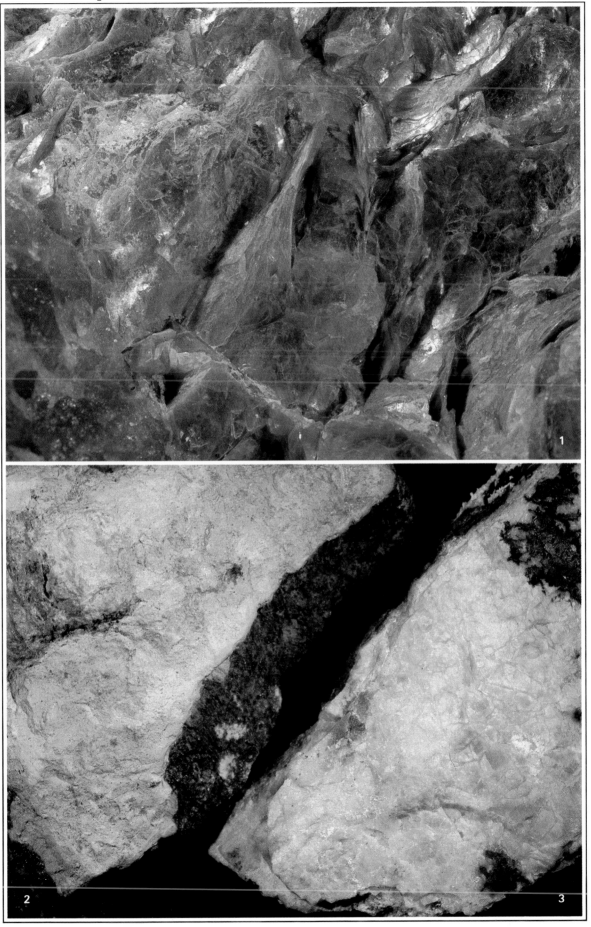

Amber (Succinite)

Organic substance
$C_{12}H_{20}O$

173

L

P

Of Ugrofinnish origin

● Hardness: 2–2.5 (brittle) ● Streak: white ● Colour: honey-yellow, orange, yellow-white to hyacinth-red ● Transparency: transparent to translucent ● Lustre: greasy ● Cleavage: absent ● Fracture: conchoidal ● Morphology: pebbles, stalactitic, impregnations ● Specific gravity: 1.0–1.1 ● Crystal system: amorphous ● Crystal form: unknown ● Luminescence: blue-white, green ● Chemical composition: variable; frequent admixture H_2S ● Chemical properties: easily fusible in a candle flame, characteristic odour, soluble in 20–25% alcohol, 18–23% ether, 9.8% benzol ● Handling: clean with soap and water ● Genesis: fossil resin in Oligocene sediments, alluvial deposits ● Occurrence: common in some places; Kaliningrad – Baltic Sea coast (Lithuania), (Romania), (Italy), (Great Britain), (Burma) ● Application: used as a precious stone, carved into ornaments (cabochons, facets).

Mellite

Organic substance
$Al_2(C_{12}O_{12}) . 18 H_2O$

174

L

From the Latin *mel* – honey
(Gmelin 1793)

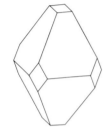

● Hardness: 2–2.5 (brittle) ● Streak: white ● Colour: honey yellow, golden-brown, brownish to reddish ● Transparency: transparent to translucent ● Lustre: vitreous, silky ● Cleavage: imperfect on (011) ● Fracture: conchoidal ● Morphology: crystals, massive and granular aggregates ● Specific gravity: 1.6 ● Crystal system: tetragonal ● Crystal form: pyramidal ● Luminescence: blue ● Chemical composition: Al_2O_3 14.3%, C 20.15%, O 20.15%, H_2O 45.4% ● Chemical properties: soluble in HNO_3, KOH, decomposes in boiling water ● Handling: clean with cold, distilled water ● Genesis: secondary ● Associated minerals: coal ● Occurrence: rare; Tatabanya (Hungary), Artern in Thuringia – in brown coal (FRG), Lužice and Valchov (Czech Republic), Malovka – in black coal (Russia), Paris basin (France).

Whewellite

Organic substance
$Ca(C_2O_4) . H_2O$

175

Named after the English natural scientist, W. Whewell (1794–1866) (Brooke 1852)

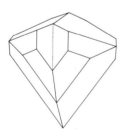

● Hardness: 2.5 (brittle) ● Streak: white ● Colour: white, yellowish ● Transparency: transparent to translucent ● Lustre: vitreous, pearly ● Cleavage: very good on (101) ● Fracture: conchoidal ● Morphology: crystals, granular aggregates ● Specific gravity: 2.23 ● Crystal system: monoclinic ● Crystal form: short prisms, isometric twinning in a heart shape ● Chemical composition: CaO 38.38%, CO_2 49.28%, H_2O 12.34% ● Chemical properties: soluble in acids, fusible ● Handling: clean with distilled water ● Similar minerals: calcite **(217)**, baryte **(240)** ● Distinguishing features: hardness, specific gravity, twin form ● Genesis: secondary in coal deposits ● Associated minerals: black coal ● Occurrence: rare; Burgk – in black coal, near Dresden and Zwickau – crystals measuring 3.5 cm (FRG), Kladno (Czech Republic), (Romania), (Hungary), (France), in oil fields near Maikop in Caucasus Mountains (Azerbaijan), Montana (USA).

---

1. Amber – yellow polished with enclosed insect (width of field 30 mm), Sopoty (Poland) **2. Mellite** – group of pyramidal crystals (20 mm); Tatabanya (Hungary) **3. Whewellite** – short prismatic crystals (4 mm) with ankerite; Kladno (Czech Republic)

Amber, mellite, whewellite

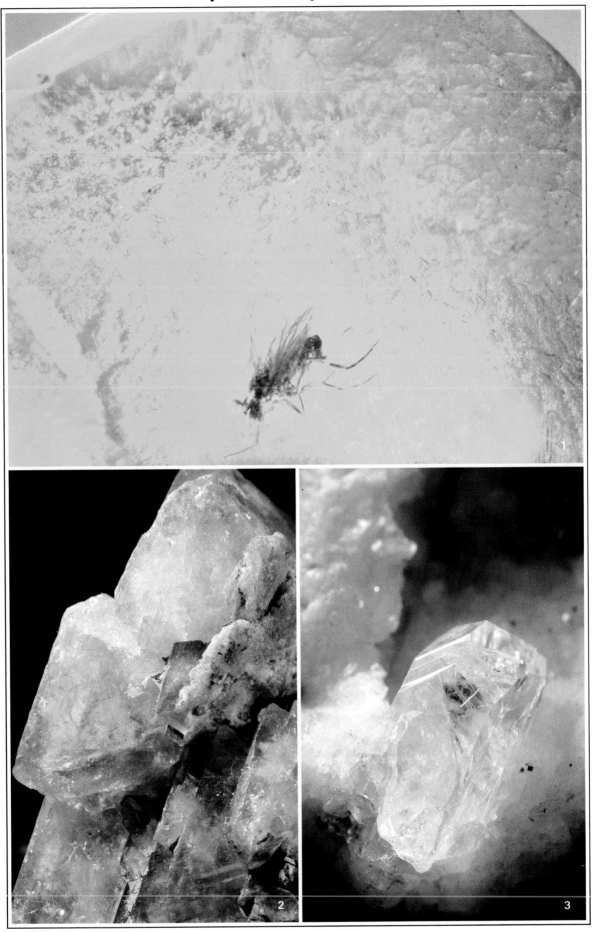

Arsenic

176

From the Greek *arse-nikós* – brave, cour-ageous
(Breithaupt 1823)

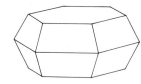

● Hardness: 3–4 (brittle) ● Streak: black ● Colour: tin-white, quickly becomes dark ● Transparency: opaque ● Lustre: metallic on fresh fracture surfaces, quickly becomes dull ● Cleavage: perfect on (0001) ● Fracture: uneven, conchoidal ● Morphology: crystals, crusty (with concentric structure), granular and earthy aggregates ● Specific gravity: 5.4–5.9 ● Crystal system: trigonal ● Crystal form: rhombohedral, pseudocubic, acicular ● Chemical composition: theoretically 100% As; admixtures: Sb, Fe, Ni ● Handling: clean with distilled water ● Similar minerals: allemontite **(177)**, antimony **(178)** ● Distinguishing features: chemical properties, X-rays ● Genesis: hydrothermal ● Associated minerals: silver **(49)**, proustite **(63)**, galena **(77)**, sphalerite **(181)**, chloanthite **(346)** ● Occurrence: rare; Schneeberg, Freiberg, Marienberg, Wittichen (FRG), Jáchymov and Příbram (Czech Republic), Kongsberg (Norway), St. Marie-aux-Mines (France), Sterling Hill – New Jersey (USA).

Allemontite

177

Named after its locality Allemont (France)
(Haidinger 1845)

● Hardness: 3–4 ● Streak: grey ● Colour: tin-white, grey to brown-black tarnish ● Transparency: opaque ● Lustre: metallic ● Cleavage: perfect in one direction ● Morphology: granular, massive, reniform aggregates ● Specific gravity: 5.8–6.2 ● Crystal system: trigonal ● Crystal form: fibres, plates ● Chemical composition: theoretically As 38.09%, Sb 61.91%; admixtures: As, Sb ● Handling: clean with distilled water ● Genesis: hydrothermal ● Associated minerals: stibnite **(51)**, arsenic **(176)**, antimony **(178)**, sphalerite **(181)** ● Occurrence: rare; Allemont (France), Příbram (Czech Republic), Marienberg (FRG), Varuträsk (Sweden), Ophir Mine – Nevada (USA).

Antimony

178

Historical name

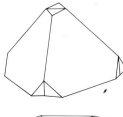

● Hardness: 3–3.5 ● Streak: lead-grey ● Colour: tin-white ● Transparency: opaque ● Lustre: metallic ● Cleavage: good on (0001) ● Fracture: uneven ● Morphology: crystals, granular and botryoidal aggregates, sometimes with radiate structure, impregnations ● Specific gravity: 6.6–6.7 ● Crystal system: trigonal ● Crystal form: rhombohedral, coarse plates ● Chemical composition: theoretically 100 % Sb; admixtures: Fe, Ag, As ● Handling: clean with distilled water ● Genesis: hydrothermal ● Associated minerals: stibnite **(51)**, berthierite **(52)**, allemontite **(177)** ● Occurrence: rare; St. Andreasberg (FRG), Allemont (France), Příbram (Czech Republic), Sala (Sweden), Mizarella (Portugal), Sarawak (Borneo), Broken Hill – N. S. Wales (Australia).

---

1. Arsenic – reniform aggregate; Příbram (Czech Republic – width of field 50 mm) **2. Allemontite** – reniform aggregates (up to 30 mm); Allemont (France)

Amalgam Ag
(Kongsbergite, Moschellandsbergite)

Native element
AgHg to Ag$_2$Hg$_3$

179

Named after its localities Kongsberg (Norway) and Moschellandsberg (FRG) (Pisani 1872, Berman 1938)

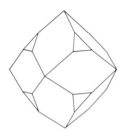

● Hardness: 3−3.5 (brittle) ● Streak: silver-white ● Colour: silver-white ● Transparency: opaque ● Lustre: metallic ● Cleavage: imperfect on (110) ● Fracture: uneven, conchoidal ● Other features of cohesion: malleable ● Morphology: crystals, granular, compact and dendritic aggregates, coatings ● Specific gravity: 13.7−14.1 ● Crystal system: cubic ● Crystal form: dodecahedral, octahedral, hexahedral ● Chemical composition: alloys of Ag and Hg; α − amalgam Ag (kongsbergite) 5−30% Hg, γ − amalgam Ag (moschellandsbergite) about 70% Hg ● Chemical properties: soluble in HNO$_3$, readily fusible, forms Ag beads ● Handling: clean with distilled water or diluted HCl; keep in the dark ● Similar minerals: silver **(49)** ● Distinctive features: hardness, specific gravity ● Genesis: secondary, hydrothermal ● Associated minerals: acanthite **(75)**, galena **(77)**, sphalerite **(181)**, cinnabar **(76)** ● Occurrence: very rare; Kongsberg − kongsbergite (Norway), Sala (Sweden), Nižná Slaná (Slovakia), Moschellandsberg − moschellandsbergite (FRG), Chalanches (France), Coquimbo (Chile).

Alabandite (Manganblende)

Sulphide
MnS

180

Named after its locality Alabanda (Turkey) (Beudant 1832)

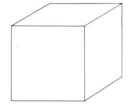

● Hardness: 3.5−4 (brittle) ● Streak: green to black-green ● Colour: black, lead-grey with brownish tint, green-black ● Transparency: opaque ● Lustre: submetallic, becomes dull ● Cleavage: perfect on (100) ● Fracture: uneven ● Morphology: crystals, granular and massive aggregates, impregnations ● Specific gravity: 4.0 ● Crystal system: cubic ● Crystal form: seldom octahedra, hexahedra ● Magnetism: slight ● Chemical composition: Mn 63.14%, S 36.86%; admixtures: Fe (ferroalabandite variety) ● Chemical properties: soluble in HCl and HNO$_3$, readily fusible ● Handling: do not clean with water (oxidizes), dry carefully and keep in the dark ● Genesis: hydrothermal ● Associated minerals: galena **(77)**, sphalerite **(181)**, rhodochrosite **(304)**, pyrite **(436)**, rhodonite **(531)** ● Occurrence: rare; Roşia Montana and Săcărâmb (Romania), Obroshiste (Bulgaria), Voberg − ferroalabandite found in phonolites (FRG), (Turkey), Morococha (Peru), Tombstone − Arizona (USA).

---

1. **Amalgam** − silver-white crust; Moschellandsberg (FRG − width of field 58 mm) 2. **Alabandite** − green-black massive aggregate in carbonates; Obroshiste (Bulgaria − width of shot 62 mm)

Amalgam Ag, alabandite

Sphalerite (Zinc blende, Mock ore, Black Jack)

Sulphide
ZnS

From the Greek *spha-leros* – misleading (Glocker 1847)

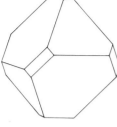

● Hardness: 3.5–4 (brittle) ● Streak: white, light brown ● Colour: light to dark brown, yellow, red, red-brown, green, yellow-green, white, black ● Transparency: transparent to translucent to opaque ● Lustre: on cleavage planes adamantine; on crystal faces vitreous; greasy to dull ● Cleavage: very good on (110) ● Morphology: crystals, granular, earthy, massive, colloform aggregates, often of differently coloured layers, sometimes in association with wurtzite **(184)** or galena **(77)** ● Specific gravity: 3.9–4.2 ● Crystal system: cubic ● Crystal form: tetrahedra, dodecahedra, often twins ● Luminescence: sometimes orange, blue, yellow, red ● Magnetism: diamagnetic ● Electric conductivity: low ● Chemical composition: Zn 67.06%, S 32.94%; admixtures: Fe (up to 26% Fe – marmatite variety **(182)** and cristophite variety), Cd (up to 2.5% Cd – pribramite variety), Sn, Pb, Ag, Hg, Mn, In, Tl, Ga, Ge. Sphalerite with a low content of Fe and Mn is called cleiophane **(183)**; white, earthy sphalerite is called brunckite; the raspberry-red, colloform variety is gumucionite ● Chemical properties: soluble in HCl and HNO_3; on charcoal forms a white sublimate of ZnO; with blowpipe crumbles, but does not fuse ● Handling: clean with distilled water or diluted acids, except HCl and HNO_3 ● Similar minerals: metacinnabar **(200)**, cassiterite **(548)**, garnet **(577)** ● Distinguishing features: hardness, specific gravity and cleavage (garnets, cassiterite), streak and specific gravity (metacinnabar), blowpipe tests, reaction to acids ● Genesis: hydrothermal, magmatic, pneumatolytic in pegmatites, sedimentary ● Associated minerals: galena, chalcopyrite **(185)**, tetrahedrite **(190)**, pyrite **(436)**; and other sulphides; calcite **(217)**, quartz **(534)** ● Occurrence: common; Schauinsland, Bensberg near Cologne-on-Rhine, Freiberg, Altenberg near Aachen and Hagendorf (FRG), Příbram – fine druses (Czech Republic), Banská Štiavnica (Slovakia), Binnental (Switzerland), Trepča – Kosovo – large crystals (Serbia), Cavnic and Rodna (Romania), Picos de Europa and Santander (Spain), Bawdwin Mine (Burma), (USA), (Australia), (Peru), (Canada), (Japan) ● Application: chief source of zinc, light coloured; transparent or translucent sphalerites are cut and polished as gemstones (facets, cabochons).

Sphalerite – druse of euhedral crystals (up to 12 mm) on quartz; Cavnic (Romania)

Sphalerite

Marmatite (Fe sphalerite variety)

Sulphide
(Zn,Fe)S

182

Named after its locality Marmato (Colombia) (Boussingault 1829)

● Hardness: 3.5−4 ● Streak: brown ● Colour: black-brown to black ● Transparency: opaque ● Lustre: adamantine ● Cleavage, fracture, morphology like sphalerite on **(181)** ● Specific gravity: 3.9−4.1 ● Crystal system: cubic ● Crystal form: dodecahedra, hexaoctahedra, tetrahedra ● Chemical composition: up to 26% Fe (cristophite) ● Chemical properties: like sphalerite ● Genesis: high-thermal ● Occurrence: Trepča (Serbia), St. Christoph (FRG), Kutná Hora (Czech Republic), Bottino (Italy), Cavnic (Romania), Alston Moor (Great Britain).

Cleiophane (A light-coloured variety of sphalerite)

Sulphide
ZnS

183

L

P

From the Greek *kleyos* − glass and *phanos* − to appear

● Hardness: 3.5−4 (brittle) ● Streak: white ● Colour: white, yellowish-white, yellowish-green, honey yellow ● Transparency: transparent to translucent ● Lustre: adamantine ● Fracture: conchoidal ● Cleavage: like sphalerite on **(181)** ● Morphology: like sphalerite ● Specific gravity: 3.9−4.1 ● Crystal system: cubic ● Crystal form: like sphalerite ● Luminescence: orange, yellow, bluish ● Chemical composition: like sphalerite, without Fe and Mn ● Chemical properties: like sphalerite ● Genesis: low-thermal ● Associated minerals: boulangerite **(55)**, galena **(77)**, calcite **(217)** ● Occurrence: Banská Štiavnica (Slovakia), Baia Sprie (Romania), Picos de Europa and Santander (Spain), Olkusz (Poland), Cananea and Sonora (Mexico), Franklin − New Jersey (USA) ● Application: often used as precious stone.

Wurtzite (Radial blende)

Sulphide
β-ZnS

184

Named after the French chemist, Ch. A. Wurtze (1817−1884) (Friedel 1861)

● Hardness: 3.5−4 (brittle) ● Streak: light brown ● Colour: light to dark brown ● Transparency: translucent to opaque ● Lustre: adamantine, greasy ● Cleavage: good on (10$\bar{1}$0) and on (0001) ● Fracture: uneven ● Morphology: crystals, radial, concentrical, tabular, colloform aggregates ● Specific gravity: 4.0 ● Crystal system: hexagonal ● Crystal form: pyramidal, plates ● Chemical composition: Zn 67.06%, S 32.94%; admixtures: Cd, Fe ● Chemical properties: soluble in HCl and HNO_3, heated on charcoal forms a white sublimate of ZnO ● Similar minerals: hübnerite **(368)** ● Distinguishing features: hardness, specific gravity, solubility in HCl ● Handling: clean with distilled water ● Genesis: hydrothermal ● Associated minerals: galena **(77)**, sphalerite **(181)**, chalcopyrite **(185)** ● Occurrence: rare; Příbram (Czech Republic), Stolberg near Aachen (FRG), Gyöngyösoroszi (Hungary), Baia Sprie (Romania), Blyava (Russia), Kirka (Greece), Butte (USA), (Peru) ● Application: Zn ore.

1. **Cleiophane** − translucent euhedral crystal (22 mm); Banská Štiavnica (Slovakia) 2. **Wurtzite** − concentrically shelled aggregate; Gyöngyösoroszi (Hungary − width of field 72 mm)

Cleiophane, wurtzite

Chalcopyrite (Copper pyrites)

Sulphide
$CuFeS_2$

From the Greek *chalkos* – copper and *pyr* – fire (Henckel 1725)

● Hardness: 3.5–4 (brittle) ● Streak: greenish-black ● Colour: brass yellow (often with a green tint), honey yellow (often tarnished) ● Transparency: opaque ● Lustre: metallic ● Cleavage: indistinct on (112) ● Fracture: conchoidal, uneven ● Morphology: crystals, granular, massive aggregates, reniform, botryoidal impregnations, encrustations on crystals of other minerals, pseudomorphs ● Specific gravity: 4.2–4.3 ● Crystal system: tetragonal ● Crystal form: pseudotetrahedral, pseudo-octahedral, often twins and multiple twins ● Chemical composition: Cu 34.5%, Fe 30.5%, S 35%; admixtures: Ag, Au, Tl, Se, Te ● Chemical properties: soluble in concentrated HNO_3 forming a green solution; in a blowpipe flame forms a magnetic bead; with soda on charcoal forms a bead of copper ● Handling: clean with distilled water (dry thoroughly, as humidity causes iridescent tarnish) and acids, except HNO_3 ● Similar minerals: gold **(50)**, pyrrhotine **(283)**, pyrite **(436)**, marcasite **(437)** ● Distinguishing features: hardness, streak, solubility in acids, very poor magnetism, very good electrical conductivity ● Genesis: magmatic, contact-metasomatic, hydrothermal, sedimentary ● Associated minerals: sphalerite **(181)**, marcasite, pyrite, calcite **(217)**, quartz **(534)** ● Occurrence: common; Freiberg, Annaberg, Johanngeorgenstadt, Mansfeld, Siegerland, Grube Clara, Wildschapbachtal and Rammelsberg (FRG), St. Agnes – Cornwall (Great Britain), Rio Tinto (Spain), Bor (Serbia), Banská Štiavnica, Smolník and Gelnica (Slovakia), Sulitelma (Norway), Falun (Sweden), La Gardette (France), Djezkazgan, Norilsk, Talnach and Monchetundra (Kazakhstan), (Poland), Recsk (Hungary), Medet, Asarel and Sedmoczislenice (Bulgaria), (Romania), Sudbury (Canada), Butte – Montana, Bingham – Maine, Clifton-Morenci – Arizona (USA), (Mexico), Chuquicamata and Braden (Chile), (Peru), (Australia), (Zambia) ● Application: the most important copper ore. Copper or copper alloys are used in brass, bronze, red brass (tombac); in electrical engineering and industries; sometimes used as a precious stone (cabochons, plates).

Chalcopyrite – druse of euhedral crystals (up to 4 mm) on quartz; Banská Štiavnica (Slovakia)

Chalcopyrite

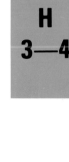

H
3—4

Luzonite

Sulphide
Cu$_3$AsS$_4$

186

Named after Luzon
Island (Philippines)
(Weisbach 1874)

● Hardness: 3.5 ● Streak: black ● Colour: pinkish-grey ● Transparency: opaque ● Lustre: metallic ● Fracture: uneven, conchoidal ● Cleavage: absent ● Morphology: crystals, granular aggregates, grains ● Specific gravity: 4.4–4.6 ● Crystal system: tetragonal ● Crystal form: short prisms, twins ● Chemical composition: Cu 48.42%, As 19.02%, S 32.56% – dimorphic with enargite **(187)**; admixtures: Sb (stibioluzonite) ● Handling: clean with distilled water ● Genesis: hydrothermal ● Associated minerals: sphalerite **(181)**, chalcopyrite **(185)**, enargite, tetrahedrite **(190)** ● Occurrence: rare; Wittichen (FRG), Bor (Serbia), Sierra de Famatina (Argentina), Cerro de Pasco (Peru), Hokuetsu (Japan), Mankayan and Luzon (Philippines), Kinkwaseki (Taiwan), Butte – Montana (USA).

Enargite

Sulphide
Cu$_3$AsS$_4$

187

From the Greek *enarges*
– obvious
(Breithaupt 1850)

● Hardness: 3.5 (brittle) ● Streak: black ● Colour: steel-grey, grey-black, black, with a fine violet tint ● Transparency: opaque ● Lustre: metallic to dull ● Cleavage: good on (110), imperfect on (100) and on (010) ● Fracture: uneven ● Morphology: crystals, rodlike, spathic, granular aggregates ● Specific gravity: 4.4 ● Crystal system: orthorhombic ● Crystal form: plates, prisms, with twinning and multiple twinning ● Chemical composition: Cu 48.42%, As 19.02%, S 32.56%; admixtures: Sb, Fe, Zn ● Chemical properties: soluble in HNO$_3$, fuses in blowpipe flame releasing characteristic garlicky odour ● Similar minerals: marmatite **(182)**, luzonite **(186)**, wolframite **(369)** ● Distinguishing features: colour, reaction in blowpipe flame ● Handling: clean with distilled water ● Genesis: hydrothermal ● Associated minerals: chalcopyrite **(185)**, luzonite, tetrahedrite **(190)**, bornite **(192)**, pyrite **(436)** ● Occurrence: rare; Wittichen (FRG), Recsk (Hungary), Bor (Serbia), Brixlegg (Austria), Butte – Montana (USA), Morococha and Cerro de Pasco (Peru), Chuquicamata (Chile), Famatina (Argentina), (Namibia), Luzon Island (Philippines) ● Application: Cu ore.

Germanite

Sulphide
Cu$_3$(Ge,Fe)S$_4$

188

Named after its content
of germanium
(Pufahl 1922)

● Hardness: 3 (brittle) ● Streak: dark grey to black ● Colour: grey with dark red tint ● Transparency: opaque ● Lustre: metallic ● Cleavage: absent ● Morphology: microscopic crystals, massive aggregates ● Specific gravity: 4.59 ● Crystal system: cubic ● Crystal form: unknown ● Chemical composition: variable; admixtures: Ga, Zn, Fe, Mo ● Chemical properties: soluble in HNO$_3$ ● Handling: clean with distilled water ● Similar minerals: enargite **(187)**, bornite **(192)** ● Distinguishing features: from bornite by chemical properties, from enargite by lack of characteristic garlicky odour of As when fused ● Genesis: hydrothermal ● Associated minerals: galena **(77)**, sphalerite **(181)**, tennantite **(189)** ● Occurrence: rare; Tsumeb (Namibia), Dastakert (Armenia) ● Application: Ge ore.

---

1. Enargite – short columnar crystals (to 20 mm); Butte (USA) **2. Luzonite** – granular crystalline aggregate; Bor (Serbia – width of field 53 mm) **3. Germanite** – grey-red massive aggregate; Tsumeb (Namibia – width of field 47 mm)

Enargite, luzonite, germanite

Tennantite

Sulphide
Cu$_{12}$As$_4$S$_{13}$

189

Named after the English chemist, S. Tennant (1761–1815) (Phillips 1819)

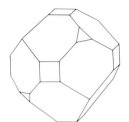

● Hardness: 3–4 (brittle) ● Streak: steel-grey with cherry-red tint ● Colour: steel-grey, black ● Transparency: opaque ● Lustre: metallic, submetallic ● Cleavage: absent ● Fracture: conchoidal, uneven, hackly ● Morphology: crystals, granular, massive aggregates, impregnations ● Specific gravity: 4.6–4.7 ● Crystal system: cubic ● Crystal form: tetrahedra, rarely octahedra ● Chemical composition: Cu 51.57%, As 20.26%, S 28.17%; forms a series with tetrahedrite **(190)**; admixtures: Bi (annivite variety), Ag,Zn (binnite variety), Fe (up to 10.9% ferrotennantite variety) ● Chemical properties: soluble in HNO$_3$; readily fusible; on charcoal forms a grey bead with a characteristic garlicky odour ● Handling: clean with distilled water ● Similar minerals: chalcocite **(68)**, tetrahedrite, bournonite **(193)** ● Distinguishing features: from bournonite by hardness, specific gravity, colouring of solution with HNO$_3$; from chalcocite by hardness and specific gravity; from tetrahedrite by garlicky odour when fused; X-rays, chemical properties ● Genesis: hydrothermal ● Associated minerals: sphalerite **(181)**, chalcopyrite **(185)**, tetrahedrite, pyrite **(436)**, arsenopyrite **(344)** ● Occurrence: common; Rammelsberg, Freiberg (FRG), Boliden (Sweden), Tsumeb (Namibia), Butte – Montana (USA), Zacatecas (Mexico) – fine crystals ● Application: Cu ore.

Tetrahedrite (Grey copper, Fahlerz)

Sulphide
Cu$_{12}$Sb$_4$S$_{13}$

190

Named after the form of its crystals (Haidinger 1845)

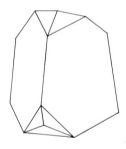

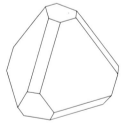

● Hardness: 3–4 (brittle) ● Streak: black ● Colour: steel-grey to black ● Transparency: opaque ● Lustre: metallic ● Cleavage: absent ● Fracture: conchoidal, uneven ● Morphology: crystals, granular and massive aggregates ● Specific gravity: 4.6–5.2 ● Crystal system: cubic ● Crystal form: tetrahedra, rarely octahedra ● Chemical composition: Cu 45.77%, Sb 29.22%, S 25.01%; forms a series with tennantite **(189)**; admixtures: Hg (schwatzite variety), Ag (freibergite variety), Fe (ferrotetrahedrite variety), Ni (frigidite variety), Te (goldfieldite variety), Sn, Zn, Bi ● Chemical properties: soluble in HNO$_3$; readily fusible; on charcoal forms a grey bead ● Handling: clean with distilled water ● Similar minerals: chalcocite **(68)**, tennantite, bournonite **(193)** ● Distinguishing features: most reliable X-rays, chemical properties ● Genesis: hydrothermal ● Associated minerals: sphalerite **(181)**, chalcopyrite **(185)**, tennantite, siderite **(306)**, pyrite **(436)**, quartz **(534)** ● Occurrence: common; Clausthal, Siegen, Dillenburg, Freiberg (freibergite), Marienberg and Annaberg (FRG), Příbram (Czech Republic), Rožňava and Rudňany (Slovakia), Cavnic (Romania), Schwaz – schwazite – Tyrol (Austria), Lizard – Cornwall (Great Britain), Berezovsk (Russia), Sunshine Mine – Idaho (USA) ● Application: Cu ore, also partly Ag ore.

Tetrahedrite – euhedral crystals (17 mm) on calcite; Cavnic (Romania)

Tetrahedrite

Chalcostibite (Wolfsbergite)

Sulphide
CuSbS$_2$

191

From the Greek *chalkos*
– copper and *stibi*
– antimony
(Glocker 1847)

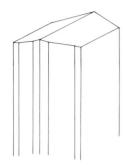

● Hardness: 3.5 (brittle) ● Streak: black ● Colour: lead-grey to black, sometimes iridescent tarnish ● Transparency: opaque ● Lustre: metallic ● Cleavage: good on (001) ● Fracture: subconchoidal to uneven ● Morphology: crystals, granular, massive aggregates ● Specific gravity: 4.8–5.0 ● Crystal system: orthorhombic ● Crystal form: plates elongated along b axis, parallel striation ● Chemical composition: Cu 25.64%, Sb 48.45%, S 25.91%; admixtures: Pb, Fe, Zn ● Chemical properties: soluble in HNO$_3$; readily fusible; on charcoal forms Sb$_2$O$_3$ sublimate ● Handling: clean with distilled water ● Similar minerals: diaphorite **(61)** ● Distinguishing features: hardness, specific gravity, chemical properties ● Genesis: hydrothermal ● Associated minerals: jamesonite **(53)**, chalcopyrite **(185)**, bornite **(192)** ● Occurrence: rare; Wolfsberg (FRG), Guajar (Spain), Pullacayo and Tapi (Bolivia), Rar el Anz (Morocco).

Bornite

Sulphide
Cu$_5$FeS$_4$

192

Named after the
Austrian mineralogist,
I. von Born (1742–1791)
(Haidinger 1845)

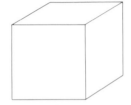

● Hardness: 3 (brittle) ● Streak: grey-black ● Colour: bronze-brown, copper-red, often iridescent tarnish (blue-violet) ● Transparency: opaque ● Lustre: submetallic to metallic ● Cleavage: imperfect on (111) ● Fracture: conchoidal to indistinct ● Morphology: crystals are rare, massive, granular, reniform aggregates ● Specific gravity: 4.9–5.3 ● Crystal system: cubic ● Crystal form: hexahedra, dodecahedra, rarely octahedra, mostly imperfect crystals, occasionally with twinning ● Chemical composition: Cu 63.33%, Fe 11.12%, S 25.55%; admixtures: Ag, Bi, In ● Chemical properties: soluble in HNO$_3$ and concentrated HCl; when fused forms a magnetic ball ● Handling: clean with distilled water and dry thoroughly; iridescent tarnish appears when exposed to the air ● Similar minerals: covellite **(6)**, germanite **(188)**, umangite **(201)**, pyrrhotine **(283)**, renierite **(285)**, niccolite **(351)** ● Distinguishing features: hardness, specific gravity, X-rays, chemical properties ● Genesis: hydrothermal, pneumatolytic, magmatic, secondary ● Associated minerals: covellite, chalcocite **(68)**, chalcopyrite **(185)** ● Occurrence: common; Mansfeld – sedimentary deposits of copper shale, Wittichen and Neubulach (FRG), Norberg (Sweden), Redruth – Cornwall – fine crystals (Great Britain), Dzhezkasgan (Kazakhstan), Butte – Montana (USA), Tsumeb (Namibia) ● Application: important Cu ore.

---

1. Chalcostibite – massive aggregate with veinlets of azurite and malachite; Rhar-el-Haur (Morocco – width of field 56 mm)
2. Bornite – massive aggregate showing variegated tarnish colours with pyrrhotine and chalcopyrite; Dzhezkasgan (Kazakhstan – width of field 76 mm)

Chalcostibite, bornite

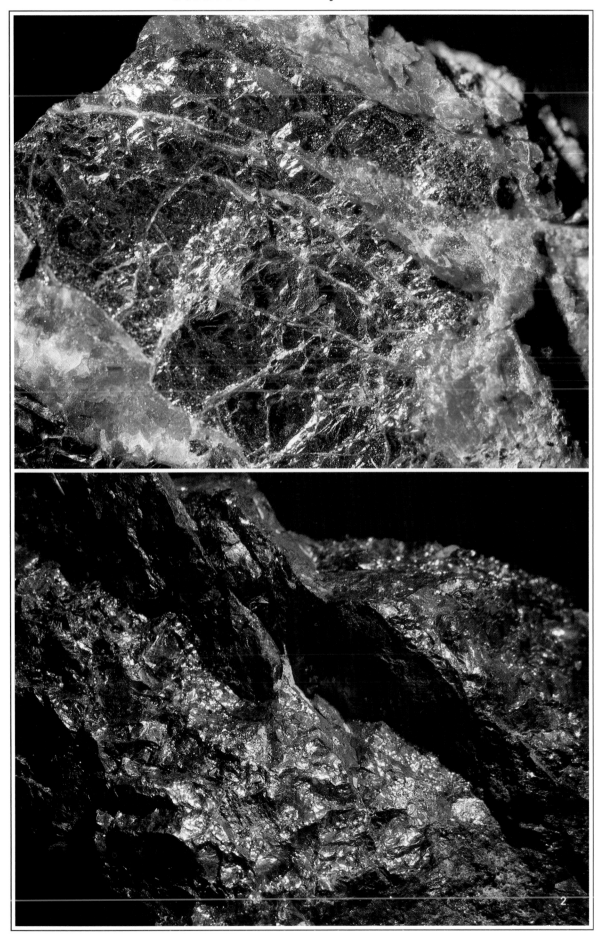

Bournonite (Wheel ore, Endellionite)

Sulphide
PbCuSbS$_3$

193

Named after the French mineralogist, J. L. de Bournon (1751–1825) (Jameson 1805)

● Hardness: 3 (brittle) ● Streak: grey ● Colour: lead-grey, black ● Transparency: opaque ● Lustre: metallic ● Cleavage: imperfect on (010) ● Fracture: conchoidal to uneven ● Morphology: crystals, granular aggregates ● Specific gravity: 5.7–5.9 ● Crystal system: orthorhombic ● Crystal form: plates, short prisms, pseudocubic, quadruplets are common; multiple twins for the famous cog-wheel twins on good specimens ● Chemical composition: Pb 42.54%, Cu 13.04%, Sb 24.65%, S 19.77% ● Chemical properties: soluble in HNO$_3$ (blue solution), readily fusible ● Handling: clean with distilled water ● Similar minerals: tetrahedrite **(190)** ● Distinguishing features: specific gravity, streak, splendent lustre ● Genesis: hydrothermal ● Associated minerals: galena **(77)**, sphalerite **(181)**, chalcopyrite **(185)**, tetrahedrite ● Occurrence: rare; Neudorf, Clausthal and Horhausen (FRG), Hütenberg (Austria), Příbram (Czech Republic), Rožňava (Slovakia), Cavnic and Săcărâmb (Romania), Cornwall (Great Britain), (Russia), Machacamarca (Bolivia), (Peru) ● Application: Pb, Cu and Sb ore.

Pentlandite

Sulphide
(Ni,Fe)$_9$S$_8$

194

Named after the Irish natural historian, J. B. Pentland (1797–1873) (Dufrenoy 1856)

● Hardness: 3.5–4 (brittle) ● Streak: green-black ● Colour: bronze-yellow ● Transparency: opaque ● Lustre: metallic ● Cleavage: good on (111) ● Fracture: conchoidal ● Morphology: crystals, granular aggregates, isolated grains ● Specific gravity: 4.6–5.0 ● Crystal system: cubic ● Crystal form: unknown ● Chemical composition: variable; admixtures: Co, Se, Te ● Chemical properties: soluble in HNO$_3$ (green solution), in blowpipe flame fuses and forms a black magnetic ball ● Handling: clean with distilled water ● Similar minerals: millerite **(195)**, pyrrhotite **(283)** ● Distinguishing features: colour, chemical properties, X-rays ● Genesis: hydrothermal, magmatic ● Associated minerals: pyrrhotine, chalcopyrite **(185)**, magnetite **(367)** ● Occurrence: rare; Horbach, Sohland (FRG), Evje (Norway), Nivala (Finland), Talnakh-Norilsk (Russia), Bushveld (RSA), Sudbury (Canada) ● Application: Ni ore.

Millerite (Hair pyrites)

Sulphide
NiS

195

Named after the English mineralogist, W. H. Miller (1801–1880) (Haidinger 1845)

● Hardness: 3.5 (brittle) ● Streak: green-black ● Colour: light yellow, yellowish-brown ● Transparency: opaque ● Lustre: metallic ● Cleavage: good on (10$\bar{1}$1) and on (01$\bar{1}$2) ● Fracture: uneven ● Morphology: crystals, radiating, fibrous, acicular, granular aggregates ● Specific gravity: 5.3 ● Crystal system: trigonal ● Crystal form: acicular, rodlike ● Chemical composition: Ni 64.67%, S 35.33%; admixtures: Co, Fe, Cu ● Chemical properties: soluble in HNO$_3$ (green solution) ● Handling: clean with distilled water ● Genesis: hydrothermal, magmatic, sedimentary ● Associated minerals: chalcopyrite **(185)**, siderite **(306)**, pyrite **(436)** ● Occurrence: rare; Freiberg, Schneeberg, Siegerland, Nassau, Saarbrücken and Oberlara – crystals measuring 7 cm (FRG), Merthyr Tydfil (Great Britain), St. Louis (USA), Sudbury (Canada) ● Application: Ni ore.

---

1. Bournonite – druse of crystals (to 10 mm); Horhausen (FRG) **2. Millerite** – group of acicular crystals (to 15 mm) in a crack in siderite; Kladno (Czech Republic)

Bournonite, millerite

Zinckenite

Sulphide
PbSb$_2$S$_4$

196

Named after the mineralogist, J. K. L. Zincken (1798–1862) (Rose 1826)

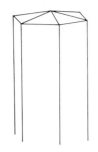

● Hardness: 3 (brittle) ● Streak: steel-grey with red-brown tint ● Colour: lead-grey to dark grey with bluish tint ● Transparency: opaque ● Lustre: metallic ● Cleavage: imperfect on (11$\bar{2}$0) ● Fracture: uneven ● Morphology: crystals, acicular, radiating-fibrous aggregates ● Specific gravity: 5.3 ● Crystal system: (pseudo)hexagonal ● Crystal form: needles, prisms with vertical striation ● Chemical composition: Pb 32.60%, Sb 44.70%, S 22.70%; admixtures: Ag, Cu, Fe, As ● Chemical properties: soluble in HNO$_3$; on charcoal fuses readily and forms yellow and white sublimates ● Handling: clean with distilled water ● Similar minerals: jamesonite **(53)**, boulangerite **(55)** ● Distinguishing features: chemical properties, X-rays ● Genesis: hydrothermal ● Associated minerals: antimonite **(51)**, jamesonite, boulangerite, galena **(77)** ● Occurrence: rare; Wolfsberg, Adlerbachtal, Welschensteinach and Sulzburg (FRG), Săcărâmb (Romania), Liptovská Dúbrava (Slovakia), Sevier Co. – Arkansas and San Juan – Colorado (USA), Oruro (Bolivia).

Pearceite

Sulphide
(Ag,Cu)$_{16}$As$_2$S$_{11}$

197

Named after the American chemist, R. Pearce (1837–1927) (Penfield 1896)

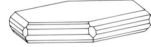

● Hardness: 3 (brittle) ● Streak: black ● Colour: black ● Transparency: opaque ● Lustre: metallic ● Cleavage: absent ● Fracture: uneven to conchoidal ● Morphology: crystals, granular aggregates ● Specific gravity: 6.1 ● Crystal system: monoclinic ● Crystal form: plates ● Chemical composition: variable ● Chemical properties: soluble in HNO$_3$; readily fusible ● Handling: clean with distilled water and ultrasonically ● Similar minerals: polybasite **(9)** ● Distinguishing minerals: silver **(49)**, argentite-acanthite **(75)** ● Occurrence: rare; Wittichen (FRG), Banská Hodruša (Slovakia), Mollie Gibson Mine – Colorado – mined as Ag ore, and Phillipsburg – Montana (USA), Argueros (Chile) ● Application: sometimes as a source of silver.

Coloradoite

Telluride
HgTe

198

Named after Colorado (USA) (Genth 1877)

● Hardness: 3 (brittle) ● Streak: black ● Colour: black ● Transparency: opaque ● Lustre: metallic ● Cleavage: absent ● Fracture: uneven ● Morphology: massive and granular aggregates ● Specific gravity: 8.0–8.1 ● Crystal system: cubic ● Crystal form: unknown ● Chemical composition: Hg 61.14%, Te 38.86% ● Chemical properties: soluble in hot HNO$_3$; in flame evaporates and tinges it light green ● Handling: clean with distilled water and acids ● Similar minerals: petzite **(82)** ● Distinguishing features: solubility in H$_2$SO$_4$; flame reaction ● Genesis: hydrothermal ● Associated minerals: tellurides of Au and Ag ● Occurrence: rare; Jílové (Czech Republic), Kalgoorlie (Australia), Boulder County – Colorado and Stanislaus Mine – California (USA).

---

1. Pearceite – tabular crystal; Jáchymov (Czech Republic – width of field 26 mm) **2. Coloradoite** – compact aggregate embedded in quartz; Kalgoorlie (Australia – width of field 56 mm)

Pearceite, coloradoite

Greenockite

Sulphide
CdS

199

Named after Ch. M. Cathcart (1783–1859), addressed as Lord Greenock (Jameson 1840)

● Hardness: 3–3.5 (brittle) ● Streak: orange-yellow, shining ● Colour: yellow, orange to reddish ● Transparency: transparent ● Lustre: adamantine, greasy ● Cleavage: imperfect on (1010) ● Fracture: conchoidal ● Morphology: rarely crystals, powdered aggregates, coatings, encrustations ● Specific gravity: 4.9–5.0 ● Crystal system: hexagonal ● Crystal form: pyramidal, less often prismatic and platy ● Chemical composition: Cd 77.81%, S 22.19% ● Chemical properties: soluble in HCl and HNO_3, on charcoal forms reddish sublimate of CdO ● Handling: clean with distilled water ● Similar minerals: wulfenite **(243)** ● Distinguishing features: hardness, specific gravity, chemical properties, X-rays ● Genesis: secondary ● Associated minerals: galena **(77)**, sphalerite **(181)**, smithsonite **(373)** ● Occurrence: rare; Bishoptown – Scotland (Great Britain), Gyöngyösoroszi (Hungary), Franklin (USA), Llallagua (Bolivia), Sibai (Russia) ● Application: of mineralogical importance, sometimes source of Cd.

Metacinnabar

Sulphide
HgS

200

From the Greek *meta* and cinnabar (similar chemical composition and association with cinnabar) (Moore 1870)

● Hardness: 3 (brittle) ● Streak: black ● Colour: grey-black, black ● Transparency: opaque ● Lustre: metallic ● Cleavage: absent ● Fracture: uneven, subconchoidal ● Morphology: crystals, granular, powdered aggregates, coatings ● Specific gravity: 7.7–7.8 ● Crystal system: cubic ● Crystal form: tetrahedra, twins ● Chemical composition: Hg 86.21%, S 13.79%; admixtures: Zn (to 4% guadalcazarite), Se (onofrite variety) ● Handling: clean with distilled water and acids ● Genesis: hydrothermal ● Associated minerals: realgar **(5)**, stibnite **(51)**, cinnabar **(76)**, calcite **(217)** ● Occurrence: Merník (Slovakia), Idria (Slovenia), Baia Sprie (Romania), Vyshkovo (Ukraine), San Onofre – onofrite variety and Guadalcazare – guadalcazarite variety (Mexico), Marysvale – Utah (USA), (China).

Umangite

Selenide
Cu_3Se_2

201

Named after Sierra de Umango (Argentina) (Klockmann 1891)

● Hardness: 3 ● Streak: black ● Colour: on a fresh fracture surface dark cherry-red with violet tint, turns to violet-grey (similar to bornite – **192**) ● Transparency: opaque ● Lustre: metallic ● Cleavage: in two directions ● Fracture: uneven ● Morphology: granular aggregates ● Specific gravity: 6.78 ● Crystal system: orthorhombic ● Crystal form: unknown ● Chemical composition: Cu 54.70%, Se 45.30%; admixtures: Ag ● Chemical properties: soluble in HNO_3; colours the flame red ● Handling: clean with distilled water ● Similar minerals: bornite ● Distinguishing features: X-rays, flame colour ● Genesis: hydrothermal ● Associated minerals: berzelianite **(74)**, tiemannite **(80)**, chalcopyrite **(185)**, bornite ● Occurrence: rare; Clausthal, St. Andreasberg, Tilkerode, Lehrbach (FRG), Předbořice, Slavkovice and Bukov (Czech Republic), Skrikerum (Sweden), Sierra de Umango (Argentina).

---

1. Greenockite – euhedral crystal (3 mm) on quartz; Llallagua (Bolivia) **2. Umangite** – granular aggregate of light violet colour; Předbořice (Czech Republic – width of field 38 mm) **3. Metacinnabar** – veinlet (1 mm thick) in calcite-cinnabar vein; Merník (Slovakia)

Greenockite, umangite, metacinnabar

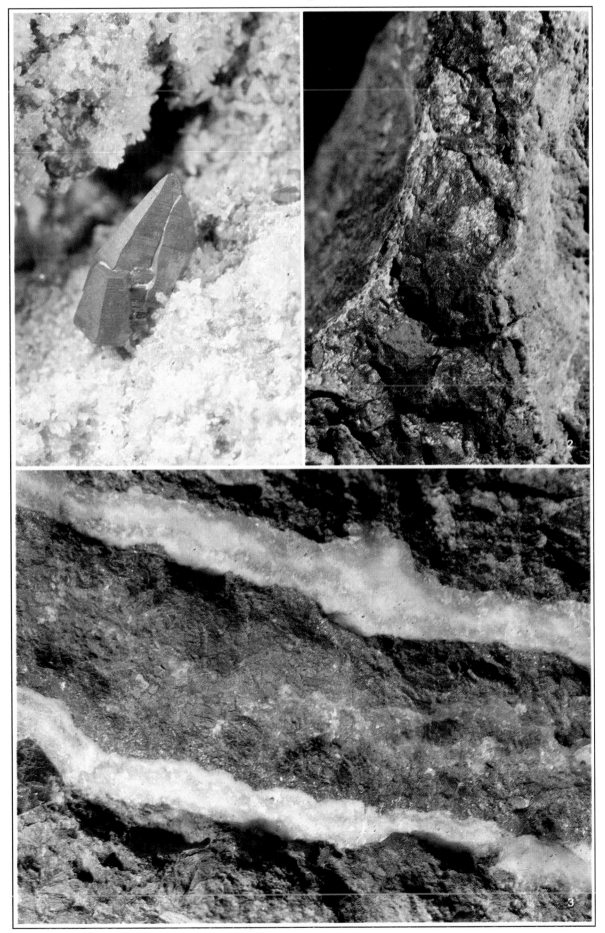

Jordanite

Sulphide
$Pb_4As_2S_7$

202

Named after H. Jordan from Saarbrücken (Rath 1864)

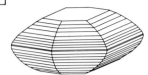

● Hardness: 3 (brittle) ● Streak: black ● Colour: dark lead-grey, often iridescent tarnish ● Transparency: opaque ● Lustre: metallic ● Cleavage: good on (010) ● Fracture: conchoidal ● Morphology: crystals, granular, globular and botryoidal aggregates ● Specific gravity: 6.4 ● Crystal system: monoclinic ● Crystal form: platy, twinning ● Chemical composition: Pb 71.90%, As 10.30%, S 17.80% ● Chemical properties: soluble in HNO_3; readily fusible on charcoal ● Handling: clean with distilled water ● Similar minerals: bournonite **(193)** ● Distinguishing features: chemical properties, X-rays ● Genesis: hydrothermal ● Associated minerals: galena **(77)**, sphalerite **(181)**, pyrite **(436)** ● Occurrence: rare; Wiesloch (FRG), Binnental – fine crystals in dolomites (Switzerland), Săcărâmb (Romania), (Russia), Kupferberg (Namibia), Mutsu – aggregates weighing 1 kg (Japan).

Domeykite

Arsenide
Cu_3As

203

P

Named after the Chilean mineralogist, I. Domeyk (1802–1889) (Haidinger 1845)

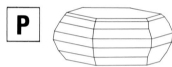

● Hardness: 3–3.5 (brittle) ● Streak: black ● Colour: tin-white, quickly becomes yellow to coppery-brown ● Transparency: opaque ● Lustre: metallic, on exposure becomes dull ● Cleavage: absent ● Fracture: uneven ● Other features of cohesion: partly ductile ● Morphology: massive, granular, coatings ● Specific gravity: 7.2–8.1 ● Crystal system: dimorphic: α – domeykite (cubic), β – domeykite (hexagonal) ● Crystal form: unknown ● Chemical composition: Cu 71.79%, As 28.21% ● Chemical properties: soluble in HNO_3; readily fusible (As fumes); on charcoal As_2O_3 sublimate ● Handling: clean with distilled water ● Similar minerals: silver **(49)**, bismuth **(48)** ● Distinguishing features: hardness, iridescent tarnish ● Genesis: hydrothermal ● Associated minerals: copper **(47)**, silver ● Occurrence: rare; Zwickau (FRG), Lautaret (France), Běloves (Czech Republic), Coquimbo and Copiapó (Chile), Mesanki (Iran) ● Application: occasionally as a precious stone.

Dyscrasite

Antimonide
Ag_3Sb

204

From the Greek *dyskrasis* – wrong mixture (Fröbel 1837)

● Hardness: 3.5 (brittle) ● Streak: silvery-white ● Colour: silvery-white with grey or golden-brown tarnish ● Transparency: opaque ● Lustre: full, metallic ● Cleavage: imperfect on (001) and (011) ● Fracture: uneven ● Other features of cohesion: easily sectile ● Morphology: crystals, compact, granular and scaly aggregates ● Specific gravity: 9.4–10.0 ● Crystal system: orthorhombic ● Crystal form: pseudohexagonal ● Chemical composition: Ag 72.66%, Sb 27.34% ● Chemical properties: soluble in HNO_3; readily fusible on charcoal; forms white sublimate of Sb_2O_3 with Ag ball ● Handling: clean with distilled water ● Similar minerals: silver **(49)**, antimony **(178)** ● Distinguishing features: hardness, ductility, X-rays, chemical properties ● Genesis: hydrothermal ● Associated minerals: silver, pyrargyrite **(64)**, galena **(77)** ● Occurrence: rare; Wolfach and St. Andreasberg (FRG), Sainte Marie aux Mines (France), Guadalcanal (Spain), Příbram (Czech Republic), Chañarcillo (Chile), (Australia) ● Application: can be source of Ag.

---

1. **Jordanite** – euhedral crystal (15 mm); Binnental (Switzerland) 2. **Domeykite** – granular aggregate in cuprite and malachite; Běloves (Czech Republic – width of field 90 mm) 3. **Dyscrasite** – druse of crystals (to 3 mm); Wolfach (FRG)

Jordanite, domeykite, dyscrasite

Connellite

Sulphate
$Cu_{19}Cl_4(SO_4)(OH)_{32} \cdot 2 H_2O$

205

Named after the Scottish chemist, A. Connell (1794–1863) (Dana 1850)

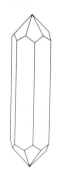

● Hardness: 3 ● Streak: light green-blue ● Colour: blue-green, light blue ● Transparency: translucent ● Lustre: vitreous ● Cleavage: absent ● Morphology: crystals, radiating-fibrous, filamentous, and crusty aggregates ● Specific gravity: 3.41 ● Crystal system: hexagonal ● Crystal form: prisms, needles ● Chemical composition: CuO 75.33%, Cl 7.07%, SO_3 3.99%, H_2O 7.63%, O 5.98% ● Chemical properties: readily soluble in acids; with blowpipe fuses and tinges the flame green ● Handling: clean with distilled water ● Similar minerals: cyanotrichite **(126)** ● Distinguishing features: chemical properties, reaction with Cl, X-rays ● Genesis: secondary ● Associated minerals: azurite **(226)**, brochantite **(228)**, malachite **(307)** ● Occurrence: rare; Grube Clara (FRG), Cornwall (Great Britain), Sardinia (Italy), Buchanan Mine – radiating crystals measuring 5 mm – California, and Ajo and Bisbee – Arizona (USA).

Atacamite

Halide
$Cu_2(OH)_3Cl$

206

Named after a province in northern Chile (Blumenbach 1805)

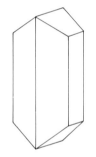

● Hardness: 3–3.5 (brittle) ● Streak: apple-green ● Colour: green, dark green to black-green ● Transparency: translucent to transparent ● Lustre: vitreous to adamantine ● Cleavage: good on (010) ● Fracture: conchoidal ● Morphology: crystals, columnar, acicular, plates, spherical and fibrous aggregates, coatings ● Specific gravity: 3.76 ● Crystal system: orthorhombic ● Crystal form: prisms, plates, rarely pseudo-octahedra, isometric ● Chemical composition: Cu 59.51%, Cl 16.60%, O 11.24%, H_2O 12.65% ● Chemical properties: readily soluble in acids and ammonia; on charcoal fuses and tinges a flame blue ● Handling: clean with distilled water ● Similar minerals: malachite **(307)**, olivenite **(257)** ● Distinguishing features: olivenite forms a white sublimate of As_2O_3; malachite in reducing flame forms Cu plates; chemical properties and X-rays ● Genesis: secondary, fumaroles ● Associated minerals: copper **(47)**, cuprite **(209)**, malachite, limonite **(355)** ● Occurrence: rare; Vesuvius (Italy), Copiapó, Chuquicamata and Taltal (Chile), Boleo near Santa Rosalia – Baja California (Mexico), Tsumeb (Namibia), Wallaroo – large crystals and Bura-Bura Mine (Australia) ● Application: Cu ore.

Boleite

Halide
$Pb_{26}Ag_9Cu_{24}Cl_{62}(OH)_{48}$

207

Named after its locality Boleo (Mexico) (Mallard, Cumenge 1891)

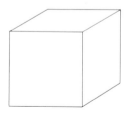

● Hardness: 3.5 ● Streak: light green, light blue ● Colour: light blue, azure-blue, dark blue ● Transparency: translucent ● Lustre: vitreous to pearly ● Cleavage: perfect on (001), good on (101) ● Morphology: crystals ● Specific gravity: 4.8–5.1 ● Crystal system: tetragonal ● Crystal form: pseudocubic, pseudododecahedral ● Chemical composition: complicated ● Chemical properties: soluble in acids; fuses in a candle flame ● Handling: clean with water ● Genesis: secondary ● Associated minerals: atacamite **(206)**, cuprite **(209)**, azurite **(226)**, malachite **(307)** ● Occurrence: rare; Boleo near Santa Rosalia – Baja California (Mexico), Mammoth Mine – Arizona (USA), Broken Hill (Australia).

---

1. **Atacamite** – spherical dark green crystals (up to 18 mm); Chuquicamata (Chile) 2. **Boleite** – dark blue euhedral crystal (12 mm); Boleo (Mexico)

Atacamite, boleite

H
3—4

Boehmite

Hydroxide
γ − AlOOH

208

Named after the German geologist and palaeontologist, J. Böhm (1857−1938) (Lapparent 1925)

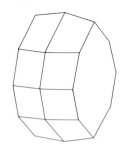

● Hardness: 3 (brittle) ● Streak: white ● Colour: white, light yellow, yellowish-green ● Transparency: translucent ● Lustre: vitreous, on cleavage planes pearly ● Cleavage: good on (010) ● Morphology: rarely crystalline, usually cryptocrystalline massive aggregates in bauxites ● Specific gravity: 3.07 ● Crystal system: orthorhombic ● Crystal form: plates ● Chemical composition: Al_2O_3 84.99%, H_2O 15.01% ● Chemical properties: insoluble in acids ● Handling: clean with water ● Similar minerals: gibbsite **(90)** ● Distinguishing features: crystal form, cleavage, hardness and specific gravity (gibbsite), X-rays ● Genesis: exogenous (weathering product), hydrothermal ● Associated minerals: kaolinite **(38)**, gibbsite, diaspore **(463)** ● Occurrence: rare; (France − in bauxites), (Germany), (Italy), (Hungary), (Russia) − seldom hydrothermal, in pegmatites in the Urals), (USA) ● Application: important Al ore.

Cuprite (Red oxide of copper)

Oxide
Cu_2O

209

L

P

From the Latin *cuprum* − copper (Haidinger 1845)

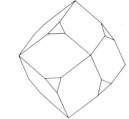

● Hardness: 3.5−4 (brittle) ● Streak: brownish-red ● Colour: brownish-red, red, lead-grey to black ● Transparency: translucent to transparent ● Lustre: adamantine, submetallic to dull ● Cleavage: imperfect on (111) ● Fracture: conchoidal, uneven ● Morphology: crystals, granular, earthy and fibrous aggregates ● Specific gravity: 6.15 ● Crystal system: cubic ● Crystal form: octahedra, hexahedra, dodecahedra, needles (chalcotrichite variety) ● Luminescence: sometimes dark raspberry red ● Chemical composition: Cu 88.82%, O 11.18% ● Chemical properties: soluble in acids and ammonia; fusible; on charcoal becomes black and copper gets separated ● Similar minerals: proustite **(63)**, pyrargyrite **(64)**, cinnabar **(76)** ● Distinguishing features: streak, hardness, reaction to copper ● Genesis: secondary ● Associated minerals: copper **(47)**, tenorite **(210)**, azurite **(226)**, malachite **(307)** ● Occurrence: Siegen, Grube Clara, Wittichen, Freudenstadt and Neubulach (FRG), Chessy (France), Cornwall (Great Britain), Tsumeb and Onganya − crystals of gemstone value (Namibia), Bisbee − Arizona (USA) ● Application: Cu ore; hardly ever used as a precious stone.

Tenorite

Oxide
CuO

210

Named after the Italian botanist, M. Tenor (1781−1861) (Semmola, 1841)

● Hardness: 3−4 (brittle) ● Streak: black, greenish ● Colour: steel-grey to black ● Transparency: opaque ● Lustre: metallic, dull ● Cleavage: indistinct ● Fracture: conchoidal to uneven ● Other properties of cohesion: thin plates are elastic ● Morphology: crystals, scaly and earthy aggregates (melaconite), encrustations ● Specific gravity: 5.8−6.4 ● Crystal system: monoclinic ● Crystal form: plates ● Chemical composition: Cu 79.89%, O 20.11% ● Chemical properties: soluble in HCl and HNO_3 ● Handling: clean with distilled water ● Similar minerals: psilomelane **(357)**, pyrolusite **(474)** ● Distinguishing features: reaction to Cu, specific gravity ● Genesis: secondary ● Associated minerals: chalcocite **(68)**, cuprite **(209)**, limonite **(355)** ● Occurrence: rare; Mansfeld, Wildschapbachtal and Siegen (FRG), Jáchymov (Czech Republic), (Romania), (Spain), (Congo), (Namibia).

Cuprite − octahedral crystal (4 mm) on quartz; Onganya (Namibia)

Cuprite

Ramsdellite

211

Named after the American mineralogist, L. S. Ramsdell (1895–1975) (Fleischer 1943)

● Hardness: 3 (brittle) ● Streak: dull black with brown tint ● Colour: steel-grey to black ● Transparency: opaque ● Lustre: metallic ● Morphology: crystals, finely granular and radiating-fibrous aggregates ● Specific gravity: 4.37 ● Crystal system: orthorhombic ● Crystal form: plates (pseudomorphs after groutite) ● Chemical composition: Mn 63.19%, O 36.18% ● Chemical properties: insoluble in HNO_3 and HCl ● Handling: clean with water ● Similar minerals: pyrolusite **(474)** ● Distinguishing features: hardness, specific gravity, X-rays ● Genesis: different in Mn ores ● Associated minerals: psilomelane **(357)**, pyrolusite ● Occurrence: rare; Horní Blatná (Czech Republic), Eregli and Mustafa Pasha (Turkey), Lake Valley – New Mexico, Butte – Montana and Chisholm – Minnesota (USA), (Egypt), (India) ● Application: Mn ore (together with other minerals).

Priceite (Pandermite)

212

L

Named after the American metallurgist, T. Price (1837–?) (Silliman 1873)

● Hardness: 3–3.5 ● Streak: white ● Colour: snow-white ● Transparency: translucent ● Lustre: dull ● Cleavage: very good on (001) ● Fracture: conchoidal, earthy ● Morphology: concretions, earthy or compact ● Specific gravity: 2.42 ● Crystal system: triclinic ● Crystal form: orthorhombic (only microscopic) ● Chemical composition: CaO 32.11%, B_2O_3 49.84%, H_2O 18.05% ● Chemical properties: soluble in acids ● Handling: clean with distilled water ● Similar minerals: ulexite **(19)**, colemanite **(301)** ● Distinguishing features: hardness, solubility in water and acids, X-rays, yellow luminescence ● Genesis: borate lakes ● Associated minerals: gypsum **(29)**, colemanite ● Occurrence: rare; Panderma and Sultan Tschair (Turkey), Chetco – Oregon and Furnace Creek Wash – California (USA) ● Application: production of boracic acid; chemical industry.

Ascharite

213

Named after Aschersleben (Saxony) – Latin *Ascharia* (Feit 1891)

● Hardness: 3–3.5 ● Streak: white ● Colour: white ● Transparency: translucent ● Lustre: silky, dull to earthy ● Cleavage: absent ● Fracture: conchoidal, earthy ● Morphology: fibrous aggregates, cross-fibrous veins, nodules ● Specific gravity: 2.65 ● Crystal system: orthorhombic ● Crystal form: unknown ● Chemical composition: MgO 47.91%, B_2O_3 41.38%, H_2O 10.71% ● Chemical properties: not readily soluble in acids; colours a flame green ● Handling: clean with distilled water ● Similar minerals: inderite **(99)**, inyoite **(100)**, chrysotile **(275)** ● Distinguishing features: hardness, specific gravity ● Genesis: borate and salt lakes, sedimentary, secondary ● Associated minerals: carnallite **(84)**, sylvite **(85)**, halite **(86)**, borax **(97)** ● Occurrence: rare; Aschersleben and Stassfurt (FRG), Inder Lake (Kazakhstan), Baiţa (Romania), Holcol (Korea), Stinson Beach – California (USA), Dougla Lake (Canada) ● Application: production of boracic acid; chemical industry.

Ramsdellite – radiating fibrous aggregates; Horní Blatná (Czech Republic – width of field 44 mm)

Ramsdellite

Hydromagnesite

Carbonate
$Mg_5(CO_3)_4(OH)_2 \cdot 4H_2O$

214

L

Named after its chemical composition (Kobell 1835)

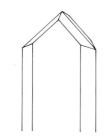

● Hardness: 3.5 ● Streak: white ● Colour: white ● Transparency: transparent ● Lustre: vitreous, in aggregates silky ● Cleavage: good ● Morphology: crystals, acicular, rose-shaped, massive aggregates ● Specific gravity: 2.2 ● Crystal system: monoclinic ● Crystal form: needles ● Luminescence: green in short-wave ultra-violet light, white to bluish in long-wave ● Chemical composition: MgO 49.93%, CO_2 27.75%, H_2O 22.32% ● Chemical properties: soluble in acids; with blowpipe turns white but does not fuse ● Handling: clean ultrasonically ● Similar minerals: artinite **(105)**, dawsonite **(215)** ● Distinguishing features: paragenesis, chemical properties, X-rays ● Genesis: secondary in serpentinites ● Associated minerals: artinite, calcite **(217)**, magnesite **(302)** ● Occurrence: rare; Kraubath and Styria (Austria), Hrubšice (Czech Republic), Jaklovce (Slovakia), Val Malenco (Italy), Limburg (FRG), Long Island – New York (USA), Dovez and Sonhan Mine (Iran).

Dawsonite

Carbonate
$NaAl(CO_3)(OH)_2$

215

L

Named after the Canadian geologist, J. W. Dawson (1820–1899) (Harrington 1874)

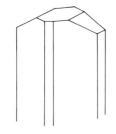

● Hardness: 3 ● Streak: white ● Colour: white ● Transparency: transparent ● Lustre: silky, in crystals vitreous ● Cleavage: good on (110) ● Morphology: crystals, spherical and crusty aggregates, rose-shaped ● Specific gravity: 2.44 ● Crystal system: orthorhombic ● Crystal form: needles, thin elongated plates ● Luminescence: dull-white, in short-wave ultra-violet light ● Chemical composition: Na_2O 21.53%, Al_2O_3 35.40%, CO_2 30.56%, H_2O 12.51% ● Chemical properties: soluble in acids, dissolves with effervescence; in a blowpipe flame swells but does not fuse ● Handling: do not clean at all ● Similar minerals: artinite **(105)**, hydromagnesite **(214)** ● Distinguishing features: chemical properties, X-rays ● Genesis: hydrothermal ● Associated minerals: calcite **(217)**, dolomite **(218)**, pyrite **(436)** ● Occurrence: rare; Monte Amiata (Italy), Terlau (Austria), Komana (Albania), Tenés (Algeria), St. Michel – Quebec (Canada), Olduvai Gorge (Tanzania).

Zaratite (Emerald-nickel, Texasite)

Carbonate
$Ni_3(CO_3)(OH)_4 \cdot 4H_2O$

216

Named after the Spanish discoverer Zarate (Casares, 1851)

● Hardness: 3–3.5 (brittle) ● Streak: light green ● Colour: emerald green ● Transparency: pellucid to translucent ● Lustre: vitreous to greasy ● Cleavage: unknown ● Fracture: conchoidal ● Morphology: encrustations, massive, powdered, stalactitic ● Specific gravity: 2.6 ● Crystal system: cubic ● Crystal form: prism ● Chemical composition: NiO 59.56%, CO_2 11.70%, H_2O 28.74% ● Chemical properties: soluble in HCl; in tube test loses water and CO_2 (grey-black, magnetic residue); in flame infusible ● Handling: do not clean ● Similar minerals: morenosite **(118)** ● Distinguishing features: hardness, specific gravity, solubility in H_2O ● Genesis: hypergenous ● Associated minerals: brucite **(91)**, millerite **(195)**, serpentine **(273)** ● Occurrence: rare; Kraubath (Austria), Kladno (Czech Republic), Cap Ortegal (Spain), Shetlands (Great Britain), Tasmania (Australia), (USA), (India).

---

1. **Hydromagnesite** – globular aggregates (size of globules 2 mm) of acicular crystals in crack in serpentinite; Valle d'Aosta (Italy) 2. **Dawsonite** – radiating fibrous crystals (10 mm) on carbonate; St. Michel (Canada) 3. **Zaratite** – emerald green compact masses; Moor Mine (USA – width of field 38 mm)

Hydromagnesite, dawsonite, zaratite

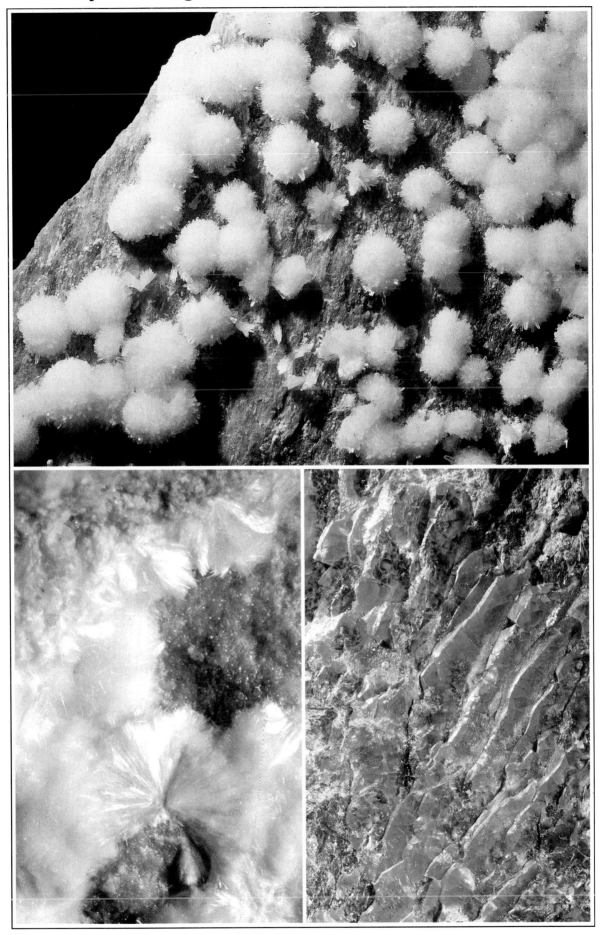

Calcite (Calc-spar, Iceland spar)

217

From the Latin *calx*
– lime
(Haidinger 1845)

L

P

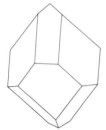
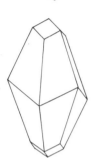

● Hardness: 3 (brittle) ● Streak: white ● Colour: colourless, white, yellow, brown, reddish, bluish to black ● Transparency: transparent to translucent ● Lustre: vitreous to pearly ● Cleavage: excellent on (10$\overline{1}$1) ● Fracture: conchoidal ● Morphology: crystals, granular, stalactitic, massive, earthy, coatings, crusts, aggregates, concretions, geodes ● Specific gravity: 2.6–2.8 ● Crystal system: trigonal ● Crystal form: rhombohedra (more than 80 forms), scalenohedra (more than 200 forms), platy, twinning, compound crystals (more than 1000 crystal forms and their combinations) ● Luminescence: white, yellowish, bluish, reddish, orange, greenish ● Chemical composition: CaO 56%, CO$_2$ 44%; admixtures: Mg, Fe, Mn, Ba, Sr, Pb, Zn. The following are some of the varieties of calcite: Iceland spar: clear, transparent; manganocalcite: admixture of up to 17% MnO; plumbo-calcite: admixture of submicroscopic cerussite (Pb); strontio-calcite: admixture of Sr ● Chemical properties: in blowpipe flame bursts and releases CO$_2$, CaO colours the flame orange; in HCl dissolves with effervescence ● Handling: clean with distilled water ● Similar minerals: dolomite **(218)**, aragonite **(221)**, baryte **(240)**, magnesite **(302)**, chabazite **(325)** ● Distinguishing features: hardness, specific gravity, solubility in HCl ● Genesis: hydrothermal, sedimentary, secondary, metamorphic and magmatic. Important rock-forming mineral ● Associated minerals: galena **(77)**, sphalerite **(181)**, dolomite, quartz **(534)**, clay minerals ● Occurrence: very common; St. Andreasberg, Freiberg, Schneeberg and Bräunsdorf (FRG), Příbram (Czech Republic), Banská Štiavnica (Slovakia), Cavnic (Romania), Rhisnes (Belgium), Derbyshire, Cornwall and Cumberland (Great Britain), Guanajuato (Mexico), Helgustadir (Iceland) – rhombohedric crystal 6 × 2 m, Joplin, Missouri and Itseberg, New Mexico – calcite of 25 tons (USA). Calcite occurs mostly in limestones, marbles, travertines forming extensive beds and long mountain ranges all over the world ● Application: in the construction of optical instruments, burnt for cement, building industry, metallurgy, for ornamental purposes. Some varieties of calcite may be cut in the form of facets and cabochons.

Calcite – druse of parallel twins (up to 6 mm) in association with pyrite; Příbram (Czech Republic – width of field 60 mm)

Calcite

Dolomite

218

Named after the French mineralogist and geologist, D. de Dolomieu (1750–1801) (Saussure 1796)

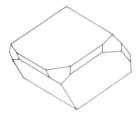

• Hardness: 3.5–4 (brittle) • Streak: white • Colour: white, grey, reddish, brownish • Transparency: transparent to translucent • Lustre: vitreous, pearly • Cleavage: excellent on ($10\bar{1}1$) • Fracture: conchoidal • Morphology: crystals, druses, granular, massive, spherical aggregates, pseudomorphs • Specific gravity: 2.85–2.95 • Crystal system: trigonal • Crystal form: rhombohedra, prisms with rhombohedral faces • Luminescence: orange, yellow, white, cream, light-green, brownish. Some dolomites show triboluminescence • Chemical composition: CaO 30.41%, MgO 21.86%, CO_2 47.73%; admixtures: Fe, Mn, Co, Pb, Zn; varieties: ferrodolomite (Fe), mangandolomite (Mn) • Chemical properties: in cold acids dissolves very slowly, bursts into flame, colours it orange • Handling: clean with distilled water • Similar minerals: calcite **(217)**, ankerite **(219)**, magnesite **(302)** • Distinguishing features: chemical properties and X-rays; calcite dissolves with effervescence in HCl, magnesite does not colour a flame • Genesis: hydrothermal, sedimentary, metasomatic • Associated minerals: galena **(77)**, sphalerite **(181)**, calcite, pyrite **(436)**, quartz **(534)** • Occurrence: very common; Freiberg (FRG), Leogang and Salzburg (Austria), Pfitsch (Italy), Binnental (Switzerland), Baiţa (Romania), Eugui (Spain), Guanajuato (Mexico). Whole mountain ranges were built of dolomite in different geological eras • Application: building industry, fertilizers, refractory furnace linings. Transparent varieties are also used as precious stones (facets).

Ankerite (Brown spar)

219

Named after the Australian mineralogist, M. J. Anker (1771–1843) (Haidinger 1825)

• Hardness: 3.5–4 (brittle) • Streak: white • Colour: white, grey, yellow, brown • Transparency: translucent to opaque • Lustre: vitreous • Cleavage: good on ($10\bar{1}1$) • Fracture: subconchoidal • Morphology: crystals, granular, massive aggregates • Specific gravity: 3.0–3.1 • Crystal system: trigonal • Crystal form: rhombohedra • Luminescence: in some localities orange in long-wave UV • Chemical composition: CaO 30.49%, FeO 39.06%, CO_2 30.45%; admixtures: Mg, Mn, Ce, La (codazite variety) • Chemical properties: dissolves slowly in acids, bursts in flame and becomes brown • Handling: clean with distilled water, dry carefully; weathers when exposed to air • Similar minerals: dolomite **(218)**, kutnohorite **(220)**, magnesite **(302)**, siderite **(306)** • Distinguishing features: specific gravity, chemical tests • Genesis: hydrothermal, metasomatic • Associated minerals: dolomite, siderite, quartz **(534)**, Cu sulphides • Occurrence: common; Eisenerz and Erzberg (Austria), Freiberg (FRG), Cavnic (Romania), Mlynky – crystals up to 5 cm (Slovakia), Traversella (Italy), Lengenbach and Binnental (Switzerland), Djelfa (Algeria) • Application: poor Fe ore.

---

1. Ankerite – light brown rhombohedral crystals (up to 10 mm); Eisenerz (Austria) **2. Dolomite** – pink-white rhombohedral crystals (up to 10 mm); Baiţa (Romania)

Ankerite, dolomite

195

Kutnohorite

Carbonate
CaMn(CO_3)_2

220

Named after its locality in the Czech Republic (Bukovský 1901)

● Hardness: 3.5−4 (brittle) ● Streak: white ● Colour: white, light yellow, light pink ● Transparency: translucent ● Lustre: vitreous, dull ● Cleavage: good on (10$\bar{1}$1) ● Fracture: conchoidal ● Morphology: granular and massive aggregates ● Specific gravity: 3.1 ● Crystal system: trigonal ● Crystal form: rhombohedra ● Chemical composition: CaO 30.64%, MnO 38.76%, CO_2 30.60% ● Genesis: hydrothermal ● Associated minerals: dolomite **(218)**, Mn minerals ● Occurrence: rare; Kutná Hora (Czech Republic), Val Malenco (Italy), Ryujima Mine (Japan), Providencia (Mexico), Franklin − New Jersey (USA).

Aragonite

Carbonate
$CaCO_3$

221

Named after its locality in Aragon (Spain) (Werner 1796)

L

P

● Hardness: 3.5−4 (brittle) ● Streak: white ● Colour: white, yellowish, bluish ● Transparency: transparent to translucent ● Lustre: vitreous, on cleavage planes pearly, dull ● Cleavage: imperfect on (010) ● Fracture: conchoidal ● Morphology: crystals, fibrous, radiating-fibrous, stalactitic, coralloidal (pistolites), crusty aggregates (sprudelstein) ● Specific gravity: 2.95 ● Crystal system: orthorhombic ● Crystal form: prisms, needles ● Luminescence: white, yellow, cream, orange, greenish ● Chemical composition: CaO 56%, CO_2 44% ● Chemical properties: dissolves with effervescence in acids ● Handling: clean with distilled water ● Similar minerals: calcite **(217)**, strontianite **[222]** ● Distinguishing features: hardness, cleavage, X-rays ● Genesis: hydrothermal, secondary ● Associated minerals: calcite, zeolites, limonite **(355)** ● Occurrence: common; Kaiserstuhl and Eisleben (FRG), Eisenerz (Austria), Podrečany (Slovakia), Karlovy Vary and Hořenec − crystals up to 30 cm (Czech Republic), Molina de Aragón (Spain), Sicily (Italy), Tsumeb (Namibia), Windcave − South Dakota and Socorro − New Mexico (USA) ● Application: often used for ornamental and decorative purposes.

Strontianite

Carbonate
$SrCO_3$

222

Named after its locality Strontian (Scotland) (Sulzer 1790)

L

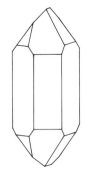

● Hardness: 3.5 (brittle) ● Streak: white ● Colour: white, grey, yellow, greenish, pink, violet ● Transparency: transparent to translucent ● Lustre: vitreous, greasy ● Cleavage: imperfect on (110) ● Fracture: uneven to subconchoidal ● Morphology: crystals, needle-shaped, fibrous, radiating aggregates ● Specific gravity: 3.7 ● Crystal system: orthorhombic ● Crystal form: prisms, acute pyramidal ● Luminescence: sometimes white, cream ● Chemical composition: SrO 70.19%, CO_2 29.81% ● Chemical properties: effervesces in acids; readily soluble; with blowpipe swells into the form of cauliflower; tinges a flame crimson ● Handling: clean with distilled water ● Similar minerals: aragonite **(221)**, natrolite **(387)** ● Distinguishing features: specific gravity, reaction in blowpipe flame, hardness ● Genesis: hydrothermal, sedimentary ● Associated minerals: calcite **(217)**, baryte **(240)** ● Occurrence: rare; Clausthal, Grund and Münster (FRG), Leogang and Oberdorf (Austria), Strontian − Scotland (Great Britain), Schoharie, New York and Strontium Hills, California (USA) ● Application: sometimes a source of Sr; in the past used in the sugar industry and for fireworks.

---

1. Aragonite − druse of long prismatic crystals attached to dolomite; Eisenerz (Austria − width of field 81 mm) **2. Strontianite** − druse of prismatic crystals (up to 20 mm); Winfield (Pennsylvania, USA)

Aragonite, strontianite

Witherite

Carbonate
$BaCO_3$

223

Named after the English natural historian, W. Withering (1741–1799) (Werner 1790)

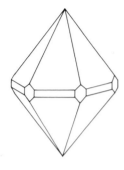

● Hardness: 3.5 (brittle) ● Streak: white ● Colour: white, yellow, grey, brownish ● Transparency: translucent to transparent ● Lustre: vitreous, greasy ● Cleavage: imperfect on (010) ● Fracture: uneven ● Morphology: crystals, granular, fibrous and massive aggregates, spherical aggregates ● Specific gravity: 4.3 ● Crystal system: orthorhombic ● Crystal form: dipyramidal, prisms, plates ● Luminescence: yellow to yellow-green, blue ● Chemical composition: BaO 77.70%, CO_2 22.30% ● Chemical properties: soluble in HCl and HNO_3, tinges a flame green ● Handling: clean with distilled water. Poisonous! ● Similar minerals: aragonite **(221)**, strontianite **(222)**, cerussite **(225)**, quartz **(534)** ● Distinguishing features: specific gravity, hardness, flame colour ● Genesis: hydrothermal ● Associated minerals: galena **(77)**, sphalerite **(181)**, siderite **(306)** ● Occurrence: rare; Fallowfield, Dufton and Alston Moor (Great Britain), Leogang and Peggau (Austria), Siberia (Russia), El Portal – California (USA) ● Application: sporadic manufacture of Ba compounds.

Otavite

Carbonate
$CdCO_3$

224

Named after its locality Otavi (Namibia) (Schneider 1906)

● Hardness: approx. 3.5–4 ● Streak: white ● Colour: white, yellowish-brown to reddish ● Transparency: translucent ● Lustre: adamantine, pearly ● Morphology: crusts, crystals ● Specific gravity: 5.03 ● Crystal system: trigonal ● Crystal form: rhombohedra ● Genesis: secondary ● Associated minerals: cerussite **(225)**, azurite **(226)**, malachite **(307)**, smithsonite **(373)** ● Occurrence: rare; Tsumeb and Otavi (Namibia), Mo Ba (Vietnam), Cally – New Mexico (USA).

Cerussite (White lead ore)

Carbonate
$PbCO_3$

225

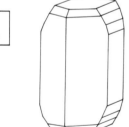

From the Latin *cerussa* – white lead (Haidinger 1845)

● Hardness: 3–3.5 (brittle) ● Streak: white ● Colour: colourless, white, yellow, brown, grey, black ● Transparency: transparent to translucent ● Lustre: adamantine ● Cleavage: imperfect on (110) and (021) ● Fracture: uneven, conchoidal ● Morphology: crystals, granular aggregates, rarely fibrous, coatings, stalactitic aggregates ● Specific gravity: 6.4–6.6 ● Crystal system: orthorhombic ● Crystal form: plates, dipyramidal, needles, twins ● Luminescence: greenish, bluish in short-wave UV, light pink-orange in long-wave UV ● Chemical composition: PbO 83.53%, CO_2 16.47% ● Chemical properties: soluble in HNO_3, in blowpipe flame bursts and fuses, colours flame yellow ● Handling: clean with distilled water ● Similar minerals: celestite **(239)**, baryte **(240)**, anglesite **(242)**, scheelite **(310)** ● Distinguishing features: hardness, specific gravity, forms twins, lustre, X-rays ● Genesis: secondary ● Associated minerals: anglesite, galena **(77)**, pyromorphite **(262)** ● Occurrence: common in oxidation zones of Pb-Zn deposits; Oberharz, Siegen, Mechernich, Badenweiler and Wildschapbachtal (FRG), Příbram and Stříbro (Czech Republic), Monteponi – Sardinia (Italy), Leadville – Colorado (USA), Tsumeb (Namibia), Kabwe (Zambia), Broken Hill (Australia) ● Application: Pb ore.

---

1. Witherite – druse of pyramidal crystals up to 20 mm; Hexham (Great Britain) **2. Cerussite** – druse of crystals (up to 20 mm) of white colour; Příbram (Czech Republic)

Witherite, cerussite

H
3—4

Azurite (Chessylite, Blue carbonate of copper)

Carbonate
$Cu_3(CO_3)_2(OH)_2$

From the Persian
lazhward – blue
(Beudant 1824)

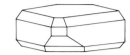

● Hardness: 3.5–4 (brittle) ● Streak: light blue ● Colour: sky blue ● Transparency: translucent to opaque ● Lustre: vitreous ● Cleavage: imperfect on (100) ● Fracture: conchoidal, uneven ● Morphology: crystals, granular, earthy, radiating-fibrous aggregates, pseudomorphs ● Specific gravity: 3.7–3.9 ● Crystal system: monoclinic ● Crystal form: plates, columns ● Chemical composition: CuO 69.24%, CO_2 25.53%, H_2O 5.23% ● Chemical properties: readily soluble in acids and ammonia, fusible in blowpipe flame ● Handling: clean with water ● Similar minerals: linarite **(110)**, vivianite **(136)**, lazurite **(392)** ● Distinguishing features: hardness, specific gravity, flame colour ● Genesis: secondary ● Associated minerals: chalcocite **(68)**, cuprite **(209)**, malachite **(307)**, limonite **(355)** ● Occurrence: very common; Mechernich, Wallerfangen and Wildschapbachtal (FRG), Chessy near Lyon (France), Nizhni Tagil (Russia), Copiapó (Chile), Tsumeb (Namibia), Bura-Bura Mine (Australia), Arizona (USA) ● Application: Cu ore, blue pigment, for ornamental purposes.

Antlerite

Sulphate
$Cu_3(SO_4)(OH)_4$

227

Named after its locality
Antler Mine (Arizona,
USA)
(Hillebrand 1889)

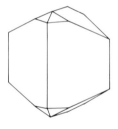

● Hardness: 3.5 ● Streak: light green ● Colour: green to dark green ● Transparency: translucent ● Lustre: vitreous ● Cleavage: good on (010) ● Morphology: crystals, granular, fibrous and powdered aggregates ● Specific gravity: 3.9 ● Crystal system: orthorhombic ● Crystal form: plates, prisms ● Chemical composition: CuO 67.28%, SO_3 22.57%, H_2O 10.15% ● Chemical properties: soluble in H_2SO_4, fuses in a blowpipe flame ● Handling: clean with distilled water ● Similar minerals: brochantite **(228)** ● Distinguishing features: solubility in acids and ammonia, X-rays ● Genesis: secondary ● Associated minerals: kröhnkite **(127)**, atacamite **(206)**, brochantite ● Occurrence: rare; Grube Clara near Oberwolfach (FRG), Špania Dolina (Slovakia), Chuquicamata (Chile), Antler Mine – Arizona (USA), Coahuila (Mexico), Kennecott (Alaska) ● Application: sometimes Cu ore.

Brochantite

Sulphate
$Cu_4(SO_4)(OH)_6$

228

Named after the French
geologist and mineralogist, A. J. M. Brochant
de Villiers (1772–1840)
(Lévy 1824)

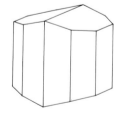

● Hardness: 3.5–4 ● Streak: light green ● Colour: emerald green, black-green ● Transparency: transparent to translucent ● Lustre: vitreous, pearly ● Cleavage: good on (100) ● Morphology: crystals, fibrous, granular and needle-shaped aggregates ● Specific gravity: 3.97 ● Crystal system: monoclinic ● Crystal form: prisms ● Chemical composition: CuO 70.36%, SO_3 17.70%, H_2O 11.94% ● Chemical properties: soluble in acids and ammonia; fuses readily in a blowpipe flame ● Handling: clean with distilled water ● Similar minerals: antlerite **(227)**, malachite **(307)** ● Distinguishing features: solubility in acids and ammonia, X-rays ● Genesis: secondary ● Associated minerals: linarite **(110)**, azurite **(226)**, antlerite, malachite ● Ocurrence: rare; Grube Clara near Wolfach, Wittichen and Neubulach (FRG), Baiţa (Romania), Lávrion (Greece), Tsumeb (Namibia), New Mexico and Arizona (USA), (Chile) ● Application: sometimes as a precious stone.

---

1. Antlerite – emerald green granular and fibrous aggregates on quartz; Chuquicamata (Chile – width of field 32 mm)
2. Azurite – aggregate of crystals (up to 4 mm); Tsumeb (Namibia) **3. Brochantite** – druse of acicular crystals in crack in quartz; Borovec (Czech Republic – width of field 18 mm)

Antlerite, azurite, brochantite

Kainite

Sulphate
$MgSO_4 . KCl . 3 H_2O$

229

From the Greek *kainós* – contemporary (Zincken 1865)

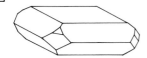

● Hardness: 3 ● Streak: white ● Colour: white, yellow, grey, reddish ● Transparency: translucent ● Lustre: vitreous ● Cleavage: good on (001) ● Morphology: crystals, granular aggregates ● Solubility: readily soluble in water ● Other properties: bitter-salty taste ● Specific gravity: 2.1 ● Crystal system: monoclinic ● Crystal form: plates, pseudomorphs ● Chemical properties: fusible ● Similar minerals: carnallite **(84)** ● Distinguishing features: hardness ● Genesis: sedimentary ● Associated minerals: sylvite **(85)**, carnallite, halite **(86)** ● Occurrence: common; Stassfurt (FRG), Hallstadt (Austria), (USA) ● Application: fertilizers, potassium salts.

Slavikite

Sulphate
$MgFe_3^{3+}(SO_4)_4(OH)_3 . 18 H_2O$

230

Named after the Czech mineralogist, F. Slavík (1876–1957) (Jirkovský 1926)

● Hardness: approx. 3.5 ● Streak: lighter than colour ● Colour: yellowish-green ● Transparency: translucent ● Lustre: vitreous ● Cleavage: unknown ● Morphology: crystals, crusts, finely granular aggregates ● Specific gravity: 2.1 ● Crystal system: trigonal ● Crystal form: plates ● Genesis: secondary ● Associated minerals: alunogen **(26)**, halotrichite **(27)** ● Occurrence: rare; Valachov (Czech Republic), (Argentina).

Kieserite

Sulphate
$MgSO_4 . H_2O$

231

Named after D. G. Kieser, President of the Academy in Jena (FRG) (1779–1826) (Reichardt, 1861)

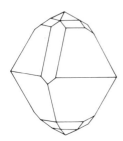

● Hardness: 3.5 ● Streak: white ● Colour: white, yellowish ● Transparency: transparent ● Lustre: vitreous ● Cleavage: excellent on (110) and (111) ● Morphology: crystals, massive and granular aggregates ● Solubility: in water ● Specific gravity: 2.57 ● Crystal system: monoclinic ● Crystal form: dipyramidal ● Chemical properties: fuses in a blowpipe flame and loses water; when exposed to air absorbs water and changes to epsomite **(111)** ● Handling: preserve in sealed bottles ● Similar minerals: epsomite ● Distinguishing features: bitter-salty taste, water-solubility ● Genesis: sedimentary ● Associated minerals: sylvite **(85)**, halite **(86)**, epsomite ● Occurrence: rare; Hallstadt (Austria), Utah (USA) ● Application: manufacture of Mg salt.

Alunite (Alum stone)

Sulphate
$KAl_3(SO_4)_2(OH)_6$

232

L

From the Latin *alunit* – alum (Beudant 1824)

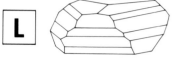

● Hardness: 3.5–4 ● Streak: white ● Colour: white, grey, yellowish, reddish ● Transparency: translucent ● Lustre: vitreous, pearly, earthy in aggregates ● Cleavage: good on (0001) ● Morphology: crystals, granular, earthy and fibrous aggregates ● Specific gravity: 2.7–2.8 ● Crystal system: trigonal ● Crystal form: rhombohedra, plates ● Luminescence: sometimes orange, white ● Chemical properties: not readily soluble in H_2SO_4 ● Handling: clean with distilled water ● Similar minerals: aluminite **(25)** ● Distinguishing features: solubility in acids, hardness, specific gravity ● Genesis: post-volcanic ● Associated minerals: halloysite **(34)**, kaolinite **(38)** ● Occurrence: rare; La Tolfa (Italy), (Hungary), (Russia), Nevada (USA) ● Application: manufacture of alum and Al sulphates.

---

1. Slavikite – crusty aggregates of yellow-brown colour; Valachov (Czech Republic) **2. Alunite** – fine granular aggregate of greyish colour; Kaluzh (Ukraine) **3. Kainite** – reddish fine granular aggregate; Stassfurt (FRG) **4. Kieserite** – white compact aggregate; Beregovo (Ukraine – width of field 85 mm)

Slavikite, alunite, kainite, kieserite

Voltaite

Sulphate
$K_2Fe_5^{2+}Fe_4^{3+}(SO_4)_{12} \cdot 18\,H_2O$

233

Named after the Italian physicist, A. G. A. A. Volta (1745–1827) (Scacchi 1841)

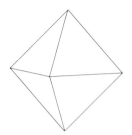

● Hardness: 3 (brittle) ● Streak: grey-green ● Colour: dark green to black ● Transparency: opaque, along crystal edges green translucence ● Lustre: silky ● Cleavage: absent ● Fracture: conchoidal ● Morphology: crystals, granular and massive aggregates ● Solubility: soluble in warm water ● Specific gravity: 2.6–2.8 ● Crystal system: cubic ● Crystal form: octahedra, dodecahedra ● Chemical composition: K_2O 4.58%, FeO 17.46%, Fe_2O_3 15.52%, SO_3 46.68%, H_2O 15.76% ● Chemical properties: soluble in acids ● Handling: do not clean, preserve in sealed bottles or plastic bags; when exposed to air changes to yellow powdered coquimbite **(121)** ● Genesis: secondary ● Associated minerals: alunogen **(26)**, halotrichite **(27)**, melanterite **(114)** ● Occurrence: rare; Rammelsberg and Waldsassen (FRG), Smolník (Slovakia), Solfatara (Italy), Huelva (Spain), Madeni Zakh (Iran).

Polyhalite

Sulphate
$K_2Ca_2Mg(SO_4)_4 \cdot 2\,H_2O$

234

From the Greek *polýs* – much and *háls* – salt (Stromeyer 1818)

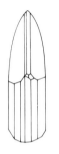

● Hardness: 3–3.5 (brittle) ● Streak: white to reddish-white ● Colour: white, yellowish, grey or flesh-pink ● Transparency: transparent to translucent ● Lustre: vitreous ● Cleavage: perfect on (101) ● Morphology: crystals, granular, fibrous, spherical or massive aggregates ● Solubility: water-soluble ● Specific gravity: 2.77 ● Crystal system: triclinic ● Crystal form: plates ● Chemical composition: K_2O 15.6%, MgO 6.6%, CaO 18.6%, SO_3 53.2%, H_2O 6.0% ● Handling: protect from humidity ● Genesis: sedimentary ● Associated minerals: gypsum **(29)**, halite **(86)**, anhydrite **(235)** ● Occurrence: common in salt deposits in northern parts of (FRG); Hallstadt and Bach Ischl (Austria), (France), (USA), (Mexico), (Russia) ● Application: manufacture of fertilizers.

Anhydrite

Sulphate
$CaSO_4$

235

From the Greek *ánhydros* – waterless (in contrast to gypsum, which contains water) (Werner 1803)

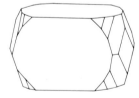

● Hardness: 3.5 (brittle) ● Streak: white ● Colour: white, bluish, grey, reddish or violet ● Transparency: translucent ● Lustre: vitreous to pearly ● Cleavage: perfect on (010), good on (100) ● Morphology: crystals, granular, fibrous, spherical aggregates, pseudomorphs ● Solubility: slightly in water ● Specific gravity: 2.9–3.0 ● Crystal system: orthorhombic ● Crystal form: plates, prisms similar to hexahedra, twins, prism faces striated ● Luminescence: sometimes red in long-wave UV ● Chemical composition: CaO 41.2%, SO_3 58.8% ● Chemical properties: in a blowpipe flame fuses to white enamel, colours flame reddish-yellow; slightly soluble in HCl and H_2SO_4 ● Handling: clean with alcohol ● Similar minerals: gypsum **(29)**, cryolite **(88)**, calcite **(217)**, baryte **(240)** ● Distinguishing features: hardness, solubility in acids, specific gravity, chemical properties, X-rays ● Genesis: hydrothermal, sedimentary, post-volcanic, magmatic ● Associated minerals: gypsum, halite **(86)**, polyhalite **(234)** ● Occurrence: common; Hannover, Stassfurt and Clausthal (FRG), (France), (Austria), (Great Britain), (India), (Russia), (USA), (Chile) ● Application: building industry; sometimes used for ornamental and decorative purposes, cut into facets or cabochons.

---

1. **Voltaite** – black fine granular aggregate; Huelva (Spain – width of field 90 mm) 2. **Polyhalite** – druse of reddish crystals; Bad Ischel (Austria – width of field 25 mm) 3. **Anhydrite** – fine crystalline aggregate in dolomite breccia; (Austria – width of field 50 mm)

Voltaite, polyhalite, anhydrite

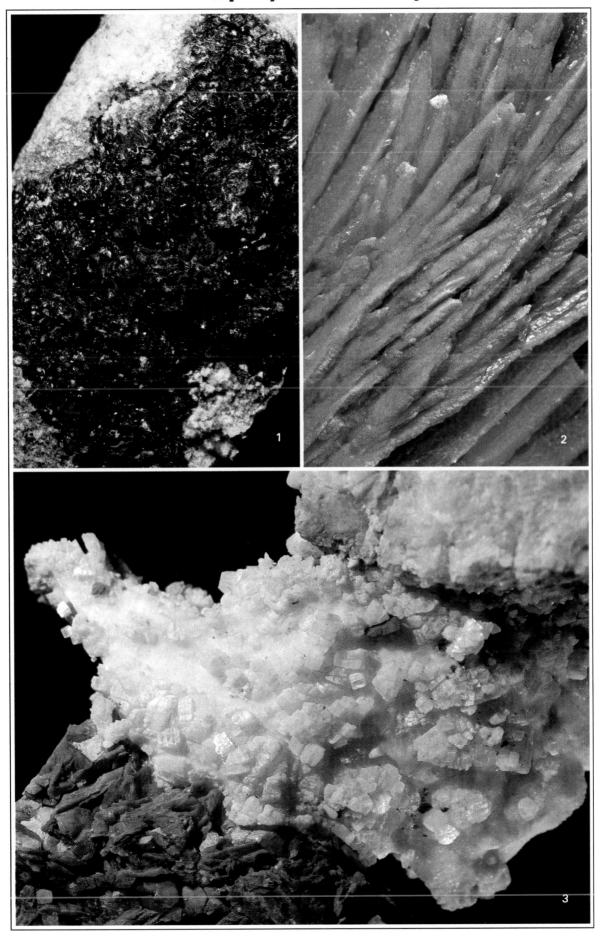

Jarosite

Sulphate
$KFe_3(SO_4)_2(OH)_6$

236

Named after its locality Barranco Jaroso (southern Spain) (Breithaupt 1852)

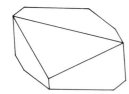

● Hardness: 3–4 (brittle) ● Streak: yellow ● Colour: yellow, brown, brownish-black, ochre yellow ● Transparency: translucent ● Lustre: vitreous ● Cleavage: imperfect on (0001) ● Morphology: crystals, granular, fibrous, scaly and earthy masses, crusts, powdered encrustments ● Other properties: feels greasy ● Specific gravity: 3.1–3.3 ● Crystal system: trigonal ● Crystal form: plates, rhombohedra ● Chemical composition: K_2O 9.41%, Fe_2O_3 47.83%, SO_3 31.97%, H_2O 10.79%; admixtures: Na, Ag, Pb ● Chemical properties: soluble in acids; when heated in test tube, it loses water ● Handling: clean with distilled water ● Similar minerals: copiapite **(123)**, limonite **(355)** ● Distinguishing features: copiapite is soluble in water, limonite feels rough; chemical properties, X-rays ● Genesis: secondary ● Associated minerals: alunite **(232)**, limonite, hematite **(472)** ● Occurrence: common; Grube Clara near Oberwolfach, Schwarzenberg (FRG), Berezovsk (Russia), Barranco Jaroso (Spain), Lávrion (Greece), Chuquicamata and Alcaparrosa (Chile), (USA), (Mexico), (Bolivia).

Natrojarosite

Sulphate
$NaFe_3^{3+}(SO_4)_2(OH)_6$

237

Named after its chemical composition and similarity to jarosite (Hillebrand 1902)

● Hardness: 3 (brittle) ● Streak: light yellow ● Colour: yellow, ochre yellow to brown ● Transparency: transparent to translucent ● Lustre: vitreous, dull (powdered aggregates) ● Cleavage: good on (0001) ● Morphology: crystals, granular and earthy aggregates, encrustations ● Solubility: slowly dissolves in HCl ● Specific gravity: 2.9–3.2 ● Crystal system: trigonal ● Crystal form: plates ● Chemical composition: Na_2O 6.40%, Fe_2O_3 49.42%, SO_3 33.04%, H_2O 11.14% ● Genesis: secondary ● Associated minerals: gypsum **(29)**, alunite **(232)**, jarosite **(236)**, limonite **(355)** ● Occurrence: rare; Wiesloch (FRG), Valachov (Czech Republic), Elba (Italy), Soda Springs – Nevada (USA), Chihuahua (Mexico), Chuquicamata (Chile).

Plumbojarosite

Sulphate
$PbFe_6^{3+}(SO_4)_4(OH)_{12}$

238

Named after its chemical composition (a variety of jarosite with Pb content) (Hillebrand 1902)

● Hardness: unknown (soft) ● Streak: lighter than colour ● Colour: yellowish-brown to dark brown ● Transparency: translucent to opaque ● Lustre: dull, vitreous ● Cleavage: imperfect on (0001) ● Morphology: crystals, crusts, massive and ochreous mounds ● Solubility: dissolves slowly in HCl ● Specific gravity: 3.6 ● Crystal system: trigonal ● Crystal form: plates ● Chemical composition: PbO 19.72%, Fe_2O_3 42.44%, SO_3 28.29%, H_2O 9.55% ● Chemical properties: soluble in HCl; with soda on charcoal forms sublimate and a lead bead ● Handling: clean with distilled water ● Similar minerals: jarosite **(236)**, natrojarosite **(237)** ● Distinguishing features: chemical properties, X-rays ● Genesis: secondary ● Associated minerals: cerussite **(225)**, jarosite, limonite **(355)** ● Occurrence: rare; Ochtiná (Slovakia), Lávrion (Greece), Cooks Peak, New Mexico and Boss Mine, Nevada (USA), Bolkardag (Turkey).

---

1. Jarosite – yellow-white granular aggregate; (USA) **2. Plumbojarosite** – yellow-brown to brown granular aggregates; Boss Mine, Clarke Co. (Nevada, USA – width of field 96 mm) **3. Natrojarosite** – orange-yellow earthy masses; Soda Springs (Nevada, USA – width of field 110 mm)

Celestite

Sulphate
SrSO$_4$

239

From the Latin *coelestis* – celestial (Werner 1798)

L

P

● Hardness: 3–3.5 (brittle) ● Streak: white ● Colour: colourless, white, blue, yellow, red ● Transparency: transparent to translucent ● Lustre: vitreous, pearly ● Cleavage: perfect on (001), good on (210) ● Morphology: crystals, granular, fibrous, compact aggregates, druses ● Specific gravity: 3.9–4.0 ● Crystal system: orthorhombic ● Crystal form: plates, prisms ● Luminescence: bluish, sometimes greenish-white ● Chemical composition: SrO 56.4%, SO$_3$ 43.6%; admixtures: Ba, Ca ● Chemical properties: soluble in H$_2$SO$_4$; in a blowpipe flame fuses and forms a white ball, colours the flame crimson ● Handling: clean with diluted acids ● Similar minerals: gypsum **(29)**, calcite **(217)**, baryte **(240)** ● Distinguishing features: hardness, specific gravity, flame colour, solubility in acids ● Genesis: sedimentary, hydrothermal ● Associated minerals: sulphur **(1)**, calcite, aragonite **(221)** ● Occurrence: common; Waldeck, Stassfurt, Bernburg and Rüdersdorf (FRG), (Poland), Bristol (Great Britain), Agrigento (Italy), Špania Dolina (Slovakia), Mokkatam (Egypt), (Libya), (Madagascar), Matehuala (Mexico) ● Application: manufacture of Sr, occasionally used as a precious stone (facets, cabochons).

Baryte (Heavy spar)

Sulphate
BaSO$_4$

240

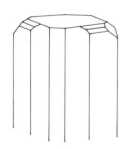

From the Greek *barys* – heavy (Karsten 1800)

L

P

● Hardness: 3–3.5 (brittle) ● Streak: white ● Colour: colourless, white, grey, yellow, blue, red, brown ● Transparency: transparent to translucent ● Lustre: vitreous, pearly ● Cleavage: excellent on (001), good on (210) ● Fracture: conchoidal ● Morphology: crystals, granular, massive, earthy aggregates, stalactitic, coatings, pseudomorphs, radiating-fibrous aggregates, nodules, concretions ● Specific gravity: 4.48 ● Crystal system: orthorhombic ● Crystal form: plates, rarely prisms ● Luminescence: white, greenish-white, yellowish green, blue-green ● Chemical composition: BaO 65.7%, SO$_3$ 34.3%; admixtures: Sr (strontiobaryte variety), Pb (hokutolite variety), Ca ● Chemical properties: slightly soluble in H$_2$SO$_4$; in a blowpipe ignites and colours a flame yellowish-green ● Handling: clean with water ● Similar minerals: calcite **(217)**, aragonite **(221)**, celestite **(239)** ● Distinguishing features: hardness, specific gravity, flame colour, often only chemical properties, X-rays ● Genesis: hydrothermal, sedimentary, hypergenous ● Associated minerals: calcite, fluorite **(291)**, quartz **(534)** and ore minerals ● Occurrence: very common; Oberwolfach, Nentershausen, Ilmenau and Meggen (FRG), Příbram (Czech Republic), Banská Štiavnica (Slovakia), Alston Moor and Egremont (Great Britain), Baia Sprie and Cavnic (Romania), Flaviac (France), Kutaisi (Russia), (Canada), (USA), (Mexico), (Algeria), (Tunisia) ● Application: Ba ore; drilling, engineering, chemical and rubber industries; occasionally used as a precious stone (facets, cabochons).

---

1. Celestite – light blue crystals (12 mm) on aragonite; Špania Dolina (Slovakia) **2. Baryte** – light blue tabular aggregates (largest size of crystals 21 mm); Baia Sprie (Romania)

Celestite, baryte

Powellite

Molybdate
CaMoO$_4$

241

(L)

Named after the American geologist, W. Powell (1834–1902)
(Melville 1891)

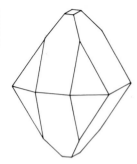

● Hardness: 3.5–4 ● Streak: light yellow to greenish ● Colour: light yellow, yellowish-green ● Transparency: transparent ● Lustre: adamantine, greasy ● Cleavage: imperfect on (112), (011) and (001) ● Fracture: uneven ● Morphology: crystals, earthy, scaly, powdered aggregates, pseudomorphs ● Specific gravity: 4.3 ● Crystal system: tetragonal ● Crystal form: pointed pyramidal, plates ● Luminescence: golden-yellow ● Chemical composition: CaO 28.48%, MoO$_3$ 71.52% ● Chemical properties: soluble in HNO$_3$ and H$_2$SO$_4$ ● Handling: clean with distilled water ● Similar minerals: scheelite **(310)** ● Distinguishing features: hardness, specific gravity, solubility in acids ● Genesis: secondary ● Associated minerals: molybdenite **(8)**, scheelite ● Occurrence: rare; Malsburg (FRG), Azegour (Morocco), Minusinsk (Russia), Seven Devils – Idaho (USA), (Turkey).

Anglesite (Lead spar, Lead vitriol)

Sulphate
PbSO$_4$

242

(L)

(P)

Named after the island of Anglesey (Wales, Great Britain)
(Beudant 1832)

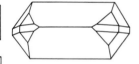

● Hardness: 3 (brittle) ● Streak: white ● Colour: white, grey ● Transparency: transparent to translucent ● Lustre: adamantine, silky ● Cleavage: imperfect on (001) and (210) ● Fracture: conchoidal ● Morphology: crystals, granular, stalactitic, rarely aggregates ● Specific gravity: 6.3 ● Crystal system: orthorhombic ● Crystal form: prisms, plates, dipyramidal ● Luminescence: yellowish-orange, yellowish-white to cream ● Chemical composition: PbO 73.6%, SO$_3$ 26.4% ● Chemical properties: soluble in hot H$_2$SO$_4$; dissolves in KOH ● Handling: clean with distilled water ● Similar minerals: phosgenite **(107)**, cerussite **(225)**, scheelite **(310)** ● Distinguishing features: specific gravity, solubility in acids and KOH, reliable X-rays ● Genesis: secondary, hydrothermal ● Associated minerals: galena **(77)**, cerussite, limonite **(355)** ● Occurrence: rare; Badenweiler, Wildschapbachtal and Einbachtal (FRG), Schwarzenbach (Austria), Monteponi – Sardinia (Italy), Anglesey, Wales and Leadhills, Scotland (Great Britain), Tsumeb (Namibia) ● Application: Pb ore; sometimes used as a precious stone.

Wulfenite (Yellow lead ore)

Molybdate
PbMoO$_4$

243

(P)

Named after the Austrian mineralogist, F. X. Wülfen (1728–1805)
(Haidinger 1841)

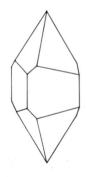

● Hardness: 3 (brittle) ● Streak: yellowish-white ● Colour: yellow, orange, reddish ● Transparency: transparent to translucent ● Lustre: adamantine, greasy ● Cleavage: imperfect on (101) ● Fracture: conchoidal ● Morphology: crystals, earthy and granular aggregates ● Specific gravity: 6.7–6.9 ● Crystal system: tetragonal ● Crystal form: plates, twins ● Chemical composition: PbO 61.4%, MoO$_3$ 38.6% ● Chemical properties: fuses in a blowpipe flame; on charcoal with soda forms a lead ball; soluble in acids ● Handling: clean with distilled water ● Similar minerals: baryte **(240)** ● Distinguishing features: specific gravity, solubility in HCl ● Genesis: secondary ● Associated minerals: galena **(77)**, calcite **(217)**, dolomite **(218)** ● Occurrence: common; Wildschapbachtal (FRG), Bleiberg (Austria), Baiţa (Romania), Mindouli (Congo), Tsumeb (Namibia), Los Lamentos (Mexico), (USA), (Morocco), (Australia) ● Application: rarely Pb ore and Mo ore.

---

1. Anglesite – euhedral crystals (to 14 mm); Monteponi (Sardinia, Italy) **2. Wulfenite** – druse of tabular crystals (up to 18 mm); Los Lamentos (Mexico)

Anglesite, wulfenite

1

2

Evansite

Phosphate
$Al_3(PO_4)(OH)_6 . 6 H_2O$

244

L

Named after the English metallurgist, B. Evans (1797–1862) (Forbes 1864)

● Hardness: 3.5–4 (brittle) ● Streak: white ● Colour: white, yellow, bluish ● Transparency: translucent ● Lustre: vitreous, pearly ● Cleavage: absent ● Fracture: conchoidal ● Morphology: coatings, stalactitic, massive, reniform and botryoidal aggregates ● Specific gravity: 1.9 ● Crystal system: amorphous ● Luminescence: sometimes green in short-wave UV, white in long-wave UV ● Chemical composition: Al_2O_3 39.60%, P_2O_5 18.40%, H_2O 42.0%; admixtures: Cu and Pb (rosieresite variety) ● Chemical properties: soluble in acids, infusible ● Handling: clean with distilled water or ultrasound ● Similar minerals: some opals **(440)**, chalcedony **(449)** ● Distinguishing features: solubility in acids ● Genesis: hypergenous ● Associated minerals: allophane **(266)**, limonite **(355)** ● Occurrence: rare; Železník and Nižná Slaná (Slovakia), (Romania), (France), (Spain), (USA), (Madagascar).

Diadochite

Phosphate
$Fe_2^{3+}(SO_4)(PO_4)(OH) . 5 H_2O$

245

From the Greek *diádochos* – substitute (Breithaupt 1837)

● Hardness: 3–4 (brittle) ● Streak: lighter than its colour ● Colour: yellow, brown, yellowish-green, cinnamon-brown, yellowish-white ● Transparency: translucent to opaque ● Lustre: dull, waxy ● Cleavage: absent ● Fracture: conchoidal, uneven, earthy ● Morphology: crusts, masses, nodules, stalactitic ● Specific gravity: 2.0–2.4 ● Crystal system: triclinic ● Crystal form: microcrystalline plates (destinezite), amorphous masses (diadochite) ● Chemical composition: Fe_2O_3 38.97%, P_2O_5 17.32%, SO_3 19.53%, H_2O 24.18% ● Chemical properties: soluble in acids; in a blowpipe flame fuses into a black mass ● Handling: clean with distilled water; dry thoroughly ● Similar minerals: bukovskyite **(376)** ● Distinguishing features: test for As, X-rays, chemical properties ● Genesis: secondary ● Associated minerals: delvauxite **(135)**, vivianite **(136)**, limonite **(355)** ● Occurrence: common; in oxidation zones of pyrite deposits in Saalfeld (FRG); Litošice (Czech Republic), Leoben (Austria), (France), (Belgium), (USA).

Cacoxenite (Kakoxen)

Phosphate
$Fe_4^{3+}(PO_4)_3(OH)_3 . 12 H_2O$

246

From the Greek *kakós* – wrong and *xénos* – guest (Steinmann 1825)

● Hardness: approx. 3 (brittle) ● Streak: straw-yellow ● Colour: yellow, ochre yellow, brown ● Transparency: translucent ● Lustre: silky, greasy ● Cleavage: absent ● Morphology: radiating-fibrous and spherulitic aggregates ● Specific gravity: 2.3 ● Crystal system: hexagonal ● Crystal form: needles ● Chemical composition: Fe_2O_3 41.18%, P_2O_5 27.46%, H_2O 31.36% ● Chemical properties: soluble in acids; in a blowpipe flame fuses into a black magnetic ball ● Similar minerals: carpholite **(401)** ● Distinguishing features: chemical properties ● Handling: clean carefully with water ● Genesis: secondary ● Associated minerals: wavellite **(247)**, strengite **(249)**, limonite **(355)** ● Occurrence: rare; Amberg-Auerbach, Hagendorf, Pleystein and Hühnerkobel (FRG), Hrbek (Czech Republic), Kirunavaara (Sweden), (USA).

---

1. Evansite – milky-white stalactitic and botryoidal crusts; Nižná Slaná (Slovakia – width of field 80 mm) **2. Cacoxenite** – yellow acicular crystals of pearly lustre in radiating fibrous aggregates in a vesicle; Weilburg (FRG – width of field 25 mm)

Evansite, cacoxenite

Wavellite

Phosphate
$Al_3(PO_4)_2(OH)_3 \cdot 5 H_2O$

247

L

Named after the English physicist, W. Wavell (Babington 1805)

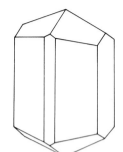

● Hardness: 3.5−4 (brittle) ● Streak: white ● Colour: white, yellow, greenish, brown, bluish ● Transparency: transparent ● Lustre: vitreous, silky ● Cleavage: good on (110) ● Fracture: uneven, subconchoidal ● Morphology: crystals, radiating-fibrous, spherical aggregates, crusts, stalactitic, coatings ● Specific gravity: 2.3−2.4 ● Crystal system: orthorhombic ● Crystal form: short prisms, long prisms ● Luminescence: greenish-white, creamy white ● Chemical composition: Al_2O_3 37.11%, P_2O_5 34.47%, H_2O 28.42% ● Chemical properties: soluble in acids; infusible in a flame ● Handling: clean ultrasonically and with water ● Similar minerals: minyulite **(248)**, prehnite **(515)** ● Distinguishing features: hardness, reaction in blowpipe flame and in HCl ● Genesis: hydrothermal, secondary ● Associated minerals: limonite **(355)**, hematite **(472)**, pyrolusite **(474)** ● Occurrence: common; Dünsberg, Langenstriegis and Waldgirmes (FRG), Cerhovice (Czech Republic), St. Austell − Cornwall (Great Britain), Ouro Preto (Brazil), Llallagua (Bolivia), Montgomery Co. − Arkansas (USA).

Minyulite

Phosphate
$KAl_2(PO_4)_2(OH,F) \cdot 4 H_2O$

248

Named after its locality Minyulo Well (western Australia) (Simpson 1933)

● Hardness: 3.5 (brittle) ● Streak: white ● Colour: white, greenish ● Transparency: transparent ● Lustre: silky ● Cleavage: perfect on (001) ● Morphology: crystals, radiating aggregates ● Specific gravity: 2.46 ● Crystal system: orthorhombic ● Crystal form: needles ● Chemical composition: complicated ● Chemical properties: soluble in hot acids and NaOH, fuses and forms a white bead ● Handling: clean with distilled water ● Similar minerals: wavellite **(247)** ● Distinguishing features: flame reaction, solubility in acids ● Genesis: secondary ● Associated minerals: phosphates ● Occurrence: rare; Pannecé (France), (Belgium), Minyulo Well and Noarlunga (Australia).

Strengite

Phosphate
$Fe^{3+}(PO_4) \cdot 2 H_2O$

249

Named after the German mineralogist, J. A. Streng (1830−1897) (Nies 1877)

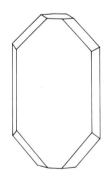

● Hardness: 3−4 (brittle) ● Streak: white ● Colour: light to dark violet, red ● Transparency: transparent to translucent ● Lustre: vitreous ● Cleavage: good on (010) ● Fracture: conchoidal ● Morphology: crystals, spherical, radiate-fibrous and spherulitic aggregates ● Specific gravity: 2.87 ● Crystal system: orthorhombic, dimorphous with phosphosiderite **(250)** ● Crystal form: octahedra, plates, prisms ● Chemical composition: Fe_2O_3 42.72%, P_2O_5 38.00%, H_2O 19.28%; admixtures: Al (barrandite variety) ● Chemical properties: readily fusible, forms a glassy black bead, soluble in HCl, insoluble in HNO_3 ● Handling: clean with distilled water ● Similar minerals: some wavellites **(247)**, phosphosiderite **(250)** ● Distinguishing features: X-rays ● Genesis: secondary ● Associated minerals: triphylite **(315)**, magnetite **(367)**, triplite **(382)**, hematite **(472)** and other phosphates ● Occurrence: rare; Pleystein, Hagendorf and Eleonora Mine near Giessen (FRG), Kiruna (Sweden), Hrbek − barrandite variety (Czech Republic), Pala − California (USA).

---

1. **Wavellite** − radiating, wheel-shaped aggregates (up to 20 mm); Cerhovice (Czech Republic) 2. **Minyulite** − radiating fibrous aggregates of grey-white colour; Pannecé (France − width of field 23 mm) 3. **Strengite** − violet-red crystals (up to 3 mm) in vesicle in quartz; Pleystein (FRG)

Wavellite, minyulite, strengite

Phosphosiderite (Metastrengite)

Phosphate
$Fe^{3+}(PO_4) \cdot 2 H_2O$

250

Named after its chemical composition (Bruhns-Bush 1890)

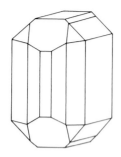

● Hardness: 3.5–4 (brittle) ● Streak: white ● Colour: reddish-violet, purple-red ● Transparency: transparent to translucent ● Lustre: vitreous ● Cleavage: good on (010) ● Fracture: uneven ● Morphology: crystals, crusts and spherical aggregates ● Specific gravity: 2.76 ● Crystal system: monoclinic, dimorphous with strengite **(249)** ● Crystal form: plates, short prisms ● Chemical composition: Fe_2O_3 42.73%, P_2O_5 37.99%, H_2O 19.28%; admixtures: Al (clinobarrandite) and Mn (vilateite) ● Chemical properties: soluble in HCl, readily fuses and forms a black magnetic ball ● Handling: clean with distilled water ● Similar minerals: strengite ● Distinguishing features: X-rays ● Genesis: secondary ● Associated minerals: pharmacosiderite **(140)**, limonite **(355)** ● Occurrence: rare; Kalterborn near Eiserfeld, Hagendorf and Pleystein (FRG), San Giovanneddu – Sardinia (Italy), La Vilase near Chanteloube (France) – vilateite variety, Bull Moose Mine – South Dakota (USA).

Phosphophyllite

Phosphate
$Zn_2Fe^{2+}(PO_4)_2 \cdot 4 H_2O$

251

Named after its chemical component and the Greek *fyllon* – leaf (Laumbmann and Steinmetz 1920)

L

P

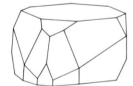

● Hardness: 3.5 (brittle) ● Streak: white ● Colour: blue-green ● Transparency: transparent ● Lustre: vitreous ● Cleavage: perfect on (100) ● Fracture: uneven ● Morphology: crystals, druses, twinning ● Specific gravity: 3.1 ● Crystal system: monoclinic ● Crystal form: long prisms, thin plates ● Luminescence: violet in short-wave UV ● Chemical composition: ZnO 36.27%, FeO 16.02%, P_2O_5 31.64%, H_2O 16.07%; admixture Mn ● Chemical properties: soluble in acids, readily fusible ● Handling: clean with distilled water ● Similar minerals: chalcophyllite **(138)** ● Distinguishing features: hardness, specific gravity, streak ● Genesis: secondary ● Associated minerals: vivianite **(136)**, sphalerite **(181)**, triplite **(382)**, apatite **(379)** ● Occurrence: rare; Hagendorf (FRG), Potosí – crystals up to 6 cm (Bolivia) ● Application: sometimes used as a precious stone (facets, cabochons).

Hopeite

Phosphate
$Zn_3(PO_4)_2 \cdot 4 H_2O$

252

Named after the Scottish chemist, T. Ch. Hope (Brewster 1823)

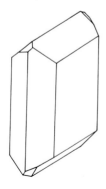

● Hardness: 3 (brittle) ● Streak: white ● Colour: white, grey, yellow ● Transparency: transparent to translucent ● Lustre: vitreous, on cleavage planes pearly ● Cleavage: very good on (100), good on (010) ● Fracture: uneven ● Morphology: crystals, granular, crusty aggregates, also massive ● Specific gravity: approx. 3 ● Crystal system: orthorhombic ● Crystal form: prisms, plates ● Chemical composition: ZnO 53.28%, P_2O_5 31.00%, H_2O 15.72% ● Chemical properties: readily fusible, forms colourless ball, soluble in HCl ● Handling: clean with distilled water ● Genesis: secondary in oxidation zones ● Associated minerals: vanadinite **(263)**, hemimorphite **(403)** ● Occurrence: rare; Altenberg near Aachen (FRG), Kabwe – crystals measuring 1 cm (Zambia), Hudson Bay Mine (Canada).

---

1. Phosphophyllite – light blue fissile aggregates; Hagendorf (FRG – width of field 28 mm) **2. Phosphosiderite** – globular aggregates (up to 3 mm); Pleystein (FRG) **3. Hopeite** – group of crystals (up to 2 mm); Nabwe (Zambia)

Phosphophyllite, phosphosiderite, hopeite

Messelite

Phosphate
$Ca_2Fe(PO_4)_2 . 2 H_2O$

253

Named after its locality Messel (FRG)
(Muthmann 1889)

● Hardness: 3.5 (brittle) ● Streak: white ● Colour: white, grey, greenish ● Transparency: transparent to translucent ● Lustre: vitreous to pearly ● Cleavage: very good on (001), good on (010) ● Fracture: uneven ● Morphology: crystals, radiating aggregates, scaly masses ● Specific gravity: 3.16 ● Crystal system: triclinic ● Crystal form: prisms, plates ● Chemical composition: CaO 30.98%, FeO 19.85%, P_2O_5 39.21%, H_2O 9.96% ● Chemical properties: soluble in acids ● Handling: clean with distilled water ● Similar minerals: muscovite **(165)** ● Distinguishing features: hardness, specific gravity, X-rays ● Genesis: hydrothermal, in bituminous clay shales ● Associated minerals: vivianite **(136)**, siderite **(306)**, triphylite **(315)** ● Occurrence: rare; Messel and Hagendorf (FRG), Semizersk (Russia), Přibyslavice (Czech Republic), Custer County – South Dakota (USA).

Scorodite

Arsenate
$Fe^{3+}(AsO_4) . 2 H_2O$

254

P

From the Greek *skórodon* – garlic
(Breithaupt 1817)

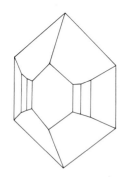

● Hardness: 3.5–4 (brittle) ● Streak: greenish-white ● Colour: yellowish-green, blue-green to black-green ● Transparency: translucent ● Lustre: vitreous, greasy ● Cleavage: imperfect on (120) ● Fracture: splintery to uneven ● Morphology: spherical, fibrous, tabular, granular, earthy aggregates ● Specific gravity: 3.1–3.3 ● Crystal system: orthorhombic ● Crystal form: dipyramidal, plates, prisms ● Chemical composition: Fe_2O_3 34.60%, As_2O_5 49.79%, H_2O 15.61% ● Chemical properties: soluble in HNO_3 and HCl; colours KOH solution reddish-brown; readily fusible; colours flame blue, releases garlicky smell ● Handling: clean with water or ultrasound ● Similar minerals: pharmacosiderite **(140)**, adamite **(258)** ● Distinguishing features: hardness, specific gravity, crystal form ● Genesis: oxidation zones of ore veins ● Associated minerals: arsenopyrite **(344)**, limonite **(355)**, pyrite **(436)** ● Occurrence: rare; Clara Mine near Oberwolfach, Johanngeorgenstadt, Schneeberg, Dernbach and Wittichen (FRG), Lölling (Austria), Cornwall (Great Britain), Nerchinsk (Russia), Tsumeb (Namibia), (Algeria), Antonio Pereira (Brazil) ● Application: occasionally used as a precious stone.

Mixite

Arsenate
$(Bi,Ca)Cu_6(AsO_4)_3(OH)_6 . 3 H_2O$

255

Named after the mining engineer, A. Mixa from Jáchymov
(Czech Republic)
(Schrauf 1879)

● Hardness: 3–4 ● Streak: lighter than colour ● Colour: green, emerald green, blue-green ● Transparency: translucent ● Lustre: crystals – adamantine; aggregates – dull ● Cleavage: unknown ● Morphology: crystals, radiate-fibrous, coatings, aggregates, also compact masses ● Specific gravity: 3.8 ● Crystal system: hexagonal ● Crystal form: needle-shaped ● Chemical composition: CuO 44.20%, BiO 10.42%, As_2O_5 31.93%, H_2O 10.85%, CaO 2.60% ● Chemical properties: soluble in acids ● Handling: clean with distilled water ● Similar minerals: cyanotrichite **(126)** ● Distinguishing features: hardness, chemical properties, X-rays ● Genesis: secondary ● Associated minerals: bismutite **(71)**, native Bi and other secondary Bi minerals ● Occurrence: rare; Wittichen, Freudenstadt and Neubulach (FRG), Jáchymov (Czech Republic), Moldava (Slovakia), Lávrion (Greece), Tintic – Utah (USA), Durango (Mexico).

---

1. Scorodite – polished crust; Brewster (USA) **2. Mixite** – fine crystals in a fissure; Jáchymov (Czech Republic – width of field 70 mm)

Scorodite, mixite

Euchroite

Arsenate
Cu₂(AsO₄)(OH) . 3 H₂O

256

From the Greek *eu* – good and *chrós* – colour (Breithaupt 1873)

● Hardness: 3.5 (brittle) ● Streak: green ● Colour: emerald green ● Transparency: transparent ● Lustre: vitreous ● Cleavage: imperfect on (101) and (110) ● Fracture: uneven, subconchoidal ● Morphology: crystals, crusts, druses ● Specific gravity: 3.45 ● Crystal system: orthorhombic ● Crystal form: prisms, plates, isometric ● Chemical composition: CuO 47.21%, As₂O₅ 34.09%, H₂O 18.70% ● Chemical properties: soluble in acids; fusible in a blowpipe flame ● Handling: clean with distilled water ● Similar minerals: dioptase **(432)** ● Distinguishing features: hardness, reaction to flame ● Genesis: secondary in oxidation zones ● Associated minerals: azurite **(226)**, olivenite **(257)**, malachite **(307)** ● Occurrence: rare; Ľubietová (Slovakia), Zapachitsa (Bulgaria), Chessy (France).

Olivenite

Arsenate
Cu₂(AsO₄)(OH)

257

Named after its colour (Jameson 1820)

● Hardness: 3 (brittle) ● Streak: yellowish-green ● Colour: olive green, yellowish-brown to dirty white ● Transparency: transparent to translucent ● Lustre: vitreous, silky, greasy ● Cleavage: imperfect on (011) and (110) ● Fracture: conchoidal ● Morphology: crystals, reniform, earthy and fibrous aggregates ● Specific gravity: approx. 4.3 ● Crystal system: orthorhombic ● Crystal form: prisms, acicular and platy ● Chemical composition: CuO 56.22%, As₂O₅ 40.60%, H₂O 3.18% ● Chemical properties: readily fusible, soluble in acids and ammonia ● Handling: clean with distilled water ● Similar minerals: atacamite **(206)**, libethenite **(319)** ● Distinguishing features: on charcoal forms a white sublimate of As₂O₃ ● Genesis: secondary in oxidation zones ● Associated minerals: tyrolite **(32)**, clinoclase **(146)**, chalcopyrite **(185)** ● Occurrence: rare; Clara Mine near Oberwolfach (FRG), Ľubietová (Slovakia), Nizhni Tagil (Russia), Utah (USA), Tsumeb (Namibia), Lávrion (Greece), (Chile).

Adamite

Arsenate
Zn₂(AsO₄)(OH)

258

Named after the French mineralogist, G. J. Adam (1795–1881) (Friedel 1866)

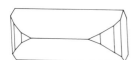

● Hardness: 3.5 ● Streak: white ● Colour: yellow, green, violet, pink ● Transparency: transparent ● Lustre: vitreous ● Cleavage: perfect on (011) ● Fracture: uneven ● Morphology: crystals, granular, druses, crusts ● Specific gravity: 4.3–4.5 ● Crystal system: orthorhombic ● Crystal form: plates, rarely prisms ● Luminescence: sometimes greenish-white, lemon-yellow ● Chemical composition: ZnO 56.77%, As₂O₅ 40.09%, H₂O 3.14%; admixture Cu (cuproadamite variety) ● Chemical properties: when heated crumbles, becomes white and porcelain-like; readily soluble in acids ● Handling: clean with distilled water ● Similar minerals: scorodite **(254)**, legrandite **(318)** ● Distinguishing features: specific gravity, streak, chemical properties, X-rays ● Genesis: secondary ● Associated minerals: limonite **(355)**, smithsonite **(373)**, hemimorphite **(403)** ● Occurrence: rare; Schwarzwald (FRG), Lávrion (Greece), Rädelgraben near Werfen (Austria), Zermatt (Switzerland), Durango (Mexico), Chañarcillo (Chile), Tsumeb (Namibia), Utah (USA).

1. **Adamite** – crystalline aggregates (crystals to 4 mm) on limonite; Mapimí (Mexico) 2. **Olivenite** – fibrous aggregate (5 mm) on quartz; St. Day (Cornwall, Great Britain) 3. **Euchroite** – group of crystals (the largest 12 mm) on limonite; Ľubietová (Slovakia)

Mottramite

Vanadate
Pb(Cu,Zn)(VO$_4$)(OH)

259

Named after its locality Mottram (Great Britain) (Roscoe 1876)

● Hardness: 3.5 (brittle) ● Streak: light brown, light green ● Colour: light green, dark green, black ● Transparency: transparent to non-transparent ● Lustre: greasy to adamantine ● Cleavage: absent ● Fracture: uneven, subconchoidal ● Morphology: crystals, radiating-fibrous, crusty aggregates ● Specific gravity: 5.9 ● Crystal system: orthorhombic ● Crystal form: prisms, plates ● Chemical composition: PbO 55.30%, ZnO 10.08%, CuO 9.86%, V$_2$O$_5$ 22.53%, H$_2$O 2.23% (when Zn:Cu = 1:1); mottramite contains more Cu than Zn ● Chemical properties: readily fusible, readily soluble in acids ● Handling: clean with distilled water ● Similar minerals: descloizite **(260)** ● Distinguishing features: chemical properties ● Genesis: secondary in oxidation zones ● Associated minerals: cerussite **(225)**, pyromorphite **(262)**, vanadinite **(263)** ● Occurrence: rare; Hofsgrund (FRG), Obir (Austria), Vrančice (Czech Republic), Mottram (Great Britain), Sardinia (Italy), California and Arizona (USA), (Argentina), Tsumeb (Namibia).

Descloizite

Vanadate
Pb(Zn,Cu)(VO$_4$)(OH)

260

Named after the French mineralogist, A.L.O.L. Des Cloizeaux (1817–1897) (Damour 1854)

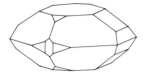

● Hardness: 3.5 (brittle) ● Streak: light brown, light green ● Colour: orange-red, brown, brownish-black, green ● Transparency: transparent to non-transparent ● Lustre: greasy to adamantine ● Cleavage: absent ● Fracture: uneven, subconchoidal ● Morphology: crystals, crystalline or crusty aggregates ● Specific gravity: 6.2 ● Crystal system: orthorhombic ● Crystal form: prisms, plates ● Chemical composition: PbO 55.30%, ZnO 10.08%, Cuo 9.86%, V$_2$O$_5$ 22.53%, H$_2$O 2.23% (when Zn:Cu = 1:1); descloizite contains more Zn than Cu ● Chemical properties: readily fusible; readily soluble in acids ● Handling: clean with distilled water ● Similar minerals: mottramite **(259)** ● Distinguishing features: chemical test ● Genesis: secondary in oxidation zones ● Associated minerals: cerussite **(225)**, pyromorphite **(262)**, vanadinite **(263)** ● Occurrence: rare; Schauinsland (FRG), Tsumeb and Otavi (Namibia), Kabwe (Zambia), Galena – South Dakota (USA) ● Application: sometimes as source of V.

Vesignieite

Vanadate
BaCu$_3$(VO$_4$)$_2$(OH)$_2$

261

Named after the French mineral collector, L. Vésignié (1870–1954) (Guillemin 1955)

● Hardness: 3–4 ● Streak: light green ● Colour: yellowish-green to olive green ● Transparency: transparent to translucent ● Lustre: vitreous ● Cleavage: good on (001) ● Morphology: crystals, lamellar aggregates, polysynthetic twinning, crusts, powdered aggregates ● Specific gravity: 4.05 ● Crystal system: monoclinic ● Crystal form: plates ● Chemical composition: BaO 25.91%, CuO 40.33%, V$_2$O$_5$ 30.72%, H$_2$O 3.04% ● Handling: clean with distilled water ● Genesis: secondary ● Associated minerals: cuprite **(209)**, calcite **(217)**, baryte **(240)** ● Occurrence: rare; Friedrichsroda (FRG), Vrančice and Horní Kalná (Czech Republic), Agalik (Uzbekistan).

1. **Mottramite** – crystals (up to 3 mm); Tsumeb (Namibia) 2. **Descloizite** – group of crystals; Tsumeb (Namibia – width of field 20 mm) 3. **Vesignieite** – lamellar aggregates; Agalik (Uzbekistan – width of field 40 mm)

Mottramite, descloizite, vesignieite

H
3—4

Pyromorphite (Green lead ore)

Phosphate
$Pb_5(PO_4)_3Cl$

262

L

From the Greek *pyr* – fire and *morfe* – form (Hausmann 1813)

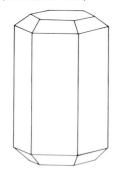

● Hardness: 3.5–4 (brittle) ● Streak: white ● Colour: green, yellow, brown, grey-white, yellowish-red ● Transparency: translucent ● Lustre: adamantine, greasy ● Cleavage: imperfect on (1011) ● Fracture: uneven, subconchoidal ● Morphology: crystals, reniform and globular aggregates ● Specific gravity: 6.7–7.0 ● Crystal system: hexagonal ● Crystal form: prisms, plates ● Luminescence: sometimes yellow in long-wave UV ● Chemical composition: PbO 82.0%, P_2O_5 15.4%, Cl 2.6% ● Chemical properties: soluble in HNO_3 and KOH; readily fusible ● Handling: clean with distilled water ● Similar minerals: mimetite **(264)**, apatite **(379)** ● Distinguishing features: chemical properties, X-rays ● Genesis: secondary ● Associated minerals: galena **(77)**, cerussite **(225)**, mimetite ● Occurrence: rare; (FRG), (Czech Republic), (Slovakia), Cornwall (Great Britain), (Zambia), (USA) ● Application: as Pb ore.

Vanadinite

Vanadate
$Pb_5(VO_4)_3Cl$

263

Named for its vanadium content (Kobell 1838)

● Hardness: 3 (brittle) ● Streak: yellow, brownish ● Colour: yellow, brown, orange, red ● Transparency: translucent ● Lustre: adamantine ● Cleavage: absent ● Fracture: conchoidal, uneven ● Morphology: crystals, granular, fibrous aggregates ● Specific gravity: 6.8–7.1 ● Crystal system: hexagonal ● Crystal form: prisms, sharply pyramidal ● Chemical composition: PbO 78.35%, V_2O_5 19.16%, Cl 2.49% ● Chemical properties: readily fusible, soluble in HNO_3 and HCl ● Handling: clean with distilled water ● Similar minerals: mimetite **(264)** ● Distinguishing features: chemical properties ● Genesis: secondary ● Associated minerals: wulfenite **(243)**, pyromorphite **(262)**, mimetite ● Occurrence: rare; Obir (Austria), (Morocco), (Namibia), Kabwe (Zambia), Los Lamentos (Mexico), Arizona (USA) ● Application: as V ore.

Mimetite (Mimetesite)

Arsenate
$Pb_5(AsO_4)_3Cl$

264

L

P

From the Greek *mímethes* – imitator (Beudant 1832)

● Hardness: 3.5–4 (brittle) ● Streak: white ● Colour: white, yellow, orange, brown, greenish, grey ● Transparency: translucent ● Lustre: adamantine, greasy ● Cleavage: imperfect on (1011) ● Fracture: conchoidal, uneven ● Morphology: crystals, granular, earthy and fibrous aggregates ● Specific gravity: approx. 7.1 ● Crystal system: hexagonal ● Crystal form: prisms, plates, dipyramidal ● Luminescence: orange-red in short-wave UV ● Chemical composition: PbO 74.59%, As_2O_5 23.04%, Cl 2.37% ● Chemical properties: soluble in H_2SO_4, HNO_3 and KOH; readily fusible, releasing garlicky smell ● Handling: clean with distilled water ● Similar minerals: pyromorphite **(262)**, vanadinite **(263)** ● Distinguishing features: chemical properties, X-rays, garlicky smell ● Genesis: secondary ● Associated minerals: galena **(77)**, pyromorphite, psilomelane **(357)** ● Occurrence: rare; Clausthal and Johanngeorgenstadt (FRG), Tsumeb (Namibia).

Campylite (Phosphomimetite, Mimetite variety)

Arsenate
$Pb_5((As,P)O_4)_3 . Cl$

265

L

From the Greek *kampé* – crooked and *líthos* – stone (Breithaupt 1841)

● Physical properties: identical with mimetite usually in barrel-shaped crystals ● Occurrence: rare; Příbram (Czech Republic), Cumberland (Great Britain), (France).

1. Pyromorphite – druse of hexagonal crystals (22 mm); Fridrichsagen Mine (FRG) **2. Vanadinite** – crystalline aggregate (the largest crystal 8 mm); Mibladen (Morocco) **3. Mimetite** – columnar crystals (up to 10 mm); Tsumeb (Namibia) **4. Campylite** – globular aggregates (up to 7 mm) with psilomelane; Cumberland (Great Britain)

Pyromorphite, vanadinite, mimetite, campylite

Allophane

Silicate
Al$_2$(SiO$_5$) . nH$_2$O

266

L

From the Greek *állos* – other and *phanos* – to appear (Stromeyer 1816)

● Hardness: 3 (brittle) ● Streak: white ● Colour: white, green, blue, yellow, brown ● Transparency: transparent to translucent ● Lustre: vitreous, greasy, waxy ● Cleavage: absent ● Fracture: conchoidal ● Morphology: crusts, coatings, stalactitic ● Specific gravity: 1.9 ● Crystal system: unknown ● Luminescence: white, cream, green and yellow-brown ● Chemical composition: variable ● Chemical properties: in a blowpipe flame crumbles but does not fuse; with HCl forms a gelatinous solution of SiO$_2$ ● Handling: clean with distilled water ● Similar minerals: variscite **(311)**, opal **(440)** ● Distinguishing features: hardness, specific gravity, solubility in HCl ● Genesis: secondary ● Associated minerals: halloysite **(34)**, limonite **(355)** ● Occurrence: rare; Wittichen, Neubulach and Badenweiler (FRG), Gross Arl (Austria), Zlaté Hory (Czech Republic), Bridestone (Great Britain), (Russia), (USA).

Thaumasite

Silicate
Ca$_3$Si(CO$_3$)(SO$_4$)(OH)$_6$. 12 H$_2$O

267

L

P

From the Greek *thaumásion* – surprising (Nordenskiöld 1878)

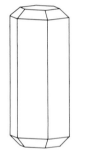

● Hardness: 3.5 (brittle) ● Streak: white ● Colour: white ● Transparency: translucent to transparent ● Lustre: vitreous, silky ● Morphology: crystals, radiating-fibrous and filamentous aggregates ● Specific gravity: 1.9 ● Crystal system: hexagonal ● Crystal form: prisms, acicular ● Luminescence: sometimes white in short-wave UV ● Chemical composition: CaO 10.98%, CO$_2$ 8.62%, SO$_3$ 15.68%, SiO$_2$ 11.77%, H$_2$O 52.95% ● Chemical properties: soluble in HCl, slightly swells, forms amorphous SiO$_2$ ● Handling: clean with distilled water ● Similar minerals: dawsonite **(215)**, garronite **(327)** ● Distinguishing features: hardness, specific gravity, solubility in acids, X-rays ● Genesis: hydrothermal ● Associated minerals: alumohydrocalcite **(104)**, laumontite **(272)**, apophyllite **(331)** ● Occurrence: rare; Haslach (FRG), Långban (Sweden), Sulitelma (Norway), New Jersey and California (USA) ● Application: sometimes used as a precious stone.

Chrysocolla

Silicate
CuSiO$_3$. nH$_2$O

268

P

From the Greek *chrysós* – gold and *kólla* – glue (Brochant 1808)

● Hardness: 2–4 ● Streak: light green ● Colour: green, blue-green to blue ● Transparency: translucent to opaque ● Lustre: vitreous, dull ● Cleavage: absent ● Fracture: conchoidal ● Morphology: coatings, stalactitic, botryoidal aggregates, crusts, massive, earthy ● Specific gravity: 2.0–2.2 ● Crystal system: amorphous (monoclinic) ● Chemical composition: variable ● Chemical properties: colours a flame green, infusible, soluble in acids, in tube-test loses water and becomes black ● Handling: clean with distilled water ● Similar minerals: aurichalcite **(106)** ● Distinguishing features: hardness, specific gravity ● Genesis: secondary ● Associated minerals: cuprite **(209)**, azurite **(226)**, malachite **(307)** ● Occurrence: common; Halsbach, Wittichen, Schauinsland and Badenweiler (FRG), Lizard – Cornwall (Great Britain), Bogoslovsk (Russia), (USA), (Mexico), (Chile), (Congo) ● Application: as a precious stone.

---

1. Allophane – reniform aggregate; Wittichen (FRG – width of field 38 mm) **2. Thaumasite** – radiating aggregates (15 mm) on calcite; West Paterson (New Jersey, USA) **3. Chrysocolla** – reniform aggregate; Novoveská Huta (Slovakia – width of field 22 mm)

Allophane, thaumasite, chrysocolla

H
3—4

Stilbite (Desmine, Bundle zeolite)

Silicate
$CaAl_2Si_7O_{18} \cdot 7 H_2O$

269

From the Greek *stilbe* – lustre (Hauy 1796)

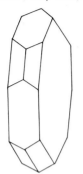

● Hardness: 3.5–4 (brittle) ● Streak: white ● Colour: white, red, yellow, brown ● Transparency: transparent to translucent ● Lustre: vitreous, pearly, silky ● Cleavage: perfect on (010) ● Morphology: crystals, radiating-fibrous, bundle-shaped aggregates ● Specific gravity: 2.1–2.2 ● Crystal system: monoclinic ● Crystal form: plates, columns ● Chemical composition: CaO 7.96%, Al_2O_3 14.47%, SiO_2 59.67%, H_2O 17.90% ● Chemical properties: soluble in HCl ● Handling: clean with distilled water ● Similar minerals: heulandite **(270)**, prehnite **(515)** ● Distinguishing features: crystal form, hardness ● Genesis: hydrothermal, post-volcanic ● Associated minerals: heulandite, laumontite **(272)**, chabazite **(325)** ● Occurrence: common; Berufjord (Iceland), (Faroe Islands), Poona (India).

Heulandite (Lamellar zeolite)

Silicate
$CaAl_2Si_7O_{18} \cdot 6 H_2O$

270

L

Named after the English mineral collector, J. H. Heuland (1778–1856) (Brucke 1822)

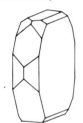

● Hardness: 3.5–4 (brittle) ● Streak: white ● Colour: white, grey, red, brown ● Transparency: transparent to translucent ● Lustre: vitreous, pearly ● Cleavage: perfect on (010) ● Fracture: uneven ● Morphology: crystals, radiating-fibrous and lamellar aggregates ● Specific gravity: 2.2 ● Crystal system: monoclinic ● Crystal form: plates, scales ● Luminescence: sometimes light blue in long-wave UV ● Chemical composition: CaO 9.2%, Al_2O_3 16.8%, SiO_2 59.29%, H_2O 14.8% ● Chemical properties: soluble in HCl ● Handling: clean with distilled water ● Similar minerals: stilbite **(269)** ● Distinguishing features: crystal form ● Genesis: hydrothermal ● Associated minerals: stilbite, chabazite **(325)** ● Occurrence: rare; Valle di Fassa (Italy), Poona (India).

Clinoptilolite

Silicate
$(Na,K,Ca)_{2-3}Al_3(Al,Si)_2Si_{13}O_{36} \cdot 12 H_2O$

271

From the Greek *klinó* – oblique, *ptylon* – feather and *líthos* – stone (Schaller 1923)

● Hardness: 3.5–4 ● Streak: white ● Colour: white, reddish ● Transparency: transparent to translucent ● Lustre: vitreous ● Cleavage: perfect on (010) ● Fracture: uneven ● Morphology: crystalline aggregates ● Specific gravity: 2.1–2.2 ● Crystal system: monoclinic ● Crystal form: plates ● Handling: clean with distilled water ● Genesis: hydrothermal ● Associated minerals: other zeolites ● Occurrence: rare; (Hungary), (Australia), (USA) ● Application: as a fertilizer.

Laumontite (Fibrous zeolite)

Silicate
$CaAl_2Si_4O_{12} \cdot 4 H_2O$

272

L

Named after the Frenchman, F.P.N. de Laumont (1747–1834) (Werner 1803)

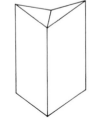

● Hardness: 3–3.5 (brittle) ● Streak: white ● Colour: white, grey, yellowish, reddish ● Transparency: translucent ● Lustre: vitreous, pearly, dull ● Cleavage: perfect ● Morphology: crystals, fibrous, compact and earthy aggregates ● Specific gravity: 2.25–2.35 ● Crystal system: monoclinic ● Crystal form: prisms ● Luminescence: white in long-wave UV ● Chemical composition: CaO 11.92%, Al_2O_3 21.67%, SiO_2 51.09%, H_2O 15.32% ● Chemical properties: soluble in HCl ● Handling: clean with water; *NB*: in dry environment it loses water and crumbles readily ● Similar minerals: bavenite **(399)** ● Distinguishing features: hardness, solubility in acids ● Genesis: hydrothermal ● Associated minerals: heulandite **(270)**, chabazite **(325)** ● Occurrence: common; (Italy), (Great Britain), (Brazil), (USA).

---

1. Stilbite – wisp-like aggregate (30 mm) with heulandite; Berufjord (Iceland) **2. Heulandite** – tabular aggregate (15 mm) of pearly lustre; Kozákov (Czech Republic) **3. Clinoptilolite** – globular crystalline aggregates (3 mm); Hončová Hůrka (Czech Republic) **4. Laumontite** – druse of prismatic crystals in fissure in andesite (7 mm); Šiatorská Bukovinka (Slovakia)

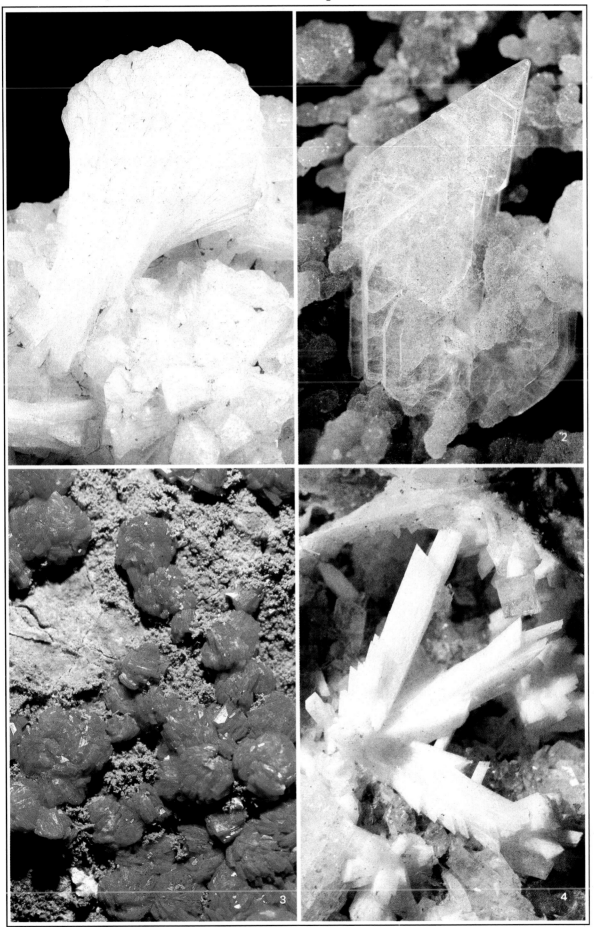

Serpentine

Silicate
$Mg_3Si_2O_5(OH)_4$

273

L

P

From the Latin *serpens* – snake (French 1753)

● Hardness: 3–4 ● Streak: white, grey ● Colour: green, yellow, brown, black and red ● Transparency: translucent ● Lustre: greasy, dull ● Cleavage: good on (001) ● Fracture: conchoidal ● Morphology: microcrystalline, massive, scaly and fibrous aggregates ● Specific gravity: 2.5–2.6 ● Crystal system: monoclinic ● Crystal form: plates, scales, fibres ● Luminescence: white in long-wave UV ● Chemical composition: MgO 43.0%, SiO_2 44.1%, H_2O 12.9% ● Chemical properties: in a blowpipe flame not readily fusible; soluble in HCl and H_2SO_4 ● Handling: clean with water ● Similar minerals: talc **(41)** ● Distinguishing features: solubility in acids, hardness ● Genesis: hydrothermal-metasomatic in ultrabasic rocks ● Associated minerals: chromite **(371)**, quartz **(534)** ● Occurrence: common; (FRG), (Czech Republic), (Slovakia), (Switzerland), (Austria), (Norway), (Great Britain), (Russia), (USA), (Iran), (Zimbabwe), (RSA) ● Application: as a precious stone.

Antigorite

Silicate
$Mg_3Si_2O_5(OH)_4$

274

P

Named after its locality Antigorio (Italy) (Schweizer 1840)

● Hardness: 3–4 (brittle) ● Streak: greenish-white ● Colour: green, grey, bluish, brown, black ● Transparency: translucent to opaque ● Lustre: vitreous, greasy ● Cleavage: very good on (001) ● fracture: scales and plates are brittle ● Morphology: crystals, massive, scaly and platy aggregates ● Specific gravity: 2.5–2.6 ● Crystal system: monoclinic ● Crystal form: plates, scales ● Chemical composition: same as serpentine **(273)** ● Chemical properties: not readily fusible; soluble in HCl and H_2SO_4 ● Handling: clean with water and diluted acids ● Similar minerals: talc **(41)**, chlorites ● Distinguishing features: solubility in acids, hardness, flexibility ● Genesis: hydrothermal (because of alteration in ultrabasic rocks) ● Associated minerals: carbonates, chromite **(371)**, titanite **(430)**, quartz **(534)** ● Occurrence: common; Antigorio (Italy), Sprechenstein (Austria), (FRG), (Norway), (Finland), (USA), (Russia), (RSA) ● Application: sometimes used as a precious stone.

Chrysotile

Silicate
$Mg_3Si_2O_5(OH)_4$

275

L

P

From the Greek *chrysos* – gold and *tilos* – fibre (Kobell 1834)

● Hardness: 3–4 ● Streak: white, grey ● Colour: grey-blue, grey-yellow, yellow, greenish ● Transparency: translucent ● Lustre: silky ● Cleavage: along fibres ● Morphology: fibrous aggregates ● Specific gravity: 2.5–2.6 ● Crystal system: monoclinic ● Crystal form: fibres ● Luminescence: cream in long-wave UV ● Chemical composition: same as serpentine **(273)** ● Chemical properties: in a blowpipe flame infusible; when heated becomes white; soluble in HCl, forming a fibrous sublimate of SiO_2 ● Handling: clean with water and ultrasonically ● Similar minerals: brucite – nemalite variety **(92)**, tremolite **(412)** ● Distinguishing features: hardness, solubility in acids, X-rays, chemical properties ● Genesis: hydrothermal by alteration of ultrabasic rocks ● Associated minerals: serpentine, tremolite, olivine **(524)** ● Occurrence: common; (Italy), (Czech Republic), (Russia), Quebec (Canada), (Zimbabwe), (RSA) ● Application: fire-proofing and insulating materials, paper industry; sometimes used as a precious stone.

---

1. **Antigorite** – fibrous aggregate; Dobamirei (Rhodopy, Bulgaria) 2. **Chrysotile** – fibrous aggregate in crack in serpentinite; Dobšiná (Slovakia – width of field 63 mm)

Zinnwaldite (Lithionite)

Silicate
K(Li,Fe^{2+},Al)$_3$(AlSi$_3$)O$_{10}$(OH)$_2$

276

Named after its locality Zinnwald (now Cínovec) (Ore Mountains, (Czech Republic) (Haidinger 1845)

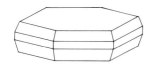

● Hardness: 2.5−4 (brittle) ● Streak: white ● Colour: light brown, silvery-white, grey, yellowish, greenish ● Transparency: transparent to translucent ● Lustre: pearly ● Cleavage: very good on (001) ● Other features of cohesion: flexible ● Morphology: crystals, scaly and platy aggregates ● Specific gravity: 2.9−3.1 ● Crystal system: monoclinic ● Crystal form: plates, scales ● Chemical composition: variable ● Chemical properties: readily fusible into dark, slightly magnetic glass; colours flame red; soluble in acids ● Handling: clean with distilled water ● Similar minerals: lepidolite (169) ● Distinguishing features: lepidolite fuses into white enamel ● Genesis: hydrothermal, pneumatolytic ● Associated minerals: fluorite (291), wolframite (369), quartz (534), cassiterite (548), topaz (595) ● Occurrence: rare; Epprechstein (FRG), Cínovec (Czech Republic), Cornwall (Great Britain), California (USA) ● Application: occasionally as source of Li.

Chamosite

Silicate
(Fe^{2+},Mg,Fe^{3+})$_5$Al(Si$_3$Al)O$_{10}$(OH,O)$_8$

277

Named after its locality Chamoson (Switzerland) (Berthier 1820)

● Hardness: 3 ● Streak: grey-green ● Colour: grey, grey-green, brown, green-black ● Transparency: opaque ● Lustre: vitreous, dull ● Cleavage: absent ● Fracture: uneven ● Morphology: massive, granular and oolitic aggregates, powdered ● Specific gravity: 3.0−3.4 ● Crystal system: monoclinic ● Chemical composition: variable ● Chemical properties: in a blowpipe flame: in oxidizing flame turns red, in reducing flame turns black (magnetic glass); soluble in HCl ● Handling: clean with distilled water ● Similar minerals: delessite (163), thuringite (164) ● Distinguishing features: X-rays and chemical properties ● Genesis: sedimentary ● Associated minerals: calcite (217), siderite (306), limonite (355), magnetite (367) ● Occurrence: common; Schmiedefeld and Wittmansgereuth (FRG), Chamoson (Switzerland), Lotharingia (France), Nučice and Chrustenice (Czech Republic) ● Application: Fe ore.

Astrophyllite

Silicate
(K$_2$,Na$_2$,Ca)Fe^{2+},Mn)$_4$(Ti,Zr)Si$_4$O$_{14}$(OH)$_2$

278

From the Greek *aster* − star and *fýllon* − leaf (Scheerer 1854)

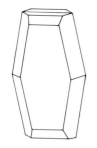

● Hardness: 3.5 (brittle) ● Streak: yellowish-brown ● Colour: brown, brownish-red ● Transparency: transparent to translucent ● Lustre: pearly to metallic ● Cleavage: perfect on (001) ● Other features of cohesion: flexible ● Morphology: crystals, platy, stellate aggregates ● Specific gravity: 3.3−3.4 ● Crystal system: triclinic ● Crystal form: plates, scales and needles ● Chemical composition: complex and variable ● Chemical properties: readily fusible into a black magnetic ball; soluble in HCl and H$_2$SO$_4$ ● Handling: clean with distilled water ● Similar minerals: lamprophyllite (170) ● Distinguishing features: fusing, X-rays and chemical properties ● Genesis: magmatic, pegmatitic, metamorphic ● Associated minerals: amphiboles, micas, zircon (587) ● Occurrence: rare; (Norway), (Russia), (Canada), (USA), (Guinea), (Greenland).

---

1. Zinnwaldite – cleavage aggregates (to 10 mm) with quartz; Cínovec (Czech Republic) **2. Chamosite** – granular to compact aggregate; Wittmansgereuth (FRG – width of field 48 mm) **3. Astrophyllite** – embedded columnar crystal (8 mm); Khibinsk (Kola Peninsula, Russia)

Zinnwaldite, chamosite, astrophyllite

Iron

279

Historical name

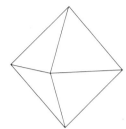

● Hardness: 4–5 ● Streak: grey, glossy ● Colour: steel-grey ● Transparency: opaque ● Lustre: metallic ● Cleavage: perfect on (001) ● Fracture: hackly ● Morphology: crystals, spongy and microcrystalline aggregates, grains, impregnations ● Specific gravity: 7.88 (native Fe) ● Crystal system: cubic ● Crystal form: unknown in nature. Terrestrial and meteoric iron are known ● Magnetism: strong ● Chemical composition: theoretically Fe 100%; admixture Ni ● Chemical properties: soluble in HCl and HNO_3 ● Handling: clean with distilled water ● Similar minerals: platinum **(281)** ● Distinguishing features: magnetism, hardness, specific gravity ● Genesis: magmatic, meteorites ● Associated minerals: pentlandite **(194)**, pyrrhotite **(283)**, olivine **(524)** ● Occurrence: rare; terrestrial – Bühl near Kassel – dendritic in pieces weighing 5 kg in basalts (FRG), Disco Island – masses of up to 25 tons (Greenland), Antrim (Northern Ireland), (New Zealand). Meteoritic – mostly iron and stony-iron meteorites.

Nickel

280

From the German *Nickel* – rogue (Ramdor 1967)

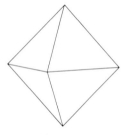

● Hardness: 4.5–5.5 ● Streak: grey-white ● Colour: grey-white, silvery-white ● Transparency: opaque ● Lustre: metallic ● Fracture: hackly ● Morphology: crystals, granules ● Specific gravity: 8.9 (Ni); 7.8–8.2 (Ni, Fe) ● Crystal system: cubic ● Chemical composition: theoretically Ni 100%; admixture Fe ● Chemical properties: slightly soluble in acids ● Genesis: ultrabasic rocks, meteorites ● Associated minerals: iron **(279)** ● Occurrence: rare; (only in New Zealand – Bogota region) in the form of idiomorphic grains in heazlewoodite; nickel with admixture of Fe occurs in meteoric glass in Henbury and in mineral samples brought from the Moon.

Platinum

281

From the Spanish *plata* – silver (Ulloa 1748)

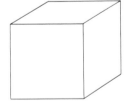

● Hardness: 4–4.5 ● Streak: steel-grey, silvery-white ● Colour: steel-grey, silvery-white ● Transparency: opaque ● Lustre: metallic ● Fracture: hackly ● Morphology: rarely crystals, grains, lumps (nuggets), irregular masses ● Other properties: ductile, malleable ● Specific gravity: 14–19 (nat. Pt 21.5) ● Crystal system: cubic ● Crystal form: rarely cubes ● Magnetism: magnetic if it contains Fe ● Chemical composition: theoretically 100% Pt; almost always admixtures: Fe, Ir, Pd, Rh, Ni, Os ● Chemical properties: soluble only in aqua regia; fuses at 1773.5 °C ● Handling: clean with acids ● Similar minerals: iron **(279)** ● Distinguishing features: solubility in acids, specific gravity ● Genesis: magmatic (ultrabasic rocks), talus piles ● Associated minerals: ilmenite **(365)**, magnetite **(367)**, chromite **(371)** ● Occurrence: rare; Nizhni Tagil, Central Urals and Norilsk (Russia), Sudbury – Ontario (Canada), Bushveld (RSA), (Colombia), (Ethiopia) ● Application: jewellery, electrotechnology and chemistry.

---

1. Platinum – alluvial nugget; Nizhni Tagil (Russia) **2. Iron and Nickel** – polished section of meteorite with Widmanstaetten figures; lighter lamellae are formed of taenite (γ – NiFe), darker lamellae of kamacite (FeNi); (width of field 45 mm)

Platinum, iron, nickel

Hauerite

Sulphide
MnS$_2$

282

Named after the Austrian geologists, J. R. Hauer (1778–1863) and F. R. Hauer (1822–1899) (Haidinger 1846)

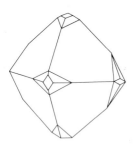

● Hardness: 4 ● Streak: red-brown ● Colour: brownish-grey, brownish-black ● Transparency: opaque to translucent ● Lustre: adamantine, submetallic, metallic ● Cleavage: perfect on (100) ● Fracture: uneven, subconchoidal ● Morphology: crystals, grains, rarely massive aggregates ● Specific gravity: 3.5 ● Crystal system: cubic ● Crystal form: octahedra, dodecahedra ● Chemical composition: Mn 46.14%, S 53.86% ● Chemical properties: fusible, soluble in HCl ● Handling: clean with water or diluted acids, except HCl ● Similar minerals: pyrite **(436)** ● Distinguishing features: test for Mn, X-rays ● Genesis: sedimentary, exhalations ● Associated minerals: sulphur **(1)**, gypsum **(29)**, pyrite, marcasite **(437)** ● Occurrence: rare; Kalinka (Slovakia), Raddusa (Italy), Chiaturi (Georgia), Texas and Louisiana (USA).

Pyrrhotite (Magnetic pyrites)

Sulphide
FeS

283

From the Greek *pyrrótes* – reddish (Breithaupt 1835)

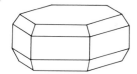

● Hardness: 4 (brittle) ● Streak: grey-black ● Colour: yellowish-brown, bronze, in air tarnishes tombac colour ● Transparency: opaque ● Lustre: metallic ● Cleavage: imperfect on (0001) and (11$\bar{2}$0) ● Fracture: uneven ● Morphology: crystals, granular, massive, platy aggregates ● Specific gravity: 4.6 ● Crystal system: hexagonal ● Crystal form: plates, seldom dipyramidal, barrel-shaped ● Magnetism: paramagnetic ● Electric conductivity: good ● Chemical composition: Fe 63.53%, S 36.47% ● Chemical properties: on charcoal fuses into black magnetic mass; soluble in HCl, and HNO$_3$ (partly) ● Handling: clean with diluted acids which should be washed off with water ● Similar minerals: chalcopyrite **(185)**, bornite **(192)** ● Distinguishing features: hardness, magnetism, chemical properties, X-rays ● Genesis: magmatic, hydrothermal, contact, metamorphic, meteoric ● Associated minerals: chalcopyrite, marcasite, pyrite **(436)** ● Occurrence: common; Freiberg, Bodenmais, Horbach, Schauinsland and Waldsassen (FRG), Trepča (Serbia), Chiusbaia (Romania), Sudbury – Ontario (Canada), Norilsk (Russia) ● Application: sometimes as Fe ore.

Stannite (Tin pyrites, Bell metal ore)

Sulphide
Cu$_2$FeSnS$_4$

284

From the Latin *stannum* – tin (Beudant 1832)

● Hardness: 4 (brittle) ● Streak: black ● Colour: steel-grey, on freshly fractured surface olive green ● Transparency: opaque ● Lustre: metallic, quickly becomes dull ● Cleavage: imperfect on (110) ● Fracture: conchoidal, uneven ● Morphology: massive, fine crystalline, crystals are rare ● Specific gravity: 4.3–4.5 ● Crystal system: tetragonal ● Crystal form: tetrahedral, scalenohedra, often twins ● Chemical composition: Cu 29.58%, Fe 12.99%, Sn 27.61%, S 29.82% ● Chemical properties: on charcoal fuses, becomes white; soluble in HNO$_3$, colouring the solution blue ● Handling: clean with distilled water ● Similar minerals: tetrahedrite **(190)** ● Distinguishing features: colour, X-rays, chemical properties ● Genesis: hydrothermal ● Associated minerals: tetrahedrite, arsenopyrite **(344)**, pyrite **(436)**, cassiterite **(548)** ● Occurrence: common; Freiberg and Zinnwald (FRG), Cínovec (Czech Republic), Cornwall (Great Britain), (Russia), Tasmania (Australia), Oruro and Llallagua (Bolivia) ● Application: sometimes as Sn ore.

---

1. **Hauerite** – octahedral crystal with sulphur (10 mm); Vigl'ašská Huta (Slovakia) 2. **Pyrrhotite** – easily cleavable pseudohexagonal crystals (to 20 mm); Chiuzbaia (Romania)

Renierite

Sulphide
Cu₃(Fe, Ge)S₄

285

Named after the Belgian geologist, A. Reniér (Vaes 1948)

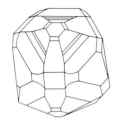

● Hardness: 4.5 (brittle) ● Streak: dark grey to black ● Colour: bronze-yellow, pink-brown ● Transparency: opaque ● Lustre: metallic ● Cleavage: absent ● Fracture: uneven ● Morphology: crystals, granular aggregates ● Specific gravity: 4.3 ● Crystal system: tetragonal ● Crystal form: tetrahedra, hexahedra, rhombododecahedra ● Magnetism: strong ● Chemical composition: variable; forms isomorphous series with germanite **(188)** in ratio Fe:Ge = 1:1, or 1:2 (germanite), or 2:1 (renierite) ● Chemical properties: soluble in HNO_3 ● Handling: clean with distilled water ● Similar minerals: germanite, bornite **(192)** ● Distinguishing features: hardness, X-rays, chemical properties ● Genesis: hydrothermal ● Associated minerals: enargite **(187)**, germanite, tetrahedrite **(190)**, bornite ● Occurrence: rare; Kipushi (Congo), Tsumeb – crystals measuring 1.5 mm (Namibia), Dastakert (Armenia).

Gudmundite

Sulphide
FeSbS

286

Named after its locality Gudmundstorp (Sweden) (Johansson 1928)

● Hardness: 4 ● Streak: black ● Colour: silvery-white ● Transparency: opaque ● Lustre: splendent, metallic ● Cleavage: absent ● Fracture: uneven ● Morphology: crystals, crystalline aggregates ● Specific gravity: 6.72 ● Crystal system: monoclinic ● Crystal form: prisms, often twins ● Chemical composition: Fe 26.83%, Sb 57.76%, S 15.41% ● Chemical properties: soluble in HNO_3 ● Handling: clean with distilled water ● Similar minerals: arsenopyrite **(344)** ● Distinguishing features: hardness, test for Sb ● Genesis: hydrothermal ● Associated minerals: stibnite **(51)**, pyrrhotite **(283)**, arsenopyrite ● Occurrence: rare; Waldsassen (FRG), Gudmundstorp and Boliden (Sweden), Sulitälma (Norway), Kutná Hora, Příbram (Czech Republic), Pezinok (Slovakia), Nikko (Japan), Broken Hill (Australia), Turhal (Turkey).

Safflorite

Sulphide
CoAs₂

287

From the German *Safflor* – dyer's saffron (Breithaupt 1835)

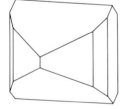

● Hardness: 4.5–5.5 (brittle) ● Streak: grey-black ● Colour: tin-white, grey-white, becomes dark after some time ● Transparency: opaque ● Lustre: metallic ● Cleavage: imperfect on (010) ● Fracture: conchoidal, uneven ● Morphology: rarely crystals, massive, granular or radiating aggregates ● Specific gravity: 6.9–7.3 ● Crystal system: monoclinic ● Crystal form: short and long prisms (similar to arsenopyrite), sometimes twins ● Electric conductivity: very good ● Chemical composition: Co 28.23%, As 71.77%; admixtures: Fe, Ni and S ● Chemical properties: on charcoal fuses; soluble in HNO_3 (pink solution) ● Handling: clean with distilled water or HCl ● Similar minerals: arsenopyrite **(344)**, chloanthite **(346)**, skutterudite **(438)** ● Distinguishing features: X-rays, chemical properties ● Genesis: hydrothermal ● Associated minerals: löllingite **(350)**, skutterudite ● Occurrence: rare; Wittichen, Schneeberg and Niederramstadt (FRG), Jáchymov (Czech Republic), (Sweden), (Italy), (Russia), Cobalt – Ontario (Canada) ● Application: sometimes as Co ore.

---

1. **Gudmundite** – granular aggregate in darker antimonite; Turhal (Turkey – width of field 46 mm) 2. **Safflorite** – radiating fibrous aggregate (20 mm); Schneeberg (FRG)

Gudmundite, safflorite

Hodrushite

$Cu_8Bi_{12}S_{22}$

288

Named after its locality Hodruša (Slovakia) (Kupčík 1968)

● Hardness: 4−4.5 (brittle) ● Streak: grey-black ● Colour: steel-grey, on a fresh fracture yellowish, bronze-yellow coating ● Transparency: opaque ● Lustre: metallic ● Cleavage: absent ● Morphology: crystals, finely granular aggregates, irregular grains ● Specific gravity ● 6.45 ● Crystal system: monoclinic ● Crystal form: needles ● Chemical composition: Cu 13.66%, Bi 67.39%, S 18.95% ● Chemical properties: soluble in ,HNO_3 ● Handling: clean with distilled water ● Similar minerals: emplectite **(69)**, bismutite **(71)** ● Distinguishing features: X-rays, chemical properties ● Genesis: hydrothermal ● Associated minerals: chalcopyrite **(185)**, hematite **(472)**, quartz **(534)**, bismutite ● Occurrence: rare; Hodruša (Slovakia).

Heyrovskyite

Sulphide
$Pb_6Bi_2S_9$

289

Called after the Czech chemist, J. Heyrovský (1890−1967) (Klomínský 1971)

● Hardness: 4−4.5 ● Streak: grey-black ● Colour: tin-white (on fresh fracture) ● Transparency: opaque ● Lustre: metallic ● Cleavage: absent ● Morphology: crystals ● Specific gravity: 7.18 ● Crystal system: orthorhombic ● Crystal form: needles ● Chemical composition: Pb 63.76%, Bi 21.44%, S 14.80% ● Chemical properties: soluble in HNO_3 ● Handling: clean with distilled water ● Similar minerals: cosalite **(72)** ● Distinguishing features: hardness, X-rays, chemical properties ● Genesis: hydrothermal ● Associated minerals: molybdenite **(8)**, galena **(77)**, pyrite **(436)**, quartz **(534)** ● Occurrence: rare; Hůrky (Czech Republic), Furka (Switzerland).

Prosopite

Halide
$CaAl_2(F,OH)_8$

290

L

From the Greek *prósopon* − mask (Scheerer 1853)

● Hardness: 4.5 (brittle) ● Streak: white ● Colour: white, greenish, reddish ● Transparency: transparent to translucent ● Lustre: vitreous, dull, greasy ● Cleavage: perfect on (111) ● Fracture: uneven, conchoidal ● Morphology: crystals, granular aggregates ● Specific gravity: 2.89 ● Crystal system: monoclinic ● Crystal form: plates ● Luminescence: when crushed exhibits golden-yellow light (Altenberg region) ● Chemical composition: Ca 16.84%, Al 22.66%, F 31.92%, OH 28.58% ● Chemical properties: soluble in hot H_2SO_4; in flame spills and quickly becomes white but does not fuse ● Handling: clean with distilled water ● Genesis: hydrothermal ● Associated minerals: fluorite **(291)**, siderite **(306)**, hematite **(472)** ● Occurrence: rare; Altenberg − crystals measuring 3 cm (FRG), Pikes Peak − Colorado (USA), Ivigtut (Greenland).

1. **Hodrushite** − aggregate of fine needles (to 2 mm) with chalcopyrite and quartz in polished section; Hodruša (Slovakia) 2. **Heyrovskyite** − crystalline aggregate; Hůrky (Czech Republic − width of field 25 mm)

Hodrushite, heyrovskyite

Fluorite (Fluor spar)

291

From the Latin *fluore* – to flow (Napione 1797)

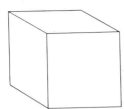

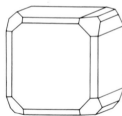

● Hardness: 4 (brittle) ● Streak: white ● Colour: white, yellow, green, violet-red, pink, exceptionally blue or black (anthozonite); some specimens change colour, when heated becomes discoloured ● Transparency: transparent ● Lustre: vitreous ● Cleavage: perfect on (111) ● Morphology: crystals, granular aggregates and earthy masses ● Specific gravity: 3.18 ● Crystal system: cubic ● Crystal form: cubes, hexahedra, octahedra and their combinations, orthorhombic dodecahedra, rarely twins ● Luminescence: blue to violet in UV light; when heated phosphoresces (thermoluminescence) ● Chemical composition: Ca 51.33%, F 48.67%; admixtures: Cl, rare earths ● Chemical properties: soluble in H$_2$SO$_4$, forming HF (*NB* etches glass and optical glass) ● Handling: clean with distilled water or diluted HCl; easily damaged when cleaned mechanically ● Similar minerals: cryolite **(88)**, senarmontite **(93)**, baryte **(240)**, apatite **(379)**, amethyst **(536)** ● Distinguishing features: hardness is high, compared with bromargyrite, cryolite, senarmontite and baryte; low, compared with apatite and amethyst; perfect cleavage ● Genesis: hydrothermal, in pegmatites, pneumatolytic, in alpine fissures, sedimentary ● Associated minerals: galena **(77)**, sphalerite **(181)**, calcite **(217)**, dolomite **(218)**, baryte, apatite, cassiterite **(548)**, tourmaline **(564)** ● Occurrence: common; Badenweiler, Wölsendorf and Freiberg – light yellow crystals (FRG), (Switzerland – octahedra in alpine fissures), Horní Slavkov, Moldava, Harrachov and Litice (Czech Republic), Durham and Cumberland – violet, etc. crystals in galena veins (Great Britain), (Norway), Bergamo (Italy), Mikhalkovo (Bulgaria), Newfoundland (Canada), Rosiclaire – Illinois, Salem – Kentucky, Westmoreland – New Hampshire and Jefferson Co. – New York (USA) (Australia), (Chile), (Mongolia) ● Application: fluorite was used by the (USA), (Australia), (Chile), (Mongolia) ● Application: fluorite was used by the ancient Greeks for the manufacture of fine vessels and vases known as *vasa murrhina*. At pressent it is used in metallurgy, chemistry, the glass industry and optics. Some types are used as precious stones (facets, cabochons), but they are soft and cleave readily.

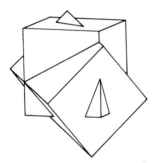

Fluorite – octahedral crystal (40 mm) composed of twin cubes developed on quartz and siderite; Horní Slavkov (Czech Republic)

Fluorite

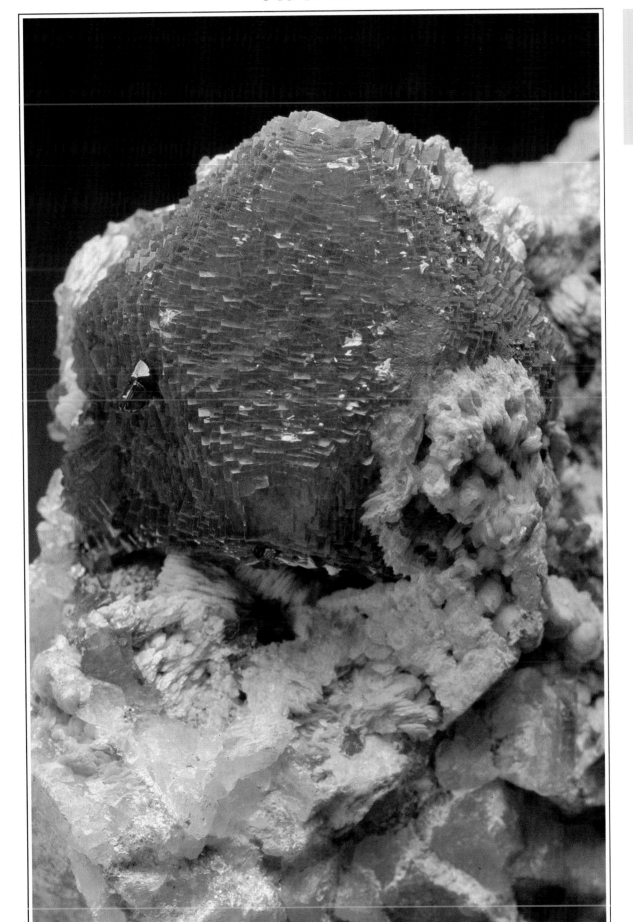

Stibiconite

Oxide
SbSb$_2$O$_6$(OH)

292

From the Latin *stibium* – antimony and the Greek *konis* – powder (Brush 1862)

● Hardness: 3–7 (varies considerably in powdered to massive aggregates) ● Streak: light yellow, white ● Colour: light yellow, yellow, white, brownish-yellow ● Transparency: transparent to translucent ● Lustre: vitreous, greasy, dull ● Cleavage: unknown ● Fracture: uneven, earthy ● Morphology: earthy, compact, crusty and powdered aggregates, pseudomorphs after stibnite ● Specific gravity: 4.1–5.8 ● Crystal system: cubic ● Chemical composition: Sb 76.37%, O 21.75%, H$_2$O 1.88% (variable) ● Chemical properties: soluble in acids; on charcoal with soda forms a white sublimate ● Handling: clean carefully with distilled water ● Similar minerals: bindheimite **(293)**, cervantite **(294)**, roméite **(361)** ● Distinguishing features: X-rays, chemical properties ● Genesis: secondary in Sb deposits ● Associated minerals: antimonite **(51)**, cervantite, romeite ● Occurrence: rare; Goldkronach and Neubulach (FRG), Sonora (Mexico), Sikwanshan (China), Algiers (Algeria), Cajamarca (Peru), (Russia), (USA), (Australia).

Bindheimite

Oxide
Pb$_2$Sb(O,OH,F,H$_2$O)$_7$

293

Named after the German chemist, J. J. Bindheim (1750–1825) (Dana 1868)

● Hardness: 4–4.5 ● Streak: lighter than colour ● Colour: yellow, greenish-yellow, green, brownish, white, grey ● Transparency: translucent to opaque ● Lustre: greasy, dull ● Cleavage: absent ● Fracture: conchoidal ● Morphology: earthy, powdered, massive, cryptocrystalline aggregates, crusts, pseudomorphs ● Specific gravity: 4.6–7.3 ● Crystal system: cubic ● Crystal form: unknown ● Chemical composition: variable ● Chemical properties: soluble in HCl and HNO$_3$; on charcoal forms a metallic ball of Pb ● Handling: clean ultrasonically ● Similar minerals: stibiconite **(292)** ● Distinguishing features: reaction to form Pb, X-rays, chemical properties ● Genesis: secondary in Pb-Sb deposits ● Associated minerals: boulangerite **(55)**, tetrahedrite **(190)**, bournonite **(193)** ● Occurrence: rare; Adlersbachtal, Wildschapbachtal and Welchensteinach (FRG), Rudník (Slovakia), Oberzeiring (Austria), San Bernardino Co. – California (USA), Broken Hill (Australia), Nerchinsk (Russia).

Cervantite

Oxide
Sb$_2$O$_4$

294

Named after its locality Cervantes (Spain) (Dana 1854)

● Hardness: 4–5 ● Streak: lighter than colour ● Colour: yellow, orange-yellow, white ● Transparency: translucent ● Lustre: greasy, dull, pearly ● Cleavage: perfect on (001) ● Fracture: conchoidal ● Morphology: finely granular, massive, earthy aggregates, rarely crystals ● Specific gravity: 6.5–6.6 ● Crystal system: orthorhombic ● Crystal form: needles ● Chemical composition: Sb 79.19%, O 20.81% ● Chemical properties: infusible, slightly soluble in HCl ● Handling: clean ultrasonically ● Similar minerals: valentinite **(94)**, stibiconite **(292)** ● Distinguishing features: specific gravity, fusibility, X-rays, chemical properties ● Genesis: secondary in Sb deposits ● Associated minerals: stibnite **(51)**, valentinite, stibiconite ● Occurrence: common; Clara Mine near Oberwolfach (FRG), Cervantes (Spain), Pereta (Italy), Baia Sprie (Romania), Pocca (Bolivia) ● Application: sometimes as Sb ore.

---

1. Bindheimite – pseudomorph after Pb-Sb sulphosalt; Nerchinsk (Russia – width of field 15 mm) **2. Stibiconite** – encrustations on antimonite; Malá Lehota (Slovakia – width of field 60 mm) **3. Cervantite** – reniform crust on antimonite crystal; Baia Sprie (Romania – width of field 36 mm)

Bindheimite, stibiconite, cervantite

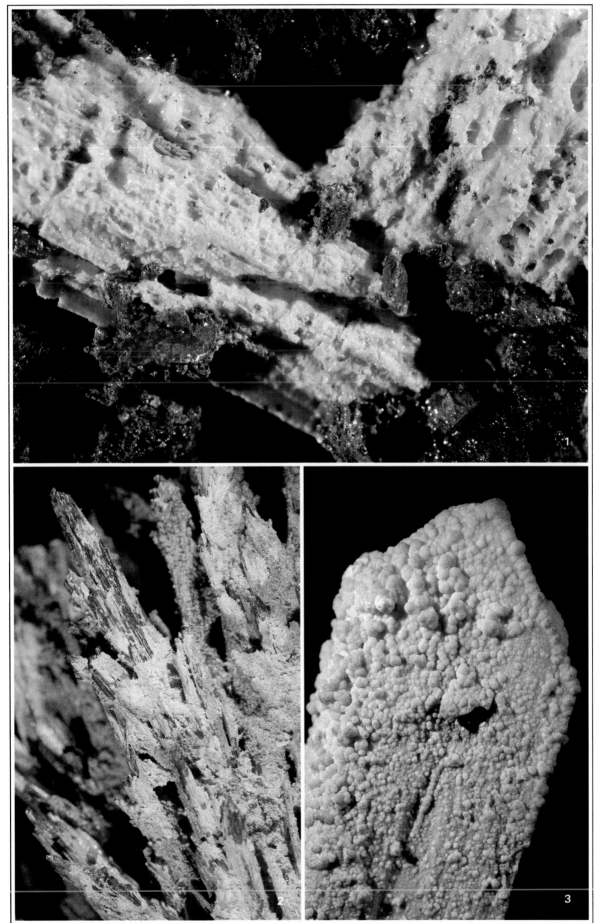

Manganite (Brown manganese ore)

Hydroxide
γ – MnOOH

295

Named after its chemical composition
(Haidinger 1827)

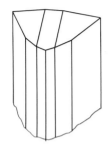

● Hardness: 4 (brittle) ● Streak: dark brown ● Colour: black, grey, brownish-black ● Transparency: opaque, in thin lamellae red translucence ● Lustre: submetallic, dull ● Cleavage: perfect on (010) ● Fracture: uneven ● Morphology: crystals, granular, earthy, acicular, radiating-fibrous aggregates, coatings, concretions ● Specific gravity: 4.3–4.4 ● Crystal system: monoclinic ● Crystal form: prisms, needles (vertically striated), twins ● Chemical composition: Mn_2O_3 89.76%, H_2O 10.24%, (Mn 62.47%) ● Chemical properties: in blowpipe flame infusible; soluble in HCl ● Handling: clean with water; black coatings cleaned ultrasonically ● Similar minerals: antimonite **(51)** ● Distinguishing features: hardness, streak ● Genesis: hydrothermal, sedimentary ● Associated minerals: calcite **(217)**, baryte **(240)**, hematite **(472**, pyrolusite **(474)** ● Occurrence: common; Clara Mine near Oberwolfach, Ilfeld (FRG), Cornwall (Great Britain), (Ukraine), Brideville (Canada), Långban (Sweden), (India), (Australia), (Brazil), (China) ● Application: Mn ore.

Zincite (Red oxide of zinc)

Oxide
ZnO

296

P

Named after its chemical composition
(Haidinger 1845)

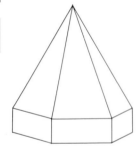

● Hardness: 4.5–5 (brittle) ● Streak: orange-yellow, brownish-yellow ● Colour: red, reddish-yellow, reddish-brown ● Transparency: translucent to opaque ● Lustre: adamantine, submetallic ● Cleavage: perfect on (0001) ● Fracture: conchoidal ● Morphology: rarely crystals, granular, lamellar aggregates ● Specific gravity: 5.4–5.7 ● Crystal system: hexagonal ● Magnetism: diamagnetic ● Chemical composition: Zn 80.34%, O 19.66% ● Chemical properties: infusible in blowpipe flame; soluble in acids ● Handling: clean with distilled water ● Similar minerals: cinnabar **(76)**, rutile **(464)** ● Distinguishing features: hardness, specific gravity, test for Zn ● Genesis: hydrothermal, contact-metamorphic ● Associated minerals: calcite **(217)**, willemite **(404)**, franklinite **(470)**, rhodonite **(531)** ● Occurrence: rare; Schneeberg (FRG), Olkusz (Poland), Bottino (Italy), Kučajna (Serbia), Franklin – New Jersey (USA) ● Application: rarely as Zn ore; also used as a precious stone.

Betafite

Oxide
$(Ca,Na,U)_2(Ti,Nb,Ta)_2O_6(OH)$

297

R

Named after its locality Betafo (Malagasy Republic)
(Lacroix 1912)

● Hardness: 3–5.5 ● Streak: yellow, white ● Colour: brown, black, brownish-green, yellow ● Transparency: opaque ● Lustre: greasy, vitreous ● Cleavage: absent ● Fracture: conchoidal ● Morphology: crystals, massive, granular and crusty aggregates ● Specific gravity: 3.7–5 ● Crystal system: cubic, a member of the pyrochlore group ● Crystal form: octahedra, dodecahedra ● Radioactivity: sometimes strong ● Chemical composition: variable and unstable ● Chemical properties: soluble in acids; edges fuse with blowpipe and it turns black ● Handling: clean with distilled water ● Genesis: pegmatites, carbonates ● Associated minerals: xenotime **(324)**, monazite **(383)**, allanite **(410)**, euxenite **(471)** ● Occurrence: rare; (Russia), (Brazil), (Canada), (USA), (Malagasy Republic).

---

1. **Manganite** – prismatic vertically striated crystals (15 mm); Ilfeld (Harz, FRG) 2. **Zincite** – granular aggregate (12 mm) in calcite; Franklin (New Jersey, USA) 3. **Betafite** – massive aggregate; Impilanti (Finland – width of field 40 mm)

Manganite, zincite, betafite

Brannerite

298

Named after the American geologist, G. Branner (1850–1922) (Hess, Wells 1920)

● Hardness: approx. 4.5 ● Streak: dark brown, green-brown ● Colour: black ● Transparency: opaque; in thin slabs translucent (brown-violet and yellow) ● Lustre: sub-metallic, adamantine, greasy ● Cleavage: unknown ● Fracture: uneven, conchoidal ● Morphology: crystals, isometric grains, pseudomorphs ● Specific gravity: 6.35 ● Crystal system: monoclinic ● Crystal form: prisms, isometric ● Magnetism: slight ● Radioactivity: strong ● Chemical composition: variable; UO$_2$ 62.83%, TiO$_2$ 37.17% (theoretically for UTi$_2$O$_6$) ● Chemical properties: soluble in hot HNO$_3$, and H$_2$SO$_4$ ● Handling: clean with distilled water ● Similar minerals: allanite **(410)** ● Distinguishing features: hardness, X-rays and chemical properties ● Genesis: magmatic, in pegmatites, talus material ● Associated minerals: ilmenite **(365)**, feldspars, apatite **(379)**, zircon **(587)** ● Occurrence: rare; Hornachuelos (Spain), Bou Azzer (Morocco), Kelley Gulch – Idaho (USA), Blind River Distr. – Ontario (Canada), (Australia), (RSA) ● Application: source of rare earths; U ore.

Bismite

299

Named after its chemical composition (Dana 1868)

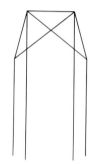

● Hardness: 4.5 ● Streak: grey-yellow, light yellow ● Colour: straw yellow, greenish-yellow, grey-white, grey-yellow ● Transparency: transparent to translucent ● Lustre: adamantine, earthy ● Cleavage: absent ● Fracture: uneven, conchoidal, earthy ● Morphology: granular, powdered, earthy, pseudomorphs ● Specific gravity: approx. 9 ● Crystal system: monoclinic ● Crystal form: prisms ● Chemical composition: Bi 89.68%, O 10.32% ● Chemical properties: soluble in HNO$_3$; on charcoal readily fusible, forming metallic Bi ● Genesis: secondary in oxidation zone ● Associated minerals: bismutite **(71)** ● Occurrence: rare; Wittichen, Schneeberg and Schwarzenberg (FRG), Jáchymov (Czech Republic), Berezovsk and Adrasman (Russia), Colavi (Bolivia).

Curite

300

Named after the French physicist, P. Curie (1859–1906) (Schoep 1921)

● Hardness: 4.5 (brittle) ● Streak: orange ● Colour: yellow, reddish-orange, brownish-yellow ● Transparency: translucent ● Lustre: adamantine ● Cleavage: good on (100) and (110) ● Morphology: crystals, fibrous, massive, granular aggregates, crusts, pseudomorphs ● Specific gravity: 7.19 ● Crystal system: orthorhombic ● Crystal form: needles ● Radioactivity: strong ● Chemical composition: PbO 22.10%, UO$_3$ 75.52%, H$_2$O 2.38% ● Chemical properties: readily soluble in acids; reacts to Pb ● Handling: clean with ultrasound ● Genesis: secondary in oxidation zones of U deposits ● Associated minerals: kasolite **(338)**, monazite **(383)**, allanite **(410)**, uraninite **(482)** ● Occurrence: rare; Wölsendorf and Menzenschwand (FRG), Puy-de-Dôme (France), Kasolo (Congo), Malakialina (Malagasy Republic), (Australia) ● Application: sometimes as U ore.

Curite – granular aggregate showing tarnish colours; Kasolo (Congo – width of field 43 mm)

Curite

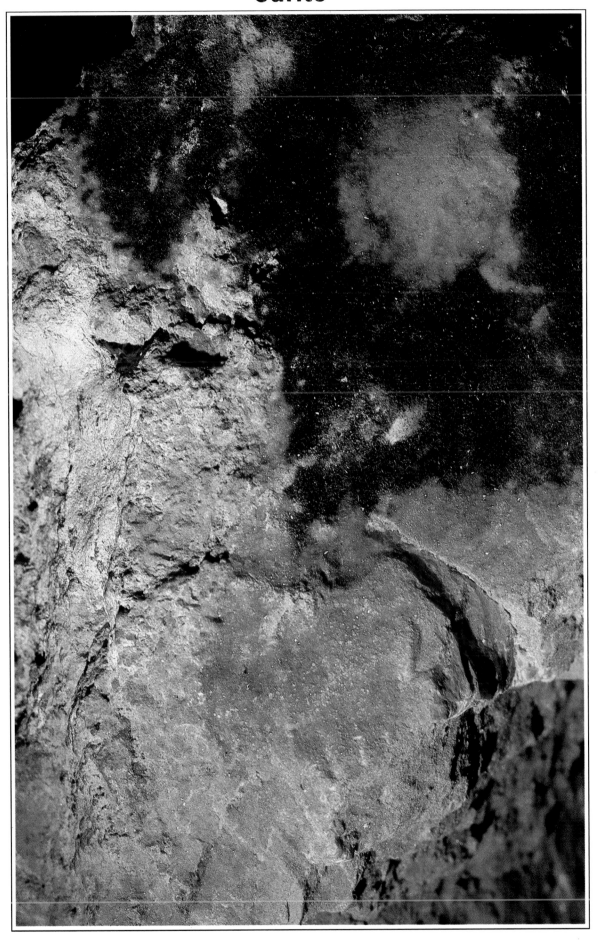

Curite

H
4—5

Colemanite

Borate
$CaB_3O_4(OH)_3 \cdot H_2O$

301

L

Named after the American businessman, W. T. Coleman (1824–1893) (Evans 1884)

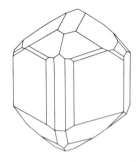

● Hardness: 4.5 ● Streak: white ● Colour: white, grey ● Transparency: transparent to translucent ● Lustre: vitreous ● Cleavage: perfect on (010), imperfect on (001) ● Fracture: uneven, subconchoidal ● Morphology: crystals, massive and granular aggregates ● Specific gravity: 2.4 ● Crystal system: monoclinic ● Crystal form: short prisms, pseudorhombohedra, isometric ● Luminescence: strong yellowish-white and greenish-white phosphorescence ● Chemical composition: CaO 27.28%, B_2O_3 50.81%, H_2O 21.91% ● Chemical properties: fusible in a blowpipe flame; soluble in hot HCl ● Handling: clean with distilled water ● Similar minerals: ulexite **(19)**, inyoite **(100)**, priceite **(212)**, datolite **(407)** ● Distinguishing features: hardness, specific gravity ● Genesis: sedimentary (borax lakes) ● Associated minerals: ulexite, gypsum **(29)**, calcite **(217)**, celestite **(239)** ● Occurrence: common; Inder (Kazakhstan), Eskisehir (Turkey), Jujuy (Argentina), Death Valley – California (USA) ● Application: borax ore.

Magnesite (Bitter spar)

Carbonate
$MgCO_3$

302

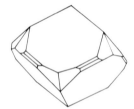

L

Named after its chemical composition (Karsten 1808)

● Hardness: 4–4.5 (brittle) ● Streak: white ● Colour: white, grey, yellow, brown, black ● Transparency: transparent to translucent ● Lustre: vitreous ● Cleavage: perfect on (10$\bar{1}$1) ● Fracture: conchoidal ● Morphology: crystals, massive, granular, porcellanic aggregates ● Specific gravity: approx. 3.0 ● Crystal system: trigonal ● Crystal form: rhombohedra, scalenohedra ● Luminescence: sometimes yellowish-white, greenish-white, blue-white; occasional triboluminescence ● Chemical composition: MgO 47.81%, CO_2 52.19%; admixtures; Ca, Mn, Fe (breunnerite variety) ● Chemical properties: breaks in blowpipe flame but does not fuse; soluble in hot acids ● Handling: clean with distilled water ● Similar minerals: calcite **(217)**, dolomite **(218)**, ankerite **(219)** ● Distinguishing features: optical and chemical properties, X-rays ● Genesis: metamorphic, hydrothermal, sedimentary ● Associated minerals: talc **(41)**, calcite, dolomite ● Occurrence: common; Zillertal, Pfitschtal, Veitsch, Kraubath and Trieben (Austria), Hrubšice (Czech Republic), Lubeník, Jelšava and Košice (Slovakia), Satka (Russia), Baldissero (Italy), (Serbia), (Norway), Euboea Island (Greece), Haicheng (China), Copley (Australia), Chewelah – Washington (USA), (Brazil) ● Application: metallurgy, rubber and paper industries.

---

1. **Colemanite** – milky-white radiating aggregates (up to 20 mm); Panderma (Turkey) 2. **Magnesite** – greyish crystals (20 mm) with dolomite and quartz; Ratkovská Suchá (Slovakia)

Colemanite, magnesite

Barytocalcite

Carbonate
BaCa(CO₃)₂

$$BaCa(CO_3)_2$$

303

L

Named after its chemical composition
(Brooke 1824)

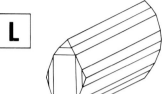

● Hardness: 4 (brittle) ● Streak: white ● Colour: white, yellow, grey, greenish ● Transparency: transparent to translucent ● Lustre: vitreous ● Cleavage: perfect on (110) ● Morphology: crystals, massive and granular aggregates ● Specific gravity: 3.66 ● Crystal system: monoclinic ● Crystal form: prisms ● Luminescence: dull, light yellow ● Chemical composition: BaO 51.56%, CaO 18.85%, CO_2 29.59% ● Chemical properties: in blowpipe flame spills; soluble in HCl ● Handling: clean with water ● Genesis: hydrothermal ● Associated minerals: calcite **(217)**, baryte **(240)**, fluorite **(291)** ● Occurrence: rare; Alston Moor (Great Britain), Badenweiler, Freiberg (FRG), Långban (Sweden).

Rhodochrosite (Manganese spar)

Carbonate
$MnCO_3$

304

L

P

From the Greek *rhódon* – rose and *chroma* – colour
(Hausmann 1813)

● Hardness: 4 (brittle) ● Streak: white ● Colour: pink, reddish-brown, grey ● Transparency: translucent ● Lustre: vitreous ● Cleavage: perfect on (10$\bar{1}$1) ● Fracture: uneven, conchoidal ● Morphology: crystals, granular, massive, reniform aggregates, encrustations ● Specific gravity: 3.3–3.6 ● Crystal system: trigonal ● Crystal form: rhombohedra, scalenohedra, plates, prismatic ● Luminescence: sometimes light pink in long-wave UV ● Chemical composition: MnO 61.71%, CO_2 38.29% ● Chemical properties: in flame becomes brown but does not fuse; soluble in warm acids ● Handling: clean with water or diluted HCl ● Similar minerals: dolomite **(218)**, rhodonite **(531)** ● Distinguishing features: hardness, specific gravity, solubility in acids ● Genesis: hydrothermal, contact-metasomatic, in pegmatites, sedimentary ● Associated minerals: galena **(77)**, sphalerite **(181)**, pyrite **(436)** ● Occurrence: common; Neubulach and Freiberg (FRG), Săcărâmb and Cavnic (Romania), Banská Štiavnica (Slovakia), Las Cabesses (France), Pasto Bueno (Peru), Colorado (USA), (Mexico), (Argentina), (Russia) ● Application: Mn source; used as a precious stone.

Bastnäsite

Carbonate
Ce[F | CO₃]

305

Named after its locality Bastnäs (Sweden)
(Huot 1841)

● Hardness: 4–4.5 ● Streak: white ● Colour: yellow, reddish-brown ● Transparency: transparent to translucent ● Lustre: vitreous, greasy ● Cleavage: imperfect on (10$\bar{1}$1), sometimes (0001) ● Fracture: uneven ● Morphology: crystals, massive and granular aggregates ● Specific gravity: 5.0 ● Crystal system: hexagonal ● Crystal form: plates ● Chemical composition: variable ● Chemical properties: infusible in flame, turns white and becomes opaque when heated; soluble in hot acids ● Handling: clean with water ● Genesis: in pegmatites, carbonates, contact-metasomatic environments ● Associated minerals: fluorite **(291)**, allanite **(410)** ● Occurrence: rare; Clara Mine near Oberwolfach (FRG), Bastnäs near Riddarhyttan (Sweden), Colorado and New Mexico (USA), (Malagasy Republic), (Burundi), (RSA), (Congo) ● Application: major source of Ce and Eu.

---

1. Barytocalcite – druse of platy crystals (up to 22 mm) attached to calcite; Stříbro (Czech Republic) **2. Bastnäsite** – massive aggregate with violet fluorite; Pikes Peak (Colorado, USA – width of field 22 mm) **3. Rhodochrosite** – scalenohedral crystals (up to 12 mm) on limonite; Horhausen (FRG)

Barytocalcite, bastnäsite, rhodochrosite

Siderite (Chalybite, Spathose iron)

Carbonate
FeCO$_3$

306

P

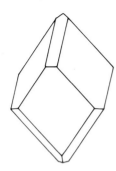

From the Greek *sideros* – iron
(Haidinger 1845)

● Hardness: 4–4.5 (brittle) ● Streak: white, yellowish ● Colour: yellowish-white, yellowish-brown, brown, grey, brownish-black, metallic coatings, deposits ● Transparency: opaque, on edges translucent ● Lustre: vitreous, pearly ● Cleavage: perfect on (10$\bar{1}$1) ● Fracture: uneven, conchoidal, sometimes splintery ● Morphology: crystals, granular, massive, oolitic, earthy to compact aggregates, botryoidal, reniform and globular pseudomorphs. Aggregates with a radiating internal structure are called spherosiderites. Concretions in argillaceous sediments are called pelosiderites ● Specific gravity: 3.7–3.9 ● Crystal system: trigonal ● Crystal form: rhombohedra, often rounded or lenticular, saddle-shaped, seldom plates, prisms, twins ● Chemical composition: FeO 62.01%, CO$_2$ 37.99%; admixtures: Mg (sideroplesite variety), Mn (oligonite variety), Ca (siderodot variety), Zn (monheimite variety) ● Chemical properties: in blowpipe flame breaks but does not fuse, turns black and becomes magnetic; soluble in hot HCl ● Handling: clean with distilled water and dry carefully ● Similar minerals: dolomite **(218)**, ankerite **(219)**, magnesite **(302)** ● Distinguishing features: X-rays, chemical properties ● Genesis: hydrothermal, metasomatic, pegmatitic-pneumatolytic, sedimentary ● Associated minerals: chalcopyrite **(185)**, tetrahedrite **(190)**, calcite **(217)**, ankerite, baryte **(240)**, pyrite **(436)**, quartz **(534)** ● Occurrence: common; Siegerland, Wildschapbachtal, Wittichen and Neudorf (FRG), Hüttenberg, Friesach, Erzberg (Austria), Rožňava, Rudňany, Nižná Slaná (Slovakia), Příbram (Czech Republic), Cornwall (Great Britain), Bilbao (Spain), Lotharingia (France), Baikal, Alapaevsk and the Urals (Russia), Roxbury – Connecticut (USA), (Algeria) ● In association with cryolite, siderite is found in Ivigtut (Greenland); oligonites are found in Ehrenfriedersdorf (FRG) and in Tisovec (Slovakia); monheimite is found in Altenberg near Aachen (FRG); pelosiderites are found in coal basins in (Great Britain), (Czech Republic) and Ruhrgebiet (FRG) ● Application: important iron ore; occasionally used as a precious stone (faceted).

Siderite – rhombohedral crystals (up to 20 mm) with pyrite; Siegen (FRG)

Siderite

Malachite

Carbonate
$Cu_2(CO_3)(OH)_2$

307

P

Historical name

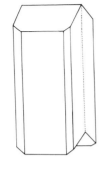

● Hardness: 4 (brittle) ● Streak: light green ● Colour: green, black-green ● Transparency: translucent to opaque ● Lustre: vitreous, silky, dull ● Cleavage: good on (001) ● Fracture: conchoidal ● Morphology: crystals, granular, massive, coatings, fibrous and earthy aggregates, crusts, impregnations, pseudomorphs ● Specific gravity: 4.0 ● Crystal system: monoclinic ● Crystal form: prisms ● Chemical composition: CuO 71.95%, CO_2 19.90%, H_2O 8.15% ● Chemical properties: soluble in HCl (effervesces), dampened with HCl it colours a flame green ● Handling: clean with water ● Similar minerals: chrysocolla **(268)**, rosasite **(308)**, pseudomalachite **(321)** ● Distinguishing features: specific gravity, X-rays and chemical properties ● Genesis: secondary ● Associated minerals: copper **(47)**, chalcopyrite **(185)**, cuprite **(209)**, azurite **(226)** ● Occurrence: common; Betzdorf and Rheinbreithbach (FRG), Chessy (France), Baiţa (Romania), Nizhni Tagil (Russia), Arizona (USA), Shaba (Congo), Tsumeb (Namibia) ● Application: Cu ore; used as a decorative and precious stone.

Rosasite

Carbonate
$(Cu,Zn)_2(CO_3)(OH)_2$

308

Named after the mine in Rosas (Sardinia) (Lovisato 1908)

● Hardness: approx. 4 ● Streak: lighter than colour ● Colour: blue-green, light blue ● Transparency: translucent to opaque ● Lustre: vitreous, silky ● Cleavage: in two directions ● Morphology: crystals, fibrous and spherulitic aggregates, crusts ● Specific gravity: 4.0–4.2 ● Crystal system: monoclinic ● Crystal form: plates ● Chemical composition: CuO 41.15%, ZnO 30.99%, CO_2 19.77%, H_2O 8.09% ● Chemical properties: soluble in acids; fusible in flame ● Handling: clean with distilled water ● Similar minerals: malachite **(307)** ● Distinguishing features: X-rays and chemical properties (test for Zn) ● Genesis: secondary ● Associated minerals: hydrozincite **(103)**, aurichalcite **(106)**, brochantite **(228)**, malachite ● Occurrence: rare; Sardinia (Italy), Kisil Espe (Kazakhstan), Tsumeb (Namibia), California and New Mexico (USA).

Beudantite

Arsenate
$PbFe_3^{3+}(SO_4)(AsO_4)(OH)_6$

309

Named after the French mineralogist, F. S. Beudant (1787–1850) (Lévy 1826)

● Hardness: 4 (brittle) ● Streak: yellow, greenish-yellow ● Colour: dark green, brown, black ● Transparency: transparent to translucent ● Lustre: adamantine, vitreous, greasy ● Cleavage: good on (0001) ● Morphology: crystals ● Specific gravity: 4.3 ● Crystal system: trigonal ● Crystal form: hexahedra, rhombohedra, pseudocubic, plates ● Chemical composition: PbO 31.35%, Fe_2O_3 33.68%, SO_3 11.24%, As_2O_5 16.14%, H_2O 7.59% ● Chemical properties: fuses in flame; soluble in HCl ● Handling: clean with distilled water ● Similar minerals: pharmacosiderite **(140)** ● Distinguishing features: hardness, specific gravity ● Genesis: secondary ● Associated minerals: pharmacosiderite, malachite **(307)**, limonite **(355)** ● Occurrence: rare; Horhausen and Clara Mine near Oberwolfach (FRG), Moldava (Czech Republic), Lávrion (Greece), Mt McGrath (Australia), Tsumeb (Namibia).

Malachite – polished section showing concentric growth patterns; Shaba (Congo – width of field 70 mm)

Malachite

Scheelite (Calcium tungstate)

310

L

P

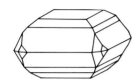

Named after the Swedish chemist, K. W. Scheele (1742–1786) (Leonhard 1821)

● Hardness: 4.5–5 (brittle) ● Streak: white ● Colour: white, yellow, brown, greenish, reddish, grey-white ● Transparency: transparent to translucent ● Lustre: adamantine, greasy ● Cleavage: imperfect on (101) ● Fracture: conchoidal ● Morphology: crystals, granular, massive aggregates, crusts, impregnations, pseudomorphs ● Specific gravity: 5.9–6.1 ● Crystal system: tetragonal ● Crystal form: dipyramidal, pyramidal, plates ● Luminescence: strong, light blue in short-wave UV ● Chemical composition: CaO 19.47%, WO$_3$ 80.53% ● Chemical properties: fuses with difficulty; soluble in HCl and HNO$_3$ ● Handling: clean with distilled water ● Similar minerals: cerussite **(225)**, baryte **(240)**, powellite **(241)**, anglesite **(242)**, quartz **(534)** ● Distinguishing features: hardness, specific gravity, luminescence, absence of Pb distinguishes it from cerussite and anglesite, X-rays ● Genesis: pegmatitic-pneumatolytic, hydrothermal, contact-metamorphic ● Associated minerals: molybdenite **(8)**, fluorite **(291)**, wolframite **(369)**, quartz ● Occurrence: common; Rossgrabeneck, Schwaigwald, Eisenbach, Zinnwald and Altenberg (FRG), Cínovec and Obří důl (Czech Republic), (Russia), (Dagestan), (Uzbekistan), Pitkäranta (Finland), Cornwall (Great Britain), Natas Mine (Namibia), Kings Island – Tasmania (Australia), Condeauque (Bolivia), (Austria), (Canada), (USA), (Korea) ● Application: W ore; sometimes used as a precious stone (facets, cabochons).

Variscite

311

L

P

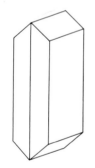

Named after Variscia, the historical name of Vogtland (FRG) (Breithaupt 1837)

● Hardness: 4–5 ● Streak: white ● Colour: white, green, blue-green ● Transparency: translucent ● Lustre: dull, greasy ● Cleavage: perfect on (010) ● Fracture: conchoidal ● Morphology: massive, crusty and reniform aggregates ● Specific gravity: 2.52 ● Crystal system: orthorhombic ● Crystal form: pseudo-octahedra, short prisms ● Luminescence: green, creamy-green ● Chemical composition: Al$_2$O$_3$ 32.26%, P$_2$O$_5$ 44.94%, H$_2$O 22.80%; admixtures: Fe and As ● Chemical properties: infusible; soluble in KOH ● Handling: clean with distilled water ● Similar minerals: wavellite **(247)** ● Distinguishing features: different crystal form, hardness, X-rays and chemical properties ● Genesis: secondary ● Associated minerals: wavellite, bolivarite, limonite **(355)** ● Occurrence: rare; Messbach (FRG), Leoben (Austria), Třenice (Czech Republic), Montgomery Co. – Arkansas and Mercur – Utah (USA), Posoconi (Bolivia) ● Application: sometimes used as a precious stone (cabochons).

Cyrilovite

312

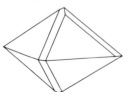

Named after its locality Cyrilov (Czech Republic) (Novotný 1953)

● Hardness: approx. 4 ● Streak: yellow ● Colour: yellow, orange-yellow, brown ● Transparency: transparent ● Lustre: vitreous ● Morphology: crystals, aggregates ● Specific gravity: 3.08 ● Crystal system: tetragonal ● Crystal form: pseudo-octahedra, tetrahedra ● Genesis: pegmatites ● Associated minerals: strengite **(249)**, graftonite **(381)** ● Occurrence: rare; Hagendorf (FRG), Cyrilov (Czech Republic), Sapucaia (Brazil).

---

1. **Scheelite** – crystal (15 mm) embayed in quartz; Fürstenberg (FRG) 2. **Variscite** – massive polished aggregate; Lewinston (Utah, USA – width of field 45 mm)

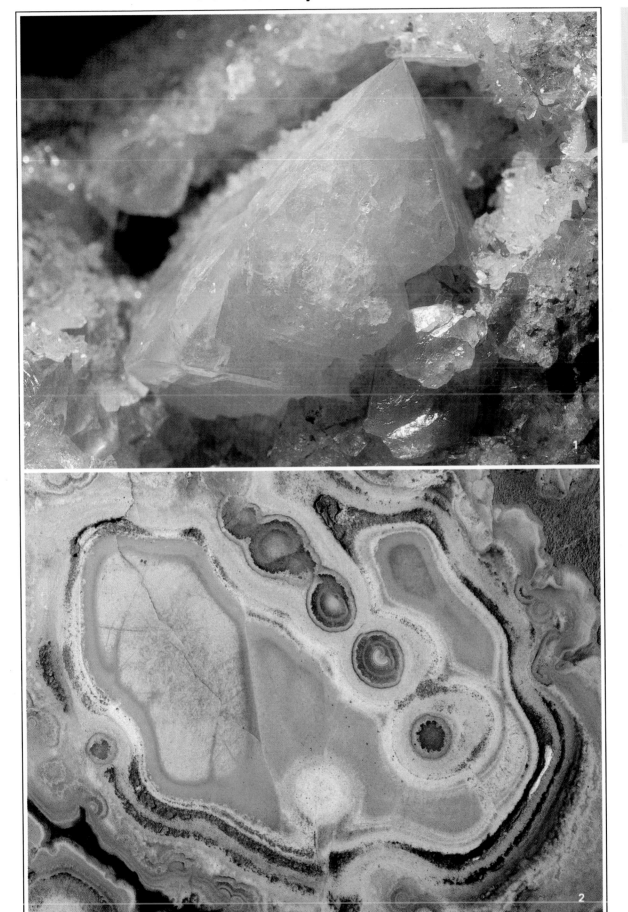

Goyazite (Hamlinite)

Phosphate
$SrAl_3(PO_4)_2(OH)_5 \cdot H_2O$

313

Named after the province of Goyaz (Brazil) (Damour 1884)

● Hardness: 4.5 ● Streak: white ● Colour: lemon-yellow, pink ● Transparency: transparent ● Lustre: vitreous, greasy ● Cleavage: perfect on (0001) ● Fracture: uneven ● Morphology: crystals, isometric grains ● Specific gravity: 3.2 ● Crystal system: trigonal ● Crystal form: rhombohedra, plates ● Chemical composition: SrO 22.45%, Al_2O_3 33.14%, P_2O_5 30.75%, H_2O 13.66%; admixtures: Ba, F ● Chemical properties: slowly soluble in acids ● Handling: clean with distilled water ● Similar minerals: apatite **(379)**, topaz **(595)** ● Distinguishing features: hardness ● Genesis: pegmatites, secondary ● Associated minerals: baryte **(240)**, apatite, pyrite **(436)**, bertrandite **(485)** ● Occurrence: rare; Fuchsbach (FRG), Lengenbach (Switzerland), Romny (Russia), Greenwood – Maine and Boulder Co. – Colorado (USA), Serra de Congonhas (Brazil).

Sicklerite

Phosphate
$Li(Mn^{2+}, Fe^{3+})[PO_4]$

314

Named after the discoverer of the Pala deposit, Sickler (California, USA) (Schaller 1912)

● Hardness: approx. 4 ● Streak: lighter than colour ● Colour: dark brown, yellow ● Transparency: opaque ● Lustre: dull ● Cleavage: good on (100) ● Fracture: uneven ● Morphology: massive aggregates ● Specific gravity: 3.4 ● Crystal system: orthorhombic ● Crystal form: unknown ● Chemical composition: variable Mn and Fe contents ● Chemical properties: readily fusible; soluble in acids ● Handling: clean with distilled water ● Similar minerals: sometimes graftonite **(381)** ● Distinguishing features: hardness, X-rays, chemical properties ● Genesis: secondary in pegmatites ● Associated minerals: triphylite **(315)**, purpurite **(316)** ● Occurrence: rare; Hühnerkobel and Hagendorf (FRG), Varuträsk (Sweden), Pala – California (USA), Wodgina (Australia) ● Application: mineralogically important.

Triphylite

Phosphate
$Li(Fe^{2+}, Mn^{2+})[PO_4]$

315

From the Greek *tri* – three and *fýlon* – family (Fuchs 1834)

● Hardness: 4–5 ● Streak: grey-white ● Colour: greenish-grey, blue-grey, brown ● Transparency: transparent to translucent ● Lustre: greasy ● Cleavage: good on (100) ● Fracture: uneven, conchoidal ● Morphology: crystals, granular and massive aggregates ● Specific gravity: 3.4–3.6 ● Crystal system: orthorhombic ● Crystal form: prisms ● Chemical composition: Li_2O 9.47%, FeO 45.54%, P_2O_5 44.99%; constant admixture: Mn (end member of the isomorphous series is lithiophilite – $LiMn(PO_4)$) ● Chemical properties: readily fusible; soluble in acids ● Handling: clean with distilled water ● Similar minerals: lithiophilite ● Distinguishing features: chemical properties ● Genesis: in pegmatites ● Associated minerals: amblygonite **(377)**, spodumene **(502)**, cassiterite **(548)**, beryl **(554)** ● Occurrence: rare; Hühnerkobel and Hagendorf (FRG), Mangualde (Portugal), Přibyslavice (Czech Republic), Norrö (Sweden), Newport – N. Hampshire (USA), Karibib (Namibia).

1. Goyazite – isolated grains (up to 5 mm); Serra de Congonhas (Brazil) **2. Triphylite** – granular aggregate; Newport (USA – width of field 44 mm)

Goyazite, triphylite

Purpurite

Phosphate
(Mn³⁺, Fe³⁺)[PO₄]

Phosphate
$(Mn^{3+}, Fe^{3+})[PO_4]$

316

P

From the Latin *pur-pureus* – purple red
(Craton 1905)

● Hardness: 4.5 ● Streak: red ● Colour: dark red to dark violet ● Transparency: translucent to opaque ● Lustre: dull ● Cleavage: perfect on (100) and on (001) ● Fracture: uneven ● Morphology: granular and massive aggregates ● Specific gravity: 3.4 ● Crystal system: orthorhombic ● Crystal form: unknown ● Chemical composition: Mn_2O_3 52.66%, P_2O_5 47.34%; admixture: Fe (end member of the isomorphous series is heterosite – $Fe^{3+}(PO_4)$) ● Chemical properties: readily fusible; soluble in HCl ● Handling: clean dark coating with diluted acids, except HCl ● Similar minerals: heterosite ● Distinguishing features: colour, chemical properties ● Genesis: secondary in pegmatites ● Associated minerals: sicklerite **(314)**, triphylite **(315)** ● Occurrence: rare; Chanteloube (France), Wodgina (Australia), Custer Co. – South Dakota and Pala – California (USA) ● Application: sometimes used as a precious stone (cabochons).

Plumbogummite

Phosphate
$PbAl_3(PO_4)_2(OH)_5 . H_2O$

317

Named after its composition: *plumbum* – lead and *gummi* – India rubber
(Laumont 1819)

● Hardness: 4–4.5 ● Streak: white ● Colour: white, grey, yellow, blue-green, reddish-brown ● Transparency: translucent ● Lustre: dull, greasy ● Cleavage: unknown ● Fracture: conchoidal ● Morphology: gelatinous, massive, deposits, stalactitic, crusty aggregates of concentric structure ● Specific gravity: 4–5 ● Crystal system: trigonal ● Crystal form: hexagonal ● Chemical composition: PbO 38.41%, Al_2O_3 26.32%, P_2O_5 24.42%, H_2O 10.85% ● Chemical properties: swells in a flame and is partly fusible; soluble in hot acids ● Handling: clean with distilled water ● Genesis: secondary in oxidation zones ● Associated minerals: cerussite **(225)**, anglesite **(242)**, wulfenite **(243)**, pyromorphyte **(262)** ● Occurrence: rare; Huelgoat and Nussiére (France), Roughten Gill (Great Britain), Diamantina (Brazil), Cerro Gordo Mine – California (USA).

Legrandite

Arsenate
$Zn_2(AsO_4)(OH) . H_2O$

318

Named after the Belgian mining engineer, Legrande
(Drugmann, Hey 1932)

● Hardness: 4.5 ● Streak: white ● Colour: yellow ● Transparency: transparent to translucent ● Lustre: vitreous ● Cleavage: imperfect on (100) ● Morphology: crystals, crystalline aggregates ● Specific gravity: 4.0 ● Crystal system: monoclinic ● Crystal form: prisms ● Chemical composition: ZnO 53.42%, As_2O_5 37.71%, H_2O 8.87% ● Handling: clean with distilled water ● Genesis: secondary ● Associated minerals: adamite **(258)**, limonite **(355)**, hemimorphite **(403)** ● Occurrence: rare; Lampazos and Mapimí (Mexico).

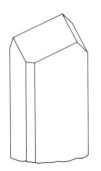

1. **Purpurite** – compact aggregate; Sandamab Mine (Namibia – width of field 90 mm) 2. **Legrandite** – columnar aggregate in limonite; Mapimí (Mexico – width of field 20 mm)

Purpurite, legrandite

Libethenite

Phosphate
$Cu_2(PO_4)(OH)$

319

Named after its locality Ľubietová (German Libethen – Slovakia) (Breithaupt 1823)

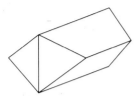

• Hardness: 4 (brittle) • Streak: light green • Colour: dark green, greenish-black • Transparency: transparent to translucent • Lustre: greasy, vitreous • Cleavage: imperfect • Fracture: uneven, conchoidal • Morphology, crystals, granular aggregates • Specific gravity: 3.9–4.0 • Crystal system: orthorhombic • Crystal form: dipyramidal, short prisms • Chemical composition: CuO 66.54%, P_2O_5 29.69%, H_2O 3.77% • Chemical properties: fuses into a black crystalline ball; readily soluble in acids and ammonia • Handling: clean with distilled water • Similar minerals: atacamite **(206)**, olivenite **(257)**, malachite **(307)** • Distinguishing features: hardness, reliable X-rays and chemical properties • Genesis: secondary • Associated minerals: cuprite **(209)**, malachite, pseudomalachite **(321)**, limonite **(355)** • Occurrence: rare; Ľubietová (Slovakia), Montebras (France), Cornwall (Great Britain), Yerington – Nevada (USA), Shaba (Congo), Nizhni Tagil (Russia).

Cornwallite (Erinite)

Arsenate
$Cu_5(AsO_4)_2(OH)_4$

320

Named after Cornwall (Great Britain) (Zippe 1846)

• Hardness: 4.5–5 (brittle) • Streak: apple green • Colour: dark green, emerald green • Transparency: translucent to opaque • Lustre: dull • Cleavage: absent • Fracture: conchoidal • Morphology: crusty aggregates of radiating-fibrous structure, encrustations • Specific gravity: 4.0–4.1 • Crystal system: monoclinic • Crystal form: plates • Chemical composition: CuO 59.97%, As_2O_5 34.63%, H_2O 5.40% • Chemical properties: fuses into black glass • Handling: clean with distilled water • Similar minerals: malachite **(307)**, pseudomalachite **(321)** • Distinguishing features: X-rays, chemical properties • Genesis: secondary • Associated minerals: tenorite **(210)**, olivenite **(257)**, malachite • Occurrence: rare; Freudenstadt, Clara Mine near Oberwolfach and Neubulach (FRG), Cornwall (Great Britain), Novoveská Huta (Slovakia), Chessy (France), Majuba Hill – Nevada (USA).

Pseudomalachite

Phosphate
$Cu_5(PO_4)_2(OH)_4$

321

P

From *pseudo* – false and malachite (Hausmann 1832)

• Hardness: 4.5 (brittle) • Streak: blue-green • Colour: dark green, emerald green • Transparency: transparent to translucent • Lustre: vitreous, greasy • Cleavage: imperfect on (010) • Fracture: conchoidal • Morphology: coatings, stalactitic, botryoidal aggregates, crystals are rare • Specific gravity: 4.34 • Crystal system: monoclinic • Crystal form: prisms • Chemical composition: CuO 69.09%, P_2O_5 24.65%, H_2O 6.26% • Chemical properties: fusible in blowpipe flame; soluble in acids • Handling: clean with distilled water • Similar minerals: malachite **(307)**, cornwallite **(320)** • Distinguishing features: X-rays and chemical properties • Genesis: secondary • Associated minerals: azurite **(226)**, malachite, limonite **(355)**, chalcedony **(449)** • Occurrence: rare; Rheinbreitbach, Hirschberg and Hagendorf (FRG), Ľubietová (Slovakia), Cornwall (Great Britain), Bogolo (Portugal), Nizhni Tagil (Russia) • Application: sometimes used as a precious stone.

---

1. **Libethenite** – euhedral crystals (up to 2 mm) on quartz; Ľubietová (Slovakia) 2. **Pseudomalachite** – reniform aggregate; Ľubietová (Slovakia – width of field 68 mm)

Libethenite, pseudomalachite

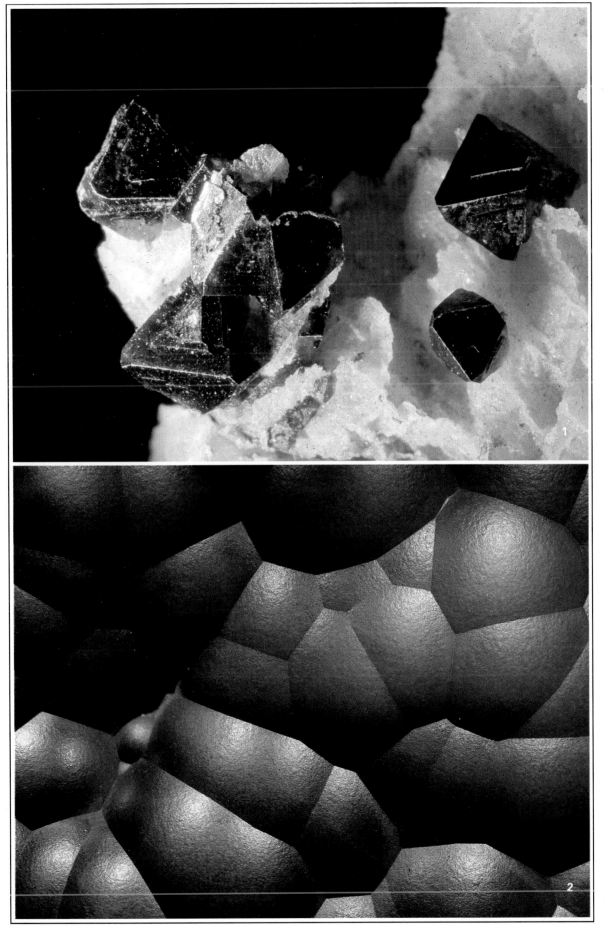

Bayldonite

Arsenate
$PbCu_3(AsO_4)_2(OH)_2$

322

P

Named after J. Bayldon (Church 1865)

● Hardness: 4.5 ● Streak: green ● Colour: yellow to green ● Transparency: translucent ● Lustre: greasy ● Cleavage: unknown ● Fracture: uneven ● Morphology: crystals, crusts, granular and powdered aggregates, pseudomorphs ● Specific gravity: 5.5 ● Crystal system: monoclinic ● Crystal form: plates ● Chemical composition: PbO 31.45%, CuO 33.62%, As_2O_5 32.39%, H_2O 2.54% ● Chemical properties: readily fusible; dissolves with difficulty in HCl ● Handling: clean with distilled water ● Similar minerals: olivenite **(257)**, malachite **(307)** ● Distinguishing features: different crystal form ● Genesis: secondary in oxidation zones ● Associated features: anglesite **(242)**, mimetite **(264)**, beudantite **(309)** ● Occurrence: rare; Clara Mine near Oberwolfach and Freudenstadt (FRG), St. Day (Great Britain), Moldava (Czech Republic), Tsumeb (Namibia), Agalik (Uzbekistan) ● Application: occasionally used as a precious stone.

Hedyphane (Mimetite variety)

Arsenate
$(Ca,Pb)_5(AsO_4)_3Cl$

323

From the Greek *hedy* – pleasant and *phan* – to appear (Breithaupt 1830)

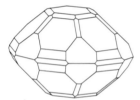

● Hardness: 4.5 ● Streak: white ● Colour: white, yellowish-white, bluish ● Transparency: translucent ● Lustre: greasy ● Cleavage: imperfect on (10$\bar{1}$1) ● Fracture: conchoidal, uneven ● Morphology: crystals, massive and granular aggregates ● Specific gravity: 5.8 ● Crystal system: hexagonal ● Crystal form: prisms ● Chemical composition: like mimetite **(264)** but contains 13.10% CaO ● Chemical properties: like mimetite ● Handling: clean with distilled water ● Genesis and associated minerals: like mimetite ● Occurrence: rare; Långban and Pajsberg (Sweden), Vrančice (Czech Republic), Franklin – New Jersey (USA).

Xenotime

Phosphate
YPO_4

324

R

From the Greek *xenos* – foreign and *time* – honour (Beudant 1832)

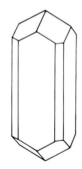

● Hardness: 4–5 (brittle) ● Streak: white, yellowish-brown ● Colour: yellowish-brown, greenish, grey, brown ● Transparency: translucent ● Lustre: greasy, vitreous ● Cleavage: perfect on (100) ● Fracture: splintery ● Morphology: crystals, granular, coarsely radiate aggregates ● Specific gravity: 4.5–5.1 ● Crystal system: tetragonal ● Crystal form: prisms, dipyramidal, plates ● Magnetism: slightly paramagnetic ● Radioactivity: sometimes radioactive ● Chemical composition: Y_2O_3 61.40%, P_2O_5 38.60%; admixtures of rare earths: Th, U and Zr ● Chemical properties: infusible in blowpipe flame; almost insoluble in acids; dampened with H_2SO_4, tinges a flame blue-green ● Handling: clean with distilled water ● Similar minerals: cassiterite **(548)**, zircon **(587)** ● Distinguishing features: hardness, specific gravity, X-rays, chemical properties ● Genesis: magmatic, in pegmatites, in alluvial deposits ● Associated minerals: apatite **(379)**, monazite **(383)**, zircon ● Occurrence: rare; Lausitz (FRG), St. Gotthard and Binnental (Switzerland), Hitterö (Norway), Ytterby (Sweden); in alluvial deposits in: (Brazil), (USA), (Australia), (Madagascar) ● Application: source of rare earths.

---

1. **Bayldonite** – fine crystalline lamellae on compact mimetite with crystals of azurite; Tsumeb (Namibia – width of field 20 mm) 2. **Hedyphane** – crystal (3 mm) embedded in pegmatite; Písek (Czech Republic) 3. **Xenotime** – idiomorphic crystal (3 mm); Binnental (Switzerland)

Bayldonite, hedyphane, xenotime

Chabazite

Silicate
$CaAl_2Si_4O_{12} \cdot 6\,H_2O$

325

L

Historical Greek name (Bosc d'Antic 1788)

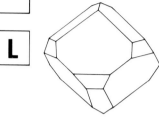

● Hardness: 4.5 (brittle) ● Streak: white ● Colour: white, yellow, reddish ● Transparency: transparent to translucent ● Lustre: vitreous ● Cleavage: imperfect on $(10\bar{1}1)$ ● Fracture: uneven ● Morphology: crystals, crystal druses ● Specific gravity: 2.08 ● Crystal system: trigonal ● Crystal form: rhombohedra, twins ● Luminescence: sometimes green in short-wave UV ● Chemical composition: CaO 14.52%, Al_2O_3 26.39%, SiO_2 31.10%, H_2O 27.99% ● Chemical properties: soluble in HCl; under blowpipe fuses with difficulty into white translucent enamel ● Handling: clean with distilled water ● Similar minerals: calcite (217), dolomite (218) ● Distinguishing features: hardness, specific gravity, X-rays, chemical properties ● Genesis: hydrothermal, post-volcanic ● Associated minerals: calcite, stilbite (269), heulandite (270), analcime (386) ● Occurrence: common; Oberstein and Vogelsberg (FRG), Řepčice, Střekov (Czech Republic), Maglovce (Slovakia), (Iceland), (Faroe Islands), Richmond (Australia), (New Zealand), (USA).

Gmelinite

Silicate
$(Na_2Ca)Al_2Si_4O_{12} \cdot 6\,H_2O$

326

Named after the German mineralogist and chemist, Ch. G. Gmelin (1792–1860) (Brooke 1825)

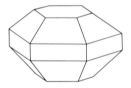

● Hardness: 4.5 (brittle) ● Streak: white ● Colour: white, yellow, reddish, pink ● Transparency: transparent to translucent ● Lustre: vitreous ● Cleavage: imperfect on $(10\bar{1}1)$ ● Fracture: uneven ● Morphology: crystals, crystalline druses ● Specific gravity: 2.03 ● Crystal system: hexagonal ● Crystal form: rhombohedra, plates, dipyramidal, occasionally twins ● Chemical composition: Na_2O 6.08%, CaO 5.50%, Al_2O_3 20.01%, SiO_2 47.19%, H_2O 21.22% ● Chemical properties: soluble in HCl; readily fuses into white enamel ● Handling: clean with distilled water ● Similar minerals: gismondite (328) ● Distinguishing features: X-rays, chemical properties ● Genesis: hydrothermal, post-volcanic ● Associated minerals: calcite (217), heulandite (270), chabazite (325) ● Occurrence: rare; Glenarm and Magee (Northern Ireland), Isle of Skye – Scotland (Great Britain), Samson Mine near St. Andreasberg (FRG), Bergen Hill – New Jersey (USA), Flinders Island (Australia).

Garronite

Silicate
$NaCa_{2.5}Al_6Si_{10}O_{32} \cdot 13.5\,H_2O$

327

Named after its locality in Garron Plateau (Northern Ireland) (Walker 1962)

● Hardness: approx. 4 ● Streak: white ● Colour: white ● Transparency: translucent to transparent ● Lustre: vitreous ● Cleavage: in two directions ● Morphology: compact fibrous aggregates and radiating aggregates ● Specific gravity: 2.1–2.2 ● Crystal system: tetragonal ● Crystal form: needles ● Chemical composition: Na_2O 2.30%, CaO 12.47%, Al_2O_3 22.67%, SiO_2 44.53%, H_2O 18.03% ● Chemical properties: readily fusible; soluble in HCl ● Handling: clean with distilled water ● Genesis: post-volcanic, hydrothermal ● Associated minerals: chabazite (325), gismondite (328), phillipsite (329), thompsonite (389) ● Occurrence: rare; several areas in Antrim (Northern Ireland), Fintice (Slovakia), (Iceland).

---

1. **Chabazite** – intergrown rhombohedral crystals (25 mm); Maglovce (Slovakia) 2. **Gmelinite** – group of crystals (to 3 mm) with quartz; Flinders (Australia)

Chabazite, gmelinite

Gismondite

Silicate
CaAl$_2$Si$_2$O$_8$. 4 H$_2$O

328

Named after the Italian mineralogist, C. G. Gismondi (1762–1824) (Leonhard 1817)

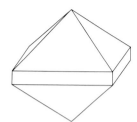

● Hardness: 4.5 (brittle) ● Streak: white ● Colour: white, grey, reddish ● Transparency: transparent to translucent ● Lustre: vitreous ● Cleavage: imperfect on (101) ● Fracture: conchoidal ● Morphology: crystals, semi-globular, wisp-like aggregates ● Specific gravity: 2.26 ● Crystal system: monoclinic ● Crystal form: pseudotetragonal bipyramids, twins ● Chemical composition: CaO 19.32%, Al$_2$O$_3$ 35.14%, SiO$_2$ 20.70%, H$_2$O 24.84% ● Chemical properties: readily fusible; soluble in HCl ● Handling: clean with distilled water ● Similar minerals: gmelinite **(326)** ● Distinguishing features: X-rays and chemical properties ● Genesis: hydrothermal, post-volcanic ● Associated minerals: other zeolites ● Occurrence: rare; Groschlattengrün, Schiffenberg and Homberg (FRG), Aci Castello – Sicily (Italy), Zálezly and Dobrná (Czech Republic), (Hawaiian Islands), (Australia).

Phillipsite (Cross stone)

Silicate
KCaAl$_3$Si$_5$O$_{16}$. 6 H$_2$O

329

Named after the English mineralogist, W. Phillips (1775–1829) (Lévy 1825)

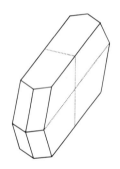

● Hardness: 4.5 (brittle) ● Streak: white ● Colour: white, yellow, reddish ● Transparency: transparent to translucent ● Lustre: vitreous ● Cleavage: good on (010) and (001) ● Fracture: uneven ● Morphology: crystals ● Specific gravity: 2.2 ● Crystal system: monoclinic ● Crystal form: crystal twins, prisms ● Chemical composition: K$_2$O 7.09%, CaO 8.44%, Al$_2$O$_3$ 23.01%, SiO$_2$ 45.19%, H$_2$O 16.27% ● Chemical properties: readily fusible; soluble in HCl ● Handling: clean with distilled water ● Similar minerals: harmotome **(332)** ● Distinguishing features: X-rays, chemical properties ● Genesis: hydrothermal, post-volcanic ● Associated minerals: calcite **(217)**, chabazite **(325),** analcime **(386)** ● Occurrence: common; Nidda, Habichtswald, Sasbach, Rossberg and Groschlattengrün (FRG), Zálezly (Czech Republic), Aci Castello – Sicily (Italy), Antrim (Northern Ireland), (Iceland).

Epistilbite

Silicate
CaAl$_2$Si$_6$O$_{16}$. 5 H$_2$O

330

From the Greek *epi* – near and the mineral, *stilbite* (Rose 1826)

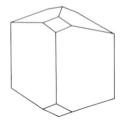

● Hardness: 4 (brittle) ● Streak: white ● Colour: white, yellowish, reddish, brownish ● Transparency: transparent to translucent ● Lustre: vitreous ● Cleavage: perfect on (010) ● Fracture: uneven ● Morphology: crystals, wisp-like and spherulitic aggregates ● Specific gravity: 2.2–2.3 ● Crystal system: monoclinic ● Crystal form: prisms ● Chemical composition: CaO 6.01%, Al$_2$O$_3$ 10.93%, SiO$_2$ 73.40%, H$_2$O 9.66% ● Chemical properties: readily fusible; soluble in HCl ● Handling: clean with distilled water ● Similar minerals: stilbite **(269)**, mesolite **(385)** ● Distinguishing features: X-rays and chemical properties ● Genesis: hydrothermal, post-volcanic ● Associated minerals: heulandite **(270)**, laumontite **(272)**, chabazite **(325),** mesolite ● Occurrence: rare; Fintice (Slovakia), Berufjord (Iceland), Isle of Skye – Scotland (Great Britain), Poona (India), (USA), (Canada).

1. Phillipsite – crystalline lining of a vesicle (crystals up to 1 mm); Limburg (FRG) **2. Epistilbite** – yellow-brown spherulitic aggregates; Fintice (Slovakia – width of field 36 mm)

Phillipsite, epistilbite

Apophyllite

Silicate
$KCa_4(Si_4O_{10})_2F \cdot 8\,H_2O$

331

From the Greek *apo-phylliso* – it flakes off
(Haüy 1806)

● Hardness: 4.5–5.0 (brittle) ● Streak: white ● Colour: colourless, white, red, green, violet ● Transparency: transparent to translucent ● Lustre: vitreous, pearly ● Cleavage: perfect on (001) ● Fracture: uneven ● Morphology: crystals, massive and granular aggregates ● Specific gravity: 2.3–2.4 ● Crystal system: tetragonal ● Crystal form: coarse plates, bipyramidal, pseudocubic ● Luminescence: sometimes yellow, greenish-white or blue green in LW ● Chemical composition: variable ● Chemical properties: in flame splits apart; soluble in HCl ● Handling: clean with distilled water ● Genesis: hydrothermal, post-volcanic ● Associated minerals: calcite **(217)**, analcime **(386)**, natrolite **(387)** ● Occurrence: rare; Sasbach, Haslach and St. Andreasberg (FRG), Ústí n/L. (Czech Republic), Valle di Fassa (Italy), Isle of Skye – Scotland (Great Britain), Poonah (India), (Brazil), (Australia), (USA) ● Application: sometimes used as a precious stone.

Harmotome

Silicate
$BaAl_2Si_6O_{16} \cdot 6\,H_2O$

332

From the Greek *harmos* – I combine and *temseis* – I cut
(Haüy 1801)

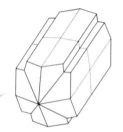

● Hardness: 4.5 (brittle) ● Streak: white ● Colour: white, grey, yellow, red ● Transparency: transparent to translucent ● Lustre: vitreous ● Cleavage: imperfect on (010) ● Fracture: uneven ● Morphology: crystals ● Specific gravity: 2.44–2.5 ● Crystal system: monoclinic ● Crystal form: prisms, plates, often twins ● Chemical composition: BaO 21.18%, Al_2O_3 14.08%, SiO_2 49.80%, H_2O 14.94%; admixture: K ● Chemical properties: fuses with difficulty; soluble in HCl ● Handling: clean with distilled water ● Similar minerals: phillipsite **(329)** ● Distinguishing features: X-rays, chemical properties ● Genesis: hydrothermal ● Associated minerals: calcite **(217)**, baryte **(240)**, phillipsite, quartz **(534)** ● Occurrence: rare; St. Andreasberg and Idar-Oberstein (FRG), Kongsberg (Norway), Old Kilpatrick – Scotland and Strontian – England (Great Britain), Westchester Co. – New York (USA).

Edingtonite

Silicate
$BaAl_2Si_3O_{10} \cdot 3\,H_2O$

333

Named after the discoverer of the mineral, Edington from Glasgow (Scotland, Great Britain)
(Haidinger 1825)

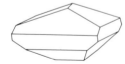

● Hardness: 4–4.5 ● Streak: white ● Colour: white, grey, pink ● Transparency: transparent to translucent ● Lustre: vitreous ● Cleavage: perfect on (110) ● Fracture: uneven ● Morphology: crystals, massive aggregates ● Specific gravity: 2.7 ● Crystal system: orthorhombic ● Crystal form: pyramidal ● Chemical composition: BaO 31.32%, Al_2O_3 20.82%, SiO_2 36.82%, H_2O 11.04% ● Chemical properties: soluble in HCl; in a blowpipe flame fuses with difficulty into clear glass ● Handling: clean with distilled water ● Similar minerals: gmelinite **(326)**, gismondite **(328)** ● Distinguishing features: X-rays, chemical properties ● Genesis: hydrothermal ● Associated minerals: calcite **(217)**, phillipsite **(329)**, harmotome **(332)** ● Occurrence: rare; Kilpatrick – Scotland (Great Britain), Bölet on Götland Island (Sweden).

---

1. Apophyllite – druse of crystals (40 mm); Poonah (India) **2. Harmotome** – crystal with growth confined on two sides (10 mm); St. Andreasberg (FRG) **3. Edingtonite** – crystals (up to 7 mm) with acicular milarite; Staré Ransko (Czech Republic)

Apophyllite, harmotome, edingtonite

273

Tugtupite

Silicate
$Na_8[Cl_2 | (BeAlSi_4O_{12})_2]$

334

Named after its locality Tugtup (Greenland) (Sörensen 1962)

● Hardness: approx. 4 (brittle) ● Streak: white ● Colour: white, pink to crimson, also blue and green ● Transparency: translucent to transparent ● Lustre: greasy, vitreous ● Cleavage: imperfect on (111) ● Fracture: uneven ● Morphology: massive aggregates ● Specific gravity: 2.36 ● Crystal system: tetragonal ● Crystal form: unknown ● Luminescence: light pink ● Chemical composition: composite ● Handling: clean with distilled water ● Genesis: low thermal ● Associated minerals: analcite **(386)**, natrolite **(387)**, nepheline **(397)**, albite **(493)** ● Occurrence: rare; Tugtup and Ilimaussag (Greenland), Lovozero and Kola Peninsula (Russia) ● Application: mineralogically important; as a precious stone (cut for ornamental purposes, cabochons, facets).

Wollastonite (Table spar)

Silicate
$CaSiO_3$

335

Named after the English mineralogist and chemist, W. H. Wollaston (1766–1828) (Leman 1818)

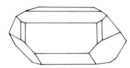

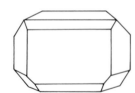

● Hardness: 4.5–5.0 (brittle) ● Streak: white ● Colour: white, yellow, grey ● Transparency: translucent ● Lustre: vitreous, silky ● Cleavage: perfect on (100) and on (001) ● Morphology: crystals, radiating-fibrous, spathic and fibrous aggregates ● Specific gravity: 2.8–2.9 ● Crystal system: triclinic ● Crystal form: plates, often elongated in one direction ● Luminescence: sometimes reddish-orange, cream ● Chemical composition: CaO 48.3%, SiO_2 51.7% ● Chemical properties: fuses with difficulty; soluble in HCl ● Handling: clean with distilled water and diluted acids, except HCl ● Similar minerals: pectolite **(400)**, tremolite **(412)** ● Distinguishing features: hardness, X-rays, chemical properties ● Genesis: in contact-metamorphic rocks ● Associated minerals: vesuvianite **(522)**, quartz **(534)**, garnet **(577)** ● Occurrence: common; Gengenbach and Auerbach (FRG), Ciclova (Romania), Pargas (Finland), Aranzazu (Mexico), Willsboro – New York (USA), Greenville (Canada), Karibib (Namibia) ● Application: ceramics manufacturing, electrical insulation, metallurgy, paper industry.

Margarite

Silicate
$CaAl_4Si_2O_{10}(OH)_2$

336

From the Greek *margaritos* – pearl (Fuchs 1823)

● Hardness: approx. 4 (brittle) ● Streak: white ● Colour: white, grey, grey-pink, reddish ● Transparency: translucent ● Lustre: pearly ● Cleavage: very good on (001) ● Other properties of cohesion: inflexible, brittle, friable ● Morphology: crystals, granular-lamellar, scaly aggregates ● Specific gravity: 3.0 ● Crystal system: monoclinic ● Crystal form: plates, twins ● Chemical composition: CaO 14.00%, Al_2O_3 51.30%, SiO_2 30.10%, H_2O 4.60%; admixtures: Na, Mg, Cr, Li, Mn, Fe ● Chemical properties: in a blowpipe flame fissile, turns white, thin edges fuse partly; slightly soluble in hot HCl ● Handling: clean with diluted acids ● Similar minerals: chlorites, micas ● Distinctive features: pearly lustre, hardness, flexibility of scales ● Genesis: metamorphic ● Associated minerals: chlorite **(158)**, diaspore **(463)**, rutile **(464)**, corundum **(598)** ● Occurrence: rare; in chlorite schists in Greiner (Austria) and Takovaya (Russia), (Greece), (Italy), (Turkey), (USA), (Japan), (RSA).

1. Tugtupite – red compact aggregate; Ilimaussag (Greenland) **2. Wollastonite** – capillary massive aggregate; Stříbrná Skalice (Czech Republic – width of field 60 mm)

Cuprosklodowskite (Jachimovite)

Silicate
$Cu(UO_2)_2Si_2O_6(OH)_2 . 5 H_2O$

337

R

Named for its composition and affinity with sklodowskite
(Buttgenbach 1933)

● Hardness: 4 ● Streak: greenish-yellow ● Colour: green, dark green ● Transparency: translucent ● Lustre: vitreous, silky ● Cleavage: good on (100) ● Morphology: crystals, radiating-fibrous, acicular, powdered aggregates, crusts ● Specific gravity: 3.8 ● Crystal system: triclinic ● Crystal form: needles ● Radioactivity: strong ● Chemical composition: CuO 9.04%, UO_3 65.02%, SiO_2 13.65%, H_2O 12.29% ● Chemical properties: soluble in acids ● Handling: clean with distilled water ● Genesis: secondary, in oxidation zones ● Associated minerals: torbernite **(149)**, uranophane **(172)**, brochantite **(228)**, kasolite **(338)** ● Occurrence: rare; Krunkelbachtal near Menzenschwand, Johanngeorgenstadt (FRG), Jáchymov (Czech Republic), Amelal (Morocco), Shaba (Congo), San Juan Co. – Utah (USA).

Kasolite

Silicate
$Pb(UO_2)(SiO_4) . H_2O$

338

R

Named after its locality Kasolo (Congo)
(Schoep 1921)

● Hardness: 4 ● Streak: light, brown-yellow ● Colour: brownish-yellow, reddish-orange, rarely green ● Transparency: translucent to transparent ● Lustre: greasy, subadamantine, dull ● Cleavage perfect on (001) ● Morphology: crystals, rose-shaped, radiating-fibrous and massive aggregates, encrustations ● Specific gravity: 6.5 ● Crystal system: monoclinic ● Crystal form: prisms ● Radioactivity: strong ● Chemical composition: PbO 37.54%, UO_3 49.26%, SiO_2 10.17%, H_2O 3.03%; admixtures: As, P, Ba ● Chemical properties: readily soluble in acids; fusible in a blowpipe flame ● Handling: clean with distilled water ● Genesis: secondary in oxidation zones ● Associated minerals: torbernite **(149)**, cerussite **(225)**, uraninite **(482)** ● Occurrence: rare; Weiler near Lahr, Menzenschwand and Wölsendorf (FRG), Lingol, Morbihan and Grury (France), Shinkolobwe (Congo), Lake Athabasca (Canada).

Thorite

Silicate
$ThSiO_4$

339

R

Named after its chemical composition
(Berzelius 1829)

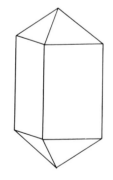

● Hardness: 4.5–5 (brittle) ● Streak: brown, orange-yellow ● Colour: brownish-yellow, reddish-brown, orange, black ● Transparency: translucent to opaque ● Lustre: vitreous, greasy ● Cleavage: imperfect on (110) ● Fracture: conchoidal ● Morphology: crystals, massive and granular aggregates, impregnations, disseminated ● Specific gravity: 4.4–6.7 ● Crystal system: tetragonal ● Crystal form: dipyramidal, prisms ● Radioactivity: alternating, according to admixtures ● Chemical composition: ThO_2 81.42%, SiO_2 18.58%; admixtures: U, Fe, Ca, P, Al, Ti ● Chemical properties: soluble in HCl ● Handling: clean with distilled water ● Similar minerals: xenotime **(324)**, zircon **(587)** ● Distinguishing features: hardness, solubility in HCl, X-rays, chemical properties ● Genesis: magmatic, in pegmatites, alluvial deposits ● Associated minerals: fluorite **(291)**, magnetite **(367)**, zircon ● Occurrence: rare; Brevik – crystals measuring 6 cm (Norway), Ilmen Mountains and the southern Urals (Russia), San Bernardino Co. – California (USA), (Nigeria – alluvial deposits), (Congo), (Australia), (Japan) ● Application: Th source.

---

1. Cuprosklodowskite – powdery coating; Great Bear Lake (Canada – width of field 25 mm) **2. Kasolite** – radiating fibrous aggregates (to 15 mm); Shinkolobwe (Congo)

Cuprosklodowskite, kasolite

Bravoite (Pyrite variety)

Sulphide
(Fe,Ni,Co)S$_2$

340

Named after the Peruvian scientist, J. J. Bravo (1874–1928) (Hillebrand 1907)

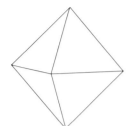

● Hardness: 5.5–6.0 ● Streak: black ● Colour: steel-grey, with Co admixture pinkish ● Transparency: opaque ● Lustre: metallic ● Cleavage: imperfect on (100) ● Fracture: conchoidal, uneven ● Morphology: crystals, granular aggregates ● Specific gravity: 4.3–4.7 ● Crystal system: cubic ● Crystal form: octahedra, hexahedra ● Chemical composition: varies within the isomorphous series: NiS$_2$ – FeS$_2$ – CoS$_2$ ● Chemical properties: soluble in HNO$_3$, partly also in HCl ● Handling: clean with distilled water ● Similar minerals: siegenite **(341)** ● Distinguishing features: X-rays, chemical properties ● Genesis: hydrothermal, magmatic, sedimentary, secondary ● Associated minerals: chalcopyrite **(185)**, millerite **(195)**, pyrite **(436)**, marcasite **(437)** ● Occurrence: rare; Mecharnich, Horbach and Wissen (FRG), Kladno (Czech Republic), Mill Close Mine (Great Britain), Sudbury – Ontario (Canada), Minas Ragra (Peru).

Siegenite

Sulphide
(Co,Ni)$_3$S$_4$

341

Named after its ore-bearing locality Siegen (FRG) (Dana 1850)

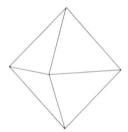

● Hardness: 5–5.5 (brittle) ● Streak: grey-black ● Colour: light grey, steel-grey with copper-red or violet-grey tarnish ● Transparency: opaque ● Lustre: metallic ● Cleavage: imperfect on (100) ● Fracture: uneven ● Morphology: crystals, granular, aggregates ● Specific gravity: 4.83 ● Crystal system: cubic ● Crystal form: octahedra ● Chemical composition: Co 29.02%, Ni 28.89%, S 42.09% (when Co:Ni = 1:1); admixtures: Se (selenosiegenite variety), Cu, Fe ● Chemical properties: soluble in HNO$_3$ ● Handling: clean with distilled water ● Similar minerals: bravoite **(340)** ● Distinguishing features: X-rays, chemical properties ● Genesis: hydrothermal ● Associated minerals: siderite **(306)**, linnaeite **(342)**, pyrite **(436)** ● Occurrence: rare; Siegen, Littfeld, Eiserfeld and Grünau (FRG), Kladno (Czech Republic), Bastnäs (Sweden), Henderson (Namibia), Shaba (Congo), Rhonda Valley – Missouri (USA).

Linnaeite

Sulphide
Co$_3$S$_4$

342

Named after the Swedish botanist, C. Linné (1707–1778) (Haidinger 1845)

● Hardness: 4.5–5.5 (brittle) ● Streak: black-grey ● Colour: white with a pink tint, red or brown tarnish ● Transparency: opaque ● Lustre: metallic ● Cleavage: imperfect on (100) ● Fracture: uneven ● Morphology: crystals, granular aggregates, impregnations ● Specific gravity: 4.8 ● Crystal system: cubic ● Crystal form: octahedra, hexahedra ● Electric conductivity: good ● Chemical composition: Co 57.96%, S 42.04%; admixtures: Ni, Cu, Fe, Se ● Chemical properties: soluble in hot HNO$_3$; colours the solution rose ● Handling: clean with distilled water ● Similar minerals: gersdorffite **(343)**, cobaltite **(345)** ● Distinguishing features: hardness, specific gravity, test for As ● Genesis: hydrothermal ● Associated minerals: galena **(77)**, chalcopyrite **(185)**, tetrahedrite **(190)** ● Occurrence: rare; Siegen, Eiserfeld, Littfeld and Grünau (FRG), Shaba (Congo), Kilembe (Uganda) ● Application: Co source.

---

1. Bravoite – fine crystals (up to 2 mm); Rico (Colorado, USA) **2. Siegenite** – euhedral crystal (2 mm) with red sphalerite in ankerite; Kladno (Czech Republic) **3. Linnaeite** – group of octahedral crystals (up to 3 mm); Müsen (FRG)

Bravoite, siegenite, linnaeite

Gersdorffite (Grey nickel pyrites, Nickel glance)

Sulphide
NiAsS

343

Named after Herr von Gersdorff, owner of Schladming Mine (Austria)
(Löwe 1842)

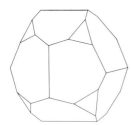

● Hardness: 5 (brittle) ● Streak: grey-black ● Colour: silvery-white, quickly becomes dull and dark ● Transparency: opaque ● Lustre: metallic ● Cleavage: perfect on (100) ● Fracture: uneven ● Morphology: crystals, granular aggregates ● Specific gravity: 5.6–6.2 ● Crystal system: cubic ● Crystal form: octahedra, hexaoctahedra or pentagon-dodecahedra ● Electric conductivity: good ● Chemical composition: Ni 35.41%, As 45.26%, S 19.33% ● Chemical properties: soluble in hot HNO_3 ● Handling: clean with distilled water and diluted acids, except HNO_3 ● Similar minerals: linnaeite (342), chloanthite (346), ullmannite (349) ● Distinguishing features: specific gravity, from ullmannite by test for Sb ● Genesis: hydrothermal ● Associated minerals: chalcopyrite (185), siderite (306), ullmannite ● Occurrence: common; Siegerland, Lobenstein and Goslar (FRG), Dobšiná (Slovakia), Mitterberg and Schladming (Austria), Cobalt – Ontario (Canada), Mina Sorpresa (Bolivia) ● Application: Ni ore.

Arsenopyrite (Arsenical pyrite, Mispickel)

Sulphide
FeAsS

344

Named after its composition
(Glocker 1847)

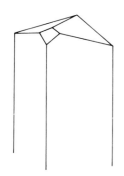

● Hardness: 5.5–6.0 (brittle) ● Streak: black ● Colour: tin-white, light steel-grey ● Transparency: opaque ● Lustre: metallic ● Cleavage: good on (110), imperfect on (001) ● Fracture: uneven ● Morphology: crystals, massive, granular and radiate aggregates ● Specific gravity: 5.9–6.2 ● Crystal system: monoclinic (pseudorhombic) ● Crystal form: prisms, pseudo-octahedra, twins ● Chemical composition: Fe 34.30%, As 46.01%, S 19.69% ● Chemical properties: soluble in HNO_3 ● Handling: clean with water and HCl ● Similar minerals: chloanthite (346), rammelsbergite (347), löllingite (350), skutterudite (438) ● Distinguishing features: X-rays, chemical properties ● Genesis: pneumatolytic, hydrothermal, metamorphic ● Associated minerals: stibnite (51), galena (77), pyrite (436) ● Occurrence: common; Sulzburg, Wittichen, Brandholz, Freiberg, Altenberg and Zinnwald (FRG), Mitterberg (Austria), Cornwall (Great Britain), Boliden (Sweden), (RSA), (USA) ● Application: As ore.

Cobaltite

Sulphide
CoAsS

345

Named after its composition
(Beudant 1832)

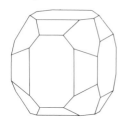

● Hardness: 5.5 (brittle) ● Streak: grey-black ● Colour: silvery-white with pinkish tint ● Transparency: opaque ● Lustre: metallic ● Cleavage: perfect on (100) ● Fracture: uneven ● Morphology: crystals, granular aggregates ● Specific gravity: 6.0–6.4 ● Crystal system: cubic ● Crystal form: octahedra, hexahedra, pentagon-dodecahedra ● Electric conductivity: good ● Chemical composition: Co 35.41%, As 45.26%, S 19.33% ● Chemical properties: soluble in hot HNO_3 ● Handling: clean with water and acids, except HNO_3 ● Similar minerals: linnaeite (342), ullmannite (349) ● Distinguishing features: test for As, X-rays, chemical properties ● Genesis: hydrothermal, contact-metasomatic ● Associated minerals: chalcopyrite (185), pyrrhotite (283), arsenopyrite (344) ● Occurrence: rare; Wittichen, Siegen, Annaberg and Schneeberg (FRG), Boliden (Sweden), (Azerbaijan), (Canada), (Australia) ● Application: Co ore.

---

1. **Gersdorffite** – coarsely tabular crystals (up to 15 mm); Lobenstein (FRG) 2. **Arsenopyrite** – crystalline aggregate (5 mm) on quartz; Příbram (Czech Republic) 3. **Cobaltite** – imperfectly developed crystals in calcite; Tunaberg (Sweden – width of field 70 mm)

Gersdorffite, arsenopyrite, cobaltite

Chloanthite (White nickel)

Sulphide
(Ni,Co)As$_3$

346

From the Greek
chloantes – greenish
(Breithaupt 1815)

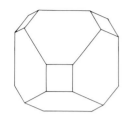

● Hardness: 5.5 (brittle) ● Streak: grey-black ● Colour: tin-white, dark grey tarnish colours ● Transparency: opaque ● Lustre: metallic ● Cleavage: absent ● Fracture: uneven ● Morphology: crystals, granular and massive aggregates ● Specific gravity: 6.4–6.6 ● Crystal system: cubic ● Crystal form: hexahedra, hexa-octahedra, dodecahedra ● Electric conductivity: good ● Chemical composition: variable (Ni greater than Co) ● Chemical properties: soluble in HNO$_3$ ● Handling: clean with HCl ● Similar minerals: safflorite **(287)**, gersdorffite **(343)**, arsenopyrite **(344)**, rammelsbergite **(347)** ● Distinguishing features: X-rays, chemical properties ● Genesis: hydrothermal ● Associated minerals: bismuth **(48)**, arsenic **(176)**, gersdorffite, skutterudite **(438)** ● Occurrence: rare; Wittichen, Nieder-Ramstadt, Annaberg and Schneeberg (FRG), Schladming (Austria), Les Chalanches (France), Bou Azzer (Morocco), (Canada) ● Application: Ni and Co ore.

Rammelsbergite

Sulphide
NiAs$_2$

347

Named after the German chemist and mineralogist, K. F. Rammelsberg (1813–1899)
(Dana 1854)

● Hardness: 5.5 (brittle) ● Streak: black ● Colour: tin-white, dark tarnish colours ● Transparency: opaque ● Lustre: full metallic ● Cleavage: indistinct ● Fracture: uneven ● Morphology: small crystals, granular, massive, radiating aggregates ● Specific gravity: 7.1 ● Crystal system: orthorhombic ● Crystal form: imperfect prisms ● Electric conductivity: good ● Chemical composition: Ni 28.15%, As 71.85% ● Chemical properties: soluble in HNO$_3$ ● Handling: clean with HCl, keep in plastic bags; oxidizes in humid air and forms coating of annabergite **(142)** ● Similar minerals: arsenopyrite **(344)**, chloanthite **(346)**, skutterudite **(438)** ● Distinguishing features: X-rays, chemical properties ● Genesis: hydrothermal ● Associated minerals: safflorite **(287)**, chloanthite, niccolite **(351)** ● Occurrence: rare; Richelsdorf, Wittichen, Schneeberg and Mansfeld (FRG), Jáchymov (Czech Republic), Turnmanntal (Switzerland), Cobalt – Ontario (Canada) ● Application: Ni ore.

Pararammelsbergite

Sulphide
NiAs$_2$

348

Named after the mineral rammelsbergite, and from the Greek *para* – similar
(Peacock 1940)

● Hardness: 5.5 ● Streak: grey-black ● Colour: silver-white, dark tarnish develops quickly ● Transparency: opaque ● Lustre: metallic ● Cleavage: perfect on (001) ● Fracture: uneven ● Morphology: crystals, massive, compact aggregates ● Specific gravity: 7.2 ● Crystal system: orthorhombic ● Crystal form: plates ● Chemical composition: Ni 28.15%, As 71.85% ● Chemical properties: soluble in HNO$_3$ ● Handling: clean with HCl ● Similar minerals: rammelsbergite **(347)** ● Distinguishing features: X-rays ● Genesis: hydrothermal ● Associated minerals: silver **(49)**, gersdorffite **(343)**, chloanthite **(346)**, niccolite **(351)** ● Occurrence: rare; Wittichen, Ölsnitz and Schneeberg (FRG), Schladming (Austria), Cobalt – Ontario (Canada) ● Application: sometimes Ni ore.

---

1. **Chloanthite** – crystalline aggregate (crystals up to 15 mm); Schneeberg (FRG) 2. **Rammelsbergite** – skeletal aggregate on calcite; Richelsdorf (FRG)

Chloanthite, rammelsbergite

Ullmannite

Sulphide
NiSbS

349

Named after the German chemist and mineralogist, J. Ch. Ullmann (1771–1821)
(Fröbel 1843)

● Hardness: 5 (brittle) ● Streak: grey-black ● Colour: silvery-white, steel-grey ● Transparency: opaque ● Lustre: metallic ● Cleavage: perfect on (100) ● Fracture: uneven ● Morphology: crystals, granular and massive aggregates ● Specific gravity: 6.7 ● Crystal system: cubic ● Crystal form: cubes, pentagon-dodecahedra, tetrahedra, twins ● Electric conductivity: good ● Chemical composition: Ni 27.62%, Sb 57.30%, S 15.08% ● Chemical properties: soluble in warm HNO_3 ● Handling: clean with water ● Similar minerals: galena **(77)**, gersdorffite **(343)**, skutterudite **(438)** ● Distinguishing features: test for Sb, X-rays, chemical properties ● Genesis: hydrothermal ● Associated minerals: chalcopyrite **(185)**, siderite **(306)**, gersdorffite, niccolite **(351)** ● Occurrence: rare; Siegerland, Harzgerode and Lobenstein (FRG), Waldenstein and Lölling (Austria), Sardinia (Italy).

Löllingite

Sulphide
$FeAs_2$

350

Named after its locality Lölling (Austria)
(Haidinger 1845)

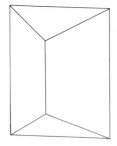

● Hardness: 5 (brittle) ● Streak: grey-black ● Colour: silvery-white, grey tarnish colours ● Transparency: opaque ● Lustre: metallic ● Cleavage: distinct on (001) ● Fracture: uneven ● Morphology: crystals, granular, massive aggregates ● Specific gravity: 7.1–7.4 ● Crystal system: orthorhombic ● Crystal form: prisms, twins ● Chemical composition: Fe 27.18%, As 72.82% ● Chemical properties: soluble in HNO_3 ● Handling: clean with water or diluted acids, except HNO_3 ● Similar minerals: arsenopyrite **(344)** ● Distinguishing features: specific gravity, X-rays, chemical properties ● Genesis: hydrothermal, pneumatolytic, in pegmatites ● Associated minerals: bismuth **(48)**, galena **(77)**, sphalerite **(181)**, arsenopyrite, chloanthite **(346)** ● Occurrence: rare; St. Andreasberg, Wittichen and Sulzburg (FRG), Złoty Stok (Poland), Lölling and Schladming (Austria), Varuträsk (Sweden), Cobalt – Ontario (Canada), Béléliéta (Algeria) ● Application: sometimes As ore.

Niccolite (Arsenical nickel)

Sulphide
NiAs

351

Named after its composition
(Beudant 1832)

● Hardness: 5.5 (brittle) ● Streak: brownish-black ● Colour: red, dark tarnish colours ● Transparency: opaque ● Lustre: metallic ● Cleavage: imperfect on (10$\bar{1}$0) and (0001) ● Fracture: conchoidal to uneven ● Morphology: individual crystals, massive, granular, rodlike and dendritic aggregates ● Specific gravity: 7.8 ● Crystal system: hexagonal ● Crystal form: prisms, pyramidal ● Electric conductivity: good ● Chemical composition: Ni 43.92%, As 56.08% ● Chemical properties: readily soluble in HNO_3 ● Handling: clean with water or diluted HCl ● Similar minerals: pyrrhotite **(283)**, native Bi ● Distinguishing features: hardness, specific gravity ● Genesis: hydrothermal, magmatic ● Associated minerals: arsenic **(176)**, safflorite **(287)**, chloanthite **(346)**, skutterudite **(438)** ● Occurrence: rare; Wolfach, Wittichen, Bieber, Schneeberg, Annaberg and Johanngeorgenstadt (FRG), Jáchymov (Czech Republic), Cobalt – Ontario (Canada) ● Application: Ni ore.

---

1. Ullmannite – crystalline aggregate (crystals up to 4 mm); Haiger (FRG) **2. Löllingite** – granular aggregate (15 mm) showing metallic lustre; Złoty Stok (Poland) **3. Niccolite** – compact aggregate with veinlet of carbonate; Bou Azzer (Morocco)

Ullmannite, löllingite, niccolite

Anatase

352

From the Greek *ánátasis*
– elongation
(Haüy 1799)

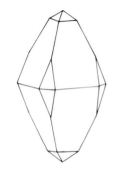

• Hardness: 5.5–6 (brittle) • Streak: white • Colour: blue, dark blue, yellow, red, brown to black • Transparency: translucent to opaque • Lustre: adamantine, greasy, submetallic • Cleavage: perfect on (101) • Fracture: conchoidal • Morphology: crystals, pseudomorphs • Specific gravity: 3.8–3.9 • Crystal system: tetragonal • Crystal form: sharp dipyramids, rarely columns and plates • Chemical composition: Ti 59.95%, O 40.05%; admixtures: Fe, Sn • Chemical properties: insoluble in acids; infusible • Handling: clean with water and diluted acids • Genesis: magmatic and metamorphic rocks, in alpine fissures, in alluvial deposits • Associated minerals: brookite **(353)**, rutile **(464)**, albite **(493)**, quartz **(534)** • Occurrence: rare; St. Gotthard, Tavetsch and Binnental (Switzerland), Bourg d'Oisans (France), Beaver Creek – Colorado (USA), Bothaville (RSA) • Application: occasionally used as a precious stone.

Brookite

353

Named after the English mineralogist, H. J. Brucke (1771–1857)
(Lévy 1825)

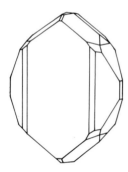

• Hardness: 5.5–6 (brittle) • Streak: yellowish-white • Colour: yellowish-brown, reddish-brown, black • Transparency: transparent to translucent • Lustre: adamantine to submetallic • Fracture: subconchoidal • Cleavage: imperfect on (110) • Morphology: crystals • Specific gravity: 4.1 • Crystal system: orthorhombic • Crystal form: plates, rarely prisms • Chemical composition: Ti 59.95%, O 40.05%; admixtures: Fe, Nb, Ta • Chemical properties: insoluble in acids; infusible • Handling: clean with water and diluted acids • Similar minerals: ilmenite **(365)** • Distinguishing features: specific gravity, very reliable X-rays, chemical tests • Genesis: in magmatic and metamorphic rocks, hydrothermal • Associated minerals: anatase **(352)**, rutile **(464)**, adularia **(487)**, albite **(493)**, quartz **(534)** • Occurrence: rare; St. Gotthard and Amsteg (Switzerland), Tremadoc – Wales (Great Britain), Bourg d'Oisans (France), Myas near Zlatoust (Russia), Magnet Cove – Arkansas (USA) • Application: occasionally used as a precious stone.

---

1. Anatase – euhedral crystal (4 mm) on albite; Binnental (Switzerland) **2. Brookite** – euhedral crystal (10 mm) on quartz; Tremadoc (Great Britain)

Goethite (Needle ironstone, Acicular iron ore)

Oxide
α – FeOOH

354

Named after the German poet, J. W. Goethe (1749–1832)
(Lenz 1806)

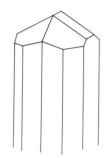

● Hardness: 5–5.5 (brittle) ● Streak: yellow ● Colour: brown, black ● Transparency: translucent to opaque ● Lustre: adamantine, submetallic, silky ● Cleavage: perfect on (010) ● Fracture: uneven to hackly ● Morphology: crystals, stalactitic, massive, earthy aggregates of radiating-fibrous arrangement, oolites, concretions, pseudomorphs ● Specific gravity: 4.3 ● Crystal system: orthorhombic ● Crystal form: prisms, fibrous ● Magnetism: paramagnetic ● Chemical composition: Fe_2O_3 89.86%, H_2O 10.14% ● Chemical properties: slowly dissolves in HCl; infusible in flame ● Handling: clean with water ● Similar minerals: manganite **(295)**, lepidocrocite **(356)**, hematite **(472)** ● Distinguishing features: streak, hardness distinguishes it from manganite and specific gravity from hematite, X-rays, chemical tests ● Genesis: secondary ● Associated minerals: siderite **(306)**, pyrite **(436)**, hematite ● Occurrence: common; Siegerland, Schwarzwald, Harz and Erzgebirge (FRG), Slovakian Ore Mountains (Slovakia), Příbram and Jáchymov (Czech Republic), Cornwall (Great Britain), (Russia), (USA), (Mexico), (Australia) ● Application: Fe ore; sometimes used as a precious stone.

Limonite
(Brown hematite, Brown ironstone, Brown iron)

Hydroxide
FeOOH . nH_2O

355

From the Latin *limus* – mud
(Hausmann 1813)

● Hardness: 5–5.5 (also lower) ● Streak: brown, yellowish-brown ● Colour: yellow, brown to black, iridescent tarnish ● Transparency: opaque ● Lustre: subvitreous, dull, silky, earthy ● Cleavage: absent ● Fracture: conchoidal, splintery ● Morphology: cryptocrystalline, fibrous, earthy, crusty, stalactitic, oolitic, massive aggregates, pseudomorphs ● Specific gravity: 3.6–3.7 ● Crystal system: orthorhombic ● Crystal form: cryptocrystalline ● Chemical composition: Fe_2O_3 89.86%, H_2O 10.14% ● Chemical properties: slowly dissolves in HCl ● Handling: clean with diluted HCl or water ● Similar minerals: hematite **(472)** ● Distinguishing features: specific gravity, hardness, streak ● Genesis: secondary ● Associated minerals: hematite, pyrolusite **(474)** ● Occurrence: common; in oxidation zones of ore deposits like goethite **(354)** ● Application: Fe ore.

Lepidocrocite

Oxide
γ – FeOOH

356

From the Greek *lepís* – scale and *krokís* – fibre
(Ullmann 1813)

● Hardness: 5 (brittle) ● Streak: dark yellow, brown ● Colour: red ● Transparency: translucent to opaque ● Lustre: adamantine, submetallic, silky ● Cleavage: perfect on (010) ● Fracture: uneven ● Morphology: crystals, scaly, fibrous, rose-shaped aggregates, also powdered ● Specific gravity: 4.0 ● Crystal system: orthorhombic ● Crystal form: plates ● Chemical composition: Fe_2O_3 89.86%, H_2O 10.14% ● Chemical properties: soluble in HCl ● Handling: clean with water ● Similar minerals: goethite **(354)** ● Distinguishing features: X-rays, crystals ● Genesis: secondary ● Associated minerals: goethite, limonite **(355)**, hematite **(472)** ● Occurrence: rare; Schneeberg, Eiserfeld, Clara Mine near Oberwolfach and Neubulach (FRG), Rožňava and Železník (Slovakia), (Italy), South Dakota and California (USA), Mapimí (Mexico).

---

1. **Goethite** – radiating aggregate; Florisant (USA) 2. **Limonite** – botryoidal aggregate; Rožňava (Slovakia – width of field 124 mm) 3. **Lepidocrocite** – finely crystalline aggregate; Rossbach (FRG – width of field 22 mm)

Goethite, limonite, lepidocrocite

Psilomelane

Oxide
(Ba,H_2O)Mn_5O_{10}

357

From the Greek *psilos* – smooth and *melas* – black
(Haidinger 1827)

● Hardness: 5 (brittle) ● Streak: black, brown ● Colour: black ● Transparency: opaque ● Lustre: submetallic, dull ● Fracture: uneven, conchoidal ● Morphology: cryptocrystalline, earthy, compact, crusty, stalactitic aggregates, dendrites ● Specific gravity: 4.4–4.7 ● Crystal system: monoclinic ● Chemical composition: variable ● Chemical properties: readily soluble in HCl, H_2SO_4, in oxalic acid and citric acid; spatters in a flame, tinges a flame green ● Handling: clean with water ● Similar minerals: hausmannite **(358)**, pyrolusite **(474)** ● Distinguishing features: specific gravity, streak ● Genesis: secondary ● Associated minerals: calcite **(217)**, baryte **(240)**, siderite **(306)**, limonite **(355)**, pyrolusite ● Occurrence: common; Schneeberg and Ilfeld (FRG), Železník (Slovakia), Nikopol (Ukraine), Cornwall (Great Britain), Ouro Preto (Brazil), (USA), (India) ● Application: Mn ore; sometimes used as a decorative stone.

Hausmannite

Oxide
Mn_3O_4

358

Named after the German mineralogist, J. F. L. Hausmann
(1782–1859)
(Haidinger 1827)

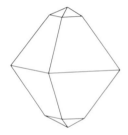

● Hardness: 5.5 (brittle) ● Streak: brown ● Colour: black ● Transparency: translucent to opaque ● Lustre: submetallic, metallic ● Cleavage: perfect ● Fracture: uneven ● Morphology: crystals, granular, massive aggregates, pseudomorphs ● Specific gravity: 4.7–4.8 ● Crystal system: tetragonal ● Crystal form: dipyramidal, pseudooctahedra, twins ● Chemical composition: Mn 72%, O 28% ● Chemical properties: infusible; soluble in HCl ● Handling: clean with water ● Similar minerals: psilomelane **(357)**, magnetite **(367)** ● Distinguishing features: specific gravity, streak, magnetism ● Genesis: metamorphic, metasomatic, hydrothermal ● Associated minerals: dolomite **(218)**, baryte **(240)**, psilomelane ● Occurrence: rare; Ilmenau and Ilfeld (FRG), Långban (Sweden), Nikopol (Ukraine), (Brazil), Arkansas (USA), (India) ● Application: Mn ore.

Pyrochlore

Oxide
$(Na,Ca)_2(Nb,Ti,Ta)_2O_6(OH,F,O)$

359

From the Greek *pyr* – fire and *chloros* – green
(Wöhler 1826)

R

● Hardness: 5–5.5 (brittle) ● Streak: brown, yellowish-brown ● Colour: brown, greenish, reddish ● Transparency: translucent to opaque ● Lustre: greasy ● Cleavage: imperfect ● Fracture: conchoidal, uneven ● Morphology: crystals, granular aggregates, impregnations ● Specific gravity: 4.3–4.5 ● Crystal system: cubic ● Crystal form: octahedra, hexahedra, twins ● Radioactivity: varying, according to the amount of admixed U ● Chemical composition: variable; often admixtures of U and of rare earths ● Chemical properties: dissolves with difficulty in HCl, H_2SO_4 and HF; thin edges fuse in a blowpipe flame ● Handling: clean with diluted acids ● Similar minerals: microlite **(360)**, perovskite **(363)** ● Distinguishing features: streak, X-rays, chemical tests ● Genesis: carbonates, pegmatites ● Associated minerals: apatite **(379)**, nepheline **(397)**, allanite **(410)**, zircon **(587)** ● Occurrence: rare; Laacher See and Kaiserstuhl (FRG), Frederiksvärn (Norway), (Tanzania), (Uganda), (Zimbabwe), (Malawi) ● Application: source of Nb and of rare earths including U.

---

1. **Hausmannite** – crystalline aggregate (the largest crystal 10 mm); Oehrenstock (FRG) 2. **Psilomelane** – dendritic aggregate lining crack in limestone; Solenhofen (FRG – width of field 66 mm) 3. **Pyrochlore** – euhedral crystal (6 mm) in feldspar; Urals (Russia)

Hausmannite, psilomelane, pyrochlore

Microlite

Oxide
$(Ca,Na)_2(Ta,Nb,Ti)_2O_6(OH,O,F)$

360

From the Greek *mikros* – small and *lithos* – stone
(Shephard 1835)

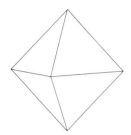

● Hardness: 5–5.5 (brittle) ● Streak: light yellow, white ● Colour: yellowish-brown, greenish-brown, reddish, grey ● Transparency: transparent to translucent ● Lustre: vitreous, greasy ● Cleavage: imperfect on (111) ● Fracture: conchoidal, uneven ● Morphology: crystals, granular aggregates ● Specific gravity: 4.3–5.7 ● Crystal system: cubic ● Crystal form: octahedra, hexahedra and their combinations ● Chemical composition: variable ● Chemical properties: slowly soluble in H_2SO_4 ● Handling: clean with diluted acids except H_2SO_4 ● Similar minerals: pyrochlore **(259)** ● Distinguishing features: X-rays, chemical tests ● Genesis: in pegmatites ● Associated minerals: lepidolite **(169)**, pollucite **(500)**, spodumene **(502)** ● Occurrence: rare; Elba (Italy), Iveland (Norway), Varuträsk (Sweden), Bikita (Zimbabwe), Wodgina (Australia), Virginia (USA) ● Application: sometimes Ta source.

Romeite (Antimony ochre)

Oxide
$(Ca,Na)Sb_2O_6(O,OH,F)$

361

Named after the French crystallographer, J. B. Romé de l'Isle (1736–1770)
(Damour 1841)

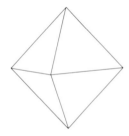

● Hardness: 5.5–6.0 ● Streak: yellow, brown ● Colour: white, yellow, yellowish-brown, brownish-red ● Transparency: opaque to translucent ● Lustre: vitreous, greasy ● Cleavage: imperfect on (111) ● Fracture: hackly, conchoidal ● Morphology: crystals, earthy crusts, powdered and massive aggregates ● Specific gravity: 4.9–5.4 ● Crystal system: cubic ● Crystal form: octahedra ● Chemical composition: variable ● Chemical properties: insoluble in HCl, HNO_3 and H_2SO_4; infusible ● Handling: clean with distilled water ● Genesis: secondary in oxidation zones ● Associated minerals: stibnite **(51)**, cinnbar **(76)**, braunite **(469)** ● Occurrence: rare; Clara Mine near Oberwolfach, Schneeberg (FRG), St. Marcel (Italy), Långban (Sweden).

Plattnerite

Oxide
PbO_2

362

Named after the German metallurgist, K. F. Plattner (1800–1858)
(Haidinger 1845)

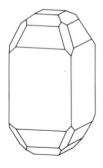

● Hardness: 5.5 (brittle) ● Streak: brown ● Colour: grey-black, black ● Transparency: opaque, in thin slabs translucent with ruby-red colour ● Lustre: full metallic, adamantine ● Cleavage: absent ● Fracture: conchoidal ● Morphology: crystals, coatings, deposits, massive and fibrous aggregates ● Specific gravity: 9.63 ● Crystal system: tetragonal ● Crystal form: prisms, dipyramids ● Chemical composition: Pb 86.62%, O 13.38% ● Chemical properties: readily soluble in HCl; in HNO_3 and H_2SO_4 dissolves with difficulty; readily fusible; in a blowpipe flame turns light yellow ● Handling: clean with distilled water ● Similar minerals: psilomelane **(357)** ● Distinguishing features: blowpipe test ● Genesis: secondary in oxidation zones in arid areas ● Associated minerals: cerussite **(225)**, jarosite **(236)**, wulfenite **(243)**, pyromorphite **(262)** ● Occurrence: rare; Leadhills – Scotland (Great Britain), Idaho – in Pb deposits: with coatings weighing up to 80 kg (USA), Mapimí (Mexico), Zaudjit (Iran).

Plattnerite – coatings on orange mimetite; Anarak (Iran – width of field 25 mm)

Plattnerite

Perovskite

Oxide
CaTiO₃

363

Named after the Russian mineralogist, L. A. Perovski (1792–1856) (Rose 1839)

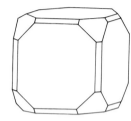

● Hardness: 5.5 ● Streak: white, grey ● Colour: black, reddish-brown, yellow ● Transparency: opaque to translucent ● Lustre: adamantine, metallic, greasy ● Cleavage: good on (100) ● Fracture: conchoidal ● Morphology: crystals, granular aggregates, reniform masses ● Specific gravity: 4.0 ● Crystal system: orthorhombic ● Crystal form: pseudohexahedra, pseudooctahedra, twins ● Radioactivity: sometimes radioactive, according to admixtures ● Chemical composition: CaO 41.24%, TiO₂ 58.76% ● Chemical properties: swells and dissolves in H₂SO₄; also soluble in cold HF; infusible ● Handling: clean with distilled water ● Similar minerals: magnetite **(367)** ● Distinguishing features: magnetism, streak ● Genesis: in ultrabasic rocks, carbonates, basalts ● Associated minerals: pyrochlore **(359)**, ilmenite **(365)**, leucite **(396)**, titanite **(430)** ● Occurrence: rare; Kaiserstuhl (FRG), Pfitsch (Austria), Zermatt (Switzerland), Akhmatovsk (Russia), Vuorijärvi (Finland), Bagagem (Brazil), Magnet Cove – Arkansas (USA) ● Application: source of rare earths and Ti.

Pyrophanite

Oxide
MnTiO₃

364

From the Greek *pyr* – fire and *fanos* – shining (Hamberg 1890)

● Hardness: 5 ● Streak: ochre yellow ● Colour: dark red, raspberry-red, black ● Transparency: translucent ● Lustre: metallic, adamantine ● Cleavage: perfect on (02$\bar{2}$1) ● Morphology: crystals, scales ● Specific gravity: 4.5 ● Crystal system: trigonal ● Crystal form: plates ● Chemical composition: MnO₂ 46.96%, TiO₂ 53.04% ● Chemical properties: dissolves with difficulty in acids ● Handling: clean with diluted acids or water ● Similar minerals: sometimes ilmenite **(365)** ● Distinguishing features: streak, X-rays, chemical tests ● Genesis: metamorphic, in pegmatites ● Associated minerals: nepheline **(397)**, titanite **(430)**, rhodonite **(531)** ● Occurrence: rare; Pajsberg (Sweden), (Norway), Lovozer Massif (Russia), Benallt Mine – Wales (Great Britain), Piquery Mine and Minas Gerais (Brazil).

Ilmenite (Titanoferrite)

Oxide
FeTiO₃

365

Named after its locality in Ilmen Mountains (southern Urals, Russia) (Kupffer 1827)

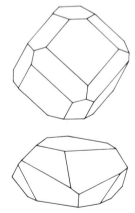

● Hardness: 5–6 ● Streak: black-brown ● Colour: black ● Transparency: opaque ● Lustre: metallic, greasy ● Cleavage: absent ● Fracture: conchoidal, uneven ● Morphology: crystals, massive, granular, rose-shaped aggregates ● Specific gravity: 4.5–5.0 ● Crystal system: trigonal ● Crystal form: plates ● Magnetism: slightly magnetic ● Radioactivity: sometimes radioactive, according to admixtures ● Chemical composition: FeO 47.34%, TiO₂ 52.66% ● Chemical properties: insoluble in acids ● Handling: clean with diluted acids or water ● Similar minerals: pyrophanite **(364)**, magnetite **(367)**, chromite **(371)**, hematite **(472)** ● Distinguishing features: streak, magnetism, X-rays, chemical tests ● Genesis: magmatic, in pegmatites, in alpine veins, in alluvial deposits ● Associated minerals: magnetite, apatite **(379)**, titanite **(430)**, hematite, rutile **(464)** ● Occurrence: common; Aschaffenburg (FRG), St. Gotthard and Binnental (Switzerland), Bourg d'Oisans (France), Cornwall (Great Britain), Kragerö (Norway), Ilmen Mountains – southern Urals (Russia), New York (USA), Quebec (Canada) ● Application: Ti ore.

1. Perovskite – euhedral crystals (up to 10 mm); Urals (Russia) **2. Ilmenite** – imperfectly-formed crystals (up to 10 mm); Pletherhorn (Sweden)

Jacobsite

Oxide
MnFe$_2$O$_4$

366

Named after its locality
Jakobsberg (Sweden)
(Damour 1869)

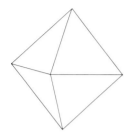

● Hardness: 5.5–6.0 (brittle) ● Streak: reddish-black ● Colour: iron-black ● Transparency: opaque ● Lustre: metallic to submetallic ● Cleavage: absent ● Fracture: uneven, conchoidal ● Morphology: crystals, massive and granular aggregates ● Specific gravity: 4.75 ● Crystal system: cubic ● Crystal form: octahedra ● Magnetism: actively magnetic ● Chemical composition: MnO 30.76%, Fe$_2$O$_3$ 69.24% ● Chemical properties: soluble in HCl; infusible ● Handling: clean with distilled water or diluted acids, except HCl ● Similar minerals: magnetite **(367)** ● Distinguishing features: chemical properties ● Genesis: metamorphic ● Associated minerals: hausmannite **(358),** magnetite, hematite **(472),** pyrolusite **(474)** ● Occurrence: rare; Jakobsberg and Långban (Sweden), Karadzhal and Dzhumart (Kazakhstan), Wibong (Australia), Kadur (India), Postmasburg (RSA) ● Application: occasionally as Mn ore.

Magnetite (Lodestone, Magnetic iron ore)

Oxide
Fe$_3$O$_4$

367

The origin of the name
is unknown
(Haidinger 1845)

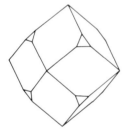

● Hardness: 5.5 (brittle) ● Streak: black ● Colour: black ● Transparency: opaque ● Lustre: metallic, greasy, dull ● Cleavage: imperfect on (111) ● Fracture: conchoidal ● Morphology: crystals, massive and granular aggregates, impregnations ● Specific gravity: 5.2 ● Crystal system: cubic ● Crystal form: octahedra, dodecahedra, twins ● Magnetism: strong ● Chemical composition: FeO 31.03%, Fe$_2$O$_3$ 68.97%; admixtures: Ti, V, Mn, Mg, Al, Cr. Titanomagnetite variety contains ilmenite **(365)** ● Chemical properties: dissolves with difficulty in HCl; infusible in flame ● Handling: clean with distilled water or diluted acids; dry thoroughly ● Similar minerals: ilmenite, jacobsite **(366),** chromite **(371),** hematite **(472)** ● Distinguishing features: streak colour, magnetism, X-rays, chemical tests ● Genesis: magmatic, metamorphic, contact-metasomatic, hydrothermal, rarely in pegmatites, sedimentary, becomes concentrated in alluvial deposits ● Associated minerals: ilmenite, apatite **(379),** augite **(429),** hematite, amphiboles ● Occurrence: common; Auerbach and Göttingen – titanomagnetites, Berggiesshübel and Pöhla (FRG), Luossavaara, Kirunavaara, Gällivaara, Dannemora and Taberg (Sweden), Otanmäki (Finland), Magnitnaya Gora, Blagodat and Dashkesan (Russia), Ocna de fier and Dagnacea (Romania), Alto Adige (Italy), Zillertal (Austria), Binnental (Switzerland), (Australia), (Brazil), (USA), (India), (Egypt – alluvial deposits in the Nile delta) ● Application: one of the most valuable ores of Fe.

Magnetite – idiomorphic octahedral crystals (20 mm) with tabular aggregates of hematite ('Alpine roses') in Alpine veins; The Alps (Switzerland)

Magnetite

297

Hübnerite

Tungstate
MnWO$_4$

368

Named after the German mining engineer, A. Hübner (Riotte 1865)

● Hardness: 5 (brittle) ● Streak: brown, greenish-grey ● Colour: brownish-red, brownish-black ● Transparency: translucent to opaque ● Lustre: submetallic, greasy ● Cleavage: perfect on (010) ● Fracture: uneven ● Morphology: crystals, parallel and hemispherical aggregates ● Specific gravity: 6.4–7.1 ● Crystal system: monoclinic ● Crystal form: prisms, thin plates ● Chemical composition: MnO 23.42%, WO$_3$ 76.58% ● Chemical properties: fuses with difficulty; not readily soluble in HCl and H$_2$SO$_4$ ● Handling: clean with water ● Genesis: in pegmatites, pneumatolytic, hydrothermal ● Associated minerals: wolframite **(369)**, cassiterite **(548)**, topaz **(595)** ● Occurrence: rare; Clara Mine near Oberwolfach, Altenberg (FRG), Horní Slavkov (Czech Republic), (France), Colorado (USA), (Bolivia), (Peru) ● Application: W ore.

Wolframite

Tungstate
(Fe,Mn)WO$_4$

369

Probably from the German *Wolf* – wolf and *Rahm* – foam (Breithaupt 1832)

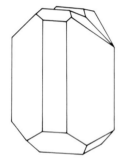

● Hardness: 5–5.5 (brittle) ● Streak: black, black-brown ● Colour: black, dark brown ● Transparency: opaque ● Lustre: metallic, greasy ● Cleavage: perfect on (010) ● Fracture: uneven ● Morphology: crystals, massive and granular aggregates ● Specific gravity: 7.1–7.5 ● Crystal system: monoclinic ● Crystal form: plates, prisms ● Magnetism: slight ● Chemical composition: FeO 11.84%, MnO 11.70%, WO$_3$ 76.46% (Fe:Mn = 1:1). Wolframite is the intermediate member of the isomorphous series: hübnerite-ferberite ● Chemical properties: fuses with difficulty; soluble in hot HCl and H$_2$SO$_4$; when fused produces a magnetic ball ● Handling: clean with water or diluted acids ● Similar minerals: niobite **(478)** ● Distinguishing features: hardness, specific gravity, solubility in acids ● Genesis: in pegmatites, pneumatolytic, hydrothermal ● Associated minerals: molybdenite **(8)**, fluorite **(291)**, scheelite **(310)**, topaz **(595)** ● Occurrence: common; Clara Mine near Oberwolfach, Altenberg, Zinnwald and Tirpersdorf (FRG), Krásno and Cínovec (Czech Republic), Caceres (Spain), Panasqueira (Portugal), (Russia), (South Korea), (Bolivia), Colorado (USA), (Japan), (Malaysia), (Thailand), (Burma), (Australia), (China) ● Application: W ore.

Ferberite

Tungstate
FeWO$_4$

370

Named after R. Ferber from Gera (FRG) (Breithaupt 1863)

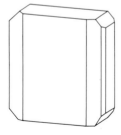

● Hardness: 5.5 (brittle) ● Streak: dark brown, black ● Colour: black, grey-black ● Transparency: opaque ● Lustre: submetallic, dull ● Cleavage: perfect on (010) ● Fracture: uneven ● Morphology: crystals, massive and granular aggregates ● Specific gravity: 6.8–7.5 ● Crystal system: monoclinic ● Crystal form: plates, prisms ● Magnetism: dull ● Chemical composition: FeO 23.65%, WO$_3$ 76.35% ● Chemical properties: readily fusible; soluble in hot HCl and H$_2$SO$_4$ ● Handling: clean with water ● Similar minerals: niobite **(478)** ● Distinguishing features: the same as for wolframite **(369)** ● Genesis: in pegmatites, pneumatolytic, hydrothermal ● Associated minerals: scheelite **(310)**, wolframite, topaz **(595)** ● Occurrence: rare; (FRG), Colorado (USA), (Bolivia), (Peru), (Greenland).

Wolframite – crystalline aggregate (30 mm) on baryte; Baia Sprie (Romania)

Wolframite

Chromite (Chromic iron, Chrome iron ore)

Oxide
$(Fe,Mg)Cr_2O_4$

371

Named after its chemical composition
(Haidinger 1845)

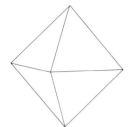

● Hardness: 5.5 ● Streak: brown ● Colour: black, brownish-black ● Transparency: opaque ● Lustre: greasy, submetallic ● Cleavage: absent ● Fracture: uneven, conchoidal ● Morphology: crystals are rare, granular and massive aggregates, impregnations, nests, pebbles in alluvial deposits ● Specific gravity: 4.5−4.8 ● Crystal system: cubic ● Crystal form: octahedra ● Chemical composition: FeO 17.26%, MgO 9.69%, Cr_2O_3 73.05% (Fe:Mg = 1:1); often contains up to 32% FeO; admixtures Al, Zn, Mn ● Chemical properties: insoluble in acids; infusible ● Handling: clean with water and diluted acids ● Similar minerals: magnetite **(367)**, franklinite **(470)** ● Distinguishing features: streak, hardness, test for Cr, solubility in acids ● Genesis: magmatic in ultrabasic rocks, meteorites ● Associated minerals: magnetite, bronzite **(427)**, olivine **(524)**, uvarovite **(581)** ● Occurrence: common; Bärenstein (FRG), Kraubath (Austria), Guleman, Dagardi and Fethyie (Turkey), (Serbia), (Bulgaria), (Albania), (Iran), Great Dyke (Zimbabwe), (RSA), (Pakistan), Luzon (Philippines), (New Caledonia), (Russia), (Brazil), (USA) ● Application: the most important chromium ore; used in metallurgy, ceramics manufacturing, glass industry and manufacture of fireproof fabrics.

Ludwigite

Borate
$(Mg,Fe^{2+})_2Fe^{3+}(BO_3)O_2$

372

Named after the Austrian chemist, E. Ludwig
(1842−1915)
(Tschermak 1874)

● Hardness: 5 (brittle) ● Streak: black-green ● Colour: black ● Transparency: opaque ● Lustre: silky, dull ● Cleavage: perfect on (001) ● Morphology: compact, massive, fibrous and radiating aggregates, crystals are rare ● Specific gravity: 3.7−4.0 ● Crystal system: orthorhombic ● Crystal form: prisms ● Chemical composition: FeO 31.67%, MgO 17.77%, Fe_2O_3 35.21%, B_2O_3 15.35% (Mg:Fe = 1:1) ● Chemical properties: slightly soluble in acids; when heated in air turns red ● Handling: clean with distilled water ● Similar minerals: ilvarte **(425)** ● Distinguishing features: solubility, fusibility, reaction when heated ● Genesis: contact-metamorphic ● Associated minerals: magnetite **(367)**, diopside **(505)** ● Occurrence: rare; Pöhla (FRG), Dognacea (Romania), Norberg and Sjögrube (Sweden), Suan (Korea), Gorman − California, Gulch − Colorado and Montana (USA), Hanayama Mine (Japan).

1. **Chromite** − granular aggregate in serpentinite; Bulquiza (Albania − width of field 128 mm) 2. **Ludwigite** − radiate fibrous aggregate; Dognacea (Romania − width of field 20 mm)

Chromite, ludwigite

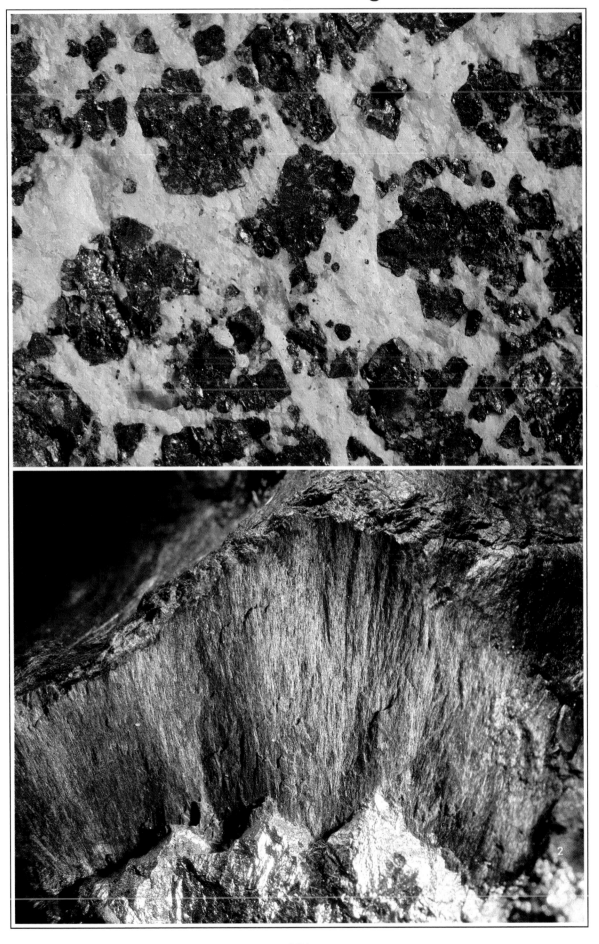

Smithsonite (Galmei, Calamine, Zinc spar)

Carbonate
$ZnCO_3$

373

Named after the English mineralogist, J. Smithson (1765–1829) (Beudant 1832)

● Hardness: 5 (brittle) ● Streak: white ● Colour: white, yellow, red, green, blue-green ● Transparency: transparent to translucent ● Lustre: vitreous, pearly ● Cleavage: perfect on (10$\bar{1}$1) ● Fracture: uneven ● Morphology: crystals, crystalline crusts, coatings, stalactitic, granular and earthy aggregates ● Specific gravity: 4.3–4.5 ● Crystal system: trigonal ● Crystal form: rhombohedra ● Luminescence: sometimes white, blue-white or greenish-white ● Chemical composition: ZnO 64.90%, CO_2 35.10% ● Chemical properties: soluble in acids; infusible ● Handling: clean with water ● Similar minerals: calcite **(217)**, hemimorphite **(403)**, chalcedony **(449)** ● Distinguishing features: hardness, specific gravity, X-rays, chemical tests ● Genesis: secondary in oxidation zones ● Associated minerals: galena **(77)**, hydrozincite **(103)**, sphalerite **(181)**, hemimorphite ● Occurrence: common; Altenberg and Wiesloch (FRG), Raibl and Bleiberg (Austria), Lávrion (Greece), Monteponi – Sardinia (Italy), Matlock (Great Britain), (Russia), Tsumeb (Namibia), (Algeria), (USA), (Vietnam), (Australia) ● Application: Zn ore; sometimes used as a precious stone.

Turquoise (Callaite)

Phosphate
$CuAl_6(PO_4)_4(OH)_8 . 4 H_2O$

374

Named after Turkey (from where it was brought to Europe) (Tavernier 1678)

● Hardness: 5–6 (brittle) ● Streak: white ● Colour: light blue to apple green ● Transparency: opaque ● Lustre: greasy ● Cleavage: good on (001) ● Fracture: uneven, conchoidal ● Morphology: cryptocrystalline, massive, compact, veins, crusts ● Specific gravity: 2.6–2.8 ● Crystal system: triclinic ● Luminescence: greenish-yellow, light blue ● Chemical composition: CuO 9.78%, Al_2O_3 37.60%, P_2O_5 34.90%, H_2O 17.72% ● Chemical properties: slightly soluble in HCl; infusible in a flame; turns brown when heated. Imitations are fusible and tinge a flame green ● Handling: clean with water ● Similar minerals: lazurite **(378)**, variscite **(311)** ● Distinguishing features: hardness, specific gravity, reaction in a blowpipe flame, solubility in HCl ● Genesis: secondary ● Associated minerals: limonite **(355)**, chalcedony **(449)** ● Occurrence: rare; Oelsnitz (FRG), (Poland), (Uzbekistan), (Iran), (Egypt), (USA), (China) ● Application: used as a precious stone.

Brazilianite

Phosphate
$NaAl_3(PO_4)_2(OH)_4$

375

Named after its first discovery in Brazil (Pough 1945)

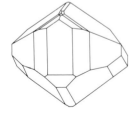

● Hardness: 5.5 (brittle) ● Streak: white ● Colour: light yellow, yellowish-green ● Transparency: transparent ● Lustre: vitreous ● Cleavage: good on (010) ● Fracture: conchoidal ● Morphology: crystals, spherulitic aggregates ● Specific gravity: 2.98 ● Crystal system: monoclinic ● Crystal form: isometric, prisms ● Chemical composition: Na_2O 8.56%, Al_2O_3 42.25%, P_2O_5 39.23%, H_2O 9.96% ● Chemical properties: slightly fusible, swells and turns white; soluble in HF and hot H_2SO_4 ● Handling: clean with water ● Similar minerals: topaz **(515)** ● Distinguishing features: hardness, specific gravity ● Genesis: in pegmatites ● Associated minerals: muscovite **(165)**, apatite **(379)**, albite **(493)** ● Occurrence: rare; Minas Gerais (Brazil), New Hampshire (USA) ● Application: used as a precious stone.

---

1. Turquoise – chamber deposits (polished section); Nishapur (Iran – width of field 25 mm) **2. Smithsonite** – aggregate of globular crystals; Broken Hill (Australia – width of field 41 mm) **3. Brazilianite** – crystal (20 mm); Minas Gerais (Brazil)

Bukovskyite

Arsenate
$Fe_2^{3+}(AsO_4)(SO_4)(OH) . 7 H_2O$

376

Named after the Czech chemist, A. Bukovský (1865–1950) (Novák 1967)

• Hardness: 5 • Streak: yellowish-white • Colour: light yellow, orange, grey-green • Transparency: translucent to non-transparent • Fracture: uneven, earthy • Morphology: nodules, bunches, microcrystalline aggregates • Specific gravity: 2.34 • Crystal system: monoclinic • Crystal form: needles, fibres • Chemical composition: Fe_2O_3 32.61%, SO_3 16.34%, As_2O_5 23.46%, H_2O 27.59% • Similar minerals: delvauxite **(135)**, diadochite **(245)** • Distinguishing features: hardness, test for As • Genesis: secondary • Associated minerals: gypsum **(29)**, arsenopyrite **(344)**, limonite **(355)** • Occurrence: rare; Kaňk near Kutná Hora (Czech Republic).

Amblygonite

Phosphate
$(Li, Na)Al(PO_4)(F, OH)$

377

From the Greek *amblys* – blunt and *góni* – angle (Breithaupt 1817)

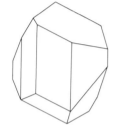

• Hardness: 5.5–6 • Streak: white • Colour: white, yellow, grey, bluish, greenish • Transparency: transparent to translucent • Lustre: vitreous, greasy, pearly • Cleavage: perfect, good on (110) • Fracture: uneven, subconchoidal • Morphology: crystals, massive • Specific gravity: 3.0–3.1 • Crystal system: triclinic • Crystal form: prisms • Luminescence: sometimes orange in long wave UV • Chemical composition: variable; the Li:Na ratio alters with F:OH • Chemical properties: readily fusible, swells and changes into opaque white ball; not readily soluble in acids • Handling: clean with distilled water • Similar minerals: albite **(493)** • Distinguishing features: specific gravity, optical properties • Genesis: in pegmatites, pneumatolytic • Associated minerals: apatite **(379)**, pollucite **(500)**, spodumene **(502)**, tourmaline **(564)** • Occurrence: rare; Varuträsk (Sweden), Montebras (France), (Burma), (Namibia), Maine and South Dakota (USA), Paraiba (Brazil). • Application: Li source; used as a precious stone.

Lazulite (Blue spar)

Phosphate
$(Mg,Fe)Al_2(PO_4)_2(OH)_2$

378

From the Arabic *azul* – sky and the Greek *líthos* – stone (Klaproth 1795)

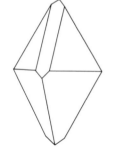

• Hardness: 5–6 (brittle) • Streak: white • Colour: blue, blue-green, blue-white • Transparency: translucent to opaque • Lustre: vitreous • Cleavage: on (001) • Fracture: uneven, splintery • Morphology: crystals, massive and granular aggregates • Specific gravity: 3.0 • Crystal system: monoclinic • Crystal form: sharp pyramidal • Luminescence: white • Chemical composition: composite • Chemical properties: slowly soluble in hot acids; infusible • Handling: clean with diluted HCl • Similar minerals: turquoise **(374)**, lazurite **(392)** • Distinguishing features: specific gravity, solubility in acids, fusibility, X-rays, chemical tests • Genesis: in pegmatites, metamorphic in quartzites • Associated minerals: muscovite **(165)**, quartz **(534)** • Occurrence: rare; Rädelgraben near Werfen and Krieglach (Austria), Zermatt (Switzerland), Nitra (Slovakia), Horrsjöberg (Sweden), Tijuco (Brazil), Bity (Madagascar), Georgia and California (USA) • Application: used as a precious stone.

Lazulite – granular nodule in quartz; Nitra (Slovakia – width of field 30 mm)

Lazulite

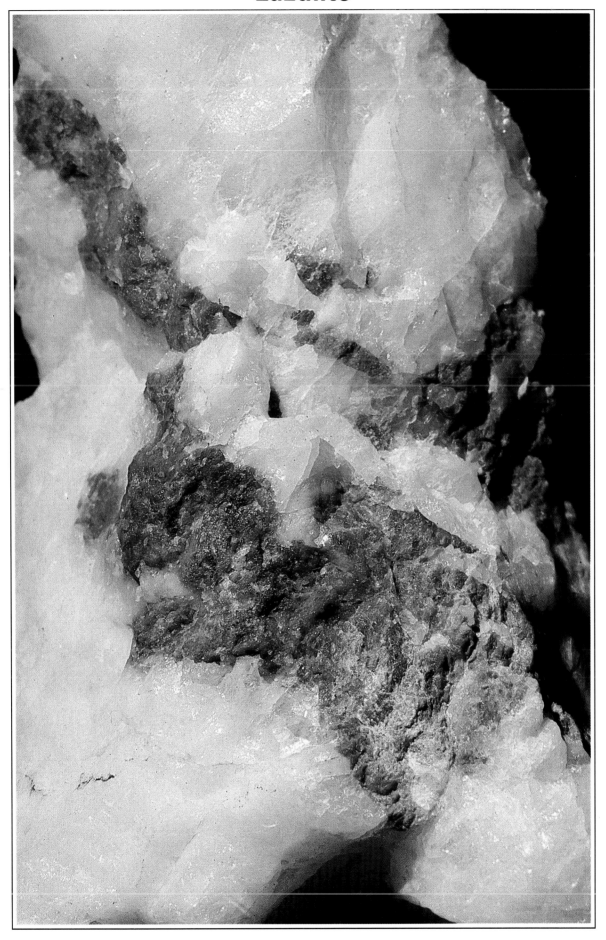

Apatite

Phosphate
$Ca_5(PO_4)_3(F,OH)$

379

L

R

P

From the Greek *apatao* – I am misleading (Werner 1786)

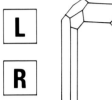

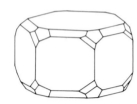

● Hardness: 5 (brittle) ● Streak: white ● Colour: white, yellowish-green, dull green, blue-green, violet, red, brownish-red ● Transparency: transparent to translucent ● Lustre: vitreous, greasy ● Cleavage: imperfect on (0001) and on (10$\bar{1}$0) ● Fracture: uneven, conchoidal ● Morphology: crystals, granular, massive, crusty, earthy, oolitic aggregates ● Specific gravity: 3.16–3.22 ● Crystal system: hexagonal ● Crystal form: short and long prisms, coarse plates ● Luminescence: yellow, yellowish-orange, pink, light green, blue and white ● Chemical composition: composite; frequent admixtures: Cl (chlorapatite), Sr and rare earths (belovite variety), Si (wilkeite variety), Ce (britholite variety), S^{6+} (allestadite variety), Mn (mangualdite variety) ● Chemical properties: soluble in acids, fusible only on edges ● Handling: clean with distilled water ● Similar minerals: nepheline **(397)**, quartz **(534)**, beryl **(554)** ● Distinguishing features: hardness, specific gravity, solubility in acids ● Genesis: magmatic, in pegmatites, pneumatolytic, hydrothermal, sedimentary ● Associated minerals: fluorite **(291)**, arsenopyrite **(344)**, cassiterite **(548)**, topaz **(595)** ● Occurrence: common; Ehrenfriedersdorf, Menzenschwand and Waldstein (FRG), Horní Slavkov (Czech Republic), Panasqueira (Portugal), Ödegarden (Norway), St. Gotthard (Switzerland), Durango (Mexico), Kola Peninsula (Russia), Kiruna (Sweden), Palabora (RSA). Apatite is an important component of phosphorites worked in Florida (USA), (Morocco), (Nauru Island) ● Application: manufacture of fertilizers, chemical industry; sometimes used as a gemstone (facets, cabochons).

Scorzalite

Phosphate
$(Fe,Mg)Al_2(PO_4)_2(OH)_2$

380

Named after the Brazilian mineralogist, E. P. Scorzu (Pecora, Fahey 1947)

● Hardness: 5.5–6 (brittle) ● Streak: white ● Colour: dark blue to blue-green ● Transparency: translucent to non-transparent ● Lustre: vitreous, dull ● Cleavage: good on (110) ● Fracture: uneven ● Morphology: massive, compact and granular aggregates ● Specific gravity: 3.27 ● Crystal system: monoclinic ● Crystal form: bipyramidal, plates ● Chemical composition: like lazulite **(378)**, but with Fe > Mg ● Chemical properties: slowly soluble in hot acids ● Handling: clean with dilute HCl or distilled water ● Similar minerals: lazurite **(392)** ● Distinguishing features: reaction in a blowpipe flame, solubility in HCl, specific gravity ● Genesis: in pegmatites ● Associated minerals: brazilianite **(375)**, apatite **(379)**, albite **(493)** ● Occurrence: rare; Corrego Frio Mine and Minas Gerais (Brazil), Victory Mine – South Dakota and Mono Co. – California (USA).

1. Apatite – crystal (20 mm) embedded in feldspar; Wibeforce (Canada) **2. Scorzalite** – blue granular aggregate; Siberia (Russia – width of field 35 mm)

Apatite, scorzalite

Graftonite

Phosphate
(Fe,Mn,Ca)₃(PO₄)₂

381

Named after its locality Grafton (New Hampshire, USA)
(Penfield 1900)

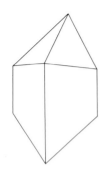

● Hardness: 5 ● Streak: white, light pink ● Colour: pink to brown ● Transparency: translucent ● Lustre: vitreous, greasy ● Cleavage: perfect on (010) ● Fracture: uneven, conchoidal ● Morphology: imperfect crystals, massive ● Specific gravity: 3.67 ● Crystal system: monoclinic ● Crystal form: short prisms ● Chemical composition: CaO 9.50%, FeO 31.51%, MnO 18.13%, P_2O_5 40.86% ● Chemical properties: readily fusible into a black magnetic ball; readily soluble in acids ● Handling: clean with distilled water ● Similar minerals: sicklerite (314) ● Distinguishing features: X-rays, chemical tests, hardness ● Genesis: in pegmatites ● Associated minerals: triphylite (315), beryl (554), tourmaline (564) ● Occurrence: rare; Brissago (Switzerland), Přibyslavice (Czech Republic), Grafton – New Hampshire and Greenwood – Maine (USA).

Triplite

Phosphate
(Mn,Fe)₂(PO₄)F

382

From the Greek *triplós* – triplex
(Hausmann 1813)

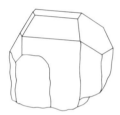

● Hardness: 5 ● Streak: yellow-grey ● Colour: brown, red to black ● Transparency: translucent to opaque ● Lustre: vitreous, greasy ● Cleavage: good on (010) and (100) ● Fracture: uneven, conchoidal ● Morphology: crystals are rare, granular and massive aggregates ● Specific gravity: 3.5–3.9 ● Crystal system: monoclinic ● Crystal form: isometric ● Chemical composition: variable; isomorphous series with end members triplite (Mn>Fe) and zwieselite (Fe>Mn) ● Chemical properties: soluble in acids; readily fusible into a steel-grey magnetic ball ● Handling: clean with distilled water ● Genesis: in pegmatites ● Associated minerals: apatite (379), quartz (534), cassiterite (548) ● Occurrence: rare; Zwiesel and Hagendorf (FRG), Cyrilov and Vídeň (Czech Republic), Branchville – Connecticut, Black Hills – South Dakota and El Paso Co. – Colorado (USA), Sierra de Córdoba (Argentina).

Monazite

Phosphate
CePO₄

383

R

From the Greek *monazeis* – sole
(Breithaupt 1829)

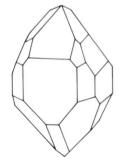

● Hardness: 5–5.5 (brittle) ● Streak: grey-white ● Colour: brown, red, yellow, orange ● Transparency: translucent to opaque ● Lustre: adamantine, greasy ● Cleavage: perfect on (001) ● Fracture: conchoidal ● Morphology: crystals, granular aggregates, loose in sands ● Specific gravity: 4.8–5.5 ● Crystal system: monoclinic ● Crystal form: plates, prisms ● Radioactivity: radioactive if it contains Th ● Chemical composition: Ce_2O_3 82.22%, P_2O_5 17.78%; constant admixtures: rare earths, Th, Ca, Si (cheralite variety contains up to 33% of Th) ● Chemical properties: fuses with difficulty; slightly soluble in acids ● Handling: clean with distilled water ● Similar minerals: allanite (410) ● Distinguishing features: reaction in a blowpipe flame, solubility in HCl ● Genesis: magmatic, in pegmatites, in alluvial deposits ● Associated minerals: ilmenite (365), rutile (464), zircon (587) ● Occurrence: rare; Tavetschtal and Binnental (Switzerland), Iveland and Narestö (Norway), (Russia), Antsirabe (Madagascar), (Australia), (USA), (Brazil), (India) ● Application: source of rare earths and Th.

---

1. Triplite – red-brown aggregates bordered with biotite in feldspar; Viitaniemi (Finland – width of field 83 mm) **2. Monazite** – crystal (10 mm) grown on feldspar; Hiterö (Norway)

Triplite, monazite

Mordenite

Silicate
$(Ca,K_2,N_2)Al_2Si_{10}O_{24} \cdot 7 H_2O$

384

Named after its locality in Morden (Canada) (How 1864)

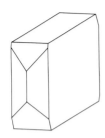

● Hardness: 5 ● Streak: white ● Colour: white, yellowish, reddish ● Transparency: transparent to translucent ● Lustre: vitreous, silky ● Cleavage: perfect on (100) ● Morphology: crystals, fibrous, acicular, reniform aggregates ● Specific gravity: 2.1 ● Crystal system: orthorhombic ● Crystal form: vertically striated needles ● Chemical composition: CaO 2.08%, Na_2O 2.30%, K_2O 3.49%, Al_2O_3 11.33%, SiO_2 66.78%, H_2O 14.02% ● Chemical properties: soluble in HCl ● Handling: clean with distilled water or ultrasonically ● Similar minerals: natrolite **(387)** ● Distinguishing features: X-rays, chemical tests ● Genesis: post-volcanic ● Associated minerals: other zeolites ● Occurrence: rare; Elba (Italy), Berufjord (Iceland), Morden (Canada), Custer Co. – Colorado and Hoodoo Mts. – Wyoming (USA).

Mesolite

Silicate
$Na_2Ca_2Al_6Si_9O_{30} \cdot 8 H_2O$

385

From the Greek *mésos* – middle (Fuchs-Gehlen 1813)

● Hardness: 5 ● Streak: white ● Colour: white, grey, yellowish ● Transparency: transparent to translucent ● Lustre: vitreous, silky, dull ● Cleavage: perfect on (101) ● Fracture: uneven, conchoidal ● Morphology: crystals, massive, spherulitic aggregates, earthy ● Specific gravity: 2.2–2.4 ● Crystal system: monoclinic ● Crystal form: needles ● Chemical composition: Na_2O 5.32%, CaO 9.63%, Al_2O_3 26.26%, SiO_2 46.42%, H_2O 12.37% ● Chemical properties: soluble in acids ● Handling: clean with distilled water ● Similar minerals: natrolite **(387)**, scolezite **(388)** ● Distinguishing features: X-rays, chemical tests ● Genesis: post-volcanic ● Associated minerals: calcite **(217)**, chabazite **(325)**, epistilbite **(330)** ● Occurrence: rare; Pflasterkaute near Eisenach (FRG), Isle of Skye – Scotland (Great Britain), (Faroe Islands), Giant's Causeway (Northern Ireland).

Analcime

Silicate
$NaAlSi_2O_6 \cdot H_2O$

386

From the Greek *análkis* – thin (Haüy 1801)

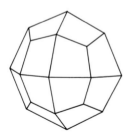

● Hardness: 5.5 (brittle) ● Streak: white ● Colour: white, yellow, red, grey ● Transparency: transparent to translucent ● Lustre: vitreous, dull ● Cleavage: very imperfect on (001) ● Fracture: uneven, conchoidal ● Morphology: crystals, massive, earthy aggregates ● Specific gravity: 2.2–2.3 ● Crystal system: cubic ● Crystal form: trapezohedra ● Chemical composition: Na_2O 14.07%, Al_2O_3 23.29%, SiO_2 54.47%, H_2O 8.17%; admixture: K ● Chemical properties: readily fusible into clear glass; when heated loses water; soluble in HCl ● Handling: clean with distilled water ● Similar minerals: leucite **(396)** ● Distinguishing features: leucite is infusible; X-rays, chemical tests ● Genesis: hydrothermal, sedimentary ● Associated minerals: zeolites, calcite **(217)** ● Occurrence: rare; St. Andreasberg (FRG), Montecchio Maggiore (Italy), Central Bohemian Highlands (Czech Republic), (Faroe Islands), (Iceland), Isle of Skye – Scotland (Great Britain), Kerguelen Islands (Indian Ocean).

---

1. Mordenite – radiating fibrous aggregate (length of fibres 33 mm); Lower Tunguzka (Russia) **2. Mesolite** – radiate aggregates to 30 mm; Monti Monzoni (Italy) **3. Analcime** – group of crystals (maximum size 7 mm); (Italy)

Mordenite, mesolite, analcime

Natrolite (Fibrous zeolite)

Silicate
Na₂Al₂Si₃O₁₀ . 2 H₂O

$Na_2Al_2Si_3O_{10} \cdot 2 H_2O$

387

From the Greek *natron* – soda and *líthos* – stone (Klaproth 1803)

● Hardness: 5–5.5 (brittle) ● Streak: white ● Colour: white, grey, reddish-white, brownish-yellow ● Transparency: transparent to translucent ● Lustre: vitreous, silky ● Cleavage: perfect on (110) ● Fracture: conchoidal to uneven ● Morphology: crystals, druses, radiating, globular, granular, massive aggregates, pulverulent ● Specific gravity: 2.2 ● Crystal system: orthorhombic ● Crystal form: needles ● Luminescence: orange ● Chemical composition: Na₂O 16.50%, Al₂O₃ 26.80%, SiO₂ 47.40%, H₂O 9.30% ● Chemical properties: readily fusible into clear glass; soluble in HCl ● Handling: clean with distilled water or ultrasonically ● Similar minerals: aragonite **(221)**, mesolite **(385)**, scolecite **(388)**, thomsonite **(389)** ● Distinguishing features: hardness, X-rays, chemical tests ● Genesis: hydrothermal, post-volcanic ● Associated minerals: other zeolites, calcite **(217)** ● Occurrence: common; Hohentwiel, Hammerunterwiesenthal (FRG), (Czech Republic), (Italy), (Faroe Islands), (Iceland), Thetford Asbestos Mine (Canada), New Jersey and California (USA).

Scolecite

Silicate
CaAl₂Si₃O₁₀ . 3 H₂O

$CaAl_2Si_3O_{10} \cdot 3 H_2O$

388

From the Greek *skolex* – worm (Fuchs, Gehlen 1813)

● Hardness: 5–5.5 (brittle) ● Streak: white ● Colour: white, yellow, brownish ● Transparency: transparent to translucent ● Lustre: vitreous, silky ● Cleavage: good on (110) ● Fracture: conchoidal, uneven ● Morphology: crystals, druses, radiating, globular, massive aggregates ● Specific gravity: 2.1–2.4 ● Crystal system: monoclinic ● Crystal form: needles, long prisms, twins ● Chemical composition: CaO 14.30% Al₂O₃ 26.00%, SiO₂ 45.90%, H₂O 13.80% ● Chemical properties: in blowpipe flame swells and twists; fuses into porous glass; soluble in HCl ● Handling: clean with distilled water or ultrasonically ● Similar minerals: aragonite **(221)**, mesolite **(385)**, natrolite **(387)** ● Distinguishing features: hardness, X-rays, chemical tests ● Genesis: post-volcanic, hydrothermal ● Associated minerals: other zeolites, calcite **(217)** ● Occurrence: rare; Berufjord (Iceland), (Faroe Islands), (USA), (Brazil).

Thomsonite

Silicate
NaCa₂Al₅Si₅O₂₀ . 6 H₂O

$NaCa_2Al_5Si_5O_{20} \cdot 6 H_2O$

389

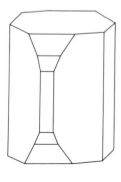

Named after the Scottish chemist, T. Thomson (1773–1852) (Brooke 1820)

● Hardness: 5–5.5 (brittle) ● Streak: white ● Colour: white, yellow, reddish ● Transparency: transparent to translucent ● Lustre: vitreous ● Cleavage: perfect on (010), good on (100) ● Fracture: uneven ● Morphology: crystals, radial, reniform and compact aggregates ● Specific gravity: 2.3–2.4 ● Crystal system: orthorhombic ● Crystal form: plates, short prisms vertically striated ● Chemical composition: Na₂O 2.42%, CaO 19.74%, Al₂O₃ 29.91%, SiO₂ 35.25%, H₂O 12.68% ● Chemical properties: soluble in HCl; in a flame swells and fuses into white glass ● Handling: clean with distilled water ● Similar minerals: natrolite **(387)** ● Distinguishing features: X-rays, chemical tests ● Genesis: hydrothermal, post-volcanic ● Associated minerals: other zeolites, calcite **(217)** ● Occurrence: rare; Pflasterkaute (FRG), Kilpatrick – Scotland (Great Britain), (Faroe Islands), (Canada).

---

1. **Natrolite** – radiating aggregates (up to 20 mm) with apophyllite; Česká Lípa (Czech Republic) 2. **Scolecite** – radiating fibrous aggregate of acicular crystals (17 mm); Šiatorská Bukovinka (Slovakia) 3. **Thomsonite** – radiating fibrous aggregate (20 mm); Central Bohemian Highlands (Czech Republic)

Okenite

Silicate
$Ca_{1.5}Si_3O_6(OH)_3 . 1 . 5 H_2O$

390

L

Named after the German natural historian, L. Oken (1779–1851) (Kobell 1828)

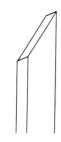

● Hardness: 5 ● Streak: white ● Colour: white, yellowish-white, blue-white ● Transparency: transparent to translucent ● Lustre: pearly ● Cleavage: good on (001) ● Fracture: conchoidal ● Morphology: massive and fibrous aggregates ● Specific gravity: 2.3 ● Crystal system: triclinic ● Crystal form: bladed ● Luminescence: sometimes creamy-white in short-wave UV ● Chemical composition: CaO 26.42%, SiO_2 56.60%, H_2O 16.98% ● Chemical properties: in a flame swells and fuses into enamel; soluble in HCl ● Handling: clean ultrasonically ● Genesis: hydrothermal, post-volcanic ● Associated minerals: zeolites, apophyllite **(331)**, chalcedony **(449)** ● Occurrence: rare; Bramburg (FRG), Antrim (Northern Ireland), Disco Island (Greenland), (Iceland), Poona (India).

Cancrinite

Silicate
$Na_6Ca_2Al_6Si_6O_{24}(CO_3)_2 . 2 H_2O$

391

Named after the Russian minister, E. F. Kankrin (1774-1845) (Rose 1839)

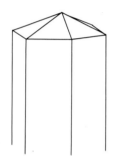

● Hardness: 5–6 ● Streak: white ● Colour: white, grey, blue, yellowish, greenish ● Transparency: translucent to opaque ● Lustre: vitreous, pearly ● Cleavage: perfect on (10$\bar{1}$0), good on (0001) ● Fracture: uneven ● Morphology: crystals, compact and granular aggregates, often found on edges of nepheline ● Specific gravity: 2.4–2.6 ● Crystal system: hexagonal ● Crystal form: short prisms, needles ● Chemical composition: variable ● Chemical properties: fuses with difficulty into bubble glass; dissolves with effervescence in HCl ● Handling: clean with distilled water ● Similar minerals: nepheline **(397)** ● Distinguishing features: cleavage, X-rays, chemical tests ● Genesis: magmatic ● Associated minerals: calcite **(217)**, nepheline, zeolites ● Occurrence: rare; Laacher See (FRG), near Oslo (Norway), Ditrău (Romania), Myas near Zlatoust (Russia), Litchfeld – Maine (USA.

Lazurite (Lapis lazuli)

Silicate
$(Na,Ca)_8(AlSiO_4)_6(SO_4,Cl,S)_2$

392

P

From the Persian *läzwärd* – blue (Brögger 1890)

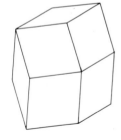

● Hardness: 5.5 (brittle) ● Streak: light blue ● Colour: dark blue, blue-green ● Transparency: opaque ● Lustre: greasy, dull ● Cleavage: imperfect on (110) ● Fracture: conchoidal ● Morphology: crystals are rare, massive, compact and finely granular aggregates ● Specific gravity: 2.38–2.42 ● Crystal system: cubic ● Crystal form: dodecahedra ● Chemical composition: variable; frequent admixtures: Cl, Ca, SO_4 ● Chemical properties: fuses into white glass; soluble in HCl; releases strong odour of H_2S ● Handling: clean with distilled water ● Similar minerals: lazulite **(378)**, sodalite **(393)**, nosean **(394)**, hauyne **(395)** ● Distinguishing features: paragenesis, streak, X-rays, chemical tests ● Genesis: contact-metamorphic ● Associated minerals: calcite **(217)**, pyrite **(436)**, diopside **(505)** ● Occurrence: rare; (Italy), Lake Baikal (Russia), Buchara – 60 kg boulders (Uzbekistan), Badakhschan (Afghanistan), (Chile), San Bernardino Co. – California (USA) ● Application: since ancient times lazurite has been mined in Badakhschan and has been used for ornamental stones and jewellery.

---

1. **Okenite** – acicular globular aggregate with apophyllite; Poona (India – width of field 60 mm) 2. **Lazurite** – granular aggregate with calcite and disseminated pyrite; Slyudyanka (Russia – width of field 40 mm)

Okenite, lazurite

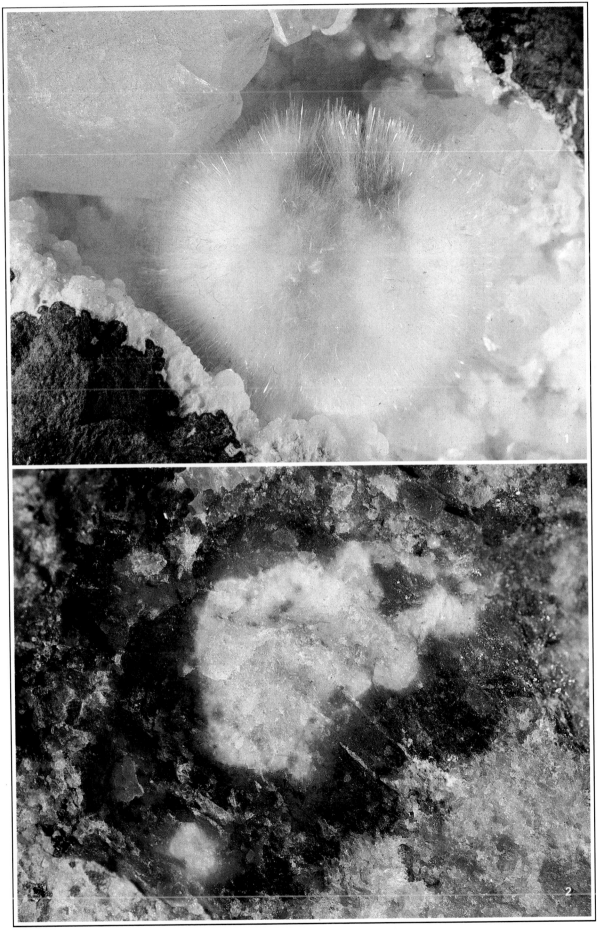

Sodalite

Silicate
$Na_8Al_6Si_6O_{24}Cl_2$

393

L

P

Named after its chemical composition
(Thomson 1811)

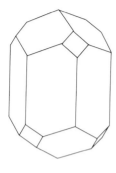

● Hardness: 5–6 ● Streak: white ● Colour: white, blue, grey, green ● Transparency: translucent to non-transparent ● Lustre: vitreous, greasy ● Cleavage: perfect on (110) ● Fracture: conchoidal, uneven ● Morphology: crystals, granular and massive aggregates ● Specific gravity: 2.3 ● Crystal system: cubic ● Crystal form: isometric, twins ● Luminescence: sometimes orange, yellow ● Chemical composition: Na_2O 25.00%, Al_2O_3 31.00%, SiO_2 37.00%, Cl 7.00% ● Chemical properties: when heated loses its blue or green colour and becomes colourless glass; soluble in acids ● Handling: clean with distilled water ● Similar minerals: lazurite **(392)**, nosean **(394)**, hauyne **(395)** ● Distinguishing features: nosean and hauyne do not change their colour when heated; streak distinguishes it from lazurite; X-rays, chemical tests ● Genesis: magmatic ● Associated minerals: nepheline **(397)**, titanite **(430)**, zircon **(587)** ● Occurrence: rare; Laacher See (FRG), Monte Somma (Italy), Ditrău (Romania), Serra de Monchique (Portugal), Kangerdluarsuk (Greenland), Cerro Sapo (Bolivia), (Russia), (Burma), (USA), (Canada) ● Application: used as a precious stone.

Nosean

Silicate
$Na_8Al_6Si_6(SO_4)O_{24}$

394

Named after the German mineralogist, K. W. Nose (1753–1835)
(Klaproth 1815)

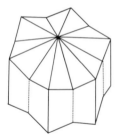

● Hardness: 5–6 ● Streak: white ● Colour: white, grey, blue, brown, black ● Transparency: transparent to translucent ● Lustre: vitreous, greasy ● Cleavage: perfect on (110) ● Fracture: conchoidal ● Morphology: crystals, compact and granular aggregates ● Specific gravity: 2.3–2.4 ● Crystal system: cubic ● Crystal form: isometric, twins ● Chemical composition: Na_2O 21.11%, Al_2O_3 26.04%, SiO_2 46.03%, So_3 6.82% ● Chemical properties: fuses in a blowpipe flame; soluble in acids ● Handling: clean with distilled water ● Similar minerals: lazurite **(392)**, sodalite **(393)**, hauyne **(395)** ● Distinguishing features: see sodalite ● Genesis: magmatic, in eruptive rocks ● Associated minerals: hauyne, leucite **(396)**, nepheline **(397)** ● Occurrence: rare; Laacher See (FRG), Monte Somma (Italy), Wolf Rock – Cornwall (Great Britain), Cripple Creek – Colorado (USA).

Hauyne

Silicate
$(Na,Ca)_{4-8}Al_6Si_6(SO_4)_{1-2}O_{24}$

395

L

P

Named after the French crystallographer, R. J. Haüy (1743–1822)
(Brunn, Neergard 1807)

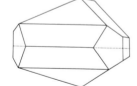

● Hardness: 5–6 ● Streak: white, bluish ● Colour: blue, green, red, yellow, grey, white ● Transparency: transparent to translucent ● Lustre: vitreous, greasy ● Cleavage: perfect on (110) ● Fracture: conchoidal ● Morphology: crystals, massive and granular aggregates ● Specific gravity: 2.4–2.5 ● Crystal system: cubic ● Crystal form: isometric, dodecahedra, twins ● Luminescence: sometimes orange ● Chemical composition: variable ● Chemical properties: fuses into blue-green glass; soluble in HCl ● Handling: clean with distilled water ● Similar minerals: lazurite **(392)**, sodalite **(393)**, nosean **(394)** ● Distinguishing features: see sodalite ● Genesis: magmatic ● Associated minerals: leucite **(396)**, nepheline **(397)**, nosean ● Occurrence: rare; Laacher See and Niedermendig (FRG), Monte Somma (Italy), Colorado (USA) ● Application: used as a precious stone.

---

1. **Sodalite** – granular aggregate; Bancroft (Canada) 2. **Nosean** – isolated embedded crystals; Laacher See (FRG) 3. **Hauyne** – granular aggregate; Niedermendig (FRG – width of field 120 mm)

Sodalite, nosean, hauyne

Leucite

Silicate
KAlS$_2$O$_6$

396

L

From the Greek *leukós* – white
(Werner 1791)

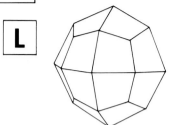

● Hardness: 5.5–6 (brittle) ● Streak: white ● Colour: white, grey ● Transparency: translucent to non-transparent ● Lustre: vitreous, greasy, dull ● Cleavage: absent ● Fracture: conchoidal, uneven ● Morphology: crystals, granular aggregates, pseudomorphs ● Specific gravity: 2.5 ● Crystal system: dimorphic, above 605 °C cubic, below 605 °C tetragonal ● Crystal form: isometric, twins ● Luminescence: sometimes orange in long-wave UV ● Chemical composition: K$_2$O 21.50%, Al$_2$O$_3$ 23.50%, SiO$_2$ 55.00% ● Chemical properties: infusible; soluble in HCl ● Handling: clean with water ● Similar minerals: analcime **(386)**, garnet **(577)** ● Distinguishing features: hardness, specific gravity, reaction in a blowpipe flame ● Genesis: magmatic ● Associated minerals: nepheline **(397),** sanidine **(488)** ● Occurrence: rare; Laacher See (FRG), Vesuvius (Italy), (Brazil), (USA), (Canada).

Nepheline

Silicate
KNa$_3$Al$_4$Si$_4$O$_{16}$

397

L

From the Greek *nefélè* – cloud
(Haüy 1800)

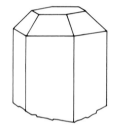

● Hardness: 5.5–6 ● Streak: white ● Colour: white, yellow, greenish, blue-green, brown, red ● Transparency: transparent to translucent ● Lustre: vitreous, greasy ● Cleavage: imperfect on (10$\overline{1}$0) and on (0001) ● Fracture: conchoidal, uneven ● Morphology: crystals, massive and granular aggregates ● Specific gravity: 2.60–2.65 ● Crystal system: hexagonal ● Crystal form: prisms, coarse plates ● Luminescence: sometimes orange-red ● Chemical composition: K$_2$O 8.06%, Na$_2$O 15.91%, Al$_2$O$_3$ 34.90%, SiO$_2$ 41.13% ● Chemical properties: fusible; tinges a flame yellow; soluble in acids ● Handling: clean with distilled water ● Similar minerals: apatite **(379),** cancrinite **(391)** ● Distinguishing features: specific gravity, X-rays, chemical tests ● Genesis: magmatic, in pegmatites ● Associated minerals: leucite **(396),** augite **(429)** ● Occurrence: common; Katzenbuckel, Löbau (FRG), Vesuvius (Italy), Larvik (Norway), (Russia), (Greenland), (Madagascar) ● Application: used in glass and ceramic industries.

Scapolite (group of minerals)

Silicate
(see below)

398

L

P

From the Greek *skápos* – rod and *líthos* – stone
(d'Andrade 1800)

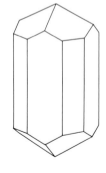

● Hardness: 5–6 (brittle) ● Streak: white ● Colour: white, grey, greenish-grey, bluish, pink, violet ● Transparency: transparent to translucent ● Lustre: vitreous, pearly ● Cleavage: perfect on (110) ● Fracture: conchoidal, uneven ● Morphology: crystals, fibrous and massive aggregates ● Specific gravity: 2.54–2.77 ● Crystal system: tetragonal ● Crystal form: columnar ● Luminescence: sometimes yellow or orange in long-wave UV ● Chemical composition: end members of the isomorphous series are marialite – Na$_4$Al$_3$Si$_9$O$_{24}$Cl and meionite – Ca$_4$Al$_6$Si$_6$O$_{24}$(CO$_3$) ● Chemical properties: fuses in a blowpipe flame, swells and changes into white glass; decomposes in HCl ● Handling: clean with water ● Similar minerals: feldspars ● Distinguishing features: hardness, solubility in HCl, reaction in blowpipe flame ● Genesis: contact-metasomatic, pneumatolytic ● Associated minerals: garnets, pyroxenes, epidote **(513),** vesuvianite **(522)** ● Occurrence: rare; Laacher See (FRG), Arendal (Norway), Tunaberg (Sweden), (Brazil), (Madagascar), (Tanzania) ● Application: precious stones.

---

1. Leucite – euhedral crystal (15 mm); Vesuvius (Italy) **2. Nepheline** – imperfectly developed crystals (10 mm) in nepheline syenite; Monte Somma (Italy) **3. Scapolite** – aggregate of columnar crystals (up to 30 mm) in quartz; Laurin Ravi (Finland)

Bavenite

Silicate
Ca$_4$Al$_2$Be$_2$Si$_9$O$_{26}$(OH)$_2$

399

Named after its locality in Baveno (Italy) (Artini 1901)

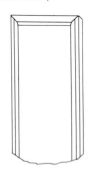

● Hardness: 5.5 (brittle) ● Streak: white ● Colour: white, green, pink, brown ● Transparency: transparent to translucent ● Lustre: silky, vitreous, pearly ● Cleavage: perfect on (100) ● Fracture: none ● Morphology: crystals, rose-shaped, radiating-fibrous and platy aggregates ● Specific gravity: 2.7 ● Crystal system: orthorhombic ● Crystal form: flat prisms, twins ● Chemical composition: CaO 23.99%, Al$_2$O$_3$ 10.90%, BeO 5.35%, SiO$_2$ 57.83%, H$_2$O 1.93% ● Chemical properties: readily fusible, swelling, insoluble in acids ● Handling: clean with diluted acids or water ● Similar minerals: laumontite **(272)** ● Distinguishing features: hardness, solubility in acids ● Genesis: in pegmatites, hydrothermal ● Associated minerals: fluorite **(291)**, albite **(493)**, beryl **(554)** ● Occurrence: rare; Tittling (FRG), Maršíkov (Czech Republic), Baveno (Italy), Strzegom (Poland), California (USA), Londonderry (Australia).

Pectolite

Silicate
NaCa$_2$Si$_3$O$_8$(OH)

400

L

P

From the Greek *pektós* – composed and *líthos* – stone (Kobell 1828)

● Hardness: 5 (brittle) ● Streak: white ● Colour: white, grey, light pink, light green ● Transparency: translucent to non-transparent ● Lustre: vitreous, pearly, silky ● Cleavage: perfect on (100) and on (001) ● Fracture: conchoidal, uneven ● Morphology: crystals, massive, compact, radiating and fibrous aggregates ● Specific gravity: 2.8 ● Crystal system: triclinic ● Crystal form: prisms, needles, twins ● Luminescence: sometimes yellow to orange in long-wave UV ● Chemical composition: Na$_2$O 9.31%, CaO 33.68%, SiO$_2$ 54.31%, H$_2$O 2.70% ● Chemical properties: soluble in HCl; readily fuses into white enamel; tinges a flame yellow ● Handling: clean with water ● Similar minerals: wollastonite **(335)**, zeolites ● Distinguishing features: flame colour ● Genesis: hydrothermal ● Associated minerals: zeolites, calcite **(217)** ● Occurrence: rare; Monte Baldo (Italy), Želechov Valley (Czech Republic), (Slovenia), New Jersey (USA) ● Application: occasionally used as a precious stone.

Carpholite

Silicate
MnAl$_2$Si$_2$O$_6$(OH)$_4$

401

From the Greek *kárfos* – straw and *líthos* – stone (Werner 1817)

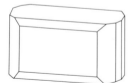

● Hardness: 5.5 (brittle) ● Streak: white ● Colour: straw-yellow, grey-green, yellowish-brown ● Transparency: translucent ● Lustre: silky ● Cleavage: imperfect on (100), (010) and (110) ● Fracture: uneven ● Morphology: crystals, fibrous, radiate-fibrous and compact aggregates ● Specific gravity: 2.9 ● Crystal system: orthorhombic ● Crystal form: acicular, fibrous ● Chemical composition: MnO 21.56%, Al$_2$O$_3$ 30.98%, SiO$_2$ 36.52%, H$_2$O 10.94% ● Chemical properties: fuses into a white or yellow-brown ball; insoluble in acids ● Handling: clean with diluted acids ● Genesis: pneumatolytic, metamorphic ● Associated minerals: fluorite **(291)**, quartz **(534)**, cassiterite **(548)** ● Occurrence: rare; Wippra (FRG), Horní Slavkov (Czech Republic), Meuville (Belgium), Prilep (Macedonia), Cornwall (Great Britain), (Japan).

1. Bavenite – lamellar rose-shaped aggregates (40 mm); Vlastějovice (Czech Republic) **2. Pectolite** – radiating fibrous aggregates (30 mm); Želechov Valley (Czech Republic) **3. Carpholite** – radiating fibrous aggregate; Horní Slavkov (Czech Republic – width of field 40 mm)

Bavenite, pectolite, carpholite

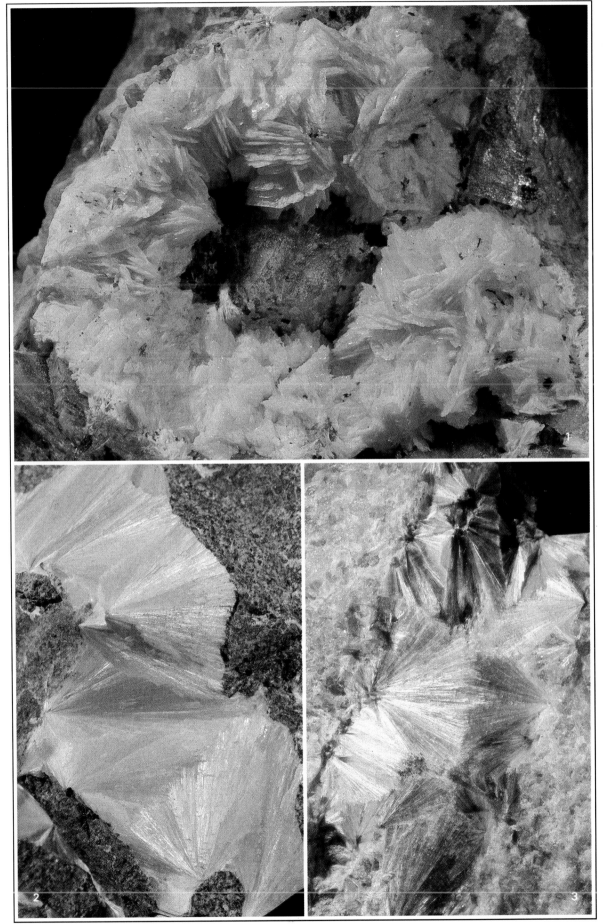

Eudialite

Silicate
$Na_4(Ca,Ce,Fe)_2ZrSi_6O_{17}(OH,Cl)_2$

402

From the Greek *eu* – well and *dialytós* – decomposable (Stromeyer 1819)

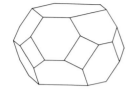

• Hardness: 5–5.5 (brittle) • Streak: white • Colour: pink, red, yellow, yellowish-brown, violet • Transparency: translucent • Lustre: vitreous • Cleavage: imperfect on (0001) • Fracture: conchoidal, uneven, splintery • Morphology: crystals, granular and massive aggregates • Specific gravity: 2.8–3.0 • Crystal system: trigonal • Crystal form: plates, rhombohedra, prisms • Chemical composition: variable, composite • Chemical properties: readily soluble in acids • Handling: clean with water • Similar minerals: some garnets • Distinguishing features: hardness, easy solubility in acids • Genesis: magmatic • Associated minerals: lamprophyllite **(170)**, nepheline **(397)**, ramsayite **(527)**, zircon **(587)** • Occurrence: rare; (Norway), (Russia), (Greenland), (Madagascar), (USA), (Canada), (RSA), (Guinea).

Hemimorphite (Calamine, Galmei, Zinc silicate)

Silicate
$Zn_4Si_2O_7(OH)_2 \cdot H_2O$

403

L

Named after its hemi-morphic form (Kenngott 1853)

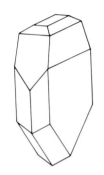

• Hardness: 5 (brittle) • Streak: white • Colour: colourless, white, bluish, greenish, grey, yellowish, brown • Transparency: transparent to translucent • Lustre: vitreous, pearly, silky • Cleavage: perfect on (110) • Fracture: conchoidal, uneven • Morphology: crystals, crusts, rose-shaped, fan-shaped and granular aggregates, deposits, stalactitic, pseudomorphs • Specific gravity: 3.3–3.5 • Crystal system: orthorhombic • Crystal form: hemimorphic, plates • Luminescence: sometimes yellow, orange, blue-white • Chemical composition: ZnO 67.59%, SiO_2 24.94%, H_2O 7.47% • Chemical properties: soluble in concentrated KOH; on charcoal forms white ZnO sublimate • Handling: clean with water • Similar minerals: smithsonite **(373)**, chalcedony **(449)**, prehnite **(515)** • Distinguishing features: hardness, solubility in acids, specific gravity • Genesis: secondary in oxidation zones • Associated minerals: sphalerite **(181)**, wulfenite **(243)**, limonite **(355)**, smithsonite • Occurrence: rare; Schauinsland and Badenweiler (FRG), Bleiberg (Austria), Olkusz (Poland), Sardinia (Italy), (Great Britain), (Russia), (Algeria), (Iran), (USA), (Mexico) • Application: Zn ore.

Willemite

Silicate
Zn_2SiO_4

404

L

P

Named after the Dutch King, William I (1772–1843) (Levy 1830)

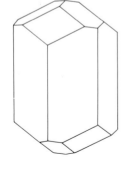

• Hardness: 5.5 • Streak: white • Colour: white, yellowish, grey, brown, blue-green • Transparency: transparent to translucent • Lustre: greasy, dull • Cleavage: perfect on (11$\bar{2}$0), imperfect on (0001) • Fracture: conchoidal, splintery • Morphology: crystals, radiate-fibrous, granular, massive and crusty aggregates • Specific gravity: 4.0 • Crystal system: trigonal • Crystal form: columnar, rhombohedra, plates • Luminescence: light green • Chemical composition: ZnO 72.96%, SiO_2 27.04% • Chemical properties: soluble in HCl; fuses with difficulty into white enamel; shines in a blowpipe flame • Handling: clean with water • Similar minerals: epidote **(513)**, olivine **(524)** • Distinguishing features: hardness, specific gravity • Genesis: secondary, metamorphic • Associated minerals: zincite **(296)**, smithsonite **(373)**, hemimorphite **(403)**, franklinite **(470)** • Occurrence: rare; Altenberg (FRG), (Zambia), (Algeria), (Namibia), (Australia), (USA) • Application: Zn ore; yellow transparent crystals are used as precious stones.

---

1. Eudialite – red granular aggregate; Kola Peninsula (Russia – width of field 30 mm) **2. Willemite** – imperfectly developed crystal (35 mm) in feldspar; Sterling Hill (New Jersey, USA) **3. Hemimorphite** – radiating aggregate in limonite (25 mm); Mapimí (Mexico)

Eudialite, willemite, hemimorphite

H
5—6

323

Gehlenite

Silicate
Ca$_2$Al(AlSi)O$_7$

405

Named after the German chemist, A. F. Gehlen (1775–1815) (Fuchs 1815)

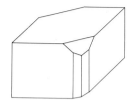

● Hardness: 5–6 ● Streak: white ● Colour: white, grey-green, brown ● Transparency: transparent to translucent to opaque ● Lustre: vitreous, greasy ● Cleavage: good on (001) ● Fracture: uneven, conchoidal ● Morphology: crystals, granular and massive aggregates ● Specific gravity: 3.0 ● Crystal system: tetragonal ● Crystal form: prisms, plates ● Chemical composition: CaO 36.96%, Al$_2$O$_3$ 16.80%, MgO 6.64%, SiO$_2$ 39.60% ● Chemical properties: fuses into grey, green or yellow glass; soluble in HCl, when previously fused ● Handling: clean with water and diluted acids ● Similar minerals: melilite **(406)**, feldspars ● Distinguishing features: hardness, specific gravity, X-rays, chemical tests ● Genesis: contact-metamorphic ● Associated minerals: calcite **(217)**, wollastonite **(335)**, vesuvianite **(522)**, garnets ● Occurrence: rare; Monzoni (Italy), Oraviţa (Romania), California (USA), (Mexico).

Melilite

Silicate
(Ca,Na)$_2$(Mg,Al,Fe)Si$_2$O$_7$

406

From the Greek *méli* – honey and *lithos* – stone (Delametherie 1796)

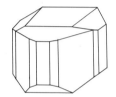

● Hardness: 5–5.5 (brittle) ● Streak: white ● Colour: white, yellowish, brown, grey, greenish ● Transparency: transparent to translucent ● Lustre: vitreous, greasy ● Cleavage: good on (001) ● Fracture: uneven, conchoidal ● Morphology: crystals, lamellar and granular aggregates ● Specific gravity: 2.9–3.0 ● Crystal system: tetragonal ● Crystal form: plates, prisms ● Chemical composition: CaO 19.17%, Na$_2$O 21.16%, MgO 4.59%, Al$_2$O$_3$ 5.81%, FeO 8.19%, SiO$_2$ 41.08% ● Chemical properties: soluble in HCl; fuses into grey, yellow or green glass ● Handling: clean with water ● Similar minerals: gehlenite **(405)**, feldspars ● Distinguishing features: hardness, specific gravity, X-rays, chemical tests ● Genesis: magmatic, contact-metamorphic ● Associated minerals: phlogopite **(168)**, perovskite **(363)**, magnetite **(367)**, olivine **(524)** ● Occurrence: common; abundant melilite basalts occur in southern and central parts of (FRG); (Italy), (Kenya), Katunga volcano (Uganda), (Russia), (USA), (RSA), (Japan).

Datolite

Silicate
CaBSiO$_4$(OH)

407

From the Greek *datéomai* – to divide and *lithos* – stone (Esmark 1805)

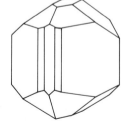

● Hardness: 5–5.5 ● Streak: white ● Colour: white, grey, yellowish ● Transparency: transparent to translucent ● Lustre: vitreous, greasy ● Cleavage: imperfect on (001) ● Fracture: uneven, conchoidal ● Morphology: crystals, massive, granular and crusty aggregates, encrustations ● Crusty aggregates with radiating-fibrous structure are called botryolites ● Specific gravity: 2.9–3.0 ● Crystal system: monoclinic ● Crystal form: plates, prisms ● Luminescence: sometimes blue or white ● Chemical composition: CaO 34.99%, B$_2$O$_3$ 21.78%, SiO$_2$ 37.63%, H$_2$O 5.60% ● Chemical properties: readily fusible, swelling; tinges a flame green; partly soluble in HCl, HNO$_3$ and H$_2$SO$_4$ ● Handling: clean with water ● Similar minerals: colemanite **(301)**, danburite **(573)** ● Distinguishing features: hardness, specific gravity, solubility in acids ● Genesis: hydrothermal, post-volcanic ● Associated minerals: zeolites, calcite **(217)**, prehnite **(515)** ● Occurrence: rare; Haslach and St. Andreasberg (FRG), (Italy), Fifeshire – Scotland (Great Britain), (Norway), (Sweden), (USA) ● Application: sometimes used as a precious stone.

1. Gehlenite – crystal aggregate (up to 10 mm); Monzoni (Italy) **2. Datolite** – euhedral crystal (7 mm) on quartz; Great Notch (USA)

Pumpellyite

Silicate
$Ca_2MgAl_2(SiO_4)(Si_2O_7)(OH)_2 \cdot H_2O$

408

Named after the American geologist, R. Pumpelly (1837–1923) (Palache, Vassar 1925)

● Hardness: 5.5 ● Streak: grey-green, green ● Colour: blue-green, olive-green, brown ● Transparency: translucent ● Lustre: vitreous ● Cleavage: perfect on (001) ● Fracture: sub-conchoidal ● Morphology: crystals, spherulitic and fibrous aggregates ● Specific gravity: 3.2 ● Crystal system: monoclinic ● Crystal form: needles, plates, twins ● Chemical composition: variable; common admixtures; Fe, Na, K, Ti ● Chemical properties: insoluble in HCl ● Handling: clean with distilled water ● Similar minerals: zoisite **(519)** ● Distinguishing features: hardness, crystal form, optical properties, X-rays, chemical tests ● Genesis: metamorphic, hydrothermal ● Associated minerals: epidote **(513)**, prehnite **(515)**, zeolites ● Occurrence: rare; Königskopf (FRG), Lotru (Romania), Keweenaw Peninsula (USA), Lake Wakatipu (New Zealand), Witwatersrand (RSA), Jordanów (Poland), Blagodat and the Urals (Russia).

Babingtonite

Silicate
$Ca_2Fe^{2+}Fe^{3+}Si_5O_{14}(OH)$

409

Named after the Irish physicist and mineralogist, W. Babington (1757–1833) (Levy 1824)

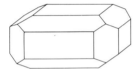

● Hardness: 5.5–6 ● Streak: green-grey ● Colour: green-black, brownish-black ● Transparency: translucent to non-transparent ● Lustre: splendent, vitreous ● Cleavage: perfect on (100) and on (001) ● Fracture: conchoidal ● Morphology: crystals, druses, fan-shaped aggregates ● Specific gravity: 3.4 ● Crystal system: triclinic ● Crystal form: short columnar, plates, often striated ● Chemical composition: CaO 19.54%, FeO 12.57%, Fe_2O_3 13.96%, SiO_2 52.36%, H_2O 1.57%; admixture: Mn ● Chemical properties: soluble in hot HF; fuses readily into a black magnetic ball ● Handling: clean with water and diluted acids ● Genesis: contact, hydrothermal ● Associated minerals: adularia **(487)**, epidote **(513)**, prehnite **(515)**, zeolites ● Occurrence: rare; Herbornseelbach (FRG), Baveno (Italy), Arendal (Norway), Yakubi Mine (Japan), Holyoke, Somerville and Westfield – Massachusetts (USA).

Allanite (Orthite)

Silicate
$(Ce,Ca,Y)_2(Al,Fe^{3+})_3(SiO_4)_3(OH)$

410

Named after the Scottish mineralogist, T. Allan (1777–1833) (Thomson 1810)

● Hardness: 5.5 ● Streak: green-grey, brown ● Colour: brown, black ● Transparency: translucent to non-transparent ● Lustre: vitreous, greasy ● Cleavage: very imperfect on (001) and on (100) ● Fracture: uneven, conchoidal ● Morphology: crystals, granular and massive aggregates, impregnations ● Specific gravity: 3.3–4.2 ● Crystal system: monoclinic ● Crystal form: plates, prisms, twins ● Radioactivity: variable ● Chemical composition: variable ● Chemical properties: soluble in HCl; readily fusible into black or brown magnetic glass ● Handling: clean with distilled water ● Genesis: magmatic, in pegmatites, contact-metamorphic, metamorphic ● Associated minerals: amphiboles, feldspars, monazite **(383)**, quartz **(534)** ● Occurrence: rare; Laacher See and Weinheim (FRG), Arendal and Hitterö (Norway), Ytterby (Sweden), Vaarala (Finland), Suhl and Ilmenau (FRG), (Czech Republic), (Russia), (Canada), (USA), (Australia) ● Application: sometimes source of rare earths.

---

1. **Pumpellyite** – spherulitic fibrous aggregate on quartz; Blagodat (Russia – width of field 38 mm) 2. **Allanite** – columnar crystal (20 mm) in albite; Rila (Bulgaria)

Pumpellyite, allanite

Amphibole (Common and basaltic hornblende)

Silicate
$(Ca,Na,K)_{2-3}(Mg,Fe^{2+},Fe^{3+},Al)_5Al_2Si_6O_{22}(OH)_2$

411

(Werner 1789)

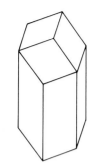

● Hardness: 5–6 ● Streak: grey-white, brown ● Colour: greenish-black, black ● Transparency: translucent to non-transparent ● Lustre: vitreous, greasy ● Cleavage: perfect on (110) ● Fracture: conchoidal ● Morphology: crystals, granular, massive or radiating aggregates, pseudomorphs ● Specific gravity: 2.9–3.4 ● Crystal system: monoclinic ● Crystal form: prisms, twins ● Chemical composition: composite, variable; the variety with a high content of Fe_2O_3 is called basaltic amphibole ● Chemical properties: fuses with difficulty into dark green glass; insoluble in acids ● Handling: clean with water and diluted acids ● Similar minerals: augite **(429)**, tourmaline **(564)** ● Distinguishing features: cleavage angle distinguishes it from augite, hardness and absence of cleavage from tourmaline ● Genesis: magmatic, metamorphic, contact-metamorphic ● Associated minerals: biotite **(167)**, magnetite **(367)**, epidote **(513)**, quartz **(534)** ● Occurrence: common; rock-forming mineral in granites, granodiorites, syenites, diorites, trachytes, phonolites, andesites and basalts (basaltic amphibole). It also occurs in crystalline schists and contact rocks and meteorites in Vesuvius (Italy), Central Bohemian Highlands (Czech Republic).

Tremolite (Amphibole group)

Silicate
$Ca_2Mg_5Si_8O_{22}(OH)_2$

412

Named after its locality in the Tremola Valley (Alps)
(Hoffner 1790)

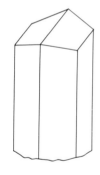

● Hardness: 5–6 (brittle) ● Streak: white ● Colour: white, grey, greenish ● Transparency: translucent to non-transparent ● Lustre: vitreous, silky ● Cleavage: perfect on (110), imperfect on (010) ● Other features of cohesion: fine needles break easily ● Morphology: crystals, granular, massive, wisp-like, radiating-fibrous aggregates, asbestos-like aggregates are called byssolite ● Specific gravity: 2.9–3.1 ● Crystal system: monoclinic ● Crystal form: long prisms, fibrous ● Luminescence: sometimes red to pink in long-wave UV or yellow, yellow-white in short-wave UV ● Chemical composition: CaO 13.80%, MgO 24.81%, SiO_2 59.17%, H_2O 2.22% ● Chemical properties: fuses with difficulty into colourless glass; insoluble in acids ● Handling: clean with water and diluted acids ● Similar minerals: chrysotile **(275)**, wollastonite **(335)**, cummingtonite **(423)**, zoisite **(519)** ● Distinguishing features: hardness, solubility in HCl, X-rays, chemical tests ● Genesis: metamorphic, contact-metamorphic ● Associated minerals: talc **(41)**, calcite **(217)**, dolomite **(218)** ● Occurrence: common; Campolungo (Italy), Złoty Stok (Poland), Zillertal (Austria), Binnental (Switzerland), Slyudyanka (Russia) ● Application: crystals are sometimes used as precious stones.

1. **Amphibole** – euhedral crystal (25 mm); Lukov (Czech Republic) 2. **Tremolite** – acicular aggregates; Campolungo (Italy – width of field 46 mm)

Amphibole, tremolite

Actinolite (Amphibole group)

Silicate
$Ca_2(Mg,Fe^{2+})_5Si_8O_{22}(OH)_2$

413

P

From the Greek *aktis* – ray and *lithos* – stone (Kirwan 1794)

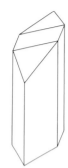

● Hardness: 5–6 (brittle) ● Streak: white ● Colour: green, grey-green, dark green, emerald green (smaragdite variety) ● Transparency: transparent to translucent to non-transparent ● Lustre: vitreous, silky ● Cleavage: perfect on (110) ● Morphology: crystals, radiate, parallel-fibrous and granular aggregates. Massive and microcrystalline aggregates are called **nephrite;** felt- and asbestos-like aggregates are known as **amianthus** ● Specific gravity: 3.0–3.2 ● Crystal system: monoclinic ● Crystal form: long prisms, needles, hair-like ● Chemical composition: CaO 12.59%, MgO 11.31%, FeO 20.15%, SiO_2 53.93%, H_2O 2.02% ● Chemical properties: fuses with difficulty into grey-green to green-black glass; insoluble in acids ● Handling: clean with water and diluted acids ● Similar minerals: acmite **(509)**, epidote **(513)**, tourmaline **(564)** ● Distinguishing features: hardness, reaction in blowpipe flame, X-rays, chemical tests ● Genesis: metamorphic, contact-metamorphic ● Associated minerals: talc **(41)**, chlorite **(158)**, serpentine **(273)**, epidote ● Occurrence: common; rock-forming in crystalline schists; Zillertal (Austria), Sobotín (Czech Republic), Val Malenco (Italy) ● Application: sometimes used as a precious stone (facets, cabochons).

Smaragdite
(Actinolite variety – Amphibole group)

Silicate
$Ca_2(Mg,Fe^{2+})_5Si_8O_{22}(OH)_2$

414

P

Named after its colour (Saussure 1796)

● Physical and chemical properties are similar to those of actinolite; differing only in colour (emerald green: admixture Cr), vitreous lustre and short needles ● Genesis: contact-metamorphic ● Associated minerals: zoisite **(519)**, quartz **(534)** ● Occurrence: rare; Zermatt-Saas Fee (Switzerland), Krautbath – in serpentinites (Austria), (Corsica), (Russia), (USA) ● Application: sometimes used as a precious stone (cabochons).

Amianthus
(Actinolite variety – Amphibole group)

Silicate
$Ca_2(Mg,Fe^{2+})_5Si_8O_{22}(OH)_2$

415

Historical name

● Physical and chemical properties are similar to those of actinolite, differing only in the felt- to asbestos-like form of crystal aggregates ● Felt and asbestos-like forms of tremolite **(412)**, are also referred to as amianthus ● Genesis: metamorphic ● Associated minerals: calcite **(217)**, albite **(493)**, epidote **(513)** ● Occurrence: rare; Teufelstal (Switzerland), Val Malenco (Italy), Sobotín (Czech Republic), Belorechka and Gruschinsk (Ukraine) ● Application: sometimes used in ceramic industry and as insulating materials.

Byssolite (Actinolite or tremolite variety – Amphibole group)

Silicate
$Ca_2(Mg,Fe^{2+})_5Si_8O_{22}(OH)_2$

416

From the Greek *býssos* – linen and *lithos* – stone (Saussure 1797)

● Physical and chemical properties are similar to those of actinolite or tremolite ● Acicular crystals resemble amianthus **(415)** ● Genesis: metamorphic, contact-metamorphic ● Associated minerals: calcite **(217)**, titanite **(430)**, albite **(493)**, epidote **(513)**, quartz **(534)** ● Occurrence: rare, but most often in the Alps; Knappenwand (Austria), Maderanertal (Switzerland), (Canada) ● Application: used in the ceramics industry and for insulating materials.

---

1. **Actinolite** – columnar crystals (up to 40 mm); Zillertal (Austria) 2. **Smaragdite** – compact aggregate; Zermatt (Switzerland – width of field 20 mm) 3. **Amianthus** – radiating fibrous aggregate (20 mm) in schist; St. Lorenzen (Austria)

Actinolite, smaragdite, amianthus

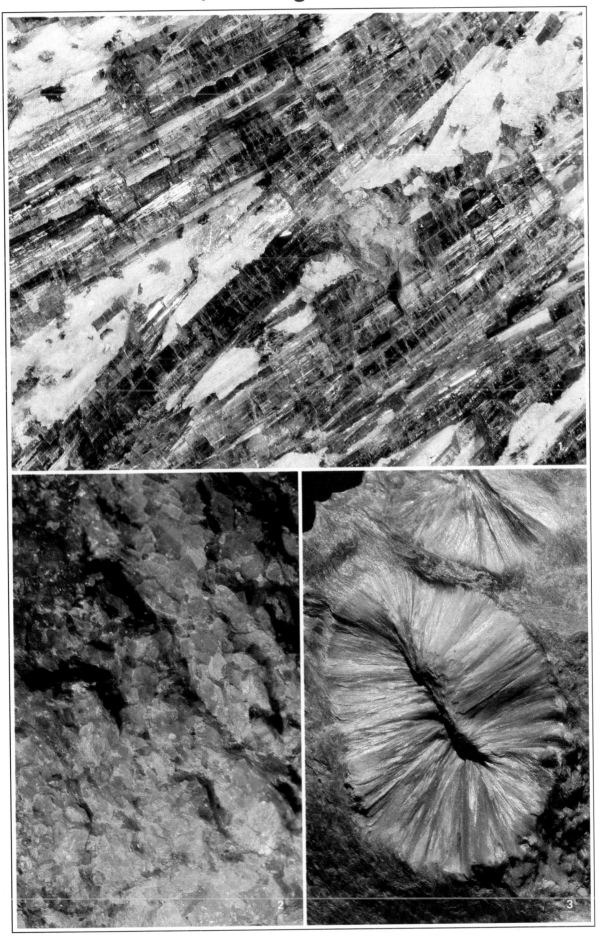

Nephrite
(Actinolite variety – Amphibole group)

Silicate
$Ca_2(Mg,Fe^{2+})_5Si_8O_{22}(OH)_2$

417

P

From the Greek *nefrós* – kidney (Werner 1780)

● Physical and chemical properties are similar to those of actinolite. It is massive (microscopically felt-like) and solid. Translucent: usually green ● Similar minerals: jadeite **(508)** ● Distinctive features: difficult fusibility, chemical tests ● Genesis: contact-metasomatic ● Associated minerals: talc **(41),** chlorite **(158)** ● Occurrence: rare; Jordanów (Poland), Chara-Zhelga, Onot river and Kunlun Mountains (Russia), Val di Poschiaro (Switzerland), Spezia (Italy), Harzburg (FRG), (New Zealand), (Taiwan), (South China), (Burma), (Alaska), British Columbia (Canada), (Australia) ● Application: since ancient times it has been used as a precious stone; for medicines and for manufacture of instruments.

Glaucophane (Amphibole group)

Silicate
$Na_2Mg_3Al_2Si_8O_{22}(OH)_2$

418

From the Greek *glaukos* – blue and *fanós* – appearing (Hausmann 1845)

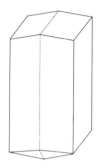

● Hardness: 6 ● Streak: blue-grey ● Colour: blue-grey, lavender blue, blue-black ● Transparency: translucent ● Lustre: vitreous ● Cleavage: good on (110) ● Fracture: uneven, conchoidal ● Morphology: crystals, radiating-fibrous, granular, fibrous aggregates ● Specific gravity: 3.0–3.1 ● Crystal system: monoclinic ● Crystal form: prisms, needles ● Chemical composition: Na_2O 7.90%, MgO 15.43%, AL_2O_3 13.01%, SiO_2 61.36%, H_2O 2.30% ● Chemical properties: fusible in a blowpipe flame; insoluble in acids ● Handling: clean with water and diluted acids ● Similar minerals: kyanite **(435)** ● Distinguishing features: cleavage, specific gravity, reaction in a blowpipe flame ● Genesis: metamorphic, in crystalline schists ● Associated minerals: chlorite **(158),** pumpellyite **(408),** epidote **(513),** garnet **(577)** ● Occurrence: rock-forming mineral; Zermatt (Switzerland), Aostatal (Italy), Euboea Island (Greece), Croix Island (France), Shikoku (Japan), California (USA).

Anthophyllite (Amphibole group)

Silicate
$(Mg,Fe)_7Si_8O_{22}(OH)_2$

419

L

From the Latin *anthophyllum* – clove (Schumacher 1801)

● Hardness: 5.5 ● Streak: white ● Colour: clove-brown, brownish-green ● Transparency: translucent ● Lustre: vitreous, pearly ● Cleavage: good on (110) ● Fracture: conchoidal ● Other features of cohesion: fibres are elastic ● Morphology: crystals, rod-like, radiating-fibrous, fibrous and granular, massive aggregates ● Specific gravity: 2.9–3.2 ● Crystal system: orthorhombic ● Crystal form: prisms, fibres ● Luminescence: sometimes light blue to white ● Chemical composition: MgO 15.83%, FeO 28.22%, SiO_2 53.93%, H_2O 2.02% (Mg:Fe = 1:1) ● Chemical properties: fuses with difficulty into a black magnetic ball; insoluble in acids ● Handling: clean with water and diluted acids ● Similar minerals: chrysotile **(275),** cummingtonite **(423)** ● Distinguishing features: hardness, specific gravity, solubility in HCl, optical properties, X-rays, chemical tests ● Genesis: metamorphic, contact-metasomatic ● Associated minerals: biotite **(167),** amphibole **(411),** feldspars ● Occurrence: rare; rock-forming mineral; Bodenmais (FRG), Kongsberg (Norway), Falun (Sweden), Heřmanov (Czech Republic), Montana (USA), Hamersley (Australia) ● Application: fibrous forms are used in the chemical industry.

---

1. **Nephrite** – polished slice; Arahura River (New Zealand – width of field 90 mm) 2. **Anthophyllite** – radiating fibrous aggregate (7 mm); Heřmanov (Czech Republic)

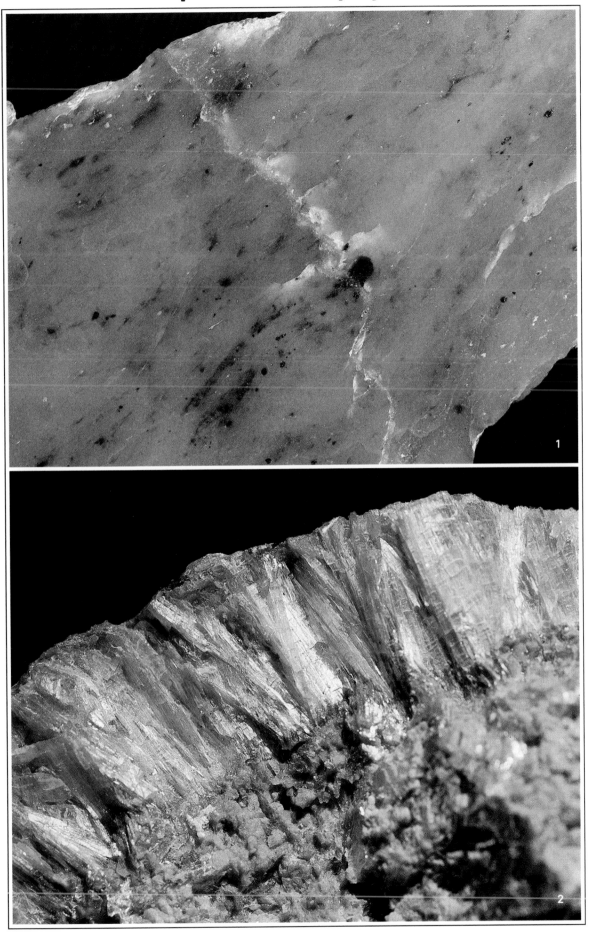

Arfvedsonite (Amphibole group)

Silicate
$Na_3Fe_4^{2+}AlSi_8O_{22}(OH)_2$

420

Named after the Swedish chemist, J. A. Arfvedson (1792–1841) (Brooke 1823)

● Hardness: 5.5–6 (brittle) ● Streak: grey-green, blue-grey, white ● Colour: black, dark blue ● Transparency: translucent to opaque ● Lustre: vitreous ● Cleavage: perfect on (110) ● Fracture: uneven ● Morphology: seldom crystals, stellate, fan-shaped fibrous and radiating-fibrous aggregates ● Specific gravity: 3.4 ● Crystal system: monoclinic ● Crystal form: prisms, plates ● Chemical composition: Na_2O 10.00%, FeO 30.90%, Al_2O_3 5.48%, SiO_2 51.68%, H_2O 1.94%; admixtures: Fe^{3+}, Mg, Ti, Mn, K ● Chemical properties: readily fusible into a magnetic ball; tinges a flame yellow; insoluble in acids ● Handling: clean with water and diluted acids ● Similar minerals: acmite **(509)** ● Distinguishing features: X-rays, chemical tests ● Genesis: magmatic (syenites), in pegmatites ● Associated minerals: sodalite **(393)**, nepheline **(397)**, zircon **(587)** ● Occurrence: rare; Katzenbuckel (FRG), Langesundsfjord (Norway), Kangerdluarsuk (Greenland), Mariupol (Ukraine), Boulder Co. – Colorado (USA) ● Application: some fibrous forms are used as insulating and acid-proof materials.

Riebeckite (Amphibole group)

Silicate
$Na_2Fe_4^{3+}Si_8O_{22}(OH)_2$

421

Named after the German traveller, E. Riebeck (1853–1885) (Sauer 1888)

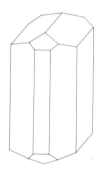

● Hardness: 5.5–6 (brittle) ● Streak: greenish-brown, yellowish-brown, white ● Colour: blue, dark blue, blue-black, dark green, black ● Transparency: translucent to non-transparent ● Lustre: vitreous, silky, dull ● Cleavage: perfect on (110) ● Morphology: crystals, fibrous, radiating-fibrous and granular aggregates ● Specific gravity: 2.9–3.4 ● Crystal system: monoclinic ● Crystal form: prisms (striated), fibrous ● Chemical composition: Na_2O 7.03%, Fe_2O_3 36.29%, SiO_2 54.63%, H_2O 2.05%; admixtures: Fe^{2+}, Ti, Mg, Al ● Chemical properties: fusible in a blowpipe flame; tinges a flame yellow; insoluble in acids ● Handling: clean with water and diluted acids ● Similar minerals: tourmaline **(564)** ● Distinguishing features: paragenesis, hardness, cleavage, reaction in a blowpipe flame, X-rays, chemical tests ● Genesis: magmatic, metamorphic ● Associated minerals: biotite **(167)**, nepheline **(397)**, arfvedsonite **(420)**, albite **(493)** ● Occurrence: rare; rock-forming mineral; in the granites of Nigeria; some American states: New Hampshire, Oklahoma, Washington and Colorado (USA), (RSA), (West Australia), Kola Peninsula and North-East Tuva (Russia), Changaj Hills – crystals measuring 15 cm (Mongolia), Poulanke (Finland), (Tanzania), (India) ● Application: fibrous forms are used as asbestos.

Crocidolite
(Riebeckite variety – Amphibole group)

Silicate
$Na_2Fe_4^{3+}Si_8O_{22}(OH)_2$

422

From the Greek *krókys* – fibre and *lithos* – stone (Hausmann 1831)

● Physical and chemical properties are similar to those of riebeckite; dark blue, silky, fibrous, acid-proof ● Genesis: contact-metasomatic ● Associated minerals: riebeckite **(421)**, cummingtonite **(423)**, albite **(493)** ● Occurrence: rare; (RSA), (Russia), (Western Australia) ● Application: insulating and acid-proof materials.

---

1. **Arfvedsonite** – embayed columnar crystals (80 mm); Mariupol (Ukraine) 2. **Riebeckite** – columnar, imperfectly developed crystal (50 mm); St. Peters Dome (USA) 3. **Crocidolite** – fibrous aggregate; Griqualand (RSA – width of field 40 mm)

Cummingtonite (Amphibole group)

Silicate
$(Mg,Fe)_7Si_8O_{22}(OH)_2$

423

Named after its locality in Cummington (Massachusetts, USA) (Dewey 1824)

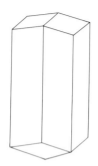

● Hardness: 5−6 ● Streak: white ● Colour: dark green, grey-green, brown, grey ● Transparency: translucent to non-transparent ● Lustre: vitreous, silky ● Cleavage: perfect on (110) ● Morphology: crystals, radiating-fibrous, fibrous and granular aggregates ● Specific gravity: 3.1−3.4 ● Crystal system: monoclinic ● Crystal form: needles, fibres, plates, twins ● Chemical composition: MgO 15.84%, FeO 28.21%, SiO_2 53.93%, H_2O 2.02%; admixtures: Mn (above 5% MnO dannemorite variety − **424**), Ca ● Chemical properties: fuses into a black magnetic ball; insoluble in acids ● Handling: clean with water and diluted acids ● Similar minerals: tremolite (**412**) ● Distinguishing features: X-rays, chemical tests ● Genesis: contact and regional metamorphosis ● Associated minerals: chlorite (**158**), magnetite (**367**), garnet (**577**) ● Occurrence: rare; Harzburg (FRG), Krivoi Rog (Ukraine), Cummington − Massachusetts and Black Hills − South Dakota (USA), (Sweden), (Finland), (Japan), (Canada).

Dannemorite (Mn variety of cummingtonite − Amphibole group)

Silicate
$(Mn,Mg,Fe)_7Si_8O_{22}(OH)_2$

424

Named after its locality Dannemora (Sweden) (Kenngott 1855)

● Physical and chemical properties are similar to those of cummingtonite (**423**) but it contains more than 5 % MnO ● Genesis: contact-metasomatic ● Associated minerals: ilvaite (**425**), adularia (**487**), garnet (**577**) ● Occurrence: rare; Chvaletice (Czech Republic), Dannemora and Silfberg (Sweden), Jacobeni (Romania), Dalnegorsk and Chivchin Mountains (Russia), (India).

Ilvaite (Lievrite)

Silicate
$CaFe_2^{2+}Fe^{3+}Si_2O_8(OH)$

425

From the Latin name *Ilva* − Elba Island (Steffens 1811)

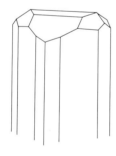

● Hardness: 5.5−6 (brittle) ● Streak: black, black-green ● Colour: brownish-black, black ● Transparency: non-transparent ● Lustre: vitreous, greasy, sub-metallic ● Cleavage: good on (010) and (001) ● Fracture: conchoidal ● Morphology: crystals, radiate, radiating-fibrous, massive and granular aggregates ● Specific gravity: 4.1 ● Crystal system: orthorhombic ● Crystal form: prisms (striated), isometric ● Magnetism: slight ● Chemical composition: CaO 13.69%, FeO 35.20%, Fe_2O_3 19.55%, SiO_2 29.36%, H_2O 2.20%; admixtures: Mg, Mn ● Chemical properties: soluble in HCl and in formic acid; readily fusible into a black magnetic ball ● Handling: clean with distilled water ● Similar minerals: ludwigite (**372**), actinolite (**413**), tourmaline (**564**) ● Distinguishing features: hardness, solubility in acids, specific gravity, streak ● Genesis: contact-metasomatic ● Associated minerals: calcite (**217**), magnetite (**367**), amphibole (**411**), augite (**429**), epidote (**513**) ● Occurrence: rare; Hernbornseelbach, Huttal (FRG), Rio Marina, Elba and Campiglia (Italy), Sérifos (Greece), Siorsuit (Greenland), Trepča (Serbia), Laxey Mine − Idaho (USA).

1. **Cummingtonite** − radiating fibrous aggregate; (New Zealand − width of field 32 mm) 2. **Dannemorite** − aggregate of fibrous crystals; Chvaletice (Czech Republic − width of field 60 mm) 3. **Ilvaite** − crystals limited in growth on two sides (5 mm) in quartz; Saxey Mine (USA)

Cummingtonite, dannemorite, ilvaite

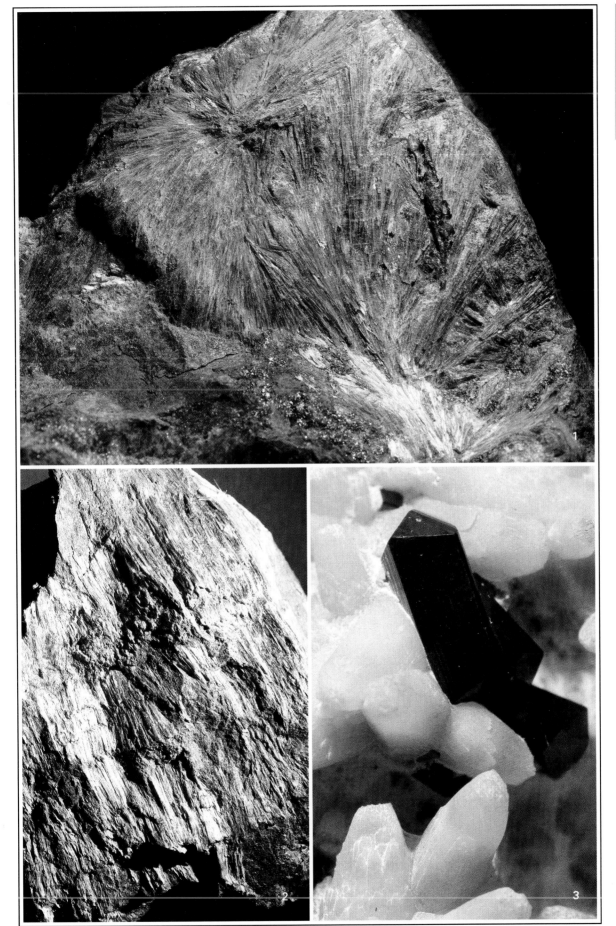

Enstatite (Pyroxene group)

Silicate
Mg$_2$Si$_2$O$_6$

426

P

From the Greek *enstates* – opponent (Kenngott 1855)

● Hardness: 5.5 ● Streak: white ● Colour: grey, green, brown ● Transparency: translucent to non-transparent ● Lustre: vitreous, pearly ● Cleavage: imperfect on (110) ● Fracture: uneven ● Morphology: imperfect crystals, massive, granular, spherulitic aggregates ● Specific gravity: 3.1–3.3 ● Crystal system: orthorhombic ● Crystal form: plates, prisms ● Chemical composition: MgO 40.16%, SiO$_2$ 59.84% ● Chemical properties: infusible; insoluble in HCl ● Handling: clean with water or diluted acids ● Similar minerals: phlogopite **(168)**, hypersthene **(428)** ● Distinguishing features: hardness, specific gravity, cleavage ● Genesis: magmatic, in pegmatites, meteorites ● Associated minerals: phlogopite, apatite **(379)**, bronzite **(427)**, olivine **(524)** ● Occurrence: common; Eifel (FRG), Bamle (Norway), (Czech Republic), (Austria), (Italy), (Russia), Arizona (USA), (Sri Lanka), (Tanzania), (Brazil), (Mexico) ● Application: clear green crystals are used as precious stones.

Bronzite (Pyroxene group)

Silicate
(Mg,Fe)$_2$Si$_2$O$_6$

427

Named after its characteristic bronze colour (Karsten 1807)

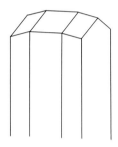

● Hardness: 5–6 (brittle) ● Streak: white, grey ● Colour: brown, bronze-brown, grey-green ● Transparency: translucent to non-transparent ● Lustre: vitreous, pearly, sub-metallic ● Cleavage: good on (110) ● Other features of cohesion: scaly cleavage ● Fracture: uneven ● Morphology: imperfect crystals, granular, massive and radial aggregates ● Specific gravity: 3.2–3.4 ● Crystal system: orthorhombic ● Crystal form: prisms ● Chemical composition: like enstatite **(426)**, but MgO is replaced by 5–15% FeO ● Chemical properties: fuses with difficulty; insoluble in HCl ● Handling: clean with water or diluted acids ● Similar minerals: enstatite, hypersthene **(428)** ● Distinguishing features: X-rays, chemical tests ● Genesis: magmatic (in basic and ultrabasic rocks), meteorites ● Associated minerals: serpentine **(273)**, magnetite **(367)**, chromite **(371)**, enstatite, olivine **(524)** ● Occurrence: common; Bad Harzburg (FRG), Kraubath (Austria), (Switzerland), Scotland (Great Britain), (Sweden), (Italy), (Russia), Bushveld (RSA), (USA).

Hypersthene (Pyroxene group)

Silicate
(Fe,Mg)$_2$Si$_2$O$_6$

428

P

From the Greek *hyper* – above and *stenos* – power (Haüy 1803)

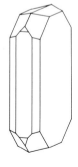

● Hardness: 5–6 (brittle) ● Streak: white, grey ● Colour: brown, grey, green, black ● Transparency: non-transparent ● Lustre: vitreous, pearly, silky, metallic ● Cleavage: perfect on (110) ● Fracture: uneven ● Morphology: imperfect crystals, granular, scaly, massive, spherulitic aggregates ● Specific gravity: 3.5–3.7 ● Crystal system: orthorhombic ● Crystal form: plates, columns ● Chemical composition: like enstatite **(426)**, but MgO is replaced by 15–34% FeO ● Chemical properties: fuses into black enamel; partly soluble in HCl ● Handling: clean with water or diluted acids ● Similar minerals: enstatite, bronzite **(427)** ● Distinguishing features: X-rays, chemical tests ● Genesis: magmatic, metamorphic (crystalline schists) ● Associated minerals: biotite **(167)**, enstatite, olivine **(524)**, feldspars ● Occurrence: common; Weiselberg, Bad Harzburg and Badenmais (FRG), Tokaj Hills (Hungary), (Romania), Scotland (Great Britain), St. Paul Island – Labrador (Canada), Demávend (Iran), (USA), (Russia), (Australia), (Japan), (Greenland) ● Application: sometimes used as a precious stone.

1. **Enstatite** – imperfectly developed columnar crystal (39 mm); Bamle (Norway) 2. **Bronzite** – polished section of a massive aggregate (52 mm); Kupferberg (FRG) 3. **Hypersthene** – embayed aggregate; Le Presse (Switzerland – width of field 21 mm)

Enstatite, bronzite, hypersthene

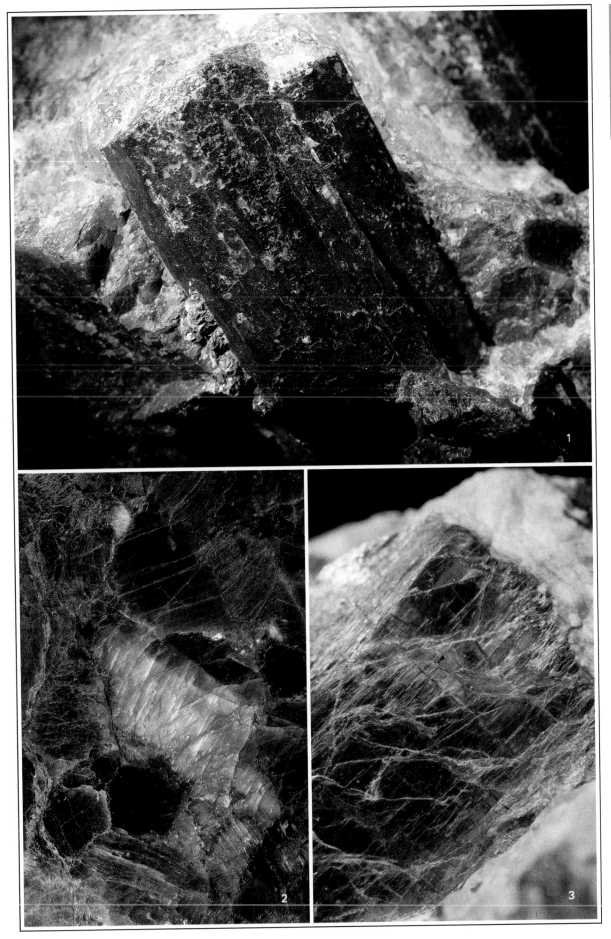

Augite (Pyroxene group)

Silicate
CaMgSi$_2$O$_6$

429

From the Greek *augé* – lustre (Werner 1792)

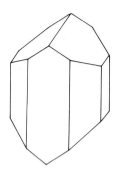

● Hardness: 5.5–6 (brittle) ● Streak: grey-green ● Colour: black, brownish-black, dark green ● Transparency: translucent to non-transparent ● Lustre: vitreous ● Cleavage: perfect on (110) ● Fracture: uneven, conchoidal ● Morphology: crystals, granular, massive aggregates, impregnations ● Specific gravity: 3.3–3.5 ● Crystal system: monoclinic ● Crystal form: short prisms, coarse plates, twins ● Chemical composition: variable, stable isomorphic admixtures Al, Fe, sometimes Ti and Na (augite, fassaite varieties) ● Chemical properties: slightly soluble in acids except HF; fuses with difficulty ● Handling: clean with distilled water ● Similar minerals: amphibole **(411)** ● Distinguishing features: crystal form, angle of cleavage (augite approx. 90°, amphibole 120°) ● Genesis: magmatic (basic eruptive rock, metamorphic) ● Associated minerals: amphibole, olivine **(524)** ● Occurrence: common; rock-forming mineral, occurs in basalts, diabases, melaphyres, tuffs: Lukov (Czech Republic), Laacher See and Kaiserstuhl (FRG), Ariccio (Italy), Auvergne (France).

Titanite (Sphene)

Silicate
CaTiSiO$_5$

430

Named after its chemical composition (Klaproth 1795)

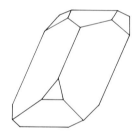

● Hardness: 5–5.5 (brittle) ● Streak: white, slightly brownish ● Colour: white, yellow, brown, reddish, greenish, black ● Transparency: transparent to translucent ● Lustre: vitreous, greasy, adamantine ● Cleavage: perfect on (110) ● Fracture: imperfect conchoidal ● Morphology: mostly crystals, granular, massive and radial aggregates ● Specific gravity: 3.4–3.6 ● Crystal system: monoclinic ● Crystal form: plates, prisms, often twins ● Chemical composition: CaO 28.60%, TiO$_2$ 40.80%, SiO$_2$ 30.60%; admixtures: Fe, Al, Y, Ce (varieties: keilhauite, grothite, alshedite) ● Chemical properties: soluble in HF and H$_2$SO$_4$; fuses only on edges into dark glass ● Handling: clean with water and diluted HCl ● Similar minerals: axinite **(523)** ● Distinguishing features: hardness, reaction in a blowpipe flame ● Genesis: magmatic, hydrothermal, metamorphic ● Associated minerals: feldspars, chlorite **(158)**, rutile **(464)**, albite **(493)**, quartz **(534)** ● Occurrence: rare; sometimes in small quantities in rocks: Plauenscher Grund near Dresden, Laacher See and Eifel (FRG), St. Gotthard, Tavetsch and Binnental (Switzerland), Zillertal and Sulzbachtal (Austria), Val Maggia and Passo di Vizze (Italy), Akhmatovsk (Russia), (Norway), (Sweden), (Canada), (USA) ● Application: transparent crystals of fine colours are used as precious stones (facets, cabochons).

---

1. Augite – embayed crystal of 22 mm; Vesuvius (Italy) **2. Titanite** – crystals (up to 20 mm); St. Gotthard (Switzerland)

Augite, titanite

Papagoite

Silicate
$CaCuAlSi_2O_6(OH)_3$

431

Named after the Indian tribe *papago* (Arizona, USA)
(Hutton 1960)

● Hardness: 5–5.5 (brittle) ● Streak: light blue ● Colour: light blue ● Transparency: transparent to translucent ● Lustre: vitreous ● Cleavage: imperfect on (100) ● Morphology: crystals, microcrystalline aggregates, coatings ● Specific gravity: 3.25 ● Crystal system: monoclinic ● Crystal form: isometric ● Chemical composition: CaO 16.80%, CuO 23.83%, Al_2O_3 15.27%, SiO_2 36.00%, H_2O 8.10% ● Chemical properties: in powdered form, soluble in hot HCl ● Handling: clean with distilled water ● Genesis: secondary ● Associated minerals: albite **(493)**, quartz **(534)** ● Occurrence: rare; occurs only in Ajo in Poma Co. (Arizona, USA).

Dioptase

Silicate
$CuSiO_3 . H_2O$

432

From the Greek *dia –* through and *optomai –* vision
(Haüy 1801)

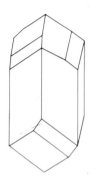

● Hardness: 5 (brittle) ● Streak: green ● Colour: emerald green, dark green ● Transparency: transparent to translucent ● Lustre: vitreous ● Cleavage: good on (10$\bar{1}$1) ● Fracture: conchoidal to uneven ● Morphology: crystals, druses, massive aggregates ● Specific gravity: 3.3 ● Crystal system: trigonal ● Crystal form: short prisms, isometric ● Chemical composition: CuO 50.48%, SiO_2 38.09%, H_2O 11.43% ● Chemical properties: soluble in HCl and HNO_3; tinges a flame green; does not fuse but becomes black when heated ● Handling: clean with distilled water ● Similar minerals: atacamite **(206)**, euchroite **(256)** ● Distinguishing features: hardness, specific gravity, crystal form, flame colour ● Genesis: secondary in oxidation zones ● Associated minerals: calcite **(217)**, chrysocolla **(268)**, malachite **(307)**, limonite **(355)** ● Occurrence: rare; Altyn Tübe (Kirgizia), (Kazakhstan), Tsumeb and Cuchab (Namibia), Kolwezi (Congo), Copiapó (Chile), Mammoth Mine – Arizona (USA), (Peru), (Iran) ● Application: sometimes used as a precious stone (facets, cabochons).

Planchéite

Silicate
$Cu_8Si_8O_{22}(OH)_2 . H_2O$

433

Named after J. Planché, who brought it from Africa
(Lacroix 1908)

● Hardness: 5.5 ● Streak: light blue ● Colour: blue, green-blue ● Transparency: translucent ● Lustre: adamantine, silky ● Cleavage: unknown ● Morphology: radial and fibrous aggregates, powdered coatings ● Specific gravity: 3.6–3.8 ● Crystal system: orthorhombic ● Crystal form: needles, fibres ● Chemical composition: CuO 54.33%, SiO_2 41.05%, H_2O 4.62% ● Chemical properties: dissolves with difficulty in HCl; tinges a flame green ● Handling: clean with distilled water ● Similar minerals: chrysocolla **(268)** ● Distinguishing features: hardness, specific gravity ● Genesis: secondary in oxidation zones ● Associated minerals: cuprite **(209)**, chrysocolla, malachite **(307)**, dioptase **(432)** ● Occurrence: rare; Tantara and Kambowe (Congo), Rioja (Argentina), Capo Calamita and Elba (Italy), Table Mountain Mine – Arizona (USA).

1. Dioptase – druse of crystals (up to 9 mm); Tsumeb (Namibia) **2. Planchéite** – radiating acicular aggregate; Kambowe (Congo – width of field 9 mm)

Dioptase, planchéite

Neptunite

Silicate
KNa$_2$Li(Fe^{2+},Mn)$_2$Ti$_2$Si$_8$O$_{24}$

434

Name derived from Roman mythology; *Neptune* – God of the sea (Flink 1893)

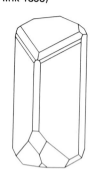

● Hardness: 5.5 ● Streak: red-brown ● Colour: black, black-brown ● Transparency: translucent to non-transparent ● Lustre: vitreous to sub-metallic ● Cleavage: perfect on (110) ● Fracture: conchoidal ● Morphology: crystals ● Specific gravity: 3.23 ● Crystal system: monoclinic ● Crystal form: prisms, twins ● Chemical composition: K$_2$O 5.48%, Na$_2$O 7.21%, Li$_2$O 3.48%, FeO 4.18%, MnO 5.06%, TiO$_2$ 18.61%, SiO$_2$ 55.98% ● Chemical properties: fuses into a black ball; soluble in HF ● Handling: clean with water or diluted acids, except HF ● Similar minerals: ilvaite **(425)**, tourmaline **(464)** ● Distinguishing features: specific gravity, paragenesis, solubility in acids ● Genesis: magmatic, metamorphic, hydrothermal ● Associated minerals: natrolite **(387)**, eudialite **(402)**, benitoite **(530)** ● Occurrence: rare; Barnavave (Ireland), Kola Peninsula (Russia), Igaliko (Greenland), San Benito Co. – California (USA), Mont St. Hilaire – Quebec (Canada).

Kyanite (Disthene)

Silicate
Al$_2$SiO$_5$

435

L

P

From the Greek *kýanos* – blue (Werner 1790)

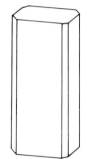

● Hardness: on prism planes, 4–4.5 along direction of elongation, 6–7 perpendicular to elongation (brittle) ● Streak: white ● Colour: white, blue, grey, greenish, yellowish ● Transparency: transparent to translucent ● Lustre: vitreous, pearly ● Cleavage: perfect on (100), imperfect on (010) ● Morphology: crystals, bunch-shaped, radial, massive aggregates ● Specific gravity: 3.6–3.7 ● Crystal system: triclinic ● Crystal form: prisms, plates, twins ● Luminescence: sometimes light red. ● Chemical composition: Al$_2$O$_3$ 62.93%, SiO$_2$ 37.07%; admixtures Fe, Cr ● Chemical properties: infusible; insoluble in acids ● Handling: clean with water or diluted acids ● Similar minerals: sillimanite **(516)** ● Distinguishing features: hardness, specific gravity, X-rays, chemical tests ● Genesis: metamorphic, in pegmatites ● Associated minerals: sillimanite, andalusite **(562)**, almandine **(585)**, staurolite **(586)**, corundum **(598)** ● Occurrence: common; Keivy in Kola Peninsula (Russia), Monte Campione (Italy), Prilep (Serbia), Zillertal (Austria), Pizzo Forno (Switzerland), Horssjöberg (Sweden), Selo Mine – North Carolina (USA), Machakos (Kenya), state of Assam (India), Mt. Margaret (Western Australia), (Brazil) ● Application: manufacture of fire-proof and acid-proof materials; clear crystals are used as precious stones (facets, cabochons).

1. **Neptunite** – euhedral crystal (20 mm); San Benito (USA) 2. **Kyanite (Disthene)** – columnar crystals (36 mm); Passo di Vizze (Italy)

Pyrite (Sulphuric pyrite, Iron pyrite)

Sulphide
FeS_2

436

P

From the Greek *pyr* – fire

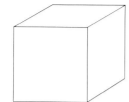

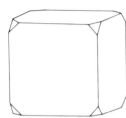

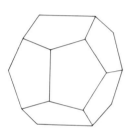

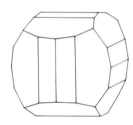

● Hardness: 6–6.5 (brittle) ● Streak: green-black ● Colour: yellow, brass-yellow, variegated tarnish colours ● Transparency: opaque ● Lustre: metallic ● Cleavage: very imperfect on (100) and on (110) ● Fracture: conchoidal, uneven ● Morphology: crystals, granular and massive aggregates, concretions, deposits, impregnations, coatings, dendrites, pseudomorphs, pulverulent (melnikovite) ● Other properties: when crushed releases sulphuric odour; produces sparks when struck with a piece of steel ● Specific gravity: 5.0–5.2 ● Crystal system: cubic ● Crystal form: cubes, showing striations; octahedra, pentagonal dodecahedra (pyritohedra), twinning ● Magnetism: sometimes slightly magnetic ● Electric conductivity: low ● Chemical composition: Fe 46.60%, S 53.40%; admixtures Ni, Co, As, Cu, Zn, Ag, Au, Tl ● Chemical properties: slightly soluble in HNO_3; fuses and forms a magnetic ball; on charcoal burns with a blue flame ● Handling: clean with distilled water; dry carefully; remove rusty stains with HCl ● Similar minerals: gold **(50)**, calaverite **(83)**, chalcopyrite **(185)**, marcasite **(437)** ● Distinguishing features: hardness, specific gravity streak, crystal form, X-rays ● Genesis: magmatic, contact-metasomatic, hydrothermal, sedimentary ● Associated minerals: galena **(77)**, sphalerite **(181)**, pyrrhotite **(283)**, arsenopyrite **(344)**, marcasite ● Occurrence: common; is the most abundant sulphide mineral; Elbingerode, Rammelsberg, Waldsassen and Meggen (FRG), Brosso, Rio Marina in Elba (Italy), Xanthe – hexahedral crystals measuring 50 cm (Greece), St. Gotthard (Switzerland), St. Just – Cornwall (Great Britain), Huelva region, Rio Tinto, Tharsis and Peña del Hierro (Spain), Alemtejo (Portugal), Grong, Lökken and Sulitelma (Norway), Falun (Sweden), Urals (Russia), Baia Sprie and Rodna (Romania), Příbram (Czech Republic), Smolník, Banská Štiavnica and Hnúšťa (Slovakia), Sain-Bel (France), Mt. Lyell (Tasmania, Australia), (Bolivia), (Peru), Arizpe and Sonora (Mexico), Central City – Colorado and French Creak – Pennsylvania (USA) ● Application: manufacture of sulphuric acid; sometimes a source of Cu, Co, Au, Se and other elements occurring as admixtures in pyrite ores. Small isolated and perfect crystals are sometimes used as precious stones (facets, cabochons).

Pyrite – perfectly developed embedded crystals (to 20 mm); Navajum (Spain)

Pyrite

Marcasite (Spear pyrites)

Sulphide
FeS$_2$

437

P

Old Arabic name for pyrites and similar minerals (Haidinger 1845)

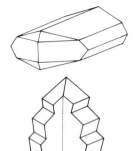

● Hardness: 6–6.5 (brittle) ● Streak: green-grey, black-grey ● Colour: light yellow, tarnish colours ● Transparency: opaque ● Lustre: metallic ● Cleavage: indistinct on (110) ● Fracture: uneven ● Morphology: crystals, druses, massive, granular, crusty aggregates, concretions, impregnations, pseudomorphs ● Other properties: when struck releases sulphuric odour ● Specific gravity: 4.8–4.9 ● Crystal system: orthorhombic ● Crystal form: plates, cockscomb, prisms, twinning ● Chemical composition: Fe 46.55%, S 53.45% ● Chemical properties: soluble in HNO$_3$; fuses into a magnetic ball; on charcoal burns with a blue flame ● Handling: do not clean ● Similar minerals: chalcopyrite **(185)**, pyrite **(436)** ● Distinguishing features: colour, crystal form, hardness, optical properties, X-rays ● Genesis: hydrothermal, post-volcanic, sedimentary, hypergenous ● Associated minerals: cinnabar **(76)**, galena **(77)**, sphalerite **(181)**, pyrite ● Occurrence: common; Freiberg, Aachen, Clausthal and Wiesloch (FRG), Most and Sokolov (Czech Republic), (Russia), (USA), (Mexico), (Chile) ● Application: manufacture of sulphuric acid, used as a precious stone.

Skutterudite (Smaltite)

Sulphide
(Co,Ni)As$_3$

438

Named after its locality Skutterud (Norway) (Haidinger 1845)

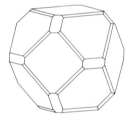

● Hardness: 6 (brittle) ● Streak: black ● Colour: light steel-grey ● Transparency: opaque ● Lustre: metallic, full ● Cleavage: very indistinct on (100) ● Fracture: conchoidal, uneven ● Morphology: crystals, massive, granular, reniform aggregates ● Other properties: when struck releases garlicky smell ● Specific gravity: 6.8 ● Crystal system: cubic ● Crystal form: cubes, octahedra, pentagonal dodecahedra ● Electric conductivity: good ● Chemical composition: variable (Co greater than Ni) ● Chemical properties: soluble in HNO$_3$; when heated the solution turns red or green ● Handling: clean with water or HCl ● Similar minerals: arsenopyrite **(344)**, chloanthite **(346)**, ullmannite **(349)** ● Distinguishing features: hardness, specific gravity, X-rays, chemical tests ● Genesis: hydrothermal ● Associated minerals: safflorite **(287)**, chloanthite, niccolite **(351)** ● Occurrence: rare; Annaberg, Schneeberg, Mansfeld, Wittichen, Richelsdorf and Spessart (FRG), Jáchymov (Czech Republic), Dobšiná (Slovakia), Schladming (Austria), Skutterud (Norway), Bou Azzer (Morocco) ● Application: Co and Ni ore.

Sperrylite

Sulphide
PtAs$_2$

439

Named after the Canadian chemist, L. J. Sperry (Wells 1889)

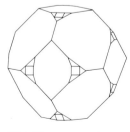

● Hardness: 6–7 (brittle) ● Streak: black ● Colour: tin-white ● Transparency: opaque ● Lustre: full metallic ● Cleavage: indistinct on (001) ● Fracture: conchoidal ● Morphology: crystals, grains ● Specific gravity: 10.6 ● Crystal system: cubic ● Crystal form: cubes, hexaoctahedra, isometric ● Chemical composition: Pt 56.58%, As 43.42% ● Chemical properties: insoluble in acids ● Handling: clean with water and diluted acids ● Similar minerals: platinum **(281)** ● Distinguishing features: hardness, crystals, specific gravity, streak ● Genesis: magmatic, in basic pegmatites, in alluvial deposits ● Associated minerals: gold **(50)**, pentlandite **(194)**, platinum, pyrrhotite **(283)**, pyrite **(436)** ● Occurrence: rare; Tweefontein (RSA), (Canada), (USA), (Russia) ● Application: Pt source.

1. **Marcasite** – aggregate of cockscomb crystals (25 mm); Komořany (Czech Republic) 2. **Skutterudite** – druses of subeuhedral crystals; Snarum (Norway – width of field 28 mm) 3. **Sperrylite** – euhedral crystal (1 mm); Trefontaine (RSA)

Marcasite, skutterudite, sperrylite

Opal

Oxide
$SiO_2 . nH_2O$

440

L

P

From the Old Indian
upala – precious stone

• Hardness: (fluctuating) 5.5–6.6 (brittle) • Streak: white • Colour: white, yellow, red, brown, green, blue, black, sometimes vari-coloured opalescence • Transparency: transparent to translucent to non-transparent • Lustre: vitreous, greasy, dull, waxy • Cleavage: absent • Fracture: conchoidal, uneven • Morphology: coatings, stalactitic, nodules, concretions, crusts, pseudomorphs, botryoidal, reniform, globular, earthy aggregates, oolites • Specific gravity: 2.1–2.2 • Crystal system: amorphous • Crystal form: unknown • Luminescence: white, yellow, yellow-green, green (depends upon admixtures, such as U) • Chemical composition: variable (content of H_2O ranges from 1 to 27%); admixtures: Mg, Ca, Al, Fe, As • Chemical properties: soluble in HF and KOH; infusible in a blowpipe flame, but becomes dull and cracks when heated • Handling: clean with distilled water • Similar minerals: chalcedony **(449)**, sometimes evansite **(244)** • Distinguishing features: hardness, solubility in acids (evansite), specific gravity, optical tests, X-rays, (chalcedony) • Genesis: volcanic, sedimentary, weathering crusts, biogenic • Associated minerals: chalcedony, cristobalite **(462)** • Occurrence: widespread; in many volcanic areas in rhyolites, andesites, trachytes, in weathering crusts, ultrabasic rocks, ore veins; is the main constituent of some sedimentary rocks, such as diatomite, radiolarite, spongilite • Application: ceramic, chemical industries, insulating and acid-proof materials; some opal varieties are used as ornamental and precious stones.

According to colour, texture and composition, opals are divided into the following varieties:

1. Precious opal **(441)**: showing a characteristic variegated opalescence;

2. Fire opal **(442)**: brick-red to hyacinth-red;

3. Milk opal **(443)**: milk-white;

4. Common opal **(444)**: yellow, brownish-yellow, brown, red; waxy lustre;

5. Wood opal **(445)**: texture of wood, displays annual ring marking, often opalized, wood;

6. Prase opal **(446)**: green because of Ni admixture;

7. Hydrophane **(447)**: dull, porous variety; when immersed in water becomes transparent; frequent opalescence;

8. Hyalite (Glassy opal) **(448)**: water-clear with glassy lustre;

9. Mossy opal;

10. Opal jasper, Cacholong, Fiorite.

Opal – polished section (size 150 mm); Nová Ves (Czech Republic)

Opal

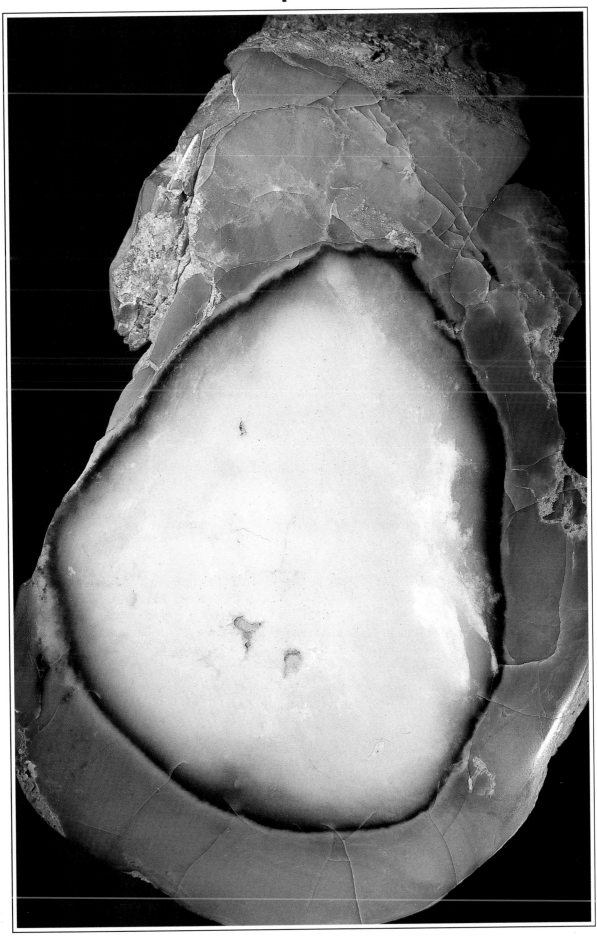

Precious opal (Opal variety)

Oxide
$SiO_2 . nH_2O$

441

L

P

● Physical and chemical properties are similar to those of opal. It differs with a characteristic variegated opalescence ● Transparent to translucent, green and brown luminescence ● Genesis: post-volcanic, sedimentary ● Associated minerals: marcasite **(437)**, hydrophane **(447)**, hyalite **(448)** ● Occurrence: rare; Dubník (Slovakia), (Faroe Islands), Humboldt Co. – Nevada (USA), Querétaro (Mexico), Gracias a Diós (Honduras), Lightning Ridge, White Cliffs, Coober Pedy, Andamooka and Tintenbar (Australia), Transbaikalia, Kamchatka (Russia), (Ukraine), (Brazil). Older literature mentions precious opals in localities in Frankfurt am Main and Leisnig (FRG) ● Application: as one of the most popular and most valuable precious stones, it is predominantly used in jewellery (cabochons).

Fire opal (Opal variety)

Oxide
$SiO_2 . nH_2O$

442

L

P

● Physical and chemical properties are similar to those of opal. It differs in its hyacinth to flame-red colour ● Transparent to translucent ● Genesis: post-volcanic ● Associated minerals: precious opal **(441)**, hyalite **(448)** ● Occurrence: rare; Steiermark and Gossendorf (Austria), Ľubietová (Slovakia), Zimapane and Querétaro (Mexico), (Faroe Islands), Simav (Turkey), (Kazakhstan), Kamchatka (Russia) ● Application: used as a precious stone (facets, cabochons).

Milk opal (Opal variety)

Oxide
$SiO_2 . nH_2O$

443

L

P

● Physical and chemical properties are similar to those of opal. It is a characteristic milk-white to yellow-white or blue-white colour, vitreous to weak lustre, translucent ● If interwoven with black dendrites of manganese and iron oxides, it is called dendritic opal ● Genesis: post-volcanic, sedimentary, hydrothermal ● Associated minerals: precious opal **(441)**, common opal **(444)**, hyalite **(448)** ● Occurrence: rare; in similar localities as precious opal, hydrothermal in serpentinites ● Application: seldom used as precious stone; most often only specimens with interesting dendritic patterns of Mn oxides are worked as cabochons.

1. Milk opal – Dubník (Slovakia) **2. Precious opal** – Coober Pedy (Australia) **3.–4. Fire opal** – Mapimí (Mexico – width of field 60 mm)

Milk opal, precious opal, fire opal

Common opal (Opal variety)

Oxide
$SiO_2 . nH_2O$

444

L

P

● Physical and chemical properties are similar to those of opal. It is mostly translucent to non-transparent, of conchoidal fracture and brittle. It occurs in different tints of yellow, brown to black ● Genesis: post-volcanic, in weathering crusts ● Associated minerals: nontronite **(36)**, hyalite **(448)**, chalcedony **(449)** ● Occurrence: common in volcanic areas, often in oxidation zones of ore veins or in weathered crusts of ultrabasic rocks; Herlany, Dargov and Badín (Slovakia), Tokaj Hills (Hungary), Transylvania (Romania), Transcarpathian area (Ukraine), Leisnig (FRG), Gleichenberg (Austria), (USA), (Mexico) ● Application: sometimes worked as a precious or ornamental stone.

Wood opal (Opal variety)

Oxide
$SiO_2 . nH_2O$

445

L

P

● Physical and chemical properties are similar to those of opal. A characteristic is the annual ring marking, composed of bands of different colour, typical of opalized tree trunks and branches ● Very brittle; conchoidal fracture ● Variable colour, from light-yellow, yellowish-brown, red up to brown-black and black, sometimes white and black stripes ● Genesis: post-volcanic ● Associated minerals: common opal **(444)**, hyalite **(448)**, chalcedony **(449)** ● Occurrence: common; Ľubietová, Antol and Zamutov (Slovakia), Holbrook – Arizona, Washington, Colorado, Idaho, Virgin Valley – Nevada (USA), (Romania), (Ukraine), Patagonia (Argentina), Dschel Moka Ham (Egypt) ● Application: sometimes used as a precious stone (cabochons.

Prase opal (Opal variety)

Oxide
$SiO_2 . nH_2O$

446

L

P

● Physical and chemical properties are similar to those of opal. Green-white to green (due to Ni admixture) ● Genesis: weathering crusts ● Associated minerals: milk opal **(443)** ● Occurrence: rare; Szklary (Poland), Křemže (Czech Republic), (New Caledonia), Hanety-Hügel (Tanzania), Nevada (USA) ● Application: sometimes used as an ornamental or precious stone (cabochons).

---

1. Wood opal – Arizona (USA) **2. Prase opal** – (Mongolia) **3. Common opal** – Třebíč (Czech Republic – width of field 72 mm)

Wood opal, prase opal, common opal

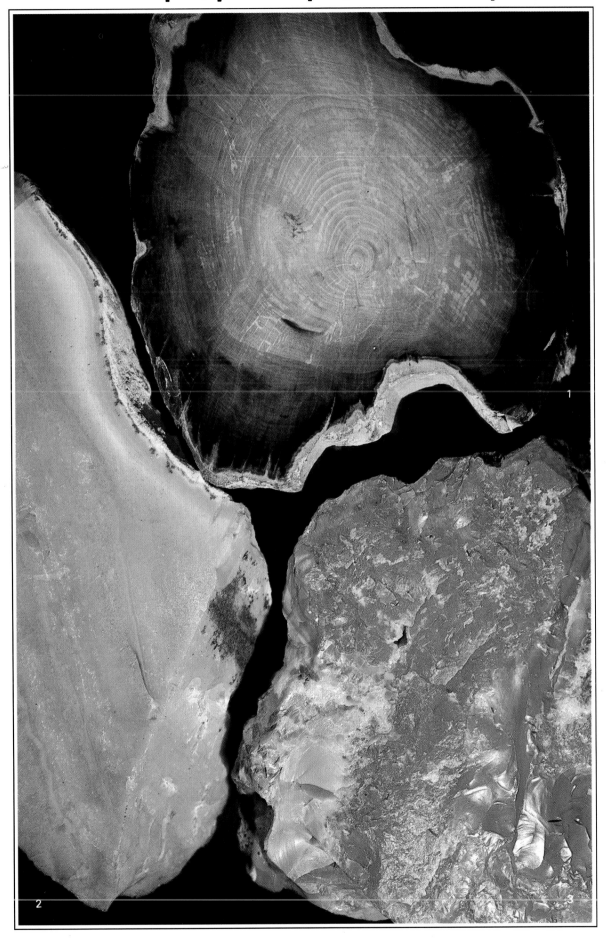

Hydrophane (Opal variety)

Oxide
$SiO_2 \cdot nH_2O$

447

From the Greek *hydor*
– water and *fános* –
appearing

L

P

• Physical and chemical properties are similar to those of opal. Dull, porous, adheres to tongue. Immersed in water acquires glassy lustre, becomes transparent and retains the play of colours as in precious opal **(441)**. In air loses its water content and becomes dull again • Genesis: post-volcanic, weathering crusts • Associated minerals: precious opal, milk opal **(443)**, hyalite **(448)** • Occurrence: rare; Hubertusburg (FRG), Dubník (Slovakia) • Application: sometimes used as a precious stone.

Hyalite (Glassy opal, opal variety)

Oxide
$SiO_2 \cdot nH_2O$

448

From the Greek *hyalos*
– glass
(Werner 1812)

L

P

• Physical and chemical properties are similar to those of opal. Characteristic is the fine blue or green tint. Transparent, splendent glassy lustre; drop-shaped, crusty, botryoidal, stalactitic, reniform aggregates, frequent green to yellow-green luminescence • Genesis: post-volcanic, weathering crusts • Associated minerals: precious opal **(441)**, milk opal **(443)**, chalcedony **(449)** • Occurrence: common; especially in young volcanic areas, such as the environment of Kaiserstuhl (FRG), Valeč (Czech Republic), Kecerovský Liptovec (Slovakia), Oberlausitz and Tharandt (FRG), San Luis Potosí (Mexico), Tatayami (Japan), (Faroe Islands), (Iceland), Klamat Falls – Oregon, North Carolina and New England (USA), (Canada), (Ukraine), (New Zealand) • Application: sometimes used as a precious or ornamental stone (individual smaller aggregates, cabochons).

---

1. Hydrophane – compact specimen with a shelly cleavage; Dubník (Slovakia – width of field 72 mm) **2. Hyalite** – crusty aggregate (26 mm); Valeč (Czech Republic)

Hydrophane, hyalite

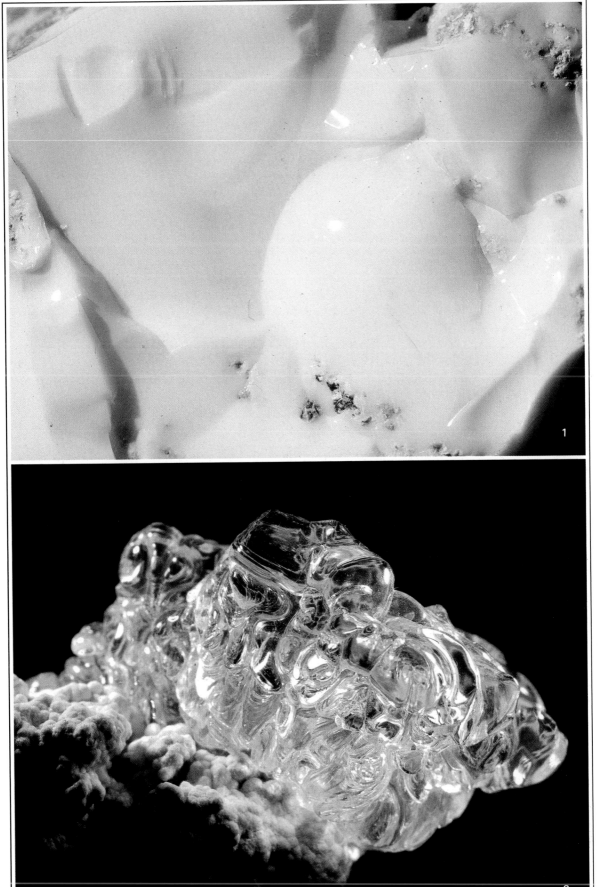

Chalcedony (Cryptocrystalline variety of quartz)

Oxide
SiO₂

449

Named after the historical town of Kalchidón (Asia Minor) (Agricola, 1546)

● Hardness: 6–7 ● Streak: white ● Colour: grey, grey-blue, grey-green, grey-white, often varicoloured by different oxides ● Transparency: translucent ● Lustre: vitreous, dull, greasy, silky ● Cleavage: absent ● Fracture: uneven, splintery, conchoidal ● Morphology: crusts, stalactitic, encrustations, pseudomorphs, nodules, geodes, reniform, amygdaloidal filling, veins ● Specific gravity: 2.59–2.61 ● Crystal system: trigonal ● Crystal form: cryptocrystalline, fibrous (microscopic crystals) ● Luminescence: yellowish-green, yellow, white ● Chemical composition: SiO_2 100%; admixtures: Fe, Al, Mg, Ca, Ni, Cr ● Chemical properties: readily soluble in alkaline solutions, especially in KOH ● Handling: clean with diluted acids or distilled water ● Similar minerals: evansite (**244**), smithsonite (**373**), hemimorphite (**403**), opal (**440**) ● Distinguishing features: hardness, specific gravity, optical properties, solubility in acids, X-rays ● Genesis: post-volcanic, from hot springs, in weathering crusts, sedimentary ● Associated minerals: calcite (**217**), quartz (**534**), zeolites ● Occurrence: widespread; in volcanic rocks (melaphyres, andesites, basalts, rhyolites); in oxidation zones of ore deposits; Idar-Oberstein (FRG), Erzberg (Austria), Tri Vody, Slanec (Slovakia), Kozákov (Czech Republic), Trieste and Sardinia (Italy), (Uruguay – large deposits), (southern Brazil), Deccan Plateau (India), Florida, Oregon, Arizona, Colorado and Idaho (USA), (Mexico), (Iceland), (Faroe Islands), (New Zealand), Caucasus and the Urals (Russia), (Arabian Peninsula), Nova Scotia and Ontario (Canada) ● Application: in chemical industry; often as an ornamental or precious stone (cabochons, facets, cameos).

Chalcedony like opal, occurs in numerous varieties, named for their textures and colours:

1. Agate (**450**) – varicoloured bands filling amygdaloidal cavities;

2. Moss agate (**451**) – green and brown with inclusions of chlorites, amphiboles and Fe and Mn oxides;

3. Onyx (**452**) – black-white-banded chalcedony;

4. Plasma (**453**) – coloured dark green by chlorites or serpentine;

5. Prase (**454**) – dark green due to inclusions of chlorite;

6. Carnelian (**455**) – dark red due to inclusions of hematite;

7. Sardonyx (**456**) – brown;

8. Chrysoprase (**457**) – green due to presence of Ni compounds;

9. Heliotrope (**458**) – green with red stains;

10. Jasper (**459**) – non-transparent chalcedony of intense colour;

11. Enhydros – **nodules of chalcedony containing water.**

Chalcedony – light blue crusts in vesicle in andesite; Banské (Slovakia – width of field 45 mm)

Chalcedony

Agate (Chalcedony variety)

Oxide
SiO_2

450

L

P

Named after its first known locality on the river Achates (southern Sicily, Italy)

● Physical and chemical properties are similar to those of chalcedony **(449)**. It has a characteristic finely banded structure of differently coloured layers in a parallel or concentric arrangement. It is found as a filling of amygdales and vesicles ● Luminescence: sometimes white, yellow-green or green ● Occurrence: widespread, especially in volcanic areas; St. Egidien, Halsbach, Schlottwitz, St. Wendel and Idar-Oberstein (FRG), Kozákov, Železnice, Rváčov and Levín (Czech Republic), Valle di Fassa (Italy), (Armenia), Urals and Siberia (Russia), (Bulgaria), (Mongolia), (China), (India), (Yemen), (Ethiopia), (Morocco), (Iceland), (Madagascar), (Mexico), Oregon, Idaho and Arizona (USA). The largest and most brilliant agates (measuring several metres) are found in (southern Brazil) and (Uruguay) ● Application: manufacture of bearings, blades in laboratory scales, mortars; popular precious stone, often artificially coloured (cabochons, plastic cutting, tumbling, fancy goods).

Moss agate (Chalcedony variety)

Oxide
SiO_2

451

L

P

Named after its appearance

● Physical and chemical properties are similar to those of chalcedony **(449)**. Its mossy appearance is derived from embedded, arborescent inclusions of chlorites, or Fe and Mn oxides. Most often fills vesicles and cavities; sometimes forming part of common agates ● Occurrence: rare; Železnice (Czech Republic), Transbaikal and the Urals (Russia), Colorado, Oregon, Utah, Washington and Wyoming (USA), (China), (India), Rio Grande do Sul (Brazil) ● Application: as an ornamental or precious stone (cabochons, tumbling).

Onyx (Chalcedony variety)

Oxide
SiO_2

452

L

P

From the Greek *onyx* – nail

● Physical and chemical properties are similar to those of chalcedony **(449)**. It shows even, parallel bands usually of black and white (onyx) or brown and white (sardonyx). With this colouring (often achieved artificially) it resembles agate ● Occurrence: (southern Brazil), (Uruguay), (India), Magnitogorsk, Urals, in the river basin of Tulda near Chita – red-brown-white to red-yellow sardonyx (Russia) ● Application: as ornamental or precious stone (cabochons, plates).

---

1. Agate – polished slice of amygdale (size 40 mm); Železnice (Czech Republic) **2. Onyx** – polished slice; (Brazil) **3. Moss agate** – polished slice; (India – width of field 75 mm)

Agate, onyx, moss agate

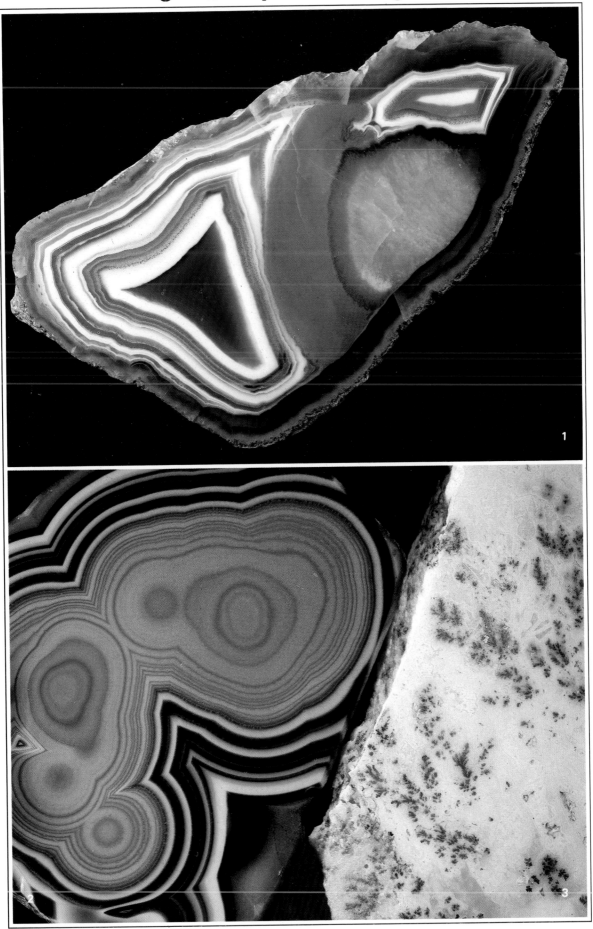

Plasma (Chalcedony variety)

Oxide
SiO_2

453

L

P

From the Italian name previously used for green gems found in the ruins of ancient Rome

- Physical and chemical properties are similar to those of chalcedony **(449)**. It is green or dark green because of inclusions of chlorites or amphiboles
- Occurrence: predominantly in weathering crusts of ultrabasic rocks; rare variety of chalcedony; Hrubšice (Czech Republic), Deccan Plateau (India)
- Application: seldom used as a precious stone.

Prase (Chalcedony or quartz variety)

Oxide
SiO_2

454

L

P

From the Greek *prasitis* – garlic-green stone

- Physical and chemical properties are similar to those of chalcedony **(449)** and quartz **(534)**. It is green to dark green because of inclusions of actinolite **(413)** • Occurrence: rare; Erzgebirge (FRG), Habachtal near Salzburg (Austria), (Finland), Scotland (Great Britain), Urals (Russia), (RSA) • Application: used as a precious stone (cabochons); in the manufacture of decorative articles.

Carnelian (Chalcedony variety)

Oxide
SiO_2

455

L

P

From the Latin *corneus* – horny
(Agricola 1546)

- Physical and chemical properties are similar to those of chalcedony **(449)**. Of red or reddish-brown colour, showing no distinct texture, translucent
- Occurrence: Nová Paka, Kozákov and Železnice (Czech Republic), (Romania), (India), (Egypt), (Arabian Peninsula) • Application: used as an ornamental or precious stone (cabochons, plates).

Sardonyx (Chalcedony variety)

Oxide
SiO_2

456

L

P

After the town Sardes in Asia Minor

- Physical and chemical properties are similar to those of chalcedony **(449)**. Colour: brown, orange-brown, reddish-brown. No distinct texture, translucent. Often grades into carnelian **(455)** • Occurrence: Transbaikal and the river basin of the Tulda (Russia), (Asia Minor) • Application: used as on ornamental or precious stone (cabochons, plates).

---

1. **Plasma** – polished slice; Hrubšice (Czech Republic) 2. **Prase** – polished slice; Urals (Russia) 3. **Carnelian** – polished slice; (India) 4. **Sardonyx** – polished slice; Minas Gerais (Brazil – width of field 62 mm)

Plasma, prase, carnelian, sardonyx

Chrysoprase (Chalcedony variety)

Oxide
SiO_2

457

L

P

From the Greek *chrysós* – gold and *práson* – to estimate

● Physical and chemical properties are similar to those of chalcedony **(449)**. It is emerald green to apple green because of the presence of Ni compounds, translucent to opaque. ● Handling: when slightly heated or exposed to sun's rays it loses its colour and becomes dull; should be stored in the dark ● Genesis: weathering crusts in ultrabasic rocks ● Associated minerals: garnierite **(157)**, serpentine **(273)**, opal **(440)** ● Occurrence: rare; Szklary, Kožmice and Wiry (Poland), Urals (Russia), Oregon and California (USA), Marlborough Creek (Australia), St. Egidien (FRG), Goyaz (Brazil), (Tanzania), (Zimbabwe), (RSA), (New Caledonia) ● Application: used as an ornamental and precious stone (cabochons).

Heliotrope (Chalcedony variety)

Oxide
SiO_2

458

L

P

From the Greek *helios* – sun and *tropos* – turn

● Physical and chemical properties are similar to those of chalcedony **(449)**. Dark green with characteristic red to brownish-red stains. Opaque ● Genesis: post-volcanic ● Associated minerals: chalcedony, plasma **(453)**, jasper **(459)** ● Occurrence: rare; Idar-Oberstein (FRG), Kozákov (Czech Republic), Scotland (Great Britain), Tyrol (Austria), Urals (Russia), Bombay area (India), (Australia), (Brazil), (USA), (China) ● Application: used as an ornamental and precious stone (cabochons, plates).

Jasper (Chalcedony variety)

Oxide
SiO_2

459

L

P

Historical name

● Physical and chemical properties are similar to those of chalcedony **(449)**; frequent admixtures of quartz and opal. Colour ranges from yellow through brown and red to green because of inclusions of chlorite and hematite. Mostly opaque, seldom translucent ● Genesis: post-volcanic, sedimentary, metamorphic ● Associated minerals: chalcedony, agate **(450)**, quartz **(534)** ● Occurrence: widespread; St. Egidien, Idar-Oberstein and Löhlbach (FRG), Kozákov (Czech Republic), Dauphiné (France), Urals (Russia), Deccan Plateau (India), Kamamba (Madagascar), (Brazil), (Egypt), (USA), (Australia), (RSA) ● Application: used as an ornamental and precious stone (cabochons).

Cacholong (Chalcedony and opal variety)

Oxide
SiO_2

460

L

Probably from the Mongolian, meaning beautiful stone

● Physical and chemical properties are similar to those of chalcedony **(449)**. Of all varieties it is the softest, of chalk-white colour, dull to pearly lustre, porous ● Genesis: secondary ● Associated minerals: opal **(440)**, chalcedony, agate **(450)** ● Occurrence: rare; Hüttenberg (Austria), Kozákov and Olomučany (Czech Republic), (Mongolia – in the steppes).

---

1. **Chrysoprase** – polished slice; Szklary (Poland) 2. **Heliotrope** – polished slice; Kozákov (Czech Republic) 3. **Jasper** – polished slice; Urals (Russia) 4. **Cacholong** – polished slice; Najat (Iraq – width of field 120 mm)

Chrysoprase, heliotrope, jasper, cacholong

Tridymite

461

From the Greek
tridymos – triplex
(Rath 1868)

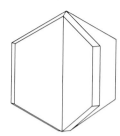

• Hardness: 6.5–7 (brittle) • Streak: white • Colour: white, yellowish-white, grey • Transparency: transparent to translucent • Lustre: vitreous • Cleavage: imperfect on (0001) and on (10$\bar{1}$0) • Fracture: conchoidal • Morphology: crystals, flabelliform and spherical aggregates • Specific gravity: 2.27 • Crystal system: dimorphous: α-tridymite orthorhombic to 117 °C, β-tridymite hexagonal (from 870 °C to 1470 °C) • Crystal form: plates, often triplets • Chemical composition: SiO$_2$ 100%; admixtures Al, Fe, Ca, Na, K • Chemical properties: soluble in hot concentrated solution of soda • Handling: clean with water and diluted acids • Similar minerals: baryte **(240)**, cristobalite **(462)** • Distinguishing features: hardness, cleavage, specific gravity, X-rays • Genesis: magmatic, post-volcanic, secondary • Associated minerals: calcite **(217)**, opal **(440)**, cristobalite • Occurrence: common in volcanic rocks as filling in cavities; Drachenfels and Perlenhardt (FRG), Monts Dore (France), Colli and Euganei (Italy), Kremnička and Vechec – crystals measuring 1 cm (Slovakia), Cerro San Cristóbal (Mexico), San Juan district – Colorado (USA), Ishigayama – crystals measuring 1.5 cm (Japan).

Cristobalite

462

Named after its locality
in Cerro San Cristóbal
(Mexico)
(Rath 1887)

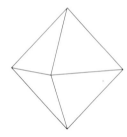

• Hardness: 6.5 (brittle) • Streak: white • Colour: white, milky-white • Transparency: translucent to transparent • Lustre: vitreous, greasy • Cleavage: absent • Fracture: conchoidal • Morphology: crystals, spherulites, fibrous (lussatite variety), crusts, cryptocrystalline • Specific gravity: 2.32 • Crystal system: dimorphic: α-cristobalite tetragonal to 270 °C, β-cristobalite cubic from 1470 °C to 1710 °C • Crystal form: dipyramidal, hexaoctahedra, plates, twinning • Chemical composition: SiO$_2$ 100%; admixtures Fe, Ca, Al, K, Na • Chemical properties: soluble in HF and hot Na$_2$CO$_3$ • Handling: clean with water and diluted acids • Similar minerals: tridymite **(461)** • Distinguishing features: X-rays • Genesis: post-volcanic, magmatic, secondary (by recrystallization of opals) • Associated minerals: calcite **(217)**, opal **(440)**, chalcedony **(449)**, tridymite • Occurrence: not as common as tridymite; in effusive rocks, in opals, agates and bentonites; Blaue Kuppe near Eschweg (FRG), Vechec (Slovakia), Nezdenice (Czech Republic), Monte Dore (France), San Cristóbal (Mexico), Hyderabad (India), (USA).

---

1. Tridymite – tabular crystals (4 mm) in vesicle in andesite; Vechec (Slovakia) **2. Cristobalite** – attached crystal (1 mm); San Cristóbal (Mexico)

Tridymite, cristobalite

Diaspore

From the Greek *dias-peireih* – to disperse (Haüy 1801)

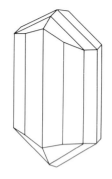

• Hardness: 6.5–7 (brittle) • Streak: white • Colour: colourless, white, yellow, pink, reddish, violet, grey • Transparency: transparent to translucent • Lustre: vitreous, pearly • Cleavage: very good on (010) • Fracture: conchoidal • Morphology: crystals, tabular aggregates, massive, crusts • Specific gravity: 3.3–3.5 • Crystal system: Orthorhombic • Crystal form: striated plates, twins • Luminescence: sometimes light yellow • Chemical composition: Al_2O_3 84.99%, H_2O 15.01% • Chemical properties: in flame spatters, but does not fuse; dissolves with difficulty in HF • Handling: clean with water or diluted acids • Similar minerals: gibbsite **(90)** • Distinguishing features: hardness, specific gravity • Genesis: metamorphic, contact-metamorphic • Associated minerals: calcite **(217)**, kyanite **(435)**, corundum **(598)** • Occurrence: common; found in bauxites and in crystalline schists; Greiner (Austria), Campolungo (Switzerland), (Greece), Langesunsdfjord (Norway), (Czech Republic), (Slovakia), (Russia), Massachusetts (USA) • Application: Al source; free-proof materials.

Rutile

From the Latin *rutilus* – reddish (Werner 1801)

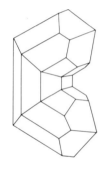

• Hardness: 6–6.5 (brittle) • Streak: yellowish-brown or brownish-red • Colour: yellow, red, brown to black (nigrine variety) • Transparency: translucent to non-transparent • Lustre: adamantine, sub-metallic, greasy • Cleavage: perfect on (110), indistinct on (100) • Fracture: uneven, conchoidal • Morphology: crystals, granular, fibrous aggregates, impregnations, disseminated, pseudomorphs • Specific gravity: 4.2–4.3 • Crystal system: tetragonal • Crystal form: prisms (often striated), needles, twinning • Chemical composition: Ti 59.95%, O 40.05% • Chemical properties: infusible, insoluble in acids • Handling: clean with water or diluted acids • Similar minerals: ilmenite **(365)**, cassiterite **(548)**, tourmaline **(564)**, zircon **(587)** • Distinguishing features: hardness, specific gravity, streak, solubility in acids • Genesis: magmatic, in pegmatites, metamorphic, in alluvial deposits • Associated minerals: anatase **(352)**, brookite **(353)**, apatite **(379)**, titanite **(430)** • Occurrence: common; Binnental and Campolungo (Switzerland), Alto Adige (Italy), Kragerö (Norway), Virginia and Arkansas (USA), Oaxaca (Mexico), (Brazil), (Australia) • Application: Ti source; sometimes used as a precious stone.

Sagenite (Rutile variety)

From the latin *sagena* – net (Saussure 1796)

• Physical and chemical properties are similar to those of rutile **(464)**. Typical is the hairlike form of its crystals forming reticulated inclusions at approx. 60 °C • Occurrence: It often forms inclusions in biotite **(167)** – Cavradi – Tavetsch (Switzerland), or in quartz crystals **(534)** in alpine fissures – Binnental and St. Gotthard (Switzerland); Modriach (Austria), northern Urals (Russia), (Brazil) • Application: quartz containing sagenite inclusions is used as a precious stone.

---

1. **Diaspore** – tabular crystals (to 13 mm); Chester Co. (USA) 2. **Rutile** – columnar doubly-terminated crystal (20 mm); Alps (Austria) 3. **Sagenite** – acicular aggregates on quartz (needles 15 mm); Hochmarr (Switzerland)

Diaspore, rutile, sagenite

H
6—7

369

Periclase

466

From the Greek *peri* – around and *kláo* – to cut (Scacchi 1841)

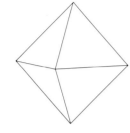

● Hardness: 6 ● Streak: white ● Colour: white, grey or green ● Transparency: transparent to translucent ● Lustre: vitreous ● Cleavage: perfect on (001) ● Morphology: crystals, isometric grains, compact ● Specific gravity: 3.7–3.9 ● Crystal system: cubic ● Crystal form: octahedra, cubes ● Luminescence: sometimes light yellow in long-wave UV ● Chemical composition: Mg 60.32%, O 39.68% ● Chemical properties: readily soluble in diluted HCl and HNO_3, infusible ● Handling: clean with distilled water ● Genesis: contact-metamorphic ● Associated minerals: brucite **(91)**, magnesite **(302)**, olivine **(524)** ● Occurrence: rare; Monte Somma and Predazzo (Italy), Långban (Sweden), Crestmore – California (USA) ● Application: sometimes used as a precious stone (facets, cabochons).

Pseudobrookite

467

From the Greek *pseudó* – I mislead, and *brookite* (name of mineral) (Koch 1878)

● Hardness: 6 (brittle) ● Streak: reddish-brown or ochre-yellow ● Colour: dark brown or black ● Transparency: translucent to non-transparent ● Lustre: sub-metallic to adamantine ● Cleavage: poor on (010) ● Fracture: uneven, conchoidal ● Morphology: crystal ● Specific gravity: 4.4. ● Crystal system: orthorhombic ● Crystal form: prisms, needles, elongated plates ● Chemical composition: Fe_2O_3 66.65%, TiO_2 33.35% ● Chemical properties: soluble in hot HCl, H_2SO_4 and HF, fuses with difficulty ● Handling: clean with distilled water ● Similar minerals: brookite **(353)**, rutile **(464)** ● Distinguishing features: X-rays, chemical tests ● Genesis: magmatic, post-volcanic or young volcanic rocks ● Associated minerals: opal **(440)**, tridymite **(461)**, hematite **(472)** ● Occurrence: rare; Katzenbuckels and Bellerberg (FRG), Uroi (Romania), Vesuvius and Etna (Italy), Havredal (Norway), Jumilla (Spain), Black Range – New Mexico (USA).

Bixbyite

468

Named after the American mineralogist, M. Bixby (Penfield, Foote 1897)

● Hardness: 6.5 (brittle) ● Streak: black ● Colour: bronze-black or black ● Transparency: opaque ● Lustre: metallic ● Cleavage: imperfect on (111) ● Fracture: uneven ● Morphology: crystals, massive aggregates ● Specific gravity: 4.9–5.0 ● Crystal system: cubic ● Crystal form: cubes with intense striation, twinning ● Chemical composition: Mn_2O_3 49.71%, Fe_2O_3 50.29% (Mn:Fe = 1:1) ● Chemical properties: dissolves with difficulty in HCl, fuses into a magnetic ball ● Handling: clean with diluted acids ● Similar minerals: jacobsite **(366)**, magnetite **(367)** ● Distinguishing features: X-rays, chemical tests ● Genesis: pneumatolytic, hydrothermal, metamorphic ● Associated minerals: braunite **(469)**, garnet **(577)**, topaz **(595)** ● Occurrence: rare; Ultevis (Sweden), Ribas and Gerona (Spain), Río Chubut (Argentina), Sitapar and Chhindwara (India), Postmasburg (RSA), Thomas Range – Utah (USA), (Mexico).

Bixbyite – euhedral crystal (4 mm); Thomas Range (Utah, USA)

Bixbyite

Braunite

Oxide
3 Mn_2O_3 . $MnSiO_3$

469

Named after K. Braun (1790–1872) from Gotha (Germany) (Haidinger 1826)

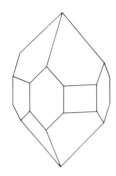

● Hardness: 6–6.5 (brittle) ● Streak: brownish-black ● Colour: black or brownish-black ● Transparency: opaque ● Lustre: metallic, greasy ● Cleavage: perfect on (111) ● Fracture: uneven, sub-conchoidal ● Morphology: crystals, granular and massive aggregates ● Specific gravity: 4.7–4.9 ● Crystal system: tetragonal ● Crystal form: pseudooctahedra, dipyramidal ● Chemical composition: Mn_2O_3 78.34%, MnO 11.73%, SiO_2 9.93%; admixtures: Fe, Ca, B, Ba ● Chemical properties: soluble in HCl, HNO_3 and hot H_2SO_4, infusible ● Handling: clean with distilled water ● Similar minerals: hausmannite **(358)**, magnetite **(367)**, franklinite **(470)** ● Distinguishing features: magnetism, reaction to Zn ● Genesis: metamorphic, hydrothermal, contact-metamorphic, sedimentary ● Associated minerals: calcite **(217)**, hausmannite, pyrolusite **(474)**, quartz **(534)** ● Occurrence: common; Ilfeld, Ilmenau and Elgersburg (FRG), Långban and Jakobsberg (Sweden), Postmasburg (RSA), Sitapar (India), Mason Co. – Texas (USA), (Brazil) ● Application: Mn ore.

Franklinite

Oxide
$(Zn,Mn,Fe^{2+})(Fe^{3+},Mn^{3+})_2O_4$

470

Named after its locality, Franklin (New Jersey, USA) (Berthier 1819)

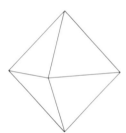

● Hardness: 6–6.5 (brittle) ● Streak: reddish-brown ● Colour: iron-black, thin slabs, a translucent red ● Transparency: opaque ● Lustre: metallic, sub-metallic ● Cleavage: imperfect on (111) ● Fracture: conchoidal ● Morphology: crystals, granular, massive aggregates ● Specific gravity: 5.0–5.2 ● Crystal system: cubic ● Crystal form: octahedra ● Magnetism: sometimes weak ● Chemical composition: variable; admixtures: Mn ● Chemical properties: soluble in HCl, infusible, becomes magnetic when heated ● Handling: clean with water and diluted acids ● Similar minerals: magnetite **(367)**, chromite **(371)** ● Distinguishing features: streak, hardness, paragenesis, chemical test for Zn ● Genesis: contact-metamorphic ● Associated minerals: calcite **(217)**, zincite **(296)**, willemite **(404)**, rhodonite **(531)** ● Occurrence: rare; Urals (Russia), Mine Hill, Sterling Hill and Franklin – New Jersey (USA).

Euxenite

Oxide
$(Y,Ce,Er,U,Th,Ca)(Nb,Ta,Ti)_2O_6$

471

From the Greek *eu* – good and *xenos* – foreigner (Scheerer 1847)

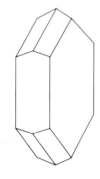

● Hardness: approx. 6 (brittle) ● Streak: reddish-brown ● Colour: brown, black-brown, yellow or olive-green ● Transparency: translucent to non-transparent ● Lustre: greasy, sub-metallic ● Cleavage: unknown ● Fracture: conchoidal, uneven ● Morphology: crystals, grains ● Specific gravity: 4.6–5.9 ● Crystal system: Orthorhombic but usually metamict ● Crystal form: prisms ● Radioactivity: strong ● Chemical composition: variable ● Chemical properties: soluble in HF and H_2SO_4, slightly soluble in KOH, infusible, spatters, shines ● Handling: clean with distilled water ● Genesis: in pegmatites ● Associated minerals: ilmenite **(365)**, monazite **(383)**, beryl **(554)**, zircon **(587)** ● Occurrence: rare; Kragerö, Hitterö, Evje and Iveland (Norway), Pitkäranta (Finland), Pomba (Brazil), Ampangabe (Madagascar) ● Applications: sometimes source of rare earths, U and Th.

---

1. Braunite – coroded crystals (up to 10 mm); Långban (Sweden) **2. Franklinite** – crystals (up to 2 mm) attached to calcite; Franklin (New Jersey, USA) **3. Euxenite** – massive aggregate; Evje (Norway – width of field 58 mm)

Braunite, franklinite, euxenite

Hematite (Iron glance, Iron mica)

Oxide
Fe₂O₃

472

P

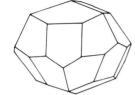

Historical name, from the Greek *haima* – blood

● Hardness: 6.5 (in earthy forms hardness 1; brittle) ● Streak: cherry-red or reddish brown ● Colour: reddish-brown, grey-black or black ● Transparency: translucent to opaque ● Lustre: metallic, dull ● Cleavage: absent, only partly due to twinning on (0001) and (10$\bar{1}$2) ● Fracture: conchoidal ● Morphology: crystals, rose-shaped, scaly, granular, massive, crusty, radiating-fibrous aggregates, oolites, pseudomorphs. The scaly variety is called specularite ● Specific gravity: 5.2–5.3 ● Crystal system: trigonal ● Crystal form: plates, scales, rhombohedra, twins ● Magnetism: slight ● Chemical composition: Fe 69.94%, O 30.06%; admixtures: Ti, Al, Mn ● Chemical properties: soluble in concentrated HCl, infusible ● Handling: clean with diluted HCl and water ● Similar minerals: goethite **(354)**, limonite **(355)**, pyrophanite **(364)**, ilmenite **(365)**, magnetite **(367)**, chromite **(371)** ● Distinguishing features: hardness, specific gravity, streak, magnetism, X-rays, chemical tests ● Genesis: magmatic, hydrothermal, metamorphic, sedimentary ● Associated minerals: siderite **(306)**, limonite, magnetite, pyrite **(436)**, quartz **(534)** ● Occurrence: common; Elbingerode, Schleiz, Lahn-Dill and Siegerland (FRG), St. Gotthard (Switzerland), (Austria), Elba (Italy), Striberg, Norberg and Blötberg (Sweden), Cumberland (Great Britain), (Romania), Wabana (Canada), Middleback Range (Australia), Boomi Hill (Liberia), Matto Grosso (Brazil), Kursk and Krivoi Rog (Ukraine) ● Application: important Fe ore; red ochre is used as the raw material for red paint and for polishing powder. Sometimes used as a precious stone (facets, cabochons).

Specularite (Hematite variety)

Oxide
Fe₂O₃

473

From the Latin *speculum* – mirror (Werner 1789)

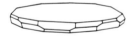

● Physical and chemical properties are similar to those of hematite. Fine scaly, splendent metallic lustre, translucent in thin slabs ● Occurrence: widely distributed in many parts of the Alps where it forms rose-shaped crystalline aggregates much sought after by collectors; St. Gotthard and Binnental (Switzerland), Zillertal (Austria), Rudňany, Rožňava and Dobšiná – hydrothermal in ore veins (Slovakia), Siegerland (FRG) ● Application: sometimes Fe ore.

1. Hematite – group of euhedral crystals (up to 20 mm) on albite; St. Gotthard (Switzerland) **2. Specularite** – scaly aggregate; Rožňava (Slovakia – width of field 50 mm)

Pyrolusite

474

From the Greek *pyr* – fire and *loýo* – washing (Haidinger 1827)

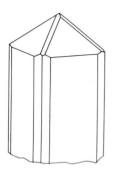

● Hardness: 6–7 (crystals), 1–2 (earthy), (brittle) ● Streak: black metallic ● Colour: grey or greyish-black ● Transparency: opaque ● Lustre: metallic, sub-metallic, dull ● Cleavage: perfect on (110) and (010) ● Fracture: uneven ● Morphology: crystals (polianite variety), massive, cryptocrystalline, earthy, granular, radiate and fibrous aggregates, crusts, oolites, dendrites, concretions, pseudomorphs, colloform masses ● Specific gravity: approx. 5 ● Crystal system: tetragonal ● Crystal form: prisms, needles ● Chemical composition: Mn 63.19%, O 36.81% ● Chemical properties: soluble in concentrated HCl, infusible ● Handling: clean with distilled water, soft forms should not be cleaned at all ● Similar minerals: stibnite **(51)**, manganite **(295)**, psilomelane **(357)**, hausmannite **(358)** ● Distinguishing features: hardness, streak, specific gravity, X-rays, chemical tests ● Genesis: secondary, weathering crusts, sedimentary, hydrothermal ● Associated minerals: manganite, psilomelane, limonite: **(355)**, braunite **(469)** ● Occurrence: common; Ilmenau, Ilfeld, Siegerland and Lindener Mark (FRG), Lanlivery – Cornwall (Great Britain), Epleny (Hungary), Tschiaturi (Georgia), Nikopol (Ukraine), Minas Gerais (Brazil), (India), (RSA) ● Application: Mn ore; in metallurgy.

Polianite (Pyrolusite variety)

475

From the Greek *poliános* – grey (Breithaupt 1844)

● Physical and chemical properties are similar to those of pyrolusite. Forms fine tetragonal crystals of submetallic to metallic lustre ● Hardness approx. 7, opaque. In Mn deposits ● Occurrence: Lostwithiel – Cornwall (Great Britain), Horní Blatná (Czech Republic), Schneeberg, Giessen and Hornhausen (FRG).

Magnesioferrite

476

Named after its chemical composition (Rammelsberg 1859)

● Hardness: 6–6.5 ● Streak: dark red ● Colour: black ● Transparency: opaque ● Lustre: metallic ● Cleavage: absent ● Fracture: uneven, sub-conchoidal ● Morphology: crystal, granular aggregates ● Specific gravity: 4.6–4.7 ● Crystal system: cubic ● Crystal form: octahedra, twins ● Magnetism: strong ● Chemical composition: MgO 20.15%, Fe$_2$O$_3$ 79.85% ● Chemical properties: soluble in HCl ● Handling: clean with distilled water ● Similar minerals: magnetite **(367)** ● Distinguishing features: hardness, specific gravity, streak ● Genesis: postvolcanic, contact-metasomatic ● Associated minerals: chlorite **(158)**, actinolite **(413)**, hematite **(472)** ● Occurrence: rare; Kaiserstuhl (FRG), Vesuvius and Stromboli (Italy), Puy de Dôme (France), (Sweden), Magnet Cove – Arkansas (USA).

Pyrolusite – radiating fibrous aggregates (15 mm); Ilfeld (FRG)

Pyrolusite

Niobite (synonym of Columbite)

Oxide
(Fe,Mn)(Nb,Ta)$_2$O$_6$

477

R

Named after its content of the element *niobium,* formerly called *columbium*
(Hatchett 1802)

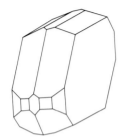

● Hardness: 6 (brittle) ● Streak: brown or brown-black ● Colour: brown-black or black ● Transparency: non-transparent ● Lustre: vitreous, greasy, sub-metallic ● Cleavage: good on (010), imperfect on (100) ● Fracture: uneven, conchoidal ● Morphology: crystals (striated), granular aggregates, compact, granular ● Specific gravity: 5.2–6.0 ● Crystal system: orthorhombic ● Crystal form: prisms, plates ● Radioactivity: sometimes weakly radioactive if U impurities are present ● Chemical composition: variable, a member of the isomorphous columbite-tantalite series ● Chemical properties: slightly soluble in H$_2$SO$_4$, infusible ● Handling: clean with water or diluted acids ● Similar minerals: wolframite **(369),** ferberite **(370),** tantalite **(479),** tapiolite **(480)** ● Distinguishing features: hardness, specific gravity, streak, X-rays, chemical tests ● Genesis: in pegmatites, alluvial deposits ● Associated minerals: spodumene **(502),** cassiterite **(548),** beryl **(554),** topaz **(595)** ● Occurrence: common; Hagendorf (FRG), Varuträsk (Sweden), Ulefoss (Norway), Myas near Zlatoust (Russia), Ribaue (Mozambique), M'buye Mine (Rwanda), Picui – Parelhas (Brazil), La Verde Mine – crystals up to 500 kg (Bolivia), (Greenland), (Australia) ● Application: important source of Nb and Ta metals.

Columbite

Oxide
(Fe,Mn)(Nb,Ta)$_2$O$_6$

478

See niobite (477)

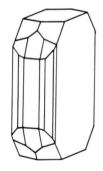

Tantalite

Oxide
(Mn,Fe)(Ta,Nb)$_2$O$_6$

479

R

Named after its chemical composition
(Ekeberg 1802)

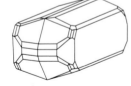

● Hardness: 6–6.5 (brittle) ● Streak: brown ● Colour: black or brown ● Transparency: opaque ● Lustre: greasy, sub-metallic ● Cleavage: imperfect on (100) ● Fracture: uneven, conchoidal ● Morphology: crystals, massive, disseminated ● Specific gravity: 8.1. ● Crystal system: orthorhombic ● Crystal form: prisms, plates ● Radioactivity: sometimes weakly radioactive according to admixtures ● Chemical composition: variable, end member of the isomorphous series (niobite-columbite-tantalite) ● Chemical properties: like columbite **(478)** ● Handling: clean with water and diluted acids ● Similar minerals: allanite **(410),** columbite ● Distinguishing features: specific gravity, chemical tests ● Genesis: in pegmatites, in alluvium ● Associated minerals: like columbite ● Occurrence: rare; Bodenmais (FRG), (Finland), (Sweden), Custer and Pennington Cos. – South Dakota (USA), (Brazil), (Australia), (Zimbabwe) ● Application: Ta source.

---

1. Columbite – euhedral crystal (11 mm); Ivigtut (Greenland) **2. Tantalite** – embedded crystal (12 mm); Turku (Finland)

Columbite, tantalite

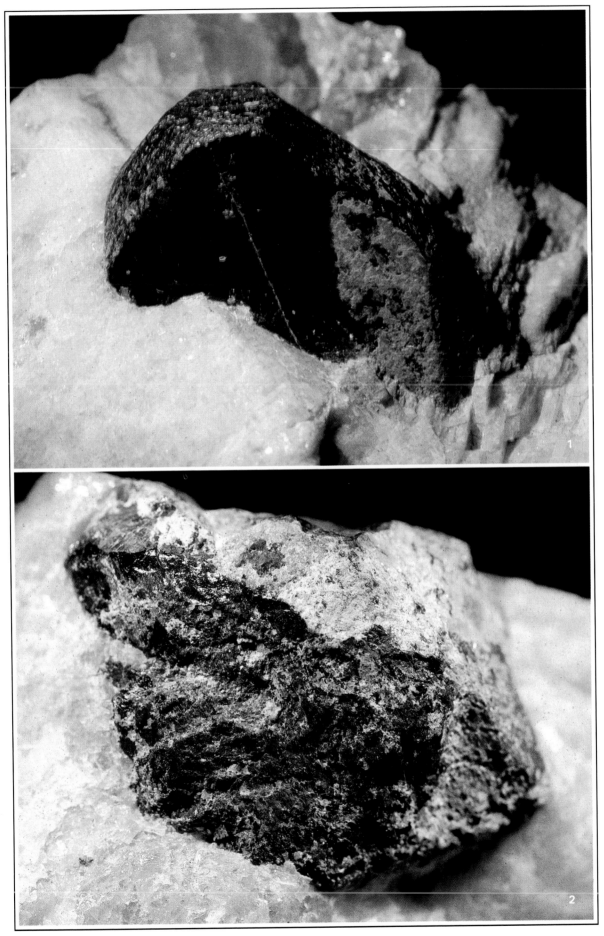

Tapiolite

Oxide
$(Fe,Mn)(Ta,Nb)_2O_6$

480

R

Named after the God *Tapio* (Finnish mythology) (Nordenskjöld 1863)

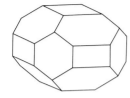

● Hardness: 6 (brittle) ● Streak: brown ● Colour: black ● Transparency: opaque ● Lustre: splendent metallic ● Cleavage: imperfect on (110) ● Fracture: uneven, conchoidal ● Morphology: crystals, granular aggregates, pebbles ● Specific gravity: 7.3–8.0 ● Crystal system: tetragonal ● Crystal form: prisms, twins ● Radioactivity: some varieties are radioactive ● Chemical composition: variable ● Chemical properties: insoluble in acids, infusible ● Handling: clean with diluted acids ● Similar minerals: columbite (478) ● Distinguishing features: twinning, X-rays ● Genesis: in pegmatites, alluvial deposits ● Associated minerals: tantalite (479), beryl (554) ● Occurrence: rare; Sukkula (Finland), Spittal (Austria), Cresciano (Italy), (Russia), Punia (Congo), (Brazil), (Morocco), (Sri Lanka), (USA).

Thorianite

Oxide
ThO_2

481

R

Named after its chemical composition (Dunstan 1904)

● Hardness: approx. 6 (brittle) ● Streak: black ● Colour: brown or black ● Transparency: opaque ● Lustre: sub-metallic, resinous ● Cleavage: imperfect on (100) ● Fracture: uneven, conchoidal ● Morphology: crystals, pebbles ● Specific gravity: approx. 10 ● Crystal system: cubic ● Crystal form: hexahedra, octahedra ● Radioactivity: strong ● Chemical composition: ThO_2 100%; constant admixtures: UO_2, UO_3 and U_3O_8 ● Chemical properties: soluble in H_2SO_4 and HNO_3, infusible, spatters ● Handling: clean with distilled water ● Similar minerals: uraninite (482) ● Distinguishing features: X-rays, chemical tests ● Genesis: in pegmatites, carbonates, in alluvial ore deposits ● Associated minerals: apatite (379), monazite (383), zircon (587) ● Occurrence: rare; in alluvial ore deposits in (Sri Lanka), (Madagascar), (Russia).

Uraninite (Pitchblende, Pitch ore)

Oxide
UO_2

482

R

Named after its chemical composition (Born 1772)

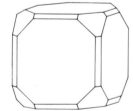

● Hardness: 6 (brittle), metamorphic uraninite 3.5 ● Streak: brown, grey or green ● Colour: black, grey or greenish ● Transparency: opaque ● Lustre: greasy, dull, sub-metallic ● Cleavage: imperfect on (111) ● Fracture: conchoidal ● Morphology: crystals, massive, earthy, reniform, granular aggregates ● Specific gravity: 10.6 (7.5–9 massive) ● Crystal system: cubic ● Crystal form: seldom cubes, octahedra ● Radioactivity: strong ● Chemical composition: U 86.86%, O 13.14%; admixtures: Th, Pb, Ra, Ac, Po, Zr ● Chemical properties: soluble in HNO_3, H_2SO_4, with difficulty in HCl, fuses on edges of grains ● Handling: clean with water and diluted HCl ● Similar minerals: psilomelane (357), thorianite (481) ● Distinguishing features: radioactivity, X-rays, chemical tests ● Genesis: in pegmatites, hydrothermal, sedimentary, contact-metasomatic ● Associated minerals: molybdenite (8), bismuth (48), galena (77), dolomite (218) ● Occurrence: common; Schneeberg, Annaberg, Aue, Wittichen and Wölsendorf (FRG), Jáchymov, Příbram (Czech Republic), La Crouzille (France), Moss (Norway), Stackebo (Sweden), South Dakota (USA), Uluguru (Tanzania), Shinkolobwe (Congo), Witwatersrand (RSA), (Canada), (Australia) ● Application: U and Ra ore.

1. **Thorianite** – disseminated crystals (to 5 mm); Balangoda (Sri Lanka) 2. **Uraninite** – reniform aggregate; Jáchymov (Czech Republic – width of field 37 mm)

Thorianite, uraninite

Petalite

Silicate
Li AlSi$_4$O$_{10}$

483

L

P

From the Greek *pétalon* – leaf
(d'Andrada 1800)

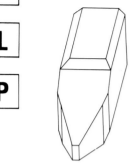

● Hardness: 6.5 ● Streak: white ● Colour: colourless, white, grey or reddish ● Transparency: transparent to translucent ● Lustre: vitreous ● Cleavage: perfect on (001), good on (201) ● Fracture: conchoidal ● Morphology: crystals, massive aggregates ● Crystal form: prisms, plates, twins ● Luminescence: orange, white, yellow ● Chemical composition: Li$_2$O 4.9%, Al$_2$O$_3$ 16.7%, SiO$_2$ 78.4% ● Chemical properties: insoluble in acids, fuses with difficulty into a ball, colours a flame red ● Handling: clean with water and diluted acids ● Similar minerals: amblygonite **(377)** ● Distinguishing features: hardness, cleavage, specific gravity, X-rays ● Genesis: in pegmatites ● Associated minerals: lepidolite **(169)**, spodumene **(502)**, tourmaline **(564)** ● Occurrence: rare; Elba (Italy), Varuträsk (Sweden), Karibib (Namibia), Bikita (Zimbabwe), (Peru), (USA), (Brazil), (Australia) ● Application: Li source; sometimes used as a precious stone.

Milarite

Silicate
KCa$_2$AlBe$_2$Si$_{12}$O$_{30}$. H$_2$O

484

P

Named after its locality in Val Milar (Switzerland)
(Kenngott 1870)

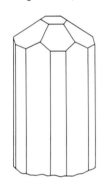

● Hardness: 6 (brittle) ● Streak: white ● Colour: colourless, yellowish or greenish ● Transparency: transparent to translucent ● Lustre: vitreous ● Cleavage: imperfect on (0001) and (1120) ● Fracture: conchoidal ● Morphology: crystals, granular ● Specific gravity: 2.52 ● Crystal system: hexagonal ● Crystal form: prisms ● Chemical composition: K$_2$O 4.81%, CaO 11.44%, BeO 5.10%, Al$_2$O$_3$ 4.05%, SiO$_2$ 73.45%, H$_2$O 1.15% ● Chemical properties: slightly soluble in HCl, fuses into spongy glass ● Handling: clean with water ● Similar minerals: apatite **(379)**, beryl **(554)** ● Distinguishing features: hardness, solubility in HCl, fusibility ● Genesis: in pegmatites, hydrothermal ● Associated minerals: apatite, adularia **(487)** ● Occurrence: rare; Tittling, Henneberg (FRG), Věžná (Czech Republic), Val Giuf (Switzerland), Tysfjord (Norway), Kola Peninsula (Russia), Swakopmund – of gem quality (Namibia), (Mexico) ● Application: occasionally as a precious stone.

Bertrandite

Silicate
Be$_4$Si$_2$O$_7$(OH)$_2$

485

Named after the French mineralogist, E. Bertrand
(Damour 1883)

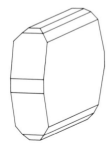

● Hardness: 6.5–7 (brittle) ● Streak: white ● Colour: colourless or light yellow ● Transparency: transparent to translucent ● Lustre: vitreous, pearly ● Cleavage: perfect on (001), good on (110) and (101) ● Fracture: conchoidal ● Morphology: crystals, granular aggregates, pseudomorphs after beryl **(554)** ● Specific gravity: 2.6 ● Crystal system: orthorhombic ● Crystal form: plates, prisms, twins ● Chemical composition: BeO 42.02%, SiO$_2$ 50.42%, H$_2$O 7.56% ● Chemical properties: soluble in HF and H$_2$SO$_4$, partly soluble in HCL, infusible, when heated becomes dull ● Handling: clean with water ● Similar minerals: albite **(493)** ● Distinguishing features: hardness, solubility in acids ● Genesis: im pegmatites, pneumatolytic, hydrothermal ● Associated minerals: bavenite **(399)**, beryl ● Occurrence: rare; Henneberg (FRG), Písek (Czech Republic), Iveland (Norway), Nantes (France), St. Gotthard (Switzerland), Maine and Virginia (USA), (Australia) ● Application: sometimes source of Be.

---

1. Milarite – long columnar crystals (up to 6 mm); Val Giuf (Switzerland) **2. Petalite** – compact aggregate; Nová Ves (Czech Republic – width of field 30 mm) **3. Bertrandite** – euhedral crystal (3 mm); Maršíkov (Czech Republic)

Milarite, petalite, bertrandite

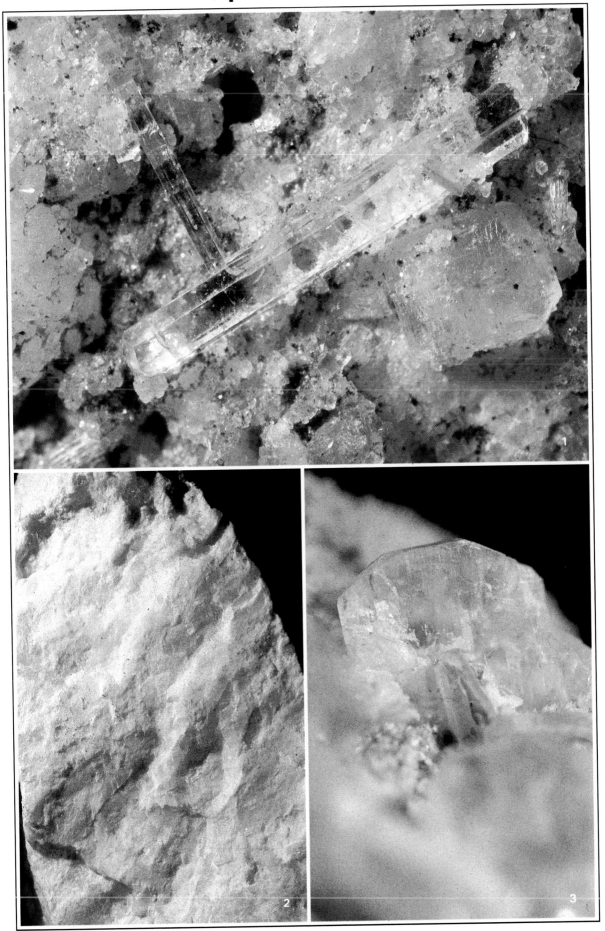

Orthoclase (Feldspar group)

Silicate
$KAISi_3O_8$

486

From the Greek *órthós* – right and *kláo* – I cleave (Breithaupt 1823)

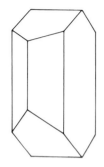

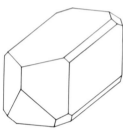

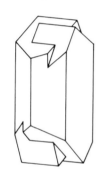

● Hardness: 6 (brittle) ● Streak: white ● Colour: colourless, white, yellowish, brownish or reddish, sometimes with a bluish tint (commonly called moonstone) ● Transparency: transparent to translucent ● Lustre: vitreous, pearly ● Cleavage: perfect on (001), good on (010) ● Fracture: uneven, conchoidal to splintery ● Morphology: crystals, compact, granular to coarse grained aggregates. Often forms inclusions with quartz resembling cuniform characters (graphic granite) ● Specific gravity: 2.53–2.56 ● Crystal system: monoclinic ● Crystal form: prisms, coarse plates, often twins ● Luminescence: sometimes yellow, cream, white, greenish ● Chemical composition: K_2O 16.93%, Al_2O_3 18.35%, SiO_2 64.72%; admixtures: Fe, Na, Rb, Ca ● Chemical properties: soluble in HF and alkaline solutions, fuses with difficulty ● Handling: clean with water and diluted acids ● Similar minerals: microcline **(490)**, plagioclase **(492)** ● Distinguishing features: optical properties, X-rays, chemical tests ● Genesis: magmatic, in pegmatites, hydrothermal ● Associated minerals: micas, plagioclases, quartz **(534)** ● Occurrence: widespread; one of most widely found rock-forming minerals, occurring in granites, granodiorites, syenites, rhyolites, in many crystalline schists (especially gneiss), arkoses; in pegmatites, alpine veins and some ore veins; in the region of Karlovy Vary – fine twins on the Carlsbad Law in weathered granites (Czech Republic); in the pegmatites near Strigom (Poland); Transbaikal (Russia), St. Pietro and Elba (Italy), Hagendorf (FRG), Itrongay – orthoclases of gem quality: transparent yellow crystals of ferriferous – orthoclase (Madagascar), (Sri Lanka – in gravels), (northern Burma), (southern India), (Tanzania), Oliver – Virginia (USA), (Brazil), (Australia) ● Application: in the ceramic and glass industries; sometimes cut as a precious stone (facets, cabochons).

Orthoclase – druse of crystals (the largest 28 mm); Baveno (Italy)

Orthoclase

385

Adularia (Orthoclase variety — Feldspar group)

Silicate
KAlSi$_3$O$_8$

487

Named after Mount Adula (Austria) (Pini 1783)

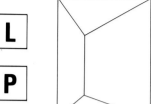

● Physical and chemical properties are identical to those of orthoclase. It is colourless, sometimes exhibiting a yellowish or bluish tint; transparent; full vitreous lustre ● Genesis: hydrothermal, in alpine cracks ● Associated minerals: chlorite **(158)**; titanite **(430)**, albite **(493)**, quartz **(534)** ● Occurrence: rare; known in several areas in the Alps: St. Gotthard, Val Cristallina — crystals up to 25 cm, Val Medel and Maderanertal (Switzerland), Zillertal and Habachtal (Austria), Val d'Isére (France); Cavnic — in ore veins (Romania), Valenciana Mine (Mexico) ● Application: sometimes used as a precious stone (cabochons).

Sanidine (Feldspar group)

Silicate
KAlSi$_3$O$_8$

488

From the Greek *sanís* — little plate and *idos* — to see (Nose 1808)

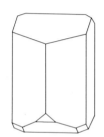

● Hardness: 6 (brittle) ● Streak: white ● Colour: grey, yellowish or reddish ● Transparency: transparent to translucent ● Lustre: vitreous, pearly ● Cleavage: perfect on (001) and (010) ● Fracture: uneven, conchoidal ● Morphology: crystals ● Specific gravity: 2.5 ● Crystal system: monoclinic ● Crystal form: plates, twins ● Chemical composition: like orthoclase **(486)**; admixture: Na ● Chemical properties: like orthoclase ● Handling: clean with water and diluted acids ● Similar minerals: orthoclase, plagioclase **(492)** ● Distinguishing features: optical properties, chemical tests and X-rays ● Genesis: magmatic — high thermal (in eruptive rocks —trachytes) ● Associated minerals: biotite **(167)**, nepheline **(397)**, quartz **(534)** ● Occurrence: in some places very common; Kaiserstuhl and Drachenfels (FRG), Pantelleria (Italy), Caucasus (Georgia), Central Bohemian Highlands (Czech Republic) ● Application: sometimes cut as a precious stone (facets, cabochons).

Hyalophane (Feldspar group)

Silicate
(K,Ba)(Al,Si)$_2$Si$_2$O$_8$

489

From the Greek *hýalos* — glass and *phanós* — to appear (Waltershausen 1855)

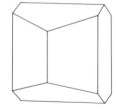

● Hardness: 6–6.5 (brittle) ● Streak: white ● Colour: colourless, white or yellow ● Transparency: transparent to translucent ● Lustre: vitreous ● Cleavage: perfect on (001) ● Fracture: uneven, conchoidal ● Morphology: crystals, compact, massive ● Specific gravity: 2.6–2.8 ● Crystal system: monoclinic ● Crystal form: prisms, rhombohedra ● Chemical composition: variable ● Chemical properties: fuses with difficulty into bubbly glass; almost insoluble in acids ● Handling: clean with water and diluted acids ● Similar minerals: adularia **(487)** ● Distinguishing features: specific gravity, X-rays, chemical tests ● Genesis: magmatic, contact-metasomatic ● Associated minerals: dolomite **(218)**, scapolite **(398)** ● Occurrence: rare; Imfeld (Switzerland), Jakobsberg (Sweden), Slyudyanka (Russia), Otjosondu (Namibia), Kaso Mine (Japan).

1. Adularia — druse of crystals; Val Medel (Switzerland — width of field 21 mm) **2. Hyalophane** — druse of crystals (the largest 5 mm) with pyrite on quartz; Binnental (Switzerland)

Adularia, hyalophane

Microcline (Feldspar group)

Silicate
KAlSi$_3$O$_8$

490

From the Greek *mikrón* – little and *klínein* – to stoop (Breithaupt 1830)

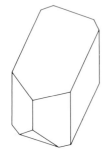

● Hardness: 6 (brittle) ● Streak: white ● Colour: white, grey, yellow or green (amazonite variety – **491**) ● Transparency: transparent to translucent ● Lustre: vitreous, pearly ● Cleavage: perfect on (010) and (001) ● Fracture: uneven ● Morphology: crystals, granular and massive aggregates ● Specific gravity: 2.5–2.6 ● Crystal system: triclinic ● Crystal form: short prisms, plates, twins ● Luminescence: sometimes blue-white ● Chemical composition: like orthoclase **(488)** ● Chemical properties: like orthoclase ● Handling: clean with water and diluted acids ● Similar minerals: orthoclase, plagioclase **(492)** ● Distinguishing features: optical properties, X-rays ● Genesis: magmatic, in pegmatites, metamorphic, hydrothermal ● Associated minerals: muscovite **(165),** biotite **(167),** orthoclase, quartz **(534)** ● Occurrence: widespread; Hagendorf and Epprechstein (FRG); Iveland and Tysfjord (Norway), Kaatiala (Finland), Strigom (Poland), Myas, Urals, Kola Peninsula (Russia), Volhynia area (Ukraine), Maine, New Hampshire, California and South Dakota (USA), (Mexico), (Brazil), (India), (Japan), (Madagascar) ● Application: ceramic and glass industries, sometimes cut as a precious stone (cabochons).

Amazonite (Amazon stone – Microcline variety, Feldspar group)

Silicate
KAlSi$_3$O$_8$

491

L

P

Named after the Amazon river (South America) (Breithaupt 1847)

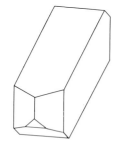

● Physical and chemical properties are similar to those of microcline. Its colour varies from green to blue-green, but when heated it loses its green colouring; translucent to non-transparent ● Luminescence: grey-green ● Genesis: magmatic, in pegmatites ● Associated minerals: microcline **(490),** quartz **(534)** ● Occurrence: rare; Packa-Alpe – in pegmatites (Austria), Pikes Peak – Colorado, Amelia Court House – Virginia – amazonites of gem quality (USA), Renfrew Co. – Ontario (Canada), Myas, Urals and Kola Peninsula (Russia), (Brazil), (Madagascar), (Mozambique), (Namibia), (India). It has also been found in Pechstein near Zwickau (FRG) ● Application: since ancient times, cut as ornamental and precious stone (cabochons).

---

1. Microcline – fissile aggregate; Strigom (Poland – width of field 56 mm) **2. Amazonite** – group of columnar crystals (to 30 mm); Pikes Peak (Colorado, USA)

Microcline, amazonite

389

Plagioclase (common name for Na-Ca feldspars)

492

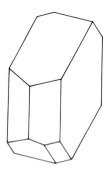

From the Greek *plágios* – oblique and *kláo* – I cleave (Breithaupt 1847)

● Hardness: 6–6.5 (brittle) ● Streak: white ● Colour: white, grey-white, bluish, reddish or greenish ● Transparency: transparent to translucent ● Lustre: vitreous, pearly ● Cleavage: very good on (001) and (010) ● Fracture: uneven ● Morphology: crystals, granular and massive aggregates ● Specific gravity: 2.61–2.76 ● Crystal system: triclinic ● Crystal form: prisms, plates, often twins ● Chemical composition: mixture of Na $AlSi_3O_8$ (albite) and Ca $Al_2Si_2O_8$ (anorthite):

mineral	proportion of Ab and An	Na_2O	CaO	Al_2O_3	SiO_2	specific gravity
		in %				
albite (Ab)	Ab_{100}	11.8	—	19.5	68.7	2.61
oligoclase	$Ab_{80}An_{20}$	9.5	4.0	22.9	63.6	2.64
andesine	$Ab_{60}An_{40}$	7.1	8.1	26.3	58.5	2.67
labradorite	$Ab_{40}An_{60}$	4.7	12.1	29.8	53.4	2.70
bytownite	$Ab_{20}An_{80}$	2.4	16.1	33.2	48.3	2.73
anorthite (An)	An_{100}	—	20.1	35.6	44.3	2.76

● Chemical properties: fuses with difficulty into a glassy mass, tinges a flame yellow (Na), insoluble in acids (except anorthite – **498**) ● Handling: clean with water and diluted acids (anorthite only with distilled water) ● Similar minerals: amblygonite **(377)**, scapolite **(398)**, gehlenite **(405)**, melilite **(406)**, orthoclase **(486)**, sanidine **(488)**, microcline **(490)** ● Distinguishing features: hardness, specific gravity, solubility in acids, X-rays, optical and chemical properties ● Genesis: magmatic, in pegmatites, in alpine veins, meteorites ● Associated minerals: muscovite **(165)**, biotite **(167)**, orthoclase, quartz **(534)** ● Occurrence: widely found; rock-forming minerals, an essential part of granites, granodiorites, diorites, gabbros, andesites. Plagioclases often form large masses in pegmatites; albite **(493)** occurs especially in alpine veins. Only seldom do they form fine crystals or crystal druses. Occurrence is given in the description of individual minerals ● Application: very occasionally in the ceramics industry; some minerals of this group are used as ornamental stones; rarely used as precious stones.

Albite (Feldspar group)

Silicate
$NaAlSi_3O_8$

493

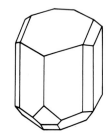

From the Latin *albus* – white (Gahn, Berzelius 1815)

● Physical and chemical properties are similar to those of other plagioclases **(492)**. Fine bladed albite is called cleavelandite ● Genesis: magmatic, in pegmatites, in alpine veins ● Associated minerals: like plagioclase ● Occurrence: common; Schmirn and the Tyrol – fine crystals (Austria), Bristenstock and Scopi (Switzerland), Strigom (Poland), Elba (Italy), Virginia – cleavelandite (USA), Bourg d'Oisans and Isère (France) ● Application: sometimes used as a precious stone (facets, cabochons).

Plagioclase – group of crystals (the largest 14 mm); Piz Valvo (Switzerland)

Plagioclase

Oligoclase (Feldspar group)

Silicate
$(Na, Ca)Al_{1-2}Si_{3-2}O_8$

494

P

From the Greek *olígos* – little and *kláo* – I cleave
(Breithaupt 1826)

● Physical and chemical properties are similar to those of other plagioclases **(492)**. Sometimes it contains hematite scales which cause a gold reflected sheen (sunstone variety) ● Genesis: magmatic, in pegmatites ● Associated minerals: like plagioclase ● Occurrence: rare; Arendal (Norway), Monte Somma (Italy), Myas and the Urals (Russia); the sunstone is found in Tvedestrand (Norway), (Canada) ● Application: sometimes used as a precious stone (facets, cabochons).

Andesine (Feldspar group)

Silicate
$(Na,Ca)Al_{1-2}Si_{3-2}O_8$

495

Named after its locality Andes (France)
(Abich 1841)

● Physical and chemical properties are identical to those of other plagioclases **(492)** ● Genesis: magmatic, metamorphic ● Associated minerals: like plagioclase ● Occurrence: widely found in andesites, diorites, syenites, cordieritegneiss; Bodenmais (FRG), Esterel (France), (Italy), (Finland), (Greenland), (South America).

Labradorite (Feldspar group)

Silicate
$(Ca,Na)Al_{1-2}Si_{3-2}O_8$

496

P

Named after the Labrador Peninsula (Canada)
(Werner 1780)

● Physical and chemical properties are similar to those of other plagioclases **(492)**. A rich play of colours is a frequent phenomenon (labradorescence) ● Genesis: magmatic, metamorphic ● Associated minerals: like plagioclase ● Occurrence: rare; Etna (Italy), Ojamo – spectrolite (Finland), Zhitomir region (Ukraine), Kangek (Greenland), Labrador Peninsula (Canada), California and South Dakota (USA) ● Application: decorative ornamental and precious stones (cabochons, facets).

Bytownite (Feldspar group)

Silicate
$(Ca,Na)Al_{1-2}Si_{3-2}O_8$

497

P

Named after Bytown (Ontario, Canada)
(Thomson 1835)

● Physical and chemical properties are similar to those of other plagioclases **(492)** ● Genesis: magmatic, meteorites ● Associated minerals: like plagioclase ● Occurrence: common; Volpersdorf and Bad Harzburg (FRG), Corsica (France), (Iceland), (Canada) ● Application: sometimes used as a precious stone (facets, cabochons).

Anorthite (Feldspar group)

Silicate
$CaAl_2Si_2O_8$

498

From the Greek *anorthos* – oblique-angled
(Rose 1823)

● Physical and chemical properties are similar to those of other plagioclases **(492)** ● Genesis: magmatic, metamorphic, in meteorites ● Associated minerals: like plagioclase ● Occurrence: rare; Monte Somma and Valle di Fassa (Italy), near Madras (India), (Japan), Franklin – New Jersey (USA).

---

1. Albite – crystals (up to 15 mm) on siderite; Rožňava (Slovakia) **2. Labradorite** – polished section; Labrador (Canada – width of field 75 mm)

Albite, labradorite

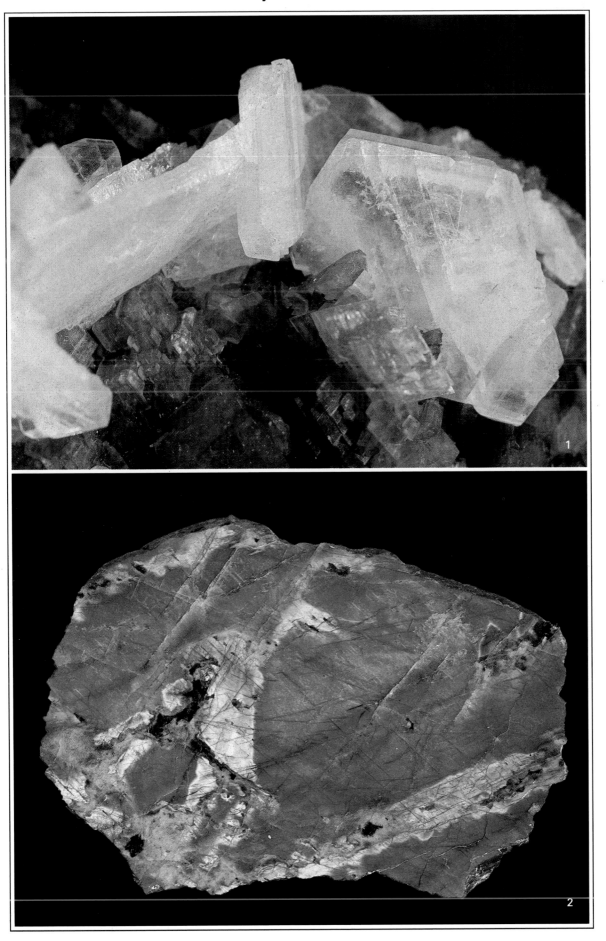

Celsian (Feldspar group)

Silicate
BaAl$_2$Si$_2$O$_8$

499

Named after the Swedish astronomer and natural scientist, A. Celsius (1701–1744) (Sjögren 1895)

● Hardness: 6–6.5 (brittle) ● Streak: white ● Colour: white or yellow ● Transparency: transparent ● Lustre: vitreous ● Cleavage: perfect on (001), good on (010) ● Fracture: uneven ● Morphology: crystals, massive and fissile aggregates ● Specific gravity: 3.1–3.4 ● Crystal system: monoclinic ● Crystal form: prisms, twins ● Chemical composition: BaO 40.83%, Al$_2$O$_3$ 27.16%, SiO$_2$ 32.01% ● Chemical properties: fuses into bubbly glass ● Handling: clean with distilled water ● Similar minerals: adularia **(487)** ● Distinguishing features: specific gravity ● Genesis: contact-metamorphic ● Associated minerals: dolomite **(218)**, quartz **(534)**, Mn minerals ● Occurrence: rare; Imfeld-Binnental (Switzerland), Candoglia (Italy), Jakobsberg (Sweden), Otjosondu (Namibia), Santa Cruz Co. – California (USA).

Pollucite (Zeolite group)

Silicate
CsAlSi$_2$O$_6$.0.5 H$_2$O

500

Named after Pollux, a figure from Greek mythology (Breithaupt 1846)

● Hardness: 6.5 ● Streak: white ● Colour: colourless, white or grey ● Transparency: transparent, dull ● Lustre: vitreous ● Cleavage: absent ● Fracture: conchoidal ● Morphology: crystals, granular and massive aggregates, grains ● Specific gravity: 2.9 ● Crystal system: cubic ● Crystal form: cubes ● Luminescence: sometimes white ● Chemical composition: Cs$_2$O 61.00%, Al$_2$O$_3$ 11.04%, SiO$_2$ 26.01%, H$_2$O 1.95% ● Chemical properties: dissolves with difficulty in hot HCl, small fragments fuse into white enamel, tinges a flame red-yellow ● Handling: clean with water ● Similar minerals: hyalite **(448)**, quartz **(534)** ● Distinguishing features: hardness, specific gravity, X-rays, chemical tests ● Genesis: in pegmatites ● Associated minerals: petalite **(483)**, albite **(493)**, beryl **(554)** ● Occurrence: rare; Elba (Italy), Varuträsk (Sweden), Karibib (Namibia), Bikita (Zimbabwe), (Canada), Maine (USA) ● Application: source of Cs, rarely used as a precious stone.

Helvite

Silicate
Mn$_4$Be$_3$(SiO$_4$)$_3$S

501

From the Greek *hélios* – sun (Werner 1816)

● Hardness: 6–6.5 (brittle) ● Streak: grey-white ● Colour: reddish-brown, yellow or green ● Transparency: translucent to non-transparent ● Lustre: greasy, vitreous ● Cleavage: imperfect on (111) ● Fracture: uneven, conchoidal ● Morphology: crystals, grains, aggregates ● Specific gravity: 3.1–3.3 ● Crystal system: cubic ● Crystal form: tetrahedra, octahedra ● Chemical composition: BeO 13.52%, MnO 48.24%, SiO$_2$ 32.46%, S 5.78% ● Chemical properties: fuses into a yellowish-brown, glassy mass, swells when heated, soluble in HCl ● Handling: clean with water ● Similar minerals: sphalerite **(181)**, vesuvianite **(522)** ● Distinguishing features: hardness, specific gravity ● Genesis: in pegmatites, scarns, hydrothermal ● Associated minerals: sphalerite, magnetite **(367)**, tourmaline **(564)** ● Occurrence: rare; Schwarzenberg and Breitenbrunn (FRG), (Sweden), Hörtekollen (Norway), Cavnic (Romania), Myas and the Urals (Russia), (USA), (Brazil) ● Application: sometimes as Be ore.

---

1. **Celsian** – compact aggregate; Slyudyanka (Russia) 2. **Pollucite** – granular aggregate; Varuträsk (Sweden – width of field 82 mm)
3. **Helvite** – isometric grains (to 3 mm); Schwarzenberg (FRG)

Celsian, pollucite, helvite

Spodumene

502

From the Greek *spòdóo*
– ashy
(D'Andrada 1800)

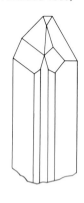

● Hardness: 6.5–7 (brittle) ● Streak: white ● Colour: yellow-white, green – hiddenite variety, pink to violet – kunzite variety, or grey ● Transparency: transparent to translucent ● Lustre: dull to vitreous ● Cleavage: good on (100), perfect on (110) ● Fracture: uneven, subconchoidal ● Morphology: crystals, massive, coarse fibrous and bowl-shaped fissile aggregates ● Specific gravity: 3.1–3.2 ● Crystal system: monoclinic ● Crystal form: long plates, prisms, twins ● Luminescence: yellow, cream, orange ● Chemical composition: Li$_2$O$_8$ 8.1%, Al$_2$O$_3$ 27.4%, SiO$_2$ 64.5% ● Chemical properties: insoluble in acids, tinges a flame red, readily fusible into white or clear glass ● Handling: clean with water and diluted acids ● Similar minerals: scapolite **(398)**, amethyst **(536)** ● Distinguishing features: hardness, specific gravity, X-rays ● Genesis: in pegmatites ● Associated minerals: lepidolite **(169)**, quartz **(534)**, beryl **(554)**, tourmaline **(564)** ● Occurrence: rare; Utö (Sweden), Petershead – Scotland (Great Britain), Killarney (Ireland), (Madagascar), Bikita (Zimbabwe), (Brazil), Black Hills – South Dakota (crystals measuring 10 m and weighing 90 tons) and Branchville – Connecticut (USA) ● Application: source of Li, sometimes used as a precious stone (facets, cabochons).

Kunzite (Spodumene variety)

503

Named after the American gem expert G. F. Kunz (1856–1932)
(Baskerville 1903)

L

P

● Physical and chemical properties are similar to those of spodumene. It is a violet, light violet or pink colour and is transparent, with a yellowish-red to orange luminescence ● Occurrence: rare; San Diego Co. – California and Maine (USA), (Madagascar), (Brazil), (Burma), (Afghanistan) ● Application: cut as a precious stone (facets, cabochons).

Hiddenite (Spodumene variety)

504

Named after the American mineralogist, W. E. Hidden (1853–1918)
(Smith 1881)

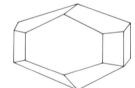

● Physical and chemical properties similar to those of spodumene. Of greenish and emerald-green colour, transparent. Very poor, red-yellow luminescence ● Occurrence: rare; Stony Point – North Carolina and California (USA), Figueira (Brazil), (Madagascar), (Burma) ● Application: cut as a precious stone (facets, cabochons).

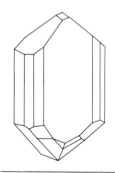

1. **Spodumene** – group of crystals (the largest 90 mm) on quartz; Dakotas (USA) 2. **Kunzite** – columnar crystal (30 mm) in kaolinite; Pala (California, USA) 3. **Hiddenite** – fragments of crystals (the largest 11 mm); Stony Point (USA)

Spodumene, kunzite, hiddenite

Diopside (Pyroxene group)

Silicate
CaMgSi$_2$O$_6$

505

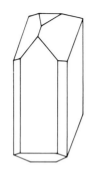

From the Greek *dis* – of two kinds and *opsis* – opinion
(Haüy 1806)

● Hardness: 6–7 (brittle) ● Streak: white ● Colour: green, green-black or grey ● Transparency: transparent to translucent ● Lustre: vitreous, greasy ● Cleavage: good on (110) ● Fracture: uneven, partly conchoidal ● Morphology: crystals, granular aggregates, also massive and radiate-fibrous ● Specific gravity: 3.3 ● Crystal system: monoclinic ● Crystal form: short prisms, sometimes long prisms, plates, twins ● Luminescence: sometimes green-white or cream ● Chemical composition: CaO 25.9%, MgO 18.6%, SiO$_2$ 55.5%; admixtures: Cr (chrome diopside variety), Fe, Mn, Zn ● Chemical properties: soluble in hot HCl, fuses with difficulty ● Handling: clean with distilled water and diluted acids ● Similar minerals: augite **(429),** fassaite **(511)** ● Distinguishing features: X-rays, chemical tests ● Genesis: rock-forming mineral, in basic and ultrabasic rocks (pyroxenites, gabbra, peridotites, diabases), in metamorphic rocks (amphiboles, metabasites, crystalline schists), in skarns and erlans ● Associated minerals: chlorite **(158),** biotite **(167),** magnetite **(367),** garnets **(577)** ● Occurrence: widespread; Mussalp – fine crystals (Italy), Zillertal (Austria), Nordmark (Sweden), Zlatoust, Southern Urals, around Baikal and Central Asia (Russia), Canaan – Connecticut and Governer – New York (USA), (Australia), (India), (Iran). Diopsides of gem quality are found in (Brazil), (Sri Lanka – gravels), (Madagascar), (Burma). Black stellate diopsides have been found in (India). When cut they exhibit four-pointed stars ● Application: sometimes used as a precious stone (facets, cabochons).

Chrome diopside
(Diopside variety – Pyroxene group)

Silicate
CaMgSi$_2$O$_6$

506

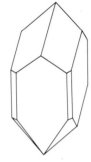

Named after its chemical composition

● Physical and chemical properties are identical to those of diopside. It is a fine emerald-green colour, transparent to translucent, contains up to 2% of Cr$_2$O$_3$ ● Occurrence: rare; Yakutia – crystals measuring 8 cm (Russia), (RSA – in kimberlites), Outokumpo (Finland), Chihuahua – in basalts (Mexico), Akita (Japan), New Zealand) – in peridotites, Moa (Cuba), (Burma) ● Application: emerald-green transparent crystals are cut as precious stones (facets, cabochons).

---

1. Diopside – group of crystals (up to 10 mm) on calcite; Nordmark (Sweden) **2. Chrome diopside** – crystal (41 mm); Outokumpu (Finland)

Diopside, chrome diopside

Hedenbergite (Pyroxene group)

Silicate
CaFeSi$_2$O$_6$

507

Named after the Swedish mineralogist, M. A. L. Hedenberg
(Berzelius 1819)

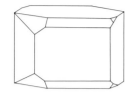

• Hardness: 6 (brittle) • Streak: white or grey • Colour: dark grey, brown, green-black or black • Transparency: non-transparent • Lustre: vitreous • Cleavage: good on (110) • Fracture: uneven • Morphology: crystals, granular and massive aggregates, radiating-fibrous aggregates • Specific gravity: 3.55 • Crystal system: monoclinic • Crystal form: prisms • Chemical composition: CaO 22.6%, FeO 29.0%, SiO$_2$ 48.4% • Chemical properties: slightly soluble in hot HCl, fuses into a black magnetic ball • Handling: clean with water or diluted acids • Genesis: contact-metasomatic, rarely magmatic • Associated minerals: magnetite **(367)**, augite **(429)**, pyrite **(436)** • Occurrence: rare; Nordmark (Sweden), Schwarzenberg (FRG), Turinsk (Russia), Elba (Italy).

Jadeite (Pyroxene group)

Silicate
NaAlSi$_2$O$_6$

508

From the Spanish *piedra de ijada* – stone relieving pain in the loins
(Damour 1863)

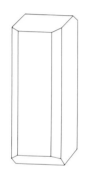

• Hardness: 6.5 • Streak: white • Colour: green-white, green, grey or yellowish • Transparency: translucent on edges • Lustre: vitreous, greasy • Cleavage: good on (110) • Fracture: uneven, hackly • Morphology: massive, granular and fibrous aggregates, crypto-crystalline • Specific gravity: 3.2–3.3 • Crystal system: monoclinic • Luminescence: grey-blue • Chemical composition: Na$_2$O 15.34%, Al$_2$O$_3$ 25.22%, SiO$_2$ 59.44% • Chemical properties: fuses into a white bead, tinges a flame light-yellow, insoluble in acids • Handling: clean with water or diluted acids • Similar minerals: nephrite **(417)** • Distinguishing features: fusible, X-rays, chemical tests • Genesis: metamorphic • Associated minerals: glaucophane **(418)**, albite **(493)**, almandine **(585)** • Occurrence: rare; Val di Susa (Italy), Tawmaw Mines (Burma), Kotaki (Japan), Tibet (China), Transbaikal, Northern Urals (Russia), California (USA), Corsica (France) • Application: precious stone.

Acmite (Aegirine – Pyroxene group)

Silicate
NaFeSi$_2$O$_6$

509

From the Greek *akmém* – spike
(Berzelius 1821)

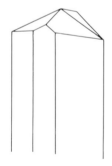

• Hardness: 6–6.5 • Streak: yellow-grey or dark green • Colour: dark green, black, reddish-brown or brownish-black • Transparency: non-transparent or slightly translucent • Lustre: vitreous, greasy • Cleavage: good on (110) • Fracture: uneven • Morphology: crystals, radiating-fibrous, fibrous and granular aggregates • Specific gravity: 3.5 • Crystal system: monoclinic • Crystal form: long prisms, twins • Magnetism: weak • Chemical composition: Na$_2$O 13.4%, Fe$_2$O$_3$ 34.6%, SiO$_2$ 52.0% • Chemical properties: fusible, tinges a flame yellow, slightly soluble in acids • Handling: clean with distilled water • Similar minerals: actinolite **(413)**, arfvedsonite **(420)** • Distinguishing features: X-rays, chemical tests • Genesis: magmatic, metamorphic, in pegmatites • Associated minerals: leucite **(396)**, nepheline **(397)**, arfvedsonite • Occurrence: rare; Langesundfjord (Norway), Scotland (Great Britain), (Greenland), (Nigeria), (Kenya), (USA), (Russia), (Canada).

1. Hedenbergite – druse of crystals (the largest 5 mm); Nordmark (Sweden) **2. Jadeite** – polished slice; Transvaal (RSA – width of field 52 mm) **3. Acmite** – radiating fibrous aggregate (needles to 10 mm) on apatite; Kola Peninsula (Russia)

Hedenbergite, jadeite, acmite

Johannsenite (Pyroxene group)

Silicate
CaMn(Si$_2$O$_6$)

510

Named after the American petrologist and geologist, A. Johannsen (1871–1962) (Schalter 1932)

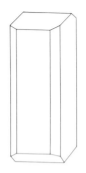

● Hardness: 6 ● Streak: greenish ● Colour: brown-grey, grey-green or brown ● Transparency: translucent to non-transparent ● Lustre: vitreous ● Cleavage: good on (110) ● Fracture: uneven, conchoidal ● Morphology: crystals, wisp-like, parallel fibres, spherulitic aggregates ● Specific gravity: 3.56 ● Crystal system: monoclinic ● Crystal form: long prisms, needles ● Chemical composition: CaO 22.69%, MnO 28.69%, SiO$_2$ 48.62%, admixtures: Fe, Mg ● Chemical properties: readily fusible, soluble in hot HCl ● Handling: clean with distilled water ● Similar minerals: actinolite (413), diopside (505) ● Distinguishing features: X-rays, chemical properties ● Genesis: contact-metasomatic ● Associated minerals: galena (77), sphalerite (181), calcite (217), rhodonite (531) ● Occurrence: rare; Madan and Borieva (Bulgaria), Campiglia (Italy), New Jersey (USA), Broken Hill – N. S. Wales (Australia), Puebla (Mexico).

Fassaite (Augite variety – Pyroxene group)

Silicate
Ca(Mg,Fe,Al)(Si,Al)$_2$O$_6$

511

Named after its locality in Valle di Fassa (Italy) (Werner 1817)

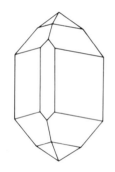

● Hardness: 6 (brittle) ● Streak: white or grey ● Colour: brownish-green, green or greenish-black ● Transparency: translucent to non-transparent ● Lustre: vitreous ● Cleavage: good on (110) ● Fracture: uneven, conchoidal ● Morphology: crystals, massive, granular aggregates, impregnations ● Specific gravity: 3.2–3.3 ● Crystal system: monoclinic ● Crystal form: short prisms ● Chemical composition: variable ● Chemical properties: soluble in hot HCl, fuses into a magnetic ball ● Handling: clean with distilled water ● Similar minerals: diopside (505) ● Distinguishing features: X-rays, chemical properties ● Genesis: contact-metasomatic ● Associated minerals: vesuvianite (522), garnet (577), spinel (590) ● Occurrence: rare; Valle di Fassa and Monte Somma (Italy), Eifel – in spinel pyroxenites enclosed in alkaline basalts (FRG), Hodruša (Slovakia), Bilimbai and Dachunur (Russia).

Piedmontite (Manganiferous epidote)

Silicate
Ca$_2$(Al,Fe^{3+})$_3$(SiO$_4$)$_3$(OH)

512

Named after the locality in Piedmont (Italy) (Kenngott 1853)

L

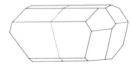

● Physical and chemical properties are similar to those of epidote (513) ● Streak: cherry-red ● Colour: red-brown, black-red to red ● Transparency: translucent ● Occurrence: rare; St. Marcel, in Val d'Aosta – Piedmont (Italy), Ultevis (Sweden), Isle de Croix (France), Glen Coe – Scotland (Great Britain), Otago (New Zealand), Annapolis – Missouri (USA).

---

1. **Johannsenite** – fissile aggregate; Madan (Bulgaria – width of field 52 mm) 2. **Fassaite** – small crystals (up to 10 mm) in calcite; Monzoni (Italy)

Johannsenite, fassaite

Epidote

Silicate
$Ca_2(Al,Fe^{3+})_3(SiO_4)_3(OH)$

513

From the Greek *epídosis* – addition (Haüy 1801)

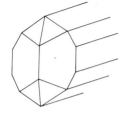

● Hardness: 6–7 (brittle) ● Streak: grey ● Colour: dark green to yellowish-green ● Transparency: translucent ● Lustre: vitreous ● Cleavage: very good on (001) to good on (100) ● Fracture: conchoidal, uneven, splintery ● Morphology: crystals, granular, radiating-fibrous, massive aggregates, pseudomorphs ● Specific gravity: 3.3–3.5 ● Crystal system: monoclinic ● Crystal form: prisms, isometric, plates, twins ● Luminescence: seldom pale dark red ● Chemical composition: CaO 23.04%, Al_2O_3 20.32%, Fe_2O_3 17.75%, SiO_2 37.04%, H_2O 1.85% (Fe^{3+}:Al = 1:2) ● Chemical properties: in a flame swells and fuses; insoluble in acids ● Handling: clean with water or diluted acids ● Similar minerals: augite **(429)**, amphibole **(411)**, actinolite **(413)**, vesuvianite **(522)**, tourmaline **(564)** ● Distinguishing features: hardness, cleavage, specific gravity, luminescence, X-rays, chemical properties ● Genesis: metamorphic, hydrothermal, contact-metasomatic ● Associated minerals: actinolite, albite **(493)**, garnet **(577)** ● Occurrence: common; Zillertal and Knappenwand (Austria), Erbendorf (FRG), Dauphiné (France), Outokumpo (Finland), Tawmaw Mines (Burma) ● Application: sometimes used as a precious stone.

Clinozoisite (Epidote group)

Silicate
$Ca_2Al_3(SiO_4)_3(OH)$

514

Named after its resemblance to zoisite and the monoclinic crystal system (Weinschenk 1896)

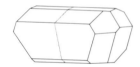

● Hardness: 6.5 ● Streak: white ● Colour: grey, yellow, greenish or light rose ● Transparency: transparent to translucent to non-transparent ● Lustre: vitreous ● Cleavage: perfect on (001) and (100) ● Fracture: uneven ● Morphology: crystals, granular, massive and fibrous aggregates ● Specific gravity: 3.2 ● Crystal system: monoclinic ● Crystal form: prisms ● Chemical composition: like epidote **(513)**, but contains very little Fe^{3+} ● Chemical properties: like epidote ● Handling: clean with water or diluted acids ● Similar minerals: epidote, zoisite **(519)** ● Distinguishing features: optical properties, X-rays, chemical tests ● Genesis: metamorphic, contact-metasomatic ● Associated minerals: amphibole **(411)**, albite **(493)**, epidote ● Occurrence: rare; (Switzerland), (Austria), (Italy), (Mexico), (Madagascar), (USA).

Prehnite

Silicate
$Ca_2Al_2Si_3O_{10}(OH)_2$

515

Named after the Dutch Colonel, H. von Prehn (1733–1785) (Werner 1790)

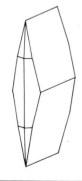

● Hardness: 6–6.5 ● Streak: white ● Colour: green, grey or yellowish-green ● Transparency: transparent to translucent ● Lustre: vitreous, pearly ● Cleavage: good on (001) ● Fracture: uneven ● Morphology: crystals, reniform, massive and granular aggregates, encrustations, pseudomorphs ● Specific gravity: 2.8–3.0 ● Crystal system: orthorhombic ● Crystal form: plates, prisms ● Chemical composition: CaO 27.1%, Al_2O_3 24.8%, SiO_2 43.7%, H_2O 4.4% ● Chemical properties: soluble in HCl, fuses, swells and forms a porous, glassy mass ● Handling: clean with water ● Similar minerals: wavellite **(247)**, stilbite **(269)**, hemimorphite **(403)** ● Distinguishing features: hardness, specific gravity, X-rays, chemical properties ● Genesis: hydrothermal ● Associated minerals: calcite **(217)**, zeolites, axinite **(523)** ● Occurrence: rare; Haslach, Harzburg and Oberstein (FRG), Valle di Fassa (Italy), Dauphiné (France), Doros (Namibia) ● Application: sometimes used as a precious stone.

---

1. **Epidote** – columnar striated crystal (20 mm) with asbestos on albite; Sulzbachtal (Austria) 2. **Prehnite** – semi-globular crystalline aggregates (up to 10 mm); Haslach (FRG)

Epidote, prehnite

405

Sillimanite (Fibrolite)

Silicate
Al$_2$SiO$_5$

516

P

Named after the American chemist and mineralogist, B. Silliman (1779–1864) (Bowen 1824)

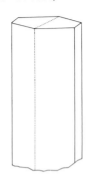

● Hardness: 6–7 (brittle) ● Streak: white ● Colour: yellow-grey, light blue, grey-green, reddish or white ● Transparency: translucent to transparent ● Lustre: vitreous, silky ● Cleavage: perfect on (010) ● Morphology: crystals, fibrous, felt-like-fibrolite, radial and compact aggregates, pebbles ● Specific gravity: 3.2 ● Crystal system: orthorhombic ● Crystal form: needles ● Chemical composition: Al$_2$O$_3$ 63.1%, SiO$_2$ 36.9% ● Chemical properties: infusible, insoluble in acids ● Handling: clean with water or diluted acids ● Similar minerals: kyanite **(435)**, mullite **(517)** ● Distinguishing features: hardness, specific gravity, X-rays and chemical tests ● Genesis: metamorphic, contact-metamorphic ● Associated minerals: cordierite **(551)**, andalusite **(562)**, spinel **(590)** ● Occurrence: widespread; Bodenmais, Freiberg (FRG), Sellrain on Juchen (Austria), Khasi Hills (India), Mogok (Burma), (Norway), (Russia), (Kenya), (Sri Lanka), (USA) ● Application: fire-proof materials, insulators, sometimes used as a precious stone.

Mullite

Silicate
Al$_6$Si$_2$O$_{13}$

517

Named after its locality on the Isle of Mull (Scotland, Great Britain) (Bowen, Greig, Zies 1924)

● Hardness: 6–7 ● Streak: white ● Colour: light rose ● Transparency: transparent to translucent ● Lustre: vitreous ● Cleavage: good on (010) ● Morphology: crystals ● Specific gravity: 3.0–3.1 ● Crystal system: orthorhombic ● Crystal form: prisms ● Chemical composition: variable ● Chemical properties: like sillimanite **(516)** ● Handling: clean with water or diluted acids ● Similar minerals: sillimanite ● Distinguishing features: X-rays, chemical properties ● Genesis: in remelted clays of tertiary basalts on the Isle of Mull – Scotland (Great Britain); usually as a result of synthetic melting of andalusite **(562)**, kyanite **(435)** or sillimanite with topaz **(595)**.

Chondrodite

Silicate
Mg$_5$(SiO$_4$)$_2$(OH,F)$_2$

518

L

P

From the Greek *chóndros* – grain (d'Ohsson 1817)

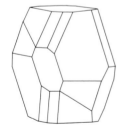

● Hardness: 6–6.5 ● Streak: white or grey ● Colour: yellow, orange, brownish, reddish or greenish ● Transparency: transparent to translucent ● Lustre: vitreous, greasy ● Cleavage: good on (100) ● Fracture: conchoidal, uneven ● Morphology: crystals, granular and massive aggregates, impregnations ● Specific gravity: 3.1–3.2 ● Crystal system: monoclinic ● Crystal form: isometric ● Luminescence: sometimes yellow, brown-orange ● Chemical composition: MgO 58.88%, SiO$_2$ 35.08%, F 7.39%, H$_2$O 1.75% (when F:OH = 2:1) ● Chemical properties: soluble in HCl and H$_2$SO$_4$, in a blowpipe flame turns white, fuses with difficulty ● Handling: clean with distilled water ● Similar minerals: olivine **(524)** ● Distinguishing features: specific gravity, solubility in acids (HCl) ● Genesis: contact-metamorphic ● Associated minerals: phlogopite **(168)**, magnetite **(367)**, apatite **(379)**, olivine ● Occurrence: rare; Wunsiedel and Passau (FRG), Pargas (Finland), Åker (Sweden), Monte Somma (Italy), Brewster – New York (USA) ● Application: rarely used as a precious stone.

---

1. **Sillimanite** – nodule (10 mm) in gneiss; Havlíčkův Brod (Czech Republic) 2. **Chondrodite** – isometric grains (9 mm) in quartz; Södal (Norway)

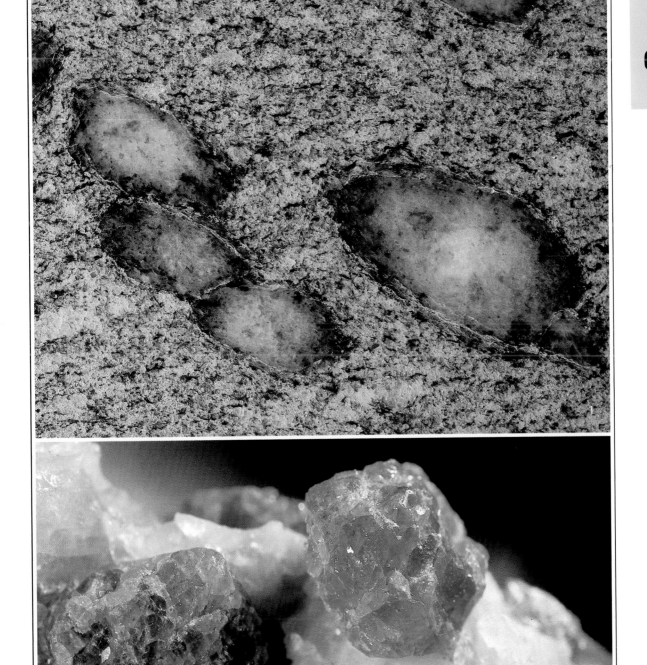

Zoisite (Epidote group)

Silicate
$Ca_2Al_3(SiO_4)_3(OH)$

519

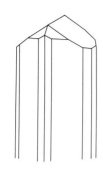

Named after the Austrian natural scientist, S. Zois (1747–1819) (Werner 1805)

● Hardness: 6–6.5 ● Streak: white ● Colour: grey-white, green – anyolite variety, brown, rose – thulite variety **(521)**, red, yellowish, blue – tanzanite variety **(520)** ● Transparency: translucent to opaque ● Lustre: vitreous, pearly ● Cleavage: perfect on (100) ● Fracture: uneven ● Morphology: crystals, radial and compact aggregates ● Specific gravity: 3.2–3.4 ● Crystal system: orthorhombic ● Crystal form: prisms ● Luminescence: sometimes light brown (thulite) ● Chemical composition: CaO 24.69%, Al_2O_3 33.66%, SiO_2 39.68%, H_2O 1.97%; admixtures: Fe, Mn, Cr, Ti, K, Na, V ● Chemical properties: insoluble in acids, fuses into a white porous mass, swells when heated ● Handling: clean with water or diluted acids ● Similar minerals: pumpellyite **(408)** ● Distinguishing features: optical properties, X-rays, chemical tests ● Genesis: metamorphic, in pegmatites ● Associated minerals: amphibole **(411)**, epidote **(513)**, vesuvianite **(522)**, quartz **(534)**, garnet **(577)** ● Occurrence: rare; Rauris and Saualpe (Austria), Zermatt (Switzerland), Vipiteno and Val Passiria (Italy), Gefrees (FRG), (Norway), Ducktown, Tennessee and New Mexico – thulite variety (USA), Longido – anyolite variety and Miralani Hills – tanzanite variety (Tanzania) ● Application: sometimes as an ornamental or precious stone.

Tanzanite (Zoisite variety – Epidote group)

Silicate
$Ca_2Al_3(SiO_4)_3(OH)$

520

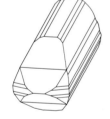

Named after Tanzania, at present the only place where it is found (Gübelin, Weibel 1976)

● Physical and chemical properties are similar to those of zoisite. It is a fine blue colour with a strong pleochroism of blue, purple-red and brown colours ● Transparent to translucent; brittle ● Genesis: rare; it occurs only in the Miralani Hills (near Arusha, Tanzania) ● Application: as a precious stone (facets).

Thulite (Zoisite variety – Epidote group)

Silicate
$Ca_2Al_3(SiO_4)_3(OH)$

521

From *Thule* the old name of Norway (Brooke 1823)

● Physical and chemical properties are similar to those of zoisite. It is a rose to rosy-red colour; opaque ● Luminescence: sometimes light brown ● Genesis: contact-metamorphic ● Associated minerals: with Mn minerals ● Occurrence: rare; Souland and Lexviken (Norway), Borzovka and the Urals (Russia), New Mexico (USA), (Western Australia), (Namibia), (eastern part of Greenland) ● Application: used as on ornamental stone.

---

1. Zoisite – columnar crystal (10 mm) in quartz; Tennessee (USA) **2. Tanzanite** – isolated crystals (size 7–9 mm); Arusha (Tanzania) **3. Thulite** – granular aggregate; Souland (Norway – width of field 56 mm)

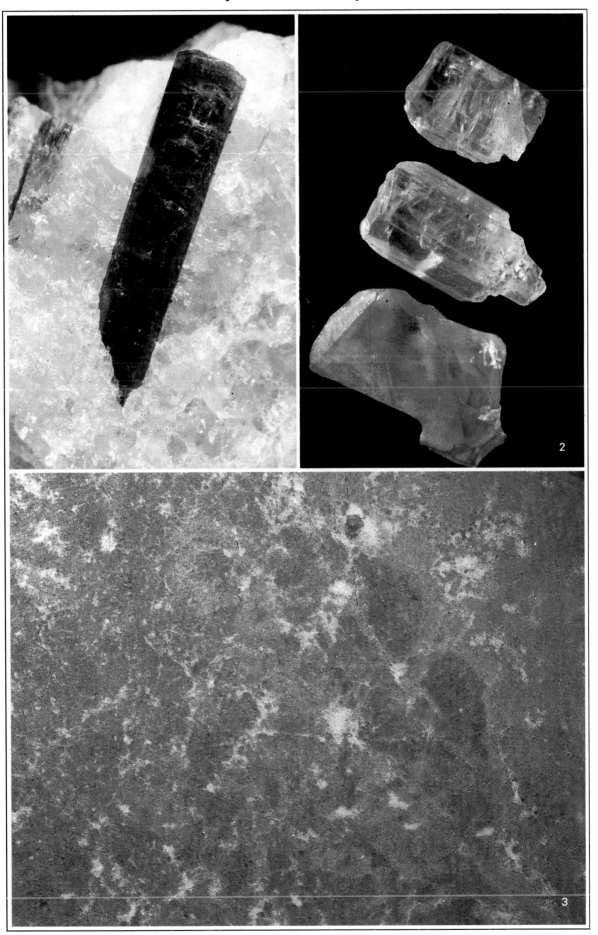

Vesuvianite (Idocrase)

Silicate
$Ca_{10}Mg_2Al_4(SiO_4)_5(Si_2O_7)_2(OH)_4$

522

P

Named after its locality on Vesuvius (Italy) (Werner 1795)

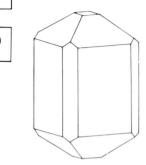

● Hardness: 6.5 ● Streak: white or grey ● Colour: brown, green, blue – cyprine variety, yellow or reddish ● Transparency: translucent ● Lustre: vitreous, greasy ● Cleavage: indistinct on (110), (100) and (001) ● Fracture: uneven, splintery ● Morphology: crystals, granular, massive and radial aggregates – egeran variety ● Specific gravity: 3.27–3.47 ● Crystal system: tetragonal ● Crystal form: prisms, needles, dipyramids, isometric crystals ● Chemical composition: variable; admixture: B_2O_3 – wiluite variety ● Chemical properties: readily fusible into yellowish-green or brown glassy mass; insoluble in acids ● Handling: clean with distilled water ● Similar minerals: epidote **(513)**, grossularite **(582)**, zircon **(587)** ● Distinguishing features: hardness, specific gravity, X-rays and chemical tests – most reliable ● Genesis: contact-metamorphic, in alpine veins ● Associated minerals: chlorite **(158)**, diopside **(505)**, garnet **(577)**, epidote ● Occurrence: widely found; Auerbach (FRG), Monzoni and Monte Somma (Italy), Dognacea and Ciclova (Romania), Hazlov and Žulová – egeran variety (Czech Republic), Zermatt (Switzerland), in the basin of the river Vilyui – wiluite variety (Russia), Chihuahua – large crystals (Mexico), Souland – cyprine variety (Norway) ● Application: sometimes used as a precious stone.

Axinite

Silicate
$Ca_3(Fe,Mg,Mn)Al_2BSi_4O_{15}(OH)$

523

L

P

From the Greek *áxine* – axe (Haüy 1799)

● Hardness: 6.5–7 (brittle) ● Streak: white ● Colour: brown, grey, violet or greenish ● Transparency: transparent to translucent ● Lustre: vitreous ● Cleavage: perfect on (010) ● Fracture: conchoidal ● Morphology: crystals, granular and massive aggregates, impregnations ● Specific gravity: 3.3 ● Crystal system: triclinic ● Crystal form: plates, clinohedra ● Luminescence: sometimes violet ● Chemical composition: variable ● Chemical properties: soluble in HF; in a blowpipe flame swells and fuses ● Handling: clean with water or diluted acids ● Similar minerals: titanite **(430)** ● Distinguishing features: hardness, specific gravity, blowpipe tests ● Genesis: contact-metamorphic, hydrothermal, in alpine veins ● Associated minerals: chlorite **(158)**, epidote **(513)** ● Occurrence: rare; St. Andreasberg, Schwarzenberg (FRG), Bourg d'Oisans (France), Scopi (Switzerland), Narodnaya and the Urals (Russia), Botallack – Cornwal (Great Britain), Franklin – New Jersey (USA) ● Application: sometimes used as a precious stone.

---

1. **Vesuvianite** – euhedral crystal (18 mm); Vilyui River (Yakutia, Russia) 2. **Axinite** – crystal (5 mm) in albite; Scopi (Switzerland)

Vesuvianite, axinite

Olivine (Peridot, Chrysolite)

Silicate
$(Mg,Fe)_2SiO_4$

Named after its colour
(Werner 1789)

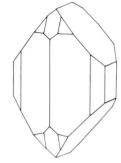

● Hardness: 6.5−7 (brittle) ● Streak: white ● Colour: yellowish-green, olive-green, greenish-black or reddish-brown ● Transparency: transparent to translucent; yellow-green transparent variety is called chrysolite (525) ● Lustre: vitreous, greasy ● Cleavage: perfect on (001) or indistinct on (010) ● Fracture: conchoidal ● Morphology: crystals, granular and massive aggregates, grains ● Specific gravity: 3.3 (forsterite 3.27, fayalite 4.20) ● Crystal system: orthorhombic ● Crystal form: short prisms ● Magnetism: paramagnetic ● Chemical composition: MgO 23.41%, FeO 41.71%, SiO_2 34.88% (when Mg:Fe = 1:1). End kinds of the isomorphous series are forsterite Mg_2SiO_4 and fayalite Fe_2SiO_4 ● Chemical properties: soluble in HNO_3; Mg kinds are soluble in warm acids; infusible; Fe kinds fuse into a magnetic ball ● Handling: clean with distilled water ● Similar minerals: willemite (404), tephroite (526), chrysoberyl (593) ● Distinguishing features: hardness, specific gravity, luminescence ● Genesis: magmatic, in basic pegmatites, contact-metasomatic, in alluvial deposits and meteorites ● Associated minerals: phlogopite (168), magnetite (367), apatite (379), diopside (505) ● Occurrence: widespread; Dreiser Weiher near Draum Maria Laach (FRG), Mourne Mts. (Northern Ireland), Mansjö (Sweden), Collobriéres (France), forsterite grains measuring 16 cm are found in pegmatitic dunites in the Urals and fayalite grains measuring 10 cm in pegmatites in the Kolyma river (Russia), Arizona – forsterite in lherzolites, Texas, Rockport – Massachusetts: fayalite (USA). Olivine is a frequent constituent in many gabbros, melaphyres, diabases, basalts, peridotites, dunites ● Application: Mg – olivines are used in the production of technical silica glass, sometimes as precious stones (peridot).

Chrysolite (Olivine variety)

Silicate
$(Mg,Fe)_2SiO_4$

From the Greek *chrysós* – gold and *líthos* – stone
(according to the Roman naturalist Pliny)

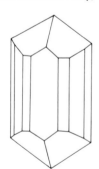

● Physical and chemical properties are similar to those of olivine (524). It is yellowish-green to green; transparent ● Occurrence: rare; Kozákov and Smrčí (Czech Republic), (Norway), (northern Burma), (Australia), (Brazil), Arizona, Hawaii and New Mexico (USA). The most beautiful chrysolites are found and cut on Zebirget Island (St. John's Island) in the Red Sea – crystals measuring 4.5 cm and weighing 70 g ● Application: cut as a precious stone (facets, cabochons).

---

1. **Olivine** – granular aggregate (53 mm) in basalt; Podmoklice (Czech Republic) 2. **Chrysolite** – grain (16 mm) in basalt; Smrčí (Czech Republic)

Olivine, chrysolite

H
6—7

413

Tephroite (Olivine group)

Silicate
Mn_2SiO_4

526

From the Greek *tephrós* – ash-grey (Breithaupt 1823)

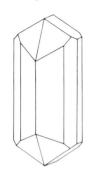

● Hardness: 6 ● Streak: grey ● Colour: grey, olive-grey, flesh pink or red-brown ● Transparency: transparent to translucent ● Lustre: vitreous, greasy ● Cleavage: perfect on (010), (001) and (110) ● Fracture: conchoidal ● Morphology: crystals, compact masses ● Specific gravity: 4.1 ● Crystal system: orthorhombic ● Crystal form: short prisms ● Chemical composition: MnO 70.25%, SiO_2 29.75%; admixtures: Zn, Ca, Mg ● Chemical properties: soluble in HCl – forms sublimate of SiO_2; fuses with difficulty ● Handling: clean with distilled water ● Similar minerals: olivine **(524)** ● Distinguishing features: X-rays and chemical tests ● Genesis: contact-metamorphic ● Associated minerals: calcite **(217)**, rhodonite **(531)**, spessartine **(584)** ● Occurrence: rare; Långban (Sweden), Mooserboden (Austria), Cornwall (Great Britain), Djumart and Kamys (Kazakhstan), Franklin and Sparta – New Jersey (USA), Himegamori (Japan).

Ramsayite (Lorenzenite)

Silicate
$Na_2Ti_2Si_2O_9$

527

Named after V. Ramsay, who pioneered the study of Khibiny and Lovozer Tundras (Kola Peninsula, Russia) (Fersman 1922)

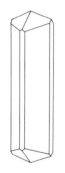

● Hardness: 6 (brittle) ● Streak: light yellow or brownish ● Colour: dark brown, reddish, yellow-brown or grey ● Transparency: transparent to translucent to opaque ● Lustre: vitreous, greasy ● Cleavage: perfect on (100) ● Fracture: uneven, conchoidal ● Morphology: crystals, granular and fibrous aggregates ● Specific gravity: 3.4 ● Crystal system: orthorhombic ● Crystal form: prisms, needles, plates ● Chemical composition: Na_2O 18.13%, TiO_2 46.74%, SiO_2 35.13% ● Chemical properties: soluble in HF, readily fusible into a black opaque ball ● Handling: clean with distilled water or diluted acids ● Genesis: magmatic (alkaline rocks), alkaline pegmatites ● Associated minerals: astrophyllite **(278)**, nepheline **(397)**, eudialite **(402)**, acmite **(509)** ● Occurrence: rare; in Larvik (Norway), Khibiny and Lovozer Tundras – Kola Peninsula (Russia), Narsarsuk (Greenland), St. Hilaire (Canada), (Canary Islands).

---

1. Tephroite – flesh-red granular aggregates with black franklinite; Franklin (New Jersey, USA) **2. Ramsayite** – columnar crystal (15 mm) with egeran, eudialite and nepheline; Kola Peninsula (Russia)

Tephroite, ramsayite

Thortveitite

Silicate
$(Sc,Y)_2Si_2O_7$

528

Named after the Norwegian engineer, O. Thortveit (Schetelig 1911)

• Hardness: 6.5 (brittle) • Streak: white or grey • Colour: brown, grey-black, black or dirty green • Transparency: translucent to opaque • Lustre: vitreous, adamantine • Cleavage: perfect on (110) • Fracture: conchoidal, uneven • Morphology: crystals, radial aggregates • Specific gravity: approx. 3.6 • Crystal system: monoclinic • Crystal form: prisms • Chemical composition: Sc_2O_3 53.5%, SiO_2 46.5%; contains up to 10% of Y_2O_3 • Chemical properties: slightly soluble in boiling HCl, fuses with difficulty • Handling: clean with distilled water • Genesis: in pegmatites • Associated minerals: ilmenite **(365)**, monazite **(383)**, beryl **(554)**, zircon **(587)** • Occurrence: rare; Iveland (Norway), Urals (Russia), Befanamo (Madagascar), Kobe (Japan), Montana (USA) • Application: source of Sc.

Chloritoid

Silicate
$Fe^{2+}Al_2SiO_5(OH)_2$

529

Named after its resemblance to chlorites (Rose 1837)

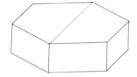

• Hardness: greater than 6 (brittle) • Streak: greenish-white • Colour: dark garlic-green, grey or greenish-black • Transparency: in thin lamellae – transparent or translucent • Lustre: vitreous, pearly • Cleavage: perfect on (001) • Fracture: uneven • Morphology: crystals, tabular, granular aggregates, grains • Specific gravity: 3.4–3.6 • Crystal system: monoclinic, sometimes triclinic • Crystal form: pseudohexagonal plates • Chemical composition: FeO 28.64%, Al_2O_3 40.64%, SiO_2 23.95%, H_2O 6.77%; admixtures: Mg – sismondine variety, Mn – ottrelite variety • Chemical properties: soluble in concentrated H_2SO_4; fuses with difficulty into black, slightly magnetic glass • Handling: clean with distilled water • Similar minerals: chlorite **(158)** • Distinguishing features: hardness, fragility; chloritoid is inflexible • Genesis: metamorphic • Associated minerals: chlorite, diaspore **(463)**, corundum **(598)** • Occurrence: rare; as a constituent in some phyllites, schists and marbles; Rörsdorf (FRG), Zermatt, Saas and Lukmanier (Switzerland), Pregraten (Austria), Kosoi Brod and the Urals (Russia), Ottrez – ottrelite variety (Belgium), Naxos (Greece).

Benitoite

Silicate
$BaTiSi_3O_9$

530

Named after its locality in San Benito County (California, USA) (Louderback 1907)

L

P

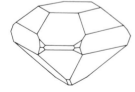

• Hardness: 6.5 (brittle) • Streak: white • Colour: colourless, blue or blue-grey; can vary in the same crystal • Transparency: translucent to opaque • Lustre: vitreous • Cleavage: indistinct on $(10\bar{1}1)$ • Fracture: conchoidal • Morphology: crystals, grains • Specific gravity: 3.7 • Crystal system: trigonal • Crystal form: dipyramidal • Luminescence: blue in short-wave UV • Chemical composition: BaO 37.09%, SiO_2 43.59%, TiO_2 19.32% • Chemical properties: soluble in HF, fuses into transparent glass • Handling: clean with diluted acids • Genesis: natrolite veins in serpentinites • Associated minerals: anatase **(352)**, natrolite **(387)**, neptunite **(437)** • Occurrence: rare; San Benito – California and in the Eocene sands – southwestern Texas (USA) • Application: sometimes used as a precious stone.

---

1. **Chloritoid** – star-shaped forms (up to 5 mm) in chloritic schist; Leoben (Austria) 2. **Thortveitite** – group of elongated embedded crystals (up to 15 mm); Aust Agder (Norway) 3. **Benitoite** – crystals (15 mm) in natrolite; San Benito Co. (California, USA)

Chloritoid, thortveitite, benitoite

Rhodonite (Manganese spar)

Silicate
CaMn₄Si₅O₁₅

531

L

P

From the Greek *rhodos* – rose-coloured (Jasche 1819)

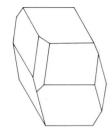

● Hardness: 5.5–6.5 (brittle) ● Streak: white ● Colour: pink, red or reddish-brown ● Transparency: translucent, but seldom transparent ● Lustre: vitreous, pearly ● Cleavage: perfect on (110) and (1$\bar{1}$0) ● Fracture: uneven ● Morphology: crystals, granular and massive aggregates ● Specific gravity: 3.73 ● Crystal system: triclinic ● Crystal form: prisms, plates ● Luminescence: sometimes dark red ● Chemical composition: CaO 8.76%, MnO 44.31%, SiO₂ 46.93% ● Chemical properties: in powder form slightly soluble in HCl; in a blowpipe flame turns black, then swells and fuses into black glass ● Handling: clean with water ● Similar minerals: rhodochrosite **(304)** ● Distinguishing features: hardness, specific gravity, soluble in acids ● Genesis: hydrothermal, contact-metasomatic, metamorphic ● Associated minerals: hausmannite **(358)**, magnetite **(367)**, spessartite **(584)** ● Occurrence: common; Elbingerode, Laasphe and Lauthental (FRG), Huelva (Spain), Långban (Sweden), Urals (Russia) ● Application: Mn ore; ornamental stone.

Inesite

Silicate
Ca₂Mn₇Si₁₀O₂₈(OH)₂ . 5 H₂O

532

From the Greek *ines* – flesh fibres (Schneider 1887)

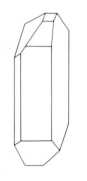

● Hardness: 6 (brittle) ● Streak: white ● Colour: pink, red or orange with a brownish coating ● Transparency: translucent ● Lustre: vitreous ● Cleavage: perfect on (010) ● Fracture: uneven ● Morphology: crystals, fan-shaped aggregates ● Other properties: when exposed to the light it loses its colour and turns brown ● Specific gravity: 3.1 ● Crystal system: triclinic ● Crystal form: prisms, plates ● Chemical composition: CaO 8.53%, MnO 37.68%, SiO₂ 45.57%, H₂O 8.22% ● Chemical properties: readily soluble in HCl ● Handling: clean with distilled water; should be protected from light ● Similar minerals: rhodonite **(531)** ● Distinguishing features: soluble in HCl ● Genesis: hydrothermal ● Associated minerals: calcite **(217)**, rhodochrosite **(304)**, rhodonite ● Occurrence: rare; Nanzenbach (FRG), Banská Štiavnica (Slovakia), Baia Mare (Romania), Långban (Sweden), (Japan), (Australia).

Pyroxmangite

Silicate
(Mn,Fe)₇Si₇O₂₁

533

Named after its resemblance to the pyroxenes (Ford, Bradley 1913)

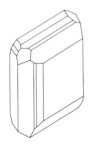

● Hardness: 6 ● Streak: white ● Colour: pink, red or brown ● Transparency: transparent to translucent ● Lustre: vitreous, pearly ● Cleavage: perfect on (110) and (1$\bar{1}$0) ● Fracture: uneven, hackly ● Morphology: crystals, granular aggregates ● Specific gravity: 3.9 ● Crystal system: triclinic ● Crystal form: plates, prisms ● Chemical composition: MnO 30.87%, FeO 23.48%, SiO₂ 45.65% (when Mn:Fe – 4:3) ● Chemical properties: insoluble in acids, fuses into a black magnetic ball ● Handling: clean with diluted acids ● Similar minerals: rhodonite **(531)** ● Distinguishing features: X-rays and chemical tests ● Genesis: metamorphic, contact-metasomatic ● Associated minerals: rhodochrosite **(304)**, rhodonite, spessartite **(584)** ● Occurrence: rare; Tunaberg (Sweden), Dürnstein (Austria), Davos (Switzerland), Iva – South Carolina (USA), Broken Hill – N. S. Wales (Australia), (Japan).

---

1. Rhodonite – tabular crystals (20 mm) with calcite and black franklinite; Franklin (New Jersey, USA) **2. Inesite** – radiate druse (20 mm); Långban (Sweden)

Rhodonite, inesite

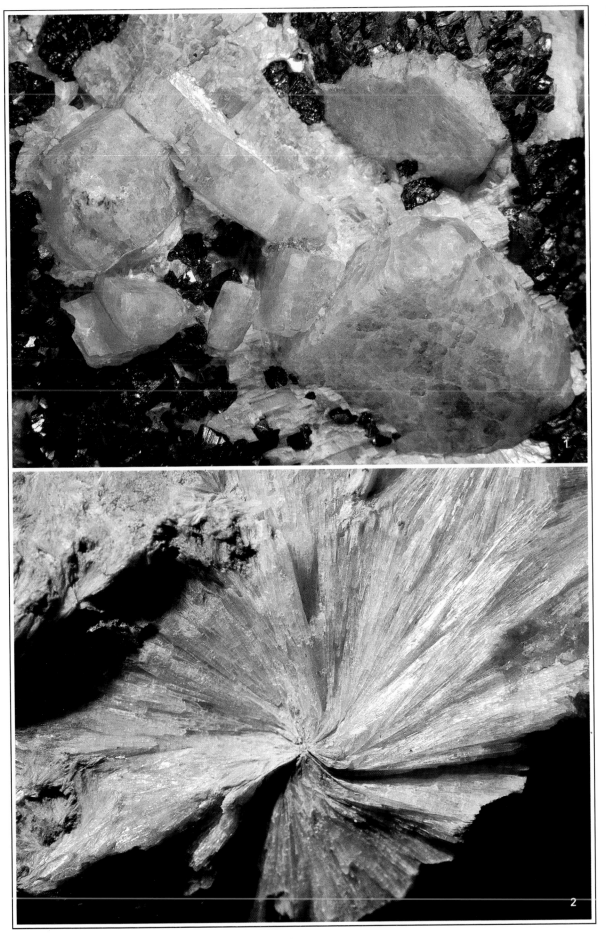

H
6—7

419

Quartz

Oxide
SiO$_2$

534

L

P

From the Greek *chrystalos* – ice

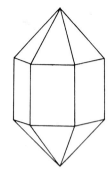

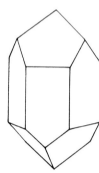

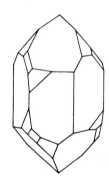

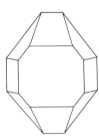

● Hardness: 7 (brittle) ● Streak: white ● Colour: colourless, white, grey, brown, black, violet, greenish, bluish, yellow or pink ● Transparency: transparent to translucent to opaque ● Lustre: vitreous, greasy ● Cleavage: indistinct on (10$\bar{1}$1) ● Fracture: conchoidal, splintery ● Morphology: crystals, granular and massive aggregates ● Specific gravity: 2.65 ● Crystal system: trigonal (α-quartz – up to 573 °C), hexagonal (β-quartz – from 573 °C to 870 °C) ● Crystal form: prisms, dipyramidal, pseudocubic, twinning is common and the types of twinning have been given names, eg Dauphinean, Brazilian, Japanese ● Electric conductivity: pyroelectric as well as piezo-electric ● Chemical composition: SiO$_2$ 100%; admixtures: Al, Li, B, Fe, Mg, Ca, Ti, K, Rb ● Chemical properties: infusible, breaks when heated, soluble in HF ● Handling: clean with water or diluted acids, except HF ● Similar minerals: apatite **(379)**, pollucite **(500)**, beryl **(554)**, topaz **(595)**, phenakite **(597)** ● Distinguishing features: hardness, specific gravity, cleavage, solubility in acids, X-rays, chemical tests, sometimes yellow, cream, orange or greenish luminescence ● Genesis: magmatic, in pegmatites, hydrothermal, metamorphic, in alpine cracks, in weathering crusts, sedimentary ● Associated minerals: feldspars, micas, amphiboles, pyroxenes ● Occurrence: important rock-forming mineral, an essential part of acidic magmatic rocks – granites, granodiorites, quartz diorites and pegmatitic masses. It forms an essential part of quartz and ore veins, is found in weathering crusts, and is found concentrated in sedimentary rocks; metamorphosed quartz may be found in alpine veins ● Occurrence: widely found; single crystals of considerable size and weight are often found (eg in Brazil – approx. 40 tons, and in Kazakhstan – approx. 70 tons).

According to its colour, texture and crystallographic development, quartz is divided into two main groups:

I phanerocrystalline varieties (visible crystalline form); and
II cryptocrystalline varieties (eg chalcedony – **449**; crystalline, but very fine grained).

Phanerocrystalline varieties are as follows:

Rock crystal **(535)** – colourless
Amethyst **(536)** – violet
Smoky quartz **(537)** – brown
Rose quartz **(538)** – pink
Morion **(539)** – black
Citrine **(540)** – yellow
Sapphire quartz **(541)** – blue
Tiger's eye **(542)** – pseudomorph of quartz from weathered crocidolite
Falcon's eye **(543)** – pseudomorph of quartz from crocidolite
Cat's eye **(544)** – pseudomorph from amianthus or asbestos minerals
Aventurine **(545)** – quartz with embedded lamellae of mica or hematite
Common quartz – grey
Milky quartz – milk-white
Ferruginous quartz – quartz containing iron oxides.

● Application: ceramic, glass and building industries, metallurgy, electrotechnics, optics, jewellery (semi-precious stone).

Quartz – compound crystals (40 mm); Sutrop (FRG)

Quartz

Rock crystal (Quartz variety)

535

L

P

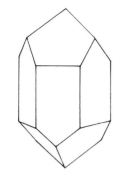

● Physical and chemical properties are identical to those of quartz **(534)** ● It is the name given to well-crystallized, colourless, transparent quartz of vitreous lustre ● Genesis: in pegmatites, hydrothermal veins, alpine veins, sedimentary ● Associated minerals: titanite **(430)**, rutile **(464)**, adularia **(487)**, albite **(493)**, epidote **(513)** ● Occurrence: rare; Aare and Gotthard Mass (Switzerland), Pfitsch (Austria), Dauphiné (France), Bavena – Elba (Italy), Strigom (Poland), Velká Kraš (Czech Republic), Hagendorf (FRG), in the Alps, crystals weighing 400–800 kg were found in 1719 in Zinngenstock (Switzerland) and 618 kg in Eiskögel (Austria). In 1965 a cavity was discovered on Granatsitze (Grossglockner, Austria), containing a crystal weighing nearly 1000 kg and measuring 120×60×75 cm. Rock crystal is found also in the pegmatites of Volhynia (Ukraine), Urals (Russia), (Kazakhstan), Auburn – Maine (USA), (Sri Lanka), (Madagascar) and Minas Gerais (Brazil). Of special interest is the clear, bipyramidal, contact-twinned quartz found in sandstones or marbles, known as *Marmarosh diamond or Herkimer quartz*; it is found in the Transcarpathian area (Ukraine) and in Herkimer – New York (USA). Similar quartz is also found in Carrara – marbles (Italy) and in Ulič and Veľký Lipník (Slovakia). In the Alps, rock crystal often contains needles or scales of other minerals, such as gold **(50)**, goethite **(354)**, amiantus **(415)**, pyrite **(436)**, rutile, hematite **(472)** or tourmaline **(564)** ● Application: in optics, used as a semi-precious stone (facets, cabochons), in the manufacture of decorative articles, such as vases, cups, figures, candle-sticks.

Amethyst (Quartz variety)

536

L

P

From the Greek *amethystos* – unintoxicating

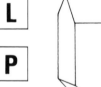

● Physical and chemical properties are identical to those of quartz **(534)**. It is a light to dark violet colour, transparent to translucent ● Genesis: magmatic, hydrothermal ● Associated minerals: chalcedony **(449)**, rock crystal **(535)** ● Occurrence: rare; in amygdaloidal cavities of effusive rocks near Oberstein and Müglitztal (FRG); in ore veins in Clara Mine near Oberwolfach, Bad Sulzburg and Freiberg (FRG); Banská Štiavnica (Slovakia), Kozákov – in melaphyres, near Bochovice and Hostákov (Czech Republic), Cavnic (Romania), Murzinsk, Berezovsk and the Urals (Russia), Serra do Mar – a geode measuring 10×5×2 m producing 70 tons of amethysts (Brazil), (Uruguay), (USA), (Madagascar), Plattveld – in dolomitic veins (Namibia), Guanajuato – in ore veins (Mexico), (Sri Lanka) – alluvial ore deposits ● Application: cut as a precious stone or for ornamental purposes (facets, cabochons, tumbling, plastic cutting, decorative articles).

1. **Rock crystal** – crystal (22 mm) embedded with calcite in marble; Carara (Italy) 2. **Amethyst** – druse of crystals (up to 32 mm); Porcura (Romania)

Rock crystal, amethyst

Smoky quartz (Quartz variety)

Oxide
SiO$_2$

537

L

P

Named after its colouring

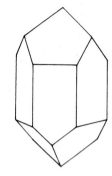

● Physical and chemical properties are identical to those of quartz **(534)**. It is a light-brown, smoky-grey or darker brown colour, sometimes altering to a colourless rock crystal **(535)** or to a dark morion **(539)**. It is transparent to translucent, of a vitreous lustre, and is often produced artificially by radioactive irradiation of rock crystal ● Genesis: in pegmatites, hydrothermal ● Associated minerals: apatite **(379)**, orthoclase **(486)**, albite **(493)**, axinite **(523)**, tourmaline **(564)**, micas ● Occurrence: rare; Hagendorf (FRG), Dolní Bory and Bobrůvka (Czech Republic), St. Gotthard – crystals weighing up to 150 kg (Switzerland); in 1946 a brilliant druse of crystals was found in Tiefengletscher measuring 90×60×40 cm and weighing 180 kg; Tessino (Italy), Sulzbachtal (Austria), Strigom (Poland). Large crystals of smoky quartz and morion are found in pegmatites in (Brazil), California, Maine, North Carolina and South Dakota (USA), (Madagascar), (Russia), (India). Valued as gems are crystals of smoky quartz from Cordoba (Spain) and from Volhynia (Ukraine), the Urals and Central Asia (Russia) and from New South Wales (Australia). Application: cut as a precious stone (facets, cabochons, tumbling, plastic cutting, decorative articles).

Rose quartz (Quartz variety)

Oxide
SiO$_2$

538

L

P

Named after its colouring

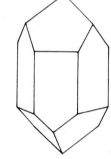

● Physical and chemical properties are identical to those of quartz **(534)**. It is a light rose to rose colour, transparent to translucent, usually compact or finely granular. It sometimes exhibits a light violet luminescence ● Genesis: in pegmatites ● Associated minerals: lepidolite **(169)**, beryl **(554)**, tourmaline **(564)** ● Occurrence: rare; Zwiesel and Bodenmais (FRG), Dolní Bory and Písek (Czech Republic), (Finland), Urals – in pegmatites (Russia), Caster – South Dakota and Maine (USA), Minas Gerais and Rio Jequitinhonha – first crystals of rose quartz were found in 1959 in Pedra Azul and Governador Valaderas (Brazil), (Madagascar), (Namibia), (RSA), Goto – Iwaki Pref. (Japan) ● Application: valued for gem and ornamental use (facets, cabochons, gemmae, plastic cutting, tumbling, decorative articles).

1. **Smoky quartz** – group of crystals (the largest 50 mm); St. Gotthard (Switzerland) 2. **Rose quartz** – crystal aggregate; Minas Gerais (Brazil – width of field 57 mm)

Smoky quartz, rose quartz

Morion (Smoky quartz variety)

Oxide
SiO$_2$

539

L

P

From the name *morion* – translucent black precious stone

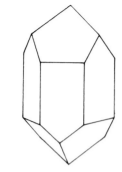

● Physical and chemical properties are identical to those of quartz **(534)**. It is a dark brown to black colour, translucent or opaque, of vitreous lustre. Many varieties of dark coloured smoky quartz **(537)** alter to morion ● Genesis: in pegmatites, hydrothermal ● Associated minerals: wolframite **(369)**, micas, feldspars, cassiterite **(548)**, topaz **(595)** ● Occurrence: rare; Dolní Bory – in pegmatites, Cínovec, Ore Mountains – in ore veins of Sn-W deposits (Czech Republic), (Russia), (Brazil), (Madagascar). Crystals of smoky quartz from alpine fissures seldom alter to morion, eg in the area of Aare and Gotthard Mass (Switzerland). The largest cavity filled with morion crystals, weighing up to 127 kg was discovered in 1867 near Tiefengletscher – Uri (Switzerland) ● Application: cut as a precious and ornamental stone (facets, cabochons, plastic cutting).

Citrine (Quartz variety)

Oxide
SiO$_2$

540

L

P

Named after its colour

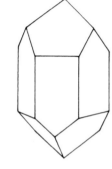

● Physical and chemical properties are identical to those of quartz **(534)**. It is a light yellow to golden-yellow colour, transparent to translucent, of vitreous lustre. Citrines are usually produced by heating amethysts **(536)** to approx. 450 °C; then they are called Madeira topaz, gold topaz, Bahia topaz or palmyra topaz ● Genesis: in pegmatites, hydrothermal ● Occurrence: rare; Cordoba and Salamanca (Spain), (France), Scotland (Great Britain), Murzinsk and the Urals (Russia), Goyaz, Bahia and Minas Gerais (Brazil), Pikes Peak – Colorado (USA), (Madagascar) ● Application: as a precious stone (facets, cabochons).

Sapphire quartz (Quartz variety)

Oxide
SiO$_2$

541

L

P

Named after its colour

● Physical and chemical properties are identical to those of quartz **(534)**. It is a blue colour because of inclusions of rutile **(464)** or crocidolite **(422)**; transparent to translucent ● Genesis: hydrothermal ● Associated minerals: amphibole **(411)**, rutile ● Occurrence: rare; Golling near Salzburg (Austria), (Scandinavia), Roseland – Virginia (USA) – in anorthosites, (RSA), (Brazil) ● Application: cut as a precious stone (cabochons, plastic cutting).

1. Morion (variety of smoky quartz) – crystal (18 mm) in marble; Monte Castelnovo (Italy) **2. Citrine** – druse of crystals (up to 15 mm); (Zimbabwe)

Morion, citrine

Tiger's eye (Quartz variety)

Oxide
SiO_2

542

L

P

Named after its characteristic colour and appearance

● A pseudomorph of quartz **(534)** and decomposed crocidolite **(422)**; of a characteristic yellow-brown or brown colour and silky lustre; translucent to opaque. Other properties are identical with those of quartz ● Occurrence: rare; in larger quantities it is found in (RSA), (India), (Mexico), (Western Australia) and California (USA) ● Application: cut as an ornamental and precious stone (cabochons, plates, plastic cutting, fancy goods).

Falcon's eye (Quartz variety)

Oxide
SiO_2

543

L

P

Named after its characteristic colour and appearance

● It is a pseudomorph of unweathered crocidolite **(422)**, which causes its fine bluish to black-blue colour and silky lustre. It is opaque ● Occurrence: rare; found in several areas in (RSA), (Australia), (Mexico) and (Sri Lanka); in Europe in the region of Salzburg (Austria) ● Application: used as an ornamental and precious stone (cabochons, plates, plastic cutting, fancy goods).

Cat's eye (Quartz variety)

Oxide
SiO_2

544

L

P

Named after its characteristic colour and appearance

● It is a pseudomorph of quartz **(534)** after amphibole **(411)**. It is a greenish-grey colour, translucent to opaque ● Occurrence: rare; in the region of Treseburg – small quantity, Bavaria and Fichtelgebirge – greenish crystals of rather poor quality (FRG), (Sri Lanka), (Burma), (Brazil), (India) ● Application: used as a precious stone (cabochons, plastic cutting).

Aventurine (Quartz variety)

Oxide
SiO_2

545

L

P

From the Italian *a ventura* – accidentally

● It is quartz with embedded lamellae of fuchsite **(166)** – green, or hematite **(472)** – reddish brown. It is translucent to opaque, sometimes exhibits red luminescence ● Occurrence: rare; stones of a good quality are found in (India), (Brazil), (Russia), (Spain) and Tibet (China). It is also found in Passo di Vizze (Italy). At the present time aventurines are produced artificially in large quantities (disseminated scales of copper in glass) ● Application: cut as a precious stone (cabochons, plates), as well as an ornamental stone (decorative articles, plastic cutting).

1. Falcon's eye – polished slice; Griqualand (RSA) **2. Aventurine** – polished slice; (India) **3. Tiger's eye** – polished slice; Griqualand (RSA – width of field 120 mm)

Falcon's eye, aventurine, tiger's eye

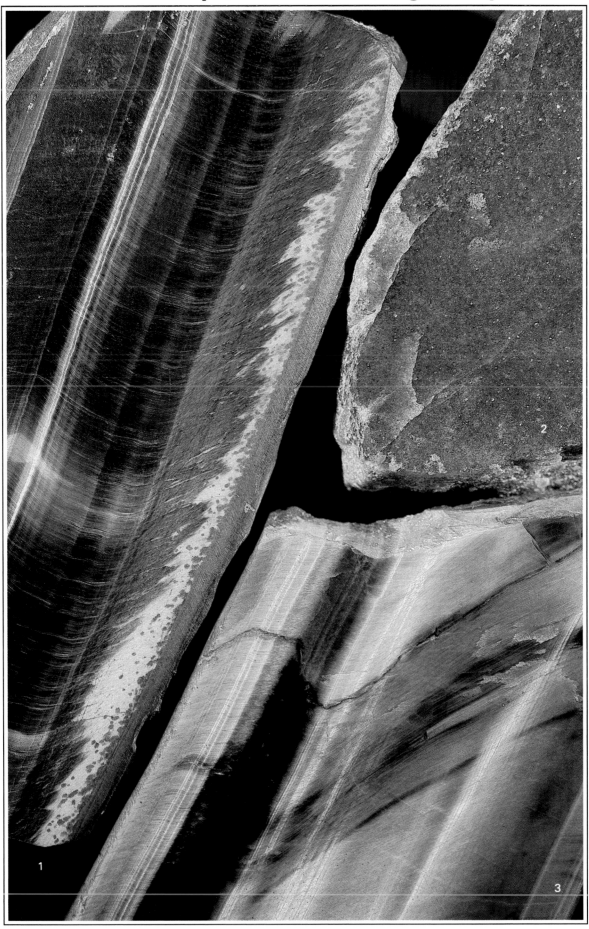

Pleonaste (Spinel variety)

Oxide
(Mg,Fe^{2+})(Al,Fe^{3+})$_2$O$_4$

546

From the Greek *pleon-asmós* – surplus (Haüy 1801)

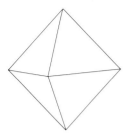

• Hardness: 7.5−8 (brittle) • Streak: white • Colour: dark green to black • Transparency: translucent to opaque • Lustre: vitreous • Cleavage: imperfect on (111) • Fracture: conchoidal • Morphology: crystals, granular aggregates • Specific gravity: 3.7−4.4 • Crystal system: cubic • Crystal form: octahedra • Chemical composition: MgO 10.78%, FeO 19.22%, Fe$_2$O$_3$ 42.72%, Al$_2$O$_3$ 27.28% • Chemical properties: insoluble in acids, infusible • Handling: clean with water and diluted acids • Similar minerals: magnetite **(367),** spinel **(590)** • Distinguishing features: magnetism, X-rays, chemical tests • Genesis: contact-metasomatic • Associated minerals: diopside **(505),** fassaite **(511)** • Occurrence: rare; Schwarzwald and Odenwald (FRG), Monzoni and Vesuvius (Italy), Routivare (Sweden), (Madagascar), (Japan), (Russia).

Hercynite

Oxide
FeAl$_2$O$_4$

547

From old Latin *Hercynia Silva* – forested mountains (Zippe 1839)

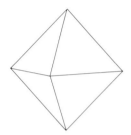

• Hardness: 7.5−8 • Streak: dark green • Colour: black • Transparency: opaque; in thin fragments exhibits dark green translucence • Lustre: vitreous • Cleavage: indistinct on (111) • Fracture: uneven, conchoidal • Morphology: crystals, granular aggregates • Specific gravity: 3.95 • Crystal system: cubic • Crystal form: octahedra • Chemical composition: FeO 41.34%, Al$_2$O$_3$ 58.66% • Chemical properties: in a blowpipe flame turns brick-red • Handling: clean with water and diluted acids • Similar minerals: magnetite **(367)** • Distinguishing features: hardness, magnetism • Genesis: magmatic • Associated minerals: titanomagnetites • Occurrence: rare; Schenkenzell (FRG), Routivare (Sweden), Poběžovice (Czech Republic), Veltlin (Italy), New York (USA).

Cassiterite (Tinstone)

Oxide
SnO$_2$

548

From the Greek *kassiteros* – tin (Beudant 1832)

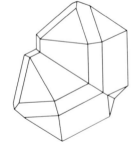

• Hardness: 7 (brittle) • Streak: white, yellow to light brown • Colour: brown, black, yellow to grey • Transparency: translucent to non-transparent • Lustre: adamantine, metallic • Cleavage: indistinct • Fracture: conchoidal • Morphology: crystals, granular and reniform aggregates, pseudomorphs, rolled grains • Specific gravity: 6.8−7.1 • Crystal system: tetragonal • Crystal form: prisms, dipyramids, needles, twinning • Chemical composition: Sn 78.6%, O 21.4% • Chemical properties: insoluble in acids, infusible • Handling: clean with water and diluted acids • Similar minerals: sphalerite **(181)** • Distinguishing features: hardness, specific gravity, solubility in acids • Genesis: pegmatitic, hydrothermal, secondary, in alluvial deposits • Associated minerals: fluorite **(291),** scheelite **(310),** wolframite **(369),** topaz **(595)** • Occurrence: widespread; Altenburg and Zinnwald (FRG), Horní Slavkov and Cínovec (Czech Republic), Cornwall (Great Britain), Brittany (France), (Russia), (USA), (Malaysia), (Thailand), (Bolivia), (Australia), (Mexico) • Application: Sn ore; sometimes used as a precious stone.

---

1. Pleonaste – crystals (up to 10 mm) embayed in quartz; Monzoni (Italy) **2. Cassiterite** – twin crystals (25 mm) with scheelite and zinnwaldite; Cínovec (Czech Republic)

Pleonaste, cassiterite

Boracite

Borate
$Mg_3B_7O_{13}Cl$

549

Named after its composition (Werner 1789)

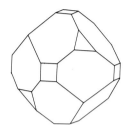

● Hardness: 7 (brittle) ● Streak: white ● Colour: colourless, white, grey, yellowish, greenish to bluish ● Transparency: transparent to translucent ● Lustre: vitreous, greasy ● Cleavage: absent ● Fracture: conchoidal ● Morphology: crystals, granular and fibrous aggregates, also cretaceous rocks (stassfurtite) ● Specific gravity: 2.9–3.0 ● Crystal system: dimorphic; below 268 °C orthorhombic, above 268 °C cubic ● Crystal form: cubes, tetrahedra, dodecahedra, twinning ● Chemical composition: MgO 29.8%, Cl 8.1%, B_2O_3 62.1%; admixtures: Ca, Fe ● Chemical properties: readily fusible into a white enamel ball, tinges a flame green, slowly dissolves in HCl ● Handling: clean quickly with distilled water ● Similar minerals: anhydrite **(235)** ● Distinguishing features: hardness ● Genesis: sedimentary (potash salt deposits) ● Associated minerals: gypsum **(29)**, carnallite **(84)**, anhydrite ● Occurrence: rare; Lüneburg, Hildesheim, Stassfurt and Westeregeln (FRG), Aislaby – Yorkshire (Great Britain), La Meurethe (France), Choctaw – Louisiana, and Otis – San Bernardino Co. – California (USA), Cristalmayu (Bolivia) ● Application: B source; production of boric acid.

Jeremejevite

Borate
$AlBO_3$

550

Named after the Russian mineralogist, P. V. Jeremejev (1830–1899) (Damour 1883)

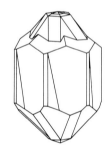

● Hardness: 7 ● Streak: white ● Colour: light yellow or bluish ● Transparency: transparent ● Lustre: vitreous ● Cleavage: absent ● Fracture: conchoidal ● Morphology: crystals ● Specific gravity: 3.31 ● Crystal system: hexagonal ● Crystal form: prisms ● Chemical composition: Al_2O_3 59.42%, B_2O_3 40.58% ● Similar minerals: beryl **(554)** ● Distinguishing features: hardness, specific gravity ● Genesis: in pegmatites ● Associated minerals: apatite **(379)**, albite **(493)**, tourmaline **(564)** ● Occurrence: rare; Soktuiberg, Adun-Chilon and Baikal – found in granite alluvium (Russia), Cape Cross – in pegmatites (Namibia) ● Application: mineralogically important; occasionally used as a precious stone (facets, cabochons).

1. Boracite – small crystals on gypsum; Schildstein (FRG – width of field 20 mm) **2. Jeremejevite** – disseminated elongated crystals (3 mm); Nerchinsk, Transbaikal (Russia)

Boracite, jeremejevite

Cordierite (Dichroite)

Silicate
$Mg_2Al_4Si_5O_{18}$

551

Named after the French mining engineer and geologist, P. L. A. Cordier (1777–1861) (Lukas 1813)

● Hardness: 7 (brittle) ● Streak: white ● Colour: blue, blue-green, grey to violet ● Transparency: transparent to translucent ● Lustre: vitreous, greasy ● Cleavage: good on (100) ● Fracture: conchoidal, uneven ● Morphology: crystals, granular and massive aggregates, rolled grains in alluvial deposits ● Specific gravity: 2.6 ● Crystal system: orthorhombic ● Crystal form: short prisms, twins ● Chemical composition: MgO 13.78%, Al_2O_3 34.86%, SiO_2 51.36% ● Chemical properties: insoluble in acids, almost infusible ● Handling: clean with water and diluted acids ● Similar minerals: quartz **(534)**, sekaninaite **(552)** ● Distinguishing features: solubility in HF, chemical tests (quartz) ● Genesis: metamorphic, magmatic, pegmatitic ● Associated minerals: tourmaline **(564)**, garnet **(577)**, spinel **(590)**, corundum **(598)** ● Occurrence: rare; Bodenmais, Wechselburg (FRG), Orijärvi (Finland), Kragerö (Norway), Cabo de Gata (Spain), Nävevsberg (Sweden), (Iceland), (Sri Lanka), (USA), (Brazil) ● Application: sometimes used as a precious stone (facets, cabochons).

Sekaninaite

Silicate
$Fe_2^{2+}Al_4Si_5O_{18}$

552

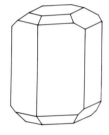

Named after the Czech mineralogist, J. Sekanina (1901–1986) (Staněk 1968)

● Hardness: 7–7.5 (brittle) ● Streak: white ● Colour: light blue to blue-violet ● Transparency: transparent to translucent ● Lustre: vitreous ● Cleavage: good on (100) ● Fracture: conchoidal, uneven ● Morphology: crystals ● Specific gravity: 2.77 ● Crystal system: orthorhombic ● Crystal form: prisms ● Chemical composition: FeO 22.18%, Al_2O_3 31.47%, SiO_2 46.35% ● Chemical properties: insoluble in acids, almost infusible ● Handling: clean with water or diluted acids ● Similar minerals: cordierite **(551)** ● Distinguishing features: X-rays, chemical tests ● Genesis: in pegmatites ● Associated minerals: orthoclase **(486)**, quartz **(534)**, tourmaline **(564)** ● Occurrence: rare; Dolní Bory (Czech Republic).

Kornerupine (Prismatine)

Silicate
$Mg_3Al_6(Si,Al,B)_5O_{21}(OH)$

553

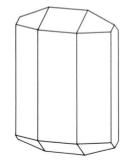

Named after the Danish geologist, A. N. Kornerup (1857–1881) (Lorenzen 1884)

● Hardness: 7 ● Streak: white ● Colour: white, brownish-yellow, green or brown ● Transparency: translucent to opaque ● Lustre: vitreous ● Cleavage: indistinct on (110) ● Morphology: crystals, rod-like to fibrous aggregates ● Specific gravity: 3.3 ● Crystal system: orthorhombic ● Crystal form: long prisms ● Chemical composition: variable ● Chemical properties: soluble only in HF, fuses with difficulty ● Handling: clean with water or diluted acids ● Similar minerals: andalusite **(562)** ● Distinguishing features: X-rays, chemical tests ● Genesis: metamorphic, alluvial deposits ● Associated minerals: biotite **(167)**, orthoclase **(486)**, cordierite **(551)** ● Occurrence: rare; Waldheim (FRG), Fiskernäs (Greenland), Betroka (Madagascar), (Canada), (Kenya), Sri Lanka), (Tanzania) ● Application: sometimes used as a precious stone (facets, cabochons).

---

1. **Sekaninaite** – columnar crystal with orthoclase; Dolní Bory (Czech Republic) 2. **Cordierite** – granular aggregate; Jihlava (Czech Republic) 3. **Kornerupine** – prismatic crystals embedded in granite; Waldheim (FRG – width of field 60 mm)

Sekaninaite, cordierite, kornerupine

H
7—8

435

From the Greek *beryllos* – precious stones of the blue-green colour of sea water (according to the Roman naturalist, Pliny)

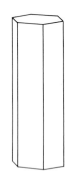

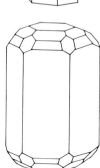

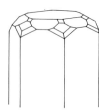

● Hardness: 7.5–8 (brittle) ● Streak: white ● Colour: colourless, white, yellowish-white, yellowish-green, green, rose, bluish, blue-green, red, golden-yellow ● Transparency: transparent to translucent ● Lustre: vitreous, dull ● Cleavage: indistinct on (0001) ● Fracture: uneven, conchoidal ● Morphology: crystals, granular, compact and radiating-fibrous aggregates (known as beryl suns), grains ● Specific gravity: 2.63–2.80 ● Crystal system: hexagonal ● Crystal form: prisms, occasionally platy ● Luminescence: sometimes green and yellow ● Chemical composition: BeO 13.96%, Al_2O_3 18.97%, SiO_2 67.07%; admixtures: Fe, Mn, Mg, Ca, Cr, Na, Li, Cs, OH ● Chemical properties: soluble in HF, infusible, when heated colourless varieties turn milky-white, emeralds form a light green bead ● Handling: clean with diluted acids, except HF ● Similar minerals: apatite **(379)**, tourmaline **(564)**, topaz **(595)** ● Distinguishing features: hardness, specific gravity, optical properties, X-rays, chemical tests ● Genesis: in pegmatites, hydrothermal-pneumatolytic, metamorphic ● Associated minerals: orthoclase **(486)**, quartz **(534)**, cassiterite **(548)**, tourmaline, topaz ● Occurrence: rare; in pegmatites: Zwiesel, Ehrenfriedensdorf (FRG), Horní Slavkov, Písek and Meclov (Czech Republic), Keystone – South Dakota – crystals measuring 9 m and weighing up to 61 tons (USA), Picui – crystals weighing 200 tons (Brazil); Chanteloube (France), Iveland (Norway), Melville (Australia), Haddam – Connecticut (USA) ● Application: Be source; in ancient times cut as lenses and used as spectacles (emerald lenses of the Emperor Nero); at present used in the production of light alloys; several of its varieties are cut as gem stones (facets, cabochons).

According to their colour and chemical composition beryls may be divided into the following varieties:

common beryl (most widely found) – Be source;

emerald **(555)** – emerald-green precious stone;

aquamarine **(556)** – blue-green and light blue precious stone;

morganite **(557)** – rose precious stone;

vorobjevite – rose to rosy-red precious stone;

golden beryl **(558)** – golden-yellow precious stone;

heliodor **(559)** – yellow to light yellowish-green precious stone;

goshenite **(560)** – transparent, colourless precious stone;

bixbite – red precious stone;

bazzite **(561)** – blue Sc beryl.

Beryl – columnar crystal (40 mm) embedded in pegmatite; Maršíkov (Czech Republic)

Beryl

Beryl

Emerald (Beryl variety)

555

L

P

Historical name, probably of Semitic origin

● Physical and chemical properties are identical to those of beryl **(554)**. It is an emerald-green colour with the admixture of Cr_2O_3, transparent to translucent ● Occurrence: rare; Habachtal (Austria), Eidsvold (Norway), Takovaya River – Central Urals (Russia), Zabarah (Egypt), Muzo and Chivor (Colombia), Sandawan (Zimbabwe), Gravelotte (RSA), Alto Ligonha (Mozambique); Lake Manjara (Tanzania), Carnaiba (Brazil), (India), (Pakistan), (Australia), (Zambia), (USA) ● Application: since ancient times used as one of the most valued of gem stones (facets, cabochons).

Aquamarine (Beryl variety)

556

L

P

From the Latin *aqua* – water, *marina* – marine (Wallerius 1747)

● Physical and chemical properties are similar to those of beryl **(554)**. It is a light blue to blue-green colour, transparent to translucent ● Occurrence: more frequent than emerald **(555)**; Mourne Mountains (Northern Ireland), Elba (Italy), Murzinsk, Takovaya River, Shaitansk Hills, Adun-Chilon and Baikal (Russia), Rössing and Kl. Spitzkopje (Namibia), Marambaya and Minas Gerais (Brazil) – in 1910 a crystal was found here measuring 48.5 cm long and weighing 110.5 kg, (Madagascar), (Zimbabwe), (Tanzania), (Kenya), (Sri Lanka), (India), (Burma), California, Colorado, Connecticut and Maine (USA), (Australia), (Pakistan), (Afghanistan) ● Application: used as a precious stone (facets, cabochons).

Morganite (Beryl variety)

557

L

P

Named after the American collector and financier, J. P. Morgan (1837–1913) (Kunz 1911)

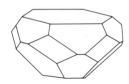

● Physical and chemical properties are similar to those of beryl **(554)**. It is a rose to rosy-red colour, transparent to translucent, sometimes exhibiting violet luminescence ● Occurrence: rare; in pegmatites in Maharitra (Madagascar), Ramona and Pala Chief – California (USA), Minas Gerais (Brazil), (Mozambique), (Zimbabwe), (Russia). In the Urals (Russia) rose beryls have been found containing up to 3.1% Cs_2O and 1.39% Li_2O. They are named after the Russian mineralogist V. I. Vorobev ● Application: used as a precious stone (facets, cabochons).

---

1. **Emerald** – columnar crystal (20 mm); Muzo (Colombia) 2. **Aquamarine** – prismatic crystal (25 mm) embedded in quartz; Minas Gerais (Brazil) 3. **Morganite** – crystal (15 mm) on albite; San Piero in Campo (Italy)

Emerald, aquamarine, morganite

Golden beryl (Beryl variety)

Silicate
$Al_2Be_3Si_6O_{18}$

558

L

P

Named after its colour

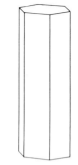

● Physical and chemical properties are identical to those of beryl **(554)**. It is a golden-yellow to lemon-yellow colour – its colour often resembles heliodor, transparent to translucent ● Occurrence: seldom in pegmatites; Minas Gerais (Brazil), (Sri Lanka), Otavi and Rossing, (Namibia); especially remarkable are dark brown beryls from Governador Valadares and Minas Gerais (Brazil), exhibiting bronze lustre and golden asterism ● Application: used as a precious stone (facets, cabochons).

Heliodor (Beryl variety)

Silicate
$Al_2Be_3Si_6O_{18}$

559

L

P

From the Greek *dóron* – gift and *hélion* – sun (Pranach 1910)

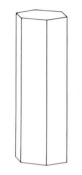

● Physical and chemical properties are identical to those of beryl **(554)**. It is yellow with a green or honey-yellow tint; transparent to translucent; bluish luminescence ● Occurrence: occasionally in pegmatites; in pneumatolytic-hydrothermal deposits; Nerchinsk (Russia), Otavi and Rossing (Namibia), Santa Maria do Suaçui and Minas Gerais (Brazil), (Madagascar) ● Application: cut as a precious stone (facets, cabochons) ● A remarkable red beryl was found in vesicles in rhyolite lavas in the Thomas Mountains – Utah (USA) in association with tridymite **(461)**, hematite **(472)**, spessartine **(584)** and topaz **(595)**. It is called bixbyite.

Goshenite (Beryl variety)

Silicate
$Al_2Be_3Si_6O_{18}$

560

Named after its locality Goshen (Massachusetts, USA) (Shepard 1844)

● Physical and chemical properties are similar to those of beryl **(554)**. It is colourless to white, transparent, of gem quality ● Occurrence: rare; Goshen – Massachusetts – in pegmatites (USA), (Brazil) ● Application: cut as a precious stone (facets).

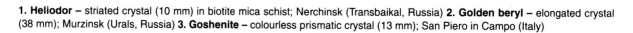

1. Heliodor – striated crystal (10 mm) in biotite mica schist; Nerchinsk (Transbaikal, Russia) **2. Golden beryl** – elongated crystal (38 mm); Murzinsk (Urals, Russia) **3. Goshenite** – colourless prismatic crystal (13 mm); San Piero in Campo (Italy)

Heliodor, golden beryl, goshenite

Bazzite

Silicate
Sc$_2$Be$_3$Si$_6$O$_{18}$

561

Named after the Italian engineer, A. E. Bazzi (Artini 1915)

● Bazzite is the scandium analogue of beryl **(554)**, having many physical and chemical properties in common. It is a blue to dark blue colour, rarely colourless; of a slightly lower hardness than beryl (6.5) ● Occurrence: very rare; in pegmatites and in alpine veins; Val Strem, St. Gotthard (Switzerland), Baveno, Lake Maggiore (Italy) – in fissures in granite, (Kazakhstan).

Andalusite

Silicate
Al$_2$SiO$_5$

562

Named after its locality in Andalusia (Spain) (Delametherie 1789)

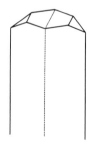

● Hardness: 7.5 (brittle) ● Streak: white ● Colour: grey, reddish-grey, brown, green, pinkish ● Transparency: transparent, translucent or opaque ● Lustre: vitreous, greasy, dull ● Cleavage: good on (110) ● Fracture: uneven ● Morphology: crystals, granular, compact, rodlike, radiating-fibrous aggregates, pebbles in alluvial deposits ● Specific gravity: 3.1–3.2 ● Crystal system: orthorhombic ● Crystal form: prisms ● Luminescence: green, yellow-green ● Chemical composition: Al$_2$O$_3$ 62.93%, SiO$_2$ 37.07%; admixture: Mn (viridine variety). Andalusite, containing inclusions of carbonaceous substances and exhibiting a characteristic cruciform dark core, is called chiastolite **(563)** ● Chemical properties: infusible, insoluble in acids ● Handling: clean with water and diluted acids ● Similar minerals: tourmaline **(564)** ● Distinguishing features: X-rays, chemical tests ● Genesis: metamorphic, in pegmatites ● Associated minerals: rutile **(464)**, quartz **(534)**, tourmaline, garnet **(577)** ● Occurrence: common; rock-forming mineral in gneiss, in mica schists, in pegmatites, in hornstones and in alluvial ore deposits; Wunsiedel, Neualbenreuth and Bergen (FRG), Lisenz-Alpe and the Tyrol (Austria), (Spain), Dolní Bory – in pegmatites (Czech Republic), Murzinsk – Urals (Russia), Standish – Maine (USA), Mt. Howden (Australia), Darmstadt – viridine variety (FRG). Andalusites from USA (California) and Brazil are of gem quality ● Application: fire and acid-proof materials; sometimes used as a precious stone (facets, cabochons).

Chiastolite (Andalusite variety)

Silicate
Al$_2$SiO$_5$

563

From the Greek *chiastos* – cruciform (Karsten 1800)

● Physical and chemical properties are similar to those of andalusite **(562)**. It is a yellow or brownish to black colour, opaque, forms characteristic cruciform inclusions on cross sections of crystal prisms ● Occurrence: rare; in metamorphic clay schists; Gefrees (FRG), Santiago de Compostela (Spain), La Carolina (France), Lancaster (Great Britain), Mankova (Russia), Bona (Algeria) ● Application: sometimes used as a precious stone (cabochons).

---

1. Bazzite – deformed crystal embedded in carbonate; Pibia (Switzerland) **2. Andalusite** – columnar crystal (20 mm); Mt. Howden (Australia) **3. Chiastolite** – polished cross section (30 mm); Lancaster (Great Britain)

Bazzite, andalusite, chiastolite

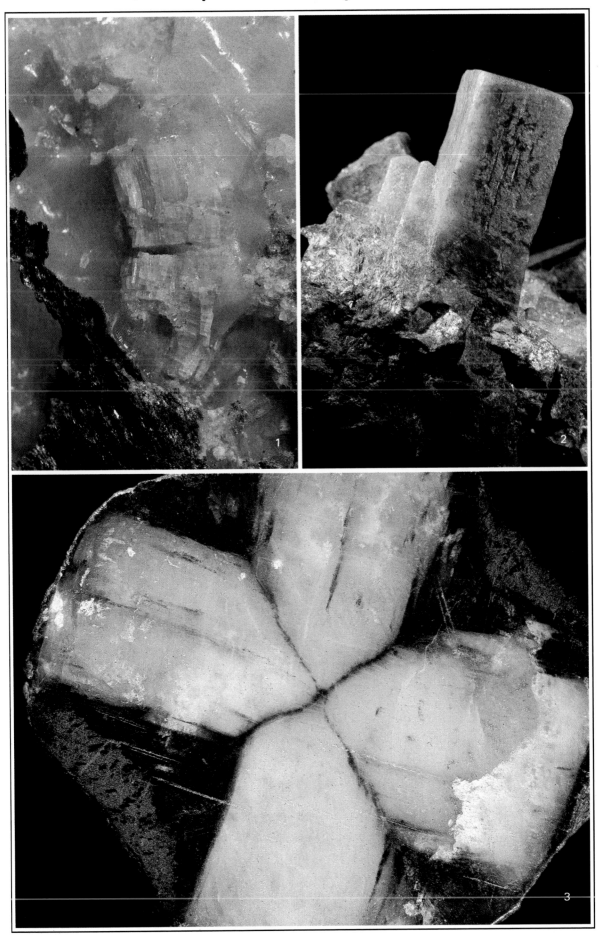

443

Tourmaline group

564

Historical name, from the Sinhalese *turmali* – special stones brought to Europe from Ceylon

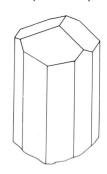

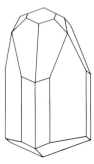

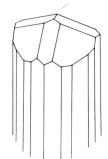

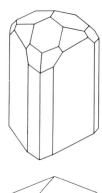

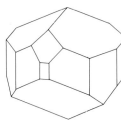

● Hardness: 7–7.5 (brittle) ● Streak: white ● Colour: black – schorl **(565)**; brown to brownish-green and brownish-black – dravite **(566)** or uvite **(572)**; rose to rosy-red – rubellite **(569)**; blue to blue-green – indicolite **(570)**; green – verdelite **(571)**; colourless – achroite **(568)**. Some tourmaline crystals are multi-coloured in cross or longitudinal sections ● Transparency: transparent to translucent to opaque ● Lustre: vitreous ● Cleavage: indistinct on $(10\bar{1}1)$ ● Fracture: uneven, conchoidal ● Morphology: crystals, granular, compact, radiating fibrous aggregates, often forming the characteristic *tourmaline suns* ● Other properties: when heated and rubbed, positive and negative electrical charges develop at the opposite ends of the tourmaline prisms ● Specific gravity: 2.9–3.2 ● Crystal system: trigonal ● Crystal form: prisms, needles ● Luminescence: yellow, green ● Electric properties: pyro-electric and piezo-electric ● Chemical composition: very variable, see below; admixtures: Mg, Fe^{3+}, Mn, Ca, sometimes also Ti, Cr, V, Li ● Chemical properties: dependent on their composition they are either fusible (poor in Fe and rich in Mg) or infusible; insoluble in acids ● Handling: clean with water and diluted acids ● Similar minerals: amphibole **(411)**, actinolite **(413)**, riebeckite **(421)**, ilvaite **(425)**, beryl **(554)**, andalusite **(562)** ● Distinguishing features: hardness, cleavage, specific gravity, X-rays, chemical properties ● Genesis: magmatic: in pegmatites; metamorphic: in alpine veins; hydrothermal ● Associated minerals: apatite **(379)**, orthoclase **(486)**, quartz **(534)**, beryl, topaz **(595)** ● Occurrence: common; widely found rock-forming minerals (granites, diorites, syenites, granulites); in contact-metamorphic deposits, in metamorphic rocks, sedimentary rocks ● Application: in electrotechnics; stones of good colour are used as gems.

The tourmaline family includes the following minerals:

elbaite – $Na(Li, Al)_3Al_6(BO_3)_3Si_6O_{18}(OH)_4$

Colour varieties:

achroite – colourless, sometimes with greenish or black terminations of crystals

rubellite – rose to rosy-red

indigolite – blue to blue-green

verdelite – green to dark green

dravite – $NaMg_3Al_6(BO_3)_3Si_6O_{18}(OH)_4$

schorl – $NaFe_3^{2+}(Al,Fe^{3+})_6(BO_3)_3Si_6O_{18}(OH)_4$

buergerite – $NaFe_3^{3+}Al_6(BO_3)_3Si_6O_{21}F$

tsilaisite – $NaMn_3Al_6(BO_3)_3Si_6O_{18}(OH)_4$

uvite – $CaMg_3(Al_5Mg)(BO_3)_3Si_6O_{18}(OH)_4$

liddicoatite – $Ca(Li,Al)_3Al_6(BO_3)_3Si_6O_{18}(OH)_4$

Tourmaline – elongated crystal (29 mm) of elbaite; Elba (Italy)

Schorl

Silicate
$NaFe_3^{2+}(Al,Fe^{3+})_6(BO_3)_3Si_6O_{18}(OH)_4$

565

L

P

Old name of unknown origin
(Mathesius 1524)

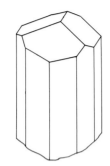

● Physical and chemical properties are similar to those of tourmaline **(564)**. It is a black colour, occasionally in brown, greenish-black or blue-black fragments, opaque ● Similar mineral: dravite **(566)** ● Occurrence: most widely found mineral of the tourmaline family; occurs in granites, diorites, gabbros, gneisses, greisens, skarns and quartz veins. In pegmatites it frequently forms large, fine crystals; Sonnenberg, Bodenmais and Spessart (FRG), Dolní Bory and Písek (Czech Republic); Arendal and Kragerö (Norway) – crystals up to 5 m, Skrumpetorp (Sweden), Spittal and St. Leonhard (Austria), Campolungo (Switzerland), Namib (Namibia), (Madagascar), (Australia), (Brazil), (USA), (Canada) ● Application: electronics.

Dravite

Silicate
$NaMg_3Al_6(BO_3)_3Si_6O_{18}(OH)_4$

566

L

P

Named after the Drava River (Austria – Drau)
(Tschermak 1883)

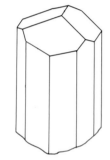

● Physical and chemical properties are similar to those of tourmaline **(564)**. It is a brown, brownish-green to brownish-black colour, but rarely yellow, dark red or grey-blue; transparent to translucent to opaque ● Similar minerals: schorl **(565)**, buergerite and uvite **(572)** ● Occurrence: rare; Unterdrauburg and Zillertal (Austria), Eibenstock (FRG), Urals, Transbaikal (Russia), (Turkmenistan), Governer – New York, Pennsylvania and Texas (USA), (Australia – large crystals), Osarora – dark red crystals in quartzites (Kenya); chromium dravites are found in Shabrakh – Urals (Russia) ● Application: occasionally used as a precious stone (facets).

Elbaite

Silicate
$Na(Li,Al)_3Al_6(BO_3)_3Si_6O_{18}(OH)_4$

567

L

P

Named after the island of Elba (Italy)
(Vernadski 1913)

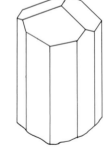

● Physical and chemical properties are similar to those of tourmaline **(564)**. It is a variety of colours, sometimes colourless with green to black terminations of crystals (achroite variety – **568**), rose to rosy-red (rubellite variety – **569**), blue to blue-green (indicolite variety – **570**), green to dark green (verdelite variety – **571**) and multi-coloured. Transparent to translucent ● Similar minerals: liddicoatite from Madagascar and tsilaisite ● Occurrence: rare; Elba (Italy), (Czech Republic), (Kazakhstan), Transbaikal and the Urals (Russia), (USA), (Brazil), (Madagascar), (Mozambique) ● Application: sometimes cut as a precious stone (facets, cabochons).

---

1. Schorl – columnar crystal (27 mm) embedded in albite; Dolní Bory (Czech Republic) **2. Dravite** – elongated crystal (20 mm) in muscovite; Dobrova (Slovenia) **3. Elbaite** – group of crystals 'Moor's heads' (the largest 21 mm) on albite and quartz; San Piero in Campo (Italy)

Schorl, dravite, elbaite

Achroite (Elbaite variety)

Silicate
$Na(Li,Al)_3Al_6(BO_3)_3Si_6O_{18}(OH)_4$

568

From the Greek *achroos* – colourless (Hermann 1845)

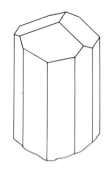

● Physical and chemical properties are similar to those of tourmaline **(564)**. It is a colourless variety of elbaite **(567),** rarely with a greenish tint or black end faces of crystals, which are called Moor's heads. Some dravites may be a similar colour. It is transparent, sometimes exhibiting a dark violet luminescence ● Occurrence: rare; in pegmatites; Elba (Italy), (Kazakhstan), Urals (Russia), (Afghanistan – in the vicinity of Dzhalalabad), Moravia (Czech Republic) ● Application: sometimes used as a precious stone (facets, cabochons).

Rubellite (Elbaite variety)

Silicate
$Na(Li,Al)_3Al_6(BO_3)_3Si_6O_{18}(OH)_4$

569

From the Latin *rubellus* – reddish (Kirwan 1794)

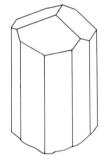

● Physical and chemical properties are identical to those of tourmaline **(564)**. It is a rose, rosy-red or red colour, but occasionally violet. Transparent to translucent. Tsilaisite and liddicoatite are a similar colour ● Occurrence: rare; in pegmatites in association with lepidolite **(169),** albite **(493)** and microcline **(490)** in San Piero (Elba, Italy); in pegmatites in Sušice, Dobrá Voda and Rožná (Czech Republic), Penig (FRG), Shaitansk, Urals, Lipovka, Murzinsk, Zolotaya Gora and Transbaikal (Russia) – red rubellites from Siberia are called Siberian rubies, Chesterfield – Massachusetts, Paris – Maine, Mesa Grande, Ramona and Pala in San Diego Co. – California (USA); fine crystals are found in pegmatites in Alto Ligonha (Mozambique), Otjimbingwe (Namibia), (Madagascar), Minas Gerais (Brazil). Many-coloured elbaites are of different colours, displaying predominantly rose, green, blue and yellow stripes in their cross or longitudinal sections. They are found in Italy, Mozambique, Madagascar and the USA. A special type of colouring shows black crystals with red end faces, which are called Turkish heads ● Application: cut as a precious stone (facets, cabochons).

---

1. Achroite – crystal (10 mm) on albite; San Piero in Campo (Italy) **2. Rubellite** – sun (diameter 70 mm); Pala Chief, San Diego Co. (California, USA)

Achroite, rubellite

Indicolite (Elbaite variety)

Silicate
$Na(Li,Al)_3Al_6(BO_3)_3Si_6O_{18}(OH)_4$

570

L

P

Named after its indigo-blue colour
(d'Andrada 1800)

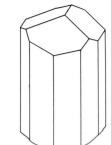

● Physical and chemical properties are identical to those of tourmaline **(564)**. It is a light blue, green-blue to dark blue colour, transparent to translucent. Also dravite, schorl and tsilaisite may be of a similar bluish colour ● Occurrence: rare; in pegmatites in Utö (Sweden), Murzinsk, Urals (Russia), Rožná (Czech Republic), Goshen – Massachusetts (USA), Minas Gerais (Brazil), Usacosa (Namibia), (Congo), (Mozambique), (Sri Lanka) – ain alluvial deposits ● Application: cut as a precious stone (facets, cabochons).

Verdelite (Elbaite variety)

Silicate
$Na(Li,Al)_3Al_6(BO_3)_3Si_6O_{18}(OH)_4$

571

L

P

From the Latin *verde* – green
(Quensel, Gabrielson 1939)

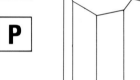

● Physical and chemical properties are identical to those of tourmaline **(564)**. It is a green to dark green colour, transparent to translucent. Also dravite, schorl, buergerite and tsilaisite may be a green-black, green-brown or green colour. These minerals may be distinguished only by a detailed mineralogical investigation ● Occurrence: rare; in pegmatites in: Penig (FRG), Varuträsk (Sweden), Rožná (Czech Republic), Murzinsk, Urals (Russia), (Kazakhstan), (Namibia), (Brazil) – Brazilian emeralds, Maine (USA) ● Application: cut as a precious stone (facets, cabochons).

Uvite

Silicate
$CaMg_3(Al_5Mg)(BO_3)_3Si_6O_{18}(OH)_4$

572

L

P

Named after the province Uva, (Sri Lanka)
(Kunitz 1920)

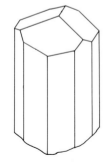

● Physical and chemical properties are similar to those of tourmaline **(564)**. It is a yellowish-brown, brown to black-brown colour, occasionally blue-black, translucent to opaque. It contains more Mg and Ca than Al. Crystals are mostly small ● Similar minerals: dravite and buergerite ● Occurrence: rare; in pegmatites and scarns; Hnúšťa (Slovakia), Palabikha, Transbaikal and South Yakutia (Russia), Uva (Sri Lanka), Essex – New York (USA), Renfrew Co. – Ontario (Canada), (China) ● Application: occasionally used as a precious stone.

1. **Indicolite** – columnar crystals (7 mm) with lepidolite; Rožná (Czech Republic) 2. **Verdelite** – crystal (15 mm) grown on albite; San Piero in Campo (Italy) 3. **Uvite** – fan-shaped aggregate; Hnúšťa (Slovakia – width of field 13 mm)

Indicolite, verdelite, uvite

Danburite

Silicate
CaB$_2$Si$_2$O$_8$

573

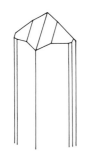

Named after its locality in Danbury (Connecticut, USA) (Shepard 1839)

● Hardness: 7–7.5 ● Streak: white ● Colour: colourless, white, yellowish, brown, grey ● Transparency: transparent to translucent ● Lustre: vitreous, greasy ● Cleavage: very indistinct on (001) ● Fracture: conchoidal, uneven ● Morphology: crystals, granular and compact aggregates ● Specific gravity: 2.9–3.0 ● Crystal system: orthorhombic ● Crystal form: prisms ● Luminescence: sometimes bluish, green-blue ● Chemical composition: CaO 22.8%, B$_2$O$_3$ 28.4%, SiO$_2$ 48.8% ● Chemical properties: readily fusible, tinges a flame green, soluble in acids ● Handling: clean with distilled water ● Similar minerals: datolite **(407)**, topaz **(595)** ● Distinguishing features: hardness, specific gravity, X-rays, chemical properties ● Genesis: contact-metamorphic, in pegmatites, greisens (pneumatolytic) ● Associated minerals: calcite **(217)**, dolomite **(218)**, augite **(429)**, tourmaline **(564)** ● Occurrence: rare; Piz Valatscha (Switzerland), Maglovec (Slovakia), Dalnegorsk (Russia), Danbury – Connecticut and Russell – New York (USA), Obira (Japan), Maharitra (Madagascar), Charcas (Mexico) ● Application: sometimes used as a gemstone (facets, cabochons).

Euclase

Silicate
AlBeSiO$_4$(OH)

574

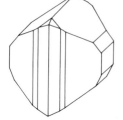

From the Greek *eu* – well and *klásis* – breaking (Haüy 1792)

● Hardness: 7.5 (brittle) ● Streak: white ● Colour: colourless, white, light green, bluish ● Transparency: transparent to translucent ● Lustre: vitreous to adamantine ● Cleavage: perfect on (010) ● Fracture: conchoidal ● Morphology: crystals, grains, radial aggregates ● Specific gravity: 3.0–3.1 ● Crystal system: monoclinic ● Crystal form: prisms with vertical striation ● Luminescence: sometimes dark red ● Chemical composition: BeO 17.28%, Al$_2$O$_3$ 35.18%, SiO$_2$ 41.34%, H$_2$O 6.20%; admixture: Zn ● Chemical properties: fuses with difficulty into white enamel, insoluble in acids ● Handling: clean with water or diluted acids ● Similar minerals: achroite **(568)**, topaz **(595)** ● Distinguishing features: cleavage, X-rays ● Genesis: hydrothermal, in alpine cracks, in pegmatites, in alluvial deposits ● Associated minerals: albite **(493)**, beryl **(554)**, phenakite **(597)** ● Occurrence: rare; Epprechstein, Dobschütz (FRG), Hocharn (Austria), Sanarka River – Urals – in alluvial deposits (Russia), Boa Vista and Villa Rica (Brazil), (Congo), (Tanzania), (India), (Zimbabwe) ● Application: sometimes used as a gemstone (facets, cabochons).

---

1. Danburite – columnar crystal (10 mm) with longitudinal striation embedded in quartz; Charcas (Mexico) **2. Euclase** – druse of crystals (the largest 6 mm); Minas Gerais (Brazil)

Danburite, euclase

Dumortierite

Silicate
Al$_7$BSi$_3$O$_{18}$

575

L

P

Named after the French palaeontologist, M. E. Dumortier (1802–1873) (Gonnard 1881)

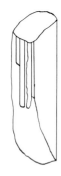

● Hardness: 7 ● Streak: bluish-white, white ● Colour: red-violet, blue, green ● Transparency: translucent ● Lustre: silky ● Cleavage: good on (100) ● Fracture: absent ● Morphology: crystals, fibrous, fan-shaped and radiating aggregates ● Specific gravity: 3.3–3.4 ● Crystal system: orthorhombic ● Crystal form: prisms, needles ● Luminescence: sometimes blue-white, violet ● Chemical composition: Al$_2$O$_3$ 62.39%, B$_2$O$_3$ 6.09%, SiO$_2$ 31.52% ● Chemical properties: infusible, when heated turns white ● Handling: clean with water or diluted acids, except HF ● Similar minerals: kyanite **(435)**, tourmaline **(564)** ● Distinguishing features: specific gravity, optical properties, X-rays ● Genesis: in pegmatites, pneumatolytic, metamorphic rocks ● Associated minerals: kyanite, cordierite **(551)**, andalusite **(562)**, tourmaline ● Occurrence: rare; in granite-aplites in Schwarzwald (FRG), Beaune (France), Kutná Hora (Czech Republic), Giant Mountains (Poland), Harlem – New York, Clip – Arizona, Madish – Montana and Riverside – California (USA), Minas Gerais (Brazil), (Madagascar), (Namibia), (India), (Kazakhstan), (Armenia), Yakutia (Russia), Aberdeen – Scotland (Great Britain), (Bulgaria), Nabekura (Japan) ● Application: insulators; ceramics; sometimes used as a gemstone (cabochons).

Sapphirine

Silicate
Mg$_{3.5}$Al$_{4.5}$(Al$_{4.5}$Si$_{1.5}$)O$_{20}$

576

P

Named after its colour (Giesecke 1819)

● Hardness: 7.5 ● Streak: white ● Colour: light blue, bluish, greenish-grey to dark green ● Transparency: transparent ● Lustre: vitreous ● Cleavage: perfect on (010) ● Fracture: uneven ● Morphology: crystals, grains, granular aggregates ● Specific gravity: 3.46–3.49 ● Crystal system: monoclinic ● Crystal form: plates ● Chemical composition: MgO 20.44%, Al$_2$O$_3$ 66.50%, SiO$_2$ 13.06%; admixture: Fe ● Chemical properties: infusible, insoluble in acids, readily soluble in KHSO$_4$ ● Handling: clean with water and diluted acids ● Similar minerals: lazulite **(378)**, kyanite **(435)** ● Distinguishing features: hardness, specific gravity, solubility in acids, X-rays, chemical properties ● Genesis: metamorphic, magmatic ● Associated minerals: kornerupine **(553)**, spinel **(590)**, corundum **(598)** ● Occurrence: rare; Waldheim (FRG), Snaresund (Norway), Lerc (France), Val Codera (Italy), Fiskernäs (Greenland), Gangurvapatti (India), Betroka (Madagascar), Transvaal (RSA), St. Urbain – Quebec (Canada), Peekskill – New York (USA), MacRobertson (Antarctic), (Greece) ● Application: sometimes used as a gemstone (facets, cabochons).

---

1. Dumortierite – radiating fibrous aggregate (needles 30 mm); Dehesa (USA) **2. Sapphirine** – crystalline aggregate in muscovite; Betroka (Madagascar – width of field 20 mm)

Dumortierite, sapphirine

Garnet group

577

Historical name, from the Latin *granatum malum* – garnet apple (Magnus 1250)

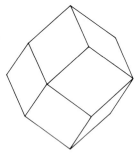

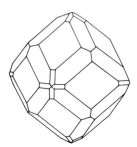

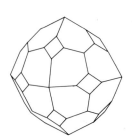

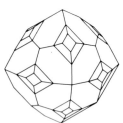

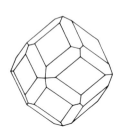

● Hardness: 6.5–7.5 (brittle) ● Streak: white or lightly coloured shades ● Colour: colourless, white, rose, light green, hyacinth-red, red-violet, dark red, dark green to emerald-green, brown, yellowish-brown, brownish-red or black ● Transparency: translucent to opaque ● Lustre: vitreous, greasy, silky ● Cleavage: very indistinct on (110) ● Fracture: uneven, conchoidal, splintery ● Morphology: crystals, granular, compact aggregates, pebbles, grains in alluvial deposits ● Specific gravity: 3.4–4.6 ● Crystal system: cubic ● Crystal form: rhombododecahedra, hexaoctahedra ● Chemical composition: variable, forms continuous isomorphous series of the following elements: Mg, Fe, Ca, Al, Cr, V, Mn, Ti, Zr, Y, etc.

According to the dominant elements in their chemical composition, garnets are classified as follows:

Al garnets: pyrope **(578)** $Mg_3Al_2(SiO_4)_3$

grossularite **(582)** $Ca_3Al_2(SiO_4)_3$

hessonite **(583)** $Ca_3Al_2(SiO_4)_3$

spessartite **(584)** $Mn_3Al_2(SiO_4)_3$

almandine **(585)** $Fe_3Al_2(SiO_4)_3$

Fe garnets: andradite **(579)** $Ca_3Fe_2^{3+}(SiO_4)_3$

demantoid **(580)** $Ca_3Fe_2^{3+}(SiO_4)_3$

majorite $Mg_3(Fe,Si)_2(SiO_4)_3$

calderite $Mn_3Fe_2(SiO_4)_3$

skiagite $Fe_3^{2+}fe_2^{3+}(SiO_4)_3$

Cr garnets: uvarovite **(581)** $Ca_3Cr_2(SiO_4)_3$

knorringite $(Ca,Mg)_3Cr_2(SiO_4)_3$

V garnets: goldmanite $Ca_3V_2^{3+}(SiO_4)_3$

yamatoite $Mn_3V_2(SiO_4)_3$

Zr garnets: kimzeyite $Ca_3Zr_2Al_2SiO_{12}$

● Chemical properties: apart from Cr garnets, they are easily fusible; when melted, soluble in acids (except andradite) ● Handling: clean with water or diluted acid ● Similar minerals: sphalerite **(181)**, leucite **(396)**, eudialite **(402)**, spinel **(590)**, ruby **(599)** ● Distinguishing features: hardness, specific gravity, cleavage, solubility in acids, X-rays ● Genesis: magmatic, pegmatitic, metamorphic, contact-metasomatic, in alluvial doposits ● Associated minerals: chlorite **(158)**, biotite **(167)**, feldspars, quartz **(534)** ● Occurrence: common; seldom in magmatic rocks, more frequent in pegmatites, especially in contact-metasomatic rocks on contact with acidic, magmatic rocks with carbonates. They are often found in crystalline schists and alluvial deposits, concentrated in the course of the weathering processes ● Application: sometimes used as gemstones (facets, cabochons); and in cutting, grinding and drilling tools.

Garnet – druse of crystals of spessartite (5 mm) on muscovite; Italy

Garnet

Pyrope (Garnet variety)

Silicate
$Mg_3Al_2(SiO_4)_3$

578

From the Greek *pyropos* – similar to fire (Werner 1800)

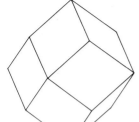

● Physical and chemical properties are similar to those of garnet **(577)**. It is a dark red, violet-red to black-red colour, transparent to translucent, known by the name of Bohemian garnet ● Occurrence: magmatic in ultrabasic rocks, in diamond deposits, in alluvial deposits; Zöblitz (FRG), Třebenice, Měrunice and Podsedlice (Czech Republic), (RSA), (Australia), (Sri Lanka), Siberia (Russia), Utah, New Mexico and Arkansas (USA) ● Application: cutting, grinding and drilling tools; as a precious stone (facets, cabochons, tumbling).

Andradite (Garnet variety)

Silicate
$Ca_3Fe_2^{3+}(SiO_4)_3$

579

Named after the Brazilian mineralogist, J. B. d'Andrada e Silva (1763–1838) (Dana 1868)

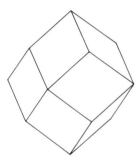

● Physical and chemical properties are similar to those of garnet **(577)**. It is colourless, yellow, green (topazolite variety), deep green (demantoid variety – **580**), brown or black (melanite variety). Transparent to opaque. It sometimes contains Ti (schorlomite variety) ● Occurrence: rare; Wurlitz – topazolite, Rieden am Laacher See, Kaiserstuhl – melanite, Schwarzenberg – topazolite (FRG), Zermatt – topazolite (Switzerland), Mussa Alp – topazolite (Italy), Podzamek – schorlomite (Poland), Kovdor – schorlomite (Russia), Ice River – melanite (Canada), Magnet Cove, Arkansas – melanite and schorlomite (USA) ● Application: some varieties are used as gemstones (facets, cabochons).

Demantoid (Andradite variety)

Silicate
$Ca_3Fe_2^{3+}(SiO_4)_3$

580

Named after its adamantine lustre (Nordenskiöld 1878)

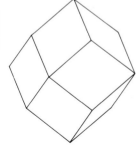

● Physical and chemical properties are similar to those of garnet **(577)** and andradite **(579)**. It is a fine green or yellow colour, of adamantine lustre, transparent ● Occurrence: rare; ultrabasic rocks, alluvial deposits; Dobšiná – in serpentinites (Slovakia), Saxony (FRG), Frascati (Italy), Nizhni Tagil – Central Urals – in alluvial deposits (Russia), (Congo) ● Application: cut as a gemstone (facets, cabochons).

---

1. Andradite – druse of crystals (the largest 3 mm); Benat (Romania) **2. Pyrope** – grains (up to 8 mm) in serpentinized peridotite; Sklené (Czech Republic) **3. Demantoid** – group of crystals (up to 10 mm); Val Malenco (Italy)

Andradite, pyrope, demantoid

Uvarovite (Garnet variety)

Silicate
$Ca_3Cr_2(SiO_4)_3$

581

Named after the Russian minister, S. S. Uvarov (1786–1855) (Hess 1832)

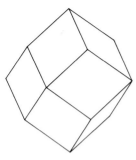

● Physical and chemical properties are similar to those of garnet **(577)**. It is a green to dark emerald-green colour, transparent to translucent ● Occurrence: rare; in chromite deposits; Jordanów (Poland), Outukumpo (Finland), Rösos (Norway), Syssert and Nizhni Tagil – Central Urals (Russia), Bushveld – Transvaal (RSA), Oxford – Quebec (Canada), Riddle – Oregon and Texas (USA) ● Application: sometimes used as a gemstone (facets, cabochons).

Grossularite (Garnet variety)

Silicate
$Ca_3Al_2(SiO_4)_3$

582

From the Latin *ribes grossularia* – gooseberry (Werner 1811)

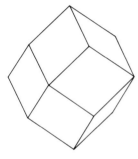

● Physical and chemical properties are similar to those of garnet **(577)**. It is a white, yellow, yellowish-green, brownish-red, orange or black colour (brownish-orange variety is called hessonite – **583**), transparent to opaque ● Occurrence: rare; contact-metasomatic deposits; Alatal, Piedmont, Elba and Monte Somma (Italy), Auerbach (FRG), Ciclova (Romania), Zermatt (Switzerland), Jordanów (Poland), Isle of Mull – Scotland (Great Britain), Vilyui and Yakutia (Russia), Morelos and Concepción del Oro (Mexico), San Diego Co. – California, Chaffe Co. – Colorado and Minot – Maine (USA), Fusodo (Korea), (RSA) ● Application: sometimes cut as a precious stone (facets, cabochons). (*NB* Another variety of grossularite is the emerald-green tsavorite named after Tsavo Park in Kenya. It is transparent to opaque.)

Hessonite (Grossularite variety)

Silicate
$Ca_3Al_2(SiO_4)_3$

583

From the Greek *hésson* – slight (of low specific gravity) (Haüy 1822)

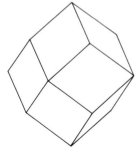

● Physical and chemical properties are similar to those of garnet **(577)** and grossularite **(582)**. It is brownish-orange, translucent to opaque ● Occurrence: rare; contact-metasomatic deposits; Žulová – large crystals (Czech Republic), Monzoni (Italy), Auerbach (FRG), Baita (Romania), (Sri Lanka), (Brazil), (Tanzania) ● Application: sometimes cut as a gemstone (facets, cabochons).

---

1. **Uvarovite** – crystals (up to 2 mm); Urals (Russia) 2. **Hessonite** – group of crystals (up to 20 mm) with carbonates; Žulová (Czech Republic) 3. **Grossularite** – crystals (up to 10 mm) embedded in quartz; Banat (Romania)

Uvarovite, hessonite, grossularite

Spessartite (Garnet variety)

Silicate
$Mn_3Al_2(SiO_4)_3$

584

P

Named after its locality
Spessart (FRG)
(Beudant 1832)

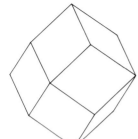

● Physical and chemical properties are identical to those of garnet **(577)**. It is a yellow, rose or orange to reddish-brown colour, translucent to opaque ● Occurrence: magmatic, in pegmatites; metamorphic; Spessart, Ilfeld (FRG), Gola (Poland), Kimito (Finland), (Sweden), Budislav (Czech Republic), Tyrol (Austria), (Russia), (Madagascar – orange-yellow crystals in Antsirabe), Quebec (Canada), Ramona – California, Rutherford Mine – Virginia, Nevada, Pennsylvania, Montana, Colorado and Oklahoma (USA), (Sri Lanka), (Japan), Ceava (Brazil), (Australia), (Tanzania – of gem quality), (northern Burma) ● Application: sometimes cut as a gemstone (facets, cabochons).

Almandine (Garnet variety)

Silicate
$Fe_3Al_2(SiO_4)_3$

585

P

Named after its locality
Alabanda in Asia Minor
(Karsten 1800)

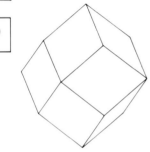

● Physical and chemical properties are similar to those of garnet **(577)**. It is a fine violet-red colour, sometimes brown or black; transparent to opaque; sporadically, rosy-reddish crystals are found which are the rhodolite variety of pyrope and almandine ● Occurrence: common; in pegmatites and metamorphic rocks; Irchenrieth – Bavaria – large crystals in pegmatites, and Saar-Pfalz – in rhyolites (FRG), Obergurgl (Austria), Přibyslavice (Czech Republic), Falun (Sweden), Bodö (Norway), North Creek – New York and Fort Wrangel – Alaska (USA), Mtoko (Zimbabwe), Ampandramaika (Madagascar), (southern India) – in alluvial deposits, (Sri Lanka). Asteriated almandines are found in Idaho (USA). Almandines are also found in Afghanistan, Brazil, Russia, Tanzania, Greenland, Japan and elsewhere. The rhodolite variety occurs in North Carolina (USA), Mexico, Sri Lanka, Brazil, Zambia and Tanzania ● Application: cut as a precious stone (facets, cabochons, tumbling); in cutting, grinding and drilling tools.

---

1. **Spessartite** – crystals (up to 10 mm); Natrop (USA) 2. **Almandine** – euhedral crystals (up to 20 mm); Iventino (Italy)

Spessartite, almandine

Staurolite

$Fe_2Al_9(Si,Al)_4O_{22}(OH)_2$

586

From the Greek, *stauros* – cross and *líthos* – stone (Delamétherie, 1792)

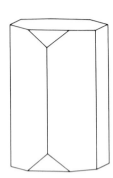

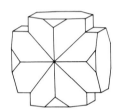

● Hardness: 7–7.5 ● Streak: grey-white ● Colour: brown to brownish-black ● Transparency: translucent to opaque ● Lustre: vitreous, dull ● Cleavage: good on (010) ● Fracture: conchoidal, splintery ● Morphology: crystals, cruciform twins, granular aggregates ● Specific gravity: 3.5–3.6 ● Crystal system: orthorhombic ● Crystal form: short prisms, long prisms, twinning, triplets ● Chemical composition: FeO 16.7%, Al_2O_3 53.4%, SiO_2 27.9%, H_2O 2.0%; admixtures: Co, Mg (lusakite variety), Zn (Zn – staurolite variety), Mn (nordmarkite variety) ● Chemical properties: infusible, partly soluble in H_2SO_4 ● Handling: clean with water ● Similar minerals: garnet **(577)** ● Distinguishing features: X-rays, chemical properties ● Genesis: metamorphic (in mica schists, phyllites, granulites, gneiss), in alluvial deposits ● Associated minerals: muscovite **(165)**, kyanite **(435)**, quartz **(534)**, almandine **(585)** ● Occurrence: rare; Aschaffenburg (FRG), Pizzo Forno, Tessin and Lago Ritom (Switzerland), Passeier Tal, Sterzing and St. Radegund (Austria), Petrov and Branná (Czech Republic), Quimper (France), Scotland (Great Britain), (Ireland), Altai, Sanarka River and the Urals – in alluvial deposits (Russia), Fannin Co. – Georgia, Lisbon – New Hampshire, Franconia and Ducktown – Tennessee (USA), Gorob Mine (Namibia), (India), (Australia). The lusakite variety occurs in the vicinity of Lusaka (Zambia); it contains up to 8.48% CoO, is a black to cobalt-blue colour, with a light-blue streak. The Zn-staurolite variety contains up to 7.44% ZnO, is of yellowish colour; among other places it occurs in mica schists in Georgia (USA). The nordmarkite variety contains up to 11.61% Mn_2O_3, is a brownish-red colour, fuses readily in a blowpipe flame into magnetic glass, with a bead of soda reacts on Mn. Nordmarkite was found in Nordmark, Sweden, in granular dolomites of gneiss formation.

Staurolite – compound crystals in mica schist (20 mm); Petrov (Czech Republic)

Staurolite

Zircon

Silicate
ZrSiO$_4$

587

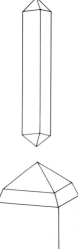

From *cerkonier* – a name used by German jewellers, altered to Cirkon and Zyrkon (Werner 1783)

● Hardness: 7.5 (brittle) ● Streak: white ● Colour: colourless, yellow (jargon variety – **589**), reddish to orange-red (hyacinth variety – **588**), greenish and bluish (starlite variety), brown ● Transparency: transparent to translucent to opaque ● Lustre: vitreous, adamantine, greasy ● Cleavage: imperfect on (100) ● Fracture: conchoidal ● Morphology: crystals, granular, earthy and radiating aggregates, grains and pebbles in alluvial deposits ● Specific gravity: 4.0−4.7 ● Crystal sytem: tetragonal ● Crystal form: prismatic, dipyramidal, isometric ● Luminescence: yellow, orange, dull red, green-yellow ● Radioactivity: sometimes slightly radioactive when it contains admixed U and Th ● Chemical composition: ZrO$_2$ 67.01%, SiO$_2$ 32.99%; admixtures: U, Th, rare earths, H$_2$O (malacon, cyrtolite varieties), Y, Nb (naegite variety), Hf (alvite variety), rare earths (oyamalite variety), etc. ● Chemical properties: infusible, partly soluble in H$_2$SO$_4$, HF and HCl. Zircons are often found in the metamict state ● Handling: clean with water ● Similar minerals: xenotime **(324)**, thorite **(339)**, garnet **(577)** ● Distinguishing features: hardness, specific gravity, X-rays, chemical properties ● Genesis: magmatic, metamorphic, pegmatitic, sedimentary, in alluvial deposits ● Associated minerals: biotite **(167)**, amphibole **(411)**, quartz **(534)**, garnet ● Occurrence: common; Laacher See, Niedermendig, Usedom (FRG), Langensundsfjord (Norway), Ilmen Mountains – crystals up to 3.5 kg, Myas, Urals, Slyudyanka – crystals up to 5 cm (Russia), Expailly – St. Marcel (France), Haddam, Connecticut and Mellen – Wisconsin – needles up to 20 cm (USA), Renfrew Co. – crystals up to 7 kg (Canada), (Madagascar), (Burma), Pailin (Cambodia), (Sri Lanka), (Australia), (Brazil) ● Application: Zr source, also used as a gemstone (facets, cabochons).

Hyacinth (Zircon variety)

Silicate
ZrSiO$_4$

588

● Physical and chemical properties are similar to those of zircon **(587)**. It is an orange-red colour, transparent, of a strong adamantine lustre ● Handling: should be protected from sunlight, otherwise it becomes dark and dull ● Occurrence: rare; in alluvial deposits in (Sri Lanka), (eastern Australia), (Thailand), (Cambodia), (Burma), (Brazil) and (Madagascar) ● Application: used as a gemstone (facets, cabochons).

Jargon (Zircon variety)

Silicate
ZrSiO$_4$

589

From the French, a name denoting the colourless, precious stone of adamantine lustre from Sri Lanka (Wallerius 1772)

● Physical and chemical properties are similar to those of zircon **(587)**. It is a light yellow colour, often colourless, transparent, of a brilliant lustre ● Occurrence: rare; in alluvial deposits in (Sri Lanka), (Thailand), (Burma) and (Brazil) ● Application: cut as a gemstone (facets, cabochons).

---

1. **Zircon** – elongated crystal (22 mm); Diana (USA) 2. **Hyacinth** – subeuhedral crystal (4 mm) in tuffaceous rock; Mayen (FRG) 3. **Jargon** – euhedral crystal (10 mm) in pegmatite; Myas (Urals, Russia)

Spinel

590

The origin of its name is unknown
(Agricola 1546)

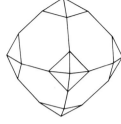
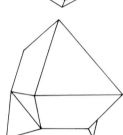

● Hardness: 8 ● Streak: white ● Colour: colourless, yellow, blue, green, red, brown ● Transparency: transparent to translucent ● Lustre: vitreous ● Cleavage: imperfect on (111) ● Fracture: conchoidal ● Morphology: crystals, grains, granular aggregates ● Specific gravity: 3.5 ● Crystal system: cubic ● Crystal form: octahedra, dodecahedra, twinning ● Chemical composition: MgO 28.34%, Al$_2$O$_3$ 71.66%; admixtures: Fe (pleonaste or hercynite variety), Cr (chrome spinel, picotite variety) ● Chemical properties: dissolves with difficulty in H$_2$SO$_4$, infusible ● Handling: clean with distilled water ● Similar minerals: garnet **(577)**, zircon **(587)**, corundum **(598)** ● Distinguishing features: hardness, specific gravity, X-rays, chemical properties ● Genesis: magmatic, contact-metamorphic, in alluvial deposits ● Associated minerals: dolomite **(218)**, magnetite **(367)**, garnet, zircon, corundum ● Occurrence: rare; Odenwald and Schwarzwald (FRG), Vesuvius (Italy), Södermanland (Sweden), Zlatoust – Urals (Russia), (Sri Lanka), (Burma), (Thailand), Amity – New York (USA) ● Application: precious stone, ceramics.

Gahnite (Zn-spinel)

591

Named after the Swedish chemist and mineralogist, J. G. Gahn (1745–1818)
(V. Moll 1807)

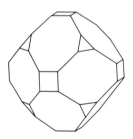

● Hardness: 8 (brittle) ● Streak: grey ● Colour: green with a bluish tint ● Transparency: translucent, but opaque on edges ● Lustre: vitreous, greasy ● Cleavage: indistinct on (111) ● Fracture: conchoidal ● Morphology: crystals, grains, granular aggregates ● Specific gravity: 4.3 ● Crystal system: cubic ● Crystal form: octahedra, dodecahedra, twins ● Chemical composition: ZnO 44.39%, Al$_2$O$_3$ 55.61% ● Chemical properties: dissolves with difficulty in hot H$_2$SO$_4$, infusible ● Handling: clean with distilled water ● Similar minerals: spinel **(590)** ● Distinguishing features: specific gravity, chemical properties ● Genesis: metamorphic, in pegmatites ● Associated minerals: galena **(77)**, sphalerite **(181)**, magnetite **(367)** ● Occurrence: rare; Bodenmais (FRG), Maršíkov (Czech Republic), Smilovne (Bulgaria), Tirolio (Italy), Falun (Sweden), New Jersey and Connecticut (USA), Minas Gerais (Brazil), (Finland), Broken Hill – N. S. Wales (Australia). Sn-variety called limaite occurs in Ponto de Lima (Portugal).

Nigerite

592

Named after Nigeria where it was first found
(Jacobson 1947)

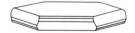

● Hardness: 8.5 (brittle) ● Streak: grey-white ● Colour: brown or reddish-brown ● Transparency: opaque ● Lustre: vitreous, greasy ● Cleavage: absent ● Fracture: hackly ● Morphology: crystals ● Specific gravity: 4.51 ● Crystal system: hexagonal ● Crystal form: plates ● Magnetism: poor ● Chemical composition: variable ● Chemical properties: insoluble in acids ● Handling: clean with water or diluted acids ● Genesis: in pegmatites ● Associated minerals: cassiterite **(548)**, gahnite **(591)**, chrysoberyl **(593)** ● Occurrence: rare; Kabba – crystals up to 1 cm (Nigeria), Liksa (Portugal), Siberia (Russia), (China).

---

1. Spinel – euhedral crystal (4 mm) embedded in feldspar; New Jersey (USA) **2. Gahnite** – crystal (5 mm); Tiziolo (Italy)
3. Nigerite – embedded crystal (5 mm) in granite; Přibyslavice (Czech Republic)

Spinel, gahnite, nigerite

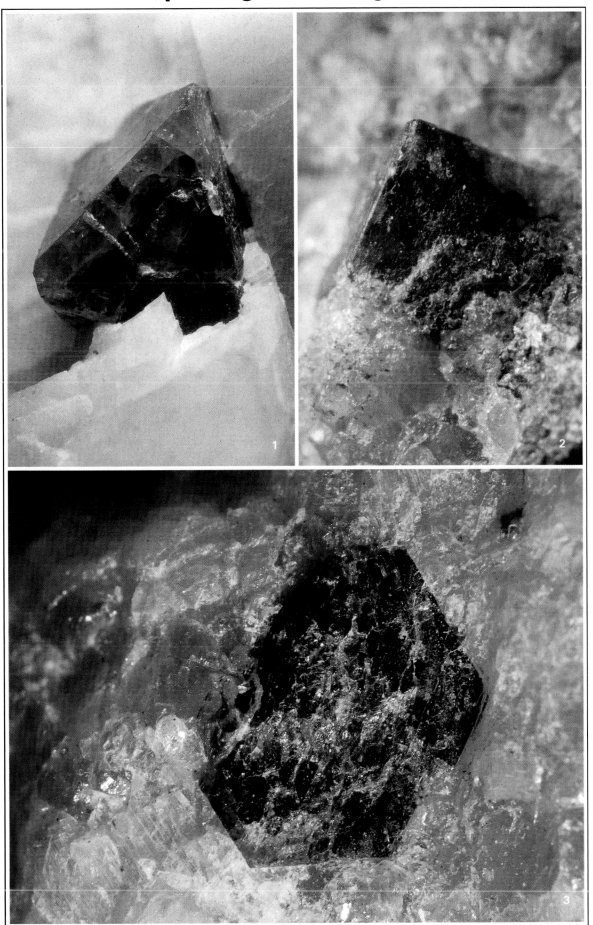

Chrysoberyl

Oxide
Al_2BeO_4

593

L

P

From the Greek *chrysos* – golden and the mineral *beryl* (Werner 1790)

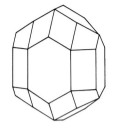

● Hardness: 8.5 ● Streak: white ● Colour: yellow, light green, emerald-green, dark green, brownish-green; the cymophane variety (chrysoberyl or cat's eye) is golden yellow with a silvery white line on the surface of the cut ● Transparency: transparent to translucent ● Lustre: vitreous, greasy ● Cleavage: good on (001) ● Fracture: conchoidal ● Morphology: crystals, grains, pebbles in alluvial deposits ● Specific gravity: approx. 3.7 ● Crystal system: orthorhombic ● Crystal form: plates, short prisms, often twins ● Luminescence: yellow-green ● Chemical composition: Al_2O_3 80.29%, BeO 19.71%; admixtures: Cr, Fe^{3+} ● Chemical properties: insoluble in acids, infusible ● Handling: clean with water or diluted acids ● Similar minerals: beryl **(554)** ● Distinguishing features: hardness, specific gravity ● Genesis: pegmatitic, metamorphic ● Associated minerals: beryl, tourmaline **(564),** garnet **(577),** spinel **(590)** ● Occurrence: rare; Maršíkov (Czech Republic), Campolungo (Switzerland), Piona (Italy), Kolsva (Sweden), (Norway), (Finland), Takovaya River, Central Urals (Russia), (Canada), Drew Hill – Colorado and Haddam – Connecticut (USA), Minas Gerais and Espírito Santo (Brazil), (Madagascar), (Ghana), (Congo), Fort Victoria (Zimbabwe), Manjara Lake (Tanzania), (Sri Lanka), Mogok and Pegu (north Burma), Radzhastan – Madras (India), (Australia). Cymophane is found in (Brazil), (China) and (Sri Lanka) ● Application: transparent and translucent varietes, **alexandrite (594)** and **cymophane** are cut as gemstones (facets, cabochons).

Alexandrite (Chrysoberyl variety)

Oxide
Al_2BeO_4

594

L

P

Named after the Russian Czar, Alexander II (Nordenskiöld 1842)

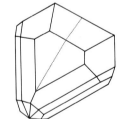

● Physical and chemical properties are similar to those of chrysoberyl **(593).** Characteristic is its colour variation which changes from light green or emerald green in daylight to red or violet in artificial light ● Luminescence: red ● Occurrence: rare; Takovaya River – Central Urals (Russia), Fort Victoria (Zimbabwe), Lake Mananjara (Tanzania), Campo Formoso – Bahia (Brazil), (Sri Lanka), (Burma), (Madagascar) ● Application: a valued precious stone (facets, cabochons).

---

1. Chrysoberyl – flat crystal (8 mm) in pegmatite; Maršíkov (Czech Republic) **2. Alexandrite** – crystal (11 mm) in daylight; Takovaya River (Central Urals, Russia)

Chrysoberyl, alexandrite

Topaz

Silicate
$Al_2SiO_4F_2$

595

L

P

Named after the To-pasos Island in the Red Sea (Boodt 1636)

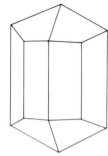

● Hardness: 8 ● Streak: white ● Colour: colourless, yellow, golden-yellow, rose, bluish, red, violet, greenish and brown ● Transparency: transparent to translucent ● Lustre: vitreous ● Cleavage: perfect on (001) ● Fracture: conchoidal, uneven ● Morphology: crystals, granular and radial aggregates (pycnite variety – **596**), impregnations, pebbles ● Specific gravity: 3.5–3.6 ● Crystal system: orthorhombic ● Crystal form: prisms, vertically striated ● Luminescence: gold-yellow, cream, green ● Chemical composition: Al_2O_3 55.4%, SiO_2 32.6%, F 20.7% (less O = F_2 8.7%); admixtures: Fe^{3+}, Cr, Mg, Ti ● Chemical properties: slowly dissolves in hot H_2SO_4, infusible, when heated turns dull ● Handling: clean with water or diluted acids; loses colour when exposed to light for a long time ● Similar minerals: brazilianite **(375)**, beryl **(554)**, phenakite **(597)** ● Distinguishing features: specific gravity, cleavage, X-rays, chemical properties ● Genesis: pneumatolytic, pegmatitic, hydrother-mal, metasomatic, in alluvial deposits ● Associated minerals: fluorite **(511)**, quartz **(534)**, cassiterite **(548)**, tourmaline **(564)** ● Occurrence: rare; Schneck-enstein, Altenberg (FRG), Horní Slavkov, Cínovec (Czech Republic), Mourne Mountains (Northern Ireland), Iveland – crystals up to 80 kg (Norway), Alabashka, Urals – blue topaz (Russia), Volhynia (Ukraine), Sanarka River, Nerchinsk, Transbaikal – rose-red crystals in alluvial deposits (Russia), San Luis Potosí and Durango (Mexico), Spitzkopje (Namibia), Tonokamiyama (Japan), Ferros (Brazil), (Pakistan), (Sri Lanka), (USA), (Nigeria), (Mongolia) ● Application: fire-proof materials; used as a gemstone (facets, cabochons).

Pycnite (Topaz variety)

Silicate
$Al_2SiO_4F_2$

596

L

From the Greek *pyknós* – solid

● Physical and chemical properties are similar to those of topaz **(595)**. Parallel or radiating fibrous aggregates, a yellow-white colour, in greisen cassiterite deposits ● Occurrence: rare; Ehrenfriedensdorf, Altenberg (FRG), Cínovec (Czech Republic).

Phenakite

Silicate
Be_2SiO_4

597

P

From the Greek *phenakos* – liar (Nordenskiöld 1833)

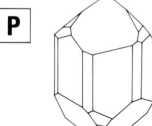

● Hardness: 8 (brittle) ● Streak: white ● Colour: colourless, bluish, white, yellow, rose, brown ● Transparency: transparent to translucent ● Lustre: vitreous ● Cleavage: indistinct on (11$\bar{2}$0) ● Fracture: conchoidal ● Morphology: crystals, granular and radiating fibrous aggregates ● Specific gravity: 3.0 ● Crystal system: trigonal ● Crystal form: flat rhombohedra, prisms vertically striated, twinning ● Chemical composition: BeO 45.53%, SiO_2 54.47% ● Chemical properties: insoluble in acids, infusible ● Handling: clean with water or dilute acids ● Similar minerals: quartz **(534)**, topaz **(595)** ● Distin-guishing features: hardness, cleavage, specific gravity, X-rays, chemical properties ● Genesis: in pegmatites, hydrothermal, in alpine fissures ● As-sociated minerals: apatite **(379)**, quartz, beryl **(554)**, topaz ● Occurrence: rare; Habachtal (Austria), Reckingen (Switzerland), Kragerö (Norway), Takovaya River – Central Urals (Russia), Minas Gerais (Brazil), (Namibia), (USA) ● Application: sometimes Be ore; also used as a gemstone (facets, cabochons).

---

1. Pycnite (a variety of topaz) – columnar aggregate; Altenberg (FRG – width of field 50 mm) **2. Topaz** – idiomorphic crystal (9 mm); Thomas Range (USA) **3. Phenakite** – columnar crystal (50 mm) in quartz; Kragerö (Norway)

Pycnite, topaz, phenakite

H
8—9

473

Corundum

598

L

P

Historical name, probably from the Old Indian *kauruntaka* (Estner 1795)

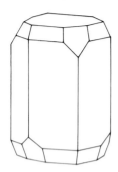

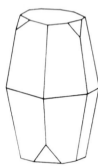

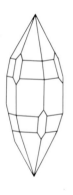

● Hardness: 9 ● Streak: white ● Colour: colourless, blue (sapphire variety – **600**), red (ruby variety – **599**), rosy-red, brown, grey, yellow, violet, blue-green, or of zonal colouring. In sapphires and rubies inclusions of asteriated rutile **(464)** may be found. Colourless corundum is called leucosapphire **(601)** ● Transparency: transparent or translucent ● Lustre: vitreous, greasy, dull ● Cleavage: on (0001) ● Fracture: conchoidal, splintery ● Morphology: crystals, granular aggregates, pebbles ● Specific gravity: 3.9–4.1 ● Crystal system: trigonal ● Crystal form: plates, bipyramids, rhombohedra, columns, twinning ● Luminescence: sometimes yellow ● Chemical composition: Al 52.91%, O 47.09%; admixtures: Cr, Fe, Ti, Mn, Ni, V ● Chemical properties: insoluble in acids, infusible ● Handling: clean with water or diluted acids ● Similar minerals: apatite **(379)**, zircon **(587)**, spinel **(590)**, topaz **(595)** ● Distinguishing features: hardness, specific gravity, cleavage, X-rays, chemical properties ● Genesis: contact and regionally metamorphic rocks, in pegmatites, in alluvial deposits ● Associated minerals: magnetite **(367)**, diaspore **(463)**, spinel, topaz ● Occurrence: rare; Unkel-on-Rhine, Bockau, Waldheim (FRG), Pokojovice (Czech Republic), Campolungo (Switzerland), Myas, Urals, Chainit and Yakutia (Russia), Aktash (Kazakhstan), Renfrew – Ontario (Canada), North Carolina, Montana, Colorado, Pennsylvania, Massachusetts, Virginia and Georgia (USA), Chittering (Australia), Assam (India), (Afghanistan), (Thailand), (Japan), Zoutpansberg, Bandolierskop, Pietersberg and Transvaal (RSA). In Transvaal crystals up to 25 cm and 150 kg have been found. Corundum, in association with magnetite, hematite and spinel, forms the rock called **emery**. It is formed by contact metamorphism of argillaceous rocks (laterites and bauxites). Emery is found in Naxos (Greece), Izmir (Turkey), Marmorskoe – Urals (Russia), Chester – Massachusetts (USA) ● Application: in cutting, grinding and drilling tools, in bearings, as a gemstone (facets, cabochons).

Corundum (Sapphire) – euhedral isolated crystal (21 mm); Ratnapura (Sri Lanka)

Corundum

H
9—10

Ruby (Corundum variety)

Oxide
Al_2O_3

599

L

P

From the Latin *rubeus* – red
(Wallerius 1747)

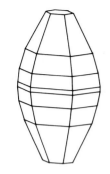

● Physical and chemical properties are similar to those of corundum (598). It is a red to dark red colour, transparent to translucent, has rhombohedral or platy crystals, exhibits a red or rosy luminescence ● Occurrence: rare; Prilep (Serbia), Kosoi Brod (Russia), Ratnapura – in alluvial deposits (Sri Lanka), Mogok (Burma), Chatnaburi – in basalts (Thailand), Phailin (Cambodia), (eastern Afghanistan), (India), Jü-nan Prov. (China), Inverell (Australia), Taita Hills – in metamorphic rocks (Kenya), Umba Valley – Longida – in zoisite-amphibolite rocks (Tanzania), (Zambia), (Angola), Montana, North and South Carolina (USA) ● Application: used as a precious stone (facets, cabochons, tumbling).

Sapphire (Corundum variety)

Oxide
Al_2O_3

600

L

P

The origin of its name is unknown
(Wallerius 1747)

● Physical and chemical properties are similar to those of corundum (598). It is a blue, light blue, green or yellow colour, transparent, forms dipyramidal or prismatic crystals, seldom plates. Often contains stellate inclusions of rutile (464), exhibiting asterism when correctly cut ● Occurrence: rare; (northern Finland), Jizerská louka (Czech Republic), Ratnapura – in alluvial deposits (Sri Lanka), Mogok (Burma), Chatnaburi (Thailand), Kasmir and Zaskar (India), Jü-nan Prov. (China), Phailin (Cambodia), Inverell (Australia), Montana (USA), Mato Grosso (Brazil), (Kenya), (Malawi), (Zambia), Umba (Tanzania), (Angola) ● Application: cut as precious stone (facets, cabochons, tumbling).

Leucosapphire (Corundum variety)

Oxide
Al_2O_3

601

L

P

From the Greek *leukos* – white and *sapphire* – the name of the mineral

● Physical and chemical properties of the mineral are similar to those of corundum (598). It is colourless and perfectly clear ● Occurrence: rare; Ratnapura – in alluvial deposits (Sri Lanka); Missouri River and Rock Creek – Montana (USA) ● Application: cut as a precious stone (facets, cabochons).

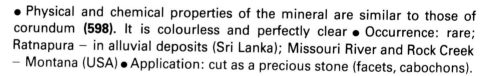

1. **Ruby** – embedded crystal (13 mm); Mysore (India) 2. **Sapphire** – nugget of 23 mm; Ratnapura (Sri Lanka) 3. **Leucosapphire** – polished alluvial nuggets (max. size 10 mm); Ratnapura (Sri Lanka)

Ruby, sapphire, leucosapphire

Diamond

Historical name, from the Greek *adamas* – invincible

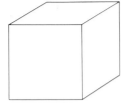

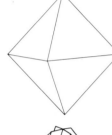

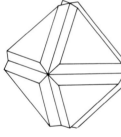

• Hardness: 10 (brittle) • Streak: white • Colour: colourless, grey, bluish, greenish, yellowish, brown and black • Transparency: transparent to opaque • Lustre: adamantine • Cleavage: perfect on (111) • Fracture: conchoidal • Morphology: crystals, twinning • Specific gravity: 3.52 • Crystal system: cubic • Crystal form: octahedra, dodecahedra, cubes • Luminescence: blue to greenish • Chemical composition: theoretically, C 100%; admixtures: Si, Al, Mg, Fe, Ti • Chemical properties: insoluble both in acids and in alkalis • Handling: clean with water or diluted acids • Similar minerals: none • Genesis: magmatic, in alluvial deposits and meteorites • Associated minerals: gold **(50)**, platinum **(281)**, magnetite **(367)**, rutile **(464)**, olivine **(524)**, pyrope **(578)**, zircon **(587)** • Occurrence: rare; in ultrabasic rocks (kimberlites) and alluvial deposits, occasionally in meteorites. The most important deposits are in RSA in the vicinity of Kimberley (in the alluvial deposits of the Vaal and Orange Rivers); in the Premier Mine the largest diamond crystal found weighed 622 gm (3,106 carats). Also in eastern part of Deccan Plateau (India), (Namibia), (Angola), Kasai Province (Congo), (Sierra Leone), (Ghana), (Borneo), (Brazil), western part of the Urals, Yakutia (Russia), (Australia), Arizona – in meteorites (USA) • Application: precious stone; for cutting, grinding and drilling tools.

Diamond varieties:

Bort – of inferior quality, granular, opaque, grey to black aggregates; occurs in Brazil, Congo, Russia, Ghana.
Ballas – fine grains of radiating-fibrous form, occurs in association with bort.
Carbonado – massive or porous aggregates of grey to black colour; occurs in Cincora, Bahia, Brazil.

The most famous diamonds:

Cullinan – colourless, found in RSA (3,106 carats; 104 gemstones were cut from the original stone, the largest 531.20 carats)
Excelsior – blue-white, RSA, 995.2 car.
Large Mogul – light blue-green, India, 787.5 car.
Woyie River – colourless, Sierra Leone, 770 car.
President Vargas – colourless, Brazil, 726.6 car.
Jonker – blue-white, India, 726 car.
Jubilee Imperial – colourless, RSA, 650.8 car.
Victoria Imperial – colourless, RSA, 469 car.
De Beers – light yellow, RSA, 440 car.
Matan – colourless, Borneo, 367 car.
Nizam – colourless, India, 340 car.
Stewart – yellowish, RSA, 296 car.
Tiffany – gold-yellow, RSA, 287.4 car.
Southern Star – colourless, Brazil, 261.88 car.
Julius Pam – yellow, RSA, 248 car.
Yakutia Star – yellowish, Russia, 232.1 car.
Orlov – colourless, India, 194.75 car.
Koh-i-Nur – Indian Diamond, 108.9 car. (set in the crown of English Queens)
Hope – the most beautiful and largest deep blue diamond, 44.5 car. (Smithsonian Institute, Washington, USA)
Dresden Diamond – rich green, 41 car.

Diamond – euhedral crystal (5 mm) in parent rock; Kimberley (RSA)

Diamond

Identification
of minerals

The exact identification of a mineral is sometimes very difficult and requires much precision and perseverance. Most minerals can be identified directly in situ. Sometimes, however, typical features are not visible. If it proves impossible to identify a mineral, a mistake has probably been made, or an unsuitable weathered or non-homogenous sample has been used. The tests must be repeated once again with a fresh piece of mineral broken off from a larger specimen. If it fails again, the mineral cannot be identified by ordinary simple means without the aid of complicated laboratory tests and measuring apparatus.

Everyone starting a collection of minerals should determine what he is going to collect initially, in what way and what identification clues he will use. There are several identification clues which can be applied, based upon some typical mineral features. Many handbooks indicate physical properties of minerals as the most important identification clues, others lay stress on optical or chemical properties, or their combinations. For a layman then the approach to be adopted is not always clear. The best clues to be obtained are those tests based on physical properties as the main identification feature, with the other tests as supplementary distinctive features. Attention is mostly paid to those properties that can be identified directly or by means of simple tests, such as hardness, streak colour, mineral colour, lustre, etc. Difficulties which may arise in their determination are described in the respective chapters.

Testing should start on the spot with more specimens of one mineral to enable identification of all its characteristic properties. Firstly, determination of its approximate hardness is made; then the streak colour (by eye or by

means of a lens), its colour, transparency, lustre, cleavage, fracture and its morphology. The mineral's solubility in water or hydrochloric acid should be determined; then the typical odour, indicating minerals containing arsenic (ie giving a garlicky smell). Having finished the identification, check the results comparing them with the data in the identification tables and the description of the individual minerals. It should not be forgotten that identical minerals can occur in several morphological forms (see Fig. 19), can exist in several colours (eg quartz varieties), some of their physical and optical properties can vary according to the degree of weathering, damage or according to the granularity of the mineral. A note should also be made of the associated minerals, as these may also be a guide to the identification of the specimen.

The distinguishing of similar minerals, such as quartz, feldspars and calcite may cause difficulties. In non-crystallized masses these minerals do not differ in colour or lustre and cannot be reliably distinguished. On the other hand, quartz and feldspars can easily be distinguished from calcite by their greater hardness. Furthermore, calcite dissolves in hydrochloric acid. Feldspars can be distinguished from quartz by their cleavage, which is excellent in feldspars but poor in quartz (ie conchoidal fracture). Dark minerals, such as biotite, amphibole and occasionally tourmaline, look very similar. Biotite can be distinguished from the columnar crystals of amphibole or tourmaline by its excellent cleavage and characteristic lamellar form. These minerals can be distinguished by their cleavages, which are perfect in amphibole (at angles of 120°), and very poor in tourmaline. Also tourmaline displays typical striations on its prism faces.

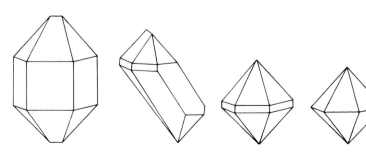

Fig. 19 Different morphological forms of quartz

In ore deposits some similar minerals occur, such as chalcopyrite, pyrite and pyrrhotite, which in granular masses can be distinguished only with difficulty. Their colour and streak are identical, although pyrrhotite displays a slight shade of tobacco brown. They can be distinguished only by their hardness, eg pyrite is harder (6−6.5) than chalcopyrite (4.5) and pyrrhotite (3). Pyrrhotite, compared with chalcopyrite and pyrite, possesses a perfect cleavage; chalcopyrite sometimes shows an iridescent surface. When heated in a blowpipe flame, it fuses readily and forms magnetic lumps.

Pyrite and marcasite are similar and both occur in coal deposits. Their hardness, colour and streak are identical. They can be distinguished, however, by their morphological features. Marcasite occurs in characteristic coxcomb forms (ie orthorhombic), pyrite in tiny cubes or granular masses (ie cubic). The granular aggregates of magnetite and chromite also look very similar. However, they can be easily distinguished by their streak, which is black in magnetite and brown in chromite. Apart from this, magnetite is much more strongly magnetic than chromite. Also, antimonite and berthierite aggregates look similar. They can be distinguished when immersed in water. Antimonite shows a splendent lustre in water, berthierite remains dark. Diamonds can be distinguished from quartz under water, this method being successfully applied by customs officers in Africa. Quartz appears to lose its shape in water, whereas diamonds display a brilliant adamantine lustre.

The final thing for a collector to do is to set up a display of minerals and place duplicate specimens in a cabinet. After trimming, identification and cleaning, each mineral specimen must be labelled. Every label should bear the name and the address of the collector, the date the mineral was collected and its number, the name of the mineral, the place where it was found, a short description, the manner of acquisition, or its price. In case of rare and valuable minerals the label should bear also the size and weight. The data on the labels should be concise. Details should be noted either on the reverse side of the label or in a catalogue or card index. In order to mark the specimen with an identical number as in the catalogue, a small label with a number can be affixed to the reverse side of the mineral specimen where it is least obtrusive; or an inconspicuous part of the mineral can be painted with a white enamel spot and the number written in black Indian ink on it.

A serious collector compiles a catalogue of his collection, where the mineral specimens are arranged according to their numbers (it is advisable to use a decimal numbering system, enabling additions to be made), mineralogical systems, individual areas or in alphabetical order. Sometimes a card index can be supplemented with photographs. In the cabinets, mineral specimens should be kept in card trays or boxes, or in special plastic boxes. There are numerous types of collections, such as systematic, crystallographic, genetic, geochemical, or collections of precious stones, ores or meteorites. Minerals easily affected by light should be preserved in the drawers of a cabinet and never be exposed to sunlight. Minerals reacting sensitively to humidity and hygroscopic minerals are kept in plastic bags or sealed glass bottles or tubes sealed with wax. Radioactive minerals should not be exhibited at all. In the home they should never be kept in large numbers, and never in living rooms.

Every collection of minerals must be carefully protected from dust, humidity and great variations in light and temperature.

Identification table according to hardness, streak, colour and lustre

		Hardness less than 2						
		Streak colour						
Lustre	Colour	white silver-white	yellow ochre-yellow orange	red violet	blue	green	grey steel-grey green-grey	black grey-black
metallic submetallic	white						3⁺, 12	
	red		7	7				
	violet						8	
	grey						3⁺, 8, 10, 13	2, 11
	black							2, 9
non-metallic	colourless	14, 18, 19, 20, 23, 24, 26, 27, 28, 29, 31, 39, 43						
	white	14, 18, 19, 20, 21, 23, 24, 25, 26, 27, 28, 29, 33, 34, 35, 38, 39, 40, 41, 42, 43	15					
	yellow	1, 14, 21, 23, 26, 27, 29, 31, 33, 34, 35, 36, 38, 39, 40, 41, 42, 43, 44	1, 4, 15, 16, 17, 30		16	37		
	orange		4, 5, 30	5				
	red	14, 21, 26, 28, 33, 34, 35,	5, 7	5, 7				
	violet	22		22	6		6	6
	blue	29, 32, 33, 34, 35			6		6	6
	green	27, 32, 33, 34, 35, 36, 38, 41, 42, 43, 44	16, 17		16	37		
	brown	21, 23, 29, 31, 33, 36, 41, 44	4, 17, 30			37		
	grey	18, 20, 21, 29, 33, 40, 42, 44	15					2
	black							2, 9

+ liquid, no streak

		Hardness 2—3							
		Streak colour							
Lustre	Colour	white silver-white	yellow ochre-yellow orange	pink red violet	blue	green	brown red-brown	grey steel-grey green-grey	black grey-black
metallic submetallic	white	49, 74, 81, 170					170	46, 48, 83, 87	69, 73, 78
	yellow	81	50					83	
	red			47, 60, 64				48	
	violet			96			96		
	blue								68, 69
	green	170					170		68
	brown	170						52, 170	

Identification table according to hardness, streak, colour and lustre — cont.

Lustre	Colour	white silver-white	yellow ochre-yellow orange	pink red violet	blue	green	brown red-brown	grey steel-grey green-grey	black grey-black
metallic submetallic	grey			45, 51, 57, 60			52	13, 51, 61, 62, 71, 77	53, 54, 55, 58, 59, 67, 68, 69, 70, 72, 73, 75, 77, 79, 80, 82
	black	49		60					54, 55, 56, 59, 62, 74, 75, 82
non-metallic	colourless	84, 108							
	white	84, 85, 86, 88, 90, 91, 92, 93, 94, 97, 98, 99, 100, 101, 102, 103, 104, 105, 107, 108, 111, 112, 113, 120, 124, 125, 136, 139, 147, 155, 156, 159, 160, 165, 169, 170, 175		169	136		170	98	
	yellow	84, 85, 97, 98, 102, 103, 104, 107, 111, 113, 120, 124, 125, 126, 139, 155, 160, 168, 170, 173, 174, 175	66, 123, 132, 133, 148, 150, 151, 153, 154, 171, 172				170	98	
	orange	86, 173	65, 66, 123, 133						
	red	85, 86, 87, 88, 90, 94, 100, 107, 111, 117, 122, 124, 125, 134, 139, 158, 168, 169, 174	66, 95, 119, 133, 135	76, 87, 122, 141, 162, 169		158	119		
	violet	84, 86, 103, 104, 121, 122, 158, 169		96, 122, 141, 169		158	96		
	blue	84, 86, 103, 104, 108, 115, 116, 121, 124, 127, 136			89, 106, 110, 126, 131, 136, 137, 138, 144, 145, 146	109, 128, 129, 130, 144, 146, 157			
	green	84, 90, 91, 92, 107, 108, 111, 112, 114, 115, 120, 121, 124, 134, 155, 158, 159, 160, 165, 166, 167, 168, 169, 170	148, 172	169	137, 144, 146	106, 109, 118, 123, 128, 129, 130, 140, 142, 143, 144, 146, 147, 149, 151, 152, 157, 158, 161, 164, 166	170	167	68
	brown	84, 88, 114, 134, 156, 165, 167, 168, 170, 174	66, 135			129, 161, 164	140, 170	167	
	grey	85, 86, 88, 90, 93, 94, 97, 102, 103, 107, 108, 124, 155, 156, 165, 168, 169		57, 60, 169				62	68, 75
	black	167	135	60, 63			167		62, 67, 74, 75

Identification table according to hardness, streak, colour and lustre — cont.

Lustre	Colour	Streak colour							
		white silver-white	yellow ochre-yellow orange	pink red violet	blue	green	brown red-brown	grey steel-grey green-grey	black grey-black
metallic submetallic	white	179, 204, 281						177, 178, 279, 280, 281	176, 203, 287, 289
	yellow	204, 278					278		185, 194, 195, 203, 283, 286, 288
	orange								285
	red		296	209			296		186, 192, 201
	violet								192, 201
	green								284
	brown	204	278				278, 282		192, 195, 203, 283, 285
	grey	281		209		180	282, 295	189, 193, 196, 279, 280, 281	176, 186, 187, 188, 190, 191, 200, 201, 202, 210, 211, 284, 287, 288
	black			209		180	282, 295, 298	177, 189, 193, 279	187, 190, 191, 197, 198, 200, 210
non-metallic	colourless	290, 301, 302, 311, 325, 328, 329, 330, 331, 332, 335							
	white	181, 183, 208, 212, 213, 214, 215, 217, 218, 219, 220, 221, 222, 223, 224, 225, 229, 231, 232, 233, 234, 235, 239, 240, 242, 244, 247, 248, 252, 253, 264, 265, 266, 267, 269, 270, 271, 272, 275, 290, 291, 292, 293, 294, 301, 302, 303, 310, 317, 323, 325, 326, 327, 328, 329, 330, 331, 332, 333, 334, 335, 336				257			176, 203
	yellow	181, 183, 208, 217, 219, 220, 221, 222, 223, 224, 225, 229, 231, 232, 234, 235, 239, 240, 244, 247, 252, 258, 262, 264, 265, 266, 269, 272, 273, 275, 292, 297, 302, 303, 305, 306, 310, 313, 317, 318, 323, 324, 325, 326, 329, 330, 332, 335	199, 230, 236, 237, 238, 241, 243, 244, 245, 246, 263, 278, 293, 294, 299, 300, 306, 312, 338	234		241, 322	263, 275, 278, 324, 339	273	203
	orange	217, 264, 265, 336	199, 243, 244, 263, 294, 300, 312, 338, 339			260	260, 263, 339		
	red	181, 217, 218, 220, 222, 224, 229, 232, 234, 235, 239, 240, 249, 250, 258, 262, 269, 270, 271, 272, 273, 290, 304, 310, 324, 325, 326, 328, 329, 330, 331, 332, 334, 336	199, 243, 263, 296, 300	209, 216, 234, 316		260	260, 263, 296, 324	273	

Identification table according to hardness, streak, colour and lustre — cont.

		Hardness 3—5							
Lustre	Colour	Streak colour							
		silver-white white	yellow ochre-yellow orange	pink to violet	blue	green	brown red-brown	grey steel-grey green-grey	black grey-black
non-metallic	violet	222,235, 249, 258, 291, 331, 333							
	blue	217, 221, 235, 239, 240, 244, 247, 251, 266, 275, 311, 317, 323			205, 207, 226, 255, 308	205, 207, 234, 254, 268, 274		275, 315	
	green	183, 208, 211, 221, 222, 247, 248, 251, 253, 258, 262, 264, 265, 266, 273, 275, 290, 291, 297, 303, 310, 311, 317, 331	241, 247, 297, 299, 309, 337, 338		205, 321	205, 206, 216, 227, 228, 230, 241, 245, 254, 255, 256, 257, 259, 260, 261, 268, 274, 293, 307, 308, 319, 320, 321, 322, 337	181, 259, 260	230, 273, 275, 277, 315	
	brown	218, 219, 221, 223, 224, 225, 240, 247, 262, 264, 265, 266, 269, 270, 273, 276, 297, 302, 304, 305, 306, 310, 317, 324, 330	236, 237, 246, 263, 278, 297, 306, 309, 312, 338, 339			257, 260, 274	181, 184, 238, 245, 260, 263, 278, 282, 293, 314, 324, 339	273, 277, 315	203
	grey	218, 219, 221, 222, 223, 225, 229, 232, 234, 235, 240, 242, 252, 253, 262, 264, 265, 270, 272, 275, 301, 302, 303, 304, 306, 310, 317, 324, 328, 332, 333, 335, 336	209, 306	209, 234		180, 274	282, 295, 324, 339	277, 315	176, 187
	black	217, 225, 273, 297, 302	297, 309, 339	209		180, 259, 274	181, 182, 233, 259, 282, 295, 298, 339	273	187

		Hardness 5—7							
Lustre	Colour	Streak colour							
		colourless white silver-white	yellow ochre-yellow orange	pink red violet	blue	green	brown red-brown	grey steel-grey green-grey	black grey-black
metallic submetallic	white								342, 343, 344, 345, 346, 347, 348, 349, 350
	yellow	363					464, 465, 471	363, 436, 437	437, 438, 439, 468
	orange								340
	red		356, 364	472			351, 356, 368, 464, 465, 470, 472	368	340, 341, 342, 345
	blue					482	482		
	green	427					471	427	

Lustre	Colour	Streak colour							
		colourless / white / silver-white	yellow / ochre-yellow / orange	pink / red / violet	blue	green	brown / red-brown	grey / steel-grey / lead-grey / grey-white	black / black-grey
metallic submetallic	brown	363, 427	354, 356, 364, 467	472			351, 356, 362, 368, 369, 371, 464, 465, 467, 471, 472, 478	363, 368, 425, 427	342, 369, 425
	grey	427		472, 473		482	370, 472, 482	425, 427, 482	340, 341, 343, 344, 346, 349, 350, 370, 425, 438, 474, 475
	black	363	354, 364, 467	366, 472, 473, 476		482	357, 358, 362, 365, 369, 370, 371, 467, 469, 470, 472, 478, 479, 480, 482	363, 425, 482	357, 367, 369, 370, 425, 468, 474, 475
non-metallic	colourless	352, 360, 373, 375, 379, 385, 386, 387, 388, 393, 396, 397, 398, 403, 404, 406, 407, 435, 440, 448, 461, 462, 463, 466, 483, 484, 486, 488, 489, 492, 493, 494, 495, 496, 497, 498, 499, 500, 502, 505, 517, 524	360						
	white	373, 377, 379, 384, 385, 386, 387, 388, 389, 390, 391, 393, 394, 395, 396, 397, 398, 399, 400, 403, 404, 405, 406, 407, 412, 430, 435, 440, 443, 445, 446, 447, 449, 450, 451, 452, 460, 461, 462, 463, 466, 483, 486, 489, 490, 492, 493, 494, 495, 496, 497, 498, 499, 500, 502, 516	361		395		361, 471		
	yellow	352, 360, 363, 373, 375, 377, 379, 383, 384, 385, 386, 387, 388, 389, 390, 391, 392, 395, 397, 401, 402, 403, 404, 406, 407, 430, 435, 440, 441, 443, 444, 445, 447, 449, 450, 451, 455, 456, 457, 459, 461, 463, 484, 485, 486, 487, 488, 489, 490, 499, 501, 502, 504, 508, 514, 515, 516, 518, 522	360, 361, 376		395		361, 464, 465	363, 368, 383, 573, 518, 522	
	orange	373, 383, 442, 449, 450, 456, 532						383	
	red	352, 360, 373, 379, 381, 383, 384, 386, 387, 389, 395, 397, 398, 399, 400, 402, 419, 430, 440, 441, 442, 445, 449, 450, 451, 452, 455, 456, 459, 463, 483, 486, 488, 492, 493, 494, 495, 496, 497, 498, 501, 503, 514, 516, 517, 518, 519, 520, 521, 522, 531, 532, 533	356, 360, 361, 364, 382, 527	381, 472	395		356, 361, 368, 464, 465, 472, 527	368, 383, 518, 522, 526	
	violet	379, 398, 402, 449, 450, 463, 502, 503, 523, 533							
	blue	352, 373, 374, 377, 378, 379, 380, 390, 391, 393, 394, 395, 397, 398, 403, 404, 420, 421, 422, 426, 435, 440, 441, 443, 447, 448, 449, 450, 484, 487, 491, 492, 493, 494, 495, 496, 497, 498, 520, 522, 530			392, 395, 418, 420, 431, 433	421, 422, 482	421, 482	420, 482, 513, 522	

Identification table according to hardness, streak, colour and lustre — cont.

		Hardness 5—7							
Lustre	Colour	Streak colour							
		colourless white silver-white	yellow ochre-yel-low orange	pink red violet	blue	green	brown red-brown black-brown	grey steel-grey lead-grey grey-white	black black-grey
non-metallic	green	373, 374, 375, 377, 378, 379, 380, 389, 391, 393, 395, 397, 398, 399, 400, 401, 402, 403, 404, 405, 406, 412, 413, 414, 415, 416, 417, 419, 421, 423, 424, 426, 427, 428, 430, 435, 440, 441, 444, 445, 446, 448, 449, 450, 453, 454, 457, 458, 459, 466, 490, 491, 492, 493, 494, 495, 496, 497, 498, 501, 502, 504, 505, 506, 507, 508, 511, 514, 515, 516, 518, 519, 522, 523, 524, 525, 528	376		392, 395, 408, 433	421, 432, 509, 510	411, 421, 471	409, 411, 427, 428, 429, 507, 509, 511, 513, 518, 522, 526, 528, 529	
	brown	352, 360, 363, 379, 381, 383, 387, 388, 389, 394, 397, 399, 401, 402, 403, 404, 405, 406, 419, 424, 425, 426, 427, 428, 430, 440, 442, 444, 445, 449, 450, 454, 456, 459, 486, 501, 507, 511, 518, 519, 520, 522, 523, 524, 528, 531, 532, 533	353, 354, 356, 359, 360, 361, 364, 382, 467, 527	381, 434, 472, 512	408	509, 510	353, 355, 356, 359, 361, 362, 368, 369, 371, 410, 434, 464, 465, 467, 469, 471, 472, 478, 527	363, 368, 383, 409, 410, 425, 427, 428, 429, 507, 509, 511, 518, 522, 526, 528,	369, 370, 425, 481,
	grey	360, 377, 385, 386, 387, 391, 393, 394, 395, 396, 397, 398, 400, 403, 404, 406, 407, 412, 413, 414, 415, 416, 417, 419, 423, 424, 426, 427, 428, 435, 444, 445, 447, 449, 450, 451, 461, 463, 466, 483, 486, 488, 490, 500, 502, 505, 507, 508, 514, 515, 519, 523, 528	360, 527	472, 477	395, 418	482	477, 482, 527	425, 427, 428, 482, 507, 526, 528, 529	425
	black	363, 394, 420, 421, 428, 430, 440, 441, 444, 445, 449, 450, 452, 505, 507, 511, 524, 528	353, 354, 364, 382, 467	434, 472, 477	420	372, 421, 482, 509	353, 355, 357, 360, 365, 369, 370, 371, 410, 411, 421, 434, 467, 469, 472, 477, 478, 479, 482	363, 409, 410, 411, 420, 425, 428, 429, 482, 509, 511, 513, 528, 529	357, 367, 369, 370, 425

487

Identification table according to hardness, streak, colour and lustre — cont.

Lustre	Colour	white silver-white	yellow ochre-yellow orange	pink red violet	blue	green	brown red-brown	grey steel-grey green-grey	black grey-black
Hardness greater than 7 — *Streak colour*									
metallic submetallic	brown	548	548				548		
	grey	548	548				548		
	black	548	548				548		
non-metallic	colourless	534, 535, 549, 550, 554, 560, 564, 567, 568, 573, 574, 577, 579, 587, 589, 590, 595, 596, 597, 598, 601, 602					548		
	white	534, 549, 553, 554, 573, 574, 575, 577, 596, 597, 602							
	yellow	534, 540, 542, 548, 549, 550, 553, 554, 558, 563, 572, 573, 577, 579, 581, 582, 584, 587, 589, 590, 593, 595, 596, 597, 598, 602	548, 577				548		
	orange	577, 583, 584, 588	577						
	red	534, 537, 538, 545, 554, 557, 562, 564, 567, 569, 577, 578, 584, 585, 587, 588, 590, 594, 595, 597, 598, 599		577					
	violet	534, 536, 537, 551, 552, 569, 575, 577, 585, 594, 595, 598		577					
	blue	534, 541, 543, 548, 549, 550, 551, 552, 554, 556, 561, 564, 567, 570, 574, 575, 576, 577, 587, 590, 595, 598, 600, 602							
	green	534, 544, 545, 546, 549, 551, 553, 554, 555, 556, 559, 564, 567, 568, 570, 571, 574, 575, 576, 577, 579, 580, 581, 587, 590, 593, 594, 595, 598, 602				577	591		
	brown	534, 538, 539, 542, 545, 548, 553, 562, 563, 564, 572, 573, 577, 579, 583, 584, 585, 587, 590, 592, 593, 595, 597, 598, 602	548				548	577, 585, 586, 592	
	grey	534, 544, 548, 549, 551, 562, 566, 573, 577, 598, 602	548				548	577	
	black	534, 539, 543, 546, 548, 563, 564, 565, 577, 579, 585, 590, 602	548				548	547, 585, 586	577

Minerals soluble in water

Hardness	No. of mineral	In cold water — Mineral	No. of mineral	In warm water — Mineral
1—2	14	sal-ammoniac	18	sassolite
	20	natron	19	ulexite
	21	nitratine	29	gypsum
	23	mirabilite	30	sideronatrite
	24	tschermigite	31	struvite
	26	alunogen	43	evenkite
	27	halotrichite		
	28	pickeringite		
	84	carnallite	100	inyoite
	85	sylvite	101	kernite
	86	halite	104	alumohydrocalcite
	87	villiaumite		
	97	borax	108	leadhillite
	98	gaylussite	174	mellite
	102	trona		
	111	epsomite		
	112	hexahydrite		
	113	goslarite		

Hardness	No. of mineral	In cold water — Mineral	No. of mineral	In warm water — Mineral
2—3	114	melanterite		
	115	pisanite		
	116	chalcanthite		
	117	bieberite		
	118	morenosite		
	120	fibroferrite		
	121	coquimbite		
	122	quenstedtite		
	123	copiapite		
	124	ferrinatrite		
	125	thenardite		
	127	kröhnkite		
	135	delvauxite		
	139	pharmacolite		
3—5	229	kainite		
	231	kieserite		
	234	polyhalite		

Identification table
according to hardness and specific gravity

Specific gravity	Hardness				
	below 2	2—3	3—5	5—7	greater than 7
below 2	14, 18, 20, 23, 24, 25, 26, 27, 28, 31, 33, 43, 44	84, 85, 97, 98, 99, 100, 101, 111, 112, 114, 115, 117, 120, 135, 173, 174	234, 244, 266, 267		
2—3	1, 2, 19, 21, 22, 29, 30, 33, 34, 35, 36, 37, 38, 39, 40, 41, 42	86, 87, 88, 90, 91, 92, 102, 104, 105, 113, 116, 118, 119, 121, 122, 123, 124, 125, 126, 127, 135, 136, 138, 139, 140, 144, 155, 156, 157, 158, 159, 160, 161, 162, 163, 165, 166, 167, 168, 169, 175	212, 213, 214, 215, 216, 217, 218, 221, 229, 230, 231, 232, 233, 234, 235, 237, 245, 246, 247, 248, 249, 250, 268, 269, 270, 271, 272, 273, 274, 275, 276, 290, 301, 311, 325, 326, 327, 328, 329, 330, 331, 332, 333, 334, 335	374, 375, 376, 384, 385, 386, 387, 388, 389, 390, 391, 392, 393, 394, 395, 396, 397, 398, 399, 400, 401, 402, 406, 407, 411, 412, 419, 421, 422, 427, 440, 441, 442, 443, 444, 445, 446, 447, 448, 449, 450, 451, 452, 453, 454, 455, 456, 457, 458, 459, 460, 461, 462, 483, 484, 485, 486, 487, 488, 489, 490, 491, 492, 493, 494, 495, 496, 497, 498, 500, 515	534, 535, 536, 537, 538, 539, 540, 541, 542, 543, 544, 545, 549, 551, 552, 554, 555, 556, 557, 558, 559, 560, 561, 564, 565, 566, 567, 568, 569, 570, 571, 572, 573
3—4	4, 5, 32	103, 106, 128, 129, 130, 131, 137, 141, 142, 143, 144, 145, 147, 148, 149, 150, 151, 152, 153, 154, 158, 161, 164, 167, 170, 171, 172	181, 182, 183, 205, 206, 208, 219, 220, 222, 226, 227, 228, 235, 236, 237, 238, 239, 251, 252, 253, 254, 255, 256, 276, 277, 278, 282, 291, 297, 302, 303, 304, 306, 312, 313, 314, 315, 316, 319, 336, 337	352, 354, 355, 372, 377, 378, 379, 380, 381, 382, 403, 405, 406, 407, 408, 409, 410, 411, 412, 413, 414, 415, 416, 417, 418, 419, 420, 421, 422, 423, 424, 426, 427, 428, 429, 430, 431, 432, 433, 434, 435, 463, 466, 499, 501, 502, 503, 504, 505, 506, 507, 508, 509, 510, 511, 512, 513, 514, 515, 516, 517, 518, 519, 520, 521, 522, 523, 524, 525, 527, 528, 529, 530, 531, 532, 533	546, 547, 549, 550, 553, 562, 563, 564, 565, 566, 567, 568, 569, 570, 571, 572, 573, 574, 575, 576, 577, 578, 579, 580, 581, 582, 583, 584, 585, 586, 590, 593, 594, 595, 596, 597, 598, 599, 600, 601, 602
4—5	6, 7, 8	45, 51, 52, 57, 132, 146, 154, 158	180, 181, 182, 183, 184, 185, 186, 187, 188, 189, 190, 191, 192, 194, 199, 207, 211, 223, 239, 240, 241, 257, 258, 261, 283, 284, 285, 292, 293, 295, 297, 307, 308, 309, 317, 318, 319, 320, 321, 324, 339	340, 341, 342, 353, 354, 356, 357, 358, 359, 360, 361, 363, 364, 365, 366, 371, 373, 383, 404, 410, 425, 437, 464, 465, 467, 468, 469, 471, 476, 526	546, 577, 578, 579, 580, 581, 582, 583, 584, 585, 587, 588, 589, 591, 592, 598, 599, 600, 601
5—6	16, 17	53, 54, 55, 58, 59, 60, 63, 64, 65, 66, 68, 89, 93, 94, 96, 109, 110	176, 177, 190, 191, 193, 194, 195, 196, 199, 207, 210, 224, 259, 292, 293, 296, 305, 310, 322, 323, 324, 339	343, 344, 360, 361, 367, 383, 436, 468, 470, 471, 472, 473, 474, 475, 477, 478	
6—8	9, 10, 11, 15	46, 55, 56, 61, 62, 67, 69, 70, 71, 72, 73, 74, 75, 77, 107, 108, 133, 134	177, 178, 179, 197, 200, 201, 202, 203, 209, 210, 225, 242, 243, 260, 262, 263, 264, 265, 279, 286, 287, 288, 289, 293, 294, 298, 300, 310, 338, 339	343, 344, 345, 346, 347, 348, 349, 350, 351, 368, 369, 370, 438, 480	548
greater than 8	3, 12, 13	47, 48, 49, 50, 76, 78, 79, 80, 81, 82, 83, 95, 134	198, 203, 204, 280, 281, 299	362, 439, 479, 480, 481, 482	

Luminescent minerals

Explanations:

○ — mineral is luminescent
● — mineral is luminescent in long-wave ultra-violet light
△ — mineral is luminescent in short-wave ultra-violet light

▲ — mineral is phosphorescent
□ — mineral shows triboluminescence
■ — mineral shows thermoluminescence

Hardness	No. of mineral	Mineral	white	yellow-white	green-white	blue-white	yellow	yellow-green	yellow-brown	orange	cream	pink to violet	red	brown	green	blue	blue-green
below 2	15	calomel								●		○	○				
	18	sassolite														○	
	19	ulexite	○														
	23	mirabilite	●▲														
	25	aluminite	▲														
	29	gypsum				●▲	○							●	○		
	33	montmorillonite	●														
	34	halloysite	●														
	41	talc	○		△	●						●		●	△	●	△
	42	pyrophyllite	●			●				●							
	43	evenkite				○											
	44	idrialine					○								○	○	
2—3	86	halite									○	○					
	90	gibbsite						△						△			
	91	brucite				○										○	
	97	borax														▲	
	98	gaylussite									○						
	100	inyoite		○													
	102	trona	○													○	
	103	hydrozincite				○										○	
	107	phosgenite					○										
	108	leadhillite					○										
	125	thenardite		●▲			●			●							
	133	crocoite												○			
	134	stolzite			△												
	141	erythrite								○							
	148	autunite						○									
	150	tyuyamunite						○									
	151	meta-autunite						○									
	155	sepiolite		△		△											
	159	clinochlore								○							
	162	kämmererite								●							
	168	phlogopite				△											
	169	lepidolite														□■	
	172	uranophane						○									
	173	amber				●									△		
	174	mellite														●	

Luminescent minerals — cont.

Hardness	No. of mineral	Mineral	Luminescence														
			white	yellow-white	green-white	blue-white	yellow	yellow-green	yellow-brown	orange	cream	pink to violet	red	brown	green	blue	blue-green
	181	sphalerite					□			□			□			□	
	209	cuprite											○				
	212	priceite					○										
	214	hydromagnesite	●				●								△		
	215	dawsonite	△														
	217	calcite	▲□■				▲□■			▲□■			▲□■		▲■	▲■	
	218	dolomite	○							○	○			○	○		
	219	ankerite								●							
	221	aragonite	○				○			○	○				○		
	222	strontianite	▲								▲						
	223	witherite					○	○								○	
	225	cerussite								●		●			△	△	
	232	alunite	○	.						○							
	235	anhydrite											○				
	239	celestite			○											○	
	240	baryte	○		○				○								○
	241	powellite					○										
	242	anglesite		○						○	○						
	244	evansite	●												△		
	247	wavellite			○							○					
3—5	251	phosphophyllite										△					
	258	adamite			○		○										
	262	pyromorphite					○										
	264	mimetite								△							
	266	allophane	○				○			○					○		
	267	thaumasite	△														
	270	heulandite														●	
	272	laumontite	●														
	273	serpentine	●				●										
	275	chrysotile												●			
	290	prosopite					○										
	291	fluorite											□■			□■	
	301	colemanite		▲	▲												
	302	magnesite		□	□	□											
	303	barytocalcite					○										
	304	rhodochrosite										●					
	310	scheelite														○	
	311	variscite													○		
	325	chabazite													△		
	331	apophyllite			●		●										●
	334	tugtupite										○					
	335	wollastonite					○			○	○	○			○	○	

Luminescent minerals — cont.

Hardness	No. of mineral	Mineral	white	yellow-white	green-white	blue-white	yellow	yellow-green	yellow-brown	orange	cream	pink to violet	red	brown	green	blue	blue-green
5—7	373	smithsonite	○		○	○		○								○	
	374	turquoise						○								○	
	377	amblygonite								●							
	378	lazulite	○														
	379	apatite	■				■			■		■			■	■	
	387	natrolite								○							
	390	okenite									△						
	393	sodalite					○			○							
	395	hauyne								○							
	396	leucite								●							
	397	nepheline						○									
	398	scapolite					△■			△■							
	400	pectolite					△□			△□							
	403	hemimorphite				□	□			□							
	404	willemite													○		
	407	datolite	○													○	
	412	tremolite		△			△					●	●				
	419	anthophyllite	○			○										○	
	435	kyanite											○				
	440	opal	○				○	○							○		
	441	precious opal												○	○		
	448	hyalite					○								○		
	449	chalcedony	○				○								○		
	450	agate	○				○								○		
	463	diaspore					○										
	466	periclase					●										
	483	petalite	○				○			○							
	486	orthoclase	○				○				○				○		
	490	microcline			○												
	491	amazonite													△		
	493	albite													○		
	500	pollucite	○														
	502	spodumene					○			○							
	503	kunzite								○							
	504	hiddenite								○							
	505	diopside			○						○						
	508	jadeite														○	
	513	epidote												○			
	518	chondrodite					○			○					○		
	519	zoisite													○		
	521	thulite													○		
	523	axinite										○					

Luminescent minerals — cont.

Hardness	No. of mineral	Mineral	Luminescence														
			white	yellow-white	green-white	blue-white	yellow	yellow-green	yellow-brown	orange	cream	pink to violet	red	brown	green	blue	blue-green
5—7	530	benitoite														△	
	531	rhodonite											○				
greater than 7	534	quartz					□			□	□				□		
	536	amethyst														□	
	538	rose quartz									□						
	545	aventurine													○		
	554	beryl					○								○		
	557	morganite										○					
	559	heliodor													○		
	562	andalusite					○								○		
	564	tourmaline					○								○		
	573	danburite														○	○
	574	euclase											○				
	575	dumortierite				○						○					
	587	zircon					○	○		○			○				
	590	spinel						○					○				
	593	chrysoberyl								○			○				
	594	alexandrite											○				
	595	topaz					○				○				○		
	598	corundum					○										
	599	ruby											○	○			
	600	sapphire								○	○						
	602	diamond													▲■	▲■	

Radioactive minerals

Hardness	No. of mineral	Constant		No. of mineral	Dependent on admixtures
		Mineral			Mineral
2—3	96	ianthinite			
	148	autunite			
	149	torbernite			
	150	tyuyamunite			
	151	meta-autunite			
	152	metatorbernite			
	153	zeunerite			
	154	carnotite			
	172	uranophane			
3—5	297	betafite		324	xenotime
	298	brannerite		339	thorite
	300	curite			
	337	cuprosklodowskite			
	338	kasolite			

Hardness	No. of mineral	Constant		No. of mineral	Dependent on admixtures
		Mineral			Mineral
5—7	359	pyrochlore		363	perovskite
	471	euxenite		365	ilmenite
	481	thorianite		379	apatite
	482	uraninite		383	monazite
				410	allanite
				477	columbite
				479	tantalite
				480	tapiolite
greater than 7				587	zircon
				588	hyacinth
				589	jargon

Mineral associations of magmatic processes
(main types of magmatic rocks)

Rock group	Rocks		Minerals		
	intrusive	effusive	main	accessory	secondary
ultra-basic	dunite		olivine	pyroxene, magnetite, ilmenite	serpentine, uralite,
	peridotite		olivine, pyroxene	chromite, spinels, pyrrhotine, platinum, pentlandite, chalcopyrite, pyrites, uvarovite	chlorites, talc
	pyroxenite		pyroxene	olivine	
	gabbro	basalt melaphyre diabase	basic plagioclases, pyroxene, olivine, common amphibole, biotite	orthoclase, quartz, apatite, titanite, ilmenite, pyrrhotine, pentlandite, chalcopyrite	albite, chlorites, uralite, sericite, agate, chalce-dony, quartz, opal, talc
inter-mediate	diorite	andesite	intermediate plagio-clases, common amphi-bole, biotite, pyroxene	quartz, orthoclase, apatite, titanite, magnetite	sericite, kaolinite, zoisite, chlorites, carbonates
	monzonite	latite	acidic plagioclase, ortho-clase, common amphi-bole, biotite	quartz, zircon, titanite, apatite	sericite, kaolinite, chlorites
	syenite	trachyte	orthoclase, acidic plagio-clase, common amphi-bole, biotite	quartz, zircon, titanite, apatite, magnetite	sericite, kaolinite, chlorites
acidic	granodiorite granite	dacite rhyolite quartz-porphyry	quartz, orthoclase, acidic plagioclase, biotite, muscovite, common amphibole	apatite, zircon, magne-tite, tourmaline, pyrites, chalcopyrite, bornite, allanite, garnet	sericite, kaolinite, chlorites
alkaline	nepheline-syenite	phonolite	orthoclase, nepheline, sanidine, alkaline pyrox-ene, alkaline amphibole, biotite	zircon, titanite, apatite, magnetite, sodalite, kan-krinite, corundum, leu-cite, eudialite, astrophyl-lite, lamprophyllite	sericite, kaolinite, chlorites, zeolites
	carbonatite[x]		calcite, dolomite, anker-ite, diopside, forsterite, phlogopite, apatite, mag-netite, vesuvianite, bar-yte, arfvedsonite, feld-spars	titanomagnetite, pyrochlore, columbite, perovskite	
	kimberlite[x]		olivine, diopside, phlogopite, pyrope	diamond, ilmenite, mag-netite, chromite, spinel, perovskite, zircon	

[x] varieties of altered peridotites or genetically associated with ultrabasic rocks

Mineral associations of the pegmatitic process

Pegmatites		Minerals	
		main	accessory
Granitic	muscovite and feldspar	oligoclase, albite, microcline, quartz, muscovite, biotite, apatite, schorl	garnet, allanite, beryl, monazite, xeno-time, zircon
	containing rare elements	albite, clevelandite, quartz, microcline, spodumene, lepidolite	muscovite, rubellite, elbaite, indicolite, beryl, amblygonite, triphylite, colum-bite, tantalite, pollucite, cassiterite, rose quartz, wolframite
	quartz	quartz, rock crystal, smoky quartz, albite, microcline, topaz, beryl	muscovite, phenakite, biotite
	in serpentinites	phlogopite, biotite, talc, chlorites, actinolite, plagioclase	common amphibole, quartz, musco-vite, fluorite, beryl, emerald, phenakite, apatite, magnetite, tourmaline, molyb-denite

Mineral associations of the pegmatitic process — cont.

Pegmatites	Minerals	
	main	accessory
Gabbroic	orthoclase, plagioclase, nepheline	lepidomelane, biotite, ilmenite, natrolite, sodalite, apatite, zircon, pyrochlore, titanite, muscovite, magnetite, cryolite, fluorite
Syenite	microcline, orthoclase, oligoclase, muscovite, biotite, titanite, augite, common amphibole	zircon, orthite, monazite, pyrochlore, corundum, ilmenite, ilmenorutile, fluorite
Nepheline-syenite	microcline, nepheline, vesuvianite, arfvedsonite, lepidomelane	titanite, ilmenite, zircon, eudialite, astrophyllite, lamprophyllite, pyrochlore, calcite

Mineral associations of post-magmatic processes

Processes	Type of mineralization		Minerals	
			main	accessory
Metasomatic (main types of metasomatic transformation of rocks)	**skarns**	magnesic	forsterite, diopside, calcite, phlogopite, magnetite, scapolite, pyrogenes, garnets, hematite, calcite, magnesite	quartz, plagioclase, spinels, serpentine, ludwigite, apatite, titanite, actinolite, chondrodite, periclase, lazurite, spinel, pyrite, pyrrhotine, chalcopyrite, sphalerite
		calcareous	grossularite, andradite, diopside, hedenbergite, vesuvianite, epidote, scapolite, magnetite, wollastonite, quartz, hematite, chlorites, calcite	plagioclases, tremolite, scheelite, datolite, molybdenite, danburite, axinite, helvite, ilvaite, fluorite, cassiterite, pyrite, chalcopyrite, cobaltite, galena, sphalerite, gold, bismutite, bismuth, skutterudite
	greisens		quartz, muscovite, zinnwaldite, topaz, fluorite	cassiterite, tourmaline, aquamarine, wolframite, scheelite, arsenopyrite, molybdenite, pyrrhotine, chalcopyrite, bismutite, cosalite, pyrite
	albitization (albitites)		albite, quartz, microcline, amazonite	muscovite, beryl, phenakite, bertrandite, wolframite, molybdenite, lepidolite, zinnwaldite, coloradoite, tantalite, microlite, spodumene, amblygonite, cassiterite, zircon, xenotime, riebeckite, monazite
	silicification (secondary quartzites)		quartz, sericite, alunite, kaolinite, andalusite, diaspore, pyrophyllite, corundum	dickite, tourmaline, dumortierite, pyrite, chalcopyrite, molybdenite, hematite, topaz
	sericitization (Cu — porphyritic ores)		quartz, sericite, chlorites, dolomite, calcite, ankerite, pyrite	tourmaline, rutile, fluorite, baryte, anhydrite, chalcopyrite, bornite, galena, sphalerite, gold, molybdenite, arsenopyrite
	propylitization (propylites)		albite, chlorites, epidote, actinolites, sericite	ankerite, calcite, pyrite, adularia, quartz
Hydrothermal	**high thermal**	Sn formation	quartz, cassiterite, zinnwaldite, fluorite, topaz, adularia	arsenopyrite, molybdenite, wolframite, ankerite, bismutite, pyrite, beryl, scheelite, gold, chalcopyrite
		Sn-W formation	quartz, adularia, cassiterite, wolframite, zinnwaldite, fluorite, topaz	pyrite, pyrrhotine, arsenopyrite, molybdenite, scheelite, bismutite, beryl, gold, chalcopyrite
		Mo formation	quartz, arsenopyrite, molybdenite, calcite, fluorite, topaz, pyrite	zinnwaldite, pyrrhotine, cassiterite, wolframite, bismutite, chalcopyrite, gold, adularia

Mineral associations of post-magmatic processes — cont.

Proces-ses	Type of mineralization	Minerals	
		main	accesory
Hydrothermal — medium thermal	Au formation	quartz, ankerite, pyrite, gold, arsenopyrite	baryte, chalcopyrite, galena, tetrahedrite, scheelite, aikinite, Au tellurides
	Co-Ni-Ag-Bi-U formation	quartz, ankerite, calcite, dolomite, nicco-lite, safflorite, skutterudite, proustite, pyrargyrite, uraninite	cobaltite, rammelsbergite, silver, tetra-hedrite, hematite, bismuth
	Polymetallic formation	quartz, calcite, rhodochrosite, baryte, fluorite, galena, sphalerite	siderite, ankerite, chalcopyrite, pyrite, pyrrhotine, gold, arsenopyrite, tetrahe-drite, bornite, boulangerite, bournonite, Ag tellurides
	Cu formation	quartz, siderite, dolomite, pyrite, chalco-pyrite, tetrahedrite	calcite, pyrrhotine, galena, sphalerite, bournonite, emplectite, wittichenite, bornite, covellite, baryte
Hydrothermal — low thermal	Sb formation	quartz, chalcedony, stibnite, pyrite, arsenopyrite	calcite, dolomite, boulangerite, jameson-ite, ferberite, realgar, cinnabar, marcasite, galena, sphalerite
	Hg formation	chalcedony, quartz, dolomite, cinnabar, marcasite	stibnite, realgar, orpiment, pyrite, arseno-pyrite, evenkite, dickite, dawsonite, opal, baryte
	As formation	dolomite, calcite, realgar, orpiment	stibnite, marcasite, baryte, chalcedony
Postvolcanic	fumaroles	calcite, dolomite, baryte, fluorite, hematite	sal-ammoniac, halite, sylvite, pyrite, tenorite, sulphur
	solfataras	tschermigite, K-ammonia, fluorite, baryte, hematite	halotrichite, gypsum, pickeringite, aluno-gen, alunite, melanterite, sulphur, sassolite, halite
	moffettes	gypsum, alunite, tschermigite	kaolinite, sulphur, thenardite, anhydrite, sassolite, halite, sylvite

Mineral associations of weathering processes

Type of process		Rock deposits	Minerals	
			main	accessory
Weathering crusts	areas of hu-mid and hot climate	Laterites (ultrabasic and basic rocks)	serpentine, nontronite, garnierite, magnesite, calcite, chlorites	Ni-nontronite, revdanskite, opal, chal-cedony, goethite, halloysite, talc, hydromagnesite, brucite
		Bauxites (basic and acidic rocks)	diaspore, boehmite, gibbsite	goethite, kaolinite, nontronite, chlorite, hydrohematite, limonite
	areas of mild climate	Kaolinites	kaolinite	halloysite, montmorillonite, chalce-dony, opal, goethite, allophane, limon-ite
Oxidation zones of sulphidic deposits — gossans		Cu — deposits	malachite, azurite, limonite, native Cu, cuprite, tenorite	melanterite, chalcanthite, brochantite, antlerite, dioptase, libethenite, chal-cophyllite, gypsum, aragonite, oliven-ite, atacamite
		Pb-Zn deposits	smithsonite, anglesite, pyromorphite, cerussite, limonite	plumbojarosite, mimetite, vanadinite, crocoite, hydrozincite, hemimorphite, auricalcite, aragonite, gypsum, adamite, goslarite, phosgenite, wulfenite, linarite
		Sb — deposits	valentinite, senarmontite, cervantite, limonite	kermesite, stibiconite, bindheimite, aragonite, gypsum, scorodite
		Ag — deposits	silver, cerargyrite, argentite, limonite	electrum, gold, chlorargyrite, acanthite
Infiltration		Fe — deposits	siderite, limonite	illite, pyrite, kaolinite, baryte, chalce-dony
		U — deposits	carnotite	roscoelite
		Cu — deposits (cementation zones)	covellite, chalcocite, bornite, chalco-pyrite	pyrite, limonite, goethite, gold

Mineral associations of sedimentary processes

Type of process	Rocks deposits	Minerals	
		main	accessory
Mechanical	Gravels, conglomerates	quartz, rock fragments, organic remains	gold, uraninite, pyrite, marcasite, galena, sphalerite
	Sands, sandstones (alluvial deposits)	magnetite, ilmenite, rutile, quartz, pyroxenes, tourmaline, titanite, Ca and Mg carbonates, plagioclase, orthoclase	gold, platinum, diamond, monazite, zircon, xenotime, cassiterite, wolframite, scheelite, ruby, sapphire, topaz, spinels, almandine, pyrope, chromite
	Clays, claystones	illite, montmorillonite, kaolinite	limonite, goethite, calcite, opal, marcasite, halloysite
Chemical and biochemical deposits of salt lakes and seas	Limestone	calcite	dolomite, chalcedony, siderite, limonite, psilomelane, baryte, celestite
	Dolomite	dolomite	calcite, baryte, limonite, psilomelane, quartz, glauconite, phosphorite
	Evaporites	gypsum, anhydrite	celestite, thenardite, mirabilite, glauberite, epsomite, halite, soda, polygorskite, sulphur, baryte, aragonite
	Salt deposits	halite, carnallite, sylvite, kainite, polyhalite	gypsum, anhydrite, dolomite, calcite, glauberite, epsomite, aragonite
	Borates	ascharite, hydroboracite, boracite, colemanite, pandermite, ulexite	inyoite, inderite, realgar, calcite, dolomite, magnesite
	Phosphorites	phosporite, apatite	glauconite, limonite, illite, quartz, pyrite
	Fe — ores	goethite, chamosite, thuringite, glauconite, siderite	pyrite, vivianite, baryte, psilomelane, rhodochrosite, hematite, apatite, chalcedony
	Mn — ores	psilomelane, pyrolusite, manganite, rhodochrosite, opal, hydrogoethite	glauconite, chamosite, baryte, marcasite, pyrite, apatite
	Bauxites	diaspore, boehmite, gibbsite	goethite, kaolinite, chlorites, limonite, hydrohematite
	Silicides	opal, quartz, chalcedony	pyrite, marcasite, calcite
	Coal	organic substances	illite, dawsonite, ankerite, quartz, pyrite, marcasite

Mineral associations of metamorphic processes

Type of metamorphosis	Rock types mineral facies	Minerals
Regional metamorphosis (main metamorphic facies)	Zeolite facies	quartz, albite, chlorites, pumpellyite, native Cu
	Green schist facies (chloritic schist)	quartz, albite, epidote, chlorites, actinolite, calcite, sericite, talc, serpentine, magnetite, hematite, graphite, chrysotile
	Glaucophane facies	quartz, spessartite, rhodonite, glaucophane, vesuvianite, jadeite, muscovite, epidote, chlorites, calcite
	Epidote — amphibolite facies (epidote amphibolites)	epidote, common amphibole, plagioclase, biotite, almandine, sillimanite, andalusite, staurolite, anthophyllite, magnetite
	Amphibolite facies (amphibolites)	common amphibole, diopside, hypersthene, basic plagioclases, orthoclase, sillimanite, forsterite, rutile
	Granulite facies (gneiss, erlans)	quartz, garnet, diopside, hypersthene, basic plagioclases, orthoclase, sillimanite, forsterite, rutile
	Eclogite facies (eclogites)	garnet, kyanite, enstatite, rutile

Mineral associations of metamorphic processes — cont.

Type of metamorphosis	Rock types mineral facies		Minerals
Hydrothermal-metamorphosis	**Serpentinites**		serpentine, antigorite, chrysotile, opal, calcite
Dislocation metamorphosis	**Alpine veins**		quartz, rock crystal, smoky quartz, dolomite, halite, ripidolite, adularia, albite, rutile, brookite, hematite, epidote, zeolites, prehnite, titanite, apatite
Thermal metamorphosis	**Contact hornfels**	with argillaceous rocks	andalusite, cordierite, biotite, plagioclase, orthoclase, microcline, quartz, corundum, spinel
		with carbonate rocks	calcite, wollastonite, grossularite, vesuvianite, phlogopite, quartz, tremolite, diopside, hedenbergite, forsterite, actino-lite, brucite, talc, spinel, periclase
		with basic and magnesic rocks	basic plagioclases, diopside, hypersthene, cordierite, biotite, epidote, actinolite, anthophyllite, forsterite, spinel

Blowpipe tests for elements producing beads

⊕ — colour when hot
◯ — colour when cold

Bead colour	Borax		Phosphor	
	oxidizing	reducing	oxidizing	reducing
colourless or white	Ag, Bi, Cd, Hg, Fe, (◯ Mo), Pb, Sb, Sn, Ti, W, Zn alkaline metals alkaline earths	(⊕ Cu), Mn, (⊕ Ni), Sn alkaline metals alkaline earths	Bi, Cd, (◯ Fe), Hg, Mo, Pb, Sb, Sn, (◯ Ti) W, Zn	
grey		Ag, Bi, Cd, Ni, Pb, Sb, Zn		Ag, Bi, Cd, Ni, Pb, Sb, Zn
black	(◯ Mn)			
green	(◯ Cr), (⊕ Cu)	(◯ Cr), Fe, U, (◯ V) (◯ Cu — blue-green)	(◯ Cr), (⊕ Cu), (⊕ Mo)	(◯ Cr), Mo, U, (◯ V), (⊕ W)
blue	Co, (◯ Cu)	Co	Co, (◯ Cu)	Co, (◯ W)
violet	Mn, (⊕ Ni)		Mn	(◯ Ti)
red or brown	(⊕ Cr), (⊕ Fe), (⊕ Mo) (◯ Ni), (⊕ U)	(◯ Cu highly saturated) (◯ Mn), Mo	(⊕ Cr), (⊕ Ni), (⊕ Fe highly saturated)	(◯ Cu highly saturated) (⊕ Cr), (⊕ Fe), (◯ Fe + Ti), (◯ Fe + W)
yellow	(⊕ Bi), (⊕ Cr), (⊕ Fe) (◯ Fe saturated), (⊕ Mo) (⊕ Pb), (⊕ Sb saturated), U	Ti, W	(⊕ Ag), (⊕ Fe), (◯ Ni), (⊕ Ti), U, V, (⊕ W)	

Analytical reactions of blowpipe tests

Symbol of element (ions)	Flame colour	Heating of minerals		Blowpipe tests on charcoal		
		in closed tube	in open tube	oxidizing	reducing	with cobalt solution
Ag				light red-brown sublimate	with soda produces white malleable metal, no sublimate or light red-brown	
Al				forms no sublimate, shines	remains white infusible oxide	blue colour (Thénard's blue)
As	light azure-blue	black sublimate, with soda forms metallic globule	white sublimate, garlic odour	white fume, garlic odour, white (bluish) sublimate	sublimate, fume with garlic odour	
Au					yellow metal bead	
Ba	yellow-green			no sublimate, shines	remains infusible oxide	
Be				no sublimate, shines		violet to blue-grey
Bi				orange sublimate when hot, lemon-yellow sublimate when cold (with white border)	reddish fragile metal, yellow sublimate	
$BO_2^{\ominus}$	green, sometimes blue-green					
Ca	orange to brick-red			no sublimate, shines	remains infusible oxide	
Cl				white sublimate		
Cd				brown fume, red-brown sublimate with variegated border	sublimate (brown) with irized border	
Co					metallic grey magnetic powder	
$CO_3^{\ominus 2}$		CO_2 is released				
Cu	emerald $CuCl_2$ — azure-blue	copper and carbonates become black, sulphates become, white				
Fe					grey magnetic metal	
Hg		with soda Hg mirror	with soda Hg mirror			
H_2O		dew-like precipitate	dew-like precipitate			
K	light violet			salts melt and soak in charcoal		
Li	crimson					
Mg				no sublimate, shines	white infusible oxide remains	beige colour
Mn	green					
Mo	yellow-green			copper-red, sometimes white or yellow sublimate	metallic grey powder	

Symbol of element (ions)	Flame colour	Heating of minerals		Blowpipe tests on charcoal		
		in closed tube	in open tube	oxidizing	reducing	with cobalt solution
Na	deep yellow			salts melt and soak in charcoal		
$NH_4^{\oplus}$		with soda forms sublimate, ammonia is released		white sublimate		
Ni					metallic grey magnetic powder	
$NO_3^{\ominus}$		swells		swells		
Pb	grey-green to bluish			when hot deep yellow, when cold light yellow sublimate	grey soft metal (smears paper)	
$PO_4^{\ominus 3}$	grey-green when wetted with H_2SO_4	wetted and fused with Mg has a hydrogen phosphide odour				
Rb	blue					
S		yellow sublimate	odour of hydrogen sulphide or yellow sublimate	hydrogen sulphide odour	hepar reaction	
Sb	light blue-green	black sublimate, with soda forms mirror	white fume, white odourless sublimate	white odourless fume, blue sublimate	fragile metal soluble in HCl, blue-white sublimate	dirty green colour
Se	deep blue	black balls with red translucence	steel-grey to red sublimate, odour of rotten radish	odour of rotten radish, grey sublimate		
Si					clear glass	
Sn				slight white sublimate in close proximity to specimen	metal reducible with difficulty, slight sublimate close to specimen, yellow when hot, white when cold	blue-green colour
Sr	crimson				infusible oxide	
Te	greenish (with oxides)	white sublimate, black globules of Te	white fume, sublimate melts in clear drops	white sublimate with red border		
Ti					transparent when hot, dull when cold	yellow-green colour
Tl	green (disappears soon)					
W					grey powdered metal	
Zn	green-blue			yellow sublimate when hot, white when cold	only sublimate	green colour

Precious Stones

Colour	Hardness	No. of mineral	Mineral	frequency	Mode of application							
					natural form	facets	cabochons	tumble polished	glyptic	plastic cut	fancy goods	decorative and ornamental stones
Colourless	2—3	107	phosgenite	III		●	●					
	3—5	183	sphalerite	III		●	●					
		217	calcite	III		●						
		218	dolomite	III		●						
		221	aragonite	III		●	●				●	●
		228	cerussite	III		●	●					
		235	anhydrite	III		●	●					
		239	celestite	III		●						
		240	baryte	III		●						
		242	anglesite	III		●	●					
		291	fluorite	II		●	●					
		331	apophyllite	III		●						
	5—7	387	natrolite	III		●						
		398	scapolite	II		●	●					
		448	hyalite	III	●	●	●					
		483	petalite	II		●	●					
		487	adularia	II		●	●(P)					
		490	microcline	III			●(P)					
		500	pollucite	III		●						
		502	spodumene	II		●						
	greater than 7	535	rock crystal	I	●	●	●(A)	●	●	●	●	●
		560	goshenite	II		●						
		568	achroite	III		●						
		573	danburite	II		●						
		582	grossularite	II		●	●		●			
		589	jargon	II		●	●					
		595	topaz	I	●	●	●					
		597	phenakite	II		●	●					
		601	leucosapphire	I		●						
		602	diamond	I	●	●						
White	below 2	19	ulexite	II			●		●			●
		29	gypsum (alabaster)	I			●			●	●	●
		41	talc (steatite)	I			●			●	●	●
		42	pyrophyllite	I			●			●	●	●
	2—3	155	sepiolite	II			●			●	●	●
	3—5	203	domeykite	III			●					
		267	thaumasite	III			●					
	5—7	400	pectolite	III			●(P)					
		443	milk opal	I			●		●			
		447	hydrophane	II			●(O)					
		486	orthoclase	II			●(P)					
Yellow	below 2	1	sulphur	III			●					
		2	orpiment	III								●
	2—3	107	phosgenite	III		●						
		173	amber	I	●	●	●	●		●	●	●
	3—5	183	sphalerite	III		●	●					
		185	chalcopyrite	III	●	●	●					
		217	calcite	III		●						

Colour	Hardness	No. of mineral	Mineral	frequency	Mode of application							
					natural form	facets	cabochons	tumble polished	glyptic	plastic cut	fancy goods	decorative and ornamental stones
Yellow	3—5	221	aragonite	I			●			●	●	●
		223	witherite	III		●	●					
		240	baryte	III		●	●					
		243	wulfenite	III		●	●					
		275	chrysotile	III			●(P)					●
		291	fluorite	II		●	●					
		310	scheelite	II		●	●					
		322	bayldonite	III		●	●					
		331	apophyllite	III		●						
	5—7	375	brazilianite	II		●	●					
		377	amblygonite	II		●	●					
		379	apatite	II	●	●	●					
		398	scapolite	II		●	●(P)					
		404	willemite	III		●						
		407	datolite	III		●						
		430	titanite	II		●	●					
		436	pyrite	II	●	●	●					
		437	marcasite	II	●	●	●					
		444	common opal	I			●		●	●	●	●
		445	wood opal	I			●			●	●	●
		466	periclase	III		●	●					
		484	milarite	III		●	●					
		486	orthoclase	II		●	●(P)					
		488	sanidine	II		●	●					
		490	microcline	III		●	●(P)					
		515	prehnite	III		●	●					
		516	sillimanite	III		●	●					
		518	chondrodite	III		●	●					
		522	vesuvianite	II		●	●					
	greater than 7	540	citrine	I	●	●	●	●	●	●	●	●
		558	gold beryl	II		●	●					
		559	heliodor	II		●	●					
		573	danburite	II		●						
		582	grossularite	II		●	●					
		584	spessartite	III		●	●					
		593	chrysoberyl	II		●	●(P)					
		595	topaz	I	●	●	●					
		597	phenakite	II		●	●					
		600	sapphire	II	●	●	●(A)					
		602	diamond	II	●	●						
Orange	below 2	4	orpiment	III								●
	2—3	133	crocoite	III		●	●					
	3—5	243	wulfenite	III		●	●					
		264	mimetite	III			●					
	greater than 7	582	grossularite	II		●	●					
		583	hessonite	II		●	●					
		588	hyacinth	II		●	●					
Violet	below 2	22	stichtite	II			●					
	2—3	169	lepidolite	II			●				●	●
	3—5	235	anhydrite	III			●					
		291	fluorite	II		●	●				●	●
	5—7	379	apatite	II		●	●					
		398	scapolite	II		●	●					
		503	kunzite	II		●	●					
		523	axinite	II		●	●					
	greater than 7	536	amethyst	I	●	●	●	●	●	●	●	●
		551	cordierite	II		●	●					
		585	almandine	I		●	●	●				
		590	spinel	II		●	●					

Precious Stones — cont.

Colour	Hardness	No. of mineral	Mineral	frequency	Mode of application							
					natural form	facets	cabochons	tumble polished	glyptic	plastic cut	fancy goods	decorative and ornamental stones
Violet	greater than 7	594	alexandrite	II		●	●					
		595	topaz	I	●	●	●					
		600	sapphire	II	●	●	●(A)					
		602	diamond	III		●						
Red	2—3	76	cinnabar	III		●						
		173	amber	I			●	●	●	●	●	
	3—5	183	cleiophane	III		●	●					
		209	cuprite	III		●	●					
		296	zincite	III		●						
		304	rhodochrosite	I		●	●	●		●	●	●
		316	purpurite	II			●					
		334	tugtupite	III		●	●					
	5—7	379	apatite	II		●	●					
		442	fire opal	I		●(O)	●(O)			●(O)		●(O)
		445	wood opal	I			●	●		●	●	●
		455	carnelian	I			●	●	●	●	●	●
		486	orthoclase	II		●	●(P)					
		521	thulite	II			●			●	●	●
		531	rhodonite	I			●	●		●	●	●
	greater than 7	554	beryl	II		●	●					
		569	rubellite	II	●	●	●					
		578	pyrope	I		●	●	●				
		584	spessartite	III		●						
		585	almandine	I		●	●(A)	●				
		588	hyacinth	II		●	●					
		590	spinel	II		●	●					
		595	topaz	II	●	●	●					
		599	ruby	I	●	●	●(A)					
		602	diamond	III		●						
Pink	3—5	291	fluorite	II		●	●					
		331	apophyllite	III		●						
	5—7	398	scapolite	II		●	●					
		483	petalite	II		●	●					
		503	kunzite	II		●						
		531	rhodonite	I			●	●		●	●	●
	greater than 7	538	rose quartz	I		●	●(A)	●	●	●	●	●
		557	morganite	II		●	●					
		569	rubellite	II	●	●	●					
		573	danburite	II		●						
		590	spinel	II		●	●					
		597	phenakite	II		●	●					
		600	sapphire	III		●						
		602	diamond	III		●						
Green	below 2	41	talc	I			●			●	●	●
		42	pyrophyllite	I			●			●	●	●
	2—3	166	fuchsite	II			●				●	●
	3—5	251	phosphophyllite	III		●	●					
		268	chrysocolla	II			●					
		273	serpentine	II			●			●	●	
		274	antigorite	III			●					
		307	malachite	I	●		●	●		●	●	●
		311	variscite	II			●					●
		321	pseudomalachite	II	●		●					●
	5—7	373	smithsonite	III			●					●
		374	turquoise	I			●	●		●		
		375	brazilianite	II		●	●					
		379	apatite	II		●	●					
		398	scapolite	II		●	●					
		407	datolite	III		●						

Colour	Hardness	No. of mineral	Mineral	frequency	Mode of application							
					natural form	facets	cabochons	tumble polished	glyptic	plastic cut	fancy goods	decorative and ornamental stones
Green	5—7	412	tremolite	III			●					
		413	actinolite	III		●	●					
		414	smaragdite	II			●					
		417	nephrite	I			●	●		●	●	●
		426	enstatite	II		●	●(A)					
		430	titanite	II		●	●					
		432	dioptase	II		●	●					
		435	kyanite	II		●	●					
		446	praseopal	I			●			●	●	●
		453	plasma	I			●	●	●	●	●	●
		454	prase	I			●	●		●	●	●
		457	chrysoprase	I			●	●		●	●	●
		458	heliotrope	I			●	●		●	●	●
		484	milarite	III		●	●					
		491	amazonite	I			●			●	●	
		495	plagioclase	II			●					
		504	hiddenite	II		●						
		505	diopside	II		●	●(A)					
		506	chrome diopside	II		●						
		508	jadeite	I			●	●	●	●	●	●
		513	epidote	II	●	●	●					
		515	prehnite	III		●	●					
		519	zoisite	II			●					
		522	vesuvianite	II		●	●					
		524	olivine	I			●					
		525	chrysolite	I		●	●	●				
	greater than 7	544	Cat's eye	II			●(P)	●(P)		●(P)	●(P)	●(P)
		545	aventurine	I			●(Av)	●(Av)		●(Av)	●(Av)	●(Av)
		553	kornerupine	II		●	●					
		555	emerald	I	●	●	●		●	●		
		556	aquamarine	I	●	●	●		●			
		562	andalusite	II		●	●					
		571	verdelite	II	●	●	●					
		574	euclase	II		●	●					
		579	andradite	II		●	●					
		580	demantoid	II		●	●					
		581	uvarovite	II		●	●					
		582	grossularia	II		●	●					
		593	chrysoberyl	II		●	●(P)					
		594	alexandrite	II		●	●					
		595	topaz	I	●	●	●					
		600	sapphire	II		●	●(A)					
		601	leucosapphire	II		●	●					
		602	diamond	II		●						
Brown	3—5	173	amber	I			●	●		●		●
		181	sphalerite	III	●		●					
		183	cleiophane	III		●	●					
		221	aragonite	I		●	●			●	●	●
		228	cerussite	III		●	●					
		240	baryte	III		●						
		306	siderite	III		●						
		310	scheelite	II		●	●					
	5—7	352	anatase	III		●	●					
		353	brookite	III		●	●					
		354	goethite	II		●	●					
		379	apatite	II		●						
		426	enstatite	III		●	●(A)					
		428	hypersthene	III		●						
		430	titanite	II		●	●					
		444	common opal	I			●			●	●	●
		445	wood opal	I			●			●	●	●
		456	sardonyx	II			●		●	●	●	●

Precious Stones — cont.

Colour	Hardness	No. of mineral	Mineral	frequency	Mode of application							
					natural form	facets	cabochons	tumble polished	glyptic	plastic cut	fancy goods	decorative and ornamental stones
Brown	5—7	464	rutile	III		●	●					
		472	hematite	II		●	●		●			
		486	orthoclase	II		●	●(P)					
		488	sanidine	III		●	●					
		523	axinite	II		●	●					
	greater than 7	537	smoky quartz	I	●	●	●	●	●	●	●	●
		542	Tiger's eye	I			●(P)	●(P)	●(P)	●(P)	●(P)	●(P)
		545	aventurine	I			●(Av)	●(Av)		●(Av)	●(Av)	●(Av)
		548	cassiterite	III		●	●					
		563	chiastolite	II			●					
		566	dravite	II		●	●					
		583	hessonite	II	●	●	●					
		584	spessartite	III		●	●					
		595	topaz	II	●	●	●					
Blue	2—3	136	vivianite	III		●	●					
	3—5	217	calcite	III		●	●					
		226	azurite	II	●	●	●				●	●
		239	celestite	III		●	●					
		251	phosphophyllite	III		●	●					
		268	chrysocolla	II			●					●
		291	fluorite	III		●						
	5—7	373	smithsonite	III			●					●
		374	turquoise	I			●	●		●		
		378	lazulite	II		●	●					
		379	apatite	II	●	●	●					
		392	lazurite	I			●	●		●	●	●
		393	sodalite	I			●	●		●	●	●
		395	hauyne	III		●	●					
		428	hemimorphite	II		●	●					
		435	kyanite	II	●	●	●					
		486	orthoclase (moonstone)	II			●(P)					
		520	tanzanite	II		●	●					
		530	benitoite	III		●	●					
	greater than 7	541	blue quartz	II			●	●		●	●	●
		543	Falcon's eye	I			●(P)	●(P)	●(P)	●(P)	●(P)	●(P)
		550	jeremejevite	III		●	●					
		551	cordierite	II		●	●					
		556	aquamarine	I	●	●	●(P)					
		570	indicolite	II	●	●	●					
		574	euclase	III			●					
		575	dumortierite	II			●					
		576	sapphirine	II		●	●					
		595	topaz	II	●	●	●					
		600	sapphire	I	●	●	●(A)	●				
		602	diamond	II		●						
Grey	2—3	51	stibnite	III	●		●					●
Black	5—7	354	goethite	III			●		●			
		357	psilomelane	III			●					
		444	common opal	I			●			●	●	●
		445	wood opal	I			●			●	●	●
		452	onyx	I			●	●	●	●	●	●
		472	hematine	II	●		●		●		●	
	greater than 7	539	morion	I	●	●	●					
		546	pleonaste	III		●	●					
		548	cassiterite	III	●		●					
		565	schorl	III	●	●	●					
Multi-coloured	3—5	291	fluorite	III		●	●					
	5—7	379	apatite	II		●	●(P)					
		440	opal	I			●		●	●	●	●

505

Colour	Hardness	No. of mineral	Mineral	frequency	Mode of application							
					natural form	facets	cabochons	tumble polished	glyptic	plastic cut	fancy goods	decorative and ornamental stones
Multicoloured	5—7	441	precious opal	I			●(O)		●(O)	●(O)		
		449	chalcedony	I			●	●	●	●	●	●
		450	agate	I			●	●	●	●	●	●
		451	moss agate	I			●	●		●	●	●
		459	jasper	I			●	●	●	●	●	●
		496	labradorite (spectrolite)	I			●(L)	●(L)		●(L)	●(L)	●(L)
	greater than 7	534	quartz	I	●	●	●(P)	●	●	●	●	●
		554	beryl	I	●	●	●					
		564	tourmaline	II	●	●	●(P)					
		567	elbaite	II	●	●	●					
		577	garnet	I	●	●	●		●			
		587	zircon	II		●	●					
		590	spinel	II		●	●					
		595	topaz	I		●	●					
		598	corundum	I		●	●					
		600	sapphire	I		●	●					
		602	diamond	I		●						

List of minerals containing metallic elements

No. of mineral	Mineral	No. of mineral	Mineral	No. of mineral	Mineral
	Al		**As**	48	bismuth
88	cryolite	4	orpiment	69	emplectite
90	gibbsite	5	realgar	70	wittichenite
104	alumohydrocalcite	176	arsenic	71	bismutite
208	boehmite	177	allemontite	72	cosalite
215	dawsonite	344	arsenopyrite	73	galenobismuthite
232	alunite	350	löllingite	255	mixite
463	diaspore			288	hodrushite
562	andalusite		**Au**	289	heyrovskyite
575	dumortierite	11	nagyagite	299	bismite
590	spinel	12	sylvanite		
598	corundum	50	gold		**Ca**
		81	krennerite	217	calcite
	Ag	82	petzite	218	dolomite
9	polybasite	83	calaverite	221	aragonite
12	sylvanite	344	arsenopyrite	235	anhydrite
13	hessite	436	pyrite	291	fluorite
16	chlorargyrite				
17	iodargyrite		**Ba**		**Cd**
49	silver	223	witherite	199	greenockite
60	miargyrite	240	baryte	224	otavite
61	diaphorite	303	barytocalcite		
62	stromeyerite	499	celsian		**Co**
63	proustite			117	bieberite
64	pyrargyrite		**Be**	141	erythrite
65	pyrostilpnite	334	tugtupite	287	safflorite
66	xanthoconite	399	bavenite	340	bravoite
67	stephanite	484	milarite	341	siegenite
75	acanthite	485	bertrandite	342	linnaeite
77	galena	501	helvite	344	arsenopyrite
81	krennerite	554	beryl	345	cobaltite
82	petzite	561	bazzite	346	chloanthite
179	amalgam	574	euclase	436	pyrite
190	tetrahedrite	593	chrysoberyl	438	skutterudite
197	pearceite	597	phenakite		
204	dyscrasite				**Cs**
207	boleite		**Bi**	500	pollucite
344	arsenopyrite	10	tetradymite		

506

No. of mineral	Mineral	No. of mineral	Mineral	No. of mineral	Mineral
	Cu	283	pyrrhotine	531	rhodonite
6	covellite	306	siderite	532	inesite
9	polybasite	354	goethite	533	pyroxmangite
32	tyrolite	355	limonite		
47	copper	356	lepidocrocite		**Mo**
62	stromeyerite	367	magnesite	8	molybdenite
68	chalcocite	472	hematite	132	ferrimolybdite
69	emplectite	473	specularite	241	powellite
70	wittichenite			243	wulfenite
74	berzelianite		**Ge**		
106	aurichalcite	188	germanite		**Na**
109	caledonite	285	renierite	20	natron
110	linarite			23	mirabilite
116	chalcanthite		**Hg**	80	halite
126	cyanotrichite	3	mercury	87	villiaumite
127	kröhnkite	15	calomel	88	cryolite
128	spangolite	57	livingstonite	102	trona
129	devilline	76	cinnabar	125	thenardite
130	langite	80	tiemannite	127	kröhnkite
131	posnjakite	179	amalgam	397	nepheline
138	chalcophyllite	190	tetrahedrite		
144	liroconite	198	coloradoite		**Nb + Ta**
145	lavendulane	200	metacinnabar	297	betafite
146	clinoclase			359	pyrochlore
147	strashimirite		**K**	360	microlite
185	chalcopyrite	84	carnallite	402	eudialite
186	luzonite	85	sylvite	471	euxenite
187	enargite	229	kainite	477	columbite
188	germanite	232	alunite	479	tantalite
189	tennantite	234	polyhalite	480	tapiolite
190	tetrahedrite	397	nepheline		
191	chalcostibite	486	orthoclase		**Ni**
192	bornite	488	sanidine	118	morenosite
193	bournonite	490	microcline	142	annabergite
197	pearceite			143	cabrerite
201	umangite		**Li**	157	garnierite
203	domeykite	169	lepidolite	194	pentlandite
205	connellite	276	zinnwaldite	195	millerite
206	atacamite	314	sicklerite	216	zaratite
207	boleite	315	triphylite	280	nickel
209	cuprite	377	amblygonite	340	bravoite
210	tenorite	483	petalite	341	siegenite
226	azurite	502	spodumene	343	gersdorffite
227	antlerite			346	chloanthite
228	brochantite		**Mg**	347	rammelsbergite
255	mixite	84	carnallite	348	pararammelsbergite
256	euchroite	91	brucite	349	ullmannite
257	olivenite	105	artinite	351	niccolite
259	mottramite	213	ascharite	438	skutterudite
260	descloizite	214	hydromagnesite		
261	vesignieite	218	dolomite		**Pb**
268	chrysocolla	229	kainite	53	jamesonite
284	stannite	302	magnesite	54	plagionite
285	renierite	466	periclase	55	boulangerite
307	malachite	524	olivine	56	semseyite
308	rosasite			58	cylindrite
319	libethenite		**Mn**	59	franckeite
320	cornwallite	180	alabandite	61	diaphorite
321	pseudomalachite	211	ramsdellite	72	cosalite
322	bayldonite	220	kutnohorite	73	galenobismuthite
431	papagoite	282	hauerite	77	galena
432	dioptase	295	manganite	78	altaite
433	plancheite	304	rhodochrosite	79	clausthalite
436	pyrite	316	purpurite	89	diaboleite
		357	psilomelane	95	minium
	Fe	358	hausmannite	107	phosgenite
164	thuringite	366	jacobsite	108	leadhillite
219	antlerite	467	braunite	109	caledonite
277	chamosite	474	pyrolusite	110	linarite
279	iron	526	tephroite	133	crocoite

List of minerals containing metallic elements — cont.

No. of mineral	Mineral	No. of mineral	Mineral	No. of mineral	Mineral
134	stolzite		**Se**	154	carnotite
193	bournonite	45	selenium	172	uranophane
196	zinckenite	74	berzelianite	297	betafite
202	jordanite	79	clausthalite	298	brannerite
207	boleite	80	tiemannite	300	curite
225	cerussite	201	umangite	337	cuprosklodowskite
242	anglesite			338	kasolite
243	wulfenite		**Si**	359	pyrochlore
259	mottramite	534	quartz	471	euxenite
260	descloizite			481	thorianite
262	pyromorphite		**Sn**	482	uraninite
263	vanadinite	58	cylindrite		
264	mimetite	59	franckeite		**V**
293	bindheimite	284	stannite	259	mottramite
309	beudantite	344	arsenopyrite	260	descloizite
322	bayldonite	548	cassiterite	261	vesignieite
323	hedyphane			263	vanadinite
362	plattnerite		**Sr**		
		222	strontianite		**W**
	Pl (platinoids)	239	celestite	134	stolzite
281	platinum	313	goyazite	310	scheelite
439	sperrylite			368	hübnerite
			Te	369	wolframite
	Sb	10	tetradymite	370	ferberite
7	kermesite	11	nagyagite		
9	polybasite	12	sylvanite		**Zn**
51	stibnite	13	hessite	103	hydrozincite
52	berthierite	46	tellurium	106	aurichalcite
53	jamesonite	78	altaite	113	goslarite
54	plagionite	81	krennerite	181	sphalerite
55	boulangerite	82	petzite	182	marmatite
56	semseyite	83	calaverite	184	wurtzite
57	livingstonite	198	coloradoite	251	phosphophyllite
58	cylindrite			252	hopeite
59	franckeite		**Th**	258	adamine
60	miargyrite	324	xenotime	259	mottramite
61	diaphorite	339	thorite	260	descloizite
62	stromeyerite	383	monazite	296	zincite
64	pyrargyrite	410	allanite	308	rosasite
65	pyrostilpnite	471	euxenite	318	legrandite
67	stephanite	481	thorianite	373	smithsonite
93	senarmontite			403	hemimorphite
94	valentinite		**Ti**	404	willemite
171	chapmanite	352	anatase	470	franklinite
177	allemontite	353	brookite	591	gahnite
178	antimony	363	perovskite		
190	tetrahedrite	364	pyrophanite		**Rare earths**
191	chalcostilbite	365	ilmenite	298	brannerite
193	bournonite	430	titanite	305	bastnasite
196	zinckenite	464	rutile	324	xenotime
204	dyscrasite	527	ramsayite	359	pyrochlore
286	gudmundite			360	microlite
292	stibiconite		**U**	363	perovskite
293	bindheimite	96	ianthinite	379	apatite
294	cervantite	148	autunite	383	monazite
349	ullmannite	149	torbernite	402	eudialite
361	romeite	150	tyuyamunite	410	allanite
		151	meta-autunite	471	euxenite
	Sc	152	metatorbernite	528	thortveitite
528	thortveitite	153	zeunerite		
561	bazzite				

Glossary

Absorption − assimilation

Accessory minerals − minerals included in a rock or ore in quantities of 1−2% of its total volume

Acidic rocks − igneous rocks containing more than 65 % SiO_2

Alkaline metals − K, Na (Li, Rb, Ca)

Alkaline rocks − eruptive rocks containing a large portion of alkalis

Amphibolite − metamorphic rock composed mainly of amphibole

Amorphous mineral − mineral devoid of regular internal structure and consequently non-crystalline

Anatexis − the highest degree of metamorphism in which rocks melt

Andesite − neovolcanic, effusive rock of an identical composition to diorite

Anisotropy − dependence of physical properties of a substance on the direction of measurement

Apophyse − stringer of a larger subsurface or deep-seated magmatic body

Arkose − sedimentary rock composed mainly of quartz and feldspar

Association − occurrence of genetically related minerals

Asterism − a star-like effect caused by the play of light reflected from tiny, regularly arranged inclusions, evident in cabochons

Aventurism − lustre caused by tiny scales of mica or hematite inclusions in quartz

Basalt − neovolcanic effusive rock of an identical composition to gabbro

Basic rocks − extrusive rocks containing less than 52% SiO_2

Bitumens − mixture of solid and liquid hydrocarbons

Breccia − a cemented mass of rock fragments

Cabochon − smooth, domed gemstone, polished but not faceted

Carat − measure of weight for precious stones, both cut and uncut (1 carat = 0.2 gm)

Carbonatites − igneous rocks containing a large portion of primary carbonates

Carbonization − metasomatic process in which SiO_2 is extruded from the silicates by CO_2

Colloform structure − characteristic texture of substances of colloidal origin

Condenser − system of lenses in a microscope concentrating the rays of light

Cementation zone − enriched zone of ore deposits

Dehydration of minerals − water removal from minerals

Diabase − palaeovolcanic rock resembling gabbro in composition

Diagenetic processes − consolidation of sediments into rock

Differentiation of magma − physical and chemical processes involved in the separation of a homogenous magma

Diorite − deep-seated magmatic rock rich in plagioclases and dark minerals (amphibole, pyroxene)

Endogenic processes − processes originating in the interior of the Earth

Erlan − calc-silicate rock formed by metamorphosis of carbonates at the contact with magma

Eruptive rocks − effusive rocks solidified on the Earth's surface

Euhedral − see idiomorphic

Exogenous process − process set in motion by some external forces

Facet cut − precious stone cut with flat polished faces

Facies − characteristic of a rock or series of rocks reflecting their appearance, composition and conditions of formation

Feldspars − an important group of alumosilicate minerals

Fumaroles − volcanic exhalations of vapour and gas of 100−800 °C

Gabbro − basic, deep-seated rock composed of basic plagioclases, pyroxene, amphibole and olivine

Genesis − origin

Geode − cavity in rock or ore vein completely or partly filled with crystallized minerals

Gossan (iron hat) − oxidation zone above ore veins

Granite − deep-seated igneous rock formed mainly of potash feldspar and quartz, with a small portion of acidic plagioclase

Greisen − granite metamorphosed by pneumatolysis

Hornstone (hornfels, chert) – siliceous rock

Hydrothermal minerals – minerals originating from hot water solutions

Hypergenous process – natural weathering process which takes place in the atmosphere or hydrosphere

Hypidiomorphic (subhedral) crystal – partly developed crystal

Hypogene minerals – deep-seated minerals

Idiomorphic (euhedral) – well-formed crystal

Impregnation – filling of fine cracks in rocks or ores with minerals

Inclusions – bodies of foreign minerals in a mineral or rock (see xenolith)

Infiltration deposits – deposits formed of minerals precipitated in the upper layers of the Earth's crust or in older surface deposits

Intrusive rocks – rocks formed of magmas cooled beneath the surface of the Earth

Isomorphism – replacement of elements and radicals of similar properties (such as Ca – Na in plagioclases, Ca – Mg in carbonates)

Isotropy – physical properties are the same in all directions

Kaolin – mixture of argilliferous minerals with kaolinite as a result of decomposition of feldspars

Labradorization – grey-blue to green-blue change of colour on cleavage planes of labradorite

Lava – magma which penetrated to the Earth's surface

Lateritic weathering – process occurring in tropical areas in which SiO_2 and alkalis are removed and Al_2O_3 is enriched

Lherzolite – ultrabasic rock composed of olivine, bronzite and diallage

Limestone – sedimentary rock containing more than 50% of calcium carbonate

Limnic – lacustrine, freshwater

Magma – liquid molten siliceous rock substance from which igneous rocks form

Magmatism – process of rock metamorphism at different depths, under different pressure and temperature accompanied by gradual chemical changes

Melaphyre – palaeovolcanic effusive rock of a similar composition to gabbro

Metamict minerals – minerals whose crystalline structure has been altered or completely destroyed by radioactive emanation from uranium or thorium contained in the mineral; frequently the external crystal form is unchanged

Metasomatism – replacement of the original mineral by another, usually less soluble

Nepheline syenite – a platonic rock composed of alkali feldspar, nepheline and a ferromagnesian component

Neovolcanic rocks – rocks of Later Cretaceous Period

Nodule – rounded body, generally harder than the surrounding sediment in rock matrix

Oolites – aggregates composed of small, predominantly rounded bodies produced by the deposition from water solutions

Ochres – name of secondary minerals of a characteristic colour

Opalization – play of fine colours exhibited especially by opals

Opaque – non-transparent

Oxidation zone – the upper part of an ore deposit resulting from the decomposition of primary minerals

Palaeovolcanic rocks – effusive rocks of Pre-tertiary Age

Paragenesis – an association of minerals, related in space and time

Peridotite – name of a group of ultrabasic rocks composed mainly of olivine

Phantom – a crystal in which an earlier stage of crystallization is outlined in the interior

Phonolite – neovolcanic effusive alkaline rock with a similar composition to nepheline syenite

Picrite – ultrabasic rock composed mainly of olivine, augite and amphibole

Piezo-electricity – pressure generated electrical charge

Pneumatolysis – the process of direct separation of minerals from hot gases and vapour escaping from magma

Polaroid – $(C_{20}H_{24}N_2O_2)_4 . 3 H_2SO_4 . 2 HI . I_4 . 6 H_2O$, substance with the property of polarizing light

Polymorphism – ability of some mineral substances to occur in more than one crystal form

Post-magmatic process – following the magmatic process

Pseudomorphs – a crystal having the outward form of another species from which it has formed by replacement or alteration

Pyroelectric – a crystal, when heated, becomes electrically charged

Quartzites – rocks composed of metamorphosed siliceous sediments

Recent minerals – minerals younger than the Pleistocene

Refractive index – the measure of deflection of a ray of light passing into or out of a transmitting substance

Secondary minerals – minerals originating from other minerals due to chemical changes caused by atmospheric oxygen, carbonic acid and water

Serpentinite – rock composed mainly of serpentine; it originated through the metamorphism of ultrabasic volcanic rocks

silicification – the process by which rocks are replaced or impregnated by silica

Skarn – metamorphosed siliceous rock rich in calcium and iron, composed mainly of garnet, hedenbergite and magnetite

Solfataras – post-volcanic emanations of gases and vapour at 100–200 °C

Spherulite – radiating-fibrous aggregates of acicular crystals

Subhedral – see hypidiomorphic

Supergene process – secondary process resulting from action of descending water on primary minerals

Syenite – a rock which lacks quartz entirely, containing more potash feldspar and less plagioclase

Trachyte – effusive rock with a similar composition to syenite

Tuff – solidified volcanic ash

Ultrabasic rocks – igneous rocks containing less than 44% SiO_2, mainly composed of olivine, pyroxene, amphibole, biotite and ore minerals

Xenolith – inclusion of foreign mineral in a rock (see inclusion)

Zeolites – group of hydrated alumosilicates

List of reference books

I. Mineralogy, Crystallography, Mineral Identification

Bancroft, P.: Minerals and Crystals. The Viking Press; New York, 1973

Bancroft, P.: Die schönsten Minerale und Kristalle aus aller Welt, 1976

Bariand, P.: Marvellous World of Minerals. Abbey Library; London, Stuttgart, 1976

Bauer, J.: Der Kosmos-Mineralienführer. Mineralien-Gesteine-Edelsteine; Praha, 1975

Betechtin, A. G.: Lehrbuch der speziellen Mineralogie. Leipzig, 1977

Blüchel, K., Medenbach, O.: Zauber der Mineralien. Ringier; Zürich, 1981

Boottley, E. P.: Rocks and Minerals. Octopus Books; London, 1972

Brauns, R., Chudoba, K. F.: Spezielle Mineralogie. Slg. Göschen; 1964

Brauns, R., Chudoba, K. F.: Allgemeine Mineralogie. Slg. Göschen; 1968

Bruhns, W., Ramdohr, P.: Kristallografie. Slg. Göschen; 1965

Buchwald, V. F.: The Mineralogy of Iron Meteorites. Royal Soc.; London, 1976

Carrob I. G.: Trattato di Mineralogia. Florenz, 1971

Chukhrov, F. V., Bonstedt-Kupletskaya, E. M. etc.: Manual of Mineralogy (in Russian), Moscow

Dana, L., Hurlbut, S.: Manual of Mineralogy. John Wiley and Sons; New York, 1952

Deer, W. A., Howie, R. A., Zussman, J.: Rock-forming Minerals, Vol. V.; 1962–1964

Desautels, P. E.: The Mineral Kingdom. New York, 1968

Fleischer, M.: Glossary of Mineral Species. Bowie; Maryland, 1975

Frondel, C.: The System of Mineralogy. Vol III; New York, 1962

Frondel, J. W.: Lunar Mineralogy. New York, 1975

Ginzburg, A. I.: Atlas mineralov i rud redkich elementov. Nedra; Moskva, 1977

Grim, R. E.: Clay Mineralogy. New York, 1953

Hey, M. H.: Chemical Index of Minerals. 2. ed.; London, 1955, Appendices 1963 and 1974

Hiller, J. E.: Grundriss der Kristallchemie. Walter de Guyter; Berlin, 1952

Hofmann, F., Karpinski, J.: Schöne und seltene Minerale. Leipzig, 1980

Hochleitner, R.: Fotoatlas der Mineralien und Gesteine. München, 1980

Hurlbut, C. S., Klein, C.: Manual of Mineralogy. New York, 1977

Kipfer, A.: Kleinmineralien. Franckh; Stuttgart, 1974

Kleber, W.: Einführung in die Kristallographie. VEB Verlag Technik; Berlin, 1965

Kostov, I.: Mineralogy. London, 1968

Kouřimský, J.: Bunte Welt der Mineralien. Artia; Praha, 1977

Kouřimský, J.: The Illustrated Encyklopedia of Minerals and Rocks. Octopus Books; London, 1977

Krebs, H.: Grundzüge der anorganischen Kristallchemie. Enke; Stuttgart, 1968

Lieber, W.: Der Mineraliensammler. Thun u. München, 1973

Mason, B.: Meteorites. New York, 1962

Milovsky, A. V., Kononov, O. V.: Mineralogiya, Nedra; Moskva, 1982

Mason, B., Berry, L. G.: Elements of Mineralogy. San Francisco; 1968

Madenbach, O., Wilk, H.: Zauberwelt der Mineralien. Sigloch Edition; Künzelsan, Thawil, Salzburg, 1977

Mitchell, R. S.: Mineral names: what do they mean? Van Nostrand Reinhold Co., New York, 1979

Moore, CH. B.: Researches on Meteorites. New York, 1962

Mottana, A., Crespi, R., Liborio, G.: Der grosse BLV Mineralienführer. BLV Verlagsgesellschaft; München, Bern, Wien, 1979

O'Donoghue, M.: Enzyklopädie der Minerale und Edelsteine. Harder; Freiburg, Basel, Wien, 1977

Palache, C., Berman, H., Frondel, C.: The System of Mineralogy. vol. I. 1944, vol. II. 1951, New York

Parker, R. L., Bambauer, H. U.: Mineralienkunde. Thun, 1975

Picot, P., Johan, Z.: Atlas des Minéraux Metalliques. Paris, 1977

Ramdohr, P.: Die Erzmineralien und ihre Verwachsungen. Berlin, 1975

Ramdohr, P., Strunz, H.: Klockmann's Lehrbuch der Mineralogie. Stuttgart, 1980

Roberts, W. L., Rapp, G. R., Weber, J.: Encyklopedia of Minerals. Van Nostrand Reinhold Co.; New York, 1974

Schumann, W.: Steine und Mineralien. München, 1975

Seim, R.: Minerale. Sammeln und Bestimmen. Leipzig, 1981

Semenova, E. I.: Mineralogicheskie tablicy. Nedra; Moskva, 1981

Simpson, B.: Minerals and Rocks. Octopus; London, 1975

Sinkankas, J.: Mineralogy for Amateurs. Van Nostrand Reinhold Co.; New York, Cincinnati, Toronto, London, Melbourne, 1964

Rössler, H. J.: Lehrbuch der Mineralogie. VEB Deutscher Verlag für Grundstoffindustrie; Leipzig, 1980

Strunz, H.: Mineralogische Tabellen. Leipzig, 1977

Winchell, A. N., Winchell, H.: Elements of Optical Mineralogy. John Wiley and Sons; New York, London, 1951

II. Mineral localities

Bernard, J. H. et all.: Mineralogie Československa. Academia; Praha, 1981

Boggild, O. B.: The Mineralogy of Greenland. Kopenhagen, 1953

Carrobi, G., Rodolico, F.: I Minerali della Toscana, Florenz, 1976

Gramaccioli, C. M.: Die Mineralien der Alpen. Kosmos; Stuttgart, 1978

Gübelin, E.: Die Edelsteine der Insel Ceylon. Luzern, 1968

Michele, V. de: Guida mineralogica d'Italia 1, 2. Instituto Geografico De Agostini, S. p. A.; Novara, 1974

Parker, R. L.: Die Mineralfunde der Schweiz. Basel, 1973

Roubault, M.: Les Minérais uraniféres Francais. Paris, 1962

Sinkankas, J.: Gemstones of North America. New York, London, 1959

Stalder, H. A., Embrey, P., Graeser, S., Nowacki, W.: Die Mineralien des Binntals. Naturhist. Museum; Berlin, 1978

Strunz, H.: Mineralien und Lagerstätten in Ostbayern. Regensburg, 1952

Vollstädt, H.: Einheimische Minerale. Dresden, 1974

Vollstädt, H., Baumgärtel, R. Einheimische Edelsteine. Dresden, 1977

Walenta, K.: Mineralien aus dem Schwarzwald. Stuttgart, 1979

Weibel, M.: Mineralien der Schweiz. Birkhäuser; Stuttgart, 1973

Weninger, H.: Die alpinen Kluftmineralien der Österreichischen Ostalpen. Der Aufschluss 25. Sonderheft; Heidelberg, 1974

Koch, S.: Magyar ásványai. Budapest, 1966

Kostov, I., Breskovska, V., Mincheva-Stefanova, J., Kirov, G. N.: Mineralite v Bolgaria. Sofia, 1964

512

Lazarenko, E. A., Lazarenko, E. A., Baryshnikov, E. K., Malygina, O. A.: Mineralogiya Zakarpatia. Lvov, 1963

Radulescu, D., Dimitrescu, R.: Mineralogia topografica a Romaniei. Bucuresti, 1966

III. Petrography, Geology, Geology of Deposits

Barth, T., Correns, C., Eskola, P.: Die Entstehung der Gesteine. Berlin, 1970

Bruhns, W., Ramdohr, P.: Petrografie. Slg. Göschen; Vol. 173; Berlin, 1972

Bülow, K. von.: Geologie für Jedermann. 1973

Deer, W. A., Howie, R. A., Zussman, J.: Rock Forming Minerals. I—V; London, 1962—1965

Lieber, W.: Bunte Welt der schönen Steine. Kosmos; Stuttgart, 1973

Lüschen, H.: Die Namen der Steine. Thun u. München, 1968

Pape, H.: Leitfaden zur Gesteinbestimmung. Enke; Stuttgart, 1971

Pape, H.: Der Gesteinsammler. Franckh; Kosmos; Stuttgart, 1974

Schneiderhöhn, H.: Erzlagerstätten. Stuttgart, 1962

Schumann, W.: Knaurs Buch der Erde. München, 1975

Winkler, G. F.: Die Genese der metamorphen Gesteine. Springer; Berlin, Heidelberg, 1979

Zeschke, G.: Mineral-Lagerstätten und Exploration. Enke; Stuttgart (Vol. I.), 1970

Smirnov, V. I.: Geologiya poleznykh iskopayemykh. Nedra, Moskva, 1976

IV. Precious Stones, Gemmology

Anderson, B. W.: Gemstones for Everyman. Faber; London, 1976

Anderson, B. W.: Gem Testing. Butterworts; London, 1980

Bank, F.: Aus der Welt der Edelsteine. Pinguin-Verlag; Innsbruck, 1971

Chudoba, K. F., Gübelin, E. J.: Echt oder syntetisch? Stuttgart, 1956

Chudoba, K. F., Gübelin, E. J.: Edelsteinkundliches Handbuch. Bonn, 1974

Copeland, L. L., Liddicoat, R. T., et all.: The Diamond Dictionary. Los Angeles, 1960

Elwell, D.: Man-made Gemstones. John Wiley and Sons; New York, Chichester, Brisbane, Toronto

Eppler, W. F.: Praktische Gemmologie. Stuttgart, 1973

Fischer, W.: Praktische Edelsteinkunde. Kettwig, 1953

Hartmann, K., Binnewies, B.: Edelsteine, Franckh, Kosmos; Stuttgart, 1975

Hurlbut, C. S., Switzer, G. S.: Gemmology. John Wiley and Sons; New York, 1979

Orlov, Yu. L.: The Mineralogy of the Diamond. New York, 1977

Rutland, E. H.: Gemstones. The Hamlyn Publishing Group Ltd.; London, New York, Sydney, Toronto, 1974

Schlossmacher, K.: Edelsteine und Perlen. Stuttgart, 1969

Schubnel, H. J.: Pierres Précieuses dans le Monde. Horizons; Paris, 1972

Schumann, W.: Edelsteine und Schmucksteine. BLV Verlagsgesellschaft; München, Bern, Wien, 1976

Shirai, S.: The Story of Pearls. Tokio, 1970

Sinkankas, J.: Gemstone and Mineral Data Book. New York, 1972

Sinkankas, J.: Gem Cutting. Van Nostrand Reinhold Co.; New York, 1963

Smirnov, V. I.: Dragocennye i cvetnye kamni kak poleznoe iskopaemoe. Nauka; Moskva, 1973

Smith, G. F. H.: Gemstones, Chapman and Hall; London, 1972

Webster, R.: Gems: Their Sources, Descriptions and Identification. Butterworts; London, 1975

Webster, R.: A. Gemmologist's compendium. Van Nostrand Reinhold Co.; New York, 1980

V. Journals

The American Mineralogist: Mineralogical Society of America; Washington, USA

The Canadian Mineralogist; Ottawa, Canada

Lapidary Journal; San Diego, California, USA

Lapis; Christan Weise Verlag; München, FRG

The Mineralogical Magazine; London, Great Britain

Mineraliensammler, Bern, Switzerland

Zeitschrift der Deutschen Gemmologischen Gesellschaft; Idar-Oberstein, FRG

The Mineralogical Record; Bowie, Maryland, USA

Minerals Index

For complete description of mineral, refer to page numbers in **bold**;
for colour photograph of mineral refer to page numbers in *italic*.

516